Socialism with Chinese Characteristics

Roland Boer

Socialism with Chinese Characteristics

A Guide for Foreigners

Springer

Roland Boer
School of Marxism
Dalian University of Technology
Dalian, China

ISBN 978-981-16-1621-1 ISBN 978-981-16-1622-8 (eBook)
https://doi.org/10.1007/978-981-16-1622-8

This Springer imprint is published by the registered company Springer Nature Singapore Pte Ltd.
The registered company address is: 152 Beach Road, #21-01/04 Gateway East, Singapore 189721, Singapore

For Domenico Losurdo (1941–2018)

Preface

Let me begin with a quotation from Mao Zedong:

> Some foreigners say that our ideological reform is brainwashing. As I see it, they are correct in what they say. It is washing brains, that's what it is! This brain of mine was washed to become what it is. After joining the revolution, it was slowly washed, washed for several decades. What I received before was all bourgeois education, and even some feudal education. (Mao Zedong, quoted in Shao 2017, 2)[1]

Mao was speaking to Chinese students studying in Moscow in 1957, but his words are still resonant today. For me at least, the in-depth study of Chinese Marxism, of socialism with Chinese characteristics, has required a washing of my brain, a washing that has taken a dozen years or more. Why? When I first came to China, I thought I was open-minded, thought that I did not assume the frameworks and assumptions with which I had been brought up and educated. How wrong I was. Like other foreigners, I had developed an opinion about China that was quite erroneous. This is particularly so for those from the small number of countries that make up the 'West' (containing about 14% of the global population). I have found that those who have grown up in socialist countries—past and present—find it much easier to understand socialism with Chinese characteristics. This is also the case for the many who come from developing countries, for there too is a living memory of the experience of colonial depredation at the hands of the 'West'. So if you are like me, having been brought up and educated in one of the few Western countries, then you may well need to engage in a process of washing your brain so as to be able to understand socialism with Chinese characteristics, or sinified Marxism.

Another way of putting it is 'liberating thought', a term that became a central feature of Deng Xiaoping's tenure and crucial in the launching the Reform and Opening-Up. For Deng, liberating thought entailed liberation from old dogmas and

[1]To set the context: the text I have quoted comes from comments Mao made on the evening of 17 November, 1957. Mao had led a delegation to Moscow, from 2 to 21 November, 1957, for a celebration of the fortieth anniversary of the October Revolution, and for two congresses of Communist and Workers' Parties. He also engaged in a whirlwind of other activities. After much anticipation, Mao arrived at Moscow University on the evening of 17 November to speak with and answer questions from more than 3,000 Chinese students studying in Moscow.

assumptions about what socialism should be and indeed what capitalism was. To be clear: this is not some liberal 'freedom of expression' that simply reinforces Western liberal frameworks. Instead, the liberation of thought is central to the correct theoretical line of Marxism itself: Marxism is not a dogma, but a guide to action, a method for analysis and a framework—in China—for the construction of socialism.

By now it should be obvious that I will have much to say concerning Marxism in this book. The simple reason is that Marxism is front and centre in the Chinese project of constructing socialism. Socialism? Yes: I agree with the vast majority of Chinese scholars and common people—along with not a few in many other parts of the world—that the Chinese project is indeed a socialist project. Thus, if you want to understand China, you need to understand Marxism, especially Chinese Marxism. Those who ignore Chinese Marxism risk profound misunderstandings of China and its path. My primary focus is the Reform and Opening-Up, launched by Deng Xiaoping and the CPC in 1978. I will also have much to say at various points on the longer Marxist tradition—especially on the development of contradiction analysis and the theory of socialist democracy. But my focus remains the distinctly Marxist project of the Reform and Opening-Up.

As I indicate in the introductory chapter, this book primarily uses research undertaken by Chinese Marxist scholars in order to understand socialism with Chinese characteristics. This research has thus far been overwhelmingly published in the Chinese language and has not been studied outside China as much it should have been studied. Although there are some notable exceptions—Domenico Losurdo, Colin Mackerras, Nick Knight, Stefano Azzarà, and Barry Sautman—I do not find much Western material on China particularly useful. Most of these latter works fall into the trap of 'using Western categories to understand China [*yixi jiezhong*]'.[2] Even more, when an occasional Western Marxist feels called upon to opine about China, we find that such an effort 'uses Western categories to understand Marx [*yixi jiema*]'. For these reasons and more, it is necessary to deploy the extraordinary depth and range of Chinese Marxist scholarship to understand socialism with Chinese characteristics.

Many are those whom I need to thank for discussing and debating the material presented in this book. They include Colin Mackerras, Stefano Azzarà, Antonis Balasopoulos, Yiannis Kokosalakis, Tamara Prosic, Carsten Boyer Thøgersen, Sean Sayers, Geoff Boucher, James Juniper, and—among local CPA branch members—Grant Osland, Peter Rønne, Brynn Lewis, Andrew Rayment, Darren Ward, and Dave. In China, my long path to understanding socialism with Chinese characteristics has included vital conversations with Yang Huilin, Zang Fengyu, Zhang Shuangli, Zhang Jing, Zhu Yanming, Yu Min, and more recently Hong Xiaonan, Fang Yumei, Liu Guixiang, Chen Xiaogui, Qu Hong, and Yan Ping. I hope I have done justice to their many insights and helpful comments, both witting and unwitting. As ever, Christina

[2]In the first Chapter (1.4.1) I provide a typology of sub-genres of many Western works on China: secular apocalypse ('China doomer'), dystopian fiction (and its associated 'atrocity propaganda'), ghost story, conspiracy theory (and its betrayal narrative), Orientalist mystery, and sectarian intolerance (a distinct feature of Western Marxism).

Petterson has heard and discussed most with me, as part of the division of labour in our common project.

The book is dedicated to Domenico Losurdo, from whom I have learnt much. Although we met on only one occasion before he died, that time was a week together in China. We participated in two conferences, one in Beijing and one in Shanghai, travelling by train between the two cities. During that time, we talked much and found much common ground. At one point, Losurdo said to me: 'You need to be patient; we are part of the mainstream'. Of course, our mutual appreciation of and desire to understand the many developments of Marxism from Russia to China, especially during the era of socialist construction after a proletarian revolution, means that we are in fact part of the mainstream. This means too that all of the developments in Chinese Marxism, and thus of socialism with Chinese characteristics, is indeed the mainstream. This book is an effort to present central features of this mainstream development to those who may know relatively little but desire to know more.

Dalian, Liaoning, China Roland Boer
February 2021

Reference

Shao, Ning. 2017. Mao zhuxi yong san zhong yuyan shuo 'shijie'. Shanghai liusu xuexi shenqing huiyi Mao Zedong 60 nian qian zai mosike daxue fabiao jianghua: 'shijie shi nimen de...' *Xinmin wanbao*, 18 November 2017: 1–2. Available at: http://newsxmwb.xinmin.cn/xinminyan/2017/11/18/31334807.html.

Contents

1 Introduction: Marxism as China's Special Skill ... 1
1.1 General ... 1
1.2 Marxism as China's Special Skill ... 1
1.2.1 Defining Marxist Philosophy ... 2
1.2.2 Philosophy and the Social Sciences ... 4
1.2.3 The General Secretary as a Thinker ... 7
1.3 Chinese Characteristics ... 8
1.4 Historical Nihilism ... 10
1.4.1 Typology of Western Genres ... 10
1.4.2 Using Western Categories to Understand China (*yixi jiezhong*) ... 13
1.5 Method ... 15
1.6 A Note on Sources ... 17
References ... 19

2 Reading Deng Xiaoping ... 25
2.1 Liberating Thought (*jiefang sixiang*) ... 27
2.1.1 Liberation From ... 27
2.1.2 Liberation For ... 29
2.2 Seek Truth from Facts (*shishiqiushi*) ... 32
2.3 Liberating the Forces of Production (*jiefang shengchanli*) ... 37
2.4 Conclusion: Laying the Foundations for Communism ... 41
References ... 44

3 Contradiction Analysis: History, Meaning, and Application ... 55
3.1 Opening Remarks ... 55
3.2 Lenin ... 57
3.3 Dialectical Materialism ... 60
3.4 Mao Zedong ... 65
3.4.1 Contradiction and Antagonism ... 67
3.4.2 Principal and Secondary Contradictions ... 71

3.4.3 Chinese Characteristics 73
3.5 Conclusion 75
References 77

4 The Marxist Basis of the Reform and Opening-Up 85
4.1 Opening Remarks 85
4.2 One Big Pot and Household Responsibility 86
4.2.1 Returning to the Countryside 86
4.2.2 Collective and Individual 87
4.2.3 Equality and Difference 88
4.3 Reform 89
4.3.1 Deepening Reform 90
4.3.2 Revolution and Reform 91
4.3.3 The Wild 90s 93
4.4 Opening up 97
4.4.1 How to Relate to Capitalist Countries 97
4.4.2 Self-Reliance and Globalisation 99
4.5 Class Analysis 100
4.5.1 Internal Class Contradictions 100
4.5.2 International Class Antagonisms 102
4.6 One Country, Two Systems 103
4.7 Conclusion: One Central Task and Two Basic Points 105
4.7.1 Reform and Opening-Up 107
4.7.2 Four Cardinal Principles 107
4.7.3 Both Hands Should Be Hard 108
References 109

5 China's Socialist Market Economy and Planned Economy 115
5.1 Opening Remarks 115
5.2 De-Linking: Planning and the Market 116
5.2.1 Deng Xiaoping and the Socialist Market Economy 116
5.2.2 Market Economies in History 118
5.3 Contradiction Analysis 120
5.3.1 From Ownership to Liberating the Forces of Production 120
5.3.2 Primary Contradiction 121
5.4 Is It Socialist? Universality and Particularity 123
5.4.1 Universality and Particularity 123
5.4.2 What Makes It Socialist? 124
5.4.3 A Basis in Marx and Engels 126
5.5 Dialectical Transcendence: Beyond Planning and Market Economies 128
5.5.1 From Temporal Narratives to Managing the Contradiction 128

5.5.2 Dialectical Transcendence 130
5.6 Conclusion and Implications 133
References 134

6 Seeking a *Xiaokang* Society, or, Socialist Modernisation 139
6.1 Opening Remarks 139
6.2 The Four Modernisations 140
6.3 Datong: From the Confucian Tradition to Mao Zedong 144
6.3.1 The Book of Rites (*Liji*) 144
6.3.2 He Xiu's Revision: *Datong* as Topos 145
6.3.3 Kang Youwei's Confucian Reformism 147
6.3.4 Mao Zedong: *Datong* and Communism 150
6.4 *Xiaokang*: From the Book of Songs (*Shijing*) to Xi Jinping 152
6.4.1 The Book of Rites and the Book of Songs (*Shijing*) 152
6.4.2 Deng Xiaoping and *Xiaokang Shehui* 154
6.4.3 The Two Centenary Goals 156
6.5 Whither *Datong*? 157
References 158

7 The Chinese Marxist Approach to Sovereignty and Human Rights 165
7.1 Opening Remarks 165
7.2 On Universals, False and Rooted 166
7.2.1 False Universals 166
7.2.2 Rooted Universals 167
7.3 The Western Liberal Tradition of Human Rights 169
7.4 Sovereignty: From Westphalia to Anti-colonialism 171
7.4.1 Westphalia and Secularised Theology 172
7.4.2 Anti-colonial Sovereignty 173
7.4.3 Anti-hegemony, Non-interference, and Peaceful Coexistence 175
7.5 The Chinese Marxist Approach to Human Rights 176
7.5.1 The Prerequisite of Anti-hegemonic Sovereignty 176
7.5.2 The Right to Socio-Economic Well-Being 177
7.5.3 Policy Implications: From the Belt and Road Initiative to Minority Nationalities 179
7.5.4 The Rooted Universal of Chinese Marxist Human Rights 183
7.6 Conclusion: Mutual Recognition in a Multi-polar World 183
References 184

8 Socialist Democracy in Practice 191
8.1 Opening Remarks 191
8.2 Electoral Democracy and the People's Congresses 193
8.3 Consultative Democracy 194

8.3.1 Philosophical and Historical Foundations: Non-Antagonistic Contradictions and the Mass Line ... 196
8.3.2 Chinese People's Political Consultative Conferences ... 197
8.3.3 Comprehensive Consultation and Democratic Supervision ... 198
8.4 Grassroots Democracy ... 199
8.4.1 History: From Engels to Pre-Liberation Red Areas ... 200
8.4.2 Two Case Studies: Miaoba and Dengzhou ... 201
8.4.3 Improving Targeted Grassroots Democracy ... 203
8.5 Minority Nationalities ... 204
8.5.1 Defining 'Minzu' ... 204
8.5.2 Preferential Policies (youhui zhengce): Economics, Culture, and Governance ... 205
8.5.3 Autonomy and Unity ... 207
8.6 Rule of Law ... 209
8.6.1 Legal System and Rule of Law ... 209
8.6.2 Rule of Law and Rule of Virtue ... 211
8.6.3 Rule of Law Versus Rule of a Person ... 212
8.6.4 Governing the Country According to Law ... 214
8.7 Leadership of the Communist Party ... 216
8.7.1 From Historical to Practical Legitimacy ... 216
8.7.2 The Statutory Procedures of Practical Legitimacy ... 217
8.7.3 The Mutual Strength of Communist Party Leadership and Socialist Democracy ... 218
8.8 Conclusion: The Superiority of a Work in Progress ... 219
References ... 220

9 Socialist Democracy in Theory ... 231
9.1 Opening Remarks ... 231
9.1.1 Historical Forms of Democracy ... 232
9.2 Engels and Marx ... 234
9.2.1 Equating the Paris Commune with the Dictatorship of the Proletariat ... 234
9.2.2 The Seeds of Democratic Centralism ... 235
9.2.3 Principles of Socialist Democracy ... 235
9.3 Lenin and the 'Highest Form of Democracy' ... 237
9.3.1 Three Meanings of Democracy ... 237
9.3.2 The Superiority of Socialist Democracy ... 239
9.3.3 Democratic Centralism ... 240
9.4 Stalin and the Leadership of the Communist Party ... 241
9.4.1 Organic Leadership of the Communist Party ... 242
9.4.2 Proactive Human Rights Based on Freedom from Economic Exploitation ... 243

9.5 Mao Zedong ... 244
9.5.1 New Democracy ... 245
9.5.2 Democratic Dictatorship ... 247
9.5.3 Democratic Centralism ... 248
9.6 From Deng Xiaoping to Xi Jinping: The Problem of Democratic Centralism ... 251
9.6.1 Inner-Party Democratic Centralism ... 251
9.6.2 Separation of Party and Government ... 254
9.6.3 The Statutory Procedures of Socialist Democracy ... 255
9.6.4 Xi Jinping: Democratic Centralism and Country-Wide Governance ... 256
9.7 Conclusion: Stability and Social Health ... 257
9.7.1 Why Not Social Democracy? ... 258
9.7.2 Stability and Social Health ... 259
References ... 260

10 Xi Jinping on Marx and Engels ... 273
10.1 Setting the Scene: Why Xi Jinping's Thought is Important ... 273
10.2 The Biography of an Engaged Intellectual ... 275
10.3 Marxism in China ... 276
10.3.1 Scientific Socialism ... 276
10.3.2 Marxism and Anti-colonial Struggles ... 277
10.4 Study Marx ... 279
10.4.1 Development of Human Society (*renlei shehui fazhan*) ... 279
10.4.2 Sticking to the People's Standpoint (*jianshou renmin lichang*) ... 281
10.4.3 Productive Forces and Relations of Production (*shengchanli he shengchan guanxi*) ... 282
10.4.4 People's Democracy (*renmin minzhu*) ... 284
10.4.5 Cultural Construction (*wenhua jianshe*) ... 286
10.4.6 Social Construction (*shehui jianshe*) ... 289
10.4.7 Human-Nature Relationship (*ren yu ziran guanxi*) ... 290
10.4.8 World History (*shijie lishi*) ... 291
10.4.9 Marxist Party Building (*makesizhuyi zhengdang jianshe*) ... 294
10.5 Conclusion: An Original Contribution to the Development of Marxism ... 296
References ... 298

11 Conclusion: On the Socialist System and Cultural Confidence ... 309
11.1 A Guide for Foreigners ... 309
11.2 Socialist System ... 310
11.3 Cultural Confidence ... 312
References ... 315

About the Author

Roland Boer is a professor in the School of Marxism Studies, Dalian University of Technology, China. His research area is (comparative) Marxist philosophy and he is the first non-Chinese citizen to be employed in a School of Marxism Studies in China. Among many publications, he has most recently published a book on Stalin (Springer, 2017) and will soon have a book published with the title of *Friedrich Engels and the Foundations of Socialist Governance.*

Chapter 1
Introduction: Marxism as China's Special Skill

1.1 General

The best way to understand China and its path is through Chinese Marxism. It is as simple and as complex as that. I should hardly need to point out that the need to understand China's path grows by the day, especially as its rejuvenation (*fuxing*) gathers pace and hits ever-new targets. In light of this situation, it seems as though nearly everyone in the world now has an opinion on China, now matter whether they know anything about the place or not. But what soon becomes apparent amongst all the various opinions and indeed scholarly works from other parts of the world is that very few of them pay any attention to Chinese Marxism, or indeed socialism with Chinese characteristics. Even less are prepared to devote themselves to the arduous but rewarding task of studying what Chinese Marxist scholars themselves have to say about China's path. This is precisely what I do in this book: I offer a careful presentation of socialism with Chinese characteristics in light of the research undertaken by Chinese Marxist scholars, research that has been overwhelmingly published in the Chinese language.

In light of this research, it is quite very that China is vigorously following the socialist road and that Marxism is in the driver's seat on that road. So let us plunge straight in and see what it means for Marxism to be the core and centre of the Chinese project. Marxism—and especially Marxist philosophy—is regarded as China's 'special skill' (Xi 2013b, 404; 2020b, 5). The four-character Chinese term—*kanjia benling*—means a stock-in-trade, a special knack, a particular and honed skill that one has for—literally—'looking after the home' (Yang M. 2016).

1.2 Marxism as China's Special Skill

Some may be surprised: how can it be that a major global power has Marxist philosophy as its special skill? Not merely philosophy, which may seem surprising enough

R. Boer, *Socialism with Chinese Characteristics*,
https://doi.org/10.1007/978-981-16-1622-8_1

in itself, but Marxist philosophy. Obviously, we need to dig deeper, so I will examine three inter-related texts by none other than Xi Jinping: the first concerns the central role of Marxist philosophy and the social sciences; the second deals with dialectical materialism; and the third concerns historical materialism (Xi 2016c, 2019a, 2020b). The first has become a much-referenced landmark text, initially delivered as a speech at a major forum on philosophy and the social sciences in May of 2016. I will give it extended attention in a moment, but before doing so we need to ask: what is meant by Marxist philosophy?

1.2.1 Defining Marxist Philosophy

The answer appears in the other two pieces mentioned: Marxist philosophy entails dialectical materialism as its method and historical materialism as its application. This is a mainstream definition of Marxist philosophy, which has its roots in Marx and Engels, was explicitly identified in Soviet Marxism, and has been developed further in Chinese Marxism. You will find some in a few small corners of the world suggesting that only 'historical materialism' is appropriate, but this is a view from a small tributary and not the mainstream.[1] As for dialectical materialism (Xi 2019a), it entails four key propositions: (1) The world is unified in matter and matter determines consciousness, so policies should be developed in light of objective reality; (2) Since the movement of contradictions is a determining feature of matter, one should strengthen one's awareness of such contradictions and seek to resolve them; (3) The fundamental method of materialist dialectics is to think dialectically and develop the ability to deal with complex situations and problems; (4) Theory has a crucial role—think of Marxist theory—in terms of the dialectical relationship between knowledge and practice, but theoretical innovation should always be based on practice, on seeking truth from facts. In sum: as a method dialectical materialism is concerned with the inherent contradictions in matter, nature, and human society, with the need for dialectical analysis of such contradictions so to develop appropriate theories, policies, and programs—including those of governance and economic planning. I will have more to say in the second chapter on 'contradiction analysis', which is another way of speaking about dialectical materialism as it has encountered the Chinese philosophical tradition.

[1] The effort to separate Engels from Marx and thus from the whole development of dialectical materialism is a wayward development in Western Marxism (see Kangal 2020, 9–42, for a comprehensive overview of this debate). The best approach to the division of labour between Marx and Engels is in terms of parallels and reciprocal work (Griese 1987; Stanley 1989). Chinese scholars agree. After comprehensive assessments of the Western debate, they point out that while the 'complete agreement' theory is careless, the 'complete opposition' theory is untenable (Zhao 2016). Instead, they prefer an approach of 'agreement based on differences', or 'co-creation and complementarity [*tongchuang hubu*]' (Huang G. 2016, 2017). After all, it it was Engels (1892, 111) who coined the term 'historical materialism', while Marx (1880, 542) spoke of 'scientific socialism'.

In regard to historical materialism (Xi 2020b), this is the specific application of a Marxist method in order to understand human social development. In this case, there are three core principles: (1) Analyse and develop policies in light of basic social contradictions, which should be understood specifically in terms of the contradictions between the means and relations of production, between the economic base and superstructure (politics, culture, philosophy, and so on); (2) Although productive forces provide the material prerequisite for all social life, so much so that the basic task of socialism is to liberate the forces of production so as to improve the lives of all, there is also a complex dialectical relation between the economic base and the superstructure, and between the means and relations of production so that constant adjustments are needed; (3) People are the makers of history, in the sense that—to gloss Marx[2]—while objective realities determine the direction of a society, initiative and innovation from the common people can bring about changes in this reality.

This twofold definition of Marxist philosophy and its method is perhaps a little abstract and may be somewhat unfamiliar to those not aware of the Marxist tradition, but I have brought this definition to the fore in my treatment here to show how important it is in China—especially during the Reform and Opening-Up.[3] Notably, the texts by Xi Jinping concerning dialectical and historical materialism were initially delivered as relatively brief contributions to collective study sessions of the CPC Central Committee's Politburo early in Xi Jinping's tenure.[4] Obviously, Xi was keen to clarify the foundations of his tenure as general secretary of the CPC and as president of the People's Republic. Much of the rest of this book will unfold various aspects of this definition, but in what follows I would like to discuss the longer and more detailed speech on philosophy and the social sciences.

---

[2]This sense is also captured by the Chinese term *mingyun* (命运), in which one can change one's destiny by concerted effort. As for Marx, 'Men make their own history, but they do not make it just as they please; they do not make it under circumstances chosen by themselves, but under circumstances directly encountered, given and transmitted from the past' (Marx 1852a, 96–97; 1852b, 103).

[3]Marxist philosophy has been given a significant boost during the Reform and Opening-Up, which has entailed a move away from what is called the 'textbook' approach (when positions were repeated ad nauseam in one work after another) to profound innovation. Although the topic itself requires another study, I cite here the main works that provide surveys of the development of Marxist philosophy, precisely during a period (since 1978) that has been very much under-studied outside China (Wang Wei 2015; Chen Xueming et al. 2016; Ren 2017; Chen S. 2018; Li X. 2018; Mei 2018; Wang H. 2018; Wang N. 2018; Yu and He 2018).

[4]A fuller list of the study sessions that dealt explicitly with Marxism is as follows: 3 December, 2013: 11th study session of the 18th CPC Central Committee Politburo, on the theme of 'The fundamental principles and methodology of historical materialism' (Xi 2020b); 23 January, 2015: 20th study session of 18th CPC Central Committee Politburo, on the theme of 'The fundamental principles and methodology of dialectical materialism' (Xi 2019a); 23 November, 2015: 28th study session of the 18th CPC Central Committee Politburo, on the theme of 'The basic principles and methodology of Marxist political economy' (Xi 2020a); 29 September, 2017: 43rd study session of the 18th CPC Central Committee Politburo, on the theme of 'Marxism in the contemporary world and its influence'; 23 April, 2018: fifth study session of the 19th CPC Central Committee Politburo, on the theme of 'The Communist Manifesto and its significance for the times'.

1.2.2 Philosophy and the Social Sciences

The text begins by emphasising that philosophy and the social sciences are as important as the natural sciences in a country's development, indeed that the former are a benchmark of a country's overall level.[5] Here Xi quotes Engels: 'a nation that wants to climb the pinnacles of science cannot possibly manage without theoretical thought for a moment' (Xi 2016c, 2; Engels 1882c, 437; 1882b, 332; 1882a, 340). Further, every great leap of human civilisation is intimately connected with the transformational knowledge and theoretical guidance of philosophy and the social sciences—as the histories of Western Europe and of China show. Already we can see how remarkable the speech is: it would be difficult to find another leader of a major country emphasising the central role of philosophy and the social sciences. From my own experience in Western countries, I have seen these disciplines not merely restricted to small university departments, but also progressively whittled down and abolished since they are seen as 'useless' and 'idle' pursuits. Not so in China and not so for Xi Jinping.

However, it is not merely philosophy as such, or indeed the social sciences as such. Xi's historical narrative concerning China moves from its ancient philosophical endeavours, through its colonial humiliation, to the arrival of Marxism in China. Indeed, it was this arrival, initially enabled by 'the report of the cannons of the October Revolution' in Russia, that ushered in the contemporary era of philosophy and the social sciences. As we have seen, it is explicitly Marxist philosophy that Xi has in mind, which has guided China's path for a century (Liu 2015). At the same time, Xi emphasises that philosophy and the social sciences in China leave much to be desired in today's rapidly changing world, so much so that they are not really living up to the calling of the era. What era? 'China is experiencing the most extensive and profound social changes in its history, and it is carrying out the most ambitious and uniquely practical innovation in human history' (Xi 2016c, 4). A tall claim, perhaps, but Xi has in mind the two centenary goals of 2021 and 2049, with the aims of achieving a moderately well-off, healthy, and peaceful country (*xiaokang*) and then a 'strong socialistically modernised country [*shehuizhuyi xiandaihua qiangguo*]'. For a socialist project, these goals are unprecedented, especially when we keep in mind that China is already the most powerful socialist country in human history. For Xi, however, the standard and level of Chinese philosophy and social sciences is not commensurate with the country's national strength and international status. The message to the philosophers and social scientists: live up the calling, stand at the forefront of these developments, guide them, innovate, and become world leaders. In short, lift your game.

When reading the text of this speech, I try to imagine what was going through the minds of those present, from well-known scholars to aspiring students. Would they be inspired by such words, or would they be daunted by the challenge of a comprehensive shakeup of the whole system in China so that philosophy and the social sciences

[5] I recommend a number of widely-read studies of the speech as a whole (Chen Xixi 2016; Jiang Q. 2016; Yang J. 2016).

would be at the forefront nationally and internationally? Add to this the fact that Marxism is to provide the overall framework and leading position for all such research and innovation and I can imagine not a few quailing at the task. On a smaller scale, I have been present at a dinner where the dean of a School of Marxism—the nerve centre of Chinese universities—stipulated to all present that their research should be focused on Marxism and that it should seek not merely to be published in the best presses and journals, but that it should also seek to contribute to society as a whole. More than one person present confided in me that this was a major call indeed.

Xi's speech provides concrete proposals for a qualitative improvement in the way Marxism should guide the development of philosophy and the social sciences: (1) The integration of Marxism's basic principles and methods with China's rich history, as well as drawing upon positive developments throughout the world, albeit within the framework of Marxism; (2) The need for profound innovation and breakthroughs in dealing with new problems; (3) The development a comprehensive system of research that includes the whole range of other disciplines, increased international engagement, and the necessary resources to attract the best talents; (4) The improvement of the CPC's leadership, not merely in enabling a whole spate of improvements in philosophy and the social sciences, but in the fabric of the Party itself so that advanced Marxist philosophy is at the core of the Party's agenda. Clearly, some hard work was needed in 2016 to ensure that Marxism would once again become the over-arching framework for all pursuits (Deng C. 2014). Concrete work began immediately,[6] and I have witnessed at many levels how this call to qualitative improvement is bearing fruit, from the transformation of Schools of Marxism into the nerve centres of universities to the growth of high-quality international journals published in English.[7]

But one may wonder: is it wise to make philosophy and the social sciences serve a specific agenda? Should they not be 'free' to pursue their various avenues for the sake of knowledge itself? Xi addresses this question specifically, pointing out that all depends on the overall framework and value system. Thus, the very terms I have used in these questions arise from the Western liberal tradition, in which such disciplines provided the means by which 'the Western world studied itself, explained its own functioning, the better to control what was happening' (Wallerstein 2011, 264). Xi points out that there is no 'pure' philosophy, for it all depends on the question, 'for whom?' For the minority or the majority, for intellectuals in ivory towers or for

[6]The speech was soon followed by a key document from the CPC Central Committee, 'Opinions on Speeding Up the Construction of Philosophy and the Social Sciences with Chinese Characteristics', along with pieces by and interviews with Chen Baosheng, Minister of Education, and Wang Weiguang, president of the Chinese Academy of Social Sciences (CASS), which itself underwent a major and well-overdue overhaul (CPC Central Committee 2017; Guo J. 2017; Chen B. 2017a; 2017b; Wang Weiguang 2017).

[7]Xi quotes Engels again to stress the point that much work is to be done: 'The development of the materialist conception in respect of even a single historical example was a scientific task requiring years of quiet research, for it is evident that mere phrases can achieve nothing here and that only an abundance of critically examined historical material which has been completely mastered can make it possible to solve such a problem' (Xi 2016c, 6; Engels 1859a, 598; 1859c, 471; 1859b, 470).

'the people as centre [*yi renmin wei zhongxin*]'? That said, Marxism is by no means a closed system, a 'dogma [*jiaoyi*]' or 'doctrine [*jiaotiao*]' that means the end of free intellectual inquiry. On the contrary, it is an open and problem-oriented system, a 'starting point for further research and a method for such research' (Xi 2016c, 7; Engels 1895b, 691; 1895a, 428; see also Xi 2011, 16–17). Indeed, a Marxist framework is arguably even more open than the liberal tradition's empty formulae.

This is all very well, but is this emphasis on Marxist philosophy and social science no more than an academic pursuit, restricted to the ivory towers of research institutes and universities? One may be tempted by this Western perspective, especially if one focuses only on the academic reforms begun by Hu Jintao that led to Marxism becoming a discipline in its own right, along with six sub-disciplines.[8] In his speech, Xi acknowledges that this had been a problem in some quarters, along with lack of competence, the devolution into jargon and textbook language, the sense that Marxism was out date and simply 'ideological', indeed that China was no longer pursuing Marxism at all (Xi 2016c, 5). Clearly, this situation was unacceptable and one of the effects of the speech was to deal with such problems through improving the quality and focus of compulsory courses in Marxism in high schools and universities, through programs to attract the best students into Marxist programs (who in the past tended to go to other disciplines), and in providing significant structural and financial support (Xi 2016a). That it entailed weeding out the relatively few liberals and anti-Marxists goes without saying, a process that I have witnessed in different quarters.

However, there is a deeper issue here that goes to the very heart of academic research in China. As Chang Gaixiang puts it, philosophy—*zhexue*, a loan word via Japanese—in China has a history of maxims from the dialogues of sages rather than the construction of abstract systems of thought. While this has led some Western philosophers to look down on the Chinese tradition, it means that philosophy is not the 'mere pursuit of intellectual understanding' or the pleasure of constructing systems of thought, but devotion to the 'activities and realities of life'. Philosophy exists as a way of life, is integrated with life and seeks to improve life (Chang Gaixiang 2018, 18; see also Qiao 2014; Wang H. 2018, 24). Or, as Xi Jinping puts it in his speech, the great achievements of philosophy and the social sciences have been created in 'answering and solving the major problems faced by humanity and society'. Researchers live in a real society, so much so that without flesh-and-blood human beings, philosophy 'would have no attraction, appeal, influence or vitality' (Xi 2016c, 6). Thus philosophy, and especially Marxist philosophy, is not seen in China

[8] There were a number of important documents produced by the CPC Central Committee in 2004 and by the Ministry of Education in 2005 that began a process of reforming the structure of Marxism education (CPC Central Committee 2004a; 2004b; Xuanchuanbu he jiaoyubu 2005; Jaioyubu 2005). One result was the establishment of what became the Academy of Marxism, within the Chinese Academy of Social Sciences, and another was the identification of five specialisations of Marxism: Basic Principles of Marxism; History and Development of Marxism; Studies of Sinified Marxism; International Marxism Studies; Ideological and Political Education. To these a sixth was added a little later: Basic Studies of Modern and Contemporary Chinese History. These now structure all Marxist educational programs in China.

as merely a 'scientific' or 'academic' pursuit, a preserve of scholars divorced from everyday realities. Indeed, this approach—so common in 'Western' academia—is seen as a distortion and weakening of Marxism itself (Chen S. 2018, 6). Instead, philosophers and social scientists are by very definition engaged or organic intellectuals, focused on solving the major problems of the day. They also have the major responsibility of training 'the builders of socialism and their successors, who will be well developed morally, intellectually, physically and aesthetically' (Xi 2018, 1–2; see also 2016a, 376). The four-character saying used here is *lide-shuren* (立德树人), with the senses of strengthening moral education and cultivating people, as well as fostering character and civic virtue (Qi R. 2018).[9] In this light, Marx's famous eleventh thesis on Feuerbach gains a whole new meaning: 'Marxism has a distinctive practical character, which is not only committed to "explaining the world" scientifically, but is also committed to actively "changing the world"' (Xi 2016c, 5; see also Cai 2018, 9).

1.2.3 The General Secretary as a Thinker

A question may linger for some: isn't all this attention to the thought of a political leader a little too much like fawning and obsequiousness, or perhaps propaganda on his behalf? The question is pertinent, since I will deal extensively with the thought of Deng Xiaoping (Chapter 2) and return to Xi Jinping (Chapter 10). On this matter, we encounter a problem to which I will return a little later: one of the roadblocks for those unfortunate enough to have been raised in a Western liberal context is the absence of any serious attention to the thought of political leaders. Even if such a leader has written and published anything of substance—a rare occurrence indeed in the West—such material is of interest to only a few for the sake of what passes as 'political analysis'. Indeed, the task of such analysis is to 'cut through' or 'look behind' the rhetoric that has been carefully crafted by professional 'spin doctors'.[10] It is assumed that such an approach is 'critical' and 'objective', but in doing so of course it becomes an ideological prop of the Western liberal system itself. In light of such assumptions, it should be no surprise that there are in Western contexts very few serious engagements with any communist leader's thought when a Communist Party has been in power.

Those familiar with the communist tradition have a somewhat different perspective. In this case, the thought of the Party's general secretary is crucial, especially works that mark a new step in the development of Marxist theory in light of changing

[9]In this sense should we understand studies that examine the implications of Xi's speech for news services (Xi 2016b; Tong 2016; Lei and Zhang 2018; Zhang and Li 2018) and education, especially ideological and political education (Peng 2018).

[10]Thus, a typical version of 'Chinese politics' from such a perspective is to speculate concerning supposed factional struggles within the CPC. This assumption is also based on the deeply entrenched Western assumption that 'politics' means struggle, which we may see—from a Marxist perspective—as arising from the class struggle that is constitutive of capitalist political systems.

circumstances. Of course, to focus on an individual leader may seem a little strange for a tradition that emphasises the collective as the foundation for a fully-rounded individual, let alone the collective role of urban and rural workers. The answer is obvious: the general secretary's work is never an isolated occurrence, but arises from a collective leadership, and especially from periods of intense study and debate. Think of Mao Zedong's study circle in Yan'an in the 1930s, from which the landmark studies on contradiction and practice arose, or the late-night discussions of Deng Xiaoping's comrades as they sought to plot a path for the Reform and Opening-Up. These actions did not take place in a vacuum, for they were part and parcel of intense debates with the Communist Party itself. Fair enough, one might think: we can see the process in the past and study it carefully. But the present? Even 'Western' Marxists baulk at such a focus. They are happy to discuss and debate leaders of the past and their legacy, but not the present. They tend to toe the line that careful study of a current general secretary's writings seems a little too obsequious, especially when—according to 'Western' liberal assumptions—one should take a journalistic approach and engage in what passes for 'criticism'. Not so for the communist tradition, in which the thought of current leaders, as well of those of the past, not merely deserves but demands careful study.

It follows from all of this that the Party's general secretary must be a thinker. Some may have spoken and written more and some less than others—Deng Xiaoping, for example, preferred to get down to work rather than write long screeds. It is simply not enough to serve one's time in the political workings of the Party, to rise through the ranks by means of experience and merit. One must also be a thinker, and preferably a thinker of some substance. How then, should their contributions be assessed? In his speech commemorating the 120th anniversary of Mao Zedong's birth, Xi Jinping identified Mao's major contributions to Chinese Marxism and China's socialist road. But he also observed: 'Revolutionary leaders are human beings, not gods … we cannot worship them like gods or refuse to allow people to point out and correct their errors just because they are great; neither can we totally repudiate them and erase their historical feats just because they made mistakes' (Xi 2013c, 8).

1.3 Chinese Characteristics

The title of this book is 'socialism with Chinese characteristics [*Zhongguo tese*]'. This is the standard term used in China, along with the 'sinification [*zhongguohua*] of Marxism'.[11] There is no mystique in such terms, despite efforts in some quarters to espy—with Orientalist assumptions—a deft concealment. Simply put, it means that Marxism has its basic principles and method, but that the method itself needs to take account of the specific historical, economic, and cultural realities of a country.

[11] Throughout this book, I translate *zhongguohua* as 'sinification', literally—from Latin—'to make Chinese'. One will often find an alternative translation as 'sinicisation'. The meaning is obviously the same.

Or, as Qi Yiming puts it, the Chinese characteristics entail China's specific practice of Marxism, the era in which China finds itself, and China's culture and history (Qi Y. 2018).

But why not simply call it socialism, rather than adding the 'Chinese characteristics'? History is important: the desire to express this reality dates back to the Zunyi Conference of January 1935. Held at the early stages of the Long March, the expanded conference of the Politburo finally brought to a head simmering tensions between Mao's circle and the Moscow-appointed leadership's[12] effort to impose the model of the Russian Revolution on China. In light of recent military disasters resulting in the need to evacuate the Jiangxi-Fujian Soviet, the former were removed by popular vote and replaced with Mao and other comrades. At last, they were able to enact a revolutionary approach that was sensitive to the specific conditions in China. Not long after this crucial event, Mao began to speak of China's 'own laws of development' and 'its own national characteristics'. In fact, there is 'no such thing as abstract Marxism, but only concrete Marxism [*juti de makesizhuyi*]', by which Mao meant Marxism that is 'applied to the concrete struggle in the concrete conditions [*juti huanjing*] prevailing in China, and not Marxism abstractly used'. Mao urged that the whole Party needed to address the question of 'the sinification of Marxism [*Makesizhuyi zhongguohua*]—that is to say, making certain that in all its manifestations it is imbued with Chinese characteristics [*Zhongguo de texing*], using it according to Chinese peculiarities [*Zhongguo de tedian*]' (Mao 1938a, 658–659; 1938b, 538–539; see also 1944, 191–192; 1959, 109). Or, as Mao put it somewhat more poetically a few years later: 'The "target" is the Chinese revolution, the "arrow" is Marxism-Leninism' (Mao 1941a, 801; 1941b, 22).

This emphasis on Chinese conditions runs all the way from the strategy of 'using the countryside to surround the cities [*nongcun baowei chengshi*]' to the socialist market economy of the Reform and Opening-Up. Alongside these historical realities are specific philosophical developments in light of dialectical materialism, with which I engage in more detail in Chapter 3. But there is an important consequence of this emphasis on China's specific conditions for the development of socialism. In the same way that the development of a 'China Model' for a proletarian revolution and the subsequent construction of socialism is not dependent on foreign templates or models, so also does China not seek to impose its approach on others. I will have more to say on this question in later chapters, but the fundamental approach of the 'China Model [*Zhongguo moshi*]' is that China will lead by example and urge others to develop approaches suitable to their own conditions (Xu 2010).[13] But is it really

[12]Especially Qin Bangxian—also known as Bo Gu—and Otto Braun.

[13]As Deng Xiaoping put it: 'The Chinese revolution was not carried out according to the model [*moshi*] of the Russian October Revolution but by proceeding from the realities in China, by using the rural areas to encircle the cities and seize power with armed force. Since the Chinese revolution succeeded by integrating the universal principles of Marxism-Leninism with the concrete practice of China, we should not demand that other developing countries carry out revolution according to the China model [*Zhongguo de moshi*], and even less demand that developed capitalist countries carry out revolution according to the China model [*Zhongguo de moshi*]' (Deng X. 1980, 318; see also 1988, 261).

socialism? Stress too much the specific characteristics and one risks losing touch with the core Marxist principles and methods. Thus, it always needs to be remembered that socialism with Chinese characteristics 'is socialism, and not some other -ism' (Xi 2013a, 22; 2019b, 1).

1.4 Historical Nihilism

It will soon become clear that I do not refer to much secondary literature of a Western provenance. The main reason is that a significant amount of this literature on China leaves much to be desired. To be clear: there are notable exceptions, from whom I have learnt much in my research. These include Domenico Losurdo's insightful Marxist work on China, the wise reflections of Colin Mackerras, the earlier careful studies of Nick Knight, and Barry Sautman's sharp pieces (Losurdo 2012, 2017a, 2017b; Mackerras 2003; Mackerras and Knight 2015; Knight 1990, 2005, 2007; Sautman 1998, 2006, 2010). More limited assistance can be found in a few other works that try at least to take China seriously but do not engage at all with Marxism (Jacques 2009; Bell 2006; Vogel 2011; Guo B. 2018). Beyond such works, one soon descends into what in China is known as 'historical nihilism [*lishi xuwuzhuyi*]', by which is meant the denial of the proletarian revolution, negating the leadership of the CPC, and ignoring Marxism or suggesting that Marxism is outdated and that China has abandoned Marxism (Zheng 2008; Zhu 2016). In a Chinese context, the disaster that befell the Soviet Union is seen as a clear example of the effects of historical nihilism. In that context there was intense ideological struggle, during which the achievements of the October Revolution and the Soviet Communist Party were denied, Lenin and Stalin were belittled, Party organisations at all levels lost their way, and the military was no longer under the leadership of the Party. The result: 'the massive Communist Party of the Soviet Union scattered like birds and beasts [*niaoshousan*], and the vast socialist state of the Soviet Union collapsed and fell apart [*fenbeng lixi*]' (Xi 2019b, 2). In short, historical nihilism is the favoured tool of those hostile to the communist project, those who seek to vilify and slander China and its path.

I suggest that the various approaches of historical nihilism can best be categorised in terms of sub-genres, some of them with vestiges of the more unsavoury aspects of the Christian tradition that has an abiding influence on Western thought forms.

1.4.1 Typology of Western Genres

Secular apocalypse: this type is also known as the 'China doomer' approach, in which someone seeks to predict yet again the apocalyptic crash of China's economic and political system. One of the earlier works that set the tone was Gordon Chang's *The Coming Collapse of China* (2001), although one can trace such fantasies back to the establishment of the People's Republic in 1949.[14] If one is fond of recycling this narrative, then it is quite easy to get such a work published in one or another less than reputable press. Every year a new title or more appears proposing a 'collapse' or 'crisis', focusing on whatever aspect takes the author's fancy, but each time recycling the old Judaeo-Christian myth of the apocalyptic end of the world. As this tradition makes clear, the weary repetition of such predictions does not seem to dampen the enthusiasm of those who propagate them.

Dystopian fiction: such works peddle old anti-communist tropes, such as 'cultural genocide' in Tibet, 'forced labour' in Xinjiang, human rights 'abuses' in Hong Kong, 'suppression' of minority nationalities, a 'surveillance state', 'authoritarian dictatorship' that suppresses freedom of the press, and so on and so on. This type of material is known as 'atrocity propaganda',[15] an old anti-communist and indeed anti-anyone-who-does-not-toe-the-Western-line approach that tries to manufacture a certain image for popular consumption. These pieces of 'atrocity propaganda' feed off one another, creating a dystopia that can only be a fiction for anyone who actually spends some time in China, let alone lives there. The only way I can make sense of this type of material is that it belongs to the genre of 'dystopian science fiction', in which another planet is created with a country called 'China'. This fictional representation has nothing to do with the real China here on earth.

Ghost story: this sub-genre postulates that the Communist Party is a secretive and paranoid outfit that is terribly afraid of its own people and seeks world domination. Here too one can be assured of a publication in a less than reputable press if one suggests, for example, that the social credit system is geared to surveillance of a restive population, or that women are indoctrinated to produce the next generation of communists, or indeed that the CPC has a long-term plan to undermine global institutions and take over the world. Much like a ghost story, really, in which one has an irrational belief in ghosts, fits bits and pieces into an apparently coherent narrative of ghostly appearances, and then denies the overwhelming weight of empirical evidence to the contrary. The result: spooks everywhere.

Conspiracy theory: this one is particularly favoured by the relatively few scholars who mostly belong to the small tributary or side-stream known as 'Western Marxism'. The theory relies on an initial 'betrayal'—think of Adam and Eve and the first sin, or Judas Iscariot with Jesus of Nazareth—of Marxism by one or another leader. In a Chinese context, the favoured 'traitor' is Deng Xiaoping, who is cast as a 'capitalist roader'[16] and who supposedly undid all of the socialist achievements of Mao

---

[14]Occasionally, one finds a self-professed 'Marxist' entertaining such views (Li M. 2008, 2016).

[15]The term 'atrocity propaganda' was coined by James Read (1976). In our time, the country subject to the most consistent atrocity propaganda is the DPRK, or North Korea (Beal 2005). It should be noted that in the tightly controlled media environment of the UK, the BBC has, since its founding in 1922, been the cultural arm of the UK government's cultural propaganda. In such a role, the BBC has been a prime exponent of atrocity propaganda. Examples include the struggles in Northern Ireland, the invasion of Iraq, the promotion of the 'White Helmets' in Syria, and more recently in relation to Xinjiang in China.

[16]Even though Mao never used the term 'capitalist roader [*zouzipai*]' to speak of Deng Xiaoping, this historical fact has not prevented more than one Western Marxist from making such an assertion.

Zedong. Now the conspiracy theory comes into play: since they believe that China has embarked on a capitalist road since the beginning of the Reform and Opening-Up (Meisner 1996; Weil 1996; Harvey 2005),[17] it follows that all of the many and detailed statements, along with all of the scholarly research projects that are based on empirical data and show that China is actually following a socialist path, must take the form of a massive conspiracy theory with an elaborately coded language.[18] How massive? It has been going for over 40 years and includes the CPC leadership, tens of thousands of scholars, tens of millions of CPC members, and hundreds of millions of Chinese citizens. Quite impressive really, but only if one believes in conspiracy theories.

Orientalist mystery: an old Western and deeply racist trope, the 'orientalist mystery' has many levels. It runs all the way from the notion of 'implacable Asian faces', through the suggestion that people 'disappear' when under police investigation, to the belief that the Communist Party is 'hiding' some horrible truth. In terms of the latter, the possibilities are endless but I am—for the purposes of the present study—particularly interested in the suggestion that the 'truth' of Mao Zedong in terms of what he said and did, of the Cultural Revolution, or Tiananmen Square in 1989, or indeed Xinjiang today, have all been concealed and kept from the public eye. Obviously, this sub-genre is closely connected with 'conspiracy theories', but the 'orientalist mystery' brings to the fore the deeply racist nature of such assumptions. It goes back to the idea of the mystery—both dangerous and sexualised—of the East hidden behind a curtain or veil.

Sectarian intolerance: once again an approach that afflicts Western Marxists, but there are many others who also respond with sectarian or ideologically-inspired intolerance and rejection. I have experienced this response on a number of occasions, when one aspect or another of the research contained in this book has been presented or published. Some listeners and readers simply block it out, suggesting that any effort to present empirical facts—such as the achievements in poverty alleviation, ecological development, promotion of rule of law and human rights, and the nature of China's socialist democracy—is 'partisan'. Indeed, the absurd suggestion that anything that is not a dismissal is 'partisan', along with the passionate denial of the realities of China today, obviously overlaps with some of the other approaches mentioned above. But it also has a distinct air of the sectarian intolerance of Christian

[17]One also finds some non-Marxist scholars peddling such a betrayal narrative and its attendant conspiracy theory (Dickson 2003; Huang Y. 2008; Walter and Howie 2011).

[18]A good example of such a perceived code is 'crossing the river by feeling for the stones [*mozhe shitou guohe*]', which is recoded to mean crossing 'from the socialist bank to the capitalist bank'. Of course, it means nothing of the sort. The saying was originally used by the Marxist economist, Chen Yun, in order to describe pilot programs that could be tested in one area and then, subject to assessment and revision, be used elsewhere. Chen Yun wrote: 'We should institute reforms slowly and carefully. This is because the reforms we will carry out are complicated, we should not be hasty. Reforms should be based on theoretical research, economic statistics and economic forecasting, but more importantly, we should set out from pilot programs and always sum up experience whenever it is necessary. That is to say, we should "cross the river by feeling for the stones." We should take small steps to advance slowly at the beginning' (Chen Y. 1980, 279).

groups, who are so often given to a 'zero-sum' approach to other groups and reject them entirely.

In all of these various sub-genres, one finds not merely a residue of Christian narrative influences—even in Marxist scholars (Losurdo 2008; 2017b)—but also a studied avoidance of Chinese Marxist scholarship. The obvious reason is that if a Western scholar did focus on such research, his or her pet narrative sub-genre would fall apart. But some may ask: is this really fair, offering a caricature of much of Western scholarship on China? What about some who try to present objective, scientific analyses?

*1.4.2 Using Western Categories to Understand China (***yixi jiezhong***)*

On this matter, we encounter what Chinese researchers call *yixi jiezhong* (以西解中), using Western frameworks or categories in an effort to understand China (Wang H. 2018, 26).[19] By this is meant not so much methods that initially had a Western provenance and have been sinified—Marxism being the most notable—but the assumed framework of Western liberalism and its perspectives on what an economy, state, and society should look like. Within this framework, the assumed categories include: civil society over against the state; politics as an antagonistic struggle between political parties or factions; democracy defined as elections between different political parties; human rights as civil and political rights; the rise and existence of a 'middle class' and indeed a working class; and that a 'market economy' is by definition a capitalist market economy—as the misleading slogan by Count Ludwig von Mises (1932, 142) would have it, 'the alternative is still either Socialism or a market economy'. From this framework arises a distortion of language, such as socialist and post-socialist, with 1978 being the turning point; the terminology of 'conservative' and 'reformer', with 'conservatives' being Communists like Deng Xiaoping and 'reformers' being the odd liberal; the student unrest of 1989 as a turning point along such 'conservative-reformer' lines; and the assumption that human beings everywhere hanker after the illusory 'freedom and democracy' of a Western provenance (Goldman and MacFarquhar 1999; Fewsmith 2008; Lampton 2014; Tsang 2014). This whole framework and its usually unquestioned assumptions produces strange works that seek to analyse China as an emerging capitalist market economy, with a rising middle class that would demand its liberal 'freedom and democracy' were it not for a repressive Communist Party that is 'conservative' to the core. It certainly leads to circular research 'results'. A good example is the search for 'evidence' of 'democracy', focusing on grassroots democratic practices. Since the whole perspective for what counts as 'democracy' is the rather thin Western liberal notion, they typically fail to find 'evidence' and so must conclude that such an absence is due to an 'authoritarian' political structure

[19]On occasion, it is also known as '*yixi shizhong* [以西释中]', 'using the West to explain China' (Qiao 2014).

that 'represses' such 'democracy'. You cannot find what is not there, especially when you ignore the reality of a relatively mature socialist democracy (see Chapters 8 and 9).

Why do these perspectives remain influential in Western efforts to misrepresent China? After all, what counts as the 'West' is a relatively few countries—perhaps 12–15—that comprise only 14 percent of the global population. A major reason can be found in the fact that all of them are former colonisers and have through such colonial endeavours been able to assert a dominant discourse that arises from Western liberalism. Of course, this is a somewhat aberrant perspective in the world. As Igor Diakonoff was fond of pointing out, the historical development of the western peninsula of the Eurasian landmass is quite unlike other parts of the world and should certainly not be seen as a model (Diakonoff 2003, 157). For Chinese scholars, those who peddle Western perspectives and models fall into the trap of *yixi jiezhong*, seeking the understand China with Western eyes. To be sure, there are a few who seek to challenge such a framework in various ways, arguing that Western frameworks will always lead to mistakes when trying to understand China (Bell 2006; Jacques 2009; Guo B. 2018).[20] Agreed, but they tend to do so through a culturalist approach that posits an inherent cultural difference.

Let us go a step further and focus for a moment on Western Marxist scholars, some of whom I have already mentioned. In this case, Chinese scholars speak of *yixi jiema* (以西解马), using Western categories to understand Marx (Ren and Wang 2010, 104; Ren 2017, 67). Isn't this a step too far, since Marx was after all a German and thus a Western scholar and communist? The point is pertinent, since there seems to be an almost constitutive inability within Western Marxism to understand socialism with Chinese characteristics. Having spent more time I should have done in the various lanes and alleys of Western Marxism, I have found that a number of factors play a role. We have already met the liking for 'betrayal narratives', with many potential candidates all the way from Engels to Deng Xiaoping, as well as the inherent deployment of 'orientalist mystery'. But here I should also mention a 'holier than though' attitude to many parts of the world deemed 'inferior' and not living up to a supposed Western standard—an attitude that reveals Western Marxism's 'tailism' to Western imperialism and colonialism;[21] the deforming effect of utopian messianism, in which the possibility of socialism, let alone communism, becomes a hoped-for dream and is used as the basis for condemning actual proletarian revolutions and efforts to construct socialism (Losurdo 2008; 2017b); a reductionism that sees class struggle only in terms of bourgeoisie and proletariat, and thus fails to see that Marx and

[20] Chinese scholars tell me that even Daniel Bell and Martin Jacques—whose work is reasonably well-known—ultimately use a Western framework in their studies.

[21] Lenin deployed the term 'tailism' when he had to deal with those who argued that a Communist Party should not take the lead in any revolutionary activity but should 'tail behind'. A succinct expression of this Western attitude is from Terry Eagleton's late effort to reassert his Marxist credentials: 'Marx himself never imagined that socialism could be achieved in impoverished conditions. Such a project would require almost as bizarre a loop in time as inventing the Internet in the Middle Ages' (Eagleton 2011, 16).

Engels also included anti-colonial struggles for liberation, as well as the struggle for women's liberation, within the complexity of class struggle (Losurdo 2013, 2016); a capitulation to the dominance of 'centrist liberalism' (Wallerstein 2011), where Marxism becomes a 'liberal Marxism' that retreats to defending bourgeois parliamentary democracy as a means for accelerated reform (Engels already struggled with such a tendency in the 1890s); and an overwhelming tendency to focus on the period 'before October', before a proletarian revolution and to dismiss any development that has come after a successful revolution, all the way from Russia to China. The outcome is an approach that is empirically false, for it does not 'seek truth from facts' as one should when using a Marxist method, and methodologically highly problematic, as the observations above concerning betrayal narratives and conspiracy theories indicate. Constitutive failure to understand Chinese Marxism—the reasons should be obvious by now.[22] Indeed, many efforts to use Western Marxist assumptions to understand socialism with Chinese characteristics are not merely a cases of *yixi jiema* (using Western categories to understand Marx), but also *shiyang buhua* (食洋不化), eating foreign food without digesting it (Ren 2017, 67).[23]

1.5 Method

In light of all of the above, what is the method I use in this book?

Simply put, the method entails a careful reading of texts, both the primary (from Mao Zedong to Xi Jinping) and secondary works of Chinese Marxism in relation to socialism with Chinese characteristics. As is my wont, the references to such works are heavy in the work that follows. But I have found it necessary to provide such copious references so as to indicate how thorough this scholarship is, how it is based on in-depth empirical research, how much it has thought through the many problems faced in the construction of socialism in China, and how it provides the major way to understanding socialism with Chinese characteristics.

To get to such a point required much work. I began with a need to dismantle most of the assumptions I had gathered in my indoctrination into Western liberalism, which I imbibed almost from my first breaths and soaked in through formal education and cultural assumptions. This process was by no means easy, producing many moments

[22]One may ask: what about the 'Maoist Leftists [*maozuo*]' or 'Maoist sectarians [*maopai*]' in China? This a very small group who have adopted Western betrayal narratives and conspiracy theories in relation to Deng Xiaoping and the Reform and Opening-Up, and who in China are regarded as following a 'Left Deviation [*zuopai pianxiang*]' that attempts to pander to Western Marxist proclivities. An example is Jiang Hongsheng's doctoral thesis on the Shanghai Commune of 1967 and the way an octogenarian Western Maoist like Alain Badiou, who has never been to China, has promoted such a work (Jiang H. 2014; Badiou 2018).

[23]Or, as Ernst Bloch observed in a different context but with pertinence for today: 'Whereby such large sections of bourgeois erudition, without any concrete knowledge-relationship to the present, either confronted this latter epoch helplessly when it demanded decision, or, in recent times, sold themselves to anti-Bolshevism, over and above all class interests, with scandalous ignorance and lack of wisdom' (Bloch 1985, 331; 1995, 284).

of deconstruction and reconstruction, many 'aha' moments. It also entailed a removal of the assumptions of Western Marxism, where I had dwelt for too long (since my youth). This process began with my work on Lenin and especially Stalin (Boer 2013, 2017), during which I encountered a crucial distinction between 'before October' and 'after October'. The reference is, of course, to the October Revolution of 1917 in Russia, the first proletarian revolution in human history, which was able to seize and consolidate power by successfully seeing off the counter-revolution. The distinction itself became clear to me at a conference on Lenin, held in Wuhan in 2012. Half of the delegates were non-Chinese and mostly Western, and half of the delegates were Chinese. Soon enough, a difference in focus began to emerge: the Western delegates were primarily interested in the Lenin before October, before the revolution; the Chinese delegates were interested in the Lenin after October, when he began to deal with the early problems of socialist construction. Obviously, the contexts of the delegates influenced their perspectives, with the Western delegates coming from situations of seeking a revolutionary seizure of power, and the Chinese delegates from a situation where Communist power was well and truly secured. But it was more than that: it struck me that nearly everything changes when a Communist Party has gained power. Planning for and pulling off a successful revolution is the relatively easy part; setting out to construct socialism is exponentially more difficult and complicated. This is the overwhelming perspective of Chinese Marxism.

What remains after one has—as far as possible—dismantled unhelpful assumptions and frameworks of analysis, when one has 'washed' one's brain as Mao Zedong put it, or 'liberated thought' as Deng Xiaoping urged? The answer: a focus on the texts in question. Here I fall back to my most basic training in classical languages and textual analysis.[24] At this level, I have found an intersection with the Chinese concern with written texts, which go back more than 3000 years. But this method entails that one must study such texts in the languages in which they were written and passed down through the tradition. In light of this earlier training and its intersection with Chinese approaches, I have long maintained the absolute necessity of studying a distinct development of Marxism in the language in which it was written: primarily German and French for Marx and Engels, Russian for Lenin and Stalin, and of course Chinese for socialism with Chinese characteristics. Some people may pick up languages more quickly; not me. It requires disciplined daily work. Despite Mao Zedong's famous quip that 'the whole world must learn Chinese [*quan shijie bixu xuexi zhongwen*]', I have found the process of learning the Chinese language both arduous and rewarding. They say it takes about ten years of daily study and practice to become fluent. I can read and write very well, and my oral-aural skills draw ever closer to the point of fluency. Thus, the reader will find frequent references to Chinese terms and efforts to explain what they mean. I have read deeply in the Chinese texts of Mao Zedong, Deng Xiaoping, and Xi Jinping, and also of Jiang Zemin and Hu Jintao. I have also—as the references should show—read very many works of Chinese Marxist scholarship. There are so many, in fact, that I have had to

[24]These languages include Greek, Latin, and Hebrew, all of which I have taught in the past, along with a number of others for research purposes, such as Syriac, Aramaic, Coptic, and Sanskrit.

restrict myself mostly to sources that are are designated 'core [*hexin*]' sources and those listed on the Chinese Social Sciences Index (CSSCI).

Language is the best insight into a distinct culture. The adage may be old, but it is nonetheless very true. So also is living in the country in question, as I do.[25] This enables me to continue engaging with scholars, members of the CPC, and work in a School of Marxism Studies—the first non-Chinese national to do so. As my old mentor, Yang Huilin, once put it: visiting China from time to time is good, but if you really want to understand China, you need to live and work here. The observation by Shirokov and Iankovskii in relation to the Soviet Union is apt:

> Foreign workers arriving in the U.S.S.R., even in a first cursory inspection, can apprehend the general character of socialist construction. ... However, to obtain a real and fruitful understanding of the working of our institutions the foreigner must penetrate into the details, must understand the special task of each institution and learn the special difficulties of each part of our socialist construction. (Shirokov and Iankovskii 1937, 214)

In sum, this approach requires that one has big ears and a small mouth, is willing to listen, learn, and understand so to build trust. Only on this basis can you begin to engage in serious discussion and debate.

1.6 A Note on Sources

I have already mentioned that by far the majority of sources used in this study are Chinese language sources. I cite these sources following East Asian naming conventions, in which the family name precedes the personal name. However, there will a reasonable number of readers who are not able to read Chinese materials but who may be interested in reading further. Part of the process of cultural confidence and 'telling China's story well' has been an increasing number of sources published in English. To begin with, I recommend works published by Springer, such as its 'China Insights' series.[26] The works in this series are written by leading Chinese scholars on a range of key issues concerning China's socialist path.[27] There are also a number of journals that now publish materials in English, the oldest of which is *Social Sciences in China*. This journal publishes translations of articles from the Chinese language version, and a good number of the translated items concern aspects of Chinese Marxism and socialism with Chinese characteristics. I would also like to

---

[25]By contrast, compare a popular quip in China in relation to Western pundits: how does one become a 'China expert' or 'China hand [*Zhongguotong*]'? Do not speak Chinese. Do not live in or visit China. Do not speak with Chinese people. Be white and Western.

[26]These works are overseen by Springer's Beijing office, which has editorial autonomy in terms of deciding what to publish.

[27]In other cases, such as the Lexington series 'Challenges Facing China's Political Development', one has to be selective: some material is useful, while other material falls into the trap of *yixi jiezhong*. To be avoided are havens for liberal ideologues and 'China bashers' such as the 'Studies on Contemporary China' series with Oxford University Press and the 'Cambridge Modern China' series.

mention *Marxist Studies in China*, a print-only annual published by the Academy of Marxism within the Chinese Academy of Social Sciences. This journal publishes major selected texts by Chinese Marxist scholars. More recent is the journal *International Critical Thought*, edited by the Academy of Marxism but published in London. The focus here is on Marxism in many parts of the world, and it is establishing itself as the leading English language journal of research in Marxism. If one wants to keep up to date with the latest from the Central Committee of the CPC, then *Qiushi* (Seeking Truth) is the place to go. While primarily published in Chinese on a bi-monthly basis, it also has an English edition (http://en.qstheory.cn/).

To return to the primary Chinese sources: where possible, I cite a source that has been carefully verified by the relevant academic authorities. This is a very ancient Chinese approach and is apparent today in all manner of ways, but it contrasts with the Western theologically-inspired idea that an 'original' text is in some way more 'authentic'. The basis of this Western approach is, of course, analysis of the Bible, to which inordinate attention continues to be directed in order to ascertain what—for example—the 'authentic' words of Jesus of Nazareth might have been. In terms of a Chinese approach to texts, a good example concerns Mao Zedong. I cite works that have been published in the *Selected Works* (*xuanji*) and *Collected Works* (*wenji*), along with other smaller collections. I avoid material that has been published in the *Maozedong wansui* (*Mao Zedong Live Forever*) in five volumes. This material was published during the Cultural Revolution by the Red Guards, but it has neither place of publication nor editor listed. In short, it is an unreliable source that cannot be verified, so one should read this material with extreme caution. This reality has not prevented the incomplete series *The Writings of Mao Zedong 1949–1976* (M.E. Sharpe), as well as parts of the series *Mao's Road to Power* (M.E. Sharpe) and occasional one-volume collections, publishing translations of much of the material from the *Wansui*. Why? It is seen as in some way 'authentic', raw even, but also includes the old anti-communist and even Orientalist racist trope that the CPC seeks to 'conceal' and 'edit' texts to make them conform to ideological orthodoxy.[28]

I close on a slightly different note: when one reads the texts I have studied for this book, one will soon encounter a distinct liking for numbering points. The list is potentially endless: two whatevers, three don'ts (don't pick on others for their faults, don't put labels on people, and don't use a big stick), three benefits, four modernisations, four cardinal principles, two inevitabilities and two impossibilities, and so on. Why such a liking? One influence is the *Yijing*, or *Book of Changes*, with its complex numbering of all manner of phenomena. But this practice enables me to make a final point via Xi Jinping. In his study of historical materialism, he cites the 'two inevitabilities [*liangge biran*]' and the 'two impossibilities [*liangge juebuhui*]'. The first is from the 'Communist Manifesto': 'The fall [of the bourgeoisie] and

---

[28] A good example of such an assumption is the introduction by Stuart Schram to a collection drawn from the *Wansui* and published in English. Schram justifies the collection by observing that 'the real flesh-and-blood Mao revealed in these uncensored utterances, Rabelaisian in speech and forthright in his criticism both of himself and of others, is not only far more believable, but far more impressive, than the plaster saint worshipped by some of his self-appointed disciples' (Schram 1974, 8). I hardly need to point out the theological and Orientalist undertones of such a statement.

the victory of the proletariat are equally inevitable' (Marx and Engels 1848a, 474; 1848b, 496). The second is from Marx's preface to *A Contribution to a Critique of Political Economy* (1859): 'No social formation is ever destroyed before all the productive forces for which it is sufficient have been developed, and new superior relations of production never replace older ones before the material conditions for their existence have matured within the framework of the old society' (Marx 1859b, 101; 1859a, 263). For Xi Jinping, the two pairs 'help us understand why capitalism has not completely died, why socialism still has twists and turns like the disintegration of the Soviet Union and the upheavals in Eastern Europe, and why the communism foreseen by Marxism still needs a long historical development to come true'. In light of this situation, Marxist dialectical and historical materialism enables a sound understanding of historical development, thus strengthening confidence in the path, theory, and system of socialism with Chinese characteristics. The whole point of such an approach is to continue improving the development of China's productive forces and people's living standards, 'so that the advantages of the socialist system continue to be revealed and enriched, and the path of socialism with Chinese characteristics will become broader' (Xi 2020b, 4).

References

Badiou, Alain. 2018. *Petrograd, Shanghai: Les deux révolutions du XXe siècle.* Paris: Fabrique.

Beal, Tim. 2005. *North Korea: The struggle against American power*. London: Pluto.

Bell, Daniel. 2006. *Beyond liberal democracy: Political thinking for an East Asian context.* Princeton: Princeton University Press.

Bloch, Ernst. 1985. *Das Prinzip Hoffnung*. In *Ernst Bloch Werkausgabe*, vol. 5. Frankfurt am Main: Suhrkamp Verlag.

Bloch, Ernst. 1995. *The principle of hope.* Translated by Neville Plaice, Stephen Plaice, and Paul Knight. Cambridge: MIT Press.

Boer, Roland. 2013. *Lenin, religion, and theology*. New York: Palgrave Macmillan.

Boer, Roland. 2017. *Stalin: From theology to the philosophy of socialism in power*. Singapore: Springer.

Cai, Yongsheng. 2018. Lun dangdai Zhongguo xianhuo de makesizhuyi de hexin yaoyi—Xi Jinping xinshidai Zhongguo tese shehuizhuyi sixiang yanjiu. *Nanjing shida xuebao (shehui kexue ban)* 2018 (1): 5–12.

Chang, Gaixiang. 2018. Zhongguo tese shehuizhuyi zhexue de jiben tezheng. *Yan'an daxue xuebao (shehui kexue ban)* 40 (6): 11–20.

Chang, Gordon. 2001. *The coming collapse of China*. New York: Random House.

Chen, Baosheng. 2017a. Fahui gaoxiao youshi, jiakuai goujian Zhongguo tese zhexue shehui kexue. *Qiushi* 2017 (10): 9–11.

Chen, Baosheng. 2017b. Jiaoyubu buzhang Chen Baosheng jiedu 'Guanyu jiakuai goujian Zhongguo tese zhexue shehui kexue de yijian'. *Xinhua News*, 21 June 2017. http://www.xinhuanet.com/politics/2017-06/21/c_1121186838.htm.

Chen, Shuguang. 2018. Zhongguo makesizhuyi yanjiu 40 nian: 1978–2018. *Jiaoxue yu yanjiu* 2018 (10): 5–16.

Chen, Xixi. 2016. Guanyu fazhan 21 shiji makesizhuyi de ruogan sikao—xuexi Xi Jinping zongshuji zai zhexue shehui kexue gongzuo zuotanhui shang de jianghua. *Sixiang lilun jiaoyu* 2016 (8): 4–10.

Chen, Xueming, Ma Yongjun, Luo Qian, and Jiang Guomin. 2016. Makesizhuyi zhexue yanjiu 'xin qimeng' hue yu 'houxiandai' hua pipan. *Zongguo shehui kexue pingjia* 2016 (1): 4–17.
Chen, Yun. 1980. Jingji xingshi yu jingyan jiaoxun (1980.12.16). In *Chen Yun wenxuan*, vol. 3:276–282. Beijing: Renmin chubanshe, 1986.
CPC Central Committee. 2004a. *Zhonggong zhongyang guanyu jinyibu fanrong fazhan zhexue shehui kexue de yijian (2004.01.05)*. Beijing: Zhongguo gongchandang zhongyang weiyuanhui.
CPC Central Committee. 2004b. *Zhonggong zhongyang guanyu jinyibu jiaqiang he gaijin daxuesheng sixiang zhengzhi jiaoyu de yijian (2004.10.14)*. Beijing: Zhongguo gongchandang zhongyang weiyuanhui.
CPC Central Committee. 2017. *Guanyu jiakuai goujian Zhongguo tese zhexue shehui kexue de yijian (2017.05.16)*. Beijing: Zhongguo gongchandang zhongyang weiyuanhui.
Deng, Chundong. 2014. Work hard to construct a discourse system in philosophy and social sciences under the guidance of Marxism. *Marxist Studies in China* 2014: 68–81.
Deng, Xiaoping. 1980. Chuli xiongdi dang guanxi de yitiao zhongyao yuanze (1980.05.31). In *Deng Xiaoping wenxuan*, vol. 2:318–319. Beijing: Renmin chubanshe, 2008.
Deng, Xiaoping. 1988. Jiefang sixiang, duli sikao (1988.05.18). In *Deng Xiaoping wenxuan*, vol. 3:260–261. Beijing: Renmin chubanshe, 2008.
Diakonoff, Igor. 2003. *The paths of history*. Cambridge: Cambridge University Press.
Dickson, Bruce. 2003. *Red capitalists in China: The party, private entrepreneurs and prospects for political change*. Cambridge: Cambridge University Press.
Eagleton, Terry. 2011. *Why Marx was right*. New Haven: Yale University Press.
Engels, Friedrich. 1859a. Ka'er·makesi 'Zhengzhijingjixue pipan. Diyi fence'. In *Makesi Engesi wenji*, vol. 2:595–606. Beijing: Renmin chubanshe, 2009.
Engels, Friedrich. 1859b. Karl Marx, A contribution to the critique of political economy. In *Marx and Engels collected works*, vol. 16:465–477. Moscow: Progress Publishers, 1980.
Engels, Friedrich. 1859c. Karl Marx, 'Zur Kritik der politischen Ökonomie'. In *Marx Engels Werke*, vol. 13:468–477. Berlin: Dietz, 1974.
Engels, Friedrich. 1882a. Dialectics of nature. In *Marx and Engels collected works*, vol. 25:313–588. Moscow: Progress Publishers, 1987.
Engels, Friedrich. 1882b. Dialektik der Natur. In *Marx Engels Werke*, vol. 20:305–570. Berlin: Dietz, 1973.
Engels, Friedrich. 1882c. Ziran bianzhengfa (jiexuan). In *Makesi Engesi wenji*, vol. 9:399–563. Beijing: Renmin chubanshe, 2009.
Engels, Friedrich. 1892. Introduction to the English edition (1892) of 'socialism: Utopian and scientific'. In *Marx Engels Gesamtausgabe*, vol. I.32:109–128. Berlin: Akademie Verlag, 2010.
Engels, Friedrich. 1895a. Engels an Werner Sombart in Breslau, London, 11.März 1895. In *Marx Engels Werke*, vol. 39:427–429. Berlin: Dietz, 1973.
Engels, Friedrich. 1895b. Zhi Wei'erna·Sangbate, Buleisilao, 1895 nian 3 yue, 11 ri yu Lundun xibei qu. In *Makesi Engesi wenji*, vol. 10:689–692. Beijing: Renmin chubanshe, 2009.
Fewsmith, Joseph. 2008. *China since Tiananmen*, 2nd ed. Cambridge: Cambridge University Press.
Goldman, Merle, and Roderick MacFarquhar, red. 1999. *The paradox of China's post-Mao reforms*. Cambridge: Harvard University Press.
Griese, Anneliese. 1987. Parallelen und Wechselwirkungen in den naturwissenschaftlichen Studien von Marx und Engels in den siebziger und frühen achtziger Jahren. *Beiträge zur Marx-Engels-Forschung* 23 (4): 249–258.
Guo, Baogang. 2018. Sino-Western cognitive differences and Western liberal biases in Chinese political studies. In *Governance innovation and policy change: Recalibrations of Chinese politics under Xi Jinping*, ed. Nele Neosselt, 73–95. Lanham: Lexington Books.
Guo, Jieyu. 2017. Zhonggong zhongyang yinfa 'Guanyu jiakuai goujian Zhongguo tese zhexue shehui kexue de yijian' (2017.05.18). *Xinhua News*, 16 May 2017. http://www.xinhuanet.com/2017–05/16/c_1120982602.htm.
Harvey, David. 2005. *A brief history of neoliberalism*. Oxford: Oxford University Press.

Huang, Guangqiu. 2016. Makesi Engesi guanxi de 'tongyi' shuo—jiyu jingji jichu yu shangceng jianzhu sixiang fenxi. *Beifang luncong* 2016 (5): 160–164.

Huang, Guangqiu. 2017. Makesi, Engesi jingji jichu yu shangceng jianzhu sixiang bijiao—'tongyi' guanxi: 'jueding' neihan, 'tongchuang hubu' guocheng. *Shanxi daxue xuebao (zhexue shehui kexue ban)* 2017 (1): 39–47.

Huang, Yasheng. 2008. *Capitalism with Chinese characteristics: Entrepreneurship and the state*. Cambridge: Cambridge University Press.

Jacques, Martin. 2009. *When China rules the world: The rise of the middle kingdom and the end of the western world*. London: Allen Lane.

Jaioyubu. 2005. *Guanyu tiaozheng zengshe makesizhuyi lilun yiji xueke ji suoshi erji xueke de tongzhi (2005.12.23)*. Beijing: Zhongguo renmin gongheguo jiaoyubu.

Jiang, Hongsheng. 2014. *La Commune de Shanghai et la Commune de Paris*. Translated by Eric Hazan. Paris: Fabrique.

Jiang, Qian. 2016. Fazhan dangdai Zhongguo makesizhuyi zhengzhijingjixue de kexue zhinan—xuexi Xi Jinpng zongshuji zai zhexue shehui kexue gongzuo zuotanhui shang de zhongyao jianghua. *Lilun shiye* 2016 (8): 9–11.

Kangal, Kaan. 2020. *Friedrich Engels and the dialectics of nature*. Cham: Palgrave Macmillan (Springer).

Knight, Nick (ed.). 1990. *Mao Zedong on dialectical materialism: Writings on philosophy, 1937*. Armonk: M.E. Sharpe.

Knight, Nick. 2005. *Marxist philosophy in China: From Qu Qiubai to Mao Zedong, 1923–1945*. Dordrecht: Springer.

Knight, Nick. 2007. *Rethinking Mao: Explorations in Mao Zedong's thought*. Lanham: Lexington.

Lampton, David. 2014. *Following the leader: Ruling China, from Deng Xiaoping to Xi Jinping*. Berkeley: University of California Press.

Lei, Yuejie, and Zhang Xinfang. 2018. Xi Jinping xinwen yulun sixiang dui makesizhuyi xinwen guan de xin fazhan. *Qingnian jizhe* 2018 (7): 16–18.

Li, Minqi. 2008. *The rise of China and the demise of the capitalist world-economy*. London: Pluto.

Li, Minqi. 2016. *China and the twenty-first-century crisis*. London: Pluto.

Li, Xiaoxiao. 2018. Shijian weiwuzhuyi de xingqi yu gaige kaifang. *Xueshu yanjiu* 2018 (9): 8–13.

Liu, Yiqiang. 2015. Xi Jinping weishenme gaodu zhongshi makesizhuyi zhexue de xuexi he yunyong. *Dang de wenxian* 2015 (3): 34–38.

Losurdo, Domenico. 2008. Wie der 'westliche Marxismus' geboren wurde und gestorben ist. In *Die Lust am Widerspruch. Theorie der Dialektik—Dialektik der Theorie. Symposium aus Anlass des 80. Geburtstag von Hans Heinz Holz*, edited by Erich Hahn and Silvia Holz-Markun, 35–60. Berlin: Trafo.

Losurdo, Domenico. 2012. *Fuga dalla storia? La rivoluzione russa e la rivoluzione cinese oggi*. Napoli: La scuola di Pitagora editrice.

Losurdo, Domenico. 2013. *La lotta di classe: Una storia politica e filosofica*. Roma-Bari: Laterza.

Losurdo, Domenico. 2016. *Class struggle: A political and philosophical history*. New York: Palgrave Macmillan.

Losurdo, Domenico. 2017a. Has China turned to capitalism?—Reflections on the transition from capitalism to socialism. *International Critical Thought* 7 (1): 15–31.

Losurdo, Domenico. 2017b. *Il marxismo occidentale: Come nacque, come morì, come può rinascere*. Rome: Editori Laterza.

Mackerras, Colin. 2003. *China's ethnic minorities and globalisation*. London: RoutledgeCurzon.

Mackerras, Colin, and Nick Knight (eds.). 2015. *Marxism in Asia*. London: Routledge.

Mao, Zedong. 1938a. Lun xin jieduan (1938.10.12–14). In *Zhonggong zhongyang wenjian xuanji*, vol. 11:557–662. Beijing: Zhonggang zhongyang xuexiao chubanshe, 1991.

Mao, Zedong. 1938b. On the new stage (12–14 October, 1938). In *Mao's road to power: Revolutionary writings 1912–1949*, vol. 6:458–541. Armonk: M. E. Sharpe, 2004.

Mao, Zedong. 1941a. Gaizao women de xuexi (1941.05.19). In *Mao Zedong xuanji*, vol. 3:795–803. Beijing: Renmin chubanshe, 2009.

Mao, Zedong. 1941b. Preface and postscript to rural surveys (March and April, 1941). In *Selected works of Mao Tse-Tung*, vol. 3:11–16. Beijing: Foreign Languages Press, 1965.
Mao, Zedong. 1944. Tong Yinguo jizhe Sitanyin de tanhua (1944.07.14). In *Mao Zedong wenji*, vol. 3:182–194. Beijing: Renmin chubanshe, 1996.
Mao, Zedong. 1959. Du Sulian 'Zhengzhijingjixue jiaokeshu' de tanhua (1959.12–1960.02). In *Mao Zedong wenji*, vol. 8:103–148. Beijing: Renmin chubanshe, 2009.
Marx, Karl. 1852a. Der achtzehnte Brumaire des Louis Bonaparte. In *Marx Engels Gesamtausgabe*, vol. I.11:96–189. Berlin: Dietz, 1985.
Marx, Karl. 1852b. The Eighteenth Brumaire of Louis Bonaparte. In *Marx and Engels collected works*, vol. 11:99–197. Moscow: Progress Publishers, 1979.
Marx, Karl. 1859a. A contribution to the critique of political economy. In *Marx and Engels collected works*, vol. 29:257–417. Moscow: Progress Publishers, 1987.
Marx, Karl. 1859b. Zur Kritik der politischen Ökonomie. In *Marx Engels Gesamtausgabe*, vol. II.2:95–245. Berlin: Dietz, 1980.
Marx, Karl. 1880. Avant-propos. In *Marx Engels Gesamtausgabe*, vol. I.27:541–543. Berlin: Dietz, 1988.
Marx, Karl, and Friedrich Engels. 1848a. Manifest der Kommunistischen Partei. In *Marx Engels Werke*, vol. 4:459–493. Berlin: Dietz Verlag, 1974.
Marx, Karl, and Friedrich Engels. 1848b. The manifesto of the communist party. In *Marx and Engels collected works*, vol. 6:477–519. Moscow: Progress Publishers, 1976.
Mei, Rongzheng. 2018. Zai gaige kaifang zhong makesizhuyi lilun xueke de chuangjian he fazhan. *Makesizhuyi lilun xueke yanjiu* 2018 (5): 37–51.
Meisner, Maurice. 1996. *The Deng Xiaoping era: An inquiry into the fate of Chinese socialism, 1978–1994*. New York: Hill and Wang.
Mises, Ludwig von. 1932. *Socialism: An economic and sociological analysis*. Translated by J. Kahane. London: Jonathan Cape, 1936.
Peng, Shouqing. 2018. Xi Jinping xinshidai zhongguo tese shehuizhuyi jiaoyu sixiang de zhexue jichu. *Xinan daxue xuebao (shehui kexue ban)* 44 (1): 12–21.
Qi, Ruqiang. 2018. Xi Jinping lideshuren sixiang de lilun yuanyuan yu jingshen shizhi. *Makesizhuyu yanjiu* 2018 (7): 35–42.
Qi, Yiming. 2018. Cong makesizhuyi zhongguohua de san ge weidu kan Xi Jinping xinshidai zhongguo tese shehuizhuyi sixiang. *Dang de wenxian* 2018 (3): 9–14.
Qiao, Qingju. 2014. Zhongguo zhexue yanjiu fansi—chaoyue 'yixi shizhong'. *Zhongguo shehui kexue* 2014 (11): 43–62.
Read, James. 1976. *Atrocity propaganda, 1914–1919*. London: Ayer.
Ren, Ping. 2017. Dangdai Zhongguo makesizhuyi zhexue chuangxin fanshi tupu. *Zhongguo shehui kexue* 2017 (1): 63–82.
Ren, Ping, and Wang Jianming. 2010. Lun chayixing shehui yu Zhongguo tese shehuizhuyi minzhu zhengzhi de weilai. *Makesizhuyi yanjiu* 2010 (5): 102–110.
Sautman, Barry. 1998. Preferential policies for ethnic minorities in China: The case of Xinjiang. *Nationalism and Ethnic Politics* 4 (1–2): 86–118.
Sautman, Barry. 2006. Colonialism, genocide, and Tibet. *Asian Ethnicity* 7 (3): 243–265.
Sautman, Barry. 2010. 'Vegetarian between meals': The Dalai Lama, war, and violence. *Positions* 18 (1): 89–143.
Schram, Stuart. 1974. Introduction. In *Chairman Mao talks to the people: Talks and letters: 1956–1971*, ed. Stuart Schram, 7–48. New York: Pantheon.
Shirokov, I., and R. Iankovskii, (eds.). 1937. *A textbook of Marxist philosophy*. London: Victor Gollancz.
Stanley, John. 1989. The Marxism of Marx's doctoral dissertation. *Journal of the History of Philosophy* 33 (1): 133–158.
Tong, Bing. 2016. Cong fanchou renzhi shenhua makesizhuyi xinwenguan yanjiu—dui Xi Jinping guanyu xinwen yulun, wangluo chuanbo he zhexue shehui kexue gongzuo jianghua tichu de shi duo fanchou de sikao. *Xinwen daxue* 2016 (5): 17–24, 146.

Tsang, Eileen Yuk-Ha. 2014. *The new middle class in China: Consumption, politics and the market economy*. Houndmills: Palgrave Macmillan.

Vogel, Ezra. 2011. *Deng Xiaoping and the transformation of China*. Cambridge: Harvard University Press.

Wallerstein, Immanuel. 2011. *The modern world-system IV: Centrist liberalism triumphant, 1789–1914*. Berkeley: University of California Press.

Walter, Carl, and Fraser Howie. 2011. *Red capitalism: The fragile financial foundation of China's extraordinary rise*. Singapore: John Wiley & Sons.

Wang, Haifeng. 2018. Dangdai Zhongguo makesizhuyi zhexue de xianshixing pingge—gaige kaifang 40 nianlai makesizhuyi zhexue yanjiu de fansi. *Zhexue dongtai* 2018 (10): 22–30.

Wang, Nanshi. 2018. Gaige kaifang 40 nian Zhongguo makesizhuyi fazhan lilu zhi zai jianshi. *Shehui kexue zhanxian* 2018 (11): 14–23.

Wang, Wei. 2015. Fanshi zhuanxing yu huayu zhuanhuan—gaige kaifang yilai Zhongguo makesizhuyi zhexue de huigu yu zhanwang. *Shanghai shifan daxue xuebao (zhexue shehui kexue ban)* 44 (5): 30–37.

Wang, Weiguang. 2017. Jiakuai goujian Zhongguo tese zhexue shehui kexue xueke tixi, xueshu tixi, huayu tixi—Zhongguo shekeyuan yuanzhang Wang Weiguang jiedu 'Juakuai goujian Zhongguo tese zhexue shehui kexue de yijian'. *Xinhua News*, 25. maj 2017. http://www.xinhuanet.com/politics/2017-05/25/c_1121036878.htm.

Weil, Robert. 1996. *Red cat, white cat*. New York: Monthly Review Press.

Xi, Jinping. 2011. Zhongguo gongchandang 90 nianlai zhidao sixiang he jiben lilun de yushijujin ji lishi qishi—zai jinian Zhongguo gongchandang chengli 90 zhounian dangjian yantaohui shang de jianghua (2011.06.20). *Dangjian yanjiu* 2011 (7): 16–21.

Xi, Jinping. 2013a. Haobu dongyao jianchi he fazhan Zhongguo tese shehuizhuyi (2013.01.05). In *Tan zhiguolizheng*, vol. 1:21–24. Beijing: Waiwen chubanshe, 2014.

Xi, Jinping. 2013b. Yikao xuexi zouxiang weilai (2013.03.01). In *Tan zhiguolizheng*, vol. 1:401–408. Beijing: Waiwen chubanshe, 2014.

Xi, Jinping. 2013c. *Zai jinian Mao Zedong tongzhi danchen 120 zhounian zuotanhui shang de jianghua (2013.12.26)*. Beijing: Renmin chubanshe.

Xi, Jinping. 2016a. Jiakuai jianshe shijie yiliu daxue he yiliu xueke (2016.12.07). In *Tan zhiguolizheng*, vol. 2:376–380. Beijing: Waiwen chubanshe, 2017.

Xi, Jinping. 2016b. Tigao dang de xinwen yulun chuanboli yindaoli yingxiangli gongxinli (2016.02.19). In *Tan zhiguolizheng*, vol. 2:331–334. Beijing: Waiwen chubanshe, 2017.

Xi, Jinping. 2016c. *Zai zhexue shehui kexue zuotanhui shang de jianghua (2016.05.17)*. Beijing: Renmin chubanshe.

Xi, Jinping. 2018. Zai Beijing daxue shisheng zuotanhui shang de jianghua (2018.05.02). *Guangming ribao*, 2018.

Xi, Jinping. 2019a. Bianzheng weiwuzhuyi shi Zhongguo gongchandangren de shijieguan he fangfalun. *Qiushi* 2019 (1): 1–3.

Xi, Jinping. 2019b. Guanyu jianchi he fazhan Zhongguo tese shehuizhuyi de jige wenti. *Qiushi* 2019 (7): 1–4.

Xi, Jinping. 2020a. Buduan kaituo dangdai makesizhuyi zhengzhijingjixue xin jingjie. *Qiushi* 2020 (16): 1–6.

Xi, Jinping. 2020b. Jianchi lishi weiwuzhuyi buduan kaipi dangdai Zhongguo makesizhuyi fazhan xin jingjie (2020.01.15). *Qiushi* 2020 (2): 1–5.

Xu, Chongwen. 2010. Certain questions on how to understand the Chinese model. *Marxist Studies in China* 2010: 153–165.

Xuanchuanbu he jiaoyubu. 2005. *Guanyu jiaqiang he gaijin gaodeng xuexiao zhexue shehui kexue xueke tixi yu jiaocai tixi jianshe de yijian (2005.05.08)*. Beijing: Zhongguo renmin gongheguo jiaoyubu.

Yang, Jinhai. 2016. Yong makesizhuyi zhidao zhexue shehui kexue fazhan de fangfalun sikao—xuexi Xi Jinping zongshuji zai zhexue shehui kexue gongzuo xuotanhui shang jianghua jingshen de jidian tihui. *Sixiang lilun jiaoyu* 2016 (7): 4–11.

Yang, Mingwei. 2016. 'Ba makesizhuyi zhexue zuowei kanjia benling'—Xi Jinping tan xuexi he yunyong makesizhuyi zhexue de ji ceng yiyun. *Dang de wenxian* 2016 (6): 42–49.

Yu, Yongcheng, and He Lai. 2018. Gaige kaifang 40 nianlai makesizhuyi zhexue yanjiu de huigu yu zhanwang. *Guangdong shehui kexue* 2018 (4): 5–16.

Zhang, Lei, and Li Cheng. 2018. Xinshidai makesizhuyi xinwen guan de zuixin fazhan—lun Xi Jinping winwen sixiang dui makesizhuyi xinwen guan de xin gongxian. *Xinwen yu chuanbo yanjiu* 2018 (7): 5–12.

Zhao, Yue. 2016. Makesizhuyi zhexue yu Deguo gudian zhexue guanxi de 'Engesishi chanshi'—chongdu 'Ludeweixi·fei'erbaha he Deguo gudian zhexue de zhongjie'. *Makesizhuyi zhexue luncong* 2016 (4): 184–196.

Zheng, Keyang. 2008. Zou Zhongguo tese shehuizhuyi yao jingto xin ziyouzhuyi, minzhu shehuizhuyi, yu lishi xuwuzhuyi san gu sichao. *Zhengzhixue yanjiu* 2008 (1): 8–11.

Zhu, Jiamu. 2016. Advancing the construction of the discourse system of Marxist theory of historiography with Chinese characteristics in the struggle with historical nihilism. *Marxist Studies in China* 2016: 18–52.

Chapter 2
Reading Deng Xiaoping

> Revolutionary spirit is a treasure beyond price. Without it there would be no revolutionary action. But revolution takes place on the basis of the need for material benefit. It would be idealism to emphasise the spirit of sacrifice to the neglect of material benefit. (Deng 1978f, 146; 1978b, 156)

Deng Xiaoping Theory (*lilun*) is a major key to understanding socialism with Chinese characteristics. However, much like Engels in relation to Marx, Deng's distinct contributions are often overshadowed by those of Mao Zedong. Or at least this is true outside China. One may find a stray quotation from Deng, usually taken out of context and twisted to say what it does not mean,[1] or one may find more or less useful biographies, histories, and political assessments (following Western models) of his all-important leadership and legacy (Goodman 1994; Shambaugh 1995; Vogel 2011; Pantsov and Levine 2015),[2] but one struggles to find outside China a careful consideration of his thought.[3] Part of the reason is that Deng was eminently a man of action rather than words. Many of his texts are short, drawn from observations and speeches. Occasionally, he penned a longer piece for a speech at a congress. This is not to say that Deng did not think. While he preferred to get down to work rather than sit and read heavy tomes of Marxist theory and write long

---

[1]A good example is the 'white cat, black cat' saying, which is often taken as an expression of 'pragmatism', or given even more sinister connotations. The original text, which concerns strategies for reviving agriculture, indicates nothing of the sort: 'When talking about fighting battles, Comrade Liu Bocheng often quotes a Sichuan proverb—"It does not matter if it is a yellow cat or a black cat, as long as it catches mice it is a good cat"' (Deng 1962c, 323). The point: taking advantage of given conditions in battle and at times coming up with unconventional methods should also be used in agriculture. See also the discussion of 'crossing the river by feeling the stones' in the Introduction.

[2]Of these studies, Vogel's is the most useful and detailed, although he pays scant attention to Deng's Marxist credentials. The most comprehensive account of Deng Xiaoping life is the multi-volume collection, *A Chronology of Deng Xiaoping: 1975–1997* (Zhonggong zhongyang wenxian yanjiushi 2004, 2009).

[3]Occasionally, one finds a non-Chinese writer admitting that they ignore Deng's texts due to the wayward 'reason' that they were produced collectively or have been 'doctored' by later editors of his published works (Whyte 1995, 107).

R. Boer, *Socialism with Chinese Characteristics*,
https://doi.org/10.1007/978-981-16-1622-8_2

screeds of his own,[4] he did take time to think through and discuss matters. This was particularly the case with the time of banishment to Nanchang, during the tumultuous years from 1969 to 1974. With a quiet rhythm of factory labour, reading and keeping up with events, Deng was able to consider the disastrous developments of the Cultural Revolution and what needed to be done (Vogel 2011, 51–57). When he shared these thoughts, he did so with close comrades and—later—in concise speeches that reflected the need to seek solutions to concrete problems, to 'seek truth from facts'. One simply cannot disconnect his thoughts from action, developing policies on the basis of actual situations. The disadvantage is that one must work harder to identify the philosophical basis of his thought. But the philosophy is there, permeating his published texts as a type of 'applied philosophy [*yingyong zhexue*]' (Pan and Yang 1999, 30; Yong 2004, 3).[5] Deng was through and through a Marxist, and the tradition—Marxism-Leninism and Mao Zedong Thought—was the horizon of his thought and action.[6]

The following focuses on what is regarded in China as the foundation of Deng Xiaoping Theory: liberating thought (*jiefang sixiang*) and seeking truth from facts (*shishiqiushi*), articulated above all in a key speech delivered at the beginning of the Reform and Opening-Up (Deng 1978f, 1978b).[7] The speech was seen at the time as a clap of 'spring thunder [*chunlei*]' (Cai and Pan 2008, 188), waking people from their ideological torpor and promising the nourishing rains of spring, especially after the chaotic aberration of the 'Cultural Revolution'. The topics that arise from the speech run like a 'red line [*hongxian*]' throughout Deng's works (Pan and Xu 2003, 49), so they determine the structure of what follows: liberation of thought from its enslavement, liberation for socialism (in terms of the correct theoretical line), the

[4]Deng was characteristically self-deprecating in a late comment: 'Practice is the sole criterion for testing truth. I haven't read too many books, but there is one thing I believe in: Chairman Mao's principle of seeking truth from facts' (Deng 1992b, 382; 1992a, 370). As Zhou Yinzu observes, Deng's approach may be described in terms of 'three positive emphases and four negative emphases', that is, 'to speak frankly [*zhiyan buhui*], to solve problems, and to speak purely scientifically [*kexue tilian*]; no talking at length, no empty words, no formulaic language [*taohua*], and no big words' (Zhou Y. 1997, 119).

[5]Thus, it erroneous to hypothesise that Deng dispensed with 'ideology' and took a 'pragmatic' approach, or indeed that he had no theoretical content for his policies (Pye 1995, 24; Chang 1988, 9–10). As Vogel observes: 'Some Westerners were so impressed with Deng's directness and pragmatism that they mistakenly thought he was a capitalist at heart and that he would lead China toward a Western-style democracy. He was always ready to learn, but in the end he believed he knew better than they what was good for China and it was not capitalism and Western-style democracy' (Vogel 2011, 5).

[6]We should always remember the fact that—despite suggestions to the contrary—Mao never personally called Deng a 'capitalist roader'. Although Mao spoke often during the Cultural Revolution of those in authority within the party who sought to 'walk down the capitalist road [*zou zibenzhuyi daolu*]'—a term that would be shortened to '*zouzipai*' and is usually translated as 'capitalist roader'—Mao never used the term to speak of Deng Xiaoping. Instead, Mao continually protected his old comrade, and it was others who spoke of Deng in such a manner in the late 1960s. During the tumultuous events of 1976, when Zhou Enlai and Mao died and when popular support was shifting decisively to Deng, the Gang of Four sought to designate Deng as a 'capitalist roader'.

[7]For an overview of the background leading up to the speech, see Wang D. and Han (2008, 10–11).

healthy exercise of democratic centralism, seeking truth from facts as an inescapable dimension of liberating thought, and the close connection with liberating the forces of production.[8]

2.1 Liberating Thought (*jiefang sixiang*)

Liberate thought, emancipate the mind, use one's brains—Deng Xiaoping uses various expressions to emphasise this central idea, which I will analyse in some detail. In his key speech from 1978 on this topic, Deng implicitly distinguishes between liberation *from* and liberation *for*.

2.1.1 Liberation From

Deng identifies four reasons why people have stopped using their brains, and then three outcomes.[9] The four reasons: (1) ideological taboos leading to 'blind faith'; (2) over-centralisation and the undermining of democratic centralism; (3) a distortion of right and wrong through a false or 'phony [*jia*]' Marxism so that people lost their bearings and stopped thinking; (4) force of habit of small production, with the suggestion of a resort to much older feudal practices of small peasant production, following old conventions and unwilling to accept anything new.

The immediate context is a need to come to terms with the disruptive deviation of the Cultural Revolution (Liu T. 1999, 21–22). While the 'Gang of Four [*sirenbang*]'—a term coined by Mao[10]—bears a good deal of the blame, especially in the last few years as Mao's health deteriorated and he retreated even more, Mao himself is not without blame.[11] As Deng puts it a little later, the Cultural Revolution witnessed an emergence of feudal, patriarchal practices in Mao's later years (Deng 1980c, 347; 1980b, 344–345). I will have more to say below concerning Deng's effort to recover the line Mao took before his later years, so let us consider the three outcomes, which have a direct bearing on liberating thought since these outcomes led people to stop using their brains, asking questions, and innovating.

---

[8]Not unexpectedly, the research in China on Deng Xiaoping Theory's philosophical foundations is immense, but one may usefully consult a number of comprehensive surveys (Wang D. and Cheng 2002; Ma J. and Tan 2004).

[9]This section is relatively brief, since I am more interested in the substantive contributions that are to come.

[10]At a Politburo meeting on 17 July, 1974, Mao warned Jiang Qing, Wang Hongwen, Zhang Chunqiao and Yao Wenyuan that they should not act like a 'Gang of Four'. The term and the association with dangerous Leftism would stick (Vogel 2011, 82).

[11]The best account is a candid interview on such matters with the Italian journalist Oriana Fallaci (Deng 1980c, 1980b).

To begin with, people had begun to act according rules and regulations, veering with the wind, and book worship.[12] 'Rules and regulations [*tiaotiao kuangkuang*]' is a pejorative term, with the sense of outmoded conventions, restrictions, and taboos. In other words, one is encircled (*kuang*) by regulations (*tiao*). Further, 'bending with the wind' comes comes from a popular saying: 'grass on top of a wall sways this way and that with the wind [*qiangtoucao, sui feng dao*]'.[13] The point is that grass on top of a wall has little soil for its roots. A tuft may find some nourishment, but it is unable to grow deep roots and so it sways this way and that way, depending on the direction of the wind. Finally, the criticism of 'book worship [*benbenzhuyi*]' is an old theme that we find consistently in Mao's works as well (see more below on 'truth from facts'). The problem is not careful study as such, but that it is does not proceed from actual conditions (*bu cong shiji chufa*). The focus here is not so much the tradition of formulaic Chinese scholarship (the proverbial 'eight-legged essay'), but more dogmatic Marxists who rely exclusively on what is said in the works of the founders, official documents or leader's statements.[14] The twist here is that despite Mao's warnings, his own works became the subject of such book worship. As Deng observes a little later: 'even if we paid constant lip-service [*koutou shang dajiang yonghu*] to Mao Zedong Thought, we would actually be going against it' (Deng 1978j, 118; 1978g, 129).

In sum, the immediate problem was coming to terms with the disruptive deviation of the Cultural Revolution, which had the consequence that thought was captured and not free. Indeed, Deng addresses the question directly a little later in the speech, insisting on thorough historical and scientific analysis. Significantly, Comrade Mao was 'not without shortcomings [*quedian*] or mistakes [*cuowu*]', for to 'demand' such of a revolutionary leader would be inconsistent with Marxism (Deng 1978f, 148–149; 1978b, 158; see also CPC Central Committee 1981, 9). Thus Mao's many

---

[12]Each begins with the phrase, *sixiang yijianghua*, where *jiang* refers to what is stiff and motionless, and thus what is ossified and stereotyped.

[13]*Sui feng dao* is literally to turn upside down (*dao*) or be inverted by the direction of the wind.

[14]One is reminded here of a parable told by Stalin (1926b, 93–94; 1926a, 97–98): 'It was at the time of the sailors' and soldiers' revolt in the Crimea. Representatives of the navy and army came to the Social-Democrats and said: "For some years past you have been calling on us to revolt against tsarism. Well, we are now convinced that you are right, and we sailors and soldiers have made up our minds to revolt and now we have come to you for advice." The Social-Democrats became flurried and replied that they couldn't decide the question of a revolt without a special conference. The sailors intimated that there was no time to lose, that everything was ready, and that if they did not get a straight answer from the Social-Democrats, and if the Social-Democrats did not take over the direction of the revolt, the whole thing might collapse. The sailors and soldiers went away pending instructions, and the Social-Democrats called a conference to discuss the matter. They took the first volume of *Capital*, they took the second volume of *Capital*, and then they took the third volume of *Capital*, looking for some instruction about the Crimea, about Sevastopol, about a revolt in the Crimea. But they could not find a single, literally not a single instruction in all three volumes of *Capital* either about Sevastopol, or about the Crimea, or about a sailors' and soldiers' revolt. They turned over the pages of other works of Marx and Engels, looking for instructions—but not a single instruction could they find. What was to be done? Meanwhile the sailors had come expecting an answer. Well, the Social-Democrats had to confess that under the circumstances they were unable to give the sailors and soldiers any instructions. And so … the sailors' and soldiers' revolt collapsed'.

achievement are indispensable and primary: his role in establishing the CPC, leading the long revolutionary struggle towards Liberation and the New China, and providing the foundations in terms of Mao Zedong Thought. His mistakes, especially in his later years, were secondary. But to assess these mistakes properly, one needs sober historical and scientific study, which takes time.[15]

2.1.2 Liberation For

After identifying what thought should be liberated *from*, Deng shifts to devote most of his attention to liberating thought *for* the socialist project, for human liberation (Tong 2017, 59–60). Deng's main points may be summarised as follows: (1) liberating thought is the correct ideological line; (2) it requires a healthy exercise of socialist democracy, both political and economic; (3) it is the basis of the proletarian world outlook and is embodied in seeking truth from facts; (4) in providing the impetus to innovation, to generating new ideas and new ways, it entails a dialectical transformation of liberating the forces of production and economic planning.

Each of these points entails a contradiction, which should be approached from the perspective of the contradiction analysis that I will examine in detail in the next chapter. For our present purposes, the following points are pertinent: each contradiction contains an opposition that is also complementary; while contradictions under a capitalist system are antagonistic and lead eventually to revolution, under socialism contradictions should be non-antagonistic; any situation has multiple contradictions and their relations to one another constantly change in light of changing circumstances, so one always needs to assess the situation carefully and scientifically so as to be able to manage these contradictions. Let us see how Deng deals with the contradictions embodied in each of the points summarised above (see also Xiang 2009, 38–44).

The first contradiction: liberating thought is all about the correct 'line of thought' or 'theoretical line [*sixiang luxian*]'. To quote Deng: the 'debate about the criterion for testing truth is really a debate about the theoretical line [*sixiang luxian*], about politics, about the future and the destiny of our Party and nation' (Deng 1978f, 143; 1978b, 153).[16] Obviously, we are far from any Western liberal free-for-all, a thought-for-thought's sake that is supposedly free from any ideological interference (except the ideology of liberalism itself). Instead, for Deng liberating thought is at one and

[15]Later assessment has made it clear that the Cultural Revolution was a potential collapse and defeat of the revolutionary path, which at the last moment was averted. It was a glimpse into the chaos of an abyss—a 'bitter struggle in the dark'—that had been China's reality for decades leading up to 1949.

[16]Or, Deng he puts it slightly later: 'What does liberating thought mean? It means that, guided by Marxism, we should break the fetters of habit, subjectivism and prejudice, and study new situations and solve new problems. In liberating thought, we should never deviate from the Four Cardinal Principles or impair the political situation marked by stability, unity and liveliness' (Deng 1980i, 279; 1980a, 278).

the same time the correct theoretical line, particularly if we keep in mind that the line in question is the living tradition of Marxism-Leninism and Mao Zedong Thought (Chen H. 2001, 63).[17] We may understand this approach in terms of three related aspects: (a) the very definition of the tradition is to liberate thought, for it is a living tradition rather than one ossified and dogmatically fixed on texts of the past; (b) one can liberate thinking only on the basis of Marxist-Leninism; (c) only through liberating thought can this tradition, this theoretical line develop even further. New problems demand new solutions, which Marx and Engels, and indeed Lenin and Stalin, did not experience and could not foresee. It is not for nothing that liberating thought is primary: 'When it comes to liberating thought, using our heads, seeking truth from facts and uniting as one in looking to the future, in the first place [*shouxian*] is liberating thought' (Deng 1978f, 141).

A specific and sharp example may help in understanding this contradiction: Deng's invocation of the Yan'an Rectification Movement of 1942–1945. As Deng writes, 'Comrade Mao Zedong said this time and again [*fanfu*] during the rectification movements [*zhengfeng yundong*]' (Deng 1978f, 143; 1978b, 153; see also Zhou E. 1963a, 407; 1963b, 427). Said what? Mao too urged repeatedly (1942g, 1942f, 1942b, 1942d) the danger of ossified thinking and book-worship, observing at one point: 'a prerequisite for maintaining close links with the masses and making fewer mistakes is to examine one's baggage, to get rid of it, and to emancipate one's spirit [*ziji de jingshen huode de jiefang*]' (Mao 1944b, 947; 1944a, 173). The anticipation of liberating thought should be obvious, although Mao uses *jingshen*, spirit or vital energy, rather than thought (*sixiang*). Let me put it even more sharply: liberating thought requires periodic rectification. Without such exercises, the correct line of thought risks being lost and thus the opportunity to liberate thought also risks being lost. In light of my earlier observations on the need to deal with the Cultural Revolution, the invocation of Mao's rectification campaigns is yet another effort to connect with Mao (and indeed the Marxist-Leninist theoretical line) before the deviation of the Cultural Revolution. In other words, Deng argues strongly that he is continuing the correct line that runs not only from Mao before his deviation, but also from Marx, Engels, Lenin and Stalin. And it is precisely this line, this tradition, which requires periodic rectification and even purging so as to provide the foundation for and foster liberated thinking, which in turn becomes the primary means for enabling the line to continue on its creative path.

The second contradiction concerns socialist democracy, which is embodied in the term 'democratic centralism [*minzhujizhongzhi*]'. Earlier, I mentioned briefly that one of the problems during the Cultural Revolution had been a breakdown of democratic centralism, in which a turn towards greater centralism—of a patriarchal and feudal nature (Deng 1980c, 347; 1980b, 344–345)—had undermined centralism itself through the waning of democracy and the reluctance of people to speak for

[17] See also: 'it is necessary to liberate thought, that is, to study new situations and solve new problems by applying the basic tenets of Marxism-Leninism and Mao Zedong Thought' (Deng 1979b, 179; 1979h, 187).

fear of offending the leadership.[18] As in the political sphere, so also in the economic, where economic management was 'over-concentrated [*guoyu jizhong*]' (Deng 1978f, 145).

Since I will discuss the history of democratic centralism in Chapter 9 Sect. (9.2.2, 9.3.3; 9.5.3 and 9.6), I focus here on Deng's constructive proposals for democratic centralism. In the speech under consideration he makes a number points, each of which may seem somewhat lapidary on the surface but actually has significant implications: (a) an over-emphasis on centralism requires a correction in the direction of greater democracy; (b) on economic democracy, greater decision making powers, and thus innovation, should be devolved to enterprises, provinces, and counties; (c) greater scope should be given for elections, management, and supervision by workers, which would lead to greater responsibility; (d) a comprehensive legal system should be developed that enshrines democratic realities and responsibilities.

To begin with, the correction towards greater democratic involvement may, on a cursory reading, suggest a 'golden mean' in which one searches for a reasonable balance between two poles of a contradiction. Not so, for Deng points out that centralism is not strengthened but weakened without a healthy dose of democracy. Therefore, 'we must exercise democracy to the full so as to enable proper centralism' (Deng 1978f, 143).[19] Obviously, we are in the territory of contradiction analysis, where the one strengthens the other by its full exercise. A little later, Deng would—again invoking Mao—elaborate on the contradictory unity of democratic centralism: 'We practise democratic centralism, which is the integration of centralism based on democracy with democracy under the guidance of centralism'. While this integral element of the socialist system focuses on the collective and the greater socialist good, it entails a unity of contradictions, a 'unity of personal interests and collective interests, of the interests of the part and those of the whole, and of immediate and long-term interests' (Deng 1979b, 175–176; 1979h, 183).

Further, the emphasis on economic democracy, on the household responsibility system (*lianchandaohu*), and on creative decision making at different levels (see also Deng 1979a, 195, 197; 1979e, 202–203; 1980i, 280; 1980a, 278–279),[20] should be seen in light of the interactions between the two components, or institutional forms, of market and planned economies in a socialist system (see Chapter 5). Here the key is that while a planned economy may give greater scope for centralised planning, a market economy has a greater tendency to foster decentralised initiative.

As for elections and responsibility, we now broach the fascinating development of non-politicised elections, which I will analyse further in the chapter on socialist democracy. By 'non-politicised' elections—a concept that derives from Marx and

[18] We already see Deng's wariness of this tendency in the rather different situation of the early 1940s (Deng 1941a, 8–11; 1941b, 21–23).

[19] This was by no means the first time Deng had emphasised the dialectical nature of democratic centralism. For example, in 1962 he observed: 'without democracy, there can be no centralism, and centralism cannot be truly or correctly realised unless it is based on democracy' (Deng 1962b, 304; 1962a, 300).

[20] For a comprehensive earlier analysis of the need for and workings of economic democracy in stimulating innovation, see Song (1999, 4–8).

Engels (Boer In press)—is meant the fact that elections are not the manifestation of class conflict in antagonistic political parties, but are based on qualifications, expertise, and merit for positions. Finally, there is the matter of a legal framework, concerning which the deeper issue is captured in Deng's observation that formerly 'what leaders say is taken as the law and anyone who disagrees is called a law-breaker'. Such a 'law changes whenever a leader's views change' (Deng 1978f, 146; 1978b, 156). The response: socialist democracy is unthinkable without a socialist legal system (Deng 1980f, 359; 1980h, 355). Here Deng is anticipating the whole development of a socialist rule of law (*fazhi*—法治), which—again—I will discuss in detail later. The key opposite term is 'rule of a human being [*renzhi*]', in which the will of the leader becomes law and which had once again come to the fore during the Cultural Revolution and by this caused untold havoc. Hence the urging for developing a comprehensive legal system.

We have reached an inflexion point: thus far, I have dealt with two features of Deng's crucial speech on liberating thought, focusing on the contradictions of liberating thought as the correct theoretical line, and the exercise of (economic and political) democracy as the means to strengthen democratic centralism. On the way, I have flagged items that will be developed further in subsequent chapters, especially since Deng in many ways set the agenda for what was to come in the development of the Reform and Opening-Up. Two topics from the speech on liberating thought remain to be analysed: seeking truth from facts, and liberating the forces of production.

2.2 Seek Truth from Facts (*shishiqiushi*)

The third contradiction brings us to truth from facts. This is an ancient[21] four-character phrase that deploys three homonymic characters. *Shíshì* (实事)[22] refers to what is an actual happening, a fact, but the word also includes the senses of action and what is practical. *Qiúshì* (求是) joins the character for 'seek', *qiú (求)* with another *shì* (是), now with the meaning of what is and so what is true. Thus, one must seek truth from actual conditions, what is actually taking place, from—as a breakthrough article in *Guangming Daily* (Hu 1978) put it—social practice.[23] Let me pause for a moment to emphasise this point: truth from facts is not a version of vulgar empiricism, in which scientific investigation must seek to conform with material reality; instead, the facts in question concern social practice (*shehui shijian*)

[21]The phrase goes back 2000 years to the Han Dynasty, although there it is more of scholarly approach (Yuan 2000, 18; Gao and Zhang 2013, 108; Li 2015, 50).

[22]I have added tone markers to indicate how the characters sound.

[23]The article was originally published anonymously ('a special commentator') and went through many revisions in order to ensure maximum impact. Later revealed to have been written by Hu Fuming, it was written as a direct challenge to the 'two whatevers'. Deng refers to the article on a number of occasions as having 'settled the question' (Deng 1978f, 152; 1978b, 152–153; 1979d, 190–191; 1979g, 197–198; 1980j, 244; 1980o, 245–246; see also Yang C. 2008, 4–5).

in all its complexity and contradictions (Chen Xixi 2008, 4). This specific concern should be kept in mind in the following elaboration.

Although the centrality of 'truth from facts' is usually attributed to Deng Xiaoping, it actually goes back to Mao Zedong, who first wrote it down while lecturing in Yan'an during the immensely creative period in the second half of the 1930s (Deng 1977a, 67; 1977d, 80; see also 1977g, 45; 1977c, 58; Li 2015, 51). In his published texts, Mao referred to this principle not infrequently, although the focus tended to be on 'a "seeking-truth-from-facts" work style' (Deng 1962b, 299; 1962a, 296). To quote Mao: 'To take such an attitude is to seek truth from facts'. In more detail, '"Facts" are all the things that exist objectively, "truth" means their internal relations, that is, the laws governing them, and "to seek" means to study' (Mao 1941a, 801; 1941c, 22; see also 1937d, 296; 1937c, 308; 1940b, 662–663; 1940a, 339; 1942a, 836, 1942e, 58). Again and again, we find an emphasis on the style of commendable Party work by cadres: hard work and plain living, upright and honest in word and deed, able to co-operate with others and resist undesirable practices, acting boldly and resolutely in an experienced and professional manner, integrating theory with practice, and seeking truth from facts through close contact with the masses (Li 2015, 50–51). This is, as Deng points out, the 'Party spirit' (Deng 1977h, 75; 1977e, 88),[24] so much so that it continues today to embody what it means to be a comrade, a member of the Communist Party.[25]

However, in the late 1970s there was a distinct shift, when truth from facts was raised from being a feature of a cadre's work-style to a central principle of not only the Reform and Opening-Up, but also the Chinese spirit (*jingshen*) and of Marxism-Leninism itself (Yuan 2000, 21–22). The moment that marks the shift was a speech at an all-army conference on political work, on 2 June, 1978 (six months before the important speech on liberating thought).[26] Here, Deng (1978j, 113–118; 1978g, 124–129) elaborates precisely on what is meant by truth from facts, and he does so by digging deep into Mao Zedong's earlier material.[27] In a slightly later

[24]As Mao puts it already in 1941, 'seeking truth from facts and closely combining theory with practice is the basic attitude of a Party member with a strong Party spirit [*dangxing*]' (Mao 1941e, 361; see also 1942c, 458, 1950, 57).

[25]This emphasis appears throughout Deng Xiaoping's texts (Deng 1950a, 170; 1950b, 173; 1956a, 247; 1956b, 248; 1961c, 287–288; 1961a, 284–285; 1961d, 293–295; 1961b, 291–292; 1962b, 298, 302, 304, 315; 1962a, 295, 298, 300, 310; 1978i, 106; 1978h, 117; 1978j, 124; 1978g, 134–135; 1979b, 159, 162; 1979h, 169, 172).

[26]See the later recap, in a discussion with Kim Il Sung, of the process—not without opposition and some struggle—of the promotion of seeking truth from facts and liberating thought (Deng 1982c, 9–10; 1982b, 20–21).

[27]The texts by Mao Zedong that are cited and discussed are, from 1929 to 1958: 'Draft Resolution of the Ninth Congress of the Communist Party in the Fourth Red Army'; 'Oppose Book Worship'; 'Problems of Strategy in China's Revolutionary War'; 'On Practice'; 'On Contradiction'; 'Preface and Postscript to *Rural Surveys*'; 'Reform Our Study'; 'Rectify the Party's Style of Work'; 'Oppose Stereotyped Party Writing'; 'Combat Bourgeois Ideas in the Party'; 'Strengthen Party Unity and Carry Forward Party Traditions'; 'Sixty Articles on Working Methods (Draft)' (Mao 1929b, 1929a, 1930a, 1930b,1936b, 1936a, 1937d, 1937c, 1937a, 1937b, 1941b, 1941c, 1941a, 1941d, 1942g, 1942f, 1942a,1942e, 1953b, 1953a, 1956f, 1956e, 1958a, 1958b).

speech, Deng provides specific historical examples of how Mao applied truth from facts, whether changing tactics to encircle the cities from the countryside (following Lenin's principle of the weakest link in a different context), or shifting from a struggle against imperialism, colonialism, and racism, to focusing on peaceful coexistence and working with other countries to ensure peace, or the change in focus from class struggle as the key to liberating the forces of production (Deng 1978c, 1978d).

A major reason for engaging so extensively with Mao's writings and his actual practice was a struggle over the legacy of Mao Zedong Thought (Yang S. 2004). Would it be letter or spirit? Would it be the 'two whatevers [*liang ge fanshi*]', as in 'we will resolutely uphold whatever policy decisions Chairman Mao made, and unswervingly follow whatever instructions Chairman Mao gave'.[28] For Deng and others this was a betrayal of Mao, as of Marxism as a whole: 'Neither Marx nor Engels put forward any "whatever" doctrine, nor did Lenin or Stalin, nor did Comrade Mao Zedong himself' (Deng 1977b, 38; 1977f, 51).[29] Instead, the key is seeking truth from facts, for Marxism is not a dogma, as Engels already observed, but a guide to action (Engels 1886a, 578; 1886b, 531–532; 1895a, 428; 1895b, 461). Only in this way is one able to restore the 'original features [*benlai mianmu*] of Mao Zedong Thought' (Deng 1979b, 165; 1979h, 175; see also 1979d, 190; 1979g, 197; 1987c, 253–254; 1987b, 249–250). So what is the relationship between Mao Zedong Thought and the Maoism of the Cultural Revolution? Mao Zedong Thought, up until the late 1950s, was a genuine development of the Marxist-Leninist tradition, but the Cultural Revolution and its attendant 'Maoism' was a deviation into 'phony' Marxism that was not really Marxism at all (Fu 2004, 5–7). Or, as the resolution on historical issues from the Sixth Plenary of the Eleventh CPC Central Committee put it, the 'Left' deviation of the Cultural Revolution 'clearly deviated from the track of Mao Zedong Thought, understood as a combination of the general principles of Marxism-Leninism and the concrete practice of the Chinese revolution'. Thus, the Cultural Revolution 'must be completely distinguished from Mao Zedong Thought' (CPC Central Committee 1981, 7).

What, then, is 'Western Maoism'—which captured a number on the European Left in the 1960s and 1970s—in light of the clarification outlined here? It is a curious amalgam of various bits and pieces of Mao's thought, from both Mao Zedong Thought and the Maoism of the Cultural Revolution, and then reframed in terms of the utopian tendencies inherent in Western Marxism. Crucially, it errs by postulating a continuity from Mao Zedong Thought to the Maoism of the Cultural Revolution, a continuity that can only be maintained by 'cherry-picking' items from Mao's thought and fitting them into such a narrative. Obviously, a full analysis of Mao's texts cannot sustain

[28]The 'two whatevers' were proposed in an editorial entitled 'Study the Documents Well and Grasp the Key Link'. It appeared simultaneously on 7 February, 1977, in three newspapers: *Renmin Ribao, Hongqi* and *Jiefangjun Bao*. It may be found at www.wendangku.net/doc/bd9fab3f27284b73f2425 0fc.html.

[29]The struggle to assert truth from facts against those who promoted the 'two whatevers' in the wake of the Cultural Revolution is discussed in some detail by Yang (2008, 4–6).

such a narrative.[30] It follows that Deng Xiaoping's recovery of Mao Zedong Thought was actually a recovery of the Marxist-Leninist line (Yu 1995; Wang W. 2014, 15–16).

As for Deng's own argument, there are a number of layers. The first is the point that socialism is also a scientific endeavour. It is nothing less than scientific socialism, as first formulated by Engels (1880b, 1880a). Thorough investigation of the data, formulation of a theoretical framework in response, and then further investigation. Nothing remarkable here, one might think: does not all modern science operate in the same way? The answer is yes and no, for everything turns—and this is the second layer—on the theoretical framework one uses to interpret the scientific data, and indeed on how the framework is transformed in the process (Chen Xixi 2008, 5–6).[31] For Engels, Lenin, Stalin, Mao, and Deng, the framework is of course Marxism.[32] As for the third layer, the method entails a constant dialectical interaction between facts and truth, between data and theory, between practice and philosophy—in short, dialectical materialism (Weng 1999, 30–31; Rao 2011, 8–9). The 'integration [*xiang jiehe*] of theory with practice' entails that the theories developed in order to solve problems should be 'tested by being applied in social practice', even to the extent that instructions from higher units—up to the Central Committee—should be integrated with 'actual conditions' (Deng 1978j, 116–118; 1978g, 127–128). In sum, this is a process of 'proceeding from reality and of integrating theory with practice in order to sum up past experience, analyse the new historical conditions, raise new problems, set new tasks and lay down new guidelines' (Deng 1978j, 118; 1978g, 128–129).

A further level entails inveighing—as did Mao (1930a, 1930b)—against the constant danger of 'book worship [*benbenzhuyi*]', which in another parlance may be called 'Marxology'. The image of those who are fond of trotting out selected texts from Marx, Engels, or even Mao himself instead of actually engaging in some serious investigation of the situation in question may seem like a caricature, but let us pause for a moment and ask: how often does a 'Western' Marxist like to cite Marx's euphoric description of the Paris commune and use it to judge the supposed 'failures' of Russian, Chinese, Vietnamese, or North Korean socialism? Not only is this habit selective and ignorant of Engels's important contribution (in which the commune is equated with the hard edge of the proletarian dictatorship), and not only is it made by those with no concrete experience in the arduous task of constructing socialism, but it so often falls into the utopian and well-nigh messianic tenor of 'Western'

---

[30] A good example is the way Mao put aside or forgot his emphasis on non-antagonistic contradictions under socialism (up to the late 1950s) and emphasised antagonistic class struggle as the key during the Cultural Revolution.

[31] This question also applies to what facts are important in the framework of social practice. In Deng Xiaoping's texts, we find the following: the mass line (Deng 1977g, 45; 1977c, 58), dealing with a comrade's mistakes (Deng 1980i, 274; 1980a, 273–274), even Mao's mistakes, although they are secondary to his major contributions (Deng 1980e, 292, 301; 1980m, 291, 300; 1980c, 347; 1980b, 344–345; 1980f, 365–366; 1980h, 360–361; CPC Central Committee 1981, 12), the realities of the capitalist systems of Hong Kong and Taiwan in formulating the one country-two systems approach (Deng 1984d, 101; 1984b, 107), and, most commonly, China's specific conditions as a whole.

[32] By now it should be obvious that the charge of unreconstructed empiricism, occasionally directed at Mao Zedong at least, is unfounded (Bulkeley 1977; Womack 1982, 32, 77; see the reply by Knight 1990, 24–30).

Marxism (Losurdo 2017). For those who would peremptorily dismiss China's effort at constructing socialism, Deng's invocation to seek truth from facts has a distinct pertinence. Or, as Mao put it in 1930: 'no investigation, no right to speak' (Mao 1930a, 109).

The final level of Deng's extended treatment is embodied best in Mao's observation: 'Our party has a tradition of seeking truth from facts, which is to combine the universal truth of Marxism-Leninism with China's reality' (Mao 1961, 237; see also 1940b, 662–663; 1955, 498; 1960).[33] In other words, truth from facts is a basic tenet of socialism with Chinese characteristics, if not its very embodiment (Ma S. 2000). To add to my observations in the Introduction: if one investigates the specific facts of a situation and seeks to develop an approach that is sensitive to these conditions and their history, then one has an approach—Marxism—that has specific characteristics. This is an obvious instance of materialist dialectics, but it needs to be asserted in light of the many mystifications surrounding socialism with Chinese characteristics. But does this approach mean we have merely an 'application' of Marxism? Not at all, for truth from facts is 'the basis [*jichu*] of the proletarian world outlook [*wuchan jieji shijieguan*] as well as the theoretical basis [*sixiang jichu*] of Marxism' (Deng 1978f, 143; 1978b, 153).[34] It is the point of departure (*chufadian*), the most fundamental point (*genbendian*), the basic component (*jiben zuchengbufen*), and what summarises (*gaikuo*) Marxism itself and thus Mao Zedong Thought.[35]

We come at last to the core of the contradiction in question: if seeking truth from facts means to integrate theory with reality, then liberating thought entails ensuring that thought conforms with reality. Some may ask: how can integrating theory with reality mean the liberation of thought? It sounds like another way of restraining thought: instead of being tied to dogmatism and book worship, it is now bound to reality, to facts. Not only is such an objection framed by an idealist and individualist approach, but it also misses the crucial point: thought needs to be liberated *from* dogmatism and *for* creative engagements with factual reality.

By now it should be obvious that the separation of liberating thought and truth from facts into two parts is actually somewhat artificial, for Deng is always keen stress their close interconnection. As Wang and Cheng (2002, 45) put it: 'Comparatively speaking, "emancipating the mind" emphasises human subjectivity, while "seeking truth from facts" includes human subjectivity while emphasising the objectivity of the world'. Deng may have said that liberating thought is 'primary [*shouxian*]', but he also connects it closely with seeking truth from facts. For example, in the quotation with I began the analysis of liberating thought, Deng says: 'Only if we liberate thought, seek truth from facts, proceed from reality [*shiji*] in everything and integrate [*lianxi*] theory with reality [*shiji*]…'. Three of the four phrases concern

[33] Or, as Deng puts it: 'What is the ideological line? To adhere to Marxism and to integrate it with Chinese realities—in other words, to seek truth from facts, as advocated by Comrade Mao Zedong, and to uphold his basic ideas' (Deng 1984c, 62; 1984a, 72).

[34] Already in 1956 Deng observed: 'To proceed from reality and seek truth from facts is our fundamental stand as materialists' (Deng 1956a, 243; 1956b, 244).

[35] These terms appear throughout Deng's texts (Deng 1978j, 114; 1978g, 126; 1980i, 278; 1980a, 277).

what is actually happening, reality and practice (*shiji* can mean both). This intimate connection is expressed even more clearly in another text:

> Liberating thought means making our thinking conform [*xiangfuhe*] to reality – making the subjective [*zhuguan*] conform to the objective [*keguan*] – and that means seeking truth from facts. Henceforth, if in all our work we want to seek truth from facts, we must continue to liberate thought. (Deng 1980f, 364; 1980h, 359)

The real problem, then, is to be locked into old ways, old dogmatisms developed under different circumstances. One might study carefully—always a useful undertaking—the texts of Marx and Engels, or indeed Lenin, Stalin, and Mao, but the risk is that one takes them as iron-clad prescriptions or models for all situations (Liu P. 2004, 35). Deng's point here is that such an approach is actually a betrayal of Marxism, for the key is the method itself rather than the specific results arising from the method in specific situations. Marx and Engels sought to analyse the situation in Europe of the second half of the nineteenth century, while Lenin and Stalin did so in Russia (and then the Soviet Union) in the first half of the twentieth century. Mao's extensive writings responded to and analysed the situation in China in the early to mid-twentieth century, while Deng Xiaoping faced new challenges as the overwhelmingly planned economy ran into contradictions (Weng 1999, 28). On the way, all of them developed not only solutions to specific problems, but did so by deploying an increasingly robust method that may be described as the dialectical and historical materialist approach of seeking truth from facts.

2.3 Liberating the Forces of Production (*jiefang shengchanli*)

In elaborating on the final contradiction—between planned and market economies—let me begin with the following quotation from another text by Deng:

> Not liberating thought is out of the question, even to the extent of including the question of what socialism is also requires the liberation of thought. If the economy remains stagnant for a long period of time, it cannot be called socialism. If the people's living standards remain at a very low level for a long period of time, it cannot be called socialism. (Deng 1980n, 312)[36]

I have begun with this quotation, since it makes clear the connection between liberating thought and liberating the forces of production, and thus the whole process

[36]My translation. See also: 'Liberating thought should be accompanied by really solving problems … We don't yet have many comrades who carefully study fresh situations and solve fresh problems and who really use their minds to think out ways of accelerating our advance, the development of the productive forces and the rise in national income or of improving the work of the leading bodies' (Deng 1980i, 279–280; 1980a, 278). Note also that once thought is liberated, 'only then can we … fruitfully reform those aspects of the relations of production and of the superstructure that do not correspond with the rapid development of our productive forces, and chart the specific course and formulate the specific policies, methods and measures needed to achieve the four modernisations under our actual conditions' (Deng 1978f, 140–141; 1978b, 151).

of the Reform and Opening-Up (Xiao and He 1999, 13–14; Wang Yingzi and Ma 2005, 13; Cai and Pan 2008, 191). I will elaborate on the nature of the socialist market economy in Chapter 5, so here I will emphasise specific features of Deng's approach in terms of liberating the forces of production. On this matter, we really should begin with a text from the 'Communist Manifesto', which I have occasion to revisit later in this book: 'The proletariat will use its political supremacy to wrest, by degrees, all capital from the bourgeoisie, to centralise all instruments of production in the hands of the State, i.e., of the proletariat organised as the ruling class; and *to increase the total of productive forces [Produktionskräfte] as rapidly as possible*' (Marx and Engels 1848a, 481; 1848b, 504).[37] I have italicised the last part of the sentence for obvious reasons.

There are two ways we may understand this sentence, one philosophical and the other historical. Philosophically, the relation between the two terms—ownership of the means of production and liberating the forces of production—should be seen in a dialectical manner. Indeed, if we take a comparative Marxist approach, then we may understand how different emphases arise. Thus, in parts of the world where productive forces are already quite developed, there is a tendency to focus on ownership, even to the point of insisting that such ownership is the very definition of socialism. By contrast, in other under-developed parts of the world—where successful proletarian revolutions have actually taken place—the emphasis usually shifts to liberating productive forces so as to lift people out of poverty and improve socio-economic well-being. The risk here, however, is to emphasise such liberation too much and lose sight of common ownership.

Historically, the relation between ownership and liberation of productive forces can be analysed in light of successful proletarian revolutions and the subsequent efforts to construct socialism. As mentioned, these realities took place in countries that were quite undeveloped, from Russia to China. In these contexts, the prior realities of bourgeois and landlord ownership of the means of production meant the primary task for a Communist Party in power has been to expropriate such owners and claim the means of production for workers (both rural and urban). This measure was also necessary in order to deal with the inevitable counter-revolution, and it enabled an economic surge in all countries that began the process of constructing socialism. However, the risk even in such places was to focus too much on the realm of the relations of production, on ownership of productive forces. This imbalance inevitably led to new contradictions between the forces and relations of production,

[37]Note also: 'The productive forces of society [*gesellschaftlichen Produktivkräfte*], which have outgrown the control of the bourgeoisie, are only waiting for the associated proletariat to take possession of them in order to bring about a state of things in which every member of society will be enabled to participate not only in production but also in the distribution and administration of social wealth, and which so increases [*steigert*] the productive forces of society [*gesellschaftlichen Produktivkräfte*] and their yield by planned operation of the whole of production that the satisfaction of all reasonable needs will be assured to everyone in an ever-increasing measure' (Engels 1877a, 109; 1877b, 193).

with stagnating economic initiative and lack of improvement (Deng 1982a, 16; 1985a, 148; Wang Yunjing and Yang 1994, 105).[38]

So Deng's emphasis was resolutely on the other—often neglected—side, on the forces of production.[39] Socialism is all about the liberation of the forces of production: 'The development of the productive forces... is the most fundamental [*zui genben*] revolution from the viewpoint of historical development' (Deng 1980n, 311; 1980p, 310; see also Cao 1998). There is no point to 'poor socialism'; socialism means nothing if it does not liberate the forces of production, stimulate the economy and the improve the living standards of all people. Later, on his famous 'Southern Tour' of 1992, Deng defined socialism in terms of what are now called the 'three benefits': 'whether it is conducive to the development of the productive forces of a socialist society, to the enhancement of the comprehensive national strength of a socialist country, and to the improvement of people's living standards' (Deng 1992b, 372).[40]

Obviously, this emphasis requires a distinct liberation of thought, a freeing of the mind from past dogmatisms so as to bring about a redefinition of socialism. Or, rather, it requires a recovery of an oft-forgotten feature of the Marxist tradition, which assumes that material productivity is the basis of all social and spiritual life. It remains to see to how this re-emphasis entails a contradiction. It does so at two levels. The first is between the forces and relations of production. In response to efforts in the early stages of socialist construction in the Soviet Union and Eastern Europe to suggest that the contradiction had been overcome and that socialism was all about the relations of production and ownership, which could determine economic development, Stalin (1952b, 1952a) argued that the contradictions between forces and relations of production continue under socialism (see also Mao 1957a, 214; 1957b, 393). Should one dimension outpace the other, economic policy required an adjustment in favour of the laggard (Weng 1999, 31–33; Xie 2008, 32). In China too, the problem had been an over-emphasis on the relations of production, which initially through a fully planned economy enabled an economic boost, but it had by the 1970s begun to stifle economic improvement. Hence Deng's emphasis on liberating the forces of production and on the 'three benefits'.

This liberation was achieved through a socialist market economy, which will be discussed in detail in Chapter 5. The point to be made here is that planned and market economies—as components or institutional forms (*tizhi*) of an overall socialist system (*zhidu*)—do not cancel each other out in a Chinese context, for both enable

---

[38] The foundations for Deng's practical efforts to stabilise the situation—from government, through the military, to civilian enterprises—were already laid during 1974–1975, when Mao had called him back to do precisely that (Vogel 2011, 94–114).

[39] We do find this emphasis from time to time in Mao's works (Mao 1945a, 1079; 1945b, 301; 1956c, 1–2; 1956d, 17–18). But note Deng's observation that Mao 'made the grave mistake of neglecting the development of the productive forces. I do not mean he didn't want to develop them. The point is, not all of the methods he used were correct' (Deng 1985c, 116).

[40] My translation. Deng's effort (1978e, 1978a) to define socialism in light of China's current conditions also acknowledged the importance of the definition first developed in the Soviet Union: from each according to ability, to each according to work (Boer 2017). Communism would then entail to each according to need.

the liberation of productive forces (Jiang 1992, 22; Song 1999, 2). How is this possible? Do not planned and market economies negate one another? This may be the assumption of Western liberalism, and indeed the Western Marxists who follow in its wake, but in doing so they share the view of the godfather of neo-liberalism, Count Ludwig von Mises (1932, 142): 'the alternative is still either Socialism or a market economy'. But not in Chinese Marxism, and certainly not in the theory and practice of Deng Xiaoping, or indeed in the further developments that followed in his wake. It is not a case of either-or, as is the tendency in the Western tradition, but both-and: 'things that contradict each other also complement one another [*xiangfan-xiangcheng*]'. Planning has by no means disappeared with the socialist market economy, but has achieved a whole new level of complexity and flexibility (Heilman and Melton 2013).

With this observation in mind, we may understand the emphasis on planning in the final section of Deng's speech on liberating thought. Deng introduces this material with the observation: 'In order to look forward, we must study the new situation and tackle the new problems in good time; otherwise, there can be no smooth progress'. He goes on: 'In three fields especially, the new situation and new problems demand attention: methods of management, structure of management, and economic policy' (Deng 1978f, 149; 1978b, 159). In what follows this quotation, we find an emphasis on overcoming bureaucratism in management methods, on strengthening the work responsibility system by not relying (and here he quotes Lenin) on collegiate excuses[41] but on rewards and penalties, and on a deliberate policy of uneven development, in which some regions would experience the benefits of liberating productive forces so as to provide role models for others.

Can one emphasise the liberation of productive forces too much? Yes indeed. As the Reform and Opening-Up unfolded, there emerged precisely such an over-emphasis on liberating productive forces at the expense of common ownership. This was particularly the case in the 'wild 90s', which I will analyse in greater detail in Chapter 4 Sect. (4.3.3). New problems, new contradictions arose, which are much-studied and well-known: decline in working conditions and absence of social security and health care; the gap between the Communist Party and the people, leading to corruption and loss of trust and thus legitimacy; environmental pollution; a rising gap between rich and poor. In other words, new contradictions had arisen between the forces and relations of production, requiring new solutions. I will examine these solutions in later chapters in terms of 'deepening reform' as a dialectical way of overcoming problems produced through reform, in terms of the drive to a moderately well-off (*xiaokang*) society in all respects, or indeed in terms of the new primary contradiction identified in 2017 as that between unbalanced and uneven development and the people's desire for a better life (*meihao shenghuo*). However, in terms of this treatment of Deng Xiaoping, it is notable that we find in the last decade or more a renewed emphasis on justice and equality, and especially the need to ensure that public ownership is the core and mainstay of China's economic system (Xi 2020, 4).

[41]Or indeed on the incentive-destroying 'iron rice bowl' or, in Chinese parlance, 'eating from the same big pot' (see the chapter on the Reform and Opening-Up).

2.4 Conclusion: Laying the Foundations for Communism

> We have advocated Marxism all our lives. Actually, Marxism is not abstruse. It is a plain thing, a very plain truth. (Deng 1992b, 382; 1992a, 370)

To sum up: liberating thought is both a liberation from book-worship, the whim of the leader, distortions of right and wrong, and liberation for socialism, which entails an extraordinary concern with innovation for the sake of socialist construction (Chen Xiaoming and Zhou 2000, 10–11). It also a thorough example of implicit contradiction analysis, in which liberating thought is the correct theoretical line, the manifestation of a healthy democratic centralism, seeking truth from facts as the basis of a proletarian world outlook and the Marxist method, and the liberation of productive forces in relation to ownership of such forces. Deng Xiaoping would return to the core theme of liberating thought on many occasions, whether in terms of education, writing and artistic production, rural policy, party and state leadership, and liberation from 'right', 'left' and 'feudal' straight-jackets (Deng 1977a, 67, 71, 1977d, 80, 84; 1979j, 208, 213; 1979f, 214, 218; 1980g, 316; 1980k, 315; 1980d, 326, 336; 1980l, 325, 334; 1980f, 355, 357; 1980h, 352, 353; 1981a, 379; 1981b, 373).

Let me close with a consideration of three topics: Chinese characteristics; the heresy of poor socialism; and Deng's relation to the Marxist tradition. Deng is of course well-known for popularising the phrase 'socialism with Chinese characteristics', although—as we have seen in the Introduction—it has its seeds in Mao Zedong (Mao 1938a, 657–659; 1938b, 537–539; 1945a, 1093–1094; 1945b, 314; 1956a, 42; 1956b, 304). To repeat my earlier point in regard to this very straightforward idea: Marxism has a universal method and principles, but it can become concrete only by taking into account the specific conditions, the particular history, culture, and social conditions. As Deng observes, in 'building socialism, each country should adopt policies commensurate with its particular conditions [*ziji de tedian*]' (Deng 1980n, 313; 1980p, 312; see also 1978j, 113; 1978g, 125). There is nothing mysterious about this approach: it applies as much to the developments of Marxism in Russia,[42] Latin America, Eastern and Western Europe, as it does to China. One cannot apply a template that may have worked elsewhere (most notably the Soviet Union) to quite distinct conditions. An obvious point, for Marxism always takes into account the specific conditions in which it takes root. This is precisely the meaning of 'truth from facts' (Tong 2017, 62–63).

Further, Deng Xiaoping was resolutely opposed to the idea of 'poor socialism' or 'poor communism'. In the more immediate context, this was the standpoint promoted by the Gang of Four (*sirenbang*), that poor socialism was better than rich capitalism. But the idea has a much longer history: in Western Europe, this was ascetic communism, with a distinctly feudal and Christian dimension, against which Marx and Engels already set themselves (Marx and Engels 1848a, 483–484; 1848b, 508;

---

[42]Deng makes precisely this point in his observations on Lenin and Russian Marxism (Deng 1983a, 1983b; see also Chen Z. 2012, 96–98).

Engels 1880b, 553; 1880a, 287). In China, with its distinct cultural history, this type of 'poor socialism' took a different path, but Deng found it absolutely unacceptable, especially for a country had already experienced more than enough poverty (Yong 2004). In his eyes, no-one would be satisfied with socialism if it entailed grinding poverty.[43] Such a situation would not be socialism at all, which is concerned with improving the material and spiritual lives of the vast majority, the rural and urban workers. Deng was very clear: 'we do not want capitalism, but neither do we want to be poor under socialism [*pinqiong de shehuizhuyi*]'. Even more: 'What we want is socialism in which the productive forces are developed and the country is prosperous and powerful' (Deng 1979c, 231; 1979i, 235; see also 1980n, 310; 1980p, 310–311; 1985c, 116; 1985b, 122; 1987c, 254; 1987b, 250). Most fully:

> There cannot be poor communism, nor can there be poor socialism. So to get rich [*zhifu*] is no sin. However, what we mean by getting rich is different from what you [the interviewer] mean. Wealth [*caifu*] in a socialist society belongs to the people. To get rich [*zhifu*] in a socialist society means common prosperity [*gongtong zhifu*] for the entire people. The principles of socialism are: first, development of production and second, common prosperity [*gongtong zhifu*]. (Deng 1986a, 172)

A few themes emerge from Deng's many criticisms of poor socialism and his proposal of the alternative, a strong socialistically modernised country. The begin with, he continuously emphasised the need to show the superiority of socialism over capitalism. A socialist system's superiority is predicated on its ability to improve the lives of the common people, rather than the relatively few under a capitalist system (Deng 1984c, 64–65; 1984a, 73–74). Deng held a long-term view of this process, which would certainly take much, much longer than his eventful lifetime. On this matter, Deng drew from the experience of the Soviet Union: by the 1930s it had become clear that the initial struggles—against counter-revolution and internal capitalist elements, for the sake of establishing a socialist economic and political system—were beginning to bear fruit. The upshot was that one could begin to see the contours of a second stage of socialism (Stalin 1939a, 335–336; 1939b, 420–421). This insight was developed from the basis of Lenin's distinction—when exegeting Marx's 'Critique of the Gotha Program'—between the stages of socialism and communism (Lenin 1917a, 1917b; Marx 1875b, 1875a). In China, by the late 1980s it had become clear that the effects of the Reform and Opening-Up were increasingly widespread, but in contrast to the Soviet Union it was agreed that—due to the very low socio-economic level—China was still in the primary or 'preliminary stage [*chuji jieduan*]' of socialism (Zhao 1987, 2–4). In discussing preparations for the Thirteenth National Congress of the CPC, Deng Xiaoping penned a piece in which he discussed changes in the countryside in terms of the household responsibility system, along with observations on the political system. He concluded: 'The Thirteenth National Party Congress will explain what stage China is in: the primary

[43] In a major speech on the four cardinal principles, Deng makes it clear that the poverty being experienced in China in the late 1970s was not due to the socialist system, but to the lingering effects of the pre-Liberation history of imperialism and feudalism (Deng 1979b, 166–167; 1979h, 176).

stage of socialism. Socialism itself is the first stage of communism, and here in China we are still in the primary stage [*chuji jieduan*] of socialism—that is, the underdeveloped stage'. This meant that in 'everything we do we must proceed from this reality, and all planning must be consistent with it' (Deng 1987d, 252; 1987a, 248). This has been the emphasis ever since, with a much greater wariness in proclaiming a second stage. Thus, Xi Jinping has emphasised time and again that China is still very much in this preliminary stage of socialism (Xi 2017, 5; 2019, 1–2; see further Dong and Wu 2011; Chen Xueming 2015, 9–10; Fang 2015, 15).

Why the wariness? A major reason is the awareness that the attainment of communism requires a very high socio-economic level. Before then, the task of constructing socialism is long and arduous, with more than one stage.[44] Let me put it this way: if communism entails the principle of 'from each according to ability, to each according to needs', then one requires the necessary socio-economic conditions for such an eventuality. In China, the reality was that the proletarian revolution took place in a country that was extremely undeveloped and exceedingly poor. In this context, 'poor socialism' was certainly no answer. Thus, 'in building socialism we must do all we can to develop the productive forces and gradually eliminate poverty, constantly raising the people's living standards'. Only when this outcome is achieved and there is significant prosperity for all will it become possible to begin the shift to communism: in the 'advanced stage of communism, when the economy is highly developed and there is overwhelming material abundance, we shall be able to apply the principle of from each according to his ability, to each according to his needs' (Deng 1982c, 10–11; 1982b, 21).[45] The point is clear: the dual liberation—of thought and the forces of production—is a necessary, albeit not exclusive, feature of the socialist stage that seeks to lay the foundations for communism (Cao 1998, 17; Wang Yuyao 1995, 50).

The final question concerns Deng Xiaoping's relation to the Marxist tradition. Already there have been enough indicators that Deng was clearly continuing the tradition: the Reform and Opening-Up was certainly not a path to a capitalist system, but rather through socialism to communism; Marxism entails not merely the lifelong study of writings by the founders, but is above all a guide to action, premised on seeking truth from facts; Mao Zedong Thought—as a continuation of Marxism-Leninism—needs to be upheld while also identifying the mistakes Mao made (and the attendant Maoism) in the 1960s and 1970s; one must always maintain the correct theoretical line, for this line is the only way to liberate thought and constantly renew the tradition. But I would like to draw on an intriguing piece from 1989, entitled 'Let Us Put the Past Behind Us and Open a New Era' (Deng 1989a, 1989b). The 'past'

[44] Already in 1959 Mao observed: 'The stage of socialism may be divided into two stages: the first stage is underdeveloped socialism, and the second stage is relatively developed socialism. The latter phase takes longer than the former. After the latter stage, when material products and spiritual wealth [*jingshen fengfu*] are extremely abundant and people's communist consciousness is greatly enhanced, can we enter into a communist society' (Mao 1959, 116).

[45] Note also: 'The main task in the socialist stage is to develop the productive forces, keep increasing the material wealth of society, steadily improve the life of the people and create material conditions for the advent of a communist society' (Deng 1986a, 171–172; 1986b, 174).

in question actually concerns the complex and difficult Sino-Soviet relations of the 1960s and 1970s, but in the process, Deng points out that we cannot expect Marx 'to provide ready answers to questions that arise a hundred or several hundred years after his death', or indeed Lenin some fifty or one hundred years after his death. Why? Conditions change, even more rapidly in the recent past, and neither Marx nor Lenin could foresee what the new conditions might be. For example, could Marx possibly 'predict that the October Revolution would take place in backward Russia', or could Lenin foresee that the Chinese revolutionaries would 'win by encircling the cities from the countryside?' As for the construction of socialism after a successful revolution, a country must not follow fixed models and conventions from elsewhere, but undertake construction in light of its own conditions (*ziji de tiaojian*). Does this mean that Marx and Lenin, or indeed Engels and Stalin are irrelevant in new circumstances? Not at all, for a 'true Marxist-Leninist must understand, carry on and develop Marxism-Leninism in light of the current situation' (Deng 1989a, 291–292; 1989b, 284–285). In this light, Zheng and Guo (2009, 24–25) observe that liberating thought and seeking from facts in Deng Xiaoping's hands constitute a 'new era [*xin shiqi*]' in the history of the sinification of Marxism. Or, as Deng himself put it: 'We'll be ashamed to go to see Marx if we fail to solve this problem well' (Deng 1979d, 193; 1979g, 200).

References

Boer, Roland. 2017. Stalin's biblical hermeneutics: From 2 Thessalonians 3 to Acts 4. *Journal of the Bible and Its Reception* 4 (1): 71–89.

Boer, Roland. In press. *Friedrich Engels and the foundations of socialist governance*. Singapore: Springer.

Bulkeley, Rip. 1977. On 'On practice'. *Radical Philosophy* 18: 3–9.

Cai, Xiaodong, and Pan Shaolong. 2008. Jiefang sixiang de 'xianyan shu'—chongdu Deng Xiaoping 'Jiefang sixiang, shishiqiushi, tuanjieyizhi xiangqian kan' jianghua de ganwu. *Anhui sheng zhexue xuehui huiyi lunwen ji* 2008 (12): 188–193.

Cao, Lujin. 1998. Shi lun Deng Xiaoping 'Gaige ye shi jiefang shengchanli' kexue lunduan de lilun yiyi he shijian yiyi. *Nanjing shehui kexue (zengkan)* 1998 (S1): 14–18.

Chang, David. 1988. *Deng Xiaoping: Political and economic reform*. New York: Palgrave Macmillan.

Chen, Honggui. 2001. Deng Xiaoping lilun dui shishiqiushi de zhexue jichu de chuangxin. *Zhongguo qingnian zhengzhi xueyuan xuebao* 20 (3): 62–64.

Chen, Xiaoming, and Zhou Hong. 2000. Shijian weiwuzhuyi: Deng Xiaoping lilun de zhexue jichu. *Nanjing zhengzhi xueyuan xuebao* 16 (6): 8–11.

Chen, Xixi. 2008. Deng Xiaoping dui dang de sixiang luxian fengfu fazhan de zai renshi—chongwen 'Jiefang sixiang, shishiqiushi, tuanjieyizhi xiangqian kan'. *Jiangxi shifan daxue xuebao (zhexue shehui kexue ban)* 41 (4): 3–7.

Chen, Xueming. 2015. Zhongguo daolu dui makesizhuyi de fazhan—lun Zhongguo daolu de makesizhuyi yiyi zhi san. *Nanjing zhengzhi xueyuan xuebao* 2015 (6): 1–12.

Chen, Zhihua. 2012. On historical materialism and history of the Soviet Union. *Marxist Studies in China* 2012: 87–116.

CPC Central Committee. 1981. Guanyu jianguo yilai dang de ruogan lishi wenti de jueyi (1981 nian 6 yue 27 ri Zhongguo gongchandang di shiyi jie zhongyang weiyuanhui di liu ci quanti huiyi tongguo). *Renmin Ribao*, 27 June 1981: 1–9.

Deng, Xiaoping. 1941a. Dang yu kangri minzhu zhengquan (1941.04.15). In *Deng Xiaoping wenxuan*, vol. 1:7–19. Beijing: Renmin chubanshe, 2008.

Deng, Xiaoping. 1941b. The party and the Anti-Japanese democratic government (15 April, 1941). In *Selected works of Deng Xiaoping*, vol. 1:19–32. Beijing: Foreign Languages Press, 1995.

Deng, Xiaoping. 1950a. Guanyu xinan shaoshu minzu wenti (1950.07.21). In *Deng Xiaoping wenxuan*, vol. 1:161–171. Beijing: Renmin chubanshe, 2008.

Deng, Xiaoping. 1950b. On the question of minority nationalities in the southwest (21 July, 1950). In *Selected works of Deng Xiaoping*, vol. 1:167–176. Beijing: Foreign Languages Press, 1995.

Deng, Xiaoping. 1956a. Guanyu xiugai dang de zhangcheng de baogao (1956.09.16). In *Deng Xiaoping wenxuan*, vol. 1:212–256. Beijing: Renmin chubanshe, 2008.

Deng, Xiaoping. 1956b. Report on the revision of the constitution of the communist party of China (16 September, 1956). In *Selected works of Deng Xiaoping*, vol. 1:217–255. Beijing: Foreign Languages Press, 1995.

Deng, Xiaoping. 1961a. Encourage thorough and meticulous work (23 October, 1961). In *Selected works of Deng Xiaoping*, vol. 1:282–287. Beijing: Foreign Languages Press, 1995.

Deng, Xiaoping. 1961b. It is important to accomplish our day-to-day work (27 December, 1961). In *Selected works of Deng Xiaoping*, vol. 1:290–293. Beijing: Foreign Languages Press, 1995.

Deng, Xiaoping. 1961c. Tichang shenru xizhi de gongzuo (1961.10.23). In *Deng Xiaoping wenxuan*, vol. 1:285–290. Beijing: Renmin chubanshe, 2008.

Deng, Xiaoping. 1961d. Zhongyao de shi zuo hao jingchang gongzuo (1961.12.27). In *Deng Xiaoping wenxuan*, vol. 1:293–296. Beijing: Renmin chubanshe, 2008.

Deng, Xiaoping. 1962a. Speech delivered at an enlarged working conference of the party central committee (6 February, 1962). In *Selected works of Deng Xiaoping*, vol. 1:294–311. Beijing: Foreign Languages Press, 1995.

Deng, Xiaoping. 1962b. Zai kuoda de zhongyang gongzuo huiyi shang de jianghua (1962.02.06). In *Deng Xiaoping wenxuan*, vol. 1:297–317. Beijing: Renmin chubanshe, 2008.

Deng, Xiaoping. 1962c. Zenyang huifu nongye shengchan (1962.07.07). In *Deng Xiaoping wenxuan*, vol. 1:322–327. Beijing: Renmin chubanshe, 2008.

Deng, Xiaoping. 1977a. Jiaoyu zhanxian de boluan fanzheng wenti (1977.09.19). In *Deng Xiaoping wenxuan*, vol. 2:66–71. Beijing: Renmin chubanshe, 2008.

Deng, Xiaoping. 1977b. 'Liang ge fanshi' bu fuhe makesizhuyi (1977.05.24). In *Deng Xiaoping wenxuan*, vol. 2:38–39. Beijing: Renmin chubanshe, 2008.

Deng, Xiaoping. 1977c. Mao Zedong thought must be correctly understood as an integral whole (21 July, 1977). In *Selected works of Deng Xiaoping*, vol. 2:55–60. Beijing: Foreign Languages Press, 1995.

Deng, Xiaoping. 1977d. Setting things right in education (19 September, 1977). In *Selected works of Deng Xiaoping*, vol. 2:79–84. Beijing: Foreign Languages Press, 1995.

Deng, Xiaoping. 1977e. Speech at a plenary meeting of the military commission of the central committee of the CPC (28 December, 1977). In *Selected works of Deng Xiaoping*, vol. 2:85–97. Beijing: Foreign Languages Press, 1995.

Deng, Xiaoping. 1977f. The 'two whatevers' do not accord with marxism (24 May, 1977). In *Selected works of Deng Xiaoping*, vol. 2:51–52. Beijing: Foreign Languages Press, 1995.

Deng, Xiaoping. 1977g. Wanzheng de zhunque de lijie Mao Zedong sixiang (1977.07.21). In *Deng Xiaoping wenxuan*, vol. 2:42–47. Beijing: Renmin chubanshe, 2008.

Deng, Xiaoping. 1977h. Zai zhongyang junwei quanti huiyi shang de jianghua (1977.12.28). In *Deng Xiaoping wenxuan*, vol. 2:72–84. Beijing: Renmin chubanshe, 2008.

Deng, Xiaoping. 1978a. Adhere to the principle 'to each according to his work' (28 March, 1978). In *Selected works of Deng Xiaoping*, vol. 2:112–113. Beijing: Foreign Languages Press, 1995.

Deng, Xiaoping. 1978b. Emancipate the mind, seek truth from facts and unite as one in looking to the future (13 December, 1978). In *Selected works of Deng Xiaoping*, vol. 2:150–163. Beijing: Foreign Languages Press, 1995.
Deng, Xiaoping. 1978c. Gaoju Mao Zedong sixiang qizhi, jianchi shishiqiushi de yuanze (1978.09.16). In *Deng Xiaoping wenxuan*, vol. 2:126–128. Beijing: Renmin chubanshe, 2008.
Deng, Xiaoping. 1978d. Hold high the banner of Mao Zedong thought and adhere to the principle of seeking truth from facts (16 September, 1978). In *Selected works of Deng Xiaoping*, vol. 2:137–139. Beijing: Foreign Languages Press, 1995.
Deng, Xiaoping. 1978e. Jianchi anlao fenpei yuanze (1978.03.28). In *Deng Xiaoping wenxuan*, vol. 2:101–102. Beijing: Renmin chubanshe, 2008.
Deng, Xiaoping. 1978f. Jiefang sixiang, shishiqiushi, tuanjieyizhi xiangqian kan (1978.12.13). In *Deng Xiaoping wenxuan*, vol. 2:140–153. Beijing: Renmin chubanshe, 2008.
Deng, Xiaoping. 1978g. Speech at the all-army conference on political work (2 June, 1978). In *Selected works of Deng Xiaoping*, vol. 2:124–136. Beijing: Foreign Languages Press, 1995.
Deng, Xiaoping. 1978h. Speech at the national conference on education (22 April, 1978). In *Selected works of Deng Xiaoping*, vol. 2:114–121. Beijing: Foreign Languages Press, 1995.
Deng, Xiaoping. 1978i. Zai quanguo jiaoyu gongzuo huiyi shang de jianghua (1978.04.22). In *Deng Xiaoping wenxuan*, vol. 2:103–110. Beijing: Renmin chubanshe, 2008.
Deng, Xiaoping. 1978j. Zai quanjun zhengzhi gongzuo huiyi shang de jianghua (1978.06.02). In *Deng Xiaoping wenxuan*, vol. 2:113–125. Beijing: Renmin chubanshe, 2008.
Deng, Xiaoping. 1979a. Guanyu jingji gongzuo de jidian yijian (1979.10.04). In *Deng Xiaoping wenxuan*, vol. 2:194–202. Beijing: Renmin chubanshe, 2008.
Deng, Xiaoping. 1979b. Jianchi sixiang jiben yuanze (1979.03.30). In *Deng Xiaoping wenxuan*, vol. 2:158–184. Beijing: Renmin chubanshe, 2008.
Deng, Xiaoping. 1979c. Shehuizhuyi ye keyi gao shichang jingji (1979.11.26). In *Deng Xiaoping wenxuan*, vol. 2:231–236. Beijing: Renmin chubanshe, 2008.
Deng, Xiaoping. 1979d. Sixiang luxian zhengzhi luxian de shixian yao kao zuzhi luxian lai baozheng (1979.07.29). In *Deng Xiaoping wenxuan*, vol. 2:190–193. Beijing: Renmin chubanshe, 2008.
Deng, Xiaoping. 1979e. Some comments on economic work (4 October, 1979). In *Selected works of Deng Xiaoping*, vol. 2:201–208. Beijing: Foreign Languages Press, 1995.
Deng, Xiaoping. 1979f. Speech greeting the fourth congress of Chinese writers and artists (30 October, 1979). In *Selected works of Deng Xiaoping*, vol. 2:213–219. Beijing: Foreign Languages Press, 1995.
Deng, Xiaoping. 1979g. The organizational line guarantees the implementation of the ideological and political lines (29 July, 1979). In *Selected works of Deng Xiaoping*, vol. 2:197–200. Beijing: Foreign Languages Press, 1995.
Deng, Xiaoping. 1979h. Uphold the four cardinal principles (30 March, 1979). In *Selected works of Deng Xiaoping*, vol. 2:168–191. Beijing: Foreign Languages Press, 1995.
Deng, Xiaoping. 1979i. We can Develop a market economy under socialism (26 November, 1979). In *Selected works of Deng Xiaoping*, vol. 2:235–239. Beijing: Foreign Languages Press, 1995.
Deng, Xiaoping. 1979j. Zai Zhongguo wenxue yishu gongzuozhe disici daibiao dahui shang de zhuci (1979.10.30). In *Deng Xiaoping wenxuan*, vol. 2:207–214. Beijing: Renmin chubanshe, 2008.
Deng, Xiaoping. 1980a. Adhere to the party line and improve methods of work (29 February, 1980). In *Selected works of Deng Xiaoping*, vol. 2:273–282. Beijing: Foreign Languages Press, 1995.
Deng, Xiaoping. 1980b. Answers to the Italian journalist Oriana Fallaci (21 and 23 August, 1980). In *Selected works of Deng Xiaoping*, vol. 2:342–349. Beijing: Foreign Languages Press, 1995.
Deng, Xiaoping. 1980c. Da Yidali jizhe Aolinaina Falaqiwen (1980.08.21, 23). In *Deng Xiaoping wenxuan*, vol. 2:344–353. Beijing: Renmin chubanshe, 1995.
Deng, Xiaoping. 1980d. Dang he guojia lingdao zhidu gaige (1980.08.18). In *Deng Xiaoping wenxuan*, vol. 2:320–343. Beijing: Renmin chubanshe, 1995.

Deng, Xiaoping. 1980e. Dui qicao 'Guanyu jianguo yilai dang de ruogan lishi wenti de jueyi' de yijian (1980.03–1981.06). In *Deng Xiaoping wenxuan*, vol. 2:291–310. Beijing: Renmin chubanshe, 2008.
Deng, Xiaoping. 1980f. Guanche tiaozheng fangzhen, baozheng anding tuanjie (1980.12.25). In *Deng Xiaoping wenxuan*, vol. 2:354–374. Beijing: Renmin chubanshe, 2008.
Deng, Xiaoping. 1980g. Guanyu nongcun zhengce wenti (1980.05.31). In *Deng Xiaoping wenxuan*, vol. 2:315–317. Beijing: Renmin chubanshe, 2008.
Deng, Xiaoping. 1980h. Implement the policy of readjustment, ensure stability and unity (25 December, 1980). In *Selected works of Deng Xiaoping*, vol. 2:350–368. Beijing: Foreign Languages Press, 1995.
Deng, Xiaoping. 1980i. Jianchi dang de luxian, gaijin gongzuo fangfa (1980.02.29). In *Deng Xiaoping wenxuan*, vol. 2:274–283. Beijing: Renmin chubanshe, 2008.
Deng, Xiaoping. 1980j. Muqian de xingshi he renwu (1980.01.16). In *Deng Xiaoping wenxuan*, vol. 2:239–273. Beijing: Renmin chubanshe, 2008.
Deng, Xiaoping. 1980k. On questions of rural policy (31 May, 1980). In *Selected works of Deng Xiaoping*, vol. 2:314–316. Beijing: Foreign Languages Press, 1995.
Deng, Xiaoping. 1980l. On the reform of the system of party and state leadership (18 August, 1980). In *Selected works of Deng Xiaoping*, vol. 2:319–341. Beijing: Foreign Languages Press, 1995.
Deng, Xiaoping. 1980m. Remarks on successive drafts of the 'Resolution on certain questions in the history of our party since the founding of the people's Republic of China' (March, 1980–June, 1981). In *Selected works of Deng Xiaoping*, vol. 2:290–309. Beijing: Foreign Languages Press, 1995.
Deng, Xiaoping. 1980n. Shehuizhuyi shouxian yao fazhan shengchanli (1980.04–05). In *Deng Xiaoping wenxuan*, vol. 2:311–314. Beijing: Renmin chubanshe, 1995.
Deng, Xiaoping. 1980o. The present situation and the tasks before us (16 January, 1980). In *Selected works of Deng Xiaoping*, vol. 2:241–272. Beijing: Foreign Languages Press, 1995.
Deng, Xiaoping. 1980p. To build socialism we must first develop the productive forces (April–May 1980). In *Selected works of Deng Xiaoping*, vol. 2:310–313. Beijing: Foreign Languages Press, 1995.
Deng, Xiaoping. 1981a. Guanyu fandui cuowu sixiang qingxiang wenti (1981.03.27). In *Deng Xiaoping wenxuan*, vol. 2:379–382. Beijing: Renmin chubanshe, 1995.
Deng, Xiaoping. 1981b. On opposing wrong ideological tendencies (27 March, 1981). In *Selected works of Deng Xiaoping*, vol. 2:373–376. Beijing: Foreign Languages Press, 1995.
Deng, Xiaoping. 1982a. Qianshinian wei houshinian zuohao zhunbei (1982.10.14). In *Deng Xiaoping wenxuan*, vol. 3:16–18. Beijing: Renmin chubanshe, 2008.
Deng, Xiaoping. 1982b. We shall concentrate on economic development (18 September, 1982). In *Selected works of Deng Xiaoping*, vol. 3:20–22. Beijing: Foreign Languages Press, 1994.
Deng, Xiaoping. 1982c. Yixin yiyi gao jianshe (1982.09.18). In *Deng Xiaoping wenxuan*, vol. 3:9–11. Beijing: Renmin chubanshe, 2008.
Deng, Xiaoping. 1983a. Jianshe shehuizhuyi de wuzhi wenming he jingshen wenming (1983.04.29). In *Deng Xiaoping wenxuan*, vol. 3:27–28. Beijing: Renmin chubanshe, 2008.
Deng, Xiaoping. 1983b. We are building a socialist society with both high material standards and high cultural and ethical standards (29 April, 1983). In *Selected works of Deng Xiaoping*, vol. 3:37–38. Beijing: Foreign Languages Press, 1994.
Deng, Xiaoping. 1984a. Building a socialism with a specific Chinese character (30 June, 1984). In *Selected works of Deng Xiaoping*, vol. 3:72–75. Beijing: Foreign Languages Press, 1994.
Deng, Xiaoping. 1984b. China will always keep its promises (19 December, 1984). In *Selected works of Deng Xiaoping*, vol. 3:107–109. Beijing: Foreign Languages Press, 1994.
Deng, Xiaoping. 1984c. Jianshe you Zhongguo tese de shehuizhuyi (1984.06.30). In *Deng Xiaoping wenxuan*, vol. 3:62–66. Beijing: Renmin chubanshe, 2008.
Deng, Xiaoping. 1984d. Zhongguo shi xinshou nuoyan de (1984.12.19). In *Deng Xiaoping wenxuan*, vol. 3:101–103. Beijing: Renmin chubanshe, 2008.

Deng, Xiaoping. 1985a. Shehuizhuyi he shichang jingji bu cunzai genben maodun (1985.10.23). In *Deng Xiaoping wenxuan*, vol. 3:148–151. Beijing: Renmin chubanshe, 2008.

Deng, Xiaoping. 1985b. We shall expand political democracy and carry out economic reform (15 April, 1985). In *Selected works of Deng Xiaoping*, vol. 3:121–124. Beijing: Foreign Languages Press, 1994.

Deng, Xiaoping. 1985c. Zhengzhi shang fazhan minzhu, jingji shang shixing gaige (1985.04.15). In *Deng Xiaoping wenxuan*, vol. 3:115–118. Beijing: Renmin chubanshe, 2008.

Deng, Xiaoping. 1986a. Da Meiguo jizhe Maike Hualaishi wen (1986.09.02). In *Deng Xiaoping wenxuan*, vol. 3:167–175. Beijing: Renmin chubanshe, 2008.

Deng, Xiaoping. 1986b. Replies to the American TV correspondent Mike Wallace (2 September, 1986). In *Selected works of Deng Xiaoping*, vol. 3:170–177. Beijing: Foreign Languages Press, 1994.

Deng, Xiaoping. 1987a. In everything we do we must proceed from the realities of the primary stage of socialism (29 August, 1987). In *Selected works of Deng Xiaoping*, vol. 3:247–248. Beijing: Foreign Languages Press, 1994.

Deng, Xiaoping. 1987b. We are undertaking an entirely new endeavour (13 October, 1987). In *Selected works of Deng Xiaoping*, vol. 3:249–252. Beijing: Foreign Languages Press, 1994.

Deng, Xiaoping. 1987c. Women gan de shiye shi quanxin de shiye (1987.10.13). In *Deng Xiaoping wenxuan*, vol. 3:253–257. Beijing: Renmin chubanshe, 2008.

Deng, Xiaoping. 1987d. Yiqie cong shehuizhuyi chuji jieduan de shiji chufa (1987.08.29). In *Deng Xiaoping wenxuan*, vol. 3:251–252. Beijing: Renmin chubanshe, 2008.

Deng, Xiaoping. 1989a. Jieshu guoqu, kaipi weilai (1989.05.16). In *Deng Xiaoping wenxuan*, vol. 3:330–332. Beijing: Renmin chubanshe, 2010.

Deng, Xiaoping. 1989b. Let us put the past behind us and open up a new era (16 May, 1989). In *Selected works of Deng Xiaoping*, vol. 3:284–287. Beijing: Foreign Languages Press, 1994.

Deng, Xiaoping. 1992a. Excerpts from talks given in Wuchang, Shenzhen, Zhuhai and Shanghai (18 January–21 February, 1992). In *Selected works of Deng Xiaoping*, vol. 3:358–370. Beijing: Foreign Languages Press, 1994.

Deng, Xiaoping. 1992b. Zai Wuchang, Shenzhen, Zhuhai he Shanghai deng di de tanhua yaodian (1992.01.18–02.21). In *Deng Xiaoping wenxuan*, vol. 3:370–383. Beijing: Renmin chubanshe, 2008.

Dong, Shaolin, and Wu Bo. 2011. Guanyu shehuizhuyi chuji jieduan de jieji jieceng jiegou jiqi neizai maodun. *Zhengzhixue yanjiu* 2011 (3): 57–63.

Engels, Friedrich. 1877a. Karl Marx. In *Marx Engels Gesamtaugabe*, vol. I.25:100–111. Berlin: Dietz, 1985.

Engels, Friedrich. 1877b. Karl Marx. In *Marx and Engels collected works*, vol. 24:183–195. Moscow: Progress Publishers, 1989.

Engels, Friedrich. 1880a. Socialism: Utopian and scientific. In *Marx and Engels collected works*, vol. 24:281–325. Moscow: Progress Publishers, 1989.

Engels, Friedrich. 1880b. Socialisme utopique et socialisme scientifique. In *Marx Engels Gesamtaugabe*, vol. I.27:541–582. Berlin: Dietz, 1985.

Engels, Friedrich. 1886a. Engels an Friedrich Adolph Sorge in Hoboken, London, 29.November 1886. In *Marx Engels Werke*, vol. 36:578–581. Berlin: Dietz, 1973.

Engels, Friedrich. 1886b. Engels to Friedrich Adolph Sorge in Hoboken, 29 November 1886. In *Marx and Engels collected works*, vol. 47:531–534. Moscow: Progress Publishers, 1995.

Engels, Friedrich. 1895a. Engels an Werner Sombart in Breslau, London, 11.März 1895. In *Marx Engels Werke*, 39:427–429. Berlin: Dietz, 1973.

Engels, Friedrich. 1895b. Engels to Werner Sombart in Breslau, London,11 March 1895. In *Marx and Engels collected works*, 50:460–462. Moscow: Progress Publishers, 2004.

Fang, Ning. 2015. *China's democratic path.* Translated by Wu Yisheng and Liu Aiyun. Springer Insights. Singapore: Springer.

Fu, Zhifang. 2004. Zhaoyue de zhengzhi zhihui, baoyue de jingshen caifu—zai du Deng Xiaoping 'Jiefang sixiang, shishiqiushi, tuanjieyizhi xiangqiang kan' de tihui. *Lilun qianyan* 2004 (15): 5–10.

Gao, Wenxin, and Zhang Chunjing. 2013. Shishiqiushi lun xi. *Jilin daxue shehui kexue xuebao* 53 (3): 107–34, 176.

Goodman, David. 1994. *Deng Xiaoping and the Chinese revolution: A political biography*. London: Routledge.

Heilman, Sebastian, and Oliver Melton. 2013. The reinvention of development planning in China, 1993–2012. *Modern China* 39 (6): 580–628.

Hu, Fuming. 1978. Shijian shi jianyan zhenli de weiyi biaozhun. *Guangming ribao* 11 May, 1978: 1.

Jiang, Yingguang. 1992. Shichang jingji gaige jiefang shengchanli—xuexi Deng Xiaoping nanxun jianghua de yidian tihui. *Shengchanli yanjiu* 1992 (4): 21–22.

Knight, Nick (ed.). 1990. *Mao Zedong on dialectical materialism: Writings on philosophy, 1937*. Armonk: M.E. Sharpe.

Lenin, V. I. 1917a. Gosudarstvo i revoliutsiia. Uchenie marksizma o gosudarstve i zadachi proletariata v revoliutsii. Avgust–sentiabr′ 1917g.; ranee 17 dekabria 1918g. In *Polnoe sobranie sochinenii*, vol. 33:1–120. Moscow: Izdatel'stvo politicheskoi literatury, 1969.

Lenin, V. I. 1917b. The state and revolution: The Marxist theory of the state and the tasks of the proletariat in the revolution. In *Collected works*, vol. 25:385–497. Moscow: Progress Publishers, 1964.

Li, Jilin. 2015. Lun shishiqiushi yu Deng Xiaoping lilun jingsui. *Mao Zedong sixiang yanjiu* 32 (2): 50–53.

Liu, Pusheng. 2004. Deng Xiaoping lilun zhexue jichi de san ceng jiegou. *Lilun shiye* 2004 (5): 34–36.

Liu, Tingya. 1999. Weida de xuanyan - Deng Xiaoping 'Jiefang sixiang, shishiqiushi, tuanjieyizhi xiangqian kan' yiwen de lilun jiazhi he lishi yiyi. *Lilun yu xiandaixin* 1999 (2): 21–23.

Losurdo, Domenico. 2017. *Il marxismo occidentale: Come nacque, come morì, come può rinascere*. Rome: Editori Laterza.

Ma, Jiesha, and Tan Yangfang. 2004. Deng Xiaoping zhexue sixiang yanjiu zongshu. *Huaiyin shifan xueyuan xuebao (zhexue shehui kexue ban)* 26 (2): 147–156.

Ma, Shuguang. 2000. Makesizhuyi zai woguo de bentuhua he minzuhua - shishiqiushi shi makesizhuyi zhexue de zhongguohua. *Zhonggong Shanxi shengwei dangxiao xuebao* 2000 (4): 49–50.

Mao, Zedong. 1929a. Draft resolution of the ninth congress of the communist party in the fourth red army (December 1929, at the Gutian Congress in Western Fujian Province). In *Mao's Road to power: Revolutionary writings 1912–1949*, vol. 3:195–230. Armonk: M. E. Sharpe, 1995.

Mao, Zedong. 1929b. Zhongguo gongchandang hongjun disi jun dijiuci daibiao dahui jueyi'an (1929.12). In *Mao Zedong wenji*, vol. 1:78–117. Beijing: Renmin chubanshe, 2009.

Mao, Zedong. 1930a. Fandui benbenzhuyi (1930.05). In *Mao Zedong xuanji*, vol. 1:373–386. Beijing: Renmin chubanshe, 2009.

Mao, Zedong. 1930b. Oppose book worship (May, 1930). In *Selected readings from the works of Mao Tsetung*, 40–50. Beijing: Foreign Languages Press, 1971.

Mao, Zedong. 1936a. Problems of strategy in China's revolutionary war (December, 1936). In *Selected works of Mao Tse-Tung*, vol. 1:179–254. Beijing: Foreign Languages Press, 1965.

Mao, Zedong. 1936b. Zhongguo geming zhanzheng de zhanlüe wenti (1936.12). In *Mao Zedong xuanji*, vol. 1:170–244. Beijing: Renmin chubanshe, 2009.

Mao, Zedong. 1937a. Maodun lun (1937.08). In *Mao Zedong xuanji*, vol. 1:299–340. Beijing: Renmin chubanshe, 2009.

Mao, Zedong. 1937b. On contradiction (August, 1937). In *Selected works of Mao Tse-Tung*, vol. 1:311–347. Beijing: Foreign Languages Press, 1965.

Mao, Zedong. 1937c. On practice (July, 1937). In *Selected works of Mao Tse-Tung*, vol. 1:295–309. Beijing: Foreign Languages Press, 1965.

Mao, Zedong. 1937d. Shijian lun (1937.07). In *Mao Zedong xuanji*, vol. 1:282–298. Beijing: Renmin chubanshe, 1952.
Mao, Zedong. 1938a. Lun xin jieduan (1938.10.12–14). In *Zhonggong zhongyang wenjian xuanji*, vol. 11:557–662. Beijing: Zhonggang zhongyang xuexiao chubanshe, 1991.
Mao, Zedong. 1938b. On the new stage (12–14 October, 1938). In *Mao's road to power: Revolutionary writings 1912–1949*, vol. 6:458–541. Armonk: M. E. Sharpe, 2004.
Mao, Zedong. 1940a. On new democracy (January, 1940). In *Selected works of Mao Tse-tung*, vol. 2:339–384. Beijing: Foreign Languages Press, 1965.
Mao, Zedong. 1940b. Xin minzhuzhuyi lun (1940.01.15). In *Mao Zedong xuanji*, vol. 2:662–711. Beijing: Renmin chubanshe, 2009.
Mao, Zedong. 1941a. Gaizao women de xuexi (1941.05.19). In *Mao Zedong xuanji*, vol. 3:795–803. Beijing: Renmin chubanshe, 2009.
Mao, Zedong. 1941b. Nongcun diaocha de xuyan he ba (1941.03, 04). In *Mao Zedong xuanji*, vol. 3:789–794. Beijing: Renmin chubanshe, 2009.
Mao, Zedong. 1941c. Preface and postscript to rural surveys (March and April, 1941). In *Selected works of Mao Tse-Tung*, vol. 3:11–16. Beijing: Foreign Languages Press, 1965.
Mao, Zedong. 1941d. Reform our study (May, 1941). In *Selected works of Mao Tse-Tung*, vol. 3:17–26. Beijing: Foreign Languages Press, 1965.
Mao, Zedong. 1941e. Zhonggong zhongyang guanyu diaocha yanjiu de jueding (1941.08.01). In *Mao Zedong wenji*, vol. 2:360–363. Beijing: Renmin chubanshe, 1993.
Mao, Zedong. 1942a. Fandui dang bagu (1942.02.08). In *Mao Zedong xuanji*, vol. 3:830–846. Beijing: Renmin chubanshe, 2009.
Mao, Zedong. 1942b. Guanyu zhengdun sanfeng (1942.04.20). In *Mao Zedong wenji*, vol. 2:411–423. Beijing: Renmin chubanshe, 1993.
Mao, Zedong. 1942c. Jingji wenti yu caizheng wenti (1942.12). In *Mao Zedong wenji*, vol. 2:458–468. Beijing: Renmin chubanshe, 1993.
Mao, Zedong. 1942d. On the rectification of the three styles (20 April, 1942). In *Mao's road to power: Revolutionary writings 1912–1949*, vol. 8:81–91. Armonk: M. E. Sharpe, 2015.
Mao, Zedong. 1942e. Oppose stereotyped party writing (8 February, 1942). In *Selected works of Mao Tse-Tung*, vol. 3:53–68. Beijing: Foreign Languages Press, 1965.
Mao, Zedong. 1942f. Rectify the party's style of work (1 February, 1942). In *Selected works of Mao Tse-Tung*, vol. 3:35–51. Beijing: Foreign Languages Press, 1965.
Mao, Zedong. 1942g. Zhengdun dang de zuofeng (1942.02.01). In *Mao Zedong xuanji*, vol. 3:811–829. Beijing: Renmin chubanshe, 2009.
Mao, Zedong. 1944a. Our study and the current situation (12 April, 1944). In *The selected works of Mao Tse-Tung*, vol. 3:163–176. Beijing: Foreign Language Press, 1965.
Mao, Zedong. 1944b. Xuexi he shiju (1944.04.12). In *Mao Zedong xuanji*, vol. 3:937–951. Beijing: Renmin chubanshe, 2009.
Mao, Zedong. 1945a. Lun lianhezhengfu (1945.04.24). In *Mao Zedong xuanji*, vol. 3:1029–1100. Beijing: Renmin chubanshe, 2009.
Mao, Zedong. 1945b. On coalition government (24 April, 1945). In *Selected works of Mao Tse-Tung*, vol. 3:255–320. Beijing: Foreign Languages Press, 1965.
Mao, Zedong. 1950. Rushi cha bao sunan zhengliang, chungeng he jiuzai qingkuang (1950.05.12). In *Mao Zedong wenji*, vol. 6:57–58. Beijing: Renmin chubanshe, 1999.
Mao, Zedong. 1953a. Combat bourgeois ideas in the party (12 August, 1953). In *Selected works of Mao Tse-Tung*, vol. 5:103–111. Beijing: Foreign Languages Press, 1977.
Mao, Zedong. 1953b. Fandui dangnei de zichanjingji sixiang (1953.08.12). In *Mao Zedong xuanji*, vol. 5:90–97. Beijing: Renmin chubanshe, 1977.
Mao, Zedong. 1955. Zai zibenzhuyi gongshangye shehuizhuyi gaizao wenti zuotanhui shang de jianghua (1955.10.29). In *Mao Zedong wenji*, vol. 6:493–503. Beijing: Renmin chubanshe, 2009.
Mao, Zedong. 1956a. Lun shi da guanxi (1956.04.25). In *Mao Zedong wenji*, vol. 7:23–49. Beijing: Renmin chubanshe, 2009.

Mao, Zedong. 1956b. On the ten major relationships (25 April, 1956). In *Selected works of Mao Tse-Tung*, vol. 5:284–307. Beijing: Foreign Languages Press, 1977.

Mao, Zedong. 1956c. Shehuizhuyi geming de mudi shi jiefang shengchanli (1956.01.25). In *Mao Zedong wenji*, vol. 7:1–3. Beijing: Renmin chubanshe, 2009.

Mao, Zedong. 1956d. Speech at the supreme state conference (Excerpt) (25 January, 1956). In *The writings of Mao Zedong 1949–1976*, vol. 2:17–19. Armonk: M. E. Sharpe, 1992.

Mao, Zedong. 1956e. Strengthen party unity and carry forward party traditions (30 August, 1956). In *Selected works of Mao Tse-Tung*, vol. 5:312–323. Beijing: Foreign Languages Press, 1977.

Mao, Zedong. 1956f. Zengqiang dang de tuanjie, jicheng dang de chuantong (1956.08.30). In *Mao Zedong wenji*, vol. 7:86–99. Beijing: Renmin chubanshe, 2009.

Mao, Zedong. 1957a. Guanyu zhengque chuli renmin neibu maodun de wenti (1957.02.27). In *Mao Zedong wenji*, vol. 7:204–244. Beijing: Renmin chubanshe, 2009.

Mao, Zedong. 1957b. On the correct handling of contradictions among the people (27 February, 1957). In *Selected works of Mao Tse-Tung*, vol. 5:384–421. Beijing: Foreign Languages Press, 1977.

Mao, Zedong. 1958a. Gongzuo fangfa liushi tiao (cao'an) (1958.01). In *Mao Zedong wenji*, vol. 7:344–365. Beijing: Renmin chubanshe, 2009.

Mao, Zedong. 1958b. Sixty points on working methods: A draft resolution from the office of the centre of the CPC (2 February, 1958). In *Selected works of Mao Tse-Tung*, vol. 8:20–34. Secunderabad: Kranti, 2004.

Mao, Zedong. 1959. Du Sulian 'Zhengzhijingjixue jiaokeshu' de tanhua (1959.12–1960.02). In *Mao Zedong wenji*, vol. 8:103–148. Beijing: Renmin chubanshe, 2009.

Mao, Zedong. 1960. Zhudongquan laizi shishiqiushi (1960.06.16). In *Mao Zedong wenji*, vol. 8:197–199. Beijing: Renmin chubanshe, 2009.

Mao, Zedong. 1961. Daxing diaocha yanjiu zhifeng (1961.01.13). In *Mao Zedong wenji*, vol. 8:233–238. Beijing: Renmin chubanshe, 2009.

Marx, Karl. 1875a. Critique of the Gotha programme. In *Marx and Engels collected works*, vol. 24:75–99. Moscow: Progress Publishers, 1989.

Marx, Karl. 1875b. Kritik des Gothaer Programms. In *Marx Engels Gesamtausgabe*, vol. I.25:3–25. Berlin: Dietz, 1985.

Marx, Karl, and Friedrich Engels. 1848a. Manifest der Kommunistischen Partei. In *Marx Engels Werke*, vol. 4:459–493. Berlin: Dietz Verlag, 1974.

Marx, Karl, and Friedrich Engels. 1848b. The Manifesto of the communist party. In *Marx and Engels collected works*, vol. 6:477–519. Moscow: Progress Publishers, 1976.

Mises, Ludwig von. 1932. *Socialism: An economic and sociological analysis*. Translated by J. Kahane. London: Jonathan Cape, 1936.

Pan, Zhide, and Xu Yanwei. 2003. Mao Zedong Deng Xiaoping shishiqiushi de sixiang bijiao yanjiu. *Jilin shifan daxue xuebao (renwen shehui kexue ban))* 2003 (1): 48–51.

Pan, Zhide, and Yang Huiqin. 1999. Deng Xiaoping zhexue fangfalun yuanze yanjiu chutan. *Songliao xuekan (shehui kexue ban)* 1999 (5): 30–32.

Pantsov, Alexander, and Steven Levine. 2015. *Deng Xiaoping: A revolutionary life*. Oxford: Oxford University Press.

Pye, Lucian. 1995. An introductory profile: Deng Xiaoping and China's political culture. In *Deng Xiaoping: Portrait of a Chinese statesman*, ed. David Shambaugh, 4–35. Oxford: Clarendon.

Rao, Zhihua. 2011. Wanzheng zhunque de lijie Deng Xiaoping de jiefang sixiang. *Qiushi* 2011 (3): 8–11.

Shambaugh, David (ed.). 1995. *Deng Xiaoping: Portrait of a Chinese statesman*. Oxford: Clarendon.

Song, Tao. 1999. Jiefang sixiang yu jingji minzhu—xuexi Deng Xiaoping 'Jiefang sixiang, shishiqiushi, tuanjieyizhi xiangqian kan' jianghua de jidian tihui. *Dangdai jingji yanjiu* 1999 (1): 1–8.

Stalin, I. V. 1926a. The seventh enlarged plenum of the E.C.C.I., November 22–December 16, 1926. In *Works*, vol. 9:1–155. Moscow: Foreign Languages Publishing House, 1954.

Stalin, I. V. 1926b. VII rasshirennyi plenum IKKI 22 noiabria–16 dekabria 1926g. In *Sochineniia*, vol. 9:3–151. Moscow: Gosudarstvennoe izdatel′stvo politicheskoi literatury, 1948.

Stalin, I. V. 1939a. Otchetnyi doklad na XVIII s"ezde partii o rabote TSK VKP(b), 10 marta 1939 goda. In *Sochineniia*, vol. 14:290–341. Moscow: Izdatel′stvo "Pisatel′", 1997.

Stalin, I. V. 1939b. Report on the work of the central committee to the eighteenth congress of the C.P.S.U.(B.) (Delivered March 10, 1939). In *Works*, vol. 14:355–429. London: Red Star Press, 1978.

Stalin, I. V. 1952a. Economic problems of socialism in the U.S.S.R. In *Works*, vol. 16:222–296. London: Red Star Press, 1986.

Stalin, I. V. 1952b. Ėkonomicheskie problemy sotsializma v SSSR. In *Sochineniia*, vol. 16:154–223. Moscow: Izdatel′stvo "Pisatel′", 1997.

Tong, Lianbo. 2017. Lun dangdai Zhongguo zhexue de ziwo lijie he shengming xingshi—'jiefang sixiang' de zhexue texing yu dangdai jiazhi. *Lilun tantao* 194: 58–64.

Vogel, Ezra. 2011. *Deng Xiaoping and the transformation of China*. Cambridge: Harvard University Press.

Wang, Dong, and Cheng Long. 2002. Deng Xiaoping lilun zhexue jichu yanjiu zongshu. *Lilun xuekan* 2002 (5): 44–47.

Wang, Dong, and Han Xiaoqing. 2008. Xin shiqi gaige kaifang xuanyan shu—Deng Xiaoping 'Jiefang sixiang, shishiqiushi, tuanjieyizhi xiangqian kan' de wenben jiedu. *Zhonggong Shijiazhuang shiwei dangxiao xuebao* 10 (11): 10–13.

Wang, Weiguang. 2014. Upholding and developing Mao Zedong thought and firmly advancing socialism with Chinese characteristics. *Marxist Studies in China* 2014: 2–20.

Wang, Yingzi, and Ma Fengqiang. 2005. Shi xi Deng Xiaoping lilun de zhexue sixiang. *Sixiang jiaoyu yanjiu* 2005 (1): 13–15.

Wang, Yunjing, and Yang Yuntai. 1994. Gaige shi jiefang he fazhan shengchanli – xuexi 'Deng Xiaoping xuanji' di san juan de tihui. *Shanghai daxue xuebao (sheke ban)* 1994 (6): 102–107.

Wang, Yuyao. 1995. Lun Deng Xiaoping zai jiefang he fazhan shengchanli wenti shang de xin gongxian. *Dang de wenxian* 1995 (3): 49–55.

Weng, Shisheng. 1999. Lun Deng Xiaoping lilun zhexue jichu de jiben tedian. *Zhonggong Fujian shengwei dangxiao xuebao* 1999 (8): 28–33.

Whyte, Martin. 1995. Deng Xiaoping: The social reformer. In *Deng Xiaoping: Portrait of a Chinese statesman*, ed. David Shambaugh, 107–127. Oxford: Clarendon.

Womack, Brantly. 1982. *The foundations of Mao Zedong's political thought*. Honolulu: University of Hawaii.

Xi, Jinping. 2017. *Juesheng quanmian jiancheng xiaokang shehui, duoqu xinshidai Zhongguo tese shehuizhuyi weida shengli (2017.10.18)*. Beijing: Renmin chubanshe.

Xi, Jinping. 2019. Bianzheng weiwuzhuyi shi Zhongguo gongchandangren de shijieguan he fangfalun. *Qiushi* 2019 (1): 1–3.

Xi, Jinping. 2020. Buduan kaituo dangdai makesizhuyi zhengzhijingjixue xin jingjie. *Qiushi* 2020 (16): 1–6.

Xiang, Qiyuan. 2009. The basic contradiction theory and China's economic reform. *Marxist Studies in China* 2008–2009: 30–47.

Xiao, Qian, and He Jinrui. 1999. Dangdai makesizhuyi shijian guan: Deng Xiaoping lilun de zhexue jichu. *Qianxian* 1999 (3): 12–16.

Xie, Lili. 2008. Deng Xiaoping 'Jiefang sixiang, shishiqiushi, tuanjieyizhi xiangqian kan' de xin jiedu—jinian gaige kaifang sanshi zhounian. *Chuzhou xueyuan xuebao* 10 (6): 32–35.

Yang, Chungui. 2008. Deng Xiaoping yu dangdai Zhongguo sixiang jiefang—jinian gaige kaifang 30 zhounian. *Kexue shehuizhuyi* 2008 (5): 4–9.

Yang, Songjian. 2004. Mao Zedong Deng Xiaoping shishiqiushi zhexue sixiang zhi yitong. *Zhonggong Fujian shengwei dangxiao xuebao* 2004 (4): 15–18.

Yong, Tao. 2004. Deng Xiaoping zhexue de kexue dingwei—jinian Deng Xiaoping danchen 100 zhounian. *Hubei shehui kexue* 2004 (8): 3–6.

Yu, Zhongliang. 1995. Cong Mao Zedong de 'shishiqiushi' dao Deng Xiaoping de 'jeifang sixiang, shishiqiushi' shilun Deng Xiaoping lilun dui Mao Zedong sixiang de jicheng, fazhan. *Xinan minzu xueyuan xuebao (zhexue shehui kexue ban)* 1995 (1): 75–78.

Yuan, Jifu. 2000. Deng Xiaoping shishiqiushi sixiang de chuangzaoxing neihan yu lishi diwe. *Zhonggong Jinan shiwei dangxiao, Jinan shi xingzheng xueyuan, Jinan shi shehuizhuyi xueyuan xuebao* 2000 (3): 18–24.

Zhao, Ziyang. 1987. *Yanzhe you Zhongguo tese de shehuizhuyi daolu qianjin—zai Zhongguo gongchandang di shisan ci quanguo daibiao dahui shang de baogao (1987.10.25)*. Beijing: Renmin chubanshe.

Zheng, Qianyu, and Gao Yanlai. 2009. Deng Xiaoping lilun de jingsui—'jiefang sixiang, shishiqiushi' de minzu tese. *Guizhou daxue xuebao (shehui kexue ban)* 27 (2): 21–25.

Zhonggong zhongyang wenxian yanjiushi, ed. 2004. *Deng Xiaoping nianpu (1975–1997)*. Beijing: Zhonggong wenxian chubanshe.

Zhonggong zhongyang wenxian yanjiushi, ed. 2009. *Deng Xiaoping nianpu (1904–1974)*. Beijing: Zhonggong wenxian chubanshe.

Zhou, Enlai. 1963a. Jiancheng shehuizhuyi zuguo, guanjian zaiyu shixian kexue jishu xiandaihua (1963.01.29). In *Zhou Enlai wenji*, vol. 2:407–411. Beijing: Renmin chubanshe, 1980.

Zhou, Enlai. 1963b. The key to building a powerful socialist country is to modernize science and technology (29 January, 1963). In *Selected works of Zhou Enlai*, vol. 2:427–431. Beijing: Foreign Languages Press, 1989.

Zhou, Yinzu. 1997. Mao Zedong he Deng Xiaoping guanyu maodun fenxi fangfa de bijiao yanjiu. *Nanjing shehui kexue (zengkan)* 1997 (1): 116–128.

Chapter 3
Contradiction Analysis: History, Meaning, and Application

3.1 Opening Remarks

> Why is it necessary to study dialectics to achieve the objective of changing China and the world? It is because dialectics is made up of the most general laws of development of nature and society; when we comprehend dialectics, we have gained a scientific weapon, and in the revolutionary practice of changing nature and society possess a theory and method suited to this practice … Consequently, all revolutionary comrades, and above all cadres, should diligently study dialectics. (Mao 1937c, 238–239; 1937f, 126–127)[1]

In the previous chapter on Deng Xiaoping, contradiction analysis (*maodun fenxi*) was mentioned on a few occasions. This chapter deals with contradiction analysis directly, since it provides another key to understanding socialism with Chinese characteristics, as well as the Reform and Opening-Up as a whole. The chapter is necessarily abstract and philosophical, but the reader needs to persevere since it indicates in more depth why—as mentioned in the Introduction—Marxist philosophy is so important in China. In order to understand the development of contradiction analysis, we need to take a step back, all the way to Lenin, the development of dialectical materialism in the Soviet Union of the 1930s, and then Mao Zedong's creative engagement with this material in the 1930s. Here we find the seeds of an approach that has become government policy, but at the same time shapes Chinese cultural assumptions concerning everyday life. For example, we find it in the careful identification of the primary contradiction that directs all government projects, in framing five-year plans, in the nature of Traditional Chinese Medicine and in cultural assumptions concerning food. Why? Contradiction analysis is not merely a contribution from Marxist philosophy, for it is also found in the long Chinese cultural tradition that was thoroughly transformed in light of Marxist dialectics. It was Mao Zedong's distinct contribution to make the creative connection between Marxist analysis and the Chinese tradition: the touchstone is contradiction analysis. Even more, through this contribution, we

[1]Where possible, I prefer to cite Knight's translation in *Mao Zedong on dialectical materialism: Writings on philosophy, 1937* (1990b).

R. Boer, *Socialism with Chinese Characteristics*,
https://doi.org/10.1007/978-981-16-1622-8_3

will find the philosophical roots of socialism with Chinese characteristics, which was to be so assiduously promoted by Deng Xiaoping and those who followed.

Explaining and analysing contradiction analysis may take three possible paths. One path would be to follow the specifically Chinese cultural and philosophical assumptions concerning the role of contradictions, all the way from the *Yijing* to Mao Zedong (Tian C. 2005). Another historical path would trace how contradictions were understood in the Marxist tradition, running from Hegel, through Marx and Engels's materialist inversion (Marx 1859b, 101; 1859a, 263–264; Engels 1880b, 579–580; 1880a, 324–325) to Lenin's awareness that contradictions also appear under socialism, albeit in a non-antagonistic form (Lenin 1914b, 1914a). I will take neither path, not merely because I have done so in earlier work (Boer 2017b, 2017a), but also because I have found the labour seems quite unnecessary in a Chinese context. To explain; a few years ago, I ran a couple of seminar series on contradiction analysis at Renmin University of China. The focus of the seminar series was Mao Zedong's 'On Contradiction' (see more below), but we began with a belaboured presentation of the historical development of Marxist dialectics and the growing realisation of the reality of (non-antagonistic) contradictions in the construction of socialism. The response from participants was: this is obvious! Contradictions exist under socialism, indeed they must, so why go over the history of the idea? I realised it was more about my own slow process of discovery. Having been imbued with the Western philosophical tradition's emphasis on either-or,[2] it took assiduous study and the further washing of my brain to understand the logic and reality of contradictions in socialist construction. But the seminar participants did not need to hear about this path of self-discovery. Instead, for them it was a given that contradictions are universal in life, that dialectical analysis entails the unity and struggle of opposites, and that even in communism contradictions would not be entirely abolished but would continue to exist in non-antagonistic form.

Thus, I will follow a third path that is less a path of personal discovery and more a history of ideas. Its focus is dialectical materialism, the philosophical method of Marxism that finds its prime application in historical materialism. For our purposes, the approach begins with Lenin's concise and insightful 'On the Question of Dialectics', which was informed by his in-depth return to Hegel through the Marxist lens provided above all by Engels's *Anti-Dühring* and *Dialectics of Nature*. Lenin and Engels—supplemented by pertinent examples from Marx and Stalin—subsequently provided the pillars for the sophisticated elaboration of dialectical materialism in the Soviet Union of the 1930s. As the most mature and thoroughly developed form of Marxist philosophy at the time, it was to this material that Mao Zedong and his comrades turned for a period of intense study in Yan'an in 1936–1937. This window of time, after the Long March and as the next phase of the Anti-Japanese War was about to begin, provided the core materials that would set in train a consistent concern with philosophical matters in the CPC, the revolutionary path to Liberation in 1949,

[2]This is not to say that the Western Marxist tradition is unable to break free from this underlying either-or assumption, for contradiction analysis actually arises from the development of dialectical analysis in the work of Marx and Engels (Haug 2017).

and the subsequently long and arduous task of constructing socialism. In particular, contradiction analysis—forged from Lenin in 1915 to Mao in 1937—became and remains a centrepiece for the many stages of the Chinese socialist project. Finally, as the analysis unfolds I will draw increasing attention to the way dialectical materialism provides the philosophical basis in Mao's hands for socialism with Chinese characteristics.

3.2 Lenin

> Believe me, the philosopher Hegel was right: life proceeds by contradictions, and living contradictions are so much richer, more varied and deeper in content than they may seem at first sight to a man's mind. (Lenin 1909a, 219; 1909b, 403)

Let us begin with a famous text by Lenin, which was quoted subsequently on many, many occasions. In a marginal note to his reading of Bukharin's book, *The Economics of the Transition Period* (1920a, 1920b). Lenin writes: 'Antagonism and contradiction are not at all the same thing. Under socialism, the first will disappear, the second will remain' (Lenin 1920, 391). In other words, contradictions are not always antagonistic, for contradiction and antagonism are two different categories. While antagonism—between classes, between the forces and relations of production—will begin to disappear in socialism, contradictions will clearly be part of the process. This comment would come into its own in the 1930s and beyond in the Soviet Union, when the category of non-antagonistic contradictions began to be elaborated. But is Lenin's observation an isolated occurrence, as some have asserted (Weston 2008, 433–434), perhaps due to the relatively brief years Lenin had left—under very difficult circumstances—after the October Revolution? Not at all, for he had already made a clear statement on the ubiquity of contradictions some years earlier, especially in the energetically condensed text, 'On the Question of Dialectics'.

The following observations by Lenin are key:

> The identity of opposites (it would be more correct, perhaps, to say their 'unity', – although the difference between the terms identity and unity is not particularly important here. In a certain sense both are correct) is the recognition (discovery) of the contradictory, *mutually exclusive*, opposite tendencies in *all* phenomena and processes of nature (*including* mind and society). The condition for the knowledge of all processes of the world in their '*self-movement*', in their spontaneous development, in their real life, is the knowledge of them as a unity of opposites. Development is the 'struggle' of opposites. (Lenin 1915a, 316–317; 1915b, 357–358)

Let us exegete this energetically condensed passage for a few moments. To begin with, Lenin emphasises the universality and ubiquity of contradictions in 'all phenomena and processes of nature', which includes within its orbit society and mind. At this basic level, there is no distinction here between nature and socioeconomic matters, between science and history. Lenin's more immediate inspiration may have been his re-engagement with Hegel's dialectics, but we should note that

Marx had developed already in his doctoral thesis an argument that may justifiably be called an earlier version of a dialectics of nature in the thought of Epicurus (Marx 1841; Stanley 1989). Even more, in the first volume of *Capital* Marx observed that Hegel's law of the transformation of a merely quantitative change into a qualitative one is 'attested by history and natural science alike' (Marx 1867a, 246; see also 1867b, 306).[3] It would of course be Engels in *Dialectics of Nature* who elaborated on the processes in natural science, with the most extensive texts concerned with motion, mathematics, and physics (Boer In press). Indeed, it was from this material that Lenin came to assume Engels's point that it is from 'the history of nature and human society that the laws of dialectics are abstracted' (Engels 1882b, 348; 1882a, 356).[4]

Further, Lenin emphasises that qualitative change happens in the process of self-movement, in the internal dynamics of a situation. Elsewhere in the same piece, he stresses that self-movement is the driving force, source, and motive of motion. The reason: the 'splitting of a single whole and the cognition of its contradictory parts ... is the *essence*... of dialectics' (Lenin 1915a, 316; 1915b, 357). If the contradiction in question arises from an initial split from one into two, it follows that the process is internal, that the driving force of contradictions is internal. Lenin contrasts this self-movement with the alternative: motion and thus change happens by means of external forces (whether God, the subject, and so on) and entails quantitative changes in terms of increase or decrease. This is not real change, for one has merely quantitative change, mere addition or subtraction, and the item in question remains qualitatively the same.[5] In contrast to this 'lifeless, pale and dry' approach, Lenin advocates the dynamic of self-movement, internal to an object. This point leads him to elaborate—via the example of Marx's approach in *Capital*—a dialectic of individual and universal, in which a single instance provides a microcosm of the dialectical contradictions of the whole. As it is with commodities (Marx's example), so it is with all aspects of life.

Finally, Lenin emphasises the simultaneous unity and struggle of opposites, so much so that in his notes on Hegel's *The Science of Logic* he observes that 'dialectics can be defined as doctrine of the unity of opposites'. This doctrine 'embodies the essence of dialectics' (Lenin 1914b, 203; 1914a, 222). This emphasis by Lenin is quite intriguing, for it entails a variation in the ordering of Engels's three laws of dialectics: the transformation of quantity into quality and vice versa; the interpenetration of

[3]See also some of the correspondence between Engels and Marx as the former was developing his thoughts concerning the dialectics of nature, as early as 1858 (Engels 1858; 1873; 1882d; Marx 1876).

[4]Citations from *Dialektik der Natur* are from the *textus receptus*, which has taken on a life of its own. One may also consult the effort, in MEGA I.26, to publish the manuscripts and notes as they were found in Engels's archives (Engels 1882c).

[5]A good example concerns the assumptions of neoclassical economics concerning the eternity of bourgeois capitalist economic relations, which change only in terms of quantity. Thus, 'capitalism' is 'found' even in the earliest forms of human society and economic activity (Shirokov and Iankovskii 1932b, 139; 1937, 153–154; see also Boer 2015, 11–18).

opposites; and the negation of the negation (Engels 1882b, 348; 1882a, 356).[6] Lenin elevates the second into the prime position, a move that would be followed by all of the Soviet-era material on dialectical materialism, as also Mao Zedong and his comrades (see below). We should also note here the extraordinary fragment from *Dialectics of Nature* (1882b, 481–490; 1882a, 492–501) where Engels undertakes a complete revolt against the Western tradition's focus on either-or, or zero-sum. At one point, he exclaims that for dialectics there is 'no unconditional, universally valid "either-or"'. Indeed, this approach 'bridges the fixed metaphysical differences', which is to say that '"either-or" recognises also in the right place "both this—and that"' (Engels 1882b, 482; 1882a, 493). This realisation entails considerable effort given the Western philosophical tradition's deep assumption of either-or: instead, Engels stresses the interpenetration of opposites.

For Lenin, the importance of what he calls the unity and struggle of opposites seems to be less of a struggle compared to Engels. He stresses that the two sides of the contradiction between unity and struggle must be seen together. But what happens when we distinguish between the two sides? Lenin implicitly identifies primary and secondary sides: 'The unity (coincidence, identity, equal action) of opposites is conditional, temporary, transitory, relative'. By contrast, the 'struggle of mutually exclusive opposites is absolute, just as development and motion are absolute' (Lenin 1915a, 317; 1915b, 358). The full unity of opposites may happen for a time, in light of circumstances, but it never lasts. By contrast, the struggle of opposites is absolute and eternal, even though it takes place in a situation of contested unity. Here again we have the universal nature of contradiction, but even more so the eternity of the struggle of opposites. When I first read this text and then the subsequent elaborations by Mao Zedong some years ago, I understood this point in terms of the absoluteness and eternity of antagonistic struggle, so much so that such struggle may overturn all the gains of a proletarian revolution and the construction of socialism. Perhaps I was subconsciously influenced by the events of 1989 in Eastern Europe, but the greater influence was a residue of the Western philosophical tradition's emphasis on either-or, against which Engels struggled so mightily. I feared that Lenin was stressing this side of contradictions and I preferred the unity of opposites as the primary feature. Of course, I was wrong, for struggle-in-unity may take an antagonistic form, as is characteristic of capitalist systems, or it may take predominantly non-antagonistic forms, as with the construction of socialism. In fact, Lenin's observation should be seen as the obvious point that the absolute and eternal struggle of opposites also continues under socialism, albeit within a qualitatively different framework.

To sum up: these concise and forceful observations by Lenin indicate that if contradictions are to be found in all phenomena, if self-movement is the mode of qualitative change, and if development is the struggle of opposites in unity, then one cannot escape the conclusion that the internal dynamics of the construction of socialism entail precisely such a struggle-in-unity. And if we include the observation

[6]For an exhaustive philosophical analysis of Engels's identification and deployment of the three 'laws', see Kangal (2020, 121–181).

by Lenin with which I began this discussion, then those contradictions are not, as a rule, antagonistic.

In this section, I have analysed two texts by Lenin, one a comment on Bakunin and the other a brief exposition of an early form of the dialectical materialist method. However, they were not published at the times of writing, but rather at important moments in the 1920s. Thus, 'On the Question of Dialectics' may have been written in the excitement of philosophical rediscovery in 1915, but it was not published until 1925. Further, the marginal notes on Bukharin were first published only a few years later, in 1929. The timing was not pure happenstance. On a historical level, they became of interest for understanding the profoundly dialectical New Economic Policy of the 1920s, but they were even more important for understanding the theoretical implications of the extraordinary socialist offensive of the 1930s, with its dual processes of industrialisation and collectivisation of agriculture. These insights by Lenin provided—in that context—a distinct philosophical framework for analysing and understanding what was happening. This philosophical framework would come to be known as dialectical materialism in the 1930s.

3.3 Dialectical Materialism

To this dialectical materialist project I now turn. In the first chapter Sect. (1.2.1), I mentioned Xi Jinping's definition of Marxist philosophy in terms of dialectical and historical materialism. There, the definition was necessarily brief, so here we have an opportunity to understand the background. Arising after the philosophical struggles of the 1920s,[7] Soviet works on dialectical materialism began to be produced in earnest in the immensely creative 1930s.[8] They tend to follow a similar structure, beginning with a detailed history of the philosophical precursors of the tradition, running all the way back to the pre-Socratic philosophers in ancient Greece and guided throughout by the observations of Marx, Engels, and Lenin. After dealing with key moments in the development of European philosophy, the accounts turn—not unexpectedly—to the breakthroughs by Marx and Engels. However, for the systematic explanation of dialectical materialism itself, a primary point of reference is Lenin, especially the text I discussed earlier, along with other material from the *Philosophical Notebooks* of 1914–1916. Engels is the other major reference, along with specific examples from Marx and Stalin. After distinguishing two lines of philosophy (following Engels) between idealism and materialism, these studies point out that a dialectical materialist method focuses on self-movement, on internal dynamics, from which perspective one may then understand the effect of external forces. As for the 'laws' of dialectics, these

[7]It is beyond my remit to delve into these struggles between the 'Deborinites' and the 'Mechanists', out of which dialectical materialism arose as a philosophical method.

[8]In our time, few in the West study such works, since they are dismissed as a form of Marxist 'scholasticism' that is given to 'historical determinism'. This erroneous attitude is a real shame, since these works are well-researched, philosophically insightful and—for me at least—have enabled a number of insights embodied in this chapter.

follow—as noted above—the revision by Lenin of Engels's initial articulation: the main law of the unity and struggle of opposites, the transition from quantity into quality and vice versa, and the negation of the negation. From here a number of subsidiary positions follow, in relation to essence and phenomenon, foundation and condition, form and content, necessity and chance, law and causality, and opportunity and reality. The texts often include a section on epistemology, but a question is left begging: what has happened to historical materialism? The answer: dialectical materialism is the philosophical and scientific method, while historical materialism is its application to historical development, specifically in terms of factors that lead up to a proletarian revolution and what is entailed in the tasks of socialist construction.[9]

I have drawn this outline from a major multi-authored entry in the first edition of the *Great Soviet Encyclopaedia*, which was overseen by M. B. Mitin (1935) and translated in China as *Xin zhexue dagang—Outline of New Philosophy* (Mitin 1936b). Many are the texts to which one can turn for further study,[10] but I would like to focus on two other works on dialectical materialism, one entitled *Materialist Dialectics* (Shirokov and Iankovskii 1932b; 1937),[11] and the other a work called *Dialectical and Historical Materialism* (Mitin 1931). Why these texts out of many others? These two works were also translated into Chinese and studied by Mao Zedong and his comrades in Yan'an (Shirokov and Iankovskii 1932a; Mitin 1936a). Since these works cover similar territory, I deal with them together.

To begin with, they emphasise the party nature or partisanship of philosophy, that it should be part and parcel of the Communist Party's project. While 'Western' observers have become used to the subterfuge in which philosophy pretends to be an exercise of liberal inquiry, unfettered by party and ideological frameworks,[12] the reality is quite different. The advantage of the Soviet philosophical studies is that they were explicit about dialectical materialism's agenda (Mitin 1941). It is not so much

[9]See also the effort by Li Chongfu (2014) to outline a total system of Marxism, in which its philosophy is dialectical materialism, its method is historical materialism with a focus on political economy, both of which uphold scientific socialism as the core, goal and guidance for the construction socialism and then communism.

[10]After a flurry of publications in the 1930s and 1940s, works on dialectical materialism continued to be published until the late 1980s (for example, Pichugun 1933; Mitin 1941; Myslivchenko and Sheptulin 1988). Some were translated into English and others were written in English (Guest 1939; Somerville 1946, 149–228; Yakhot 1965; Boguslavsky et al. 1978).

[11]In relation to this work, a little confusion has arisen over the names of the editors and the book title. The Russian text has I. Shirokov and R. Iankovskii as the editors, and then includes a list of names of collaborators, of which the first is A. Aizenberg. The Chinese translation by Li Da simply lists the surnames of Shirokov and Aizenberg, adding 'et cetera [*deng*]' and 'co-authors [*hezhu*]'. The English translation, which replaces the first part on the history of philosophy with a rewritten text, lists only 'M. Shirokov' as overseeing the project at the Leningrad Institute of Philosophy. It seems that the English translation's mistake has influenced the use of M. Shirokov instead of I. Shirokov in citations of this text. I have standardised my references based on the Russian source. As for the title, the Russian has *Materialist Dialectics*, with a later note, 'A Manual for Colleges and Socioeconomic Universities'—hence the Chinese title, *Bianzhengfa weiwulun jiaocheng* (*A Course on Dialectical Materialism*).

[12]For example, this assumption bedevils the otherwise useful survey by Wetter (1958a; 1958b), and even Knight's (2005) otherwise excellent study is nervous about such matters.

that philosophy is class struggle in theory, but that the path to a genuine and rooted universal in philosophy is—analogous to Lenin's argument for the partisanship of freedom and democracy as the path to true freedom—precisely through an explicit awareness of, and indeed promotion of, its partisan nature.

As for the three laws of dialectics, they draw from Lenin and argue that the 'materialist dialectic of Marx-Engels-Lenin-Stalin sees in the unity and struggle of opposites the fundamental law of dialectical development' (Mitin et al. 1935, 150–151; see also Mitin 1931, 198–221; Shirokov and Iankovskii 1932b, 129–168; 1937, 133–176).[13] These works elaborate on Lenin's brief exposition at some length, stressing the split of a unitary item into contradictory parts and thus the primacy of self-movement, or the primacy of change as an internal process through contradictions in all relations of nature and society. Drawing from these lengthy discussions, I would like to focus on three points: the interpenetration of opposites, especially in terms of the conditional nature of unity and absoluteness of struggle; the differences between contradiction and antagonism; and dialectic of quality and quantity.

In regard to the interpenetration of opposites, we find a range of examples, such as the contradictions of the New Economic Policy, the 'preferential policies' of the Soviet Union in relation to minority nationalities, and strengthening the state (understood in terms of the dictatorship of the proletariat) as the condition for the state's withering away. Concerning minority nationalities, the reference point is Stalin, who observed that, during the long 'transition period' of the construction of socialism, national cultures would flourish—and indeed did so with the world's first 'preferential policies'—in terms of economic well-being, language, culture, education, and literature. In other words, national identity would become even stronger. Why? At this point he argues that such a process was necessary for developing socialist culture as a preparation for the eventual withering away of nationalities. A comparable point is made in the very same text concerning the enhancement of state power (proletarian dictatorship) for the sake of preparing—in the context of a future global socialism—for the eventual withering away of the state (Stalin 1930d, 368–370; 1930c, 379–381; see also Mitin et al. 1935, 123–124; Boer 2017c, 47–57).

Regarding the absoluteness of struggle and the temporary nature of unity, the preferred example concerns the relations between bourgeoisie and proletariat under capitalism (Mitin et al. 1935, 152). While the bourgeoisie and proletariat are inextricably linked through the structures of capitalism, so much so that the existence of one entails the existence of the other, the struggle between them is absolute and can be resolved only through revolution. At this point, the distinction between contradiction and antagonism comes into play, now in terms of a dialectic between the two (thus moving somewhat beyond Lenin). Thus, in the early stages of the struggle against feudal lords and serfdom, the nascent bourgeoisie and workers, along with the peasants, focused their struggle against the old system. Class contradictions were undeveloped and the bourgeoisie and proletariat were yet to become antagonistic.

[13]These laws would be reframed as four 'principal features' in the section on 'Dialectical and Historical Materialism' in the *Short Course* (Stalin 1938b, 101–104; 1938a, 106–109), with the unity and struggle of opposites culminating the list.

With the bourgeois revolutions in Europe and elsewhere, the alignments shifted: the proletariat and the bourgeoisie became increasingly antagonistic, while the remnants of the old nobility aligned themselves with their former enemy, the bourgeoisie, and the growing proletariat began to draw non-proletarian workers into their common cause. By this time, the long process of exacerbating antagonisms sets the stage for an eventual proletarian revolution (Mitin et al. 1935, 153).

This argument is insightful, but it runs into a potential problem when we focus on the construction of socialism. In this case, the favoured example concerns the relations between workers and peasants, or, more strictly speaking, between the working class and the peasantry (since rural workers were not necessarily class conscious). Again and again, we find an emphasis on the 'commonality of the fundamental interests of the vast mass of the peasantry with the interests of the proletariat' (Mitin et al. 1935, 152), on 'two friendly classes' that are no longer antagonistic' (Stalin 1936a, 128; 1936b, 167), on 'contradictions *within the bond* [*vnutri smychki*]' of the working class and the main mass of the working people, especially the main mass of the working peasantry (Stalin 1930b, 20; 1930a, 21).

It seems as though the unity of opposites has come to the fore and is no longer conditional, while the universality and absoluteness of struggle has fallen into the background. In short, does this mean that in the construction of socialism the struggle of opposites is now conditional and that their unity is absolute? The answer has two levels. The first concerns the need to deal with the remnants of capitalist and even landlord elements, which may indeed form the major contradiction of the early phase of the construction of socialism.[14] This contradiction appeared most clearly in the contrast between the rich or 'big' peasants and the development of large-scale socialist industry, and its solution was enacted through the collectivisation of agriculture and the elimination of the kulaks as a class.[15] More generally, as Stalin put it in orthodox Marxist terms: in the immediate aftermath of a proletarian revolution, the new state—as the dictatorship of the proletariat and peasantry—would deploy all means available for suppressing and crushing the bourgeoisie and landlords, if not also also the hooligan and laggard elements at the fringes of the working class, and

[14]Here they echo Lenin's observations, made in regard to the role of trade unions during the transition period. Lenin identifies a number of contradictions: between persuasion-education and coercion; protecting the interests of workers and wielding state power—in terms of the dictatorship of proletariat—for the construction of socialism; adapting to the masses and seeking to lift the masses out of prejudice and backwardness. Are these contradictions a passing phase, especially in the context of the New Economic Policy? They are no accident, observes Lenin, for they 'will persist for several decades … as long as survivals of capitalism and small production remain, contradictions between them and the young shoots of socialism are inevitable throughout the social system' (Lenin 1921b, 349–350; 1921a, 382–383). This assumption was of course due to Marx's brief reflections concerning what he called an initial stage of communism, in which 'bourgeois right' would continue for some time, and Lenin's detailed exegesis of this text in terms of the stages of socialism and communism (Marx 1875b, 13–15; 1875a, 85–87; Lenin 1917a, 86–102; 1917b, 464–179).

[15]The example may be specific to the Soviet Union, but the theoretical point is obvious, for the transition period can indeed last a long time indeed, so much so that a new mode of production will not completely abolish those that have gone before but continue to embody some elements in a transformed manner within the new (Losurdo 2017; Boer 2017b).

defending the new socialist project from efforts at foreign intervention. Thus, it is not enough to remove the former ruling class from power and expropriate the means of production from the former owners; a further step is needed, and for this the new form of governance must use persuasion and force to deal with potential counter-revolution (Stalin 1939a, 333–336; 1939b, 418–422). Obviously, in this situation class conflict continues until the bourgeoisie and landlord remnants are completely destroyed or absorbed.

To put it in terms of contradiction and antagonism, the struggle during at least the early period of socialist construction is indeed sharp, focused on dealing with the counter-revolution in its many aspects. But is it antagonistic? At this point, the second level kicks in and we need to turn to the treatments of quality and quantity. All of the texts stress—drawing heavily on Engels's *Dialectics of Nature*—the dialectical relation between quality and quantity, while at the same time pointing out that qualitative difference is determinative. While quantitative change may provide the conditions for a qualitative shift, the qualitative context determines the limits of how much can be achieved in terms of quantitative development.[16] For example, socialist forms of production are ultimately impossible under the conditions of feudalism or capitalism, given the qualitative differences between them (Mitin et al. 1935, 156–157). The same point applies to contradictions: those internal to a process are qualitatively different to contradictions within another self-moving process. Thus, the primary contradiction of capitalism (see above) is ever more antagonistic, moving through periodic crises that function as landmarks of further intensification toward a revolutionary confrontation as the way to solve such a contradiction. In fact, a proletarian revolution entails an 'abolition of the formerly dominant opposite and the establishment of a new contradiction' that is qualitatively different (Shirokov and Iankovskii 1932b, 150; 1937, 174; see also Mitin 1931, 212). How so? Invoking Lenin, the texts point out that the new contradictions are primarily non-antagonistic,[17] in the sense that they do not lead to a revolutionary confrontation. But this does not mean they are without struggle. Let us return to the example of the proletariat and the peasantry, now in terms of the middle and small peasants and not the big peasants

[16]Each of the texts discusses the question of the 'leap' in quality, stressed by Lenin in his notes on Hegel. But they point out that such a leap—as Lenin recognised elsewhere—is rarely sudden and is more often long and drawn out. In the main text I do not discuss the third law of dialectics, the negation of negation, although it is worth noting that the texts use the NEP as a key example, as well as the following insight: 'Primitive communism is negated by class society, and the subsequent communist formation negates class society. But modern communism is not a simple return to primitive communism. It represents the highest step in social development, incomparably superior to primitive communism in terms of productive forces, the organisation of labour, ideology, etc' (Mitin et al. 1935, 163).

[17]Usually, they are content to quote Lenin and elaborate, but Mitin elsewhere offers the following gloss: 'Ulianov pointed out to Bukarin that it was wrong to treat contradiction and antagonism as the same thing. In socialism, for instance, the conflict between classes will be eliminated, yet the contradictions between nature and society, between the forces of production and the means of production, will remain' (Mitin 1931, 211).

(kulaks).[18] While there is an underlying common ground—in which the peasant is a rural worker—the struggle itself moves forward in steps, but now each stage in the contradiction entails a further step towards its resolution.

Shirokov and Iankovskii sum up this approach as follows:

> If in developed socialism there were *no* contradictions—contradictions between productive forces and relations in production, between production and demand, no contradictions in the development of technique, etc.—then the development of socialism would be impossible, then instead of movement we would have stagnation. Only in virtue of the internal contradictions of the socialist order can there be development from one phase to another and higher order (Shirokov and Iankovskii 1932b, 150; 1937, 175).[19]

3.4 Mao Zedong

It was precisely the material discussed in the previous section that Mao Zedong and his comrades came to study in the second half of the 1930s. But let us step back for a moment and set the scene. In October, 1935, the Long March came to an end, with the various depleted sections of the Red Army meeting up in the Red Area based in Yan'an, Shaanxi Province. What was to follow was an immensely creative period of socialist construction and theoretical development.[20] True, the Chinese Communists had already gained significant experience in Jinggang Shan in the late 1920s and with the Jiangxi-Fujian Soviet in the early 1930s,[21] but now they could set out to provide the real foundations for the New China. In the relatively brief period before the Anti-Japanese War resumed in earnest, they engaged in avid study, lectures, translation, and publication. Mao Zedong—freed for a time from too many other pressures—immersed himself in study, ushering in one of the 'most significant chapters in his development as a Marxist theorist' (Knight 2005, 147). His focus was Marxist philosophy and the most mature and fully developed form of this philosophy was to be found in Soviet works (see above). As Edgar Snow observes: 'Once when I

---

[18]This is where the Trotskyite misunderstanding arises (all these texts often contrast dialectical materialism with Trotskyism). Not only does a Trotskyite approach take the elimination of kulaks as a class as the primary form of struggle (which they see as being of the same form as worker-bourgeois struggle under capitalism), but it also sees all contradictions as antagonistic, thereby not recognising the qualitative difference entailed with socialist construction (Weston 2008). Further, such an approach is monolithic rather than dialectical, for it sees a capitalist system as monolithic and determinative on a global level. This approach may be described as a type of Marxist fundamentalism, according to which it is all-or-nothing, either-or: either you have global capitalism or global socialism.

[19]Or as Stalin observed already in 1927: 'After all, our development does not proceed in the form of a smooth, all-round ascent. No, comrades, we have classes, we have contradictions within the country ... Our advance takes place in the process of struggle, in the process of the development of contradictions, in the process of overcoming these contradictions, in the process of bringing these contradictions to light and eliminating them' (Stalin 1927b, 330–331; 1927a, 339).

[20]For a broader context, see Joseph Liu (1971, 72–75).

[21]As Mao writes in 1957, 'Our People's Republic was not built overnight, but developed step by step out of the revolutionary base areas' (Mao 1957a, 217; 1957b, 396).

was having nightly interviews with him on Communist history, a visitor brought him several new books on philosophy, and Mao asked me to postpone our engagements. He consumed those books in three or four nights of intensive reading, during which he seemed oblivious to everything else' (Snow 1968, 88). Of course, Mao was not alone and he did not step into a vacuum. He was part of a study circle that met three nights a week and included Ai Siqi, Zhou Yang, He Sijing, Ren Beige, He Peiyuan, and Chen Boda, and he was actively involved in the many educational activities and lectures at the time (giving no less than 110 lectures at the Anti-Japanese Military and Political University). Further, the ground had been laid for an intense engagement with Marxist philosophy by the pioneering works of Qu Qiubai in the 1920s, and then the extensive writings of Ai Siqi and the uncompromising rigour of Li Da in the late 1920s and especially the 1930s.[22] As Knight observes (2005, 7), these precursors were persuaded *philosophically* by Soviet developments in dialectical materialism (the 'New Philosophy') and sought to explain and analyse this material in light of Chinese conditions.

Yet it fell to Mao Zedong, whose inclination was seek understanding of the world intellectually and philosophically, to think through and write some of the most important philosophical works on Chinese Marxism, with their essence expressed in two essays, 'On Contradiction' and 'On Practice'. However, I will not begin with these texts, preferring to go back to the initial marginal notes made by Mao in his study of Soviet material and key Chinese works,[23] which I will supplement with points from the extensive lecture notes on dialectical materialism, from July-August 1937, and 'On Contradiction' itself. Why begin with the marginal notes?[24] Here one can see a creative engagement, identifying and immediately sharpening core principles,

[22]Ai Siqi's knowledge of Russian, German, Japanese, and English also placed him in a unique position as translator of key works, while Li Da's translations relied on Japanese versions.

[23]From late 1936 to the middle of 1937, Mao made often extensive notes on Chinese translations of the works by Shirokov and Iankovskii (1932a), and Mitin (1936a). Or at least these notes survive, unlike the ones he made on the Chinese translation of the major entry in the *Great Soviet Encyclopaedia* overseen by Mitin (1936b). Soon after writing the lecture notes on dialectical materialism in July-August 1937, he also made notes on works by Li Da and Ai Siqi, especially the former's *Elements of Sociology* (Li Da 1937) and the latter's *Philosophy and Life* (Ai 1937). These notes and annotations are gathered in the core Chinese source, *Mao Zedong zhexue pizhuji* (1988), which includes notes made through to the 1960s. Translations of the relevant sections can be found in Knight and volume six of *Mao's Road to Power* (Mao 1937k, 1937l, 1937d, 1937a, 1937h, 1937b). Mao also studied, among other works, Ai Siqi's *Philosophy for the Masses* (1936a), but Mao's copy of the book has not survived, so we are unable to determine any notes he may have made. For a full list of the works on Marxist philosophy studied by Mao, see Li Ji (1987), as well as the insightful study by Li Yongtai (1985).

[24]By far the best study in English of Mao's engagement with these texts and others is by Nick Knight (2005, 149–196; see also Gong, Pang, and Shi 1986; Tian S. 1986; Wang J. 1998). For the complex relations between the reading notes, the lectures on dialectical materialism, and the essays 'On Contradiction' and 'On Practice', see Knight's introduction (1990a) to the first and still best translation of Mao's philosophical works from the 1930s (Knight 1990b). To be avoided is the culturally arrogant and orientalist dismissal by Werner Meissner (1990), as also a number of other non-Chinese works (Glaberman 1968; Gray 1973, 32–69; Wakeman 1973; Schram 1969; 1989; Lee 2002).

as well as providing specific Chinese examples from philosophy, history, and the immediate revolutionary tasks at hand.[25] Through the thousands of characters he wrote in the margins, one can almost see Mao's thoughts leaping out from the pages he was studying. At the same time, there is an intriguing familiarity with the material, not so much because he had studied it before, but because it seems to resonate in many ways with Chinese cultural assumptions. Mao studied carefully the material concerning the history of Western philosophy from ancient Greece onward and the emergence of a dialectical materialist outlook,[26] he saw as obvious the universality of contradictions in nature and society, and he was instinctively drawn to the sections on the unity and struggle of opposites, as well as the interpenetration of opposites and the relations between quality and quantity. In what follows, I draw out three pertinent topics: the main topic of the unity-in-struggle of opposites; the way he goes beyond the texts he is studying on the question of primary and secondary contradictions; and how he emphasises—in the context of the dialectic of quality and quantity—the material concerning the qualitatively distinct nature of the self-movement of genuine change, since this emphasis provides the philosophical background for socialism with Chinese characteristics.[27]

3.4.1 Contradiction and Antagonism

Mao was particularly drawn to the material on the unity and struggle of contradictions, as well as the closely related interpenetration of opposites.[28] He begins with a principle: 'The so-called unity of opposites is the dissociation of a unified entity to become mutually exclusive opposites, and includes the mutual connections between these opposites. This is the source of the so-called principal contradiction, and of

[25] 'Mao's annotations indicate that he was an active reader, one who interrogated the texts in a critical manner, seeking to understand the general principles of dialectical materialism, their appropriate formulation, and how these might be applied to an understanding of China's particular problems' (Knight 2005, 100).

[26] This is particularly the case with his notes on Li Da's *Elements of Sociology* (Mao 1988, 205–231). See further Knight's detailed study of Li Da (1996).

[27] Beyond my remit are both the criticisms of formal logic (especially in the notes to Ai Siqi's *Philsophy and Life*) and the fascinating treatment of dialectical epistemology based on social practice, which would come to fruition with 'On Practice' and later with 'Where Do Correct Ideas Come From?' (Mao 1988, 22–33; 1963a, 1963b; see also Knight 2005, 157–158). Note, however, his observation: 'Reflection is not a passive absorption of the object, but an active process. In production and class struggle, knowledge is an active element which leads to the transformation of the world' (Mao 1988, 15–16; 1937k, 267).

[28] While this is also Lenin's emphasis (see above), the notes make it very clear that Mao saw the value of all three laws (Mao 1988, 113–136; 1937h, 752–764; see also Knight 1990a, 15–24). This reality belies the suggestions by some that Mao dismissed the other laws and focused only on the unity and struggle of opposites (Wang N. 2011; Schram 1989, 65, 140).

so-called self-movement' (Mao 1988, 72; 1937k, 271).[29] Or more directly in 'On Contradiction', which arose from this study: 'The law of the contradiction in things, that is, the law of the unity of opposites, is the basic law [*genben faze*] of materialist dialectics' (Mao 1937g, 299; 1937i, 311). While in the lectures on dialectical materialism and in the influential essay this 'basic law' develops a life of its own, let us stay with the reading notes and focus on the relations between contradiction and antagonism.

A long note begins with: 'Although contradiction exists universally, antagonism only emerges when the contradictions of certain processes have developed to a definite stage' (Mao 1988, 83; 1937k, 272; see also 1988, 174). Already there is a difference in emphasis from the Soviet works, which tend to speak of the way contradictions, under certain circumstances, may become antagonistic or non-antagonistic. For Mao, the key point is that contradictions—which is to say non-antagonistic contradictions—are obviously universal, while antagonism is not. This point may have been present in the Soviet works, but Mao immediately sharpens it in terms of the development of contradictions, which reach antagonism only at a definite stage. There follow some examples of antagonistic situations, drawn by and large from capitalist systems: between oppressing and oppressed classes and nationalities, between state and state, between political parties, as well as antagonisms that take the forms of oppression, war, clash, and conflict.

However, Mao is keener to move onto non-antagonistic contradictions (in the texts on which he is commenting the *locus classicus* of Lenin's observation appears here). Many are the examples offered, from the Communist movement, through culture, economy, and nature, to conditions 'under socialism'. Of specific interest here are the examples of the Communist Party and the construction of socialism. In the notes, Mao identifies the basic contradiction as that between the forces and relations of production (see also Mao 1957a, 214; 1957b, 393),[30] but let us supplement this material with the essay 'On Contradiction', where we find the following:

---

[29]With few exceptions, I use the translations of Knight from *Mao Zedong on Dialectical Materialism* (1990b).

[30]The reality of the non-antagonistic contradiction between forces and relations of production would be emphasised in Stalin's 'Economic Problems of Socialism in the U.S.S.R' (1952b, 196–204; 1952a, 266–274). Stalin points out that there may be periods when the relations of production conform to productive means—periods that lead to the rapid growth of production and living conditions—but one should expect that at different periods either the productive relations or productive forces may lag behind and act as a brake on the other. In these situations, the task becomes one of reforming the laggard and bring it into conformity with the one leaping ahead. At times, it may be the productive relations that take the lead, while at other times it may the productive forces, which in turn requires a reshaping of the productive relations. Importantly, this constant adjustment is not merely an objective process that would happen anyway, for it also entails specific policies to correct the imbalance: 'Given a correct policy on the part of the directing bodies, these contradictions cannot grow into antagonisms, and there is no chance of matters coming to a conflict between the relations of production and the productive forces of society' (Stalin 1952b, 203; 1952a, 273). Mao and a reading circle, which met from December 1959 to February 1960, studied intensely this text and other works of political economy, leading to a collection of annotations and talks (Mao 1998; see also Zhou X. 2016).

> For instance, the contradiction between the proletariat and the bourgeoisie is resolved by the method of socialist revolution; the contradiction between the great masses of the people and the feudal system is resolved by the method of democratic revolution; the contradiction between the colonies and imperialism is resolved by the method of national revolutionary war; the contradiction between the working class and the peasant class in socialist society is resolved by the method of collectivisation and mechanisation in agriculture; contradiction within the Communist Party is resolved by the method of criticism and self-criticism; the contradiction between society and nature is resolved by the method of developing the productive forces. (Mao 1937g, 311; 1937i, 321–322)

The first three examples—socialist revolution, bourgeois revolution, and anti-colonial liberation—are obviously antagonistic contradictions that require a revolutionary resolution. But the next three examples are qualitatively different: working class and peasants, within the Communist Party, and the liberation of productive forces. The solutions offered indicate that these three contradictions are primarily non-antagonistic, taking place within the socialist-communist context. As Mao's notes on Shirokov and Iankovskii observe: 'The method for the resolution of contradictions and that for the resolution of antagonism are different' (Mao 1988, 85; 1937k, 273).[31]

Despite the quotation from 'On Contradiction' above, in general the concern in that essay with antagonism in contradiction seems somewhat muted, appearing almost as an appendix. Nonetheless, there is one significant development: instead of an abstract formula, Mao observes that in light of concrete developments, 'some contradictions which were originally non-antagonistic develop into antagonistic ones, while others which were originally antagonistic develop into non-antagonistic ones' (Mao 1937g, 335; 1937i, 344). Notably, he goes on to focus on ideological struggles within the Communist Party[32] and the town-country relation. In the latter case, the contradiction is antagonistic under capitalism, as well under the rule of the Guomindang, in which foreign imperialism and the 'big comprador bourgeoisie' ruthlessly plundered the countryside. However, 'in a socialist country and in our revolutionary base areas, this antagonistic contradiction has changed into one that is non-antagonistic; and when communist society is reached it will be abolished' (Mao 1937g, 336; 1937i, 345). Even so, a question remains: is it possible that such contradictions may become antagonistic during socialist construction? If so, what is to be done? Mao offers only the principle that the methods for resolving contradictions will differ according to the specific nature of each contradiction.

We need to wait almost twenty years for a more comprehensive assessment of this problem, in 'On the Correct Handling of Contradictions Among the People' (Mao 1957a, 1957b). Obviously, the question had come to the fore once again during the

[31] The next sentence anticipates my treatment of specific characteristics: 'This is the particularity of contradiction and the particularity of the method for the resolution of contradiction, a question which requires distinctions to be made' (Mao 1988, 85; 1937h, 723).

[32] Initially, such contradictions may not be antagonistic, but they risk and can indeed become so. Mao gives examples from the Communist Party of the Soviet Union (Lenin and Stalin versus Trotsky) and then the Communist Party of China, in which incorrect thinking can avoid antagonism if those guilty of such positions correct themselves. Obviously, the Party should enable such a process, but if those comrades insist on errors, the situation may lead to antagonism.

first few years of socialist construction after Liberation, and it is no coincidence that this was also the time when Mao laboured over revisions to 'On Contradiction'.[33] Immediately in the 'Correct Handling' piece, Mao assumes a position he had hammered out twenty years earlier: the qualitative difference in contradictions depending on their circumstances. Here the difference refers to contradictions with anti-socialist enemies of the people and contradictions among the people. The two are, he writes, 'totally different in nature' (Mao 1957a, 204; 1957b, 384; see also 1956a, 164). The main concern of the essay is contradictions among the people, but if we expected that such contradictions might have been somewhat simplified in the context of socialist construction, then we will be sorely disappointed. In this context, there are even more contradictions: within and between workers, peasants and intelligentsia, between governance and people, centralism and democracy, collective and individual, and so on (see also Mao 1956b, 1956c). He devotes considerable attention to practical matters in relation to a number of these contradictions, but the basic point is that contradictions among the people need to be managed carefully so that they do not become antagonistic and can be resolved in a non-antagonistic manner. In other words, Mao does not assume that internal contradictions are always non-antagonistic, that they can always be resolved amicably. There is always a risk that they may become antagonistic and that counter-revolutionary forces—internal and external—may seek to exacerbate such antagonism. Thus, policies should always be concerned to avoid such developments, to direct contradictions in a non-antagonistic direction, and seek to resolve them in this manner. Mao writes that in 'ordinary circumstances, contradictions among the people are not antagonistic'. However, 'if they are not handled properly, or if we relax our vigilance and lower our guard, antagonism may arise' (Mao 1957a, 211; 1957b, 391; see also Zhou X. 2018, 15).[34] To reinforce this point, Mao reverts to his initial insights from the 1930s. While some may have expected that the unity of opposites would become paramount during socialist construction, he reminds us of the core insight from dialectical materialism—now described as 'Marxist philosophy'—that the unity of contradictions is temporary and transitory, but the struggle is absolute. In light of this primacy of

[33]So long did the revisions take him that the essay's initial publication appeared in the second volume of his *Selected Works* (subsequent editions would place the essay in the first volume). For a comprehensive presentation of the similarities and differences between the lecture notes from 1937 and the final publication of 'On Contradiction', see Knight's translation (Mao 1937e). Other philosophical texts appeared during the 1960s, but our only source is the unverified and therefore unreliable *Mao Zedong sixiang wansui*, published by some Red Guards (Mao 1964b, 1964a).

[34]The CPC Central Committee's resolution of 1981 expands further: 'Having eliminated the exploiting classes as classes, class struggle is no longer the principal contradiction. Owing to domestic factors and international influences, class struggle will continue to exist within a certain scope for a long time and may intensify under certain conditions. We must oppose both the idea of enlarging class struggle and the idea that it has been extinguished. We must be on high alert and wage effective struggle against all kinds of destructive activities carried out politically, economically, ideologically, culturally and socially by elements hostile to socialism. We must have a correct understanding of a large number of social contradictions in our society that do not fall within the scope of class struggle and adopt methods different from class struggle to solve them correctly' (CPC Central Committee 1981, 17).

struggle, 'socialist society grows more united and consolidated through the ceaseless process of correctly handling and resolving contradictions' (Mao 1957a, 213; 1957b, 393).

3.4.2 Principal and Secondary Contradictions

In regard to principal and secondary contradictions and their aspects, Mao devotes a significant annotation to the topic, going well beyond his source text (Mao 1988, 87–90; 1937k, 273–275). That text speaks only of the relation between a dominant aspect of a contradiction and its secondary aspect (see more below). By contrast, Mao immediately makes the distinction between principal and secondary contradictions, and then observes: 'Because the development of the principal contradiction determines the development of the various secondary contradictions, if one cannot distinguish between the principal and secondary contradictions, between the determining contradiction and those that are determined, one cannot seek out the most essential thing of a process' (Mao 1988, 87; 1937k, 273). As Knight suggests (2005, 156), there is a direct path from this annotation to the lectures and then the essay 'On Contradiction', so much so that we can see the structure of the later work already emerging as Mao was studying the Soviet sources. Even more, the need to identify the principal contradiction, as formulated by Mao, has come to guide CPC policy and the development of the New China until today; indeed, the determining feature of all government policy turns on identifying the principal contradiction to which all the other secondary contradictions relate. Importantly, it arose during Mao's close study of Shirokov and Iankovskii in 1936–1937, but it could arise only through Mao's sharpening of the point in response to Soviet treatments of dialectical materialism, a sharpening that simultaneously did so in light of the Chinese tradition and challenged its assumptions.

As for the notes, the long annotation that is my focus is by no means the first time Mao had spoken of principal and secondary contradictions. Thus, in the initial treatment of the unity and struggle of contradictions, Mao picks up a relatively minor point in the source text concerning the need to identify a basic or fundamental contradiction in a process. Mao pounces: 'it is necessary also to know the fundamental contradiction which allows development of the process, for that is the source of movement of the process' (Mao 1988, 66; 1937k, 270–271). Thus, the fundamental contradiction of capitalism is between the forces and relations of production, as manifested in the tension between the social character of production and the private character of ownership. From here, Mao moves to the contemporary situation in China, where the principal contradiction is between China and Japan, and thus the way to solve this contradiction is through a united front against the Japanese imperialist invasion (see also Mao 1988, 73–74; 1937k, 271–272).[35] Of most interest for my purposes

[35] Within a couple of years, Mao would elaborate: 'The contradiction between imperialism and the Chinese nation and the contradiction between feudalism and the great masses of the people are the

is the third principal contradiction, which is focused on the transition from capitalism to socialism. Mao simply assumes—along with the text he is studying—that contradictions will indeed be a feature of socialist construction. The contradiction: between the relics of capitalism, embodied above all in big peasants who exploit others, and large-scale socialist industry and the working class. The solution: further industrialisation and socialisation of agriculture, and—if necessary—internal force (Mao 1988, 67–69; 1937k, 271).

With respect to the principal and secondary aspect internal to a contradiction, Mao moves well beyond the source text by Shirokov and Iankovskii. They stipulate a more static view concerning the foundational role of value in relation to use value, and of production in relation to consumption (drawing on Marx's *Capital*), but also of practice in relation to theory. Mao recognises these points, but then asks 'which aspect is principal'? He observes: 'It is necessary to observe the situation of the development of a process, and it will be determined under definite conditions' (Mao 1988, 88; 1937k, 274). He goes on to provide a long series of examples, including military (China-Japan, forces in the revolutionary struggle, strategy and tactics, mobile and positional warfare, and so on), classes and economic realities (bourgeoisie and proletariat, proletariat and peasantry, manual and mental labour, and so on), and those between capitalism, feudalism, imperialism, and socialism.[36] But who is to decide which aspect is primary and which is secondary? When a process attains a definite stage of development, 'the strength of the two sides in the struggle will determine it'. Even more, the 'dominant and the non-dominant change from one to the other' (Mao 1988, 90; 1937k, 275). In fact, this is precisely the point with which Mao began the whole analysis of primary and secondary aspects, framing it in terms of the results of a struggle between the two aspects, leading to a 'change of mutual interpermeation', which entails not merely a 'transformation to achieve identity', but even more a 'transformation to its opposing aspect'. This reality is not a case of simple identity, for precisely through this transformation can one find the 'indivisible interconnection of the two opposed aspects' (Mao 1988, 87; 1937k, 273).

As commentators point out (Yang and Yang 2007, 17–18; Wang N. 2011; Sun 2017, 17), this emphasis is a distinct contribution from Mao: apart from constant need to identify the primary contradiction that determines the many secondary contradictions, within each contradiction is a primary and a secondary aspect. The relation between the two will change in light of circumstances. In the notes, Mao initially developed this analysis in the context of his study of the unity and struggle of contradictions, but by the time he came to write the lecture notes on dialectical materialism and then revise the text of 'On Contradiction', the whole question of primary and secondary became a topic in its own right (Mao 1937c, 259–265; 1937j, 643–650; 1937g, 320–327; 1937i, 331–337).

---

basic contradictions in modern Chinese society. Of course, there are others, such as the contradiction between the bourgeoisie and the proletariat and the contradictions within the reactionary ruling classes themselves. But the contradiction between imperialism and the Chinese nation is the principal one' (Mao 1939b, 631; 1939a, 313).

[36]Compare the astute analysis—in 'On Contradiction'—of the changing relations between principal and secondary aspects in the long Chinese anti-colonial and revolutionary struggle (Mao 1937g, 320–321; 1937i, 331–332).

3.4.3 Chinese Characteristics

The final point to be drawn from the notes is the philosophical background for what later became known as socialism with Chinese characteristics. In the first chapter Sect. (1.3), I provided some historical background (the Zunyi Conference of 1935) and in the previous chapter Sect. (2.5) I noted how Deng Xiaoping promoted the idea and its practice, so here I am concerned with the philosophical foundations. The philosophical key is to be found in both the self-movement of qualitative change and the qualitative difference between processes and their contradictions. The first point is obvious: if internal processes are the primary contexts for qualitative transformations (Mao 1988, 64; 1937k, 270), then it follows logically that the Chinese revolution, as well as the arduous task of constructing socialism, have their own particular characteristics. Of course, Mao denies neither the role of external causes, nor the internal-external dialectic, as the notes on Ai Siqi's *Philosophy and Life* and 'On Contradiction' make clear (Mao 1937d, 1937g, 301–303; 1937i, 313–315). But he does agree with his source texts that 'internal cause determines the necessity of change in things, not external cause' (Mao 1988, 201; 1937d, 262; see also 1937g, 301; 1937i, 313).[37] Thus, it is only through the 'intrinsic attributes of each stage that the nature of the process will develop' (Mao 1988, 49; 1937h, 705).[38]

In regard to quality and quantity,[39] Mao almost immediately observes: 'In knowing a process, we must first determine its quality, and the differences between it and other processes, that is, know its special characteristics' (Mao 1988, 41; 1937h, 700; see also 1988, 165; 1937a, 786–787). Special or particular characteristics—*tedian* or *texing* (Mao uses both terms)—would of course come into its own soon enough to designate the specific characteristics in China—*Zhongguo tese*. But let us stay with the question of contradictions. Mao elaborates that the first step is to 'indicate all of the particular characteristics of a process', especially the 'fundamental particularity'. Here we touch on the need to identify a principal contradiction, now meshed with the specific characteristics of a context. In the same note, Mao goes on to indicate the second step of the process: 'only then is it possible to know the laws of development of a process, because the laws [*faze*] are contained in the development of the contradictions of the basic particularity' (Mao 1988, 44; 1937k, 269). In other words, the fundamental or basic characteristics of a process of development are contradictory;

[37] Later in the notes, in the discussion of the relativity of unity and the absoluteness of struggle, Mao further emphasises the primacy of the internal process of contradictions. In this light, he offers a series of examples, mainly drawn from the revolutionary struggle in China along with some Chinese sayings, such as—from *Lu shi chunqiu*—'a door hinge is never worm eaten, but a piece of wood from a door hinge will be' (Mao 1988, 107–109; 1937h, 748–750).

[38] We may find a precursor to this philosophical argument, albeit with less detail, in relation to the development of socialism in one country (Shirokov and Iankovskii 1932b, 166–167; 1937, 203–205). At the same time, this was by no means a new idea propagated suddenly in the Soviet Union in the 1930s, for it has a much longer history in the socialist tradition (Van Ree 1998; 2015).

[39] In what follows, I emphasise a distinct feature of Mao's notes on quality and quantity, but it should be noted that he acknowledges the dialectical relation between the two. This is so particularly in his notes on Mitin's *Dialectical and Historical Materialism* (Mao 1988, 181–187; 1937l, 279–280).

and this principal contradiction is a contradiction particular to a specific context. Such contexts necessarily differ, whether one considers Western Europe, the Soviet Union, or China. Indeed, if one studies a specific course of development such as China in its more recent past, multiple contradictions emerge, each of which has its own particularity (Mao 1937g, 311–312; 1937i, 322–323). A little later in the notes, Mao points out that a dialectical materialist approach enables one to identify the 'particularity of contradictions' within a process, but also that it is necessary to know the 'contradictions of the various aspects of a process' (Mao 1988, 74; 1937k, 272). It is not enough to identify the specific nature of a basic contradiction in a particular context, for it also needs a careful awareness of the way such a contradiction changes in light of developments. By now, the connection with the interpermeation and indeed transformation of principal and secondary aspects of a contradiction throughout an internal process should be clear (see also Mao 1988, 46; 1937k, 269).

Given Mao's interest in the particularity or specific characteristics of a contradictory process, it should be no surprise that in the lectures on dialectical materialism and then in 'On Contradiction' this emphasis too would become an important section in its own right, entitled 'The Particularity of Contradiction' (Mao 1937c, 241–255; 1937j, 631–643; 1937g, 308–320; 1937i, 319–330). Noticeable in this material are the extensive examples, which begin with science and nature, move onto the Russian Revolution, and then focus extensively on China's specific context. As for the notes, Mao enthusiastically seeks to identify a host of contradictions, not only from the immediate context of the Communist revolutionary struggle in China, but also from the Chinese tradition (Mao 1988, 77–78, 80; 1937h, 727–730). Our situation is unique, he wants to say, not only in terms of the contrast with capitalist contexts, but also with other socialist projects, of which the Soviet Union was—in the 1930s—the prime example. On a theoretical level, Mao observes: 'Qualitatively different contradictions require different methods for their resolution' (Mao 1988, 73; 1937k, 271). On a practical level, as 'On Contradiction' puts it: 'Why is it that the Chinese revolution can avoid a capitalist future and be directly linked with socialism without taking the old historical road of Western countries, without passing through a period of bourgeois dictatorship? The sole reason is the concrete conditions [*juti tiaojian*] of the time' (Mao 1937g, 331–332; 1937i, 341).[40]

Time to sum up: I have emphasised the way Mao Zedong's creative engagement with this material from Soviet Marxist philosophy provided him with the philosophical framework for the development of the key idea that the Communist struggle in China had its own distinct characteristics. It should be no surprise that a year later, in 1938, he observes in a key work, 'The New Stage':

> The history of this great nation of ours goes back several thousand years. It has its own laws of development, its own national characteristics, and many precious treasures. As regards all this, we are mere schoolboys. Today's China is an outgrowth of historic China. We are Marxist historicists; we must not mutilate history. From Confucius to Sun Yatsen, we must sum it up critically, and we must constitute ourselves the heirs to this precious legacy. Conversely,

[40]In English language works, Knight's efforts (1983, 1990c, 2005, 165–169, 205–209) to understand Mao's sinification of Marxism are the most insightful, even though they are still caught at times in the either-or logic of Western thought.

> the assimilation of this legacy itself becomes a method that aids considerably in guiding the present great movement. A Communist is a Marxist internationalist, but Marxism must take on a national form [*minzu xingshi*] before it can be put into practice. There is no such thing as abstract Marxism, but only concrete Marxism [*juti de makesizhuyi*]. What we call concrete Marxism is Marxism that has taken on a national form [*minzu xingshi*], that is, Marxism applied to the concrete struggle in the concrete conditions [*juti huanjing*] prevailing in China, and not Marxism abstractly used. If a Chinese Communist, who is a part of the great Chinese people, bound to his people by his very flesh and blood, talks of Marxism apart from Chinese peculiarities [*Zhongguo tedian*], this Marxism is merely an empty abstraction. Consequently, the sinification of Marxism [*makesizhuyi zhongguohua*]– that is to say, making certain that in all its manifestations it is imbued with Chinese characteristics [*Zhongguo de texing*], using it according to Chinese peculiarities [*Zhongguo de tedian*]– becomes a problem that must be understood and solved by the whole Party without delay. (Mao 1938a, 658–659; 1938b, 538–539)

It is no coincidence that in the same year we find Ai Siqi—Mao's close conversation partner on philosophical matters—urging: 'Now there is a need for a sinified [*zhongguohua*], actualised [*xianshihua*] movement of philosophical research' (Ai 1938, 387).[41] But let us turn to Deng Xiaoping's pithy re-articulation at the opening of the CPC's twelfth national congress in 1982:

> We must integrate the universal truth of Marxism with the concrete realities of China, blaze a path of our own and build a socialism with Chinese characteristics – that is the basic conclusion we have reached after reviewing our long history. (Deng 1982b, 2–3; 1982a, 14)

3.5 Conclusion

This chapter has entailed a step back, before the Reform and Opening-Up, in order to identify the philosophical background of the contradiction analysis that remains today a core feature of socialism with Chinese characteristics. This task has entailed working through Lenin's initial succinct deliberations, the extensive development of dialectical materialism in the Soviet Union of the 1930s, and Mao Zedong's creative engagement with this material in light of Chinese conditions. My focus has been on the themes of the unity and struggle of opposites, the quality-quantity dialectic, contradiction and antagonism, as well as the philosophical basis for socialism with Chinese characteristics, or the sinification of Marxism. Importantly, this basis emerged in Mao Zedong's creative and critical engagement with Soviet and Chinese works on dialectical materialism in the 1930s, specifically in terms of the priority of self-movement and in the qualitative difference of contradictions.[42] Thus,

[41] This was a recurring theme in Ai Siqi's thought, already appearing in *Sixiang fangfalun* (Ai 1936b, 160), but always with the warning: 'Sinification does not mean abandoning the Marxist position' (Ai 1940, 481; see also Ni 2016, 28–29). Further, Ai's formidable organisational and editorial ability ensured, after his arrival in Yan'an, that Mao would entrust him with establishing the institutional structures to ensure the widespread dissemination of these philosophical developments (Knight 2005, 197–214).

[42] By now it should be obvious that the wayward hypotheses that Mao was not so much a Marxist philosopher but a Chinese one, or that he inverted dialectical materialism in favour or 'voluntarism'

the path of revolutionary struggle and—after Liberation—the task of constructing socialism would be determined primarily by the internal and qualitatively distinct contradictions of the Chinese context. Of course, such a Marxist approach could not work without the universal principles of Marxism, but these principles had to be concretised. However, it was not merely these features of dialectical materialism that supplied Mao and others with the philosophical basis, for contradiction analysis as a whole comes into play: Marxism is at one and the same time thoroughly universal, as a philosophical method and revolutionary program, *and* concretely specific in light of local conditions, for Marxism is not Marxism without such scientific rigour. Without one you do not have the other. This dialectical reality of universal and particular is embodied in the phrase 'socialism with Chinese characteristics' (Zhou Y. 1997, 120).

Let me close with a brief survey of government policy in light of contradiction analysis since the founding of the New China and in the process of socialist construction. In more than 70 years, there have been only three principal contradictions.[43] To begin with, at the Eighth National Congress of the CPC in 1956, it was resolved that 'the principal contradiction facing Chinese society has become the one between the need for building a modern industrial country and the reality of the backward agricultural country, and that between the needs of the people for rapid economic and cultural development and the failure of current economic and cultural supplies to meet their needs'. After the chaos and loss of direction during the Cultural Revolution, a second principal contradiction was identified at the Sixth Plenary Session of the Eleventh Central Committee in 1981: 'between backward social production and the ever-growing material and cultural needs of the masses' (CPC Central Committee 1981, 16).[44] The third principal contradiction came 36 years later, identified by Xi Jinping at the Nineteenth Congress of the CPC in 2017. Pointing out that socialism with Chinese characteristics has made major developments, a new principal contradiction has emerged, 'between unbalanced and inadequate development and the people's ever-growing needs for a better life [*meihao shenghuo*]' (Xi 2017a, 5; 2017b, 9–10).[45] One can see the similarities and differences between the

---

or 'idealism', are without foundation (Schram 1969, 71–73; 1989, 67; Wakeman 1973; Meisner 2007, 146–149).

[43]One may ask: what about Mao's emphasis on class struggle as the principal contradiction during the Cultural Revolution? For Chinese scholars, this was clearly an incorrect assessment of the situation and thus of the principal contradiction (Xiao 2004, 63; see also CPC Central Committee 1981, 10–11). We may go further: Mao had seemingly forgotten or pushed aside his earlier emphases on both the necessity of managing contradictions among the people in a socialist system so that they do not become antagonistic, and on the core need for liberating the forces of production (Zhou Y. 1997, 123, 126). This deviation was rectified by the late 1970s and early 1980s.

[44]This final agreement had a lengthy gestation, since it was first proposed at the Third Plenary Session of the Eleventh Central Committee in December, 1978, as—in Deng Xiaoping's words—the 'level of our productive forces is very low and is far from meeting the needs of our people and country' (Deng 1979a, 182; 1979b, 189). Discussion, debate, and refinement eventually came up with the wording of the Sixth Plenary Session in 1981.

[45]For a full overview of the principal contradictions from Mao Zedong to Xi Jinping, see Jin Zhenglian (2017).

three principal contradictions: structurally, they all share an emphasis on production (supply-side) and on the people's needs.[46] Each differs as well: as productive forces have been liberated ever further, the emphasis shifts, moving from an absence and then backwardness in production to unbalanced and inadequate development in 2017.[47] In terms of the people's needs, these move from material and cultural needs to the need for a better life (*meihao shenghuo*), which encapsulates material, cultural, political, public, and environmental life.

Obviously, contradiction analysis is alive and well, but so is the dialectical materialism that provides its philosophical framework. For those who have taken the time to work their way through this chapter, this point should be obvious, although it is a dialectical materialism updated and refitted for the times (Wang L. and Wang Q. 2015; Su 2017; Jiang 2018, 2; Liu H. 2018; Xie 2018). One can hardly begin to understand China's Marxist project, or indeed the worldview and methodology of the CPC, without understanding the central role that dialectical materialism continues to play, and thus of Marxist philosophy as a whole (see also Sect. 1.2). Further, one does not toss out ever new contradictions on a whim; only three have been identified since the foundation of the New China, with each one requiring assiduous research and assessment by multiple government departments and research institutes. One more dialectical twist: the three principal contradictions are not seen in terms of either evolution or revolution, but rather in terms of the dialectical interaction of change and not-change. Thus, each new principal contradiction indicates a new era (*xin shidai*), whether in 1956, 1981, or 2017, but—as we saw in the previous chapter—the fact that socialism is still in its initial or primary stage has not changed (Liu H. 2018, 42).

References

Ai, Siqi. 1936a. Dazhong zhexue. In *Ai Siqi wenji*, vol. 1:129–182. Beijing: Renmin chubanshe, 1980.

Ai, Siqi. 1936b. *Sixiang fangfalun*. 4th edn. Shanghai: Shenghuo shudian.

Ai, Siqi. 1937. *Zhexue yu shenghuo*. Shanghai: Dushu shenghuoshe.

Ai, Siqi. 1938. Zhexue he xianzhuang he renwu. In *Ai Siqi wenji*, vol. 1:384–388. Beijing: Renmin chubanshe, 1980.

Ai, Siqi. 1940. Lun Zhongguo de teshuxing. In *Ai Siqi wenji*, vol. 1:471–487. Beijing: Renmin chubanshe, 1980.

Boer, Roland. 2015. *The sacred economy of ancient Israel*. Library of Ancient Israel. Louisville: Westminster John Knox.

Boer, Roland. 2017a. From Berne to Yan'an: The theoretical breakthroughs of Lenin and Mao. *Crisis and Critique* 4 (2): 60–84.

[46]They also echo the definitions of socialism and indeed communism: from each according to ability, to each according to work (socialism) or according to need (communism).

[47]Evidence for such imbalance and inequality in production is abundant, although it has improved already since the 1990s and early 2000s: eastern and western development, urban and rural income gaps, and indeed differences between regions in incomes and provision of services such as education and health.

Boer, Roland. 2017b. Shehuizhuyi maodunlun xintan. In *Qimeng, lishiguan yu makesi bianzhengfa*, edited by Zang Fengyu, 140–156. Guizhou: Guizhou renmin chubanshe.
Boer, Roland. 2017c. *Stalin: From theology to the philosophy of socialism in power*. Singapore: Springer.
Boer, Roland. In Press. Motion, matter, and dialectics: From Marx's doctoral thesis to Engels's *Dialectics of Nature*. *Science & Society*.
Boguslavsky, B. M., V. A. Karpushin, A. I. Rakitov, V. Y. Chertikhin, and G. I. Ezrin. 1978. *ABC of historical and dialectical materialism*. Translated by Lenina llitskaya. Moscow: Progress Publishers.
Bukharin, Nikolai. 1920a. *Ėkonomika perekhodnogo perioda*. Letchworth-Herts: Prideaux Press, 1980.
Bukharin, Nikolai. 1920b. *The politics and economics of the transition period*. Translated by Oliver Field. London: Routledge, 2003.
CPC Central Committee. 1981. Guanyu jianguo yilai dang de ruogan lishi wenti de jueyi (1981 nian 6 yue 27 ri Zhongguo gongchandang di shiyi jie zhongyang weiyuanhui di liu ci quanti huiyi tongguo). *Renmin Ribao*, 27 June 1981: 1–9.
Deng, Xiaoping. 1979a. Jianchi sixiang jiben yuanze (1979.03.30). In *Deng Xiaoping wenxuan*, vol. 2:158–184. Beijing: Renmin chubanshe, 2008.
Deng, Xiaoping. 1979b. Uphold the four cardinal principles (30 March, 1979). In *Selected works of Deng Xiaoping*, vol. 2:168–191. Beijing: Foreign Languages Press, 1995.
Deng, Xiaoping. 1982a. Opening speech at the twelfth national congress of the communist party of China (1 September, 1982). In *Selected works of Deng Xiaoping*, vol. 3:13–16. Beijing: Foreign Languages Press, 1994.
Deng, Xiaoping. 1982b. Zhongguo gongchandang di shier ci quanguo daibiao dahui kaimuci (1982.09.01). In *Deng Xiaoping wenxuan*, vol. 3:1–4. Beijing: Renmin chubanshe, 2008.
Engels, Friedrich. 1858. Engels an Marx in London. Manchester, 14.Juli 1858. In *Marx Engels Werke*, vol. 29:337–339. Berlin: Dietz, 1973.
Engels, Friedrich. 1873. Engels an Marx in Manchester. London, 30.Mai 1873. In *Marx Engels Werke*, vol. 33:80–81. Berlin: Dietz, 1973.
Engels, Friedrich. 1880a. Socialism: Utopian and scientific. In *Marx and Engels collected works*, vol. 24:281–325. Moscow: Progress Publishers, 1989.
Engels, Friedrich. 1880b. Socialisme utopique et socialisme scientifique. In *Marx Engels Gesamtaugabe*, vol. I.27:541–582. Berlin: Dietz, 1985.
Engels, Friedrich. 1882a. *Dialectics of nature*. In *Marx and Engels collected works*, vol. 25:313–588. Moscow: Progress Publishers, 1987.
Engels, Friedrich. 1882b. *Dialektik der Natur*. In *Marx Engels Werke*, vol. 20:305–570. berlin: dietz, 1973.
Engels, Friedrich. 1882c. *Dialektik der Natur (systematische Anordnung der Manuskripte)*. In *Marx Engels Gesamtausgabe*, vol. I.26:293–554. Berlin: Dietz, 1985.
Engels, Friedrich. 1882d. Engels an Marx in Ventnor. London, 23.Nov. 1882. In *Marx Engels Werke*, vol. 37:118–119. Berlin: Dietz, 1973.
Glaberman, Martin. 1968. Mao as a dialectician. *International Philosophical Quarterly* 8: 94–112.
Gong, Yuzhi, Pang Xianzhi, and Shi Zhongquan. 1986. *Mao Zedong de dushu shenghuo*. 2nd edn. Beijing: Sanlian shudian, 2014.
Gray, Jack. 1973. *Mao Tse-tung*. Guildford: Lutterworth.
Guest, David. 1939. *A textbook of historical materialism*. London: Lawrence and Wishart.
Haug, Wolfgang Fritz. 2017. On the contradictions of Marxism. *Contradictions: A Journal for Critical Thought* 1 (2): 13–22.
Jiang, Xi. 2018. Bianzheng weiwuzhuyi fangfalun shiyu xia Xi Jinping xin shidai Zhongguo tese shehuizhuyi sixiang dui xin maodun de fenxi he jiejue. *Xinyu xueyuan xuebao* 23 (5): 1–3.
Jin, Zhenglian. 2017. Jindai yilai Zhongguo shehui zhuyao maodun de yanhua yu Xi Jinping 'xin shidai' de luoji guanxi. *Yancheng gongxueyuan xuebao (shehui kexue ban)* 30 (4): 18–22, 35.

Kangal, Kaan. 2020. *Friedrich Engels and the dialectics of nature*. Cham: Palgrave Macmillan (Springer).
Knight, Nick. 1983. The form of Mao Zedong's 'sinification of Marxism'. *The Australian Journal of Chinese Affairs* 9: 17–33.
Knight, Nick. 1990a. Introduction: Soviet Marxism and the development of Mao Zedong's philosophical thought. In *Mao Zedong on dialectical materialism: Writings on philosophy, 1937*, edited by Nick Knight, 3–83. Armonk: M.E. Sharpe.
Knight, Nick. 1990b. ed. *Mao Zedong on dialectical materialism: Writings on philosophy, 1937*. Armonk: M.E. Sharpe.
Knight, Nick. 1990c. Soviet philosophy and Mao Zedong's 'sinification of Marxism'. *Journal of Contemporary Asia* 20 (1): 89–109.
Knight, Nick. 1996. *Li Da and Marxist philosophy in China*. Boulder: Westview.
Knight, Nick. 2005. *Marxist Philosophy in China: From Qu Qiubai to Mao Zedong, 1923–1945*. Dordrecht: Springer.
Lee, Feigon. 2002. *Mao: A reinterpretation*. Chicago: Ivan R. Dee.
Lenin, V. I. 1909a. A. M. Gor′komu. 3 (16) noiabriai 1909g. In *Polnoe sobranie sochinenii*, vol. 47:219–220. Moscow: Izdatel'stvo politicheskoi literatury, 1970.
Lenin, V. I. 1909b. To Maxim Gorky, November 16, 1909. In *Collected works*, vol. 34:403–404. Moscow: Progress Publishers, 1966.
Lenin, V. I. 1914a. Conspectus of Hegel's book *The science of logic*. In *Collected works*, vol. 38:85–237. Moscow: Progress Publishers, 1968.
Lenin, V. I. 1914b. Konspekt knigi Gegelia 'Nauka Logiki'. In *Polnoe sobranie sochinenii*, vol. 29:77–218. Moscow: Izdatel'stvo politicheskoi literatury, 1973.
Lenin, V. I. 1915a. K voprosu o dialektike. In *Polnoe sobranie sochinenii*, vol. 29:316–322. Moscow: Izdatel'stvo politicheskoi literatury, 1979.
Lenin, V. I. 1915b. On the question of dialectics. In *collected works*, vol. 38:355–361. Moscow: Progress Publishers, 1968.
Lenin, V. I. 1917a. Gosudarstvo i revoliutsiia. Uchenie marksizma o gosudarstve i zadachi proletariata v revoliutsii. Avgust–sentiabr′ 1917g.; ranee 17 dekabria 1918g. In *Polnoe sobranie sochinenii*, vol. 33:1–120. Moscow: Izdatel'stvo politicheskoi literatury, 1969.
Lenin, V. I. 1917b. The state and revolution: The Marxist theory of the state and the tasks of the proletariat in the revolution. In *Collected works*, vol. 25:385–497. Moscow: Progress Publishers.
Lenin, V. I. 1920. Zamechaniia na knigu N. I. Bukharina 'Ėkonomika perekhodnogo perioda'. In *Leninskii Sbornik*, vol. 40:383–432. Moscow: Institute of Marxism-Leninism, 1985.
Lenin, V. I. 1921a. Tenth congress of the R.C.P.(B.), March 8–16, 1921. In *Collected works*, vol. 32:165–271. Moscow: Progress Publishers, 1965.
Lenin, V. I. 1921b. X s"ezd RKP (b) 8–16 marta 1921g. In *Polnoe sobranie sochinenii*, vol. 43:1–127. Moscow: Izdatel'stvo politicheskoi literatury, 1970.
Li, Chongfu. 2014. A study on the totality of Marxism from the perspective of scientific socialism. *Marxist Studies in China* 2014: 43–57.
Li, Da. 1937. *Shehuixue dagang*. Shanghai: Bigengtang shudian.
Li, Ji. 1987. Mao Zedong you gemingjia zhuanbian wei gemingjia jian zhexuejia de biaozhi. *Mao Zedong Deng Xiaoping lilun yanjiu* 1987 (4): 37–43.
Li, Yongtai. 1985. Mao Zedong tongzhi dui zhexue de xuexi he changdao. *Xinan daxue xuebao (renwen shehui kexue ban)* 1985 (2): 9–16.
Liu, Hao. 2018. Xin shidai Zhongguo tese shehuizhuyi zhuyao maodun fenxi. *Nei Menggu daxue xuebao (zhexue kexue shehui ban)* 50 (5): 42–56.
Liu, Joseph. 1971. Mao's 'On contradiction'. *Studies in Soviet Thought* 11 (2): 71–89.
Losurdo, Domenico. 2017. Has China turned to capitalism?—Reflections on the transition from capitalism to socialism. *International Critical Thought* 7 (1): 15–31.
Mao, Zedong. 1937a. Annotations on dialectical materialism and historical materialism by M. B. Mitin and others (before July 1937). In *Mao's road to power: revolutionary writings 1912–1949*, vol. 6:767–807. Armonk: M. E. Sharpe, 2004.

Mao, Zedong. 1937b. Annotations to Li Da's *Outline of sociology*. In *Mao's road to power: Revolutionary writings 1912–1949*, vol. 6:808–826. Armonk: M. E. Sharpe, 2004.
Mao, Zedong. 1937c. Bianzheng weiwu lun. In *Mao Zedong ji, Bujuan*, edited by Minoru Minoru, vol. 5:187–280. Tokyo: Sōsōsha, 1983–1986.
Mao, Zedong. 1937d. Extracts from Ai Siqi's *Philosophy and life* (September 1937). In *Mao Zedong on dialectical materialism: Writings on philosophy, 1937*, translated and edited by Nick Knight, 230–266. Armonk: M. E. Sharpe, 1990.
Mao, Zedong. 1937e. The law of the unity of contradictions (On contradiction). In *Mao Zedong on dialectical materialism: Writings on philosophy, 1937*, translated and edited by Nick Knight, 154–229. Armonk: M. E. Sharpe, 1990.
Mao, Zedong. 1937f. Lecture notes on dialectical materialism. In *Mao Zedong on dialectical materialism: Writings on philosophy, 1937*, translated and edited by Nick Knight, 230–266. Armonk: M. E. Sharpe, 1990.
Mao, Zedong. 1937g. Maodun lun (1937.08). In *Mao Zedong xuanji*, vol. 1:299–340. Beijing: Renmin chubanshe, 2009.
Mao, Zedong. 1937h. Notes on *A course in dialectical materialism* by M. Shirokov and others (November 1936–April 1937). In *Mao's road to power: revolutionary writings 1912–1949*, vol. 6:671–766. Armonk: M. E. Sharpe, 2004.
Mao, Zedong. 1937i. On contradiction (August, 1937). In *Selected works of Mao Tse-Tung*, vol. 1:311–347. Beijing: Foreign Languages Press, 1965.
Mao, Zedong. 1937j. On dialectical materialism (Lecture Notes). In *Mao's road to power: Revolutionary writings 1912–1949*, vol. 6:573–667. Armonk: M. E. Sharpe, 2004.
Mao, Zedong. 1937k. Philosophical annotations and marginalia: Annotations on M. Shirokov and A. Aizenberg et al., *A course on dialectical materialism*, translated by Li Da and Lei Zhongjian (third edition). In *Mao Zedong on dialectical materialism: Writings on philosophy, 1937*, translated and edited by Nick Knight, 266–277. Armonk: M. E. Sharpe, 1990.
Mao, Zedong. 1937l. Philosophical annotations and marginalia: Annotations on M.B. Milin et al., *Dialectical materialism and historical materialism*, translated by Shen Zhiyuan (Volume I). In *Mao Zedong on dialectical materialism: Writings on philosophy, 1937*, translated and edited by Nick Knight, 278–280. Armonk: M. E. Sharpe, 1990.
Mao, Zedong. 1938a. Lun xin jieduan (1938.10.12–14). In *Zhonggong zhongyang wenjian xuanji*, vol. 11:557–662. Beijing: Zhonggang zhongyang xuexiao chubanshe, 1991.
Mao, Zedong. 1938b. On the new stage (12–14 October, 1938). In *Mao's road to power: Revolutionary writings 1912–1949*, Vol. 6:458–541. Armonk: M. E. Sharpe, 2004.
Mao, Zedong. 1939a. The Chinese revolution and the Chinese communist party (December 1939). In *Selected works of Mao Tse-tung*, vol. 2:305–334. Beijing: Foreign Languages Press, 1965.
Mao, Zedong. 1939b. Zhongguo geming he Zhongguo gongchandang (1939.12). In *Mao Zedong xuanji*, vol. 2:621–656. Beijing: Renmin chubanshe, 2009.
Mao, Zedong. 1956a. Gei Huang Yanpei de xin (1956.12.04). In *Mao Zedong wenji*, vol. 7:164–166. Beijing: Renmin chubanshe, 2009.
Mao, Zedong. 1956b. Lun shi da guanxi (1956.04.25). In *Mao Zedong wenji*, vol. 7:23–49. Beijing: Renmin chubanshe, 2009.
Mao, Zedong. 1956c. On the ten major relationships (25 April, 1956). In *Selected works of Mao Tse-Tung*, vol. 5:284–307. Beijing: Foreign Languages Press, 1977.
Mao, Zedong. 1957a. Guanyu zhengque chuli renmin neibu maodun de wenti (1957.02.27). In *Mao Zedong wenji*, vol. 7:204–244. Beijing: Renmin chubanshe, 2009.
Mao, Zedong. 1957b. On the correct handling of contradictions among the people (27 February, 1957). In *Selected works of Mao Tse-Tung*, vol. 5:384–421. Beijing: Foreign Languages Press, 1977.
Mao, Zedong. 1963a. Ren de zhengque sixiang shi cong nali lai de? (1963.05). In *Mao Zedong wenji*, vol. 8:320–322. Beijing: Renmin chubanshe, 2009.
Mao, Zedong. 1963b. Where do correct ideas come from? (May, 1963). In *Four essays on philosophy*, 134–136. Beijing: Foreign Language Press, 1966.

Mao, Zedong. 1964a. Guanyu bantian wenzhang de tanhua (1964.08.24). In *Mao Zedong sixiang wansui*, vol. 5:158–161. Beijing: Hongweibing, 1968.
Mao, Zedong. 1964b. Guanyu zhexue wenti de jianghua (1964.08.18). In *Mao Zedong sixiang wansui*, vol. 5:148–154. Beijing: Hongweibing, 1968.
Mao, Zedong. 1988. *Mao Zedong zhexue pizhuji*. Beijing: Zhongyang wenxian chubanshe.
Mao, Zedong. 1998. *Mao Zedong du shehuizhuyi zhengzhijingjixue pizhu he tanhua*. Beijing: Zhonghua renmin gongheguo guoshi xuehui.
Marx, Karl. 1841. Differenz der demokritischen und epikureischen Naturphilosophie nebst einem Anhange. In *Marx Engels Gesamtausgabe*, vol. I.1:5–92. Berlin: Dietz, 1975.
Marx, Karl. 1859a. A contribution to the critique of political economy. In *Marx and Engels collected works*, vol. 29:257–417. Moscow: Progress Publishers, 1987.
Marx, Karl. 1859b. *Zur Kritik der politischen Ökonomie*. In *Marx Engels Gesamtausgabe*, vol. II.2:95–245. Berlin: Dietz, 1980.
Marx, Karl. 1867a. *Das Kapital. Kritik der politischen Ökonomie. Erster Band. Hamburg 1867*. In *Marx Engels Gesamtausgabe*, vol. II.5. Berlin: Dietz, 1983.
Marx, Karl. 1867b. Marx an Engels in Manchester, London, 22.Juni 1867. In *Marx Engels Werke*, vol. 31:305–307. Berlin: Dietz, 1973.
Marx, Karl. 1875a. Critique of the Gotha programme. In *Marx and Engels collected works*, vol. 24:75–99. Moscow: Progress Publishers, 1989.
Marx, Karl. 1875b. Kritik des Gothaer Programms. In *Marx Engels Gesamtausgabe*, vol. I.25:3–25. Berlin: Dietz, 1985.
Marx, Karl. 1876. Marx an Engels in Ramsgate. London, 25.Mai 1876. In *Marx Engels Werke*, vol. 34:14–16. Berlin: Dietz, 1973.
Meisner, Maurice. 2007. *Mao Zedong: A political and intellectual portrait*. London: Polity.
Meissner, Werner. 1990. *Philosophy and politics in China: The debate over historical materialism in the 1930s*. Translated by Richard Mann. Stanford: Stanford University Press.
Mitin, M. B. 1931. *Dialekticheskii i istoricheskii materializm*. Moscow: MLRD "Rabochii put′", 2018.
Mitin, M. B. 1936a. *Bianzhengweiwulun yu lishiweiwulun*. Translated by Shen Zhiyuan. n. p.: Shangwu yinshuguan.
Mitin, M. B. ed. 1936b. *Xin zhexue dagang*. Translated by Ai Siqi and Zheng Yili. Shanghai: Dushu shenghuo chubanshe.
Mitin, M. B. 1941. *Dialekticheskii materializm—mirovozzrenie marksistsko-leninskoi partii*. Moscow: OGIZ Gospolitizdat.
Mitin, M. B., V. Raltsevich, A. Saradzhev, G. Adamian, M. Konstantinov, A. Shcheglov, B. Bykhovski, et al. 1935. Dialekticheskii materializm. In *Bolshaia sovietskaia entsiklopediia*, vol. 22:45–235. Moscow: Gosudarstvennyi institut "sovetskaia ėntsiklopediia".
Myslivchenko, A. G., and A. P. Sheptulin, ed. 1988. *Dialekticheskii i istoricheskii materializm*. Moscow: Izdatel'stvo Politicheskoi Literatury.
Ni, Zhi'an. 2016. Guanyu makesizhuyi zhexue zhongguohua de sikao. *Shandong shehui kexue* 2016 (1): 26–31.
Pichugun, O., ed. 1933. *Dialekticheskii materializm—Marks, Engels, Lenin, Stalin*. Moscow: Partiinoe Izdatel'stvo.
Schram, Stuart. 1969. *The political thought of Mao Tse-tung*. New York: Praeger.
Schram, Stuart. 1989. *The thought of Mao Tse-tung*. Cambridge: Cambridge University Press.
Shirokov, I., and R. Iankovskii, eds. 1932a. *Bianzhengfa weiwulun jiaocheng*. Translated by Li Da. Shanghai: Bigengtang shudian.
Shirokov, I., and R. Iankovskii, eds. 1932b. *Materialisticheskaia dialektika*. 3 vols. Moscow: Partizdat.
Shirokov, I., and R. Iankovskii, ed. 1937. *A textbook of Marxist philosophy*. London: Victor Gollancz.
Snow, Edgar. 1968. *Red star over China*. New York: Grove.
Somerville, John. 1946. *Soviet philosophy: A study of theory and practice*. New York: Philosophical Library.

Stalin, I. V. 1927a. The Fifteenth Congress of the C.P.S.U.(B.), December 2–19, 1927. In *Works*, 10:275–382. Moscow: Foreign Languages Publishing House.

Stalin, I. V. 1927b. XV s"ezd VKP (b) 2–19 dekabria 1927g. In *Sochineniia*, vol. 10:271–371. Moscow: Gosudarstvennoe izdatel´stvo politicheskoi literatury, 1949.

Stalin, I. V. 1930a. Letters to comrade Ch. In *Works*, 13:21–23. Moscow: Foreign Languages Publishing House.

Stalin, I. V. 1930b. Pis′ma tov. Ch-e. In *Sochineniia*, vol. 13:20–22. Moscow: Gosudarstvennoe izdatel´stvo politicheskoi literatury.

Stalin, I. V. 1930c. Political report of the Central Committee to the sixteenth congress of the C.P.S.U.(B.), June 27, 1930. In *Works*, vol. 12:242–385. Moscow: Foreign Languages Publishing House, 1954.

Stalin, I. V. 1930d. Politicheskii otchet Tsentral′nogo Komiteta XVI s"ezdu VKP(b), 27 iiunia 1930g. In *Sochineniia*, vol. 12:235–373. Moscow: Gosudarstvennoe izdatel´stvo politicheskoi literatury, 1949.

Stalin, I. V. 1936a. O proekte konstitutsii soiuza SSR: Doklad na chrezvychaĭnom VIII vsesoiuznom s"ezde sovetov, 25 noiabria 1936 goda. In *Sochineniia*, vol. 14:119–147. Moscow: Izdatel′stvo "Pisatel′", 1997.

Stalin, I. V. 1936b. On the draft constitution of the U.S.S.R.: Report delivered at the extraordinary eighth congress of Soviets of the U.S.S.R., November 25, 1936. In *Works*, vol. 14:151–197. London: Red Star Press, 1978.

Stalin, I. V. 1938a. *History of the communist party of the Soviet Union (Bolsheviks): Short course.* New York: International Publishers.

Stalin, I. V. 1938b. *Istoriia Vsesoiuznoĭ Kommunisticheskoĭ Partii (Bol′shevikov): Kratkii kurs.* Moscow: OGIZ Gospolitizdat, 1946.

Stalin, I. V. 1939a. Otchetnyi doklad na XVIII s"ezde partii o rabote TSK VKP(b), 10 marta 1939 goda. In *Sochineniia*, vol. 14:290–341. Moscow: Izdatel′stvo "Pisatel′", 1997.

Stalin, I. V. 1939b. Report on the work of the Central Committee to the eighteenth congress of the C.P.S.U.(B.) (Delivered March 10, 1939). In *Works*, vol. 14:355–429. London: Red Star Press, 1978.

Stalin, I. V. 1952a. Economic problems of socialism in the U.S.S.R. In *Works*, vol. 16:222–296. London: Red Star Press, 1986.

Stalin, I. V. 1952b. Ėkonomicheskie problemy sotsializma v SSSR. In *Sochineniia*, vol. 16:154–223. Moscow: Izdatel′stvo "Pisatel′", 1997.

Stanley, John. 1989. The Marxism of Marx's doctoral dissertation. *Journal of the History of Philosophy* 33 (1): 133–158.

Su, Wei. 2017. Zailun maofun fenxifa zhong de 'wuding' yaojue—jinian 'maodun lun' fabiao 80 zhounian. *Mao Zedong sixiang yanjiu* 34 (2): 21–26.

Sun, Li. 2017. Zhuyao maodun fenxi fangfa shi Zhongguo gongchandang de lilun chuangxin. *Mao Zedong Deng Xiaoping lilun yanjiu* 2017 (12): 15–20.

Tian, Chenshan. 2005. *Chinese dialectics: From Yijing to Marxism.* Lanham: Lexington.

Tian, Songnian. 1986. Dui jiben zhexue shuji de pizhu. In *Mao Zedong de dushu shenghuo*, edited by Gong Yuzhi, Pang Xianzhi, and Shi Zhongquan, 2nd edn., 55–64. Beijing: Sanlian shudian, 2014.

Van Ree, Erik. 1998. Socialism in one country: A reassessment. *Studies in East European Thought* 50 (2): 72–117.

Van Ree, Erik. 2015. *Boundaries of Utopia—Imagining communism from Plato to Stalin.* London: Routledge.

Wakeman, Frederic. 1973. *History and will: Philosophical perspectives of Mao Tse-tung's thought.* Berkeley: University of California Press.

Wang, Jionghua. 1998. *Mao Zedong dushu shenghuo.* Wuhan: Changjiang chubanshe.

Wang, Lisheng, and Wang Qingtao. 2015. Zhongguo tese shehuizhuyi lilun de luoji qidian yu Zhongguo shehui zhuyao maodun de chongxin queli. *Shandong shifan daxue xuebao (renwen shehui kexue ban)* 60 (2): 46–64.

Wang, Nanshi. 2011. Mao Zedong's dialectics in the comparative perspective of Chinese and Western modes of thinking. *Social Sciences in China* 32 (1): 80–95.

Weston, Thomas. 2008. The concept of non-antagonistic contradiction in Soviet philosophy. *Science and Society* 72 (4): 427–454.

Wetter, Gustav. 1958a. *Der dialektische Materialismus. Seine Geschichte und sein System in der Sowjetunion.* 4th edn. Vienna: Herder.

Wetter, Gustav. 1958b. *Dialectical materialism: A historical and systematic survey of philosophy in the Soviet Union.* Translated by Peter Heath. London: Routledge and Kegan Paul.

Xi, Jinping. 2017a. *Juesheng quanmian jiancheng xiaokang shehui, duoqu xinshidai Zhongguo tese shehuizhuyi weida shengli (2017.10.18).* Beijing: Renmin chubanshe.

Xi, Jinping. 2017b. *Secure a decisive victory in building a moderately prosperous society in all respects and strive for the great success of socialism with Chinese characteristics for a new era: Report to the 19th National Congress of the Communist Party of China, October 18, 2017.* Beijing: Foreign Languages Press.

Xiao, Haiying. 2004. Maodun fenxifa—Deng Xiaoping lilun chuangxin de jishi. *Jinggangshan shifan xueyuan xuebao* 25 (Zengkan): 63–65.

Xie, Fusheng. 2018. Ruhe lijie Zhongguo tese shehuizhuyi xinshidai shehui zhuyao maodun de zhuanhua. *Jiaoxue yu yanjiu* 2018 (9): 5–14.

Yakhot, O. 1965. *What is dialectical materialism?* Translated by Clemens Dutt. Moscow: Progress Publishers.

Yang, Huanzhang, and Yang Xiaomei. 2007. Maodun lun: cong Heige'er dao Mao Zedong. *Guangzhou daxue xuebao (shehui kexue ban)* 6 (8): 14–20.

Zhou, Xincheng. 2016. Jingjixue yanjiu yinggai you zhexuejia de tounao—xuexi 'Mao Zedong du shehuizhuyi zhengzhijingjixue pizhu he tanhua'. *Mao Zedong sixiang yanjiu* 33 (2): 1–10.

Zhou, Xincheng. 2018. Bixu yunyong maodun fenxi fangfa lai yanjiu gaige de genben wenti. *Wenhua ruanshili* 2018 (4): 13–17.

Zhou, Yinzu. 1997. Mao Zedong he Deng Xiaoping guanyu maodun fenxi fangfa de bijiao yanjiu. *Nanjing shehui kexue (zengkan)* 1997 (1): 116–128.

Chapter 4
The Marxist Basis of the Reform and Opening-Up

4.1 Opening Remarks

> What constitutes dialectical movement is the coexistence of two contradictory sides, their conflict and their fusion into a new category. (Marx 1847a, 103; 1847b, 168)

On the 24th of November, 1978, representatives from the 18 families of Xiaogang Village, of Fengyang County in Anhui Province, met and signed what was then a secret document. In 79 characters, the document stated that each family would subdivide their collective land, work their allocated plots to meet government quotas, and then sell any surplus for their own benefit. The reason: back in 1958 the village population was 120, but 67 died from hunger during 1958–1960 (in the midst of the 'Great Leap Forward'). Starvation had haunted them once again in 1978 and they feared for the future. The result of the secret agreement: in the following year, the farmers of Xiaogang village produced six times the amount of grain compared to the previous year, and the per capita income of the farmers increased from 22 to 400 RMB. Why was the document a secret? With the fully collectivised system in force, any form of buying and selling was regarded as a 'capitalist' exercise and thus punishable. The farmers knew they were taking a risk, but they were fortunate that the local and provincial CPC officials were sympathetic to their endeavour. So also was the new leadership of the country, with Deng Xiaoping at the head. By the next spring, the word of Xiaogang's move was out. While some accused them of undermining socialism, the country's leadership saw it very differently: this would be the beginning of the household responsibility system and thus of the rural reform that drove the first period of the Reform and Opening-Up. By 1984, the household responsibility system had been implemented across the country.

I have begun with this specific example since it reveals the democratic origins of the Reform and Opening-Up, and I will return to its immediate implications in a moment. But let us step back for a moment: the concern of this chapter is the Reform and Opening-Up, which can be understood only in light of the contradiction analysis presented in the previous chapter. In other words, if we deploy dialectical analysis,

R. Boer, *Socialism with Chinese Characteristics*,
https://doi.org/10.1007/978-981-16-1622-8_4

we can see clearly that the Reform and Opening-Up is a socialist project. Some of the background to the Reform and Opening-Up has already been considered in previous chapters, whether in terms of liberating thought, seeking truth from facts, and liberating the forces of production (Xi 1999, 24; Li C. 2009, 146–149), or the contradiction between productive forces and relations of production during socialist construction (Deng 1979a, 182; 1979c, 189; CPC Central Committee 1981, 17). In this chapter, my concern is with the way contradiction analysis appears at every turn of the Reform and Opening-Up. I book-end the analysis with the questions of the resultant household responsibility system and the 'one country, two systems' breakthrough. In between, the bulk of the chapter concerns the nature of the reform in terms of the 'wild 90s' and deepening reform, and then the question of opening up to developed capitalist countries while maintaining self-reliance and sovereignty. The discussion of opening-up also enables a treatment of the recalibration of class analysis in terms of internal and external dynamics (dealing also with the wayward hypothesis concerning the rise of a 'middle class' and a new 'working class').

4.2 One Big Pot and Household Responsibility

To return to the pioneering act of Xiaogang village: as far as narratives of origin go, it is not quite up to the grandeur of the Long March. Humbler and simpler, but it is an origin narrative nonetheless, and being of such a genre it expresses both a historical truth and bears the necessary embellishments and simplifications of a retelling that has a specific ideological point. It is precisely for this reason that the story of Xiaogang village is so important, raising for my purposes three initial questions concerning the Reform and Opening-Up: the relation of rural and urban; collective and individual (expressed in terms of 'eating from one big pot' and the 'household responsibility system'); and equality and inequality under socialism.

4.2.1 Returning to the Countryside

To begin with, the impetus from the countryside was by no means new. Mao Zedong had already begun formulating the strategy of the 'surrounding the cities from the countryside [*nongcun baowei chengshi*]' in the late 1920s. Given that China was an overwhelmingly rural country with undeveloped industry and a fledgling urban working class, Mao realised that the Chinese revolution needed to begin with rural workers and then liberate the cities. From Jinggang Shan, through the Jiangxi-Fujian Soviet based in Ruijin, to the key Red Area around Yan'an (Shaanxi Province), this turned out to be a successful revolutionary strategy. Analogously, a major impetus for the Reform and Opening-Up began in the countryside rather than in the cities

(Wang Yunjing and Yang 1994, 106–107),[1] with the exercise at Xiaogang village expressing Mao's democratic adage: 'from the masses, to the masses' (Li C. 2009, 151–152). The timing was fortuitous, for the post-1976 leadership was looking for initiatives to get the socialist project back on track (Deng 1985b, 117; 1985a, 123). In doing so, this leadership circle around Deng Xiaoping reveals a continuity-in-discontinuity with Mao's initial revolutionary strategy, which should be understood in the dialectical terms of contradiction and *Aufhebung*, or *yangqi* (Zhou Y. 1997, 116).

4.2.2 Collective and Individual

The more substantive philosophical question concerns the contradiction between collective and individual, which is expressed in the Chinese context in terms of 'eating from one big pot [*daguofan*]' and 'household responsibility system [*lianchan-daohu*]'. The first image is of a large pot, in which the meal for everyone is cooked. People help themselves to how much they want, irrespective of the contribution each person has made to the food in the pot. The second term—household responsibility system—is obvious: each household takes responsibility for the production of agricultural produce, meeting the government's quota and then being able to sell any surplus for their own benefit. It was precisely the shift from one to the other that the 18 households in Xiaogang village enacted in 1978, a system that was extended to the whole country by 1984.

Is this a shift from socialist collectivism to capitalist individuality? Not at all, unless we assume the facile equations of socialism = collective and capitalism = individual. The equations may take other forms, such as Asian societies being collectively oriented, while Western European societies are individual. Not only are these equations facile, they are also undialectical: the whole liberal (and capitalist) tradition sees the collective formed through the individual, who contributes to the social reality through his or her selfish endeavours (so Adam Smith). By contrast, the Communist tradition assumes that the full flourishing and fulfilment of the individual can take place only through the collective. This is the philosophical point that the household responsibility system reflects: it seeks to enact not a capitalist path to vast income

[1] As Deng Xiaoping put it: 'In our democratic revolution, we had to act in accordance with China's specific situation and follow the path discovered by Comrade Mao Zedong of encircling the cities from the rural areas. Now, in our national construction, we must likewise act in accordance with our own situation and find a Chinese path to modernisation' (Deng 1979a, 163; 1979c, 172–173). Or as Xi Jinping observes: 'Comrade Deng Xiaoping warmly praised the creation of farmers in Xiaogang Village, Fengyang County, Anhui Province, and affirmed the socialist nature of the family contract responsibility system. Under the leadership of our country, the great creation of farmers in China led to the comprehensive implementation of the household contract responsibility system throughout the country, which greatly liberated agricultural productivity, significantly improved the living standards of farmers, and changed the outlook of the countryside' (Xi 1999, 22).

differentiation, but a socialist path to socio-economic well-being for all (Fang J. 2014, 59).

Note carefully two points: first, it speaks of households and not individuals; second, as with the initial impetus in Xiaogang village, villages today continue to own their land collectively. Decisions concerning how the land is used by households are up to the village itself. For example, Xiaogang village flourished during the 1980s, but found it had to shift to leasing land in the 1990s when young people began going to the cities to work. By the 2000s, with the deployment of a new generation of technologies, the village once again began pooling resources to make the most of the new situation.

4.2.3 Equality and Difference

All of this brings us to the question of egalitarianism, which has been a repeated trap of the Communist movement. As Stalin already observed in the early 1930s, the idea of radical equality has more to do with primitive peasant 'communism', religious ascetics, or petty-bourgeois misconceptions. Socialism is not about the same wages for all, wearing the same clothes, or eating the same food in the same quantity (Stalin 1931a, 118–119; 1931b, 120–121; 1934c, 354–357; 1934d, 361–364). Skills, tastes, and needs vary. It is not for nothing that socialism has been defined already from Lenin's time as, 'from each according to ability, to each according to work'. In terms of the collective-individual relation, Stalin observed that 'socialist society alone can most fully satisfy … and firmly safeguard the interests of the individual' (Stalin 1934a, 28; 1934b, 27).

We do not need to rely only on Stalin, for Marx and Engels already castigated the crude notion of radical equality found in utopian socialism. So too, for Deng Xiaoping 'eating from one big pot' was a formula for poverty, suffering and disaster, and it would certainly not liberate the productive forces and improve the lives of all (Deng 1985b, 115; 1985a, 121; 1986b, 155; 1986a, 158).[2] In this sense, it should be no surprise that 'eating from one big pot' should take on the figuratively negative sense of indiscriminate egalitarianism. Finally, the development of the household responsibility system was seen clearly as an exercise in enabling socialist democracy (Fang J. 2014, 60). It would not do to have every decision made by the centre, for this would be a betrayal of democratic centralism; instead, centralisation works only with healthy decentralisation, with initiatives coming from the masses. And if they work, they can then be implemented country-wide—as happened with the initiative from Xiaogang village.

[2]In an insightful article, Zhu Jiamu (2013, 103–105) points out that Mao Zedong began to see some of the same points in the late 1950s and early 1960s, including a critique of petty-bourgeois egalitarianism. Note here Zhou Enlai's observation in his government work report at the first National People's Congress of 1954: 'Egalitarianism is a petty-bourgeois concept that encourages backwardness and hinders progress. It has nothing in common with Marxism and a socialist system' (Zhou E. 1954a, 142; 1954b, 152).

4.3 Reform

From the micro to the macro: on the 12th of November, 2013, the Third Plenary Session of the CPC Central Committee produced a significant document entitled 'Decision of the CPC Central Committee on Several Issues Concerning the Comprehensive Deepening of Reform' (CPC Central Committee 2013b).[3] I will address the content of the decision in a moment, but first we need to ask: why was this document produced at this time? Much had changed since the initiative of Xiaogang village and the initial steps of the Reform and Opening-Up under Deng Xiaoping's tenure. From personal experience in China in the first decade of the twenty-first century, I witnessed much debate about the direction in which China was going. It seemed as though everything was on the table: the CPC's legitimacy was at an all-time low, corruption was rampant, the gap between rich and poor was growing, and many schools of thought vied to get their views aired. Did the loss of a moral compass require a recovery of hierarchical Confucian values, as the renaissance of Confucian studies proposed? Should the achievements of the CPC be denied ('historical nihilism') and the path of bourgeois liberalisation be pursued? Should Marxist political economy be pushed aside and neoclassical economics, and indeed neoliberalism, be embraced? Should China shift to a Western model of democratic socialism, or should it return to the values and practices of the Cultural Revolution? These and more were the questions being asked and proposals being made, not least by a swathe of Chinese thinkers and policy makers who had returned to the country from abroad in the 1990s. All these questions turned on the perceived shortcomings of the Reform and Opening-Up.

As I write, these questions have been resolved and the country's direction is very clear indeed, with more than ninety percent of the population confident about China's direction. A decade or more ago, I would talk with older CPC members and they would say they were embarrassed about the Party, but that at least conditions in China had improved. These days, I talk with even more with CPC members: the young members say they see no other path for China and hope to make their contribution to the greater project; the older members are once again proud of a hard-working and unified Party. Much of this change has to do with the decision from 2013 and what has been enacted since then. Notably, the document was produced after the first year of Xi Jinping's tenure as chairman of the CPC.[4]

---

[3]Although I cite the original Chinese version in the main text, one may also consult the English translation (CPC Central Committee 2013a).

[4]For a collection of 72 articles by Xi Jinping on deepening reform, from 2012 to 2018, see *On Persevering in Comprehensively Deepening Reform* (Xi 2018a).

4.3.1 Deepening Reform

Let us consider the document on deepening reform in a little more detail. It is certainly comprehensive, dealing with: the integration of rural and urban development[5]; international engagement with a focus on the Belt and Road Initiative; developing further the socialist democratic political system in order to 'give full play to the superiority of the socialist political system in China'; comprehensively enhancing rule of law; restricting and supervising the exercise of power (*quanli*); socialist cultural power, with a balance of cultural openness and cultural confidence; social programs, which include education, employment and entrepreneurship, income distribution, an equitable and sustainable social security system, medicine and health care; social governance focused on peace and stability, as well as public security in terms of food, drugs, disaster, and national security; ecological civilisation; and national defence, which includes civilian-military integration. Of these, pride of place is given to economic matters (the focus of three sections at the beginning). The initial point is that the 'basic economic system [*jiben jingji zhidu*]' will be enhanced, with a clear focus on state-owned enterprises as the core (Cheng 1997). In other other words, public ownership is the key, side-by-side with other diverse forms of ownership. I will have more to say on this matter in the next chapter, suffice to point out here that the 'basic economic system' (*zhidu* refers to an over-arching system) is clearly socialist, within which one finds a socialist market economy playing a 'decisive role [*juedingxing zuoyong*]' in the allocation of resources and distribution, along with the comprehensive enhancement of government planning. These two—market and planning—are components (*tizhi*) of the overall socialist system.

The essence of the document appears in its opening section, where it speaks of the Reform and Opening-Up being a 'great new revolution [*xin de weida geming*] led by the Party under the new conditions of the new era'. Further, there will be 'no end [*yongyuan zhijing*] to practice, no end to emancipating the mind and no end to the Reform and Opening-Up'. The first two phrases recall Deng Xiaoping's emphasis (see Sects. 2.2 and 2.3) on liberating thought and seeking truth from facts. Since these are the philosophical foundations of the Reform and Opening-Up, the latter too will have no end. And the overall goal of comprehensively deepening reform is not only to improve socialism with Chinese characteristics and modernise China's system and capacity for governance, but also to enable China to become a socialistically modernised society that is strong, democratic, culturally advanced, and harmonious.

The text addresses directly the question as to whether China is following a socialist or capitalist path: in implementing the Party's basic line, it is necessary to 'reject the old and ossified path of closure and rigidity, and reject any attempt to abandon socialism and take an erroneous path'. The erroneous path is of course capitalism. By contrast, 'we will stay committed to the path of socialism with Chinese characteristics, and ensure that reform is carried out in the right direction'. I will have more

[5]Of relevance for the treatment of the initial rural focus of the Reform and Opening-Up (see above), this point includes the modernisation of agriculture and people-centred urban development, which also entails an orderly process for enabling migrant workers to become urban residents.

to say on this point below, which is usually described as distinguishing between two paths of reform. But let me close this identification of the key points of the 2013 decision by asking: why deepen reform? The initial response is that the decision attests to the sense that the Reform and Opening-Up is by no means 'complete', although to put it that way suggests that it will at some point come to an end. Instead, in the current context there is to be no end to such a process. More significantly, the text addresses implicitly the many problems that had arisen during what may be called the 'wild 90s'. These problems relate to all of the topics mentioned in the document that need further reform, from the economy, through social, cultural, and environment problems, to national defence. We do find a more explicit reference to these deep problems in the treatment of social governance: here are mentions of the 'root causes' and 'symptoms' of social problems, and for more effective and efficient measures to prevent and resolve social conflicts. The purpose is to ensure social harmony, peace, and stability (CPC Central Committee 2013b, 8). This question too will be a focus in what follows, but let me close this discussion by observing that the problems of the past are but one motivation for the decision. As the text makes clear, more are anticipated: it is not merely a case of 'crossing the river by feeling the stones' (Chen Y. 1980, 279), but that reform has entered a new 'deep-water zone'. By pooling the wisdom of the whole Party and society to the greatest extent, the need for the future is to 'ford dangerous rapids' by promoting the self-improvement and development of the socialist system with Chinese characteristics (CPC Central Committee 2013b, 1; Xiao and Qiao 2018, 21–22).

4.3.2 Revolution and Reform

Two issues requiring further analysis arise from the decision: the relation between revolution and reform, and the 'wild 90s'. As for revolution and reform, this is an old question in the communist movement, a question that was initially framed in terms of either a comprehensive revolutionary process that sweeps away the old system, or working to reform that system to the point where quantitative change would lead to qualitative change. But the opposition is a false one, as Lenin already observed in an insightful solution: 'either revolutionary class struggle, of which reforms are always a by-product … or no reforms at all' (Lenin 1917a, 282; 1917b, 213). In other words, reform should always be enacted in terms of revolution and not as a path to socialism. How does this work? Before a revolution, a Communist Party should advocate reforms that temporarily improve the conditions of workers, but the Party should always make it perfectly clear that a revolution and its resultant socialist system is the only real answer.[6] Reform for the sake of reform—'tinkering

[6] As Lenin recommends to public speakers and the Social-Democratic representatives in the Russian Duma, 'five minutes of every half-hour speech are devoted to reforms and twenty-five minutes to the coming revolution' (Lenin 1916b, 221; 1916a, 159).

with washbasins' (Lenin 1906a, 263; 1906b, 189)—under a capitalist system ultimately benefits that system and weakens the working class. By contrast, in a socialist system—especially one under construction—reform is absolutely necessary in order to construct socialism. The relics of the former capitalist system need to be overcome and more and more socialist features need to be established in light of conditions. But the context is always revolution.

It is in this light that we should understand the statement in the 'Decision on Deepening Reform' that the Reform and Opening-Up is a 'great new revolution'. Of course, it was Deng Xiaoping who initially observed that the Reform and Opening-Up, with its liberation of the forces of production and modernisation, is also a revolution (Deng 1979b, 231; 1979d, 235; 1980c, 311; 1980d, 310; 1992b, 370; 1992a, 358). In other words, if a Communist revolution aims to establish a different socio-economic system with the aim of improving the lives of all workers, then reform is a crucial component of this aim (Chen X. 2015, 5). A socialist system does not emerge ready-made when power is in the hands of rural and urban workers through a Communist Party. Much needs to be done in light of the specific conditions of a country, especially if it is relatively 'backward' in economic terms. Indeed, a distinctive feature of proletarian revolutions is that—unlike bourgeois revolutions—they have mostly not been able to set up conditions beforehand, in terms of cultural framework, social assumptions, and economic realities. All of this reforming work needs to be done after a Communist Party is able to gain power through a revolution. And what is the aim of all this reform? Communism, of course (see Sect. 2.5), but this means that the lengthy stages within socialism require constant reform as preparation for the ultimate goal (Zhu J. 2016, 35).[7]

At the same time, revolution and reform are distinct processes. Chinese material distinguishes between two dialectically related stages: the period from 1949 to 1978, with its fully planned economy, becomes the stage of revolution, while the period from 1978 to the present is the stage of reform (Wang Yunjing and Yang 1994, 102–103). Distinct, yes, but also intimately connected with one another in light of seeking truth from the facts of specific conditions. As Xi Jinping (2013, 2019) observes, there are three important aspects to this understanding this crucial economic and political question. First, the period before 1978 laid the necessary groundwork for socialist construction, while the period after 1978 enabled a far greater development so that China has not fallen into the disaster the befell the Soviet Union. Second, 'although the two historical phases are very different in their guiding thoughts, principles, policies, and practical work, they are by no means separated from or opposed to each other'. In this light, many good proposals were put forward in the initial period, but they were executed poorly at the time and required the Reform and Opening-Up for their realisation. Third, the two periods require proper evaluation. Thus, the pre-reform period should not be used to deny the experience of the reform period itself, and vice versa. Instead, the conditions for the reform can be found in the pre-reform period, so much so that the 'exploration of socialist practice after the Reform and

[7]It is with this goal in mind that Ha Si (1989, 17) speaks of the whole process of reform being the 'embodiment of the spirit of Marxist philosophy'.

Opening-up is the persistence, reform, and development of the previous period' (Xi 2013, 22–23; see also 2019, 2–3; Wang W. 2014, 16–17).

4.3.3 *The Wild 90s*

The second matter that arises from the 2013 decision on deepening reform concerns the spate of problems and contradictions that emerged particularly in the 1990s, which may be designated as the 'wild 90s'. The new contradictions that arose were indeed profound and multiple. In terms of the economic base, a disjuncture emerged between the productive forces and relations of production. As Zan Jiansen (2015, 43) summarises: the leading role of the public economy (SOEs) began to be weakened; labour conditions took a turn for the worse, with a significant rise in labour unrest; income distribution became unbalanced, with a rapidly rising Gini coefficient; the resolute emphasis on economic growth began to have disastrous effects on the health of land, water, and air. At a superstructural level, a break emerged between the Communist Party and the people, with widespread corruption, ignorance of the basics of Marxism among some leading cadres, and deep mistrust.[8] Further, there was a large grey area between the letter of the law and actual practice. One could get away with much, but as long it did not lead to social unrest, the police would let the situation be. As Zan (2015, 44) observes: 'These problems have seriously eroded the mass base and the foundation of political power of our Party, seriously damaging the Party's image and the relationship between cadres and the masses'. Strong medicine was needed.

There was also the rise of ideological diversity in light of these problems, dominated by right and left tendencies. The most significant was what Chinese scholars call 'historical nihilism' (see Sect. 1.4), which entails the following suggestions: Marxism was outdated and socialism had 'failed' (after 1989 in Eastern Europe and the Soviet Union); the CPC was an aberration in Chinese history; fawning on foreign powers; and the denial of or 'farewell' to the revolution (Wang H. 2009; Zheng K. 2008, 9–10; Zhu J. 2016, 32). In sum, this was a moment of historical amnesia. While there were concerted efforts to show that such historical nihilism was another face of bourgeois liberalism, with its roots in the soil of historical idealism (Thesis Group 2009, 95–96), it also had a number of offshoots.

These included challenges to Marxist political economy as the guide for China's development, and its replacement by Western neoclassical economic theories (known as 'neoliberalism' in its more recent incarnation). Indeed, there was a time when more and more economics departments in universities turned away from Marxism and

[8] A story from Xi Jinping's early days as a regional governor illustrate the problem. Xi and other local cadres were heading to a meeting and their car became bogged in a field. The farmers initially came over to help, but when they saw it was a car with local CPC cadres, the farmers began throwing rocks. Obviously, this experience indicated that deep-seated reform of the Party was needed.

taught neoclassical economic theory as the basis for China's Reform and Opening-Up. The landmark article that challenged the drift and set in train a wholesale restoration of Marxist economic theory was by Liu Guoguang (2005). At the same time, there was a comprehensive assessment of the failures of neoliberal economic policies. Studies noted the ten years of economic destruction in Russia and Eastern Europe, the lost ten years for South America, Japan's creeping decade, slowdowns in the United States and Europe, all of which led to the initial crash of to 2007–2008—to which we can now add the massive crash of 2020 (Thesis Group 2009, 94–95).

In terms of political ideology, there were pushes to adopt the trappings of a Western capitalist state, with its antagonistic political parties and bourgeois 'civil society' (Wang Yicheng 2013). But the idea that had most traction for a time was democratic socialism.[9] Although the term may seem appealing, with its conjunction of 'democracy' and 'socialism', Chinese Marxist scholars saw its danger. It was, they argued, a capitalist ideology, with a mixture of economic components based on private property. Apparent political and ideological pluralism ensured that the capitalist system remained the basis, so that it should really be called 'social capitalism' (Gao 2007). Ultimately, it denied the guiding position of Marxism and negated the leadership of the Communist Party, and asserted the eternity of capitalism. In short, democratic socialism has nothing to do with socialism, let alone scientific socialism as the basis of socialism with Chinese characteristics (Thesis Group 2009, 97–98; Wang F. 2015, 35).

Many were the other proposals, whether 'universal values', which involve a recoding of bourgeois class interests and are thus anti-communist (CPC Central Committee 2006; Thesis Group 2009, 98–99; Ren and Wang 2010, 104); or a 'new enlightenment' humanistic reading of the young Marx with a focus on depoliticised 'human liberation'; or the dead-end of post-modernism (Dirlik and Zhang 2000), which not only reflected the decline of the West through the search for a utopian and individualistic 'poetic dwelling-place' and its associated 'identity politics', but also—through its suspicions of science and the state—implicitly denied the path of Chinese modernisation and rejuvenation (Chen X. et al. 2016, 13–17). Conversely, there was also a response in a rather different direction, entailing a recuperation of traditional Confucian values in order to fill what was felt to be a vacuum of 'values'. While the wave of new Confucian studies emphasised harmony as the key component, critics pointed out that such harmony also entailed feudal hierarchies (Wang F. 2015, 29). Indeed, as Wang Fumin (2015, 34) also points out, many of these proposals took as their underlying aim the need 'save' China. One wonders, of course, from what China needed to be saved.

The problems—or, rather, contradictions—of the 'wild 90s' were many and deep, and Chinese scholars and policy makers were certainly not afraid to address them directly. But it was precisely these contradictions that led many in the West to assume

[9] Although the debate goes back to the post-1989 period and the collapse of socialist states in Eastern Europe, it was given a new lease of life by an article published in the monthly magazine *Yanhuang chunqiu*, in which Xie Tao (2007) argued that China must adopt a peaceful transition to democratic socialism.

that China was following a capitalist and bourgeois liberal path (Zhou X. 2016, 3). Marxists, liberals, and conservatives seemed to be on the same page, although their judgements differed. Foreign and mostly Western Marxists bemoaned or denounced what they saw as China's 'capitalist' path, deploying all manner of betrayal narratives and conspiracy theories with their coded languages (see Sect. 1.4.1).[10] Not a little Orientalism, with its deeply racist undertones, infused such misperceptions. Liberals, on the other hand, sought to cheer China onward, assuming that the supposedly 'capitalist' direction of China would eventually lead to what they saw as the necessary corollary of a capitalist political system and bourgeois democracy.

They were and are wrong, but why? The answer has three dimensions, the first of which concerns the distinction between two paths of reform. One path is to move from socialism to capitalism, which is what happened in Eastern Europe in the 1980s (even if it was not initially intended); the other path is reform on a socialist trajectory (Jiang Z. 1989, 71; Xue 1995, 33).[11] The latter path was clearly the one to take, but this involves both reform and socialism. As Zhou Xincheng (2018, 16) observes: 'If we talk only about socialism without reform, socialism will become lifeless and have no future. If we talk only about reform and do not adhere to socialism, socialism will lose its inherent essential characteristics and turn into capitalism'. An insightful way of putting this distinction between two paths of reform is in terms of 'what to change' and 'what not to change': what should be reformed are contradictions within the task of socialist construction; what should not be changed is the overall socialist system. However, reform is not an end in itself: 'We do not reform for reform's sake', for 'reform is to adjust the relations of production with the aim of promoting the development of productive forces' (Zhou X. 2016, 6). In other words, reform is the way to deal with the internal contradictions—between forces and relations of production, between economic base and superstructure—of socialist construction (Zan 2015, 42).

This leads to the second part of the answer in terms of contradiction analysis. I would like to focus on the insight from dialectical materialism on the primacy of internal contradictions and the need for such contradictions to be resolved through internal processes (Jiang Y. 1990, 9; Chi 2018, 8–9). As we saw in the second chapter (Sect. 2.4), the initial problems in China were those of stagnating economic performance after a few decades of an exclusively planned economy. While such an approach initially enabled the liberation of the forces of production by removing the ownership of productive forces from former landlord and capitalist bosses, after time it led to new bottlenecks that had to be addressed in light of China's internal conditions. More specifically, the relations of production entailed in an exclusively

[10] Here we find all manner of curious and wayward hypotheses, such as 'capitalist socialism', 'bureaucratic capitalism', 'neoliberalism with "Chinese characteristics"', and 'state capitalism' (Žižek 2018; Meisner 1996; Harvey 2005; Weil 1996).

[11] If one assumes the framework of a capitalist path – as seen in Eastern Europe – then one may discern its own internal contradiction, between the 'left', which seeks to resist the supposed capitalist path by advocating a winding back of reform and a return to a 'socialist era' (the Cultural Revolution), and the 'right', which advocates a complete process of capitalist transformation and bourgeois liberalisation (Lu 2005, 60–61).

planned economy no longer met the needs of developing productive forces, so that the latter began to stagnate. Hence the Reform and Opening-Up, which sought not only to release the forces of production from their restrictions, but also to adapt the relations of production to new productive developments. In turn, this process led to new contradictions as productive forces leapt ahead. This was the case particularly in the 'wild 90s', which continued to have implications into the early 2000s. The answer, however, was not a winding back of the Reform and Opening-Up, but a deepening of the process itself (Zan 2015, 43).

Further, the emphasis on the Reform and Opening-Up as an internal dialectical process enables us to understand the role of external factors. These include the shock dismantling of the Soviet Union, which posed—at many levels—the question, 'Whither socialism?' (Zheng Y. and Hong 2014, 4), as well as the developments of capitalist countries that had adopted neoliberal policies from the late 1970s. While these developments no doubt had an influence, with Chinese researchers studying them in great detail, they were not determinative of China's own socialist path.[12]

Third and specifically in relation to the 'wild 90s', there is a crucial distinction between incidental (or cyclical) contradictions and those that are systemic. The mistake made by those who saw China's path as capitalist was to confuse incidental or cyclical problems with those that are systemic (Lo 2007, 121–122, 129, 149). Thus, the problems of social and labour unrest, rural migrant workers in the cities, the gap between rich and poor, disjunction between the CPC and the masses (with associated corruption), environmental degradation—these and more were of an incidental nature at a certain stage of the Reform and Opening-Up. They were certainly not systemic. Thus, the way to solve these problems was not to wind back the Reform and Opening-Up, but to take it further, to deepen it. In this light, we can see the logic of deepening reform as an answer to the internal and incidental contradictions of the 'wild 90s'. As Zhou Xincheng observes:

> Acknowledging that there are still contradictions in socialist society, it logically follows that they must be solved through reform. Moreover, once a contradiction is resolved, new contradictions will arise, which need to be solved through reform. It is in the process of constantly emerging contradictions and resolving them through reform that socialist society has developed. Therefore, reform is an eternal topic in socialist society. Reform is only ongoing, not complete. (Zhou X. 2018, 14; see also Fang J. 2014, 62)[13]

The facts speak for themselves: a decreasing Gini coefficient in light of the resolute poverty alleviation program and closing the gap between rural and urban development (Wei 2015; Xiao and Qiao 2018, 18, 20); the growth of a middle-income

---

[12]Thus, the Western Marxist hypothesis (Brink 2008; Panitch and Gindin 2013) that a monolithic global capitalism determined China's moves from the late 1970s misses the dialectical point arising from contradiction analysis.

[13]By now it should be obvious that the Reform and Opening-Up is not an extended version of the Soviet Union's brief step backwards with the New Economic Policy (NEP) of the 1920s. However, it may be argued that the 'new democratic' period from the mid-1940s to the early 1950s constituted a form of the NEP. In order to overcome the economic devastation of Japanese imperialism and civil war, a limited range of private capital was encouraged (Mao 1945b, 1060; 1945c, 281; 1945a, 275; 1949b, 1431–1432; 1949a, 367–368).

group of more than 500 million; the most extensive anti-corruption campaign since Mao Zedong; the rolling out of a comprehensive social security system on a sound economic basis (Fang J. 2014, 65), which is set to be completed with the Fourteenth Five-Year Plan of 2021–2024; the restoration of the unity, focus, and Marxist orientation of the CPC, which has re-earned public trust; levels of trust and confidence in governance and China's direction ranging from 80% to over 90%; and the comprehensive project of ecological civilisation, in which China—through typical 'Chinese speed'—is now leading the world (Xiao and Qiao 2018, 19). The list can go on, but now we are witnessing a whole new development of productive forces, in which government, SOEs, and private enterprises are instigating a synergised technological transformation that simply cannot be found anywhere else in the world. Yet, in China they do not celebrate too much, for the decision on deepening reform warns that China has entered 'deep waters', requiring concerted effort as it moves forward.

4.4 Opening up

Let us now turn to the 'opening-up [*kaifang*]' part of the slogan. In this case, the emphasis is mostly on the international dimension, although it has ramifications for internal processes. My focus is on the relations between socialism and capitalism, which will lead to a treatment of how Marxist class analysis has been redeployed.

4.4.1 How to Relate to Capitalist Countries

Recalling that contradiction analysis emphasises both unity and struggle, I draw on two perceptive articles that identify the layers of such an analysis in relation to the international dimension entailed in opening-up (Rong 2002; Shang 2004). They begin by pointing out that in terms of international relations between socialist systems like that of China and capitalist systems, one must always keep in mind that the two systems are fundamentally opposed. Ultimately this opposition comes out in favour of socialism, which is both better than a capitalist system and the only way that China can be saved and develop (Deng 1979a, 166–167; 1979c, 175–176). We should not, however, jump to the conclusion that on a global level we can have either socialism or capitalism, and not both. This assumption would entail deploying a typical Western either-or perspective. Instead, the Chinese approach is to argue that the two systems also have distinct connections.

The most obvious of these concerns science and technology: already with Deng Xiaoping, we find the arguments that science and technology are also forces of production, and that China should learn as much as possible from scientific and technological developments in capitalist countries to as to advance its own interests (Deng 1979a, 167–168; 1979c, 176–177; 1992b, 373; 1992a, 361–362). Crucially, science and technology may have made significant progress within capitalist systems in the nineteenth and twentieth centuries, but this historical reality does not make them 'capitalist' by nature (Deng 1980b, 351; 1980a, 348). Here our authors—following Deng Xiaoping—deploy a version of the old *zhongti-xiyong* saying: Chinese substance, Western know-how. Proposed in the second half of the nineteenth century,[14] it was an effort to deal with the intractable problems of how to relate to a technologically more advanced 'West' while not betraying China's richer cultural and historical heritage. The relatively few countries that comprised the 'West' (all former colonisers and comprising only 14% of the world's population) were seen to have little to no cultural substance worth adopting, but much technical knowledge and experience. The problem already then was how to avoid the corrosive and corrupting influences that came from the West while making the most of its then more advanced science and technology. As one would expect, the problem itself and its succinct four-character expression have been the topic of immense debate in China for more than a century.

With Deng Xiaoping we find the beginnings of a new approach to this old problem. Deng clarifies again and again that engagements with Western capitalist countries would include science and technology, controlled levels of foreign investment, and opening up trade with those countries, but that all of these these would would take place in terms of the socialist road. Here Fang Keli's well-known recalibration of the saying is pertinent, since it brings out what Deng Xiaoping was seeking to express. For Fang Keli (2006, 2015), it should be not merely *zhongti xiyong*, Chinese substance and Western know-how, but *mahun zhongti xiyong*: the spirit of Marxism, the system of China, and the application of the West. In other words, Marxism provides the overarching spirit and framework in which one can understand the role of Chinese substance and Western technological prowess. To be added here is the fact that Fang Keli was responding to debates raging in the 'wild 90s'. On the one side were the modern neo-Confucians (Fang Keli was a Confucian specialist), who urged a minimisation of Marxism and a recovery of the Confucian value of harmony, even though this included its attendant hierarchy. On the other side were those who argued that capitalism was better than socialism and that China should embrace capitalist modernisation and bourgeois liberalisation. These approaches we have already encountered, but it was Fang Keli's proposal—initially made in 2006—that won wide approval and is seen to have resolved the debate.

That was the debate in the 1990s and into the early 2000s, when it was still assumed that China lagged behind Western capitalist countries—due to China beginning the process of modernisation far behind the West. As I write, however, it has become increasingly apparent that the former colonisers known as the 'West' have lost their innovative edge, which was actually based on plundering technological advances from other countries (a colonialist model), or at least seeking to clone or crush

[14]The fuller version initially came from Zhang Zhidong (in his *Quanxue pian* of 1898) as *zhongxue wei ti, xixue wei yong*: Chinese learning as the fundamental structure, Western learning for practical use. The formulae expressed an effort to mediate a debate that had been raging for some time between those who sought to reject Western models and those who wanted a fuller 'Westernisation'.

competition. In our time, technological innovation has clearly shifted East, so much so that Western countries are increasing lagging behind and even backward.

4.4.2 Self-Reliance and Globalisation

A further dimension of international engagement with capitalist countries leads to another contradiction, now between self-reliance and globalisation. In the early days of the People's Republic, the reality of economic blockades led to Mao's emphasis on independent and self-reliant socialist construction, relying on the strength of the Chinese people (Shang 2004, 12). At least this was true in relation to capitalist countries with their relatively advanced technologies. China did have close connections with the Soviet Union and other socialist countries, until the Sino-Soviet split of the 1960s. However, the turn inward led to an exacerbation of China's economic stagnation and backwardness. From the late 1970s, the emphasis was that China could not rebuild itself behind closed doors and so it sought closer cooperation with developed capitalist countries so as to make up for the widening gap in economic development and technological innovation. 'The modern world is an open world', observed Deng Xiaoping (1984d, 64; see also 1985b, 117), and the path of history is for ever greater integration and interaction.

At the same time, China will never again depend on another country for its socialist development, since it will rely on its own efforts, hard work, and creativity. The point here is both retrospective and prospective: the long history of humiliation and semi-colonisation by foreign powers in the nineteenth and twentieth centuries has made China resolute in maintaining its sovereignty and brooking no interference. This position also entails no interference by China in any other country's internal system, a principle embodied in the Belt and Road Initiative. Prospectively, the increasing cooperation with other countries—including capitalist ones—is mutual: as China develops, its increasing economic strength will benefit others and contribute to global economy and culture (Deng 1984j, 78–79; 1984g, 86). We may put it this way: global interaction through self-reliance; win–win (*gongying*) through anti-colonial sovereignty; 'neither dependent [*yifu*] on others, nor plundering [*lüeduo*] others' (Xi 2018b, 11; see also Rong 2002, 23; Shang 2004, 12).

That said, China still has a long way to go in its international engagement. As Chen Shuguang (2018, 11, 15) observes, China's economic strength may now be the main driver of global economies, but its cultural and discursive power remains relatively weak (see further Sect. 11.3). To deploy the Marxist distinction between base and superstructure, mutual cooperation at the economic level is relatively easier and follows a global path (as Marx and Engels already saw) of ever greater integration. By contrast, mutual understanding at a superstructural level—politics, culture, ideology—is more difficult and will take much longer (Boer 2020, 1).

4.5 Class Analysis

Closely related to the question of opening-up to developed capitalist countries is that of class analysis. A casual observer may feel that China has put aside class analysis, especially since the chaotic and traumatic Cultural Revolution's emphasis on class conflict as the primary contradiction. The decision of the CPC Central Committee (2006) on a 'harmonious socialist society [*shehuizhuyi shehui hexie*]' may add to this impression, especially if one assumes that harmony is incompatible with contradiction. Internationally, peaceful co-existence, win–win cooperation, and a community of common destiny for humankind, may suggest that the struggle between socialist and capitalist systems is over, or at least that the desire is to relegate this struggle to the past. These perceptions are mistaken, for class analysis remains an important feature of Chinese Marxist analysis, both internally and externally.

4.5.1 Internal Class Contradictions

Internally, class analysis is deployed to understand developments during the Reform and Opening-Up. To set the scene: in the aftermath of the 'wild 90s' it became reasonably common to see international observers—including some Marxists—suggest that China was seeing the rise of a new 'bourgeoisie' or 'middle class'. Led by an increasing number of wealthy entrepreneurs, this group's numbers swelled quickly and they would—so it was hypothesised—at some point enact a bourgeois revolution and seize power, turning China into a capitalist state with bourgeois democracy. This perception gained China significant support among capitalist countries, giving it space to grow at 'Chinese speed', but it it is a profound misreading.

The reality is quite different: the almost 600 million people whose living standards have been drastically improved are urban and rural workers. These improvements are the result of liberating the forces of production and its associated targeted poverty alleviation program. The latter has lifted more than 800 million people out of poverty, which constitutes 7 out of 10 worldwide who have escaped poverty (World Bank 2019, 1). By the dawn of 2021 absolute poverty (based on the less than 0.1% in poverty) had been eradicated. Being lifted out of poverty is one step, but seeing one's livelihood improve to the level of *xiaokang*—moderately well-off, healthy, and secure—is another. It is these people who are now called in China the 'middle-income' group, with immense capacity as an internal economic driver. As I write during the extraordinary year of 2020 and into 2021, this reality has enabled China to become the global recovery engine after the COVID-19 pandemic.

But do they comprise a new 'bourgeoisie' or 'middle class'? No, for the terms are redolent with the history of capitalist systems in Western Europe. In that part of the world, the bourgeoisie arose in towns where they engaged in manufacture and trade. While they pressured governments—many of them absolute monarchies—to enact legal reforms, construct infrastructure, and establish firm borders with uniform policies, they were ultimately opposed to such forms of governance (Boer 2019). Through a series of bourgeois revolutions—from the sixteenth-century Netherlands onward—they took political power, established secular capitalist states, and gradually introduced bourgeois parliamentary democracy, or the dictatorship of the bourgeoisie. This history is not China's history, which has followed its own path. In China, the middle-income group is clearly aware of the core role of CPC policies in improving their livelihoods and they are overwhelmingly supportive of the CPC and confident in the direction in which China is going. Indeed, a sizeable portion of them are members of the almost 100 million strong CPC.

Questions remain, concerning the wealthy private entrepreneurs, party officials who leveraged their positions for corrupt gain, and low-paid migrant workers (Dong and Wu 2011, 60). During the 'wild 90s' and into the early 2000s, there was increasing concern that private entrepreneurs, many of them new billionaires, would form a new political force outside the CPC. Not only have they never become a class 'in itself', with associated class consciousness, but they have by and large become CPC members or non-party supporters. Further, the overwhelming expectation in Chinese society is that if one has benefited from wider support (family and society), then one's turn must come to contribute to the well-being of others. We may call this philanthropy with Chinese characteristics, since it is not based on individual will or a guilty conscience, but on an inescapable social and cultural assumption. As for corrupt CPC officials, these are being comprehensively eradicated in an ongoing 'tigers and flies' anti-corruption campaign that is the most resolute since the time of Mao Zedong. Migrant workers: while my earlier observations on rural and urban workers being lifted out of poverty applies here, the problem of 'migrant workers [*nongmingong*]' and their 'left-behind children [*liushou ertong*]' in rural areas has been a topic of major research projects and thus a focus of social policy concern (Hu and Li 2009; Lv 2014). The solution: with a refocus on rural regeneration, the countryside has begun to provide more and more opportunities, so much so that a good number of technically trained and educated young people—agricultural specialists, teachers, medical professionals, and so on—have been increasingly moving to the countryside for work. At the same time, the migrant workers who have so many jobs in the cities are now the focus of policies ranging from safe and convenient transport, housing, adequate care for their children, and reform of the residency system (*hukou*) to enable their families to move to cities where needed. In short, in the same way that there is no European-style 'bourgeoisie' in China, so also there is no 'working class' opposed to them. In fact, according to classifications in China, everyone is a 'labourer [*laodongzhe*]', with each type of work carefully specified. A 'worker [*gongren*]' is one who works in a factory, which is one type of labourer.

Let us turn to the underlying philosophical questions, shaped in terms of contradiction analysis. The first step is to recall Mao Zedong's (1957b, 1957c) distinction between contradictions among the people and with external hostile forces. Internal contradictions are primarily non-antagonistic, but also—due to emerging problems and stirred on by external forces—need to be managed so they remain non-antagonistic. Further, given that contradictions will be a feature of the long socialist stage, these contradictions will be manifested in terms of different classes for a long time to come (Dong and Wu 2011, 62), or what may be called a 'differential society [*chayixing shehui*]' (Ren and Wang 2010). But they are not to lead to polarisation and class conflict, upon which capitalist states and their political systems are erected. It is for this reason that we find the development not of the antagonistic political parties typical of capitalist states, but of 'consultative multi-party democracy' in China, operating through consultation, cooperation, and debate (see Sect. 8.3).

4.5.2 International Class Antagonisms

Ensuring non-antagonistic contradictions between classes may be the emphasis within China today, but this does not mean that antagonistic class struggle has disappeared. Internally, we see such struggle in the agitations in the Hong Kong SAR, whose capitalist system means that class struggle dominates, or in the Xinjiang and Tibet autonomous regions, or indeed on Taiwan island, where externally supported separatism, extremism, and terrorism rise and fall in a cyclical manner. But these are 'cards' played by both former European colonial powers and especially the last European colonial power, the United States. In their efforts to stir up trouble and vainly hope for the breaking up of China, they engage in class struggle on an international level. While Chinese analysts are keen to emphasise peaceful coexistence and development (Chen X. 2015, 3), based on a community of common destiny for humankind, they are under no illusions concerning the agenda of some external capitalist forces.[15]

From the founding of the People's Republic, there have been waves of attempts to restrict China's rejuvenation, keep it in a 'backward' and subservient state, or dismantle it as a whole. Witness the economic and political blockade by former colonisers in the 1950s and 1960s, or the round of sanctions after the attempted 'colour revolution' in Tiananmen Square after 1989 (Losurdo 2015, 191–194), or the desperate last-ditched efforts by a rapidly fading United States in the 2020s. Obviously, the Chinese are well-accustomed to such efforts and know well how to deal with them. But let us distinguish between the economic base and superstructural elements. Economically, colonial capitalist powers have alternated between trying to restrict or contain China, or to cajole it into following a capitalist path (for example, admitting China to the World Trade Organisation). In terms of superstructure, some of the items mentioned earlier under the 'wild 90s' are applicable. These include the promotion of 'universal values', an unchangeable 'human nature', historical nihilism, and democratic socialism—all of which may be summed up as 'bourgeois liberalisation'. The assumption by former colonisers that Chinese people hanker after such

[15]Xi Jinping observes: 'We should have a deep understanding of the self-regulation capacity of capitalist society, fully appreciate the objective reality that the Western developed countries have a long-term advantage in economy, science, technology, and military affairs, and make every effort to prepare for the long-term cooperation and struggle between the two social systems' (Xi 2019, 4).

liberalisation and its elusive values is a profound misreading of the Chinese situation, for the simple fact is that Chinese people can see that liberal freedoms actually constitute 'a community of the free and its dictatorship over peoples unworthy of liberty' (Losurdo 2011, 248). Both economic and superstructural efforts continue to fail, although China remains on guard against their potentially corrosive influences.

This is where class analysis comes to the fore, since these struggles are ultimately class struggles (Zhu J. 2016, 38–39; Mei 2018, 38–39). International bullying, 'waging a world war without gun smoke', seeking neo-colonial hegemony—these and more are the weapons of class struggle waged periodically by a few capitalist countries on China, among others. China's refusal to be intimidated or deviate from its path comes from a long experience of dealing with such international class oppression against socialism (Deng 1989d, 1989c, 1989b, 1989a; Xi 2019, 4). Where does this leave the core philosophical category of the identity and struggle of opposites? Obviously, it is not simply a shift from struggle to identity, from anti-colonial struggle to 'peaceful coexistence'. Identity may have an increased emphasis, both internally and externally (Chen X. 2015, 3), but it cannot be separated from the reality of struggle.

4.6 One Country, Two Systems

Earlier, I intimated that Hong Kong SAR (and indeed Taiwan island) are manifestations of class struggle, both internally and externally. Both parts of China have capitalist systems, in which class struggle is inescapable. Both are also sites of Western efforts to interfere with China's internal affairs and are thus manifestations of international class struggle. At the same time, Hong Kong SAR and Taiwan island, along with Macao SAR, embody another deployment of contradiction analysis, now in terms of 'one country, two systems'. Since Deng Xiaoping was the architect of this unique policy, my primary references are to his explication of the practice, albeit with an eye on the philosophical implications.

To begin with, Deng Xiaoping specifies (1984m, 101; 1984c, 107; 1987a, 218; 1987b, 217) that the 'one country, two systems' concept 'should be attributed to Marxist dialectical materialism and historical materialism', as this tradition has been developed in China. More specifically, contradiction analysis is the key, in terms of the way socialist and capitalist systems can work together non-antagonistically within one country. Here some terminological clarification is needed: the four-character phrase reads *yiguo-liangzhi* (一国两制). This is a shortened version of the original formula, *yi ge guojia, liang zhong zhidu*, or one country, two types of systems (Deng 1984k, 1984f). The 'one country' refers to China as a distinct sovereign state, with its inviolable borders, political structure, and social structure; 'two types of systems [*zhidu*]' means specifically two socio-economic systems. *Zhidu (制度)* is the key, for it has the senses of system, or an over-arching framework with a primarily economic reference. Thus, China has a socialist system, while Hong Kong SAR, Macao SAR and Taiwan island have capitalist systems. It is important to understand this specific terminology, for it is often misunderstand outside China. For example, former colonisers such as the UK misinterpret 'one country, two systems' as referring to two political structures, two forms of governance. Thus, Hong Kong—they believe—follows a Western bourgeois model, while the mainland does not (as we will see in Chapter 8, it follows a system of socialist democracy).[16] Clearly, this is a mistake: for Deng Xiaoping and his comrades, the systems (*zhidu*) refer primarily to socio-economic realities, and not to the political and territorial questions of a state.

However, the systems do not have equal status in two respects: first, socialist China permits a few 'special regions [*teshu diqu*]' to retain their capitalist systems for quite some time, perhaps even for a century; second, the main part of the country continues under socialism (Deng 1987a, 219; 1987b, 218; see also 1984k, 59; 1984f, 69). In other words, a sovereign one country is the dominant and determining category,[17] and this one country follows a socialist system (*zhidu*) within which the capitalist systems (*zhidu*) of Hong Kong SAR, Macao SAR, and Taiwan island play a subordinate role. The philosophical point that arises here concerns the internal relations between the opposites of a dialectic: as Mao Zedong already specified, one side of a contradiction is always dominant, while the other is subordinate. Even so, this contradiction must be managed not only so that damage from the subordinate side is contained, but also so that it can contribute the socialist whole of China (Li L., Zhang, and Li 1994, 59). This point is even more pertinent to Taiwan island, 'which the United States regards as its unsinkable aircraft carrier' (Deng 1984l, 86; 1984h, 93). While the proposal for the policy in relation to Taiwan indicates even greater flexibility, so much so that the island could even keep its armed forces for a time, Deng also indicates what became a consistent policy: the mainland would never give up the option—if necessary—of using non-peaceful means for normalising the situation with Taiwan island (Deng 1984i, 49; 1984a, 59; 1984l, 86–87; 1984h, 93).

Deng also deliberated at length on questions of governance and potential disturbances in Hong Kong SAR. He was fully aware that Hong Kong as a colony never had a Western-style bourgeois democracy. Further, such a parliamentary approach, which arose in the specific conditions of Europe, does not transfer well to other parts of the world: 'no Western system can be copied in toto', and one should certainly not judge whether Hong Kong is 'democratic' or not in terms of whether or not it has copied such a model (Deng 1987a, 220; 1987b, 218–219). We can now see that the efforts to impose bourgeois democracy on former colonies has either failed or

---

[16]We can see such a mistake in the perceptions of the 2020 national security law for Hong Kong SAR, with Anglophone countries that were part of the British Empire misinterpreting it in purely political terms (Quanguo renmin daibiao dahui 2020). By contrast, in China and in many formerly colonised countries, the national security law is described as Hong Kong's 'second return'. This understanding should come as no surprise, since the British stole Hong Kong from China as part of the Opium Wars and tried to prevent and booby-trap the whole process during negotiations in the 1980s. For a detailed history of the negotiations, see the long footnote in the third volume of Deng Xiaoping's selected works (pp. 373–376).

[17]In the chapter on sovereignty and human rights, we will see that such sovereignty is a distinctly new anti-colonial form, predicated on inviolability and non-interference. Deng asserted this position very clearly in negotiations over Hong Kong SAR (Deng 1982b, 12; 1982a, 23; 1984l, 84; 1984h, 91).

led to another form that may be called 'colonial democracy'. More of that elsewhere (Sect. 9.1), suffice to note here that Deng also specifies that the administrators of Hong Kong SAR should be competent, committed to China as a whole, and that the process of selecting such administrators should undergo a twofold process involving initial elections and then appointment by the central government (Deng 1984b, 74; 1984e, 82; 1987a, 220; 1987b, 219).

In regard to potential disturbances, another feature of contradiction analysis arises, now in terms of the identity and struggle of opposites. While the 'one country, two systems' approach focuses on identity (Fan 2000, 2), on mutual benefit in which things that oppose each other also complement one another (*xiangfan-xiangcheng*), Deng knew well enough that the struggle of opposites would not disappear (Zhou Y. 1997, 127). Concretely, he knew that external and internal forces may well seek to create trouble in the period leading up to Hong Kong's return to China, as well as afterwards. Apart from the British negotiators threatening a 'disastrous effect [*zainanxing de yingxiang*]', he also foresaw anti-communist forces within and without seeking to use Hong Kong SAR as a lever to cause trouble elsewhere on the mainland—as had already happened in the nineteenth and twentieth centuries. The answer: if needed, intervention from the central government would be more than appropriate to maintain peace and stability, especially if such disturbances involved sabotage and separatism (Deng 1982b, 14; 1982a, 25; 1984b, 73–75; 1984e, 81–83; 1987a, 220–221; 1987b, 219–220).

As I write, the 'one country, two systems' approach to Hong SAR, Macao SAR, and Taiwan island may seem like a well-established practice—albeit misinterpreted by some former colonisers. At the time, it was clearly a breakthrough, 'something new, without precedent in world history'. Deng saw it as a unique deployment of contradiction analysis, in contrast to capitalist countries that play a zero-sum game in relation to socialism and seek imperialist hegemony (Quan 2008, 23). Indeed, Deng hoped that this policy would have global ramifications, especially for other developing countries with whom China has a particularly close connection (Deng 1987a, 215; 1987b, 214; 1984k, 59; 1984f, 69; 1990b, 352; 1990a, 340).

Throughout this brief explication of the breakthrough 'one country, two systems' policy, I have sought to draw out the philosophical points arising from contradiction analysis. These include the reality of two systems functioning within one distinct entity, the primacy of one aspect of a contradiction over the other, and the reality of both identity and struggle between the opposites. As is so often the case with Deng Xiaoping, these philosophical points arise from between the lines, from the practical considerations of Chinese reunification, although he was aware of the precedent set and its potentially global ramifications.

4.7 Conclusion: One Central Task and Two Basic Points

In this chapter, I have presented Chinese research on the Reform and Opening-Up by using contradiction analysis as the key. We began with the return to the countryside and found that the household responsibility system was a way of recovering the socialist principle, 'from each according to ability, to each according work'. In terms of reform itself, Lenin's principle came into play, in which reform should always be undertaken in light of revolution—especially during the long and arduous task of constructing socialism. This led to a treatment of the dialectic of reform itself, in which the answer to the internal and incidental contradictions of the 'wild 90s' was to deepen reform itself as an ongoing process. When it came to opening up to the rest of the world, I examined how a socialist country relates to capitalist countries, which then led to an exploration of how class analysis has been recalibrated in terms of the international dynamics of class conflict and the internal realities of managing contradictions between classes so that they remain non-antagonistic. The final specific example was the unprecedented 'one country, two systems' policy, with the one country being China and the two systems being a dominant socialism on the mainland and capitalism in the SARs of Hong Kong and Macao, as well as Taiwan island.

This one-two example leads me to a final point concerning a Chinese Marxist formulation in relation to the Reform and Opening-Up: 'one central task and two basic points [*yi ge zhongxin, liang ge jibendian*]' (Deng 1992b, 370; 1992a, 358–359; see also Jiang Z. 1992, 2–3, 5). To wit: the central task is to focus on economic development and improvement of people's lives, while the two basic points concern adherence to the Four Cardinal Principles and adherence to the Reform and Opening-Up (Zhao 1987, 4–5). Obviously much is contained in this brief formulation, but before elaborating on its dialectical features, let me note a slight reformulation in terms of 'two aspects and one key point [*liangdianlun he zhongdianlun*]' (Jiang X. 2018, 2; Li C. 2009, 150). Why the change? It indicates a clearer continuity with Mao Zedong's explication of dialectics at the intersection between Chinese tradition and Marxist philosophy. Not only did he speak of 'two aspects [*liangdianlun*]' in relation to the *yin-yang* relationship in Chinese philosophy (Mao 1956b, 320; 1956a, 340), albeit as a metaphysical precursor to the materialist dialectics of Marxism, but he also invoked the essence of dialectics in terms of 'one divides into two [*yifenweier*]' (Mao 1957d, 332–333; 1957a, 516; see also 1937a; 1937b; Xia and Chen 2009, 1379).[18] We may identify two traditions behind this formulation. One stems from traditional Chinese philosophy, clearly expressed by Zhu Xi (1130–1200 CE) of the Song dynasty: 'The master thinks that one divides into two [*yiweifener*], two into four, four into eight … He pointed to the heart of the fan with his hand, and said, "There is only one principle, divided into two [*fen wei liangge*]"' (Zhu X. 1986, 105).[19] The other comes from Lenin's engagement with Hegel in 1914, where he

[18]During the 1960s there was a somewhat heated debate over 'one divides into two' versus 'two unites into one'. A useful summary from the *Beijing Review* is provided by Li Xue (1972). The concept has a two-edged dimension in Mao's thought: although he spoke it being the essence of philosophy, he also deployed it in launching the Cultural Revolution in order to focus on 'class struggle as the key'. Our sources in relation this material, however, are unreliable since they were published by Red Guards at unknown locations (Mao 1964a, 1964b, 1965b, 1965a).

[19]Precursors may be found in the *Xici* 1.11 section of the *Yijing* (available at https://ctext.org/book-of-changes/xi-ci-shang).

writes of the 'splitting of a single whole and the cognition of its contradictory parts ... is the *essence* ... of dialectics' (Lenin 1915a, 316; 1915b, 357). As we saw in the previous chapter, it was primarily from Lenin and the Soviet development of dialectical materialism that Mao Zedong developed the idea in the 1930s. As he did so, Mao turned Chinese philosophy over and placed it firmly on its materialist feet—to borrow a metaphor Marx used in relation to Hegel.

4.7.1 Reform and Opening-Up

To return to Deng Xiaoping: the 'one central task' is to focus on economic development by liberating the forces of production. Since I have discussed this topic in the second chapter (Sect. 2.4) and will return to it (from another angle) in the next, I will not address it here. My concern is with the 'two basic points', with the Reform and Opening-Up and the Four Cardinal Principles. These two prongs aim to counter 'leftist' and 'rightist' tendencies in relation to the project of economic development. The Reform and Opening-Up itself (the topic of the present chapter as a whole) sought to counter the leftist risk, which was very fresh in everyone's memory due to the chaos and turmoil of the Cultural Revolution. Trying to make a hasty and impractical leap to full communism, this leftist deviation meant nothing more than 'universal poverty [*pubian pinqiong*]' (Deng 1979a, 165; 1979c, 174). Such leftism neglected the realities of socialist construction in terms of liberating the forces of production, from each according to ability and to each according to work, the importance of initiative and innovation, and the observance of economic laws—in short, the scientific socialism that was a necessary and patient preparation for communism.

4.7.2 Four Cardinal Principles

The Four Cardinal Principles were targeted at the 'rightist' risk. In a key speech delivered in the context of the all-important Third Plenary Session of the CPC's Eleventh Central Committee, Deng touched on liberating thought, seeking truth from facts, and the focus on socialist modernisation. But his main concern was to identify four ideological and political principles:

1. We must keep to the socialist road [*shehuizhuyi daolu*].
2. We must uphold the dictatorship of the proletariat.
3. We must uphold the leadership of the Communist Party.
4. We must uphold Marxism-Leninism and Mao Zedong Thought (Deng 1979a, 164; 1979c, 174).

None of these points are particularly new, as Deng points out. They are part and parcel of the socialist project. But why identify and emphasise them at this crucial juncture? In the speech, Deng identifies the 'rightist' deviation as their target:

the Reform and Opening-Up may be seen by some as a path to capitalism and bourgeois liberalisation, and thus an abandonment of Marxism-Leninism. While this assumption may come from those of a 'leftist' bent, who would see the new project as a turn to the 'capitalist road', it was more likely to come from the 'rightist' deviation, which would urge full bourgeois liberalisation. In the hindsight of four decades of the Reform and Opening-Up, we can also see the 'rightist' deviation is a recurring problem among international observers (unfortunately, with some Marxist among them), who have urged and assumed that China was indeed going down the capitalist road. The Four Cardinal Principles are a clear statement to the contrary: China will not and cannot deviate from the socialist road, which focuses on improving the socio-economic conditions of the masses and is thus ultimately superior to capitalism; the dictatorship of the proletariat as the broadest and thus a higher form of democracy; the leadership of the Communist Party, since without a Party integrated with the masses socialist construction of the New China would be impossible; and the fine tradition of Marxism-Leninism and Mao Zedong Thought (and not its deviation into Maoism during the Cultural Revolution). It should be no surprise that the Four Cardinal Principles have been a touchstone ever since Deng's speech, especially since their affirmation in the crucial declaration from 1981, which was the culmination of a few years arduous work (CPC Central Committee 1981, 11, 16).

4.7.3 Both Hands Should Be Hard

Thus, the 'two basic points' emphasise the need to manage the contradiction between 'leftist' and 'rightist' deviations, between ill-advised efforts to ignore China's specific conditions in constructing socialism and the dangers of the capitalist road. I close on a related note, which captures Deng Xiaoping's practical approach to the dialectics of contradiction analysis. It concerns the concrete image of the 'two hands' (Lu 2005, 62). Deng used this image on a number of occasions,[20] but I am interested in how it relates to the 'two aspects' of the Reform and Opening-Up and the Four Cardinal Principles (Deng 1989e, 306). For Deng, it will not do for one hand to be 'hard [*ying*]' and the other 'soft [*ruan*]', for 'both hands should be hard [*liang zhi shou dou yao ying*]' (Deng 1992b, 378).[21]

[20]For example, one hand should grasp the improvements of the Reform and Opening-Up, while the other hand should 'deal a crushing blow [*yanlidaji*]' to economic crimes (Deng 1989e, 306). Or in relation to economic construction and the legal system, one hand should grasp (*zhua*) each side (Deng 1986c, 154). The same can be said for material and 'spiritual civilisation [*jingshen wenming*]' (Deng 1992b, 379).

[21]By the 14th congress of the CPC, 'both hands' would become part of government policy (Jiang Z. 1992, 3).

References

Boer, Roland. 2019. The Christian state. In *Bloomsbury companion to Marx*, ed. Jeff Diamanti, Andrew Pendakis, and Imre Szeman, 107–119. London: Bloomsbury.

Boer, Roland. 2020. Women xuedao le shenme, shijie jiang hui zenyang? *Guangming ribao*, 12 May. https://news.gmw.cn/2020-05/12/content_33821736.htm.

Brink, Tobias ben. 2008. *Global political economy and the modern state system*. Leiden: Brill.

Chen, Shuguang. 2018. Zhongguo makesizhuyi yanjiu 40 nian: 1978–2018. *Jiaoxue yu yanjiu* 2018 (10): 5–16.

Chen, Xueming. 2015. Zhongguo daolu dui makesizhuyi de fazhan – lun Zhongguo daolu de makesizhuyi yiyi zhi san. *Nanjing zhengzhi xueyuan xuebao* 2015 (6): 1–12.

Chen, Xueming, Ma. Yongjun, Luo Qian, and Jiang Guomin. 2016. Makesizhuyi zhexue yanjiu 'xin qimeng' hue yu 'houxiandai' hua pipan. *Zongguo shehui kexue pingjia* 2016 (1): 4–17.

Chen, Yun. 1980. Jingji xingshi yu jingyan jiaoxun (1980.12.16). In *Chen Yun wenxuan*, vol. 3:276–282. Beijing: Renmin chubanshe, 1986.

Cheng, Enfu. 1997. Guoyou jingji de gongneng diwei yu fazhan zhanlüe – guoyou jingji de zhudao gongneng yu zhidu chuangxin. *Xueshu yuekan* 1997 (10): 11–13.

Chi, Chenyong. 2018. Xi Jinping quanmian shenhua gaige zhongyao sixiang de makesizhuyi zhexue yiyun – jinian Zhongguo gaige kaifang 40 zhounian. *Jiangnan shehui xueyuan xuebao* 20 (4): 7–12.

CPC Central Committee. 1981. Guanyu jianguo yilai dang de ruogan lishi wenti de jueyi (1981 nian 6 yue 27 ri Zhongguo gongchandang di shiyi jie zhongyang weiyuanhui di liu ci quanti huiyi tongguo). *Renmin Ribao*, 27 June: 1–18.

CPC Central Committee. 2006. *Zhonggong zhongyang guanyu goujian shehuizhuyi shehui hexie ruogan zhongda wenti de jueding*. Beijing: Zhongguo gongchandang zhongyang weiyuanhui.

CPC Central Committee. 2013a. *Decision of the Central Committee of the Communist Party of China on some major issues concerning comprehensively deepening the reform*. Beijing: Zhongguo gongchandang zhongyang weiyuanhui.

CPC Central Committee. 2013b. *Zhonggong zhongyang guanyu quanmian shenhua gaige ruogan zhongda wenti de jueding (2013.11.12)*. Beijing: Zhongguo gongchandang zhongyang weiyuanhui.

Deng, Xiaoping. 1979a. Jianchi sixiang jiben yuanze (1979.03.30). In *Deng Xiaoping wenxuan*, vol. 2:158–184. Beijing: Renmin chubanshe, 2008.

Deng, Xiaoping. 1979b. Shehuizhuyi ye keyi gao shichang jingji (1979.11.26). In *Deng Xiaoping wenxuan*, vol. 2:231–236. Beijing: Renmin chubanshe, 2008.

Deng, Xiaoping. 1979c. Uphold the Four Cardinal Principles (30 March, 1979). In *Selected Works of Deng Xiaoping*, vol. 2:168–191. Beijing: Foreign Languages Press, 1995.

Deng, Xiaoping. 1979d. We can develop a market economy under socialism (26 November, 1979). In *Selected works of Deng Xiaoping*, vol. 2:235–239. Beijing: Foreign Languages Press, 1995.

Deng, Xiaoping. 1980a. Answers to the Italian Journalist Oriana Fallaci (21 and 23 August, 1980). In *Selected Works of Deng Xiaoping*, vol. 2:342–349. Beijing: Foreign Languages Press, 1995.

Deng, Xiaoping. 1980b. Da Yidali jizhe Aolinaina Falaqiwen (1980.08.21, 23). In *Deng Xiaoping wenxuan*, vol. 2:344–353. Beijing: Renmin chubanshe, 1995.

Deng, Xiaoping. 1980c. Shehuizhuyi shouxian yao fazhan shengchanli (1980.04–05). In *Deng Xiaoping wenxuan*, vol. 2:311–314. Beijing: Renmin chubanshe, 1995.

Deng, Xiaoping. 1980d. To build socialism we must first develop the productive forces (April–May 1980). In *Selected works of Deng Xiaoping*, vol. 2:310–313. Beijing: Foreign Languages Press, 1995.

Deng, Xiaoping. 1982a. Our basic position on the question of Hong Kong (24 September, 1982). In *Selected works of Deng Xiaoping*, vol. 3:23–25. Beijing: Foreign Languages Press, 1994.

Deng, Xiaoping. 1982b. Women dui Xianggang wenti de jiben lichang (1982.09.24). In *Deng Xiaoping wenxuan*, vol. 3:12–15. Beijing: Renmin chubanshe, 2008.

Deng, Xiaoping. 1984a. A new approach to stabilizing the world situation (22 February, 1984). In *Selected works of Deng Xiaoping*, vol. 3:59–60. Beijing: Foreign Languages Press, 1994.
Deng, Xiaoping. 1984b. Baochi Xianggang de fanrong he wending (1984.10.03). In *Deng Xiaoping wenxuan*, vol. 3:72–76. Beijing: Renmin chubanshe, 2008.
Deng, Xiaoping. 1984c. China will always keep its promises (19 December, 1984). In *Selected works of Deng Xiaoping*, vol. 3:107–109. Beijing: Foreign Languages Press, 1994.
Deng, Xiaoping. 1984d. Jianshe you Zhongguo tese de shehuizhuyi (1984.06.30). In *Deng Xiaoping wenxuan*, vol. 3:62–66. Beijing: Renmin chubanshe, 2008.
Deng, Xiaoping. 1984e. Maintain prosperity and stability in Hong Kong (3 October, 1984). In *Selected works of Deng Xiaoping*, vol. 3:80–84. Beijing: Foreign Languages Press, 1994.
Deng, Xiaoping. 1984f. One country, two systems (22–23 June, 1984). In *Selected works of Deng Xiaoping*, vol. 3:68–71. Beijing: Foreign Languages Press, 1994.
Deng, Xiaoping. 1984g. Our magnificent goal and basic policies (6 October, 1984). In *Selected works of Deng Xiaoping*, vol. 3:85–87. Beijing: Foreign Languages Press, 1994.
Deng, Xiaoping. 1984h. Speech at the third plenary session of the Central Advisory Commission of Communist Party of China (22 October, 1984). In *Selected works of Deng Xiaoping*, vol. 3:90–99. Beijing: Foreign Languages Press, 1994.
Deng, Xiaoping. 1984i. Wending shijie jushi de xin banfa (1984.02.22). In *Deng Xiaoping wenxuan*, vol. 3:49–50. Beijing: Renmin chubanshe, 2008.
Deng, Xiaoping. 1984j. Women de hongwei mubiao he genben zhengce (1984.10.06). In *Deng Xiaoping wenxuan*, vol. 3:77–80. Beijing: Renmin chubanshe, 2008.
Deng, Xiaoping. 1984k. Yi ge guojia, liang zhong zhidu (1984.04.22–23). In *Deng Xiaoping wenxuan*, vol. 3:58–61. Beijing: Renmin chubanshe, 2008.
Deng, Xiaoping. 1984l. Zai zhongyang guwen weiyuanhui di san ci quanti huiyi shang de jianghua (1984.10.22). In *Deng Xiaoping wenxuan*, vol. 3:83–93. Beijing: Renmin chubanshe, 2008.
Deng, Xiaoping. 1984m. Zhongguo shi xinshou nuoyan de (1984.12.19). In *Deng Xiaoping wenxuan*, vol. 3:101–103. Beijing: Renmin chubanshe, 2008.
Deng, Xiaoping. 1985a. We shall expand political democracy and carry out economic reform (15 April, 1985). In *Selected works of Deng Xiaoping*, vol. 3:121–124. Beijing: Foreign Languages Press, 1994.
Deng, Xiaoping. 1985b. Zhengzhi shang fazhan minzhu, jingji shang shixing gaige (1985.04.15). In *Deng Xiaoping wenxuan*, vol. 3:115–118. Beijing: Renmin chubanshe, 2008.
Deng, Xiaoping. 1986a. Let the facts speak for themselves (28 March, 1986). In *Selected works of Deng Xiaoping*, vol. 3:158–159. Beijing: Foreign Languages Press, 1994.
Deng, Xiaoping. 1986b. Na shishi lai shuohua (1986.03.28). In *Deng Xiaoping wenxuan*, vol. 3:155–156. Beijing: Renmin chubanshe, 2008.
Deng, Xiaoping. 1986c. Zai zhongyang zhengzhiju dangwei hui shang de jianghua (1986.01.17). In *Deng Xiaoping wenxuan*, vol. 3:152–154. Beijing: Renmin chubanshe, 2008.
Deng, Xiaoping. 1987a. Huijian Xianggang tebie xingzhengqu jibenfa qicao weiyuanhui weiyuan shi de jianghua (1987.04.16). In *Deng Xiaoping wenxuan*, vol. 3:215–222. Beijing: Renmin chubanshe, 2008.
Deng, Xiaoping. 1987b. Speech at a meeting with the members of the committee for drafting the basic law of the Hong Kong special administrative region (16 April, 1987). In *Selected works of Deng Xiaoping*, vol. 3:214–220. Beijing: Foreign Languages Press, 1994.
Deng, Xiaoping. 1989a. No one can shake socialist China (26 October, 1989). In *Selected works of Deng Xiaoping*, vol. 3:318–319. Beijing: Foreign Languages Press, 1994.
Deng, Xiaoping. 1989b. Shehuizhuyi de Zhongguo shei ye dongyao buliao (1989.10.26). In *Deng Xiaoping wenxuan*, vol. 3:328–329. Beijing: Renmin chubanshe, 2010.
Deng, Xiaoping. 1989c. We are confident that we can handle China's affairs well (16 September, 1989). In *Selected works of Deng Xiaoping*, vol. 3:314–317. Beijing: Foreign Languages Press, 1994.
Deng, Xiaoping. 1989d. Women you xinxin ba Zhongguo de shiqing zuo de geng hao (1989.09.16). In *Deng Xiaoping wenxuan*, vol. 3:324–327. Beijing: Renmin chubanshe, 2010.

Deng, Xiaoping. 1989e. Zai jiejian shoudu jieyan budui jun yishang shi de jianghua (1989.06.09). In *Deng Xiaoping wenxuan*, vol. 3:302–308. Beijing: Renmin chubanshe, 2010.

Deng, Xiaoping. 1990a. The basic law of the Hong Kong special administrative region is of historic and international significance (17 February, 1980). In *Selected works of Deng Xiaoping*, vol. 3:340. Beijing: Foreign Languages Press, 1994.

Deng, Xiaoping. 1990b. Xianggang jibenfa juyou lishi yiyi he guoji yiyi (1990.02.19). In *Deng Xiaoping wenxuan*, vol. 3:352. Beijing: Renmin chubanshe, 2008.

Deng, Xiaoping. 1992a. Excerpts from talks given in Wuchang, Shenzhen, Zhuhai and Shanghai (18 January–21 February, 1992). In *Selected works of Deng Xiaoping*, vol. 3:358–370. Beijing: Foreign Languages Press, 1994.

Deng, Xiaoping. 1992b. Zai Wuchang, Shenzhen, Zhuhai he Shanghai deng di de tanhua yaodian (1992.01.18 – 02.21). In *Deng Xiaoping wenxuan*, vol. 3:370–383. Beijing: Renmin chubanshe, 2008.

Dirlik, Arif, and Zhang Xudong, eds. 2000. *Postmodernism and China*. Durham: Duke University Press.

Dong, Shaolin, and Wu. Bo. 2011. Guanyu shehuizhuyi chuji jieduan de jieji jieceng jiegou jiqi neizai maodun. *Zhengzhixue yanjiu* 2011 (3): 57–63.

Fan, Wenzhou. 2000. Lüelun Deng Xiaoping dui Mao Zedong maodun fenxifa jicheng he fazhan. *Fujian caihui gongli ganbu xueyuan xuebao* 2000 (4): 1–5.

Fang, Jianguo. 2014. Gaige kaifang yilai Zhongguo gongchandang minsheng jingji sixiang de zhongda fazhan – yi makesizhuyi zhexue fangfa wei fenxi zhuxian. *Makesizhuyi yanjiu* 2014 (10): 58–67, 120.

Fang, Keli. 2006. Guanyu wenhua tiyong wenti. *Shehui kexue zhanxian* 2006 (4): 16–23.

Fang, Keli. 2015. *Mahun, zhongti, xiyong: Zhongguo wenhua fazhan de xianshi daolu*, ed. Xie Qingsong. Beijing: Renmin chubanshe.

Gao, Fang. 2007. Bainian lai kexue shehuizhuyi yu minzhu shehuizhuyi guanxi de yanbian – jian tan 'zhiyou shehuizhuyi minzhu caineng jiu Zhongguo.' *Lilun xuekan* 2007 (6): 15–22.

Ha, Si. 1989. Lun makesizhuyi zhexue chansheng de lishi biranxing jiqi dui gaige kaifang de zhidao yiyi. *Neimenggu shida xuebao (hanwen zhexue shehui kexue ban)* 1989 (4): 13–18.

Harvey, David. 2005. *A brief history of neoliberalism*. Oxford: Oxford University Press.

Hu, Feng, and Li Shantong. 2009. Fumu waichu wugong dui nongcun liushou ertong jiaoyu de yingxiang – jiyu 5 chengshi nongmingong diaocha de shizheng fenxi. *Guanli shijie* 2009 (2): 67–74.

Jiang, Xi. 2018. Bianzheng weiwuzhuyi fangfalun shiyu xia Xi Jinping xinshidai Zhongguo tese shehuizhuyi sixiang dui xin maodun de fenxi he jiejue. *Xinyu xueyuan xuebao* 23 (5): 1–3.

Jiang, Yonggui. 1990. Lüelun gaige kaifang de shijian yu makesizhuyi zhexue de yunyong. *Zhejiang shehui kexue* 1990 (2): 9–12.

Jiang, Zemin. 1989. Xin Zhongguo sishi nian lishi de jiben jielun (1989.09.29). In *Jiang Zemin wenxuan*, vol. 1:70–73. Beijing: Renmin chubanshe, 2006.

Jiang, Zemin. 1992. Jiakuai gaige kaifang he xiandaihua jianshe bufa, duoqu you Zhongguo tese shehuizhuyi shiye de geng da shengli (1992.10.12). In *Jiang Zemin wenxuan*, vol. 1:210–254. Beijing: Renmin chubanshe, 2006.

Lenin, V. I. 1906a. Peresmotr agrarnoi programmy rabochei partii. Vtoraia polovina marta 1906 g. In *Polnoe sobranie sochinenii*, vol. 12:239–270. Moscow: Izdatel'stvo politicheskoi literatury, 1968.

Lenin, V. I. 1906b. Revision of the agrarian programme of the Workers' Party. In *Collected works*, vol. 10:165–195. Moscow: Progress Publishers, 1962.

Lenin, V. I. 1915a. K voprosu o dialektike. In *Polnoe sobranie sochinenii*, vol. 29:316–322. Moscow: Izdatel'stvo politicheskoi literatury, 1979.

Lenin, V. I. 1915b. On the question of dialectics. In *Collected works*, vol. 38:355–361. Moscow: Progress Publishers, 1968.

Lenin, V. I. 1916a. Principles involved in the war issue. In *Collected works*, 23:152–160. Moscow: Progress Publishers, 1964.

Lenin, V. I. 1916b. Printsipial′nye polozheniia k voprosu o voine. Dekabr′ 1916 g. In *Polnoe sobranie sochinenii*, 30:212–222. Moscow: Izdatel'stvo politicheskoi literatury, 1974.
Lenin, V. I. 1917a. Chernovoi proekt tezisov obrashcheniia k Internatsional′noi sotsialisticheskoi komissii i ko vsem sotsialisticheskim partiiam. Dekabr′, ranee 25, 1916 g. (7 ianvaria 1917 g.). In *Polnoe sobranie sochinenii*, 30:273–285. Moscow: Izdatel'stvo politicheskoi literatury, 1974.
Lenin, V. I. 1917b. Theses for an appeal to the international socialist committee and all socialist parties. In *Collected works*, 23:205–216. Moscow: Progress Publishers, 1964.
Li, Chongfu. 2009. Creative application and deepened development of historical materialism in the great practice of reform and opening-up. *Marxist Studies in China* 2008–2009: 144–164.
Li, Liuying, Zhang Zhong, and Li Hongwen. 1994. Mao Zedong guanyu maodun teshuxing wenti de fenxi yu Deng Xiaoping jianshe you Zhongguo tese shehuizhuyi lilun. *Heihe xuekan* 1994 (2): 58–60.
Li, Xue. 1972. The theory of two points. *Bejing Review* 15 (2): 9–10.
Liu, Guoguang. 2005. Dui jingjixue jiaoxue he yanjiu zhong yixie wenti de kanfa. *Gaoxiao lilun zhanxian* 2005 (9): 23–29.
Lo, Chi. 2007. *Understanding China's growth: Forces that drive China's economic future*. Houndmills: Palgrave Macmillan.
Losurdo, Domenico. 2011. *Liberalism: A counter-history*, trans. Gregory Elliott. London: Verso.
Losurdo, Domenico. 2015. *Non-violence: A history beyond the myth*, trans. Gregory Elliott. Lanham: Lexington.
Lu, Jianjie. 2005. Deng Xiaoping dui xinshiqi sixiang zhanxian maodun de fenxi he duice de xuanze. *Mao Zedong Sixiang Yanjiu* 22 (1): 59–64.
Lv, Lidan. 2014. Cong 'liushou ertong' dao 'xinshengdai nongmingong' – gaozhong xueling nongcun liushou ertong xueye zhongzhi yi yingxiang yanjiu. *Renkou yanjiu* 38 (1): 37–50.
Mao, Zedong. 1937a. Maodun lun (1937.08). In *Mao Zedong xuanji*, vol. 1:299–340. Beijing: Renmin chubanshe, 2009.
Mao, Zedong. 1937b. On contradiction (August, 1937). In *Selected works of Mao Tse-Tung*, vol. 1:311–347. Beijing: Foreign Languages Press, 1965.
Mao, Zedong. 1945a. Dui 'lun lianhezhengfu' de shuoming (1945.03.31). In *Mao Zedong wenji*, vol. 3:272–279. Beijing: Renmin chubanshe, 1996.
Mao, Zedong. 1945b. Lun lianhezhengfu (1945.04.24). In *Mao Zedong xuanji*, vol. 3:1029–1100. Beijing: Renmin chubanshe, 2009.
Mao, Zedong. 1945c. On coalition government (24 April, 1945). In *Selected works of Mao Tse-Tung*, vol. 3:255–320. Beijing: Foreign Languages Press, 1965.
Mao, Zedong. 1949a. Report to the second plenary session of the Seventh Central Committee of the Communist Party (5 March, 1949). In *Selected works of Mao Tse-Tung*, vol. 4:361–375. Beijing: Foreign Languages Press, 1969.
Mao, Zedong. 1949b. Zai Zhongguo gongchandang di qi jie zhongyang weiyuanhui di er ci quanti huiyi shang de baogao (1949.03.05). In *Mao Zedong xuanji*, vol. 4:1424–1439. Beijing: Renmin chubanshe, 2009.
Mao, Zedong. 1956a. Speech at the second plenary session of the Eighth Central Committee of the Communist Party of China (15 November, 1956). In *Selected works of Mao Tse-Tung*, vol. 5:332–349. Beijing: Foreign Languages Press, 1977.
Mao, Zedong. 1956b. Zai Zhongguo gongchandang di ba jie zhongyang weiyuanhui di er ci quanti (1956.11.15). In *Mao Zedong xuanji*, vol. 5:313–329. Beijing: Renmin chubanshe, 1977.
Mao, Zedong. 1957a. A dialectical approach to inner-party unity (18 November, 1957). In *Selected Works of Mao Tse-Tung*, vol. 5:514–516. Beijing: Foreign Languages Press, 1977.
Mao, Zedong. 1957b. Guanyu zhengque chuli renmin neibu maodun de wenti (1957.02.27). In *Mao Zedong wenji*, vol. 7:204–244. Beijing: Renmin chubanshe, 2009.
Mao, Zedong. 1957c. On the correct handling of contradictions among the people (27 February, 1957). In *Selected works of Mao Tse-Tung*, vol. 5:384–421. Beijing: Foreign Languages Press, 1977.

Mao, Zedong. 1957d. Zai Mosike gongchandang he gongrendang daibiao huiyi de jianghua (1957.11.18). In *Mao Zedong wenji*, vol. 7:321–335. Beijing: Renmin chubanshe, 2009.

Mao, Zedong. 1964a. Guanyu zhexue wenti de jianghua (1964.08.18). In *Mao Zedong sixiang wansui*, vol. 5:148–154. n. p.: Hongweibing, 1968.

Mao, Zedong. 1964b. Talk on questions of philosophy (18 August, 1964). In *Chairman Mao talks to the people: Talks and letters: 1956–1971*, ed. Stuart Schram, 212–330. New York: Pantheon Books, 1974.

Mao, Zedong. 1965a. Speech at Hangchow (21 December, 1965). In *Chairman Mao talks to the people: Talks and letters: 1956–1971*, ed. Stuart Schram, 234–241. New York: Pantheon Books, 1974.

Mao, Zedong. 1965b. Zai Hangzhou huiyi shang de jianghua (1965.12.21). In *Mao Zedong sixiang wansui*, vol. 5:246–48. n. p.: Hongweibing, 1968.

Marx, Karl. 1847a. *Misère de la Philosophie. Réponse a la Philosophie de la Misère de M. Proudhon.* Paris and Bruxelles: A. Frank and C.G. Vogler.

Marx, Karl. 1847b. The poverty of philosophy: Answer to the *Philosophy ofpoverty* by M. Proudhon. In *Marx and Engels collected Works*, 6:104–212. Moscow: Progress Publishers.

Mei, Rongzheng. 2018. Zai gaige kaifang zhong makesizhuyi lilun xueke de chuangjian he fazhan. *Makesizhuyi lilun xueke yanjiu* 2018 (5): 37–51.

Meisner, Maurice. 1996. *The Deng Xiaoping era: An inquiry into the fate of Chinese socialism, 1978–1994*. New York: Hill and Wang.

Panitch, Leo, and Sam Gindin. 2013. The integration of china into global capitalism. *International Critical Thought* 3 (2): 146–158.

Quan, Lizhi. 2008. Deng Xiaoping dui maodun fenxifa de yunyong yu fazhan. *Lilun Tansuo* 2008 (4): 21–23.

Quanguo renmin daibiao dahui. 2020. *Zhonghua renmin gongheguo xianggang tebier xingzhengqu weihu guojia'anquan fa*. Beijing: NPC.

Ren, Ping, and Wang Jianming. 2010. Lun chayixing shehui yu Zhongguo tese shehuizhuyi minzhu zhengzhi de weilai. *Makesizhuyi Yanjiu* 2010 (5): 102–110.

Rong, Kaiming. 2002. Deng Xiaoping zai maodun fenxi he gaige fangfalun shang de xin gongxian. *Xiaogan xueyuan xuebao* 21 (4): 22–25.

Shang, Hongyin. 2004. Shi xi Deng Xiaoping jingji zhexue de hexin – maodun fenxifa. *Zhuzhou shifan gaodeng zhuanke xuexiao xuebao* 9 (6): 11–13, 24.

Stalin, I. V. 1931a. Beseda s nemetskim pisatelem Ėmilem Liudvigom, 13 dekabria 1931 g. In *Sochineniia*, vol. 13:104–123. Moscow: Gosudarstvennoe izdatel′stvo politicheskoi literatury, 1951.

Stalin, I. V. 1931b. Talk with the German author Emil Ludwig, December 13, 1931. In *Works*, 13:106–25. Moscow: Foreign Languages Publishing House, 1954.

Stalin, I. V. 1934a. Beseda s angliiskim pisatelem G.D. Uėllsom 23 iiulia 1934 goda. In *Sochineniia*, vol. 14:24–39. Moscow: Izdatel′stvo "Pisatel′", 1997.

Stalin, I. V. 1934b. Marxism versus liberalism: An interview with H. G. Wells. In *Works*, 14:21–44. London: Red Star Press, 1978.

Stalin, I. V. 1934c. Otchetnyĭ doklad XVII s"ezdu partii o rabote TSK VKP(b), 26 ianvaria 1934 g. In *Sochineniia*, 13:282–379. Moscow: Gosudarstvennoe izdatel′stvo politicheskoi literatury, 1951.

Stalin, I. V. 1934d. Report to the seventeenth party congress on the work of the Central Committee of the C.P.S.U.(B.), January 26, 1934. In *Works*, 13:288–388. Moscow: Foreign Languages Publishing House, 1954.

Thesis Group, Marxism Research Institute of CASS. 2009. The 30 most influential events in marxist theoretical development during the 30 years of China's reform and opening-up. *Marxist Studies in China* 2009: 71–102.

Wang, Fumin. 2015. Zai xin de gaige kaifang jincheng zhong jianchi yu fazhan makesizhuyi. *Zhonggong fujian shengwei dangxiao xuebao* 2015 (1): 28–36.

Wang, Hui. 2009. *The end of the revolution: China and the limits of modernity*. London: Verso.

Wang, Weiguang. 2014. Upholding and developing Mao Zedong thought and firmly advancing socialism with Chinese characteristics. *Marxist Studies in China* 2014: 2–20.
Wang, Yicheng. 2013. On the nature of 'civil society.' *Marxist Studies in China* 2013: 187–211.
Wang, Yunjing, and Yang Yuntai. 1994. Gaige shi jiefang he fazhan shengchanli – xuexi 'Deng Xiaoping xuanji' di san juan de tihui. *Shanghai daxue xuebao (sheke ban)* 1994 (6): 102–107.
Wei, Liangyi. 2015. Deng Xiaoping gongtong fuyu lilun jiqi dui woguo quanmian jianshi xiaokang shehui de qishi. *Mao Zedong sixiang yanjiu* 32 (4): 68–71.
Weil, Robert. 1996. *Red cat, white cat*. New York: Monthly Review Press.
World Bank. 2019. *China systematic country diagnostic: Towards a more conclusive and sustainable development*. Washington: World Bank Group.
Xi, Jinping. 1999. Jiefang sixiang, shishiqiushi yao yiyiguanzhi – chongdu Deng Xiaoping tongzhi 'Jiefang sixiang, shishiqiushi, tuanjieyizhi xiangqian kan.' *Qiushi* 1999 (1): 21–24.
Xi, Jinping. 2013. Haobu dongyao jianchi he fazhan Zhongguo tese shehuizhuyi (2013.01.05). In *Tan zhiguolizheng*, vol. 1:21–24. Beijing: Waiwen chubanshe, 2014.
Xi, Jinping. 2018a. *Lun jianchi quanmian shenru gaige*. Beijing: Zhongyang wenxian chubanshe.
Xi, Jinping. 2018b. *Zai jinian makesi danchen 200 zhounian dahui shang de jianghua (2018.05.04)*. Beijing: Renmin chubanshe.
Xi, Jinping. 2019. Guanyu jianchi he fazhan Zhongguo tese shehuizhuyi de jige wenti. *Qiushi* 2019 (7): 1–4.
Xia, Zhengnong, and Chen Zhili, eds. 2009. *Cihai*, 6th ed. Shanghai: Shanghai cishu chubanshe.
Xiao, Guiqing, and Qiao Huibo. 2018. Gaige kaifang 40 nian yu xiaokang shehui jianshe. *Makesizhuyi zhongguohua yanjiu* 2018 (5): 14–22.
Xie, Tao. 2007. Minzhu shehuizhuyi moshi yu Zhongguo qiantu. *Yanhuang chunqiu* 2007 (2): 1–8.
Xue, Jiulin. 1995. Deng Xiaoping de gaige kaifang guan. *Ningxia daxue xuebao (shehui kexue ban)* 17 (1): 30–35.
Zan, Jiansen. 2015. Shehui jiben maodun yu quanmian shenhua gaige. *Lilun tansuo* 2015 (4): 42–45.
Zhao, Ziyang. 1987. *Yanzhe you Zhongguo tese de shehuizhuyi daolu qianjin – zai Zhongguo gongchandang di shisan ci quanguo daibiao dahui shang de baogao (1987.10.25)*. Beijing: Renmin chubanshe.
Zheng, Keyang. 2008. Zou Zhongguo tese shehuizhuyi yao jingto xin ziyouzhuyi, minzhu shehuizhuyi, yu lishi xuwuzhuyi san gu sichao. *Zhengzhixue yanjiu* 2008 (1): 8–11.
Zheng, Yishi, and Hong Yanni. 2014. Dangdai eluosi zhexue yu gaige kaifang yilai Zhongguo makesizhuyi zhexue bijiao yanjiu. *Shehui kexuejia* 2014 (10): 3–7.
Zhou, Enlai. 1954a. Ba woguo jianshe chengwei qiangda de shehuizhuyi de xiandaihua de gongye guojia (1954.09.23). In *Zhou Enlai wenji*, vol. 2:132–145. Beijing: Renmin chubanshe, 1980.
Zhou, Enlai. 1954b. Turning China into a powerful, modern, socialist, industrialized country (23 September, 1954). In *Selected Works of Zhou Enlai*, vol. 2:142–154. Beijing: Foreign Languages Press, 1989.
Zhou, Xincheng. 2016. Jingjixue yanjiu yinggai you zhexuejia de tounao – xuexi 'Mao Zedong du shehuizhuyi zhengzhijingjixue pizhu he tanhua.' *Mao Zedong sixiang yanjiu* 33 (2): 1–10.
Zhou, Xincheng. 2018. Bixu yunyong maodun fenxi fangfa lai yanjiu gaige de genben wenti. *Wenhua ruanshili* 2018 (4): 13–17.
Zhou, Yinzu. 1997. Mao Zedong he Deng Xiaoping guanyu maodun fenxi fangfa de bijiao yanjiu. *Nanjing shehui kexue (zengkan)* 1997 (1): 116–128.
Zhu, Jiamu. 2013. Mao Zedong's exploration of and answers to the questions of 'what socialism is and how to build it.' *Marxist Studies in China* 2013: 83–111.
Zhu, Jiamu. 2016. Advancing the construction of the discourse system of marxist theory of historiography with Chinese characteristics in the struggle with historical nihilism. *Marxist Studies in China* 2016: 18–52.
Zhu, Xi. 1986. *Zhuxi yulei*, ed. Li Jingde. Beijing: Zhonghua shuju.
Žižek, Slavoj. 2018. Will our future be Chinese 'capitalist socialism'? *Russia Today*, 18 October 2018. www.rt.com/op-ed/441873-china-socialism-capitalism-zizek/.

Chapter 5
China's Socialist Market Economy and Planned Economy

5.1 Opening Remarks

A constituent feature of the Reform and Opening-Up is the socialist market economy. Much is the mystification around this concept, especially by those outside China, and much is the ignorance concerning its true nature. Most importantly, China has by no means moved from a planned economy to a market economy, for these are both components of the fundamental economic system and the overall socialist system. I will have more to say about the relationship between planned and market economies later, but the primary concern of this chapter is the socialist market economy. The reason: when one engages seriously with the topic of China's socialist market economy, one soon notices a distinct disjunction: in China, key issues in the debate have largely been settled some time ago, while outside China significant misunderstanding remains. A major reason for this ignorance is that non-Chinese researchers remain disconcertingly uninformed concerning Chinese-language scholarship (see Sect. 1.4). Thus, my purpose here is to present the major developments and breakthroughs of this scholarship.

The chapter is structured as follows: it begins (5.2) with the need to de-link a market economy from a capitalist system, and so also a planned economy from a socialist system. This entails an initial engagement with Deng Xiaoping, who—as should be obvious by now—is so important for understanding the Reform and Opening-Up as a whole. I also include in this treatment of de-linking a historical survey—beginning with Marx—on market economies throughout human history. In the following Sect. (5.3), I delve into Chinese scholarship and its deployment of Mao Zedong's contradiction analysis. Here the concern is to identify the primary contradiction in the context of the construction of socialism; or, rather, the manifestation of the contradiction between the forces and relations of production. For Chinese researchers, this manifestation is in terms of the overall socio-economic system and its specific components, or what may be called institutional forms, which include planned and market economies. Given that a primary purpose of socialism is to liberate the forces of production, the question now concerns what institutional form

R. Boer, *Socialism with Chinese Characteristics*,
https://doi.org/10.1007/978-981-16-1622-8_5

enables such a liberation. Initially, a planned economy was able to liberate productive forces, but later and in light of its unfolding contradictions a market institutional form becomes necessary—although planning does not disappear. The next Sect. (5.4) concerns the dialectic of universality and particularity, in which a market economy has universal or common features but its nature is determined by the particular socio-economic system of which it is a component. In this way, this section also seeks to answer the question as to whether the market economy in the context of socialism is indeed socialist, an answer that entails a return to Marx and Engels. The final Sect. (5.5) deals with more recent developments concerning the dialectical sublation or transformation of both market and planned economies. Obviously, planning has not been abandoned, but it has been transformed to a qualitatively new level—as has the socialist market economy. I hardly need to remind readers by this stage that the framework for all this analysis is resolutely Marxist, with a distinct bent for applying Marxist philosophy to economic questions.

5.2 De-Linking: Planning and the Market

The first step, to which all of the Chinese scholars I have consulted devote more or less space, involves de-linking a market economy from capitalism, and a planned economy from socialism. While this task may seem to be relatively easy and able to be dealt with quickly, it requires some more attention. The reason: the assumed link remains remarkably persistent in our own day, not least because of the initially exasperated—due to the viability of socialism when it was written—slogan of Count Ludwig von Mises (1932, 142): 'the alternative is still either Socialism or a market economy'. Since he is one of godfathers of an increasingly defunct neoliberalism, von Mises's deceptive slogan has become a commonplace all the way from neoliberal true believers to many Western Marxists: socialism inescapably entails a planned economy, while a market economy is by definition capitalist.

In this light, I begin with Deng Xiaoping and his circle, since the narrative of his steady efforts, against recurring opposition, to lay the groundwork and set the agenda for a socialist market economy raises a number of important questions for the discussion that follows. Second, I deal with the historical question concerning different market economies in human history.

5.2.1 Deng Xiaoping and the Socialist Market Economy

In 1979, Deng Xiaoping observed:

> It is wrong to maintain that a market economy exists only in capitalist society and that there is only 'capitalist' market economy. Why can't we develop a market economy under socialism? Developing a market economy does not mean practising capitalism ... We cannot say that market economy exists only under capitalism. Market economy was in its embryonic stages

as early as feudalist society. We can surely develop it under socialism. (Deng 1979a, 236; 1979b, 239)

This is the basic de-linking move, to which Deng would return on a number of occasions over the next dozen years, depending on the audience and the need to remind doubters and dogmatists that it was not the beginning of the 'capitalist road', and certainly not a 'heresy [*yiduan*]' (Deng 1984b, 91; 1984a, 97–98). Instead, as nearly all the Chinese scholars I have consulted make clear, the whole approach relies on the Marxist basis of liberating thought and seeking truth from facts (see Sects. 2.2 and 2.3), thereby overcoming the 'two rigid dogmas' of traditional economics (Gui 2006). At the same time, there was a distinct development in Deng's thought and in the related resolutions of the Central Committee and CPC National Congress. Here I follow the account of Yang Zhiping (2010, 11–13; see also Gao and Zheng 1996; Zhou S. 2017), who identifies three stages: the breakthrough, in which socialism can also engage in a market economy (1979–1982); the transition, in which planning and the market are combined (1982–1989); and the establishment of a socialist market economy (1989–1993).

The initial breakthrough is credited to the quiet-spoken scholar, Yu Zuyao, who published in March of 1979 a paper entitled 'An Attempt to Discuss a Socialist Market Economy' (Yu Z. 1979). Here we find the first distinct effort at de-linking, the proposal that a market economy can be based on public ownership, and a recognition of the importance of the law of value (see further below). Although Yu's proposal was not widely appreciated at the time, Deng Xiaoping clearly picked up its import and began to speak openly for such a position in only a few months. Initially, a market economy was seen was to have an 'auxiliary role [*fuzhu zuoyong*]' and function 'as a supplement [*weifu*]'—as early resolutions put it—to the planned economy, to which 'priority [*weizhu*]' would still be given (Deng 1979a, 236; 1979b, 239). Next came an effort to find a balance or symbiosis between planning and market, particularly in light of the evident contradictions arising in the planned economy, which had begun to stifle economic performance (Deng 1982b, 16; 1982a, 26–27; 1985c, 148; 1985d, 151). While earlier resolutions moved somewhat cautiously (CPC Central Committee 1984), the means of production moved more swiftly.[1] Increasing market functions led to further theoretical reflection. Thus, in 1985 Deng Xiaoping observed in response to questions, 'There is no fundamental contradiction between socialism and a market economy', and a little over a year later, he observed that 'we should no longer say' that—in an echo of his comment in 1979—'a planned economy is primary [*weizhu*]' (Deng 1985c, 148; 1985d, 151; 1987a, 203; 1987b, 203). Note the shift: it was no longer a case of an overall planned economy warily shaping the direction of a market or commodity economy, but the fact that there was no fundamental contradiction (*genben maodun*) between them, that a market economy did not necessarily violate the principles of socialism. To provide the theoretical justification for this position, Deng deployed two positions: first, one should see a market economy or a planned economy as a 'method [*fangfa*]'; second, this method has the primary purpose of

[1]For example, see the slightly later study, which has been translated into English, of the first 20 years of development in Zhejiang province (Li X. et al. 2002a, 2002b).

'liberating the forces of production [*jeifang shengchanli*]'. We will return to both points later, but the whole argument would lead to the Thirteenth National Congress of the CPC of 1987 adopting a distinct combination of planned and market economies in terms of an 'internal unity [*neizai tongyi*]' (Zhao 1987, 7; Yang Z. 2010, 12).

Even so, this breakthrough in 1987 still spoke of the 'state regulating the market and the market guiding enterprises' (Zhao 1987, 7), so there was still some way to go. The third stage culminated in the report of the CPC's Fourteenth National Congress in 1992 and of the Third Plenary Session of the Fourteenth Central Committee of the Party, in November 1993. The latter stated: 'The socialist market economic institutional form is integrated with the basic socialist system. The establishment of a socialist market economic institutional form is to make the market play a fundamental role in the allocation of resources under the state's macro-control' (CPC Central Committee 1993, 2; Yang Z. 2010, 13). The lead-up to this decision required on Deng's part both reiteration of earlier statements on de-linking and some further development: planning happens under capitalism as well; both planning and market economies should be seen as economic 'means [*shouduan*]'; and they function to 'serve [*fuwu*]' a larger system (Deng 1990b, 363–364; 1990a, 351; 1991b, 367; 1991a, 354). As to how it so serves, Deng spoke in his 'southern tour' of what became known as the 'three benefits [*san ge you liyu*]': the essence of socialism is the 'liberation and development of the productive forces, elimination of exploitation and polarisation, and the ultimate achievement of prosperity for all' (Deng 1992b, 373; 1992a, 361).

Let us summarise the main points that have arisen: (1) de-linking itself; (2) description of a market as a 'method [*fangfa*]' and then a 'means [*shouduan*]' that is distinguished from and determined by the larger socio-economic system; (3) this means 'serves [*fuwu*]' the larger system; (4) the essence of socialism is to liberate the productive forces, eliminate polarisation, and enable prosperity for all. Importantly, the de-linking move was by no means original to Deng, for it had already been established in the debates of the 1930s in Eastern Europe (Lange 1936, 1937). Further, and in relation to the second point, in Eastern Europe the market was widely understood as a neutral tool or economic mechanism that could be used by different socio-economic systems (see further below). The third and fourth items begin to indicate precisely what such differences might be, with the concept of serving a larger system indicating that a market economy is a component or institutional form of such a socio-economic system, as well as the proposal that socialism's major concern is with liberating the forces of production. I will return to these points in greater detail a little later, for now I turn to the historical point.

5.2.2 *Market Economies in History*

This point is rather straightforward: market economies have existed in many periods of human history, but they have by no means been capitalist market economies. This reality was already foreshadowed in the text I quoted earlier, from 1979, where Deng

Xiaoping (1979a, 236; 1979b, 239) observed that a 'market economy was in its embryonic stages as early as feudalist society'. Further, on a number of occasions he offered the comparative point that a planned economy is also part of capitalism, the more so during times of economic difficulties. While most Chinese scholars make similar observations, neither they nor Deng were the first in the Marxist tradition to deploy historical arguments in relation to market economies.

The first was actually Marx, in the third volume of *Capital* (1894b, 583–599; 1894a, 588–605), where he examines the market economy of ancient Rome. His concern is to trace the effects of 'usurer's capital'. Found in the 'most diverse economic formations of society', in Rome a portion of this capital led to commodities, money, trade, borrowing, surplus, and profit. In other words, we have some of the core components of a 'market economy'. But is it a capitalist market economy? Not at all. It is a slave economy, for its primary purpose was to find, transport, and buy the labour of others as slaves. The whole market economy of ancient Rome (and indeed ancient Greece) was geared for and subordinated to this purpose. Marx subsequently outlines the way some of these components worked: usury, interest, surplus, money, labour, and so on, were arranged quite differently and functioned in ways that are far from a capitalist market economy.[2] Or, if they do at times seem similar, they function in 'altered conditions', without a capitalist framework (Marx 1894b, 587, 590; 1894a, 592, 595). Marx moves on to outline how some elements of feudal markets worked, and then how the different constellation of a capitalist mode of production overturned and reconfigured many of these earlier features (especially usury). For Marx at least, market economies are not all the same and do not function in exactly the same way. They may have some components in common, and to a casual observer such market economies may appear to be similar, but it is both the arrangement of the parts in relation to each other and the overall purpose or function of the market economy in question that indicates significant differences between them.

We may add to Marx's initial thoughts that it was precisely a slave market economy that was a major component of the Ancient mode of production of both Greece and Rome (Boer and Petterson 2017), and that the ancient Persians of the first millennium BCE developed a military market economy by deploying the relatively recent invention of coinage (Boer 2015), and that the European feudal market economy was primarily focused on the estate's own production and well-being (Kula 1976). I mean not local peasant produce markets, but state-wide and even empire-wide socio-economic systems of which market economies formed an important component. As Chinese scholars routinely point out, market economies have existed throughout human history and constitute one of the significant creations by human societies (Yang J. 2009, 174). But they also point out that these market economies are by no means capitalist in nature, since they are shaped by the socio-economic system of

[2] Or, as Kula (1976, 17) points out: 'in the pre-capitalist economy, market phenomena are governed by completely different laws in many cases, and … these phenomena have an altogether different effect on the remaining sectors of the economy'.

which they are a component: to assert otherwise is—as Deng Xiaoping made clear—to become dogmatic, or to fall into what we may also call 'economics imperialism', in which the assumptions of a capitalist market economy (and its economic theory) are de-historicised, de-socialised, universalised, and superimposed on any historical market economy, thereby skewing analysis (Milonakis and Fine 2009; Fine and Milonakis 2009).

5.3 Contradiction Analysis

While Deng Xiaoping and his circle may have laid some of the foundations for a socialist market economy, there was wide recognition of the need to develop the argument further. A key move was to deploy contradiction analysis (see Chapter 3) more extensively, especially the concern with the need to identify the primary contradiction in any situation, which is the key to dealing with secondary contradictions. More specifically, researchers picked up the point that the main contradiction during the construction of socialism is between the forces and relations of production, as well as the established point that the nature of contradictions under socialism is qualitatively different from that of a capitalist system, since they are primarily non-antagonistic contradictions (*feiduikangxing de maodun*).

5.3.1 From Ownership to Liberating the Forces of Production

To see how this approach is deployed in relation to the socialist market economy, I begin with the influential work of Huang Nansen (1994), which is widely regarded as having settled the question. Huang points out that while Mao was correct on his main points, he made one crucial mistake concerning the manifestation of the main contradiction between the forces and relations of production. Let us be clear: the assumed position, which was by now well established in the Marxist tradition since Stalin (1952b, 1952a), is that during the construction of socialism contradictions continue to exist between the forces and relations of production. The question, however, concerned how such contradictions manifest themselves. Mao reasoned that since the contradiction was manifested in a capitalist system between the socialised nature of production and the private ownership of the means of production, a socialist system would seek to solve this contradiction by ensuring the social or public ownership of the means of production. Thus, both the process of production and the means of production would become socialised. So we find that Mao and those around him rapidly and even artificially raised the levels of public ownership, hoping to solve the inherent contradiction they had inherited. However, this approach—argues Huang—is ultimately non-dialectical on two related counts: there would seem to be an absence of contradictions after this one is solved; and this result would negate the point that under socialism the contradiction between forces and relations of production would continue, albeit in a distinctly different manner.

Let me emphasise this point for moment: the resolute focus on ownership of the means of production was far too one-sided, for it relegated to second place, if not not ignoring altogether, the forces of production. Mao and those around him were certainly not the only ones who pressed heavily on public ownership. It has become a staple for many in the Communist movement, and even today in the midst of bourgeois states the nationalisation of a bank or a rail network is regarded as 'socialist'. A one-sided reading of Marx and Engels in the 'Communist Manifesto' assists with such an assumption, where centralisation, nationalisation, and the abolition of bourgeois private property are seen to be the core project for Communism immediately after a successful proletarian revolution. But is this really the case? We need to remind ourselves of a text that I have quoted in an earlier chapter (Sect. 2.4): 'The proletariat will use its political supremacy to wrest, by degrees, all capital from the bourgeoisie, to centralise all instruments of production in the hands of the State, i.e., of the proletariat organised as the ruling class; and *to increase the total of productive forces [Produktionskräfte] as rapidly as possible*' (Marx and Engels 1848a, 481; 1848b, 504). I have added the italics for good reason, since for Marx and Engels the issue was both ownership *and* liberation of the productive forces.

What happens when the forces of production are returned to the dialectic? As we have seen (Sect. 2.4), this was a key feature of Deng Xiaoping's emphasis: again and again, he insisted that the main project of socialism in his era was to liberate the forces of production, rather than settle for 'poor socialism'. Only by liberating productive forces, which also required a significant liberation of thought, would it be possible to eliminate exploitation and attain prosperity for all, or what he would come to call a *xiaokang* society—one that is moderately well-off, healthy, peaceful, and secure (see Chapter 6). All of the Chinese scholars I have consulted emphasise this feature of Deng's approach, even to the point of observing that it is central to the Marxist method itself, in which the productive forces are the ultimate determinant of social relations—also in the process of socialist construction (Peng 1994, 11).

5.3.2 Primary Contradiction

On this basis, Huang Nansen reassesses the manifestation of the primary contradiction between the forces and relations of production. Instead of seeing it—as Mao did—in the form of productive forces and the ownership of such forces, Huang proposes that it is actually manifested in terms of the forces of production and the economic institutional form (*tizhi*). To non-Chinese readers, this may seem to be an unfamiliar way of formulating the question, so let me explain. The argument deploys specific technical terminology: in Huang's usage, the term for the overall or basic system is *zhidu* (制度), while that used for the specific institutional form is *tizhi* (体制). However, if one casts a cursory glance at a Chinese dictionary, one finds both terms translated as system, although *tizhi* is also a structure, setup, or way of organisation. By contrast, the usage in Huang and others is quite specific,[3] so I have translated *zhidu* as the overall or basic system, while I have used a term from '*Régulation* Theory' (Boyer and Saillard 2002) to translate *tizhi*: an 'institutional form' is a specific building block or component of a larger system, and is it one among others.[4] Thus a socialist system includes the institutional forms of planned and market economies. Another sense in the semantic field of *tizhi* is a way or mode of organisation. Thus, the institutional form of a market economy organises in a particular way the means and relations of production, so as to allocate resources and distribute products by means of the law of value, price signals, and competition. However, a planned economy organises the forces and relations of production in a somewhat different way, by means of regulation, long-term calculation of means and ends, dealing with challenges, and setting perimeters for what can and cannot be done. How these two institutional forms work together in a socialist system continues to be the focus of considerable Chinese research, to which I return later. To reiterate the key point here: an institutional form (*tizhi*) is a component of and shaped by the whole system (*zhidu*). Thus, to identify a market economy institutional form with a capitalist system is a category mistake, as it is to identify a planned economy institutional form with a socialist system. Instead, the logic is that if the system is capitalist, then we have a capitalist market economy; but if it is socialist, then the market economy will be shaped by that overall system.

To return Huang Nansen's identification of the primary contradiction's manifestation: he argues that it appears between the overall system (*zhidu*) and the institutional form (*tizhi*), which in a socialist context must enable the liberation of the forces of production. If an institutional form enables such a liberation, then the contradiction is resolved for a time. But if the institutional form hobbles the liberation of productive forces (as happened after a while with the planned economy), then it is necessary to bring another institutional form into play, such as a socialist market economy.

---

[3]Most of the references on the socialist market economy use such terminology, but one also finds that *zhidu* is used to speak—for example—of the political system of socialist democracy. As we will see in Chapter 8, this system also has a number of components or institutional forms.

[4]The specificity of these terms had already begun to emerge when Deng Xiaoping reflected on the 'Decision by the CPC Central Committee on Reform of the Economic Institutional Form' (CPC Central Committee 1984; Deng 1984b, 91; 1985c, 148–149). However, the most explicit example comes from his famous 'Southern Tour': 'After the basic socialist system [*shehuizhuyi jiben zhidu*] has been established, it is necessary to fundamentally change the economic institutional form [*jingji tizhi*] that has hampered the development of the productive forces and to establish a vigorous socialist economic institutional form [*tizhi*] that will promote their development' (Deng 1992b, 370; 1992a, 358). By this time, the terminology was clearly in place, as we see with Jiang Zemin (1992).

5.4 Is It Socialist? Universality and Particularity

A further feature of contradiction analysis concerns the relation between universality (*pubianxing*) and particularity (*teshuxing*), or commonality (*gongxing*) and individuality (*gexing*). In this light, the institutional form of a market economy is a universal or common reality, while its integration within a socio-economic system evinces the particularity of each type of market economy. But it raises the question as to what is socialist about both the overall socialist system and the particular form that a market economy takes within the system. It also entails an analysis of whether and how the universal institutional form of the market economy is shaped and determined by the particular system.

5.4.1 Universality and Particularity

A number of earlier works broach the question of universality and particularity (Huang 1994; Peng 1994; Zhang H. and Zhuang 1994; Yang X. 1994), although to understand how the dialectic works, we need some further discussion of technical terminology. As we have seen, a market economy is an institutional form (*tizhi*), a component of a larger and overall socio-economic system (*zhidu*). Now it is precisely the institutional form that becomes the universal term, found in quite a number of human societies throughout history (see Sect. 5.2.2). The socio-economic system becomes the particular or individual term, for each is distinguished from the other by specific features.

Further, many describe both market and planned economies as 'methods [*fangfa]*', 'means [*shouduan*]' and more technically as a 'mechanisms [*jizhi*]'—all of which already appear in the important report from the CPC's thirteenth national congress (Zhao 1987). However, their usage tends towards seeing a market economy as a neutral tool or piece of machinery. At this level, it is easy to see how it can be seen as a universal feature, a tool that is found in many societies and economic systems. This approach was by no means new, for—as mentioned earlier—it was already the majority position in the Eastern European experiments with market economies, where they spoke of an 'economic mechanism' (Kornai 1957; Szamuely 1982, 1984; Kozma 1989). The gain was that it enabled them to de-link a market economy from a capitalist system, and this also appears to be the reason for earlier Chinese deployment of such terms. The negative side was that risked seeing market economies under different systems as identical with one another, with no distinguishing features. The logical outcome of this line of thought is that the only difference between capitalist and socialist systems is the political structure and perhaps the cultural tradition.

Chinese arguments explicitly recognise this problem, for to emphasise that a market economy is merely a method, means, or mechanism is to fall too heavily on the universal or common side of the dialectic. This is where the relations between institutional form (*tizhi*) and overall system (*zhidu*) come into play. Thus, both planning and market are seen as institutional forms, with the former often designated as a 'regulatory institutional form [*tiaokong tizhi*]' and the latter as a 'market economy institutional form [*shichang jingji tizhi*]'.[5] As for the system itself, it is variously described as a 'basic socialist system [*shehuizhuyi jiben zhidu*]' and a 'basic socialist economic system [*shehuizhuyi jiben jingji zhidu*]' (Peng 1994, 13). Should one have any lingering doubts, the consistent usage of 'basic', or 'foundational [*jiben*]' indicates precisely how the system functions. As to how they relate to one another, Huang Nansen (1994, 4) observes: 'a market economy can become the commonality [*gongxing*] of the capitalist economic institutional form [*tizhi*] and the socialist economic institutional form [*tizhi*], and capitalism and socialism are their individualities [*gexing*]'. Or in more detail from Peng Lixun: 'A socialist market economy is the organic combination of the market economy and the basic socialist system [*shehuizhuyi jiben zhidu*]'. Further, the 'difference between it and the capitalist market economy is not the generality of the market economy, but the particularity of combining it with the basic socialist system' (Peng 1994, 13). Thus, to confuse an overall system with an institutional form is a category mistake, now in terms of universality and particularity.[6]

The outcome of this detailed terminology and the necessity of a dialectical relation between common institutional forms and particular systems is that the nature of the institutional form in question is shaped by that system. Not merely shaped, for this way of putting it suggests that a market economy is in some way an independent entity—'the market' as the neoclassical ideologues like to suggest. Huang Nansen (1994, 5) answers: 'There is no market economy institutional form that is independent of the basic economic system of society'. One cannot have the institutional form of the market economy separate from the system of which it forms a part. But how is this institutional form determined by the system with which it is integrated? One may begin by asking how a market economy can 'serve [*fuwu*]' either capitalism or socialism, or indeed any other system as a whole, but this is only the first step.

5.4.2 What Makes It Socialist?

The more elaborate answer addresses directly how the system as a whole shapes the nature of a market economy. Let us begin with the 'three benefits [*san ge you liyu*]', mentioned by many, that can be used to judge any institutional form: 'whether it is conducive to the development of the productive forces of a socialist society, to the enhancement of the comprehensive national strength of a socialist country, and to

[5] To make matters even more interesting, both are also regarded as forms of regulation. Not only do we have a 'regulatory institutional form [*tiaokong tizhi*]', but also a 'market regulation mechanism [*shichang tiaojie jizhi*]'. Integrating their types of regulation into the overall system becomes even more complicated.

[6] It follows that to confuse a market economy with a capitalist system entails a confusion between commonality and particularity.

the improvement of people's living standards' (Deng 1992b, 372; Yang X. 1994, 6). The first point picks up a core feature of socialism noted earlier: it should seek to liberate the productive forces. Not for the sake of such liberation in and of itself, but for the sake of socio-economic well-being—the core human right in the Chinese Marxist tradition, as I will show in Chapter 7 (Sun 2014; Wan 2017). The second arises from the long Chinese experience of humiliation and semi-colonisation by Western powers, as well as the experiences of constructing socialism in different parts of the world, where international blockades, outright military aggression, and the external sponsoring of internal destabilisation and plots were (and indeed continue) to be common. In this context, comprehensive national strength—specifically of an economic nature—is a must. The third, concerning the improvement of people's lives in all respects, is now expressed in terms of the people's desire for '*meihao shenghuo*', for 'a beautiful and good life' (Xi 2017, 2). These three systemic benefits relate not merely to the institutional form of a socialist market economy, but also to other components of the whole system.

Another way of indicating how a market economy may 'serve society [*gongtongti fuwu*]' appears in Huang Nansen's contribution.[7] He identifies five features of the foundational socialist system to which a market economy must contribute: (1) the system contains a multiplicity of components, but public ownership remains the core economic driver; (2) while both state owned and private enterprises must be viable, their main purpose is not profit at all costs, but social benefit and meeting the needs of all people—in short 'people-centred' (Li W. 1992, 55); (3) it deploys the old socialist principle of from each according to ability and to each according to work, limiting exploitation and wealth polarisation, and seeking common prosperity; (4) the guide for action (to parse Engels) always remains Marxism; (5) the primary value should always be socialist collectivism (*shehuizhuyi de jitizhuyi*) rather than individualism.

Public ownership as the basis of course harks back to the other side of the dialectic in the 'Communist Manifesto' (see above). While I have emphasised the liberation of the forces of production, Chinese scholars by no means ignore the importance of public ownership (see further Chapter 10). Added to public ownership is social benefit, seeking common prosperity, socialist collectivism, and Marxism as the guide. A concrete example drawn from today can illustrate: the social responsibility reports (*shehui zeren baogao*) (Feng and Zhang 2019). Each enterprise, whether state-owned, private, or foreign, must produce annual reports of this type. They are primarily the responsibility of the local Communist Party branch in the enterprise—any enterprise, Chinese or foreign, with three or more Party members must have a branch. While it is the task of governing board to ensure economic viability, the social responsibility reports focus on social benefit, poverty alleviation, environmental improvement, education, guidance and improvement of public opinion, core socialist values, Party building, and contribution to socialism with Chinese characteristics. These are not

[7] All of the other Chinese scholars used in this study offer very similar proposals. For example, Gao and Zheng (1996, 3–4) propose, now in terms of a contrast: 'A capitalist market economy is based on private ownership, which will inevitably bring about polarisation. A socialist market economy must adhere to the primacy of public ownership, and so to the road of common prosperity. These two basic characteristics of socialism cannot be lost in a socialist market economy'.

secondary to profit-making, seeking to show a compassionate face for the enterprise in question; instead they are central to the enterprise's activities in serving the common good (*gongtongti fuwu*).

A final comment: if, after reading this section, a reader still has in mind government 'interference' in an independent 'market', then this is a mistake. Such an assumption arises from a saturation in a capitalist system and the influence of its ideologues who maintain that 'the market' is in some way an independent entity with its own way of functioning, in which a government more or less 'intervenes'. Why a mistake? A Chinese Marxist approach does not assume this framework. To quote Huang Nansen (1994, 5) once again: 'There is no market economy institutional form that is independent of the basic economic system of society'.

5.4.3 A Basis in Marx and Engels

Another way of broaching the question of socialist identity is to ask how it arises from the work of Marx and Engels.[8] Earlier material assumed that one could not find the basis of a socialist market economy in their works, but that it was the outcome of using Marxism as a guide for action and seeking truth from facts in the actual construction of socialism (Deng 1984b, 91; 1984a, 97–98; 1988a, 260; 1988c, 255). Thus, Marx and Engels could not have had access to vital empirical data in order to seek truth from facts (Huang 1994, 1; Peng 1994, 15; Gao and Zheng 1996, 1).[9] My earlier resort to Marx's historical point concerning the quite different market economy of ancient Rome may now be seen as an effort to address this concern from another angle.

Others have also made the effort, with two tendencies: a search for Marxist methodological underpinnings; and more detailed examinations of the founders' texts to identify substantive features. As for the former, we have already encountered the emphasis on forces of production as the ultimately determining factor of social relations, specifically in terms of the need to liberate productive forces rather than an imbalanced concern with ownership (Peng 1994, 11). More recent is a return to Marx's 'Theses on Feuerbach' as the basis of both Mao Zedong's 'On Practice' (1937) and his slogan, 'seek truth from facts', which became a cornerstone of Deng Xiaoping's approach (Han 2000). In a Chinese Marxist framework, this entails the

[8]Without falling into one of the three traps of book worship (*benbenzhuyi*), seeing Marxism as out-of-date (*wanquan guoshi lun*), or vulgar imminent practicality (*yongsu shiyong lun*) (Li et al. 2002b, 65).

[9]As Marx (1875, 22) points out, such questions can be answered 'only scientifically [*nur wissenschaftlich*]' from evidence and experience, while Engels (1890, 447) observes: 'So-called "socialist society" is not, in my view, to be regarded as something that remains crystallised for all time [*allemal fertiges Ding*], but rather being in process of constant change and transformation [*in fortwährender Verändrung und Umbildung*] like all other social conditions'.

obvious point that the Marxist method must be combined with the actual historical, cultural, and socio-economic conditions in China to make any sense.[10]

More detailed efforts began to appear later, with a focus on the content of human nature, practice, and history. Since I have already mentioned practice, let me focus on human nature. The starting point is the well-known text from the Manifesto: 'In place of the old bourgeois society, with its classes and class antagonisms, we shall have an association, in which the free development of each is the condition for the free development of all' (Marx and Engels 1848a, 482; 1848b, 506). Other texts, from *The German Ideology* to *Capital* also appear in a similar vein, but they are connected with the three stages of human development outlined briefly in the *Grundrisse* (Marx 1858c, 90–91; 1858a, 95). The first entails limited human productivity and human dependence, while the second is one of relative independence, in which there is the social exchange of matter, universal relations, requirements, and capacities. For these Chinese scholars, the first is pre-capitalist and the second not so much capitalist, but one of a market economy (as an institutional form). This stage creates, as Marx observes (1858c, 91; 1858a, 95), the conditions for the third: 'free individuality, based on the universal development of the individuals and the subordination of their communal, social productivity, which is their social possession … is the third stage'. For these scholars, the final stage is the same as that envisaged in the Manifesto, namely, communism, with its all-round development of individuals (Zhang X. 2009, 137–138; Yang Z. 2010, 13).[11] This particular example (there are others into which I cannot delve here) reveals a development in some areas of Chinese scholarship. Let me put it this way: since the common institutional form of a market economy is not necessarily capitalist, but is shaped by the larger socio-economic system of which it is a component, it becomes possible to examine the texts of Marx and Engels in relation to the commonality of market economy in order to identify how it works. This approach is neither undertaken naively nor in a way to justify veering onto the capitalist road, but rather to identify both the benefits and shortcomings of a market economy. The ideal, of course, is to draw on its its benefits within a socialist system, while being wary and preventing its dangers. That this is an arduous task, requiring constant diligence and adjustment, goes without saying.

[10]A point suggested in Marx's reflections concerning earlier modes of production in which a particular form of production 'determines the position and importance of all the others', like a 'general light tingeing all other colours and modifying them in their specific quality (Marx 1858c, 41; 1858a, 43).

[11]It is worth noting here that the German '*die universelle Entwicklung der Individuen*' becomes in the Chinese translation '*geren quanmian fazhan*', the comprehensive or 'all-round development of individuals' (Marx 1858b, 52).

5.5 Dialectical Transcendence: Beyond Planning and Market Economies

Thus far, most references to Chinese scholarship have come from the 1990s, when the debate was strongest and there was a need to examine the Marxist underpinnings of the socialist market economy. However, this material comes from two or more decades ago, and while it reflects the reality that most of the core issues were settled in the 1990s (albeit still largely unknown outside China), there have been subsequent developments in light of the significant progress of the Reform and Opening-Up. The most significant is a further elaboration of the dialectical argument, now in terms of the sublation or transcendence of the distinction between planning and market economies. I distinguish three steps: the earlier temporal narrative; the effort achieve a balance; and transcendence itself.

5.5.1 *From Temporal Narratives to Managing the Contradiction*

As for the temporal narrative, it is not the case that a planned economy as such has been superseded during the Reform and Opening-Up—even though this is a common assumption outside China. Instead, what has passed is a highly centralised and rigidly planned economy, which has been replaced with a flexible combination of both planning and market (Liao 2008; Gu 2019).[12] In more detail (see Sect. 2.4): while a largely planned economy immediately after a successful communist revolution is a necessity—with its nationalisations, collectivisation, and crushing or transformation of the former bourgeois-landlord owners of the means of production—it leads after a few decades to new contradictions that stifle economic efficiency and improvement (Liao 2008). From the perspective of liberating the forces of production, there is no case in socialist countries where the old form of the planned economy failed to give their economies a boost and develop productive forces. But only for a while. At this point, a new arrangement of institutional forms is needed and a market economy begins to be introduced—as was tentatively attempted in some parts of Eastern Europe (Boer In press).

Through the whole process of the Reform and Opening-Up, planning has clearly not been abandoned. But how planned and market economies might work together within an overall system is the concern of much of the material I have studied. The effort arises from contradiction analysis (in terms of the unity of contradictions and their non-antagonistic interaction) and the move to designating both as institutional forms within a socialist system. Apart from earlier positions that allotted planning

[12]For example, Yang (2009, 170–171) offers a longer narrative: (1) 1848–1917, from the Communist Manifesto to the Russian Revolution; (2) 1917 to 1978, from utopia to science, with the singular planned economy as the initial liberation of productive forces; (3) 1978 to the present, with the combination of planning and the market as modern socialism.

the primary role, later proposals include an organic combination and complementary interaction of planning in terms of macro-control and a market economy's micro-management, with both seen as methods of economic management. Thus, 'the market is the foundation and national macro-control is the guide' (Peng 1994, 14; Yang X. 1994, 6), both of which—to gloss Deng Xiaoping (1992b, 378)—must have 'hard hands'.

A more extended effort to seek a balance comes from Yang Jinhai (2009) in an article published in English. Assuming Mao's contradiction analysis (see Sect. 3.4), specifically in terms of the unity of contradictions—captured by the phrase, 'what is contradictory is also complementary [*xiangfan-xiangcheng*]'—Yang proposes a contradiction between justice (or equality) and efficiency, which must be managed to avoid antagonism. Thus, justice appears in terms of a planned economy, public ownership, equal distribution of resources, and fair recompense according to work (the definition of socialism already developed in the Soviet Union in the 1930s (Boer 2017)); and efficiency is a feature of a market economy, with it logistical capabilities and fostering of innovation. The challenge is to ensure that justice and efficiency function in a both-and manner, rather than—as in the Western European tradition—as an either-or option. Under a capitalist system, the contradiction is seen as either a market economy or a planned economy, either bourgeois private ownership of the means of production or public ownership. Opting for the former, the market economy under capitalism is like a 'wild horse without reins', producing crises, social polarisation, and injustice, without being able to address the burning question of justice. By contrast, in a socialist system we find a rather different situation, with both the efficiency of a market economy and the justice of a planned economy with its public ownership. They are, Yang suggests (2009, 175), like 'the two wheels of a cart and the two wings of a bird', which function in terms of the unity of contradictions. Too much of the market economy leads to a lack of equity and potential conflict; too much of public ownership and a planned economy stifles efficiency and weighs heavily on the people. Historically, one can see that earlier the emphasis was far too much on equality, but it was an equality of poverty. In the middle period of the Reform and Opening-Up, efficiency was paramount, but it led to income disparity, widespread corruption, protests, flouting of the rule of law, lack of trust, and potential conflict, during what I have called earlier the 'wild 90s' (see Sect. 4.3.3). Yang points out at the time of writing (2009) that the urgent problem was to focus on justice and equality—an emphasis that is even greater a decade later, with a noticeable decline in corruption, protests, and the Gini-coefficient, as the rule of law is being enforced, and with a concomitant concern with poverty alleviation, prosperity for all, and ecological civilisation. Yang concludes that ensuring the non-antagonistic relation between the contradiction of justice and efficiency needs constant work, but that China has certainly not abandoned public ownership in light of developing a socialist market economy (see also Zhou N. 2017, 29).

5.5.2 Dialectical Transcendence

Nonetheless, seeking a balance between two institutional forms in tension with one another is only a half-way house, mirroring the middle stage of the development of Deng Xiaoping's thought (see Sect. 5.2.1). More significant are some who argue that China's overall system is in the process of achieving a dialectical sublation (*yangqi*) or transcendence (*chaoyue*) of planned and market economies, or more broadly of the traditional socialist economic model and that of a capitalist system. As a way of dealing with this proposal, I begin by asking what features of a market economy are seen as appropriate. Again and again one encounters the point that nearly all aspects of a market economy need to be developed. For example, Yang Xiaojie (1994, 6) observes that the general laws of the market economy include 'a method and means of allocating social resources, such as the law of value and the relationship between supply and demand, price signals, and the role of competition mechanisms in resource allocation'. A more detailed list appears in Gao and Zheng (1996, 4): market resource allocation plays a fundamental role; economic activities should follow the law of value; these activities should adapt to changes in supply and demand; price leverage and competition will enable efficient connections between resource allocation and benefits, as well as putting pressure on enterprises for the sake of innovation; economic signals should coordinate production and demand; and 'hard budget constraints' and even 'survival of the fittest' should not be avoided.

Noticeably, these proposals appear relatively early in the debate. Chinese scholars had studied the Eastern European experiments in great detail (Wang Y. 1995, 51; Yu W. 2011) and noted that the latter had not been willing to deploy fully the market realities of hard budget constraints (entry, exit, and bankruptcy), price signals, and—most importantly—the law of value (*jiazhi guilü*). The conclusion, from early on, was that if a market economy in a modern context is to function properly, it should include these features as well.[13] As Zhang and Zhuang (1994, 5) point out, a Chinese approach should 'give full play to the role of the law of value in optimising the allocation of resources and regulating the circulation of commodities', since the 'objective necessity of following the law of value is the internal premise' of a market institutional form. Without the law of value, a market economy would become 'a tree without roots and water without a source'.[14]

Clearly, the law of value is not restricted to analysing capitalist market economies, but is applied and developed as a central feature of a socialist market economy (Cheng 1996; Yang Y. 2001; Zhang G. 2010; Huo 2011). Simply put, without the law of value you cannot have a market economy. As to its specific function, two approaches appear

[13] This was by no means a sudden innovation, for by the late 1950s Mao Zedong had also begun to speak of the necessity of the 'law of value [*jiazhi faze*]' and the 'necessity for exchange at equal value [*dengjia jiaohuan*]' during the construction of socialism (Mao 1959b, 10; see also 1959a; Zhu 2013, 102). By the mid-1980s, Deng Xiaoping also began referring to the necessity of the law of value (Deng 1985a, 130; 1985b, 134; 1988b, 262; 1988d, 257).

[14] In fact, the decision to enable the law of value had already been made in 1984 the 'Decision by the CPC Central Committee on Reform of the Economic Institutional Form' (1984).

in the critical literature. The first and majority position is that the law of value applies only to the institutional form, to the component, of a market economy. It does not apply to the basic socialist system as a whole, let alone to other components such as culture, politics and law, which are determined by the 'three benefits' (see above) that constitute the domain of planning. By contrast, the minority position entails an effort to reinterpret both the law of value and Marx's theory of labour in a socialist context: on the one hand, the category of labour must be expanded to include a much wider variety, from rural to urban, and from manager to employee; on the other hand, the surplus value of a socialist market economy is not focused on profit at all costs, but directed at innovating the conditions of production, as well as education, medical improvements, poverty alleviation, and other public welfare programs. In other words, this 'social value' is focused on the cause of socialist construction and the common prosperity of all (Li X. et al. 2002b, 65–74). This is a minority position, but the implication is that the 'three benefits' are not merely the responsibility of planning, but may also be found in the socialist market economy itself.

Both approaches, however, indicate that the Chinese approach entails the full deployment of a market economy—a 'going all the way'. Thus, in 2013 Xi Jinping was instrumental in revising a position that had been standard since 1992: the market economy in the socialist system was no longer to play a 'basic role [*jichuxing zuoyong*]' but a 'decisive role [*juedingxing zuoyong*]' in allocating resources (CPC Central Committee 2013, 1). However, going all the way with a socialist market economy is only one side of the picture. It is, after all, an 'institutional form [*tizhi*]' in the 'basic economic system [*jiben jingji zhidu*]', as the text of the 2013 decision clarifies. The same text stipulates that such a process also entails going all the way with a planned economy (CPC Central Committee 2013, 3). This is not a return to old-style planned economies that sought to ban any market activity, but a qualitative transformation of planning itself. Thus, planning works with and through a market economy—since both are forms of economic management—to prevent the polarisation, chaos, economic disruption, and the pattern of boom and bust typical of capitalist market economies. Positively, it works to ensure the well-being of all, strengthening the country and making it secure and harmonious, achieving a moderately well-off society, to which may be added the complete removal of absolute poverty, ecological civilisation, and promoting core socialist values—summed up the phrase, 'people-centred development [*yi renmin wei zhongxin de fazhan*]' (Zhou Z. and Wang 2019, 41). In this light, planning has undergone a qualitative transformation, deploying all of the sophisticated technologies available (now including artificial intelligence), setting both long-term plans, and being flexible enough to deal with specific challenges (Heilman and Melton 2013).

Now we can begin to understand how the full deployment of planning and market is increasingly seen in terms of dialectical transcendence. As Zhou and Wang (2019, 41) put it, 'China's practice has proved that the combination of a market economy and socialism is a new form of exploring socialist practice, which overcomes the dual disadvantages of a traditional planned economy and a capitalist market economy, and which realises the twofold transcendence [*shuangchong chaoyue*] of a traditional planned economy and a capitalist market economy'. What does this mean?

Simply put, it means going all the way through with a market economy in all respects, and it also means giving full play to the planned economy, so as to—in Hegelian terminology—realise their mutual *Aufhebung*. Only in this way can their roles be coordinated and unified. A little earlier, Zhang Xuekui (2009, 139) elaborated on the Chinese model as a 'new form of socialist practice', for the 'combination of a market economy and socialism overcomes the dual disadvantages of a traditional planned economy and a capitalist market economy'. At the same time, it also 'makes good use of the dual advantages' of the institutional forms of planned and market economies, so as to achieve 'organic unity in equity and efficiency, market regulation and government regulation, private economy and public economy, distribution according to work and distribution according to production factors, and so on'. In short, it is the 'dual sublation [*yangqi*] and transcendence [*chaoyue*] of a traditional planned economy and a capitalist market economy'.[15] Transcendence (*chaoyue*) has a longer background in Chinese thought, but *yangqi* is the translation of Hegel's *Aufhebung*, the leap to another dialectical level that overcomes the problems and blockades of the two previous terms. Or, in Chinese parlance, it is to develop what is useful and healthy and discard what is not.

Lest we dismiss such formulations as mere philosophical wordplay, there is indeed substance to this approach. Think of China's extraordinary development in the last forty years, the move from being one of the poorest countries in the world to one of its most prosperous, lifting 800 million people out of poverty (7 out of 10 in the world), a rate of innovation that leaves everyone else behind, global technological leadership in more and more areas, the 'Chinese speed' of ecological civilisation, the growth of cultural confidence on the global stage—all of which may be captured not in terms of finally 'catching up' but a dialectical leap into the future. Some simple statistics indicate what is at stake: at the time of Liberation, 97% of the population lived in poverty and life expectancy at 35, while 72 years later the last vestige of absolute poverty has been eradicated and life expectancy is in the high 70s.

One more example, with a return to the old opposition of public and private ownership. To begin with, state-owned enterprises (SOEs) have seen a further deepening of reform in terms of mixed ownership. However, this approach to public-private ownership should not be seen in light of capitalist SOEs, which are geared to be 'stabilisers' during economic crises and line further the pockets of big capitalists (He 2016, 105–106). Instead, in a socialist system SOEs are 'owned by the whole people' and focus on achieving prosperity for all (CPC Central Committee 2013, 1). How does this work when private enterprises are involved? At a basic level, the state and collectives maintain control in both macro and micro terms, that is, through the State-Owned Assets and Control Commission and through the reality of public ownership. More dialectically, to focus purely on relations of production is one-sided, for the mixed ownership approach is ultimately to spur the development of productive forces. Ultimately, the purpose is not to weaken SOEs in terms of

[15]Or as Fang Jianguo (2014, 63) puts it, this process enacts the third law of dialectics, the negation of the negation. Precursors to such arguments already appeared in the late 1990s (Jiang G. 1998, 3–4).

capitalist privatisation, but to strengthen them as core economic drivers (Xiang and He 2014, 89–97). Already we can see results, with SEOs contributing to the lion's share of economic development, becoming hubs of innovation, winning contracts throughout the world with their superior technology, efficiency, and lower costs. Further, the multiplying of 'private' enterprises—now as a major feature of 'targeted poverty reduction' (Wang F. 2019)—may be seen as a 'people-based economy', in which the vast majority common people, or the rural and urban workers in their many different forms, involved in the socialist project are the owners (Li X. et al. 2002b, 40–42). As mentioned earlier, all enterprises, whether 'private' or 'public'—Chinese and foreign, village or local government-owned enterprises, new economic organisations, start-ups, and so on—with three or more CPC members must establish a local Party branch, elect a secretary, and engage in Party building. The larger the company, the larger the Party membership. For example, the world's leading online retailer, Alibaba, has more than 7,000 CPC members, with significant Party building as part of its core mandate. While these Party organisations do not interfere with management decisions, they do ensure that the company adheres to 'social responsibility' principles (see Sect. 5.4.2).

5.6 Conclusion and Implications

I have moved from Deng Xiaoping's initial forays into a socialist market economy, through the hard work of the 1990s with its focus on liberating the forces of the production and the primary contradiction between overall socio-economic system (*zhidu*) and institutional form (*tizhi*), to the beginnings of a dialectical sublation of both planning and market. Throughout much of the material, Mao Zedong's contradiction analysis has framed the form of the arguments, a reality that counters the idea entertained in some quarters that Deng Xiaoping departed from or even 'betrayed' Mao. We have also encountered the need to avoid some category mistakes: between a system and an institutional form, and between universal and particular—both with relevance to the tendency among some to confuse a market economy with capitalism and a planned economy with socialism. I would like to add another category mistake: seeking to analyse China's socialist system and its institutional forms by assuming that it is a capitalist system and thus using methods—including Marxist—for the analysis of capitalism. As I have emphasised on a number of occasions, China's socialist project is guided and driven by Marxist political economy (Xi 2020), so much so that it is the process of filling a gap in this approach: how to achieve a modernised socialist economic system (Wei 2018, 144).

References

Boer, Roland. In press. Socialism and the market: Revisiting the East European debate. *New Political Economy*.

Boer, Roland. 2015. *The sacred economy of Ancient Israel*. Library of Ancient Israel. Louisville: Westminster John Knox.

Boer, Roland. 2017. Stalin's biblical hermeneutics: From 2 Thessalonians 3 to Acts 4. *Journal of the Bible and Its Reception* 4 (1): 71–89.

Boer, Roland, and Christina Petterson. 2017. *Time of troubles: A new economic framework for early Christianity*. Minneapolis: Fortress.

Boyer, Robert, and Yves Saillard (eds.). 2002. *Régulation theory: The state of the art*. London: Routledge.

Cheng, Enfu. 1996. Makesi jingjixue yu jingji siwei fangfa—yu Zhang Wuchan xiansheng shangque sisan. *Xueshu yuekan* 1996 (10): 32–39.

CPC Central Committee. 1984. *Zhonggong zhongyang guanyu shichang jingji gaige de jueding*. Beijing: Zhongguo gongchandang zhongyang weiyuanhui.

CPC Central Committee. 1993. *Zhonggong zhongyang guanyu jianli shehuizhuyi shichang jingji tizhi ruogan wenti de jueding*. Beijing: Zhongguo gongchandang zhongyang weiyuanhui.

CPC Central Committee. 2013. *Zhonggong zhongyang guanyu quanmian shenhua gaige ruogan zhongda wenti de jueding (2013.11.12)*. Beijing: Zhongguo gongchandang zhongyang weiyuanhui.

Deng, Xiaoping. 1979a. Shehuizhuyi ye keyi gao shichang jingji (1979.11.26). In *Deng Xiaoping wenxuan*, vol. 2:231–236. Beijing: Renmin chubanshe, 2008.

Deng, Xiaoping. 1979b. We can develop a market economy under socialism (26 November, 1979). In *Selected works of Deng Xiaoping*, vol. 2:235–239. Beijing: Foreign Languages Press, 1995.

Deng, Xiaoping. 1982a. In the first decade, prepare for the second (14 October, 1982). In *Selected Works of Deng Xiaoping*, vol. 3:26–28. Beijing: Foreign Languages Press, 1994.

Deng, Xiaoping. 1982b. Qianshinian wei houshinian zuohao zhunbei (1982.10.14). In *Deng Xiaoping wenxuan*, vol. 3:16–18. Beijing: Renmin chubanshe, 2008.

Deng, Xiaoping. 1984a. Speech at the third plenary session of the central advisory commission of communist party of China (22 October, 1984). In *Selected Works of Deng Xiaoping*, vol. 3:90–99. Beijing: Foreign Languages Press, 1994.

Deng, Xiaoping. 1984b. Zai zhongyang guwen weiyuanhui disanci quanti huiyi shang de jianghua (1984.10.22). In *Deng Xiaoping wenxuan*, vol. 3:83–93. Beijing: Renmin chubanshe, 2008.

Deng, Xiaoping. 1985a. Gaige kaifang shi hen da de shiyan (1985.06.29). In *Deng Xiaoping wenxuan*, vol. 3:130. Beijing: Renmin chubanshe, 2008.

Deng, Xiaoping. 1985b. Reform and opening to the outside world are a great experiment (29 June, 1985). In *Selected works of Deng Xiaoping*, vol. 3:134. Beijing: Foreign Languages Press, 1994.

Deng, Xiaoping. 1985c. Shehuizhuyi he shichang jingji bu cunzai genben maodun (1985.10.23). In *Deng Xiaoping wenxuan*, vol. 3:148–151. Beijing: Renmin chubanshe, 2008.

Deng, Xiaoping. 1985d. There is no fundamental contradiction between socialism and a market economy (23 October, 1985). In *Selected works of Deng Xiaoping*, vol. 3:151–153. Beijing: Foreign Languages Press, 1994.

Deng, Xiaoping. 1987a. Jihua he shichang dou shi fazhang shengchanli de fangfa (1987.02.06). In *Deng Xiaoping wenxuan*, vol. 3:203. Beijing: Renmin chubanshe, 2008.

Deng, Xiaoping. 1987b. Planning and the market are both means of developing the productive forces (6 February, 1987). In *Selected works of Deng Xiaoping*, vol. 3:203. Beijing: Foreign Languages Press, 1994.

Deng, Xiaoping. 1988a. Jiefang sixiang, duli sikao (1988.05.18). In *Deng Xiaoping wenxuan*, vol. 3:260–261. Beijing: Renmin chubanshe, 2008.

Deng, Xiaoping. 1988b. Lishun wujia, jiasu gaige (1988.05.19). In *Deng Xiaoping wenxuan*, vol. 3:262–263. Beijing: Renmin chubanshe, 2008.

Deng, Xiaoping. 1988c. We must emancipate our minds and think independently (18 May, 1988). In *Selected works of Deng Xiaoping*, vol. 3:255–256. Beijing: Foreign Languages Press, 1994.

Deng, Xiaoping. 1988d. We must rationalize prices and accelerate the reform (19 May, 1988). In *Selected works of Deng Xiaoping*, vol. 3:257–258. Beijing: Foreign Languages Press, 1994.

Deng, Xiaoping. 1990a. Seize the opportunity to develop the economy (24 December, 1990). In *Selected works of Deng Xiaoping*, vol. 3:350–352. Beijing: Foreign Languages Press, 1994.

Deng, Xiaoping. 1990b. Shanyu liyong shiji jiejue fazhan wenti (1990.12.24). In *Deng Xiaoping wenxuan*, vol. 3:362–365. Beijing: Renmin chubanshe 2008.

Deng, Xiaoping. 1991a. Remarks made during an inspection tour of Shanghai (28 January–18 February, 1991). In *Selected works of Deng Xiaoping*, vol. 3:353–355. Beijing: Foreign Languages Press, 1994.

Deng, Xiaoping. 1991b. Shicha Shanghai shi de tanhua (1991.01.28–02.18). In *Deng Xiaoping wenxuan*, vol. 3:366–367. Beijing: Renmin chubanshe, 2008.

Deng, Xiaoping. 1992a. Excerpts from talks given in Wuchang, Shenzhen, Zhuhai and Shanghai (18 January–21 February, 1992). In *Selected works of Deng Xiaoping*, vol. 3:358–370. Beijing: Foreign Languages Press, 1994.

Deng, Xiaoping. 1992b. Zai Wuchang, Shenzhen, Zhuhai he Shanghai deng di de tanhua yaodian (1992.01.18–02.21). In *Deng Xiaoping wenxuan*, vol. 3:370–383. Beijing: Renmin chubanshe, 2008.

Engels, Friedrich. 1890. Engels an Otto v. Boenigk in Breslau, Folkestone bei Dover, 21/8/90. In *Marx Engels Werke*, vol. 37:447–448. Berlin: Dietz, 1968.

Fang, Jianguo. 2014. Gaige kaifang yilai Zhongguo gongchandang minsheng jingji sixiang de zhongda fazhan—yi makesizhuyi zhexue fangfa wei fenxi zhuxian. *Makesizhuyi yanjiu* 2014 (10): 58–67, 120.

Feng, Feng, and Zhang Yannan. 2019. Shehui zeren chengdan dui qiye fazhan de yingxiang: Hangye jingzheng de tiaojie zuoyong. *Shandong daxue xuebao (zhexue shehui kexue ban)* 2019 (5): 93–101.

Fine, Ben, and Dimitris Milonakis. 2009. *From economics imperialism to freakonomics: The shifting boundaries between economics and other social sciences*. London: Routledge.

Gao, Jingwen, and Zheng Min. 1996. Deng Xiaoping shehuizhuyi shichang jingji lilun de zhexue jichu. *Xinjiang jiaoyu xueyuan xuebao* 31 (12): 1–4.

Gu, Yumin. 2019. Cong chuantong jihua jingji dao Zhongguo tese shehuizhuyi shichang jingji. *Gaoxiao makesizhuyi lilun yanjiu* 2019 (3): 65–71.

Gui, Qiquan. 2006. Guanyu Deng Xiaoping 'jingjixue budengshi' de zhexue sikao—jian tan shehuizhuyi shichang jingji lilun de luoji xietiaoxing wenti. *Dongnan daxue xuebao (zhexue shehui kexue ban)* 2006 (6): 5–9.

Han, Xuefeng. 2000. Shehuizhuyi shichang jingji de zhexue jichu—chongdu 'Guanyu Fei'erbaha de tigang'. *Chongqing shehui kexue* 2000 (1): 12–15.

He, Bingmeng. 2016. Firmly grasping value orientation of developing mixed economy. *Marxist Studies in China* 2016: 98–112.

Heilman, Sebastian, and Oliver Melton. 2013. The reinvention of development planning in China, 1993–2012. *Modern China* 39 (6): 580–628.

Huang, Nansen. 1994. Shehuizhuyi shichang jingji lilun de zhexue jichu. *Makesizhuyi yu xianshi* 1994 (11): 1–6.

Huo, Bingsheng. 2011. Shi lun shehuizhuyi shichang jingji taiojian xia jiazhi guilü de zuoyong yu hongguantiaokong. *Caizhi* 2011 (27): 226–227.

Jiang, Guolin. 1998. Deng Xiaoping shichang jingji siwei de maodun tuiyan luoji—makesizhuyi jingjixue zhong maodun fenxifa de yunyong. *Shehui kexue* 1998 (5): 2–5, 10.

Jiang, Zemin. 1992. Jiakuai gaige kaifang he xiandaihua jianshe bufa, duoqu you Zhongguo tese shehuizhuyi shiye de geng da shengli (1992.10.12). In *Jiang Zemin wenxuan*, vol. 1:210–254. Beijing: Renmin chubanshe, 2006.

Kornai, János. 1957. *Overcentralization in economic administration*. Oxford: Oxford University Press.

Kozma, Ferenc. 1989. The market mechanism in the socialist system. *Acta Oeconomica* 40 (3–4): 243–248.

Kula, Witold. 1976. *An economic theory of feudalism: Towards a model of the polish economy, 1500–1800*. Trans. Lawrence Garner. London: New Left Books.

Lange, Oskar. 1936. On the economic theory of socialism: Part one. *The Review of Economic Studies* 4 (1): 53–71.

Lange, Oskar. 1937. On the economic theory of socialism: Part two. *The Review of Economic Studies* 4 (2): 123–142.

Li, Wencheng. 1992. Cong makesizhuyi zhexue de yangqi guankan zhongguo dangqian de gaige kaifang. *Jiangxi shehui kexue* 1992 (1): 52–56.

Li, Xingshan, Cao Xin, Zhao Zhenhua, and Han Baojiang. 2002a. The successful practice and implementation of the socialist market economy: An investigative research report on Zhejiang's economy. *Part I. The Chinese Economy* 35 (4): 6–38.

Li, Xingshan, Cao Xin, Zhao Zhenhua, and Han Baojiang. 2002b. The successful practice and implementation of the socialist market economy: An investigative research report on Zhejiang's economy, Part II. *The Chinese Economy* 35 (4): 39–72.

Liao, Xinwen. 2008. Cong jihua jingji tizhi xiang shehuizhuyi shichang jingji tizhi de zhuanbian—shi lun Mao Zedong, Deng Xiaoping dui woguo jingji tizhi de tansuo. *Dang de wenxian* 2008 (6): 50–55.

Mao, Zedong. 1937. Shijian lun (1937.07). In *Mao Zedong xuanji*, vol. 1:282–298. Beijing: Renmin chubanshe, 1952.

Mao, Zedong. 1959a. Jiazhi faze shi yige weida de xuexiao (1959.03–04). In *Mao Zedong wenji*, vol. 8:34–37. Beijing: Renmin chubanshe, 2009.

Mao, Zedong. 1959b. Zai Zhengzhou huiyi shang de jianghua (jiexuan) (1959.02.27). In *Mao Zedong wenji*, vol. 8:9–13. Beijing: Renmin chubanshe, 2009.

Marx, Karl. 1858a. *Economic manuscripts of 1857–1858 (first version of Capital) [Grundrisse]*. I *Marx and Engels collected works*, vol:28. Moscow: Progress Publishers, 1986.

Marx, Karl. 1858b. *Zhengzhijingjixue pipan (1857–1858 nian shougao) zhai xuan*. In *Makesi Engesi wenji*, vol. 8:37–209. Beijing: Renmin chubanshe, 2009.

Marx, Karl. 1858c. *Ökonomische Manuskripte 1857/1858*. In *Marx Engels Gesamtausgabe*, vol. II.1. Berlin: Dietz, 1976.

Marx, Karl. 1875. Kritik des Gothaer Programms. In *Marx Engels Gesamtausgabe*, vol. I.25:3–25. Berlin: Dietz, 1985.

Marx, Karl. 1894a. *Capital: A critique of political economy, Vol. III*. In *Marx and Engels collected works*, vol. 37. Moscow: Progress Publishers, 1998.

Marx, Karl. 1894b. *Das Kapital. Kritik der politischen Ökonomie. Dritter Band. Hamburg 1894*. In *Marx Engels Gesamtausgabe*, vol. II:15. Berlin: Akademie Verlag, 2004.

Marx, Karl, and Friedrich Engels. 1848a. Manifest der Kommunistischen Partei. In *Marx Engels Werke*, vol. 4:459–493. Berlin: Dietz Verlag, 1974.

Marx, Karl, and Friedrich Engels. 1848b. The manifesto of the communist party. In *Marx and Engels collected works*, vol. 6:477–519. Moscow: Progress Publishers, 1976.

Milonakis, Dimitris, and Ben Fine. 2009. *From political economy to economics: Method, the social and the historical in the evolution of economic theory*. London: Routledge.

Mises, Ludwig von. 1932. *Socialism: An economic and sociological analysis*. Trans. J. Kahane. London: Jonathan Cape, 1936.

Peng, Lixun. 1994. Deng Xiaoping shehuizhuyi shichang jingji lilun de zhexue jichu. *Xueshu yanjiu* 1994 (2): 11–16.

Stalin, I. V. 1952a. Economic problems of socialism in the U.S.S.R. In *Works*, vol. 16:222–296. London: Red Star Press, 1986.

Stalin, I. V. 1952b. Ėkonomicheskie problemy sotsializma v SSSR. In *Sochineniia*, vol. 16:154–223. Moscow: Izdatel′stvo "Pisatel′", 1997.

Sun, Pinghua. 2014. *Human rights protection system in China*. Heidelberg: Springer.

Szamuely, László. 1982. The first wave of the mechanism debate (1954–1957). *Acta Oeconomica* 29 (1–2): 1–24.

Szamuely, László. 1984. The second wave of the mechanism debate in Hungary and the 1968 reform in Hungary. *Acta Oeconomica* 33 (1–2): 43–67.

Wan, Qianhui. 2017. Zhongguo tese renquan guan de lishi fazhan yu neizai luoji. *Renquan* 2017 (5): 33–52.

Wang, Fanyu. 2019. Gaige kaifang yilai Zhongguo tese fupin daolu: mailuo shuli yu jingyan zongjie. *Xibei minzu daxue xuebao (zhexue shehui kexue ban)* 2019 (12): 1–10.

Wang, Yuyao. 1995. Lun Deng Xiaoping zai jiefang he fazhan shengchanli wenti shang de xin gongxian. *Dang de wenxian* 1995 (3): 49–55.

Wei, Jian. 2018. Xi Jinping xinshidai Zhongguo tese shehuizhuyi jingji sixiang: makesizhuyi zhengzhijingjixue guanyu shehuizhuyi xiandaihua jianshe de chuangxin fazhan. *Gaige* 2018 (11): 139–146.

Xi, Jinping. 2017. *Juesheng quanmian jiancheng xiaokang shehui, duoqu xinshidai Zhongguo tese shehuizhuyi weida shengli (2017.10.18)*. Beijing: Renmin chubanshe.

Xi, Jinping. 2020. Buduan kaituo dangdai makesizhuyi zhengzhijingjixue xin jingjie. *Qiushi* 2020 (16): 1–6.

Xiang, Qiyuan, and He Ganqiang. 2014. Scientifically understanding and vigorously developing mixed economy—A dialogue on reforming and strengthening state-owned enterprises. *Marxist Studies in China* 2014: 82–105.

Yang, Jinhai. 2009. The historical significance of the combination of socialism and the market economy. *Science and Society* 73 (2): 170–176.

Yang, Xiaojie. 1994. Lishi weiwuzhuyi de lilun jidian yu bianzheng tongyi de sixiang fangfa—tan shehuizhuyi shichang jingji de zhexue jichu. *Xue lilun* 1994 (5): 6.

Yang, Yusheng. 2001. Jiazhi guilü yu shehuizhuyi shichang jingji. *Zhonggong Shenyang shiwei dangxiao xuebao* 2001 (5): 30–33.

Yang, Zhiping. 2010. Lun shichang jingji yu shehuizhuyi xiang jeihe de lishi guocheng he zhexue jichu. *Zhongwai qiyejia* 2010 (5): 11–14.

Yu, Wenlie. 2011. Zhongguo jingji moshi yu Zhongguo moshi jiqi jiben tezheng. *Shehui kexue yanjiu* 2011 (1): 26–30.

Yu, Zuyao. 1979. Shi lun shehuizhuyi shichang jingji. *Jingji yanjiu cankao ziliao* 50 (3): 1–7.

Zhang, Guoyun. 2010. Lun jiazhi guilü yu jianshe shehuizhuyi shichang jingji. *Tianshui shifan xueyuan xuebao* 2010 (3): 77–81.

Zhang, Hui, and Zhuang Zejun. 1994. Shilun shehuizhuyi shichang jingji lilun de zhexue jichu. *Jingji yu guanli* 1994 (1): 3–7.

Zhang, Xuekui. 2009. Shichang jingji yu shehuizhuyi xiang jiehe de sange mingti jiqi zhexue jichu—30 nian gaige kaifang de jingji zhexue sikao. *Shehui kexue yanjiu* 2009 (3): 134–140.

Zhao, Ziyang. 1987. *Yanzhe you Zhongguo tese de shehuizhuyi daolu qianjin—zai Zhongguo gongchandang di shisan ci quanguo daibiao dahui shang de baogao (1987.10.25)*. Beijing: Renmin chubanshe.

Zhou, Nan. 2017a. Weiwu shiguan: Zhongguo tese shehuizhuyi zhengzhijingjixue de zhexue jichu. *Haipai jingjixue* 15 (4): 22–30.

Zhou, Shulian. 2017b. Wo dui Zhongguo jihua jingji zhuanbian wei shehuizhuyi shichang jingji de yanjiu. *Zhongguo pudong ganbu xueyuan xuebao* 2017 (5): 39–55.

Zhou, Zhishan, and Wang Xing. 2019. Chanyang xinshidai Zhongguo tese shehuizhuyi zhengzhijingjixue de zhexue jichu. *Zhejiang shifan daxue xuebao (shehui kexue ban)* 44 (2): 36–43.

Zhu, Jiamu. 2013. Mao Zedong's exploration of and answers to the questions of 'what socialism is and how to build it'. *Marxist Studies in China* 2013: 83–111.

Chapter 6
Seeking a *Xiaokang* Society, or, Socialist Modernisation

6.1 Opening Remarks

> The so-called four modernisations are aimed at changing the poor and backward situation in China, gradually raising the living standards of the Chinese people, restoring China to a position in international affairs commensurate with its status, and making more contributions to humankind. The four modernisations we are going to achieve are those with a Chinese style [*zhongguoshi*]. Our concept of the four modernisations is not a concept of modernisation like yours, but a concept of a 'moderately well-off family [*xiaokang zhi jia*]'. (Deng 1979i, 237)

I have begun with this quotation from Deng Xiaoping, since it captures the topic of this chapter: a *xiaokang* society that would result from the four modernisations. This was the first time that *xiaokang* was used in such a sense in China since Liberation. But it has an ancient pedigree: *xiaokang* comes from the Confucian classics and designates a moderate or acceptable time of health, well-being, prosperity, and peace. Deng sought to reinterpret the term, also used in everyday parlance, within a Marxist framework. In other words, it was yet another example of the sinification of Marxism (*makesizhuyi zhongguohua*), or Marxism made concrete and set on its feet in a Chinese context. There is another feature of Deng's observation: his reference to the 'four modernisations [*sige xiandaihua*]'. It is precisely these modernisations that he seeks to define in terms of a 'Chinese style', or a *xiaokang* society. Why this specific reference? It entails a distinct emphasis on continuity, for the four modernisations stem from Zhou Enlai in 1963 and were affirmed by Mao Zedong. In other words, Deng clearly appropriates the four modernisations for the project of the Reform and Opening-Up, which would achieve a 'moderately well-off family [*xiaokang zhi jia*]', or—as he clarifies a little later in the same text—a 'moderately well-off country [*xiaokang de guojia*]' (Deng 1979i, 238).

The following analysis sets out to explain the inter-related terms of the four modernisations and *xiaokang* society. It begins with an analysis of the four modernisations—in agriculture, industry, national defence, and science and technology—through the initial proposals of Mao Zedong and especially Zhou Enlai, and then

R. Boer, *Socialism with Chinese Characteristics*,
https://doi.org/10.1007/978-981-16-1622-8_6

its explication with Deng Xiaoping. The crucial question here is what gives these modernisations their distinctive Chinese characteristics. In order to answer this question, I analyse the reinterpretation of *xiaokang*, which will be left in transliterated form since it is almost impossible to translate. This task entails what may initially seem like a detour: an examination of the Confucian tradition's notion of *datong*, or 'great harmony'. As the highest stage of social development, it would come to be reinterpreted—through Mao Zedong—in light of communism. Before the stage of *datong* comes *xiaokang*, a more moderate and achievable middle ground, above chaos and disorder but not at the same level as the great harmony. It was specifically Deng Xiaoping who reclaimed the term *xiaokang* and reinterpreted it in light of socialism, the stage—according to orthodox Marxism since Lenin—before communism. The analysis closes with a consideration of the 'comprehensive *xiaokang* society', which has become a core feature of Chinese government policy.

6.2 The Four Modernisations

In early 1963 at a meeting in Shanghai, Zhou Enlai proposed: 'If we want to build a powerful socialist country, we must modernise agriculture, industry, national defence, science and technology' (Zhou E. 1963a, 387; 1963b, 427). This statement would become the recognised form of the 'four modernisations [*sige xiandaihua*]'. Yet, this was by no means the first occasion at which 'modernisation' or indeed their numbering were mentioned, for both Zhou Enlai and Mao Zedong had been developing the idea since the 1950s.[1] It is not my task here to delve into a detailed history of their emergence and clarification (Xu Z. and Chen 1998; Han 2006). Instead, I am interested in how they are articulated, in how they are different from 'modernisations' elsewhere. In other words, what gives these four modernisations their distinctly Chinese characteristics?

The answer to this question already appeared almost ten years earlier, in Zhou Enlai's work report—since then a typical task for the premier—at the inaugural National People's Congress of 1954. In his presentation, which offered a preliminary list of four modernisations,[2] Zhou points out that the task before the New China is to overcome backwardness and poverty (*luohou he qiongkun*), brought about by the 'three mountains' of imperialism, feudalism, and bureaucratic capitalism. The

[1]In the lead up to the constitution adopted at this National People's Congress, Mao had spoken more generally of 'socialist industrialisation' and the 'socialisation and mechanisation of agriculture' in order to make China a 'great socialist country' (Mao 1954a, 326, 329; 1954b, 143, 145–146). A few years later, he spoke of developing a 'socialist country with modern industry, modern agriculture, and modern science and culture' (Mao 1957a, 207; 1957b, 387). By 1959, 'modern national defence [*xiandai guofang*]' had returned to the list (Zhou E. 1959, 408; Mao 1960, 162).

[2]Here they are industry, agriculture, communications and transport, and national defence. This speech is the beginning of a process of clarifying the more general theme of modernisation, which was central to Zhou Enlai's economic writings (1993). The references in relation to this process of clarification are comprehensively cited by Xu and Chen (1998, 432–434).

method: to 'liberate productive forces [*jiefang shengchanli*]' and focus on economic development. The aim: to improve the 'people's material life [*weiwu shenghuo*] and cultural life' and strengthen the 'nation's independence and security [*anquan*]' (Zhou E. 1954a, 132; 1954b, 142; see also Xu Z. and Chen 1998, 443–445). We may summarise as follows: the purpose of the four modernisations was to overcome China's chronic poverty through liberating the forces of production so as to raise the level of material and cultural (or 'spiritual [*jingshen*]') life so as to secure China's strength.[3] Or, as Zhou Enlai puts it later in the same speech (1954a, 142; 1954b, 152): 'the sole aim [*weiyi mudi*] of a socialist economy is to satisfy the people's material and cultural needs'.

Turning to Deng Xiaoping, it is striking how his renewed emphasis on the four modernisations is in marked continuity with Zhou Enlai (and Mao Zedong) from the 1950s. By now this continuity should not be a surprise: we have already seen how Deng and his comrades strove to pick up and enhance the line of Marxism-Leninism and Mao Zedong Thought from the late 1950s. By contrast, the 'Maoism' of the 'Cultural Revolution' was a deviation. A comparable point applies to the four modernisations, which the Gang of Four in particular disparaged. They saw the modernisations as a path to capitalism, opposed developments in science and technology, and advocated 'poor socialism' in their place (Deng 1978h, 86; 1978f, 98–99; 1979c, 233; 1979g, 237; 1980g, 311–312; 1980i, 310–311). In the wake of the 'Cultural Revolution', Deng and his comrades strove mightily to recover the four modernisations and take them to a whole new level.[4]

In his many invocations of the four modernisations, Deng connects a wide range of topics,[5] so much so that the modernisations become an alternative term for the Reform and Opening-Up. But what is the point of the whole process? The four modernisations mean 'changing the poor and backward situation in China, gradually raising the living standards of the Chinese people, restoring China to a position in international affairs commensurate with its status, and making more contributions

[3]This core theme would be reiterated in later elaborations of the four modernisations, with further details on how they are integrated, on the role of science and technology, on the necessary stages, and on showcasing the creativity and superiority of China's socialist system (Zhou E. 1963a, 1963b, 1964a, 1964b, 1975b, 1975a).

[4]The methods to achieve the four modernisations may have differed due to circumstances. Mao Zedong and Zhou Enlai advocated a highly centralised planned economy, along with collectivised industry and agriculture. This approach—as we have seen earlier (Sect. 2.4 and Sect. 5.3.1)—was needed in the early stages of the construction of socialism and produced remarkable economic results. However, by the 1970s bottlenecks had begun to appear and the economy was stagnating, to which the Reform and Opening-Up was the answer. But the aim remained the same in terms of the four modernisations.

[5]Too many are the references to cite here, but if one reads through the second and third volumes of Deng Xiaoping's *Selected Works*, one will find—in relation the four modernisations—mentions of education (science and technology), unity in the CPC and countrywide, trade unions and the working class, socialist democracy, the legal system, nationalities, writers and artists, a new generation of cadres with professional knowledge, enthusiasm, and energy.

to humankind' (Deng 1979i, 237).[6] The continuity with Zhou Enlai's identification of the nature and purpose of the four modernisations should be obvious, with an added emphasis on an international dimension in relation to China's status in world affairs—especially as a socialist country with a deep affinity for developing countries that were formerly colonised (Deng 1978e, 112; 1978d, 123). In fact, in the sentence preceding the text I have quoted, Deng explicitly invokes Mao Zedong and Zhou Enlai. Elsewhere, Deng stressed similar themes in relation to the four modernisations: China's backward economic condition and the need to overcome poverty (Deng 1978h, 91; 1978f, 103; 1979b, 164; 1979f, 173), the resolute focus on economic construction and the productive forces (Deng 1978b, 134–139; 1978g, 145–149; 1979a, 194–195; 1979d, 201; 1980e, 240–241; 1980h, 242–243), and the need for a materially advanced socialist civilisation with a 'rich and diversified [*fengfu-duocai*] cultural life inspired by high ideals [*gaoshang*]' (Deng 1979h, 208; 1979e, 214).

When he came to provide more specific details, Deng spoke of China's advantageous conditions, notably the abundance of natural resources in terms of minerals and energy, a firm material foundation in the development of industry (despite earlier follies), the hard work, wisdom, and creativity of Chinese people who are experienced in struggle, and an opening-up policy that will enable principled engagement with other countries that are more advanced in terms of science and technology (Deng 1978e, 111–112; 1978d, 122–123; 1979c, 232–234; 1979g, 236–237). Further, when addressing the modernisation of science and technology, he specifies that these are productive forces in their own right. In this case, Deng invokes not only China's achievements in this area in the past, but also the need to develop this core area in the modern world so that China would once again take the lead, albeit in light of a socialist system in which mental labour is of service to rural and urban workers (Deng 1978h, 86–91; 1978f, 99–103). None of this would be easy—far from it. The modernisations would entail much toil and struggle, especially in light of the need to keep to the socialist road. In a more philosophical vein, he observes that the 'four modernisations represent a great and profound revolution in which we are moving forward by resolving one new contradiction after another' (Deng 1978c, 152–153; 1978a, 162). In order to enable the four modernisations, Deng specifies the struggle involved in structural reform, in constructing a socialist civilisation with a high cultural and ideological level, in combating economic crime and corruption, and rectifying the CPC's work style, organisation, and leadership (Deng 1982c, 403–404; 1982b, 395).

Clearly, Deng Xiaoping took the four modernisations to a whole new level (as we have already seen with other policies from Mao Zedong Thought, from before the deviation of the 'Cultural Revolution'). He was also resolute on the role of the CPC as the vanguard of the New China, which required a firm and consistent political line, political stability and unity, hard struggle and a pioneering spirit, as well cadres who

[6]Similarly: 'In sum, the political line of the Party at the present stage is to work with one heart and one mind for our country's four modernisations… The growth of the economy, increasing the national income, gradually improving the people's standard of living, and the corresponding consolidation and strengthening of our national defence – all these hinge on the success of the four modernisations' (Deng 1980d, 276; 1980a, 274–275).

had both resolute socialist orientation and professional competence (Deng 1980e, 248–265; 1980h, 249–265; see also 1978h, 96–100; 1978f, 108–111). Deng was also clear that the four modernisations would eventually prove the superiority of a socialist system (Deng 1980g, 311; 1980i, 310; 1980b, 322; 1980f, 321) and that they would enable China—and indeed other countries—to counter 'hegemonism [*baquan*]' or to 'struggle against hegemony [*fanba douzheng*]' (Deng 1978e, 112; 1978d, 123; 1980e, 239–240; 1980h, 241; 1980d, 275; 1980a, 274; 1982d, 415–417; 1982a, 407–409). I will return to this theme in the next chapter, suffice to note here that 'countering hegemonism' functions as a replacement for the anti-colonial struggle. China has had more enough of bullying and hegemonism by countries that followed the European model of colonial depredation, and it is certainly not going to allow such a situation again.

In closing this analysis of the four modernisations, let me return to the key question: how do they evince a Chinese 'style [*shi*]' or Chinese 'characteristics [*tese*]'? For Zhou Enlai, these characteristics entailed overcoming China's backwardness through economic development so as to improve material and cultural life. We may rephrase this answer as follows: the purpose of capitalist modernisation—enabled through imperialist plunder and colonial domination—is to enrich a small percentage of the population, specifically those who hold the reins of industry and trade, and who monopolise scientific and technological development. The vast majority of rural and urban workers continue to struggle, mostly missing out on the gains made. By contrast, socialist modernisation is—in the long term—for the improvement of the material and cultural lives of this vast majority. As we have seen (Sect. 2.5), Deng Xiaoping agrees,[7] elaborating much further as he sought to identify the four modernisations with the Reform and Opening-Up itself. But Deng also made a distinctly new contribution as to what gives the four modernisations their distinctive Chinese characteristics. Initially, he observes, the aim was to realise the four modernisations by the end of the twentieth century. However, Deng and his comrades realised that this aim was too ambitious: 'Later we changed the goal to "Chinese-style [*zhongguoshi*]" modernisations, intending to lower the standard a little' (Deng 1979a, 194).[8] A lapidary answer, is it not? But it contains a more profound meaning. This lowering of the standards entails the deployment of a term hitherto not used: *xiaokang*. As the quotation with I began this chapter makes clear, modernisation in China means a *xiaokang* family, a *xiaokang* country. Or as Deng observes elsewhere: 'The primary task we have set is to achieve by the end of this century the initial goal of modernisation, that is to say, to reach the level of *xiaokang*' (Deng 1982d, 416–417). It is to the meaning of *xiaokang* that I now turn.

---

[7]As Deng observed in 1986: 'Since our victory in the revolution, in the course of construction we have again integrated the fundamental principles of Marxism with the concrete practice of China. We are striving for the four modernisations, but people tend to forget that they are four socialist modernisations' (Deng 1986a, 173; 1986b, 175).

[8]Deng uses an idiom here, contrasting '*dakou*' with '*xiaokou*'. Literally, they mean 'large mouth' and 'small mouth' with the senses of a large or small mouthful of food. A comparable English idiom for '*dakou*' may be 'bite off more than one can chew'.

6.3 Datong: From the Confucian Tradition to Mao Zedong

In order to understand *xiaokang* and why Deng Xiaoping appropriated this term from the Chinese tradition, we need to step back and deal with the question of *datong*—with the core meaning of great unity, togetherness, or harmony. The tradition relating to this term is notable not for its lengthy discourses, but for the briefness and sparseness of its key moments. It is as though the weight of the moments has increased precisely because of this brevity.

*6.3.1 The Book of Rites (*Liji*)*

The first articulation of *datong*—and thereby its locus classicus—appears in the 'Cycle of Rites [*Liyun*]' chapter of *The Book of Rites* (*Liji*), compiled in the third to second centuries BCE:

> When the Great Way [*dadao*] was practiced, all-under-heaven was as common [*tianxia wei gong*]. They chose men of worth and ability [for public office]; they practiced good faith and cultivated good will [*xiumu*]. Therefore, people did not single out only their parents to love, nor did they single out only their children for care. They saw to it that the aged were provided for until the end, that the able-bodied had employment, and that the young were brought up well. Compassion was shown to widows, orphans, the childless, and those disabled by disease, so that all had sufficient support. Men had their portion [of land], and women, their homes after marriage. Wealth they hated to leave unused, yet they did not necessarily store it away for their own use. Strength they hated not to exert, yet they did not necessarily exert it only for their own benefit. Thus selfish scheming was thwarted before it could develop. Bandits and thieves, rebels and traitors did not show themselves. So the outer gates [*waihu*] were left open. This was known as the period of the Great Unity [*datong*]. (translation by Nylan 2001, 196)[9]

A few observations are in order. To begin with, the Chinese text is very concise, with one character often functioning as a whole word. Translators are tempted to fill in the meaning for readers. For example, *dadao* is literally the big road, but metaphorically the Great Way—think of Daoism or *daojiao*, the teaching of The Way. One may seek to expand the meaning by calling it the Great Way of Virtue (so Legge), but this adds even more layers of interpretation. The text explains *dadao* as one in which 'all under heaven [*tianxia*]' was—literally—'as common [*weigong*]'. How one interprets the phrase, which comes down to us through millennia of interpretations, says as much about the translator as the text. It may be expanded to mean that something serves or acts as common, or the common good. Some translations go further, offering 'public good', 'a public and common spirit', 'public-spirited' or 'one community'. All may offer angles on the initial phrase, but it is important to

[9] I have chosen the translation by Nylan for the sake of consistency, with one modification in the first sentence. Each translation has of course its benefits and drawbacks. One may compare James Legge's classic translation (1885, 364–366), which may also be found at https://ctext.org/liji/li-yun, and that of Watson (1960, 176).

keep in mind that the focus of the text is primarily on the common, so I have rendered the two characters in terms of 'as common'.

Further, this social reality is simultaneously envisaged as an expanded family and one that undermines the family by focusing on the common good. Thus, the primary concern is not one's immediate parents and children, but all in society—including the widowed, childless, orphans, and sick. All should have opportunities in life and appropriate care, although distinct roles were still appropriate for men and women. The text reinforces this common good with a powerful image: the 'outer gates' of the family compound were left open. The character for gate or door—*hu* (户)—also bears the meaning of family or household. If the 'outer gate [*waihu*]' is open, it means not merely that households are connected with another, but that the very sense of household expands well beyond the gates so that the family itself is not primary.[10] While the vision may be an ideal, the overall framework is from a ruling perspective. This appears initially with the phrase *tianxia*, a traditional imperial term for all under the ruler's sway. In this context, it meant China, however large or small it may have been, although it also came to be seen as encompassing the known earth. Further, the setting for this brief description of *datong* has Confucius saying the words to a certain Yan Yan as they stood on a balcony after a ritual. Confucius sighs over the current State of Lu (in Shandong province), offering his vision of what it had been like and what it might be.[11] The discourse is primarily for rulers' ears, who should be worthy (*xian*) and have ability (*neng*), exerting power not for their own advantage but for others, able to bring about the common good, or—as the final word has it—*datong*.

6.3.2 *He Xiu's Revision:* **Datong** *as Topos*

Crucially, in *Liji* the *datong* is viewed as a past era, as the opening phrase of the following stanza indicates: the way has 'fallen into disuse and obscurity [*jiyin*]'. *Datong* lay in the past, so one had to do the best in the current circumstances. The next significant moment in the tradition reworks this assumption, appearing in a commentary on a commentary. More precisely, it is the commentary of a certain He Xiu (129–82 CE) on one of three commentaries (*Gongyang*) on the Spring and Autumn Annals (*Chunqiu*). While the annals themselves are sparse indeed,[12] the commentaries explore every possible implication, based on the assumption articulated by Mencius that Confucius was the author or editor and had compiled the annals according to specific criteria, embedded through 'subtle phrasing [*weiyan*]', which had to be unearthed through careful exegesis. Of the three commentaries—by

[10]Further, the phrase for cultivating harmony or good will (*xiumu*) means to cultivate friendship with neighbours, which entails peace and harmony.

[11]The State of Lu was a vassal of the State of Zhou. Given Lu's relatively long history (c. 1042–249 BCE), Confucius could in the sixth century BCE look back on its history.

[12]The annals record events of the state of Lu (concerning which Confucius uttered his reflections on *datong*), from 722 BCE to 481 BCE.

Guliang, Gongyang, and Zuo—the one by Gongyang is the most intriguing.[13] It is this tradition, which came to be called 'New Text' (see more below), to which He Xiu added his layer of commentary.

Briefly put, He Xiu distinguished three ages, with one superseding the other: the 'decayed and disordered [*shuailuan*]' world; one of 'rising peace [*shengping*]'; and one of the 'great peace [*daping*]' (Li X. and Ma 1999, 25–26).[14] At this point we need to be careful, since He Xiu is not commenting on the *Liji* and its mention of *datong*. Instead, he is adding a layer of commentary to the Spring and Autumn Annals. Thus, he does not speak of *datong* directly, but instead refers to *daping*, the great peace (later to become *taiping*, the greatest peace). We may equate *datong* and *daping* in light of later developments with Kang Youwei (see Sect. 6.3.3), especially since they speak of a very similar desired reality, but this is a later development. More importantly, He Xiu identifies three ages, moving through chaos, rising peace, to the greatest peace. In other words, he reverses the sequence: Confucius may have seen *datong* as in the past, as a lost world that provides the model to which one should aspire; He Xiu sees *daping* as yet to come. At the same time, there is a risk that He Xiu's three-age sequence takes on a purely evolutionary sense, rising from chaos and disorder to the great peace. Scholars have been keen to stress other criteria, such as legitimacy, virtue, and ethics rather than inheritance as the criterion for office, a cyclical process in which the closer one comes to *datong* the greater is the risk of chaos, or—relatedly—the possibility of moving in either direction, especially if one juxtaposes Confucius's sense of loss in *Liji* to the progressive schema in He Xiu's interpretation (Li J. 2013; Chen H. 2016).[15]

Nonetheless, the most important contribution of He Xiu's commentary lies elsewhere: the world of great peace is not of the imagination, of rumour and innuendo, but one that can be seen and is thus verifiable. To explain: He Xiu follows an earlier interpreter, Dong Zhongshu, who distinguished between two types of meaning: inner and outer. In He Xiu's hands, this becomes a threefold schema of words and worlds that are 'rumoured [*suochuanwen*]', heard of or 'recorded [*suowen*]' and 'seen [*suojian*]' (Li J. 2013, 58–59). Now for the breakthrough: for He Xiu, these become the characteristic features of the three eras.[16] Thus, what is 'rumoured' becomes the 'decayed and disordered [*shuailuan*]' world, one of chaos in which the heart is 'course and unrefined [*cucu*]', the country is broken up into small states and the records virtually non-existent. Rumours abound of skulduggery, assassination, intrigue, and inappropriate behaviour in light of established rituals. By contrast, the 'recorded [*suowen*]' or reported world has records and it unites all of the Chinese people while outside are the foreign tribes (*Yidi*). This is known as the time of 'rising peace [*shengping*]':

---

[13]For a useful introduction to the three commentaries and thus of the central role of *Chunqiu* in Chinese tradition, see Nylan (2001, 257–306).

[14]The text may also be found on a number of websites, such as www.guoxue123.com/jinbu/ssj/gyz/index.htm.

[15]The notion of cycles or up-down movements is a feature of the Confucian tradition.

[16]As one would expect, scholarship on the development of He Xiu's 'three worlds' is immense, so I cite here only some of the more notable recent works (Jiang Q. 1995; Chen Q. 2007; Wang 2007; Xu X. 2011; Gao and Chen 2014; Chen H. 2016).

although not ideal, for it still has leaders and people engaging in less than appropriate behaviour, it is a distinct improvement. The 'seen [*suojian*]' world, one directly experienced, becomes the great or indeed greatest peace and tranquillity (*daping* and *taiping*). Here the world is one, whether distant or nearby, large or small, while the heart (*xin*) or inner being is now deep and thoroughly known (*xiang*).

This insight provides a significant contrast between Chinese and 'Western' philosophical assumptions concerning 'utopia'. Let me put it this way: He Xiu's interpretation valorises the 'seen' as the most ideal world, in contrast to what is 'rumoured' and for which no records exist. The ideal world is precisely the one that is fully recorded; in short, it is a world that one experiences directly and can thus be empirically verified and studied. The unrecorded and unseen world, of which only rumours and hearsay exist, is the world of chaos and disorder. This approach is in contrast with 'Western' theological and philosophical assumptions concerning ontological or external transcendence (*waizaichaoyue*),[17] for here it is precisely what is unseen and unknown that is the ideal world, of which the known world is only a poor copy. This external ontological transcendence, with its polar opposite in immanence, runs through Western European assumptions at many levels (from religion, through politics, to culture), but how does it influence perceptions of utopia? To put it sharply, for a 'Western' tradition the ideal world is a transcendent one, a utopia so distant that it is beyond human experience and knowability; by contrast, for the Chinese tradition examined thus far, *datong* and *taiping* constitute a topos, a known and verifiable place.[18] While the 'Western' tradition assumes that the unreachable 'no' place (*utopia*) is also the 'best' place (*outopia*), the Chinese tradition should—if we use such terminology—be called a 'topian' one, focused on a verifiable *topos*.

6.3.3 Kang Youwei's Confucian Reformism

The next major step would come many centuries later with Kang Youwei (1858–1927). In order to understand the path to his core text, *The Book of Datong* (*Datongshu*), let us return for a moment to the two main traditions that arose out of the commentaries on the Spring and Autumn Annals.[19] As mentioned earlier, the

[17]In Chinese scholarship, the contrast with 'Western' external transcendence (for which God, or at least a placeholder for God, is the ultimate cause) is 'internal transcendence [*neizaichaoyue*]', which is 'life-focused' and seeks to improve one's current social situation through an ethical order. This 'internal transcendence' and its related 'heaven and human beings are one [*tianren heyi*]' are quite distinct from the transcendence-immanence opposition in 'Western' philosophy (Ren 2012; Shen 2015; Guo X. 2016; Xu T. 2016).

[18]Noteworthy here is that while the Chinese tradition obviously has perceptions of a better world (as I have been examining), the Western concept of 'utopia/outopia' required a loan-word adaption into Chinese, as *wutuobang*, which bears both the meaning and sound structure of the original. Intriguingly, 'dystopia' becomes *fanwutuobang*, 'anti-utopia'—a distinctly different opposition.

[19]It is well-nigh impossible to do justice to the centuries of detailed commentary concerning the *Gongyang* tradition's 'three worlds' in a few sentences (Tong and Lin 2002; Xu L. and Wang 2008).

Gongyang commentary became the source of the 'New Text' tradition, which came into favour during the early Han Dynasty, only to fall into disfavour due to a perceived esoterism. From the late Han (25–220 CE) the more rationalist 'Old Text' school, based on the commentary by Guliang, was at the forefront, forcing the 'New Text' tradition into the background for a while. The rival traditions were nearly always at loggerheads, with one or the other dominating for a time, and rulers keen to see that neither was completely dominant for long (Nylan 2001, 262). However, with the imminent collapse of the whole dynastic system and ensuing profound turmoil, the 'New Text' tradition gained a new lease of life in the work of the Confucian reformer, Kang Youwei (Wong 2000).

This was precisely the tradition to which He Xiu had made his daring contribution many centuries earlier. The following quotation from Kang Youwei will indicate both how much he is indebted to and how he seeks to reinterpret this tradition:

> The divine sage-king, Confucius, reflected on and worried over this problem from early on. Therefore, he established the law of three governments [*santong*][20] and three ages [*sanshi*]: after a world according to disorder [*luan*] it will change into ascending peace [*shengping*], and then into the greatest peace [*taiping*]; after *xiaokang* it will advance to *datong*. (Kang 1935a, 6)[21]

Once again, the text is brief indeed, although Kang Youwei offers later a comprehensive table of the main features of each age (Kang 1935a, 43–52, 60–62). Yet, this sentence makes the profoundly influential connection between the Confucian text of *Liji* and the *Gongyang* commentary by He Xiu. The latter's terms appear first, with the three ages of disorder, ascending peace, and greatest peace; immediately following are the two terms that appear in the *Liyun* chapter of the *Liji*: *xiaokang* and *datong*.[22] Indeed, Kang makes explicit the slight shift from the 'great peace [*daping*]' of He Xiu's commentary and the 'greatest peace [*taiping*]' by which it is usually known.[23] The connection between Confucius and He Xiu is crucial: ascending peace (*shengping*) is thus explicitly connected with *xiaokang*, while the greatest peace (*taiping*) expands upon *datong*.[24]

Kang Youwei's influence lies primarily with these connections, but there are two further relevant issues. First, the major problem to be overcome concerns the current world's many boundaries. The bulk of the work is devoted to the method of overcoming the boundaries of nation, class, race, sex, family, occupation and private ownership, unequal laws, and suffering itself. The question that arises is

---

[20] *Tong* (统) has the sense of uniting, interconnecting, and governing.

[21] My translation. Lawrence's translation (Kang 1935b) of the work as a whole is patchy at best, expanding some parts significantly while skipping large sections elsewhere, with only summaries in their place.

[22] Kang adheres closely to the texts in question, for only two terms appear in *Liji* and there is no equivalent for the age of disorder.

[23] The Chinese differs only by one small point: from 大平 (*daping*) to 太平 (*taiping*).

[24] As the argument of *The Book of Datong* proceeds, the threefold schema is reiterated on a number of occasions: disorder (*luan*), rising peace (*shengping*), and great harmony (*datong*) or greatest peace (*taiping*) (Kang 1935a, 17, 54, 65, 78–79, 92, 97–99, 124, 133–134, 136–137, 139).

whether the resulting age of *datong* is one of homogeneous commonality, without any differences. His answer is no, but he comes at the problem through competition (*jingzheng*), which is both necessary for improvement and potentially destructive. Without competition laziness ensues, but competition also leads to strife and a return to disorder. Further, if everyone receives equal pay and is equal on all counts, little incentive would be found for further innovation. Kang concludes:

> Now, the way of heaven [*tiandao*] is not peaceful; not being peaceful it is disorderly [*luan*]. The human way [*rendao*] is afflicted by the misfortunes of disorder [*luan huo*]; therefore, they decide to assist one another and make every effort to achieve peace. But having arrived at the time of peace, then misfortunes also arise! (Kang 1935a, 127)[25]

The problem concerns not only the cyclical—or better dialectical—risk that the closer one comes to *datong* the greater is the risk of chaos returning, but also the need for differences. Kang seeks a way to continue the fostering of competition and innovation, offering as a solution three criteria: striving for excellence; encouraging knowledge; and encouraging *ren*. But the very need to foster competition indicates the continued need for differences even in the era of *datong*. How such differences might relate to one another is a problem he did not solve. For that we need to await Mao Zedong and the category of non-antagonistic contradictions.

Second, assessments of Kang Youwei's overall project vary considerably. Those keen to see Kang as a preeminent reformer and visionary do so from the perspective of Western liberalism and bourgeois ideals (Hsiao 1975; Tay 2010; A. Chen 2014). The underling reason for this praise should indicate an alternative and persuasive assessment from a Chinese Marxist perspective. In this case, we find a greater emphasis on Kang's 'Western' influences (Ding 2008), particularly the liberal tradition in which bourgeois parliamentary democracy is the highest order. Indeed, Kang equates at a political level the age of *datong* with this historical form of democracy, seeing constitutional monarchy—which he advocated for China at the time—as the achievement of *xiaokang* (Lin 2001; Fang 2016). Philosophically, Kang may have espoused Confucian reformism, but this was infused with liberal idealism so that even the core category of '*ren* [仁]'—with the basic sense of 'two-person mindedness' (Sun 2014, 4)—was equated with 'universal love [*ai*]' as the condition for *datong* (Kang 1935a, 136; Hu L. 2000). Needless to say, these liberal evolutionary assumptions put Kang Youwei at odds with not merely the Republican movement of Sun Zhongshan (Yat-Sen), but especially the revolutionary Communist movement (Tong and Lin 2002, 73–74).

To sum up, while Kang Youwei's connection between the text of *Liji* and the contribution of He Xiu has been deeply influential, his legacy in China and abroad is quite mixed. Perhaps we may put it this way: Kang repeatedly deploys the four-character phrase *tianxia wei gong*, all under heaven is as common. As the short-hand definition of *datong*, the phrase is from the initial articulation of *datong* in *Liji*. But Kang's understanding of this term was very much in the imperial tradition, in which the emperor viewed all under his sway. By contrast, Sun Zhongshan (Yat-sen) also

[25] My translation.

invoked the term, but in a rather different way: he drew it towards socialism in light of the terminology found in the *Liji*, with its image of education of the young, care of the old, and appropriate work for all (Xu Y. 2014, 29). Kang Youwei and Sun Zhongshan were by no means the only ones propagating such ideas at the time. As the last imperial dynasty stumbled into oblivion and as China still felt the sting of colonial humiliation, many such ideas and their interpretations flourished. For example, another influential piece of literature was Cai Yuanpei's short story, 'New Year's Dream' (Cai 1904; see also Liu T. 2010; Li G. 2013).[26] The story, with its revolutionary tone and invocation of the Confucian three eras—as mediated by He Xiu—became widely popular, even if it was the only fictional text published by its author.

6.3.4 Mao Zedong: Datong *and Communism*

It would fall to Mao Zedong to reinterpret *datong* in light of Communism, although he was not the only one to do so. For instance, in 1925 the Communist writer Guo Moruo published a short story entitled 'Marx Enters a Confucian Temple'. It tells of a conversation between Marx and Confucius, in which Marx is asked to explain his idea of a Communist society, Marx does so, after which Confucius is unable to contain himself, clapping his hands and crying out: 'Your ideal society and my world of *datong* coincide with each other'. Thereupon, he quotes the text from *Liji* (see Sect. 6.3.1). In reply, Marx calls Confucius an old comrade (*lao tongzhi*) and observes, 'Your opinion is completely consistent with mine' (Guo M. 1925, 164, 166; see also Yan 2013).

Given this wider context, it should be no surprise that Mao Zedong also favoured the use of *datong* in his writings, although he took somewhat longer to connect it explicitly with Communism. In his pre-communist phase, he writes 'the great harmony [*datong*] is our goal'. Confucius, Mao acknowledges, explored this idea, setting up 'the great peace [*taiping*] as his goal', although he 'did not do away with the two realms of chaos [*luan*] and ascending peace [*shengping*]' (Mao 1917, 89). Clearly, the language is not that of Confucius but of He Xiu and Kang Youwei, although they both assumed that they were explicating the thought of Confucius.[27] After Mao's turn to Communism, *datong* continues to appear, although now he begins to elaborate further: acknowledging that it was a central aspect of the revolutionary

---

[26]It was first published in 1904 as 'Xinnian meng' in the magazine, *Eshi jingwen* [Alarming news about Russia], in the February issue, pages 1–20 and 24–25.

[27]In 1917, Mao could not have read Kang Youwei's *The Book of Datong*, since it was published posthumously in 1935. However, Kang had already elaborated such ideas in *Zhongyong zhu*, *Mengzi wei* and *Liyun zhu* (Kang 1987), although the ideas were relatively widespread at the time and Mao may have encountered them elsewhere, such as the work of Cai Yuanpei, author of 'A New Year's Dream' (see above). Cai became president of Beijing University, revised its educational philosophy and structure, appointed Chen Duxiu and set up the work-study program in France. Mao's notes the influence of Cai on the 'Strengthen Learning Society' (Mao 1919).

program of Sun Zhongshan (Mao 1926, 144), he observes that it must be built on the national self-determination of all Asian countries afflicted by colonialism (Mao 1920, 560). Further, the relation between a 'movement for world *datong*' and the national anti-colonial struggle in China is not a contradiction, but a dialectic in which the only way for China to participate in the international movement is through being independent and liberated (Mao 1937, 484).[28]

Finally, on the eve of liberation, Mao makes the clearest connection with Communism. Explicitly acknowledging Kang Youwei's Book of *Datong*,[29] Mao points out that Kang's reformism was unable to find a way to *datong* (Mao 1949, 1471). How does Mao define *datong*? It entails working towards the 'conditions in which classes, state power, and political parties will die out very naturally [*ziran de guiyu xiaomie*]', so that humanity can enter *datong* (Mao 1949, 1469). The allusion is to Engels's phrase, 'dying away of the state', in the third edition (1894) of the deeply influential *Anti-Dühring*: 'The state is not "abolished". It dies out [*er stirbt ab*]' (Engels 1894, 535; see further Boer, in press). But Mao also follows what was by now Marxist orthodoxy: since Lenin (1917a, 1917b) it has become received practice to distinguish between the stages of socialism and Communism. The latter may eventually lead to such a natural dying out, but socialism is a time of struggle and development, needing to deal with internal and external foes. This entails a dialectic of strengthening the state, for only when all opposition had been overcome on a global scale could one begin to move to Communism, or *datong* (Mao 1949, 1475–1476).

The reflections in Mao's 1949 text open up the role of contradiction analysis and thus dialectics.[30] There is no need to reiterate the whole framework of such analysis, since I have already done so in the third chapter, but the invocation of contradiction analysis here relates directly to Mao's engagement with Kang Youwei. As we saw earlier, Kang had been keen to avoid the abolition of all differences and competition, although he was fearful of the risks posed: the planning for *datong* may unleash forces that would lead to its undoing and thus return to chaos and disorder. While we may see this effort in terms of a nascent dialectical analysis, Kang is unable to solve the problem. For that solution he would have required the whole category of non-antagonistic contradictions, which Mao derived from the Soviet Marxist philosophy he was studying in the 1930s. Of course, he took it to a whole new level in light of the Chinese tradition, which he was able to stand on its feet in light of Marxism.

[28]Occasionally, Mao would use the term in a low-key way to designate cooperation, whether in terms of the anti-colonial struggle (Mao 1940, 676) or labour unions (Mao 1921, 6).

[29]See also a brief note from 1967, where Mao acknowledges Kang Youwei, but also the *Liyun* chapter of the *Liji* (Mao 1967, 308). As noted earlier, caution must be exercised with these Red Guard publications during the 'Cultural Revolution', since it is difficult indeed to verify the text.

[30]An intriguing foreshadowing of this development may found in Mao's pre-communist marginal notes on Friedrich Paulsen, which had been translated by none other than Cai Yuanpei. Here Mao invokes *datong* and *ping'an*, peace. But he observes that under *datong* competition (*jingzheng*) and resistance (*dikang*) would arise, so much so that an era of greatest peace would be unbearable. Cycles of order and disorder (*luan*), war and peace, are more creative and the norm (Mao 1918, 184–186). The notes on Paulsen constitute a crucial transformative period for Mao, for he would soon throw his heart into Communism.

My point here is that *datong* too would not entail an abolition of all differences and contradictions, not a utopian 'perfect world' characteristic of 'Western' traditions in which difference and struggle is overcome. Instead, contradictions would be very much present in *datong*, but they will need to be managed so as to be non-antagonistic, or—as the term itself suggests—harmonious. Perhaps it is only then that unity will prevail over the struggle of opposites, in terms of a dialectical *yangqi*, or *Aufhebung* (Bu 2016).

6.4 *Xiaokang*: From the Book of Songs (*Shijing*) to Xi Jinping

All the same, the age of *datong* is not yet, and will not be for quite some time to come. As the third era of *taiping*, as a topian *datong*, as a dialectical *Aufhebung* of the struggle of opposites, or indeed as Communism, it requires far more preparation than most are willing to admit. Would this realisation lead to disappointment, to abandoning the whole project as simply too difficult, or indeed falling into a 'Western' utopianism in which the project becomes too ideal, too unknown, and thus impossible? The Chinese tradition in particular has an answer and it was Deng Xiaoping's genius that drew upon that tradition for the sake of Marxism. Let us return to the lapidary observation from 1979: 'Later we changed the goal to "Chinese-style [*zhongguoshi*]" modernisations, intending to lower the standard a little' (Deng 1979a, 194). This Chinese style or characteristic, this slight lowering of the standard, was expressed as *xiaokang*. To understand this term, we need once again to return to the beginning of the tradition, to *The Book of Rites* no less. As we do so, it is worth noting that Mao Zedong never refers to *xiaokang* in his many writings.[31] This was Deng Xiaoping's distinct move.

*6.4.1 The Book of Rites and the Book of Songs (*Shijing*)*

The pertinent section of *Liji* is the paragraph following the one concerning *datong*. Confucius is reported to have said:

> Now the Great Way [*dadao*] has fallen into obscurity, and all under heaven is as family [*tianxia wei jia*]. Each loves only his own parents and cares only for his own children. Wealth and strength they consider to exist only for their own advantage. Hereditary succession among the great men [the lords of the land], they take to be a sufficient rite. Inner and outer walls, ditches, and moats, they take to be adequate defenses. As for the rites and duties, they think them the main structures by which to rectify relations between ruler and subject, to consolidate relations between father and son, to induce concord between elder and younger sibling, to induce loving harmony between husband and wife. By them, they set

[31] As noted above, on one occasion in 1917 Mao referred to 'ascending peace [*shengping*]', found in He Xiu and Kang Youwei, but he does not mention *xiaokang*.

> up institutions and measures; by them, they lay out fields and hamlets; by them, they judge men of courage and understanding to be worthy; by them, they consider merit to accrue to men's personal advantage. Thus selfish schemes are invented. Warfare derives also from this … This was known as the period of *xiaokang*. (translation by Nylan 2001, 196)[32]

According to this text, the difference between *datong* and *xiaokang* may be captured by the contrast between two four-character sayings: in contrast to 'all under heaven is as common [*tianxia wei gong*]', we now find 'all under heaven is as family [*tianxia wei jia*]'. For those who would charge Confucian thought with an overwhelming emphasis on (wider) family, the contrast is instructive. Under *datong*, the family is subordinate to the common good of society, even if the latter is conceived in extending family terms to the social whole. By contrast, under *xiaokang*, one focuses primarily on one's family—a lesser good, for it leads to the pursuit of personal gain, to a focus on inheritance, moats, and ditches. Ordering society according to appropriate relations between ruler and subject, elder and younger, husband and wife—all these lead not to peace, but to personal advantage (*wei ji*), scheming, and war.

Not a particularly positive image, even if this seems to be the time when Confucius promoted his ethics. Is this what Deng Xiaoping had in mind when he first invoked *xiaokang* in 1979? Perhaps not, for an even earlier text from the tenth century BCE—the *Book of Songs* (*Shijing*)—presents a somewhat different picture (Gu 2015, 62). In the section called 'The People are Hard Pressed [*Minlao*]', from Part III, Book 9, it presents five stanzas stressing the alleviation of intolerable burdens on the people. I quote the first eight characters of each stanza:

> The people indeed are heavily burdened,
> But perhaps a little ease [*xiaokang*] may be got for them.
> The people indeed are heavily burdened,
> But perhaps a little rest [*xiaoxiu*] may be got for them.
> The people indeed are heavily burdened,
> But perhaps a little relief [*xiaoxi*] may be got for them.
> The people indeed are heavily burdened,
> But perhaps a little repose [*xiaokai*] may be got for them.
> The people indeed are heavily burdened,
> But perhaps a little tranquillity [*xiao'an*] may be got for them. (translation by Legge 1871, 495–498)[33]

The purpose of quoting these lines is to indicate the meanings attached to *xiaokang*. The repetition of the lines enhances the variation, which is only with the final character. That is, each of the following stanzas begins with the exactly the same characters, with only the last character changing: *kang, xiu, xi, kai, an,* or ease, rest, relief, repose, and peace or tranquillity. Even so, to give single translations of the terms loses their richness. For example, *kang* can mean health, well-being, prosperity, and

---

[32] As with the previous quotation from *Liji*, I have followed Nylan's translation (apart from the last sentence, which I have added). One may compare those of Watson (1960, 176) and Legge (1885, 366–367), which may also be found at https://ctext.org/liji/li-yun.

[33] Legge's translation may also be found at https://ctext.org/book-of-poetry/min-lu.

peace, while *an* has the senses of peace, calm, stillness, contentment, safety, and security. The remainder of the stanzas speak of robbers and oppressors, the wily and obsequious, the unconscientious, noisy braggarts, the multitudes of evil, and the parasites—from whom the people seek at least some relief. In short, for the *Book of Songs*, *xiaokang* is clearly a distinct improvement on tough lives.

Clearly, the *Book of Songs* provides a more positive image, of people relieved from the burdens of struggle and from those seeking to deceive and rob them (rulers included). Yet, the differences between the two explications of *xiaokang* may in part be explained by their different foci: *The Book of Rites* sees this time as a decline from *datong*, while the earlier *Book of Songs* sees *xiaokang* as a noticeable improvement. Clearly, Deng Xiaoping's invocation draws more from the sense of the most ancient picture of *xiaokang*.

6.4.2 Deng Xiaoping and Xiaokang Shehui

Now we can return to the text with which I began this chapter, quoting it more fully. Deng had been asked by the Japanese prime minister, Masayoshi Ohira, concerning the four modernisations. He replied:

> The objective of achieving the four modernisations was set by Chairman Mao and Premier Zhou Enlai. The so-called four modernisations are aimed at changing the poor and backward situation in China, gradually raising the living standards of the Chinese people, restoring China to a position in international affairs commensurate with its status, and making more contributions to humankind. Backwardness will leave us vulnerable to bullying.
>
> The four modernisations we are going to achieve are those with a Chinese style [*zhongguoshi*]. Our concept of the four modernisations is not a concept of modernisation like yours, but a concept of a 'moderately well-off family [*xiaokang zhi jia*]'. Even if we realise the four modernisations by the end of this century, our per capita GNP will still be very low. If we want to reach the level of a relatively wealthy country of the Third World with a per capita GNP US $1,000 for example, we have to make an immense effort. Even if we reach that level, we will still be a backward nation compared to Western countries. However, at that point China will be a country with a moderately well-off condition [*xiaokang de zhuangtai*] and our people will enjoy a much higher standard of living than they do now…
>
> Some people are worried that if China becomes richer, it will be too competitive in world markets. Since China will be a moderately well-off country [*xiaokang de guojia*] by that time, this will not be the case. (Deng 1979i, 237–238)

Three features of this important text should be noted. To begin with, Deng sees *xiaokang* as a distinct improvement from woeful conditions. He speaks of China suffering from poverty, backwardness, and bullying, with a clear allusion to China's long humiliation at the hands of foreign powers. Such humiliation had continued after 1949, with international sanctions, destruction of new industrial facilities, and refusal to acknowledge the People's Republic. Only a few years earlier in the 1970s had the situation begun to change, suggesting that the arduous task of achieving *xiaokang* had begun.

Further, Deng uses *xiaokang* in three formulations: 'a moderately well-off family [*xiaokang zhi jia*]', 'moderately well-off condition [*xiaokang de zhuangtai*]' and 'moderately well-off country [*xiaokang de guojia*]'. The initial use of 'family [*jia*]' here is not so much an invocation of the Confucian *Liji* with its focus on the primacy of family relations during the era of *xiaokang*, when 'all under heaven was as family [*tianxia wei jia*]'; rather, *jia* stands in as a shorthand for 'country [*guojia*]'. There is also a clear reference to the popular or folk (*minjian*) understanding *xiaokang* as having enough food, clothing, and shelter (Xiao and Qiao 2018, 14–15). Thus, for Deng the concern is the country as a whole. As he puts it in 1987, the Reform and Opening-Up seeks nothing less than a '*xiaokang* China' (Deng 1987f, 226). The reinterpretation is significant, although to put it this way suggests that Deng's approach is determined by the framework of the Confucian heritage. As Lv Shuzheng emphasises (2000, 48), the concept may have come from this tradition and it may have been a phrase used among the common people, but Deng's primary framework was not Confucianism (or indeed Kang Youwei's liberal reformism), but Marxism and the long road to Communism. In this light, the Confucian tradition was stood on its feet.

Finally, Deng's concern in the text quoted above is resolutely economic. He speaks of the four modernisations (agriculture, industry, national defence, and science and technology), quadrupling output and raising per capita GNP to US $1000 (later modified to $800) by the end of the century, of making life relatively comfortable even if China would remain a relatively backward and developing country. It is precisely this primary concern that distances Deng's reinterpretation of *xiaokang* from that of Confucius in *The Book of Rites* and from Kang Youwei's liberal Confucianism (Feng 2009, 14). Instead, it is directly related to a number of systemic emphases specific to a socialist system (Huang 2017, 46) that I already identified in previous chapters: a) socialism has nothing to do with poverty; b) liberating the forces of production and economic development are crucial to the socialist project in a developing country; c) the transition to Communism requires a significant level of prosperity for all; d) the Chinese Marxist approach to human rights sees the right to economic well-being as the core (see Chapter 7), a right that remains a key driver of the Reform and Opening-Up. At the same time, Deng was fully aware that while socio-economic well-being is the basis, it is not the only criterion: as Gu Hailiang (2015, 64–65) indicates, Deng paid also close attention to what may be loosely translated as 'spiritual civilisation [*jingshen wenming*]'.[34] This term includes the intangible influence of a long tradition, as well as cultural and social life, ecological realities, and the need for peace and stability—what would later become known as 'in an all-round way [*quanmian*]' (Xu Y. 2014, 31; Xiao 2015, 63).

[34] Here translation breaks down somewhat: *jingshen* (精神) embraces what gives a culture its vitality, essence, and socio-psychological structure, while *wenming* (文明) refers not to the 'citification' entailed in 'civilisation' but the clarity of wisdom produced by a written tradition.

6.4.3 The Two Centenary Goals

Deng Xiaoping's preferred usage was 'moderately well-off level [*xiaokang shuiping*]',[35] but it was not this phrase that would enter into the lexicon of the CPC. Instead, it was a relatively minor usage by Deng, 'moderately well-off society [*xiaokang shehui*]' that would become the norm (Deng 1984a, 54; 1984b, 64; 1986c, 161; 1987b, 216; 1987f, 226; 1988, 278).[36] Even so, it was not until Jiang Zemin's speech at the sixteenth congress of the CPC in 2002 that it became part of official policy positions (Jiang Z. 2002b; see also 2002a). Jiang broke ground by using the phrase *xiaokang shehui* in the title of his speech, now adding comprehensive or 'in an all-round way [*quanmian*]'.[37] So central did the full term—well-off society in an all-round way—become that we also find it in Hu Jintao's speeches at the seventeenth and eighteenth congresses of the CPC (Hu J. 2007, 2012), and in Xi Jinping's major speech at the CPC's nineteenth congress (Xi 2017; see also 2012).

A detailed comparison of the speeches and decisions is beyond the remit of this study (Zhang H. 2015; Xiao and Qiao 2018, 14–16), save to emphasise a particular item: the gradual fixing of dates. From Deng Xiaoping's initial 'three steps'[38] to Xi Jinping's detailed clarity (Shi 2018),[39] we find the following:

2000: The achievement of basic *xiaokang*, focused on economic conditions.

2021: Attainment of a *xiaokang shehui* in an all-round way by the centenary of the founding of the CPC.

2049: A strong 'socialistically modernised country [*shehuizhuyi xiandaihua guojia*]' on the centenary of the People's Republic of China.

The Confucian three ages have been entirely reframed in terms of Marxism. Thus, rising from chaos and disorder to *xiaokang* (and ascending peace, *shengping*) becomes a significant feature of the long period of constructing socialism. But most interesting is the clear fixing of dates. Is this not unwise for politicians, who in the West routinely have the habit of failing to achieve stated goals? This clarity may be quite difficult to understand for those steeped in the Euro-American bourgeois tradition. In this tradition, politicians are wary of any targets, not merely because they know opponents will undo them at the first opportunity, but also because political

[35] So frequent is the usage that I can give only a sample of references (Deng 1980e, 259; 1980c, 356; 1982d, 417; 1984b, 64; 1984d, 77; 1984e, 88–89; 1984c, 98; 1984f, 102; 1985b, 105; 1985a, 109; 1985d, 117; 1985c, 143; 1987g, 210; 1987b, 218; 1987c, 224; 1987d, 250; 1987e, 256).

[36] On one occasion, Deng uses the full combination, 'the level of a moderately well-off society [*xiaokang shehui de shuiping*]' (Deng 1987a, 233).

[37] For a study of how the term developed, from the 'adequate food and clothing [*wenbao*]' or the basic necessities of life, through an 'overall [*zongtixing*]' *xiaokang* society', to an all-round or 'comprehensive [*quanmian*]' *xiaokang* society, see Zhang Yi (2014).

[38] While most of Deng's focus was on achievements by the turn of the century, he also spoke of 30 and 50 years into the twenty-first century in a number of steps or stages, when China would have reached the level of a moderately developed country and the superiority of socialism would become apparent (Lv 2000, 50–51; Xiao 2014; Shi 2015).

[39] The detail may be found in the three volumes published thus far of *The Governance of China*.

spin entails that one promises nothing while pretending to promise everything. More to the point, this tradition is wary indeed of any project that seems too 'utopian', too transcendent and thereby unknown and vague.

In order to understand the very different approach of the Chinese government, we need to remember not merely the great emphasis on continuity and stability of long-term plans, but even more the point first made by He Xiu: both the greatest peace (*taiping*) and ascending peace (*shengping*) are eras that can be seen and recorded. They are empirically verifiable, rather than falling into the realm of vague promises and rumour. The 'two centenary goals [*liangge yibainian*]' should be understood in this light: as the end of 2020 drew nearer, we found ever greater detail concerning what a *xiaokang shehui* in an all-round way means and what needed to be done to ensure it had been achieved. Earlier, Jiang Zemin had interpreted 'all-round way' to mean socialist democracy, the legal system, ideological and ethical standards, and sustainable development. By the time of Xi Jinping's speech in 2017, we find advanced science and education, thriving culture, greater social harmony,[40] a better quality of life, poverty alleviation, medical cover for all, improved education, and environmental health. In speech after speech, Xi Jinping continues to elaborate on what these items entail, with the ensuing resources, detailed and tailored planning,[41] implementation, and assessment. All of the many resources available have been deployed in such a process, with research, plans, assessments for the sake of improvement, and ways to deal with obstacles (Feng 2009, 13–14; Gu 2015; Zhou S. and Fu 2015; Huang 2017, 48–50; Xiao and Qiao 2018, 17–18). If one seeks to 'change the world'—as Marx famously put in his eleventh thesis on Feuerbach—then such detailed planning is necessary (Li B. 2004). For what purpose is the world to be changed? Xiao Guiqing puts it best:

> Whether a *xiaokang* society can be completed in an all-round way depends not only on the proof of the per capita data, but also on the personal experience of the broad masses of the people and their satisfaction arising from a happy life [*xinfu shenghuo*]. The ultimate goal of completing the building of a *xiaokang* society is to realise the people's all-round development, and to realise and protect the fundamental interests of the overwhelming majority of the people. (Xiao 2015, 64)

6.5 Whither *Datong*?

A final question: what has happened to *datong*, which since Mao Zedong has been reinterpreted in light of Communism? Has it been replaced by a strong socialistically modernised society, thereby relegating *datong* to an imaginary 'utopian' future? The

---

[40]It is beyond my remit to analyse here the complex meanings of security (*anquan*), harmony (*hexie*), and stability (*wending*), which run through all material since Deng Xiaoping. On the connection between *xiaokang* and harmony (*hexie*), see Liu Chunlan (2010).

[41]For example, in regional areas—such as Xinjiang—that have lagged behind due to uneven and imbalanced development, the nature of planning for a *xiaokang* society must take local conditions as the basis (Hu A. and Wang 2013).

answer lies elsewhere: socialism precedes Communism, which will take a long time indeed to achieve. Thus, the Chinese Marxist logic is that socialism includes the achievement of *xiaokang*, which is characteristic of the primary or initial stage of socialism (Fang 2016, 15). Let me put it this way: Xi Jinping has identified three core issues as markers of attaining *xiaokang*: managing profound risks, poverty alleviation, and ecological civilisation. Without these, one cannot speak of a moderately well-off, healthy, and peaceful society. With them, one may speak of a 'new era [*xin shidai*]' of socialism, a socialistically modernised society. But even this is not yet a verifiable and carefully recorded Communism.

References

Boer, Roland. In press. *Friedrich Engels and the foundations of socialist governance*. Singapore: Springer.

Bu, Desheng. 2016. Shehuizhuyi hexin jiazhiguan zhexue fenxi. *Qingdao keji daxue xuebao (shehui kexue ban)* 32 (3): 79–82.

Cai, Yuanpei. 1904. Xinnian meng. In *Cai Yuanpei quanji*, vol. 1:230–241. Beijing: Zhonghua shuju, 1984.

Chen, Albert. 2014. The concept of 'datong' in Chinese philosophy as an expression of the idea of the common good. In *The common good: Chinese and American perspectives*, ed. David Solomon and P.C. Lo, 85–102. Dordrecht: Springer.

Chen, Hui. 2016. Gongyang 'sanshi shuo' de yanjin guocheng ji qi sixiang yiyi. *Kongzi yanjiu* 2016 (2): 110–121.

Chen, Qitai. 2007. Chunqiu gongyang 'sanshishuo': dushuyizhi de lishi zhexue. *Shixue shi yanjiu* 2007 (2): 11–13.

De Bary, William Theodore, Wing-tsit Chan, and Burton Watson, trans. 1960. *Sources of Chinese tradition, volume 1*. New York: Columbia University Press.

Deng, Xiaoping. 1978a. Emancipate the mind, seek truth from facts and unite as one in looking to the future (13 December 1978). In *Selected works of Deng Xiaoping*, vol. 2:150–163. Beijing: Foreign Languages Press, 1995.

Deng, Xiaoping. 1978b. Gongren jieji yao wei shixian si ge xiandaihua zuochu youyi gongxian (1978.10.11). In *Deng Xiaoping wenxuan*, vol. 2:134–139. Beijing: Renmin chubanshe, 2008.

Deng, Xiaoping. 1978c. Jiefang sixiang, shishiqiushi, tuanjieyizhi xiangqian kan (1978.12.13). In *Deng Xiaoping wenxuan*, vol. 2:140–153. Beijing: Renmin chubanshe, 2008.

Deng, Xiaoping. 1978d. Realise the four modernisations and never seek hegemony (7 May 1978). In *Selected works of Deng Xiaoping*, vol. 2:122–123. Beijing: Foreign Languages Press, 1995.

Deng, Xiaoping. 1978e. Shixian sihua, yongbu chengba (1978.05.07). In *Deng Xiaoping wenxuan*, vol. 2:111–112. Beijing: Renmin chubanshe, 2008.

Deng, Xiaoping. 1978f. Speech at the opening ceremony of the national conference on science (18 March 1978). In *Selected works of Deng Xiaoping*, vol. 2:98–111. Beijing: Foreign Languages Press, 1995.

Deng, Xiaoping. 1978g. The working class should make outstanding contributions to the four modernisations (11 October 1978). In *Selected works of Deng Xiaoping*, vol. 2:145–149. Beijing: Foreign Languages Press, 1995.

Deng, Xiaoping. 1978h. Zai quanguo kexue dahui kaimushi shang de jianghua (1978.03.18). In *Deng Xiaoping wenxuan*, vol. 2:85–100. Beijing: Renmin chubanshe, 2008.

Deng, Xiaoping. 1979a. Guanyu jingji gongzuo de jidian yijian (1979.10.04). In *Deng Xiaoping wenxuan*, vol. 2:194–202. Beijing: Renmin chubanshe, 2008.

Deng, Xiaoping. 1979b. Jianchi sixiang jiben yuanze (1979.03.30). In *Deng Xiaoping wenxuan*, vol. 2:158–184. Beijing: Renmin chubanshe, 2008.
Deng, Xiaoping. 1979c. Shehuizhuyi ye keyi gao shichang jingji (1979.11.26). In *Deng Xiaoping wenxuan*, vol. 2:231–236. Beijing: Renmin chubanshe, 2008.
Deng, Xiaoping. 1979d. Some comments on economic work (4 October 1979). In *Selected works of Deng Xiaoping*, vol. 2:201–208. Beijing: Foreign Languages Press, 1995.
Deng, Xiaoping. 1979e. Speech greeting the fourth congress of Chinese writers and artists (30 October 1979). In *Selected works of Deng Xiaoping*, vol. 2:213–219. Beijing: Foreign Languages Press, 1995.
Deng, Xiaoping. 1979f. Uphold the four cardinal principles (30 March 1979). In *Selected works of Deng Xiaoping*, vol. 2:168–191. Beijing: Foreign Languages Press, 1995.
Deng, Xiaoping. 1979g. We can develop a market economy under socialism (26 November 1979). In *Selected works of Deng Xiaoping*, vol. 2:235–239. Beijing: Foreign Languages Press, 1995.
Deng, Xiaoping. 1979h. Zai Zhongguo wenxue yishu gongzuozhe disici daibiao dahui shang de zhici (1979.10.30). In *Deng Xiaoping wenxuan*, vol. 2:207–214. Beijing: Renmin chubanshe, 2008.
Deng, Xiaoping. 1979i. Zhongguo ben shiji de mubiao shi shixian xiaokang (1979.12.06). In *Deng Xiaoping wenxuan*, vol. 2:237–238. Beijing: Renmin chubanshe, 2008.
Deng, Xiaoping. 1980a. Adhere to the party line and improve methods of work (29 February 1980). In *Selected works of Deng Xiaoping*, vol. 2:273–282. Beijing: Foreign Languages Press, 1995.
Deng, Xiaoping. 1980b. Dang he guojia lingdao zhidu gaige (1980.08.18). In *Deng Xiaoping wenxuan*, vol. 2:320–343. Beijing: Renmin chubanshe, 1995.
Deng, Xiaoping. 1980c. Guanche tiaozheng fangzhen, baozheng anding tuanjie (1980.12.25). In *Deng Xiaoping wenxuan*, vol. 2:354–374. Beijing: Renmin chubanshe, 2008.
Deng, Xiaoping. 1980d. Jianchi dang de luxian, gaijin gongzuo fangfa (1980.02.29). In *Deng Xiaoping wenxuan*, vol. 2:274–283. Beijing: Renmin chubanshe, 2008.
Deng, Xiaoping. 1980e. Muqian de xingshi he renwu (1980.01.16). In *Deng Xiaoping wenxuan*, vol. 2:239–273. Beijing: Renmin chubanshe, 2008.
Deng, Xiaoping. 1980f. On the reform of the system of party and state leadership (18 August 1980). In *Selected works of Deng Xiaoping*, vol. 2:319–341. Beijing: Foreign Languages Press, 1995.
Deng, Xiaoping. 1980g. Shehuizhuyi shouxian yao fazhan shengchanli (1980.04.05). In *Deng Xiaoping wenxuan*, vol. 2:311–314. Beijing: Renmin chubanshe, 1995.
Deng, Xiaoping. 1980h. The present situation and the tasks before us (16 January 1980). In *Selected works of Deng Xiaoping*, vol. 2:241–272. Beijing: Foreign Languages Press, 1995.
Deng, Xiaoping. 1980i. To build socialism we must first develop the productive forces (April–May 1980). In *Selected works of Deng Xiaoping*, vol. 2:310–313. Beijing: Foreign Languages Press, 1995.
Deng, Xiaoping. 1982a. China's foreign policy (21 August 1982). In *Selected works of Deng Xiaoping*, vol. 2:407–409. Beijing: Foreign Languages Press, 1995.
Deng, Xiaoping. 1982b. Combat economic crime (10 April 1982). In *Selected works of Deng Xiaoping*, vol. 2:394–396. Beijing: Foreign Languages Press, 1995.
Deng, Xiaoping. 1982c. Jianjue daji jingji fanzui yundong (1982.04.10). In *Deng Xiaoping wenxuan*, vol. 2:402–404. Beijing: Renmin chubanshe, 1995.
Deng, Xiaoping. 1982d. Zhongguo de duiwai zhengce (1982.08.21). In *Deng Xiaoping wenxuan*, 2:415–417. Beijing: Renmin chubanshe, 2008.
Deng, Xiaoping. 1984a. Fazhan zhongri guanxi yao kan de yuan xie (1984.03.25). In *Deng Xiaoping wenxuan*, vol. 3:53–55. Beijing: Renmin chubanshe, 2008.
Deng, Xiaoping. 1984b. Jianshe you Zhongguo tese de shehuizhuyi (1984.06.30). In *Deng Xiaoping wenxuan*, vol. 3:62–66. Beijing: Renmin chubanshe, 2008.
Deng, Xiaoping. 1984c. Jundui yao fucong zhengge guojia jianshe daju (1984.11.01). In *Deng Xiaoping wenxuan*, vol. 3:98–100. Beijing: Renmin chubanshe, 2008.
Deng, Xiaoping. 1984d. Women de hongwei mubiao he genben zhengce (1984.10.06). In *Deng Xiaoping wenxuan*, vol. 3:77–80. Beijing: Renmin chubanshe, 2008.

Deng, Xiaoping. 1984e. Zai zhongyang guwen weiyuanhui disanci quanti huiyi shang de jianghua (1984.10.22). In *Deng Xiaoping wenxuan*, vol. 3:83–93. Beijing: Renmin chubanshe, 2008.

Deng, Xiaoping. 1984f. Zhongguoshi xinshou nuoyan de (1984.12.19). In *Deng Xiaoping wenxuan*, vol. 3:101–103. Beijing: Renmin chubanshe, 2008.

Deng, Xiaoping. 1985a. Gaige keji tizhi shi weile jiefang shengchanli (1985.03.07). In *Deng Xiaoping wenxuan*, vol. 3:107–109. Beijing: Renmin chubanshe, 2008.

Deng, Xiaoping. 1985b. Heping he fazhan shi dangdai shijie de liang da wenti (1985.03.04). In *Deng Xiaoping wenxuan*, vol. 3:104–106. Beijing: Renmin chubanshe, 2008.

Deng, Xiaoping. 1985c. Zai Zhongguo gongchandang quanguo daibiao huiyi shang de jianghua (1985.09.23). In *Deng Xiaoping wenxuan*, vol. 3:141–147. Beijing: Renmin chubanshe, 2008.

Deng, Xiaoping. 1985d. Zhengzhi shang fazhan minzhu, jingji shang shixing gaige (1985.04.15). In *Deng Xiaoping wenxuan*, vol. 3:115–118. Beijing: Renmin chubanshe, 2008.

Deng, Xiaoping. 1986a. Da Meiguo jizhi Maike Hualaishi wen (1986.09.02). In *Deng Xiaoping wenxuan*, vol. 3:167–175. Beijing: Renmin chubanshe, 2008.

Deng, Xiaoping. 1986b. Replies to the American TV correspondent Mike Wallace (2 September 1986). In *Selected works of Deng Xiaoping*, vol. 3:170–177. Beijing: Foreign Languages Press, 1994.

Deng, Xiaoping. 1986c. Zhengqu zhengge zhonghua minzu de da tuanjie (1986.09.23). In *Deng Xiaoping wenxuan*, vol. 3:161–162. Beijing: Renmin chubanshe, 2008.

Deng, Xiaoping. 1987a. Gaige kaifang shi Zhongguo zhenzheng huoyue qilai (1987.05.12). In *Deng Xiaoping wenxuan*, vol. 3:232–235. Beijing: Renmin chubanshe, 2008.

Deng, Xiaoping. 1987b. Huijian Xianggang tebie xingzhengqu jibenfa qicao weiyuanhui weiyuan shi de jianghua (1987.04.16). In *Deng Xiaoping wenxuan*, vol. 3:215–222. Beijing: Renmin chubanshe, 2008.

Deng, Xiaoping. 1987c. Shehuizhuyi bixu baituo pinqiong (1987.04.26). In *Deng Xiaoping wenxuan*, vol. 3:223–225. Beijing: Renmin chubanshe, 2008.

Deng, Xiaoping. 1987d. Woguo fangzhen zhengce de liang ge jiben dian (1987.07.04). In *Deng Xiaoping wenxuan*, vol. 3:248–250. Beijing: Renmin chubanshe, 2008.

Deng, Xiaoping. 1987e. Women gan de shiye shi quanxin de shiye (1987.10.13). In *Deng Xiaoping wenxuan*, vol. 3:253–257. Beijing: Renmin chubanshe, 2008.

Deng, Xiaoping. 1987f. Xiqu lishi jingyan, fangzhi cuowu qingxiang (1987.04.30). In *Deng Xiaoping wenxuan*, vol. 3:226–229. Beijing: Renmin chubanshe, 2008.

Deng, Xiaoping. 1987g. You lingdao you zhixu de jinxing shehuizhuyi jianshe (1987.03.08). In *Deng Xiaoping wenxuan*, vol. 3:210–212. Beijing: Renmin chubanshe, 2008.

Deng, Xiaoping. 1988. Zhongyang yao you quanwei (1988.09.12). In *Deng Xiaoping wenxuan*, vol. 3:277–278. Beijing: Renmin chubanshe, 2008.

Ding, Tao. 2008. Kang Youwei zhengzhi sixiang lilu ji jiagou zhi tantao. *Tonghua shifan xueyuan xuebao* 29 (11): 4–7.

Engels, Friedrich. 1894. *Herrn Eugen Dührings Umwälzung der Wissenschaft. 3. Auflage*. In *Marx Engels Gesamtausgabe*, vol. I:27:485–538. Berlin: Dietz, 1988.

Fang, Ying. 2016. Deng Xiaoping xiaokang shehui sixiang de lilun yuanyuan ji dangdai jiazhi. *Lilun guancha* 2016 (10): 14–16.

Feng, Feilong. 2009. Deng Xiaoping xiaokang shehui sixiang yu quanmian jianshe xiaokang shehui lujing xuanze. *Makesizhuyi lilun yanjiu* 2009 (5): 13–15.

Gao, Jiyi, and Chen Xubo. 2014. Lun dong, He de 'sanshi yi ci' shuo. *Anhui daxue xuebao (zhexue shehui kexue ban)* 2014 (1): 36–45.

Gu, Hailiang. 2015. Deng Xiaoping 'xiaokang shehui' sixiang de kexue chansi jiqi yiyi. *Deng Xiaoping yanjiu* 2015 (2): 60–69.

Guo, Moruo. 1925. Makesi jin wenmiao. In *Guo Moruo quanji*, vol. 10:161–168. Beijing: Renmin wenxue chubanshe, 1985.

Guo, Xiaojun. 2016. Lun rujia zhexue de lunli jingshen – yi 'neizaichaoyue' wei shijie. *Jiangsu shehui kexue* 2016 (6): 31–36.

Han, Yaguang. 2006. Zhou Enlai yu si ge xiandaihua mubiao de tichu. *Dangdai zhongguo shi yanjiu* 2006 (1): 65–70, 126.

Hsiao, Kung-chuan. 1975. *A modern China and a new world: K'ang Yu-wei, reformer and utopian, 1858–1927*. Seattle: University of Washington Press.

Hu, Angang, and Wang Hongchuan. 2013. Quanmian jiancheng xiaokang shehui de zhanlüe xuanze – yi Xinjiang weili. *Xinjiang shifan daxue xuebao (zhexue shehui kexue ban)* 34 (4): 1–10.

Hu, Jintao. 2007. *Gaoju zhongguo tese shehuizhuyi weida qizhi, wei daoqu quanmian jianshe xiaokang shehui shengli er fendou (2007.10.15)*. Beijing: Renmin chubanshe.

Hu, Jintao. 2012. *Jianding bu yi yanzhe Zhongguo tese shehui zhuyi daolu, qianjin wei quanmian jiancheng xiaokang shehui er fendou (2012.11.08)*. Beijing: Renmin chubanshe.

Hu, Liangqiong. 2000. Kang Youwei 'shehui datong sixiang' de zhexue fenxi. *Hubei daxue chengren jiaoyu xueyuan xuebao* 18 (3): 13–17.

Huang, Zhibin. 2017. Lun Deng Xiaoping xiaokang shehui jianshe sixiang yu quanmian xiaokang shehui de jiancheng. *Deng Xiaoping yanjiu* 2017 (5): 44–50.

Jiang, Qing. 1995. *Gongyangxue yinlun*. Shenyang: Liaoning jiaoyu chubanshe.

Jiang, Zemin. 2002a. Mingque tichu quanmian jianshe xiaokang shehui de mubiao (2002.01.14). In *Jiang Zemin wenxuan*, vol. 3:413–417. Beijing: Renmin chubanshe, 2006.

Jiang, Zemin. 2002b. Quanmian jianshe xiaokang shehui, kaichuang Zhongguo tese shehuizhuyi shiye xin jumian (2002.11.08). In *Jiang Zemin wenxuan*, vol. 3:528–575. Beijing: Renmin chubanshe, 2006.

Kang, Youwei. 1935a. *Datongshu*. Beijing: Zhongguo renmin daxue chubanshe, 2010.

Kang, Youwei. 1935b. *Ta T'ung Shu: The one-world philosophy of K'ang Yu-wei*. Translated by Lawrence Thompson. London: Routledge, 1958.

Kang, Youwei. 1987. *Kang Youwei xueshu zhuzuo xuan: Mengzi wei; Liyun zhu; Zhongyong zhu*. Beijing: Zhonghua shuju.

Legge, James. 1871. *The Chinese classics: Vol. 4, Part 2: The She King, or the book of poetry*. Hong Kong: London Missionary Society.

Legge, James. 1885. *The sacred books of China: The texts of Confucianism. Part III: The Li Ki, I-IX*. Oxford: Clarendon.

Lenin, V. I. 1917a. Gosudarstvo i revoliutsiia. Uchenie marksizma o gosudarstve i zadachi proletariata v revoliutsii. Avgust–sentiabr′ 1917g.; ranee 17 dekabria 1918g. In *Polnoe sobranie sochinenii*, vol. 33:1–120. Moscow: Izdatel'stvo politicheskoi literatury, 1969.

Lenin, V. I. 1917b. The state and revolution: The Marxist theory of the state and the tasks of the proletariat in the revolution. In *Collected works*, vol. 25:385–497. Moscow: Progress Publishers, 1964.

Li, Bing. 2004. Quanmian jianshe xiaokang shehui yu gaibian shijie de makesizhuyi zhexue. *Zhonggong Yunnan shengwei dangxiao xuebao* 5 (4): 38–40.

Li, Guanyi. 2013. 'New year's dream': A Chinese anarcho-cosmopolitan utopia. *Utopian Studies* 24 (1): 89–104.

Li, Jing. 2013. 'Chunqiu gongyangzhuan' zhi sanshi. *Chang'an daxue xuebao (shehui kexue ban)* 15 (4): 58–63.

Li, Xueqin, and Ma Xinmin (eds.). 1999. *Shisan Jing zhushu: Chunqiu gongyangzhuan zhushu*. Beijing: Beijing daxue chubanshe.

Lin, Jiling. 2001. Kang Youwei dui gongyang sanshishuo de gaizao. *Guanzi xuekan* 2001 (3): 86–90.

Liu, Chunlan. 2010. Cong xiaokang dao hexie – Zhongguo tese shehuizhuyi xiandaihua mubiao moshi de chuangxin. *Qianyan* 2010 (21): 27–30.

Liu, Tao. 2010. Yi xiaoshuo wei zhongguo lifa – Cai Yuanpei 'xinnian meng' jie. *Hanyu yan wenxue yanjiu* 2010 (4): 64–70.

Lv, Shuzheng. 2000. Deng Xiaoping xiaokang shehui sixiang de kexue neihan. *Dang de wenxian* 2000 (2): 47–52.

Mao, Zedong. 1917. Zhi Li Jinxi xin (1917.08.23). In *Mao Zedong zaoqi wengao, 1912.6-1920.11*, 84–91. Changsha: Hunan chubanshe, 1990.

Mao, Zedong. 1918. 'Lunlixue yuanli' pizhu (1917–1918). In *Mao Zedong zaoqi wengao, 1912.6-1920.11*, 116–285. Changsha: Hunan chubanshe, 1990.

Mao, Zedong. 1919. Jian xuehui zhi chengli ji jinxing (1919.07.21). In *Mao Zedong zaoqi wengao, 1912.6-1920.11*, 362–372. Changsha: Hunan chubanshe, 1990.

Mao, Zedong. 1920. Zhi Zhang Guoji xin (1920.11.25). In *Mao Zedong zaoqi wengao, 1912.6-1920.11*, 559–561. Changsha: Hunan chubanshe, 1990.

Mao, Zedong. 1921. Suo xiwang yu laogonghui de (1921.11.21). In *Mao Zedong wenji*, vol. 1:6–7. Beijing: Renmin chubanshe, 2009.

Mao, Zedong. 1926. Guomindang youpai fenli de yuanyin ji qi duiyu geming qiantu de yingxiang (1926.01.10). In *Mao Zedong ji, Bujuan*, edited by Takeuchi Minoru, 2:143–149. Tokyo: Sōsōsha, 1983–1986.

Mao, Zedong. 1937. Zhongri wenti yu Xi'an shibian – he Shimotelai tanhua (1937.03.01). In *Mao Zedong wenji*, vol. 1:479–494. Beijing: Renmin chubanshe, 2009.

Mao, Zedong. 1940. Xin minzhuzhuyi lun (1940.01.15). In *Mao Zedong xuanji*, vol. 2:662–711. Beijing: Renmin chubanshe, 2009.

Mao, Zedong. 1949. Lun renmin minzhu zhuanzheng: jinian Zhongguo gongchandang ershi ba zhounian (1949.06.30). In *Mao Zedong xuanji*, vol. 4:1468–1482. Beijing: Renmin chubanshe, 2009.

Mao, Zedong. 1954a. Guanyu Zhonghua renmin gongheguo xianfa cao'an (1954.06.14). In *Mao Zedong wenji*, vol. 6:324–331. Beijing: Renmin chubanshe, 2009.

Mao, Zedong. 1954b. On the draft constitution of the People's Republic of China (14 June 1954). In *Selected works of Mao Tse-Tung*, vol. 5:141–147. Beijing: Foreign Languages Press, 1977.

Mao, Zedong. 1957a. Guanyu zhengque chuli renmin neibu maodun de wenti (1957.02.27). In *Mao Zedong wenji*, vol. 7:204–244. Beijing: Renmin chubanshe, 2009.

Mao, Zedong. 1957b. On the correct handling of contradictions among the people (27 February 1957). In *Selected works of Mao Tse-Tung*, vol. 5:384–421. Beijing: Foreign Languages Press, 1977.

Mao, Zedong. 1960. Zhong Ni bianjie yao yongyuan heping youhao (1960.03.18). In *Mao Zedong wenji*, vol. 8:155–162. Beijing: Renmin chubanshe, 2009.

Mao, Zedong. 1967. Dui 'Hongqi' zazhi, 'Renmin ribao' liang bianjibu yijiuliuqi nian wuyue bari wenzhang '(Xiuyang) de yaohai shi beipan wuchan jieji zhuanzhang' yiwen suo jia de liang duan hua (1967.05.09). In *Mao Zedong sixiang wansui*, vol. 5:308. n. p.: Hongweibing.

Nylan, Michael. 2001. *The five 'Confucian' classics*. New Haven: Yale University Press.

Ren, Jiantao. 2012. Neizaichaoyue yu waizaichaoyue: zongjiao xinyang, duode xinnian yu zhixu wenti. *Zhongguo shehui kexue* 2012 (7): 26–46.

Shen, Shunfu. 2015. Shengcun yu chaoyue: lun Zhongguo zhexue de jiben tedian. *Xueshujie* 2015 (1): 151–160.

Shi, Zhongquan. 2015. Deng Xiaoping 'san bu zou' fazhan zhanlüe yu dang de san da lishi zhongren. *Deng Xiaoping yanjiu* 2015 (1): 24–33.

Shi, Zhongquan. 2018. Xinshidai xin zhengcheng lishi yuanqi he zhanlüe anpai. *Dangshi yu wenxian yanjiu* 2018 (1): 28–32.

Sun, Pinghua. 2014. *Human rights protection system in China*. Heidelberg: Springer.

Tay, Wei Leong. 2010. Kang Youwei, The Martin Luther of Confucianism and his vision of Confucian modernity and nation. In *Secularization, religion and the state*, ed. Masahi Haneda, 97–109. Tokyo: University of Tokyo Center for Philosophy.

Tong, Xigang, and Lin Jikuo. 2002. Gongyang sanshishuo zhi bianyi yu gaizao. *Qilu wenhua yanjiu* 2002 (1): 69–74.

Wang, Gaoxin. 2007. He Xiu de gongyang 'sanshi' shuo de lilun goujian. *Shaanxi shifan daxue xuebao (zhexue shehui kexue ban)* 36 (1): 21–26.

Wong, Young-tsu. 2000. Philosophical hermeneutics and political reform: A study of Kang Youwei's use of Gongyang Confucianism. In *Classics and interpretations: The hermeneutic traditions in Chinese culture*, ed. Tu Ching-i, 383–407. New Brunswick: Transaction.

Xi, Jinping. 2012. Jinjin weirao jianchi he fazhan Zhongguo tese shehuizhuyi, xuexi xuanchuan guanche dang de shibada jingshen (2012.11.17). In *Tan zhiguolizheng*, vol. 1:6–20. Beijing: Waiwen chubanshe, 2014.

Xi, Jinping. 2017. *Juesheng quanmian jiancheng xiaokang shehui, duoqu xinshidai Zhongguo tese shehuizhuyi weida shengli (2017.10.18)*. Beijing: Renmin chubanshe.

Xiao, Guiqing. 2014. Deng Xiaoping xiaokang sixiang yu dangdai Zhongguo xiandaihua fazhan zhanlüe. *Shandong shehui kexue* 2014 (9): 38–42, 135.

Xiao, Guiqing. 2015. Quanmian jianshe xiaokang shehui de neihan, zhanlüe diwei he zhidu baozhang. *Sixiang lilun jiaoyu dao kan* 2015 (9): 62–67.

Xiao, Guiqing, and Qiao Huibo. 2018. Gaige kaifang 40 nian yu xiaokang shehui jianshe. *Makesizhuyi zhongguohua yanjiu* 2018 (5): 14–22.

Xu, Liang, and Wang Qingyu. 2008. Gongyang sanshishuo zhi liubian. *Yanshan daxue xuebao (zhexue shehui kexue ban)* 9 (2): 21–24.

Xu, Tao. 2016. Zhongxi zhexue huitong shiyu zhong de 'neizaichaoyue' yu 'tianren heyi'. *Xueshu yuekan* 2016 (6): 166–176.

Xu, Xuetao. 2011. He Xiu gongyang sanshishuo jiqi jie jing fangfa. *Xueshu yanjiu* 2011 (4): 22–28.

Xu, Youlong. 2014. Deng Xiaoping xiaokang shehui sixiang de lishi yuanyuan jiqi quanmianxing. *Guancha yu sikao* 2014 (3): 28–31.

Xu, Zhenqiu, and Chen Shisong. 1998. Shi lun Zhou Enlai dui Zhongguo si ge xiandaihua de lilun gongxian. In *Zhou Enlai bai zhounian jinian – quanguo Zhou Enlai shengping he sixiang yantaohui lun wenji (shang)*, 432–446. Beijing: Zhongyang wenxian chubanshe.

Yan, Lianjun. 2013. 1925, Makesi yu Kongzi duihua – yi Guo Moruo xiaoshuo 'Makesi jin wenmiao' wei zhongxin. *Xiandai zhongwen xuekan* 2013 (1): 16–26.

Zhang, Hui. 2015. Shilun quanmian jianshe xiaokang shehui de zhanlüe mubiao. *Shandong shehui kexue* 2015 (7): 24–29.

Zhang, Yi. 2014. Cong 'xiaokang shehui' dao 'Zhongguo meng'. *Hebei shehui kexue* 2014 (11): 5–11.

Zhou, Enlai. 1954a. Ba woguo jianshe chengwei qiangda de shehuizhuyi de xiandaihua de gongye guojia (1954.09.23). In *Zhou Enlai wenji*, vol. 2:132–145. Beijing: Renmin chubanshe, 1980.

Zhou, Enlai. 1954b. Turning China into a powerful, modern, socialist, industrialized Country (23 September 1954). In *Selected works of Zhou Enlai*, vol. 2:142–154. Beijing: Foreign Languages Press, 1989.

Zhou, Enlai. 1959. Muqian shehuizhuyi jianshe si xiang renwu (1959.12.24). In *Zhou Enlai jingji wenxuan*, 403–408. Beijing: Zhongyang wenxian chubanshe, 1993.

Zhou, Enlai. 1963a. Jiancheng shehuizhuyi zuguo, guanjian zaiyu shixian kexue jishu xiandaihua (1963.01.29). In *Zhou Enlai wenji*, vol. 2:407–411. Beijing: Renmin chubanshe, 1980.

Zhou, Enlai. 1963b. The key to building a powerful socialist country is to modernize science and technology (29 January 1963). In *Selected works of Zhou Enlai*, vol. 2:427–431. Beijing: Foreign Languages Press, 1989.

Zhou, Enlai. 1964a. Fazhan guomin jingji de zhuyao renwu (1964.12.21). In *Zhou Enlai wenji*, vol. 2:433–436. Beijing: Renmin chubanshe, 1980.

Zhou, Enlai. 1964b. Major tasks for developing the national economy (21 December 1964). In *Selected works of Zhou Enlai*, vol. 1:458–461. Beijing: Foreign Languages Press, 1989.

Zhou, Enlai. 1975a. Marching forward to the splendid goal of the four modernizations (13 January 1975). In *Selected works of Zhou Enlai*, vol. 1:504. Beijing: Foreign Languages Press, 1989.

Zhou, Enlai. 1975b. Xiang si ge xiandaihua de hongwei mubiao qianjin (1975.01.13). In *Zhou Enlai wenji*, vol. 2:452. Beijing: Renmin chubanshe, 1980.

Zhou, Enlai. 1993. *Zhou Enlai jingji wenxuan*. Beijing: Zhongyang wenxian chubanshe.

Zhou, Sijun, and Fu Weihong. 2015. Dao 2020 neng woguo quanmian jiancheng xiaokang shehui ma? *Jingji shuxue* 32 (1): 58–64.

Chapter 7
The Chinese Marxist Approach to Sovereignty and Human Rights

7.1 Opening Remarks

> The history of the Communist Party of China is the history of its struggle for human rights on behalf of Chinese people. (Sun P. 2014, 56)

Although human rights are considered in China as a component of the overall socialist democratic system (the concern of the next chapter), they also comprise a topic on their own. I have opted for the latter approach in this chapter. One reason for doing so is that the Chinese approach to human rights reveals very clearly the role of Marxism; another reason, of course, is that since the 1980s 'human rights' have become an obsession by a small number of Western countries in relation to any country that does not follow the Western liberal view of the world. Immediately, this point raises the question: what 'human rights'?

In answering this question, I distinguish between two approaches to human rights: one is the Western liberal tradition, which is based on individual mastery over private property, leads to a core concern with civil and political rights, and has an end-run in identity politics; another is the Chinese Marxist approach, which has its prerequisite in anti-hegemonic (or anti-colonial) sovereignty, entailing non-interference by other countries. This prerequisite leads to the core right of socio-economic well-being, from which flow civil, political, cultural, and environmental rights. Obviously, this chapter differs from the others in that it presents a contrast between Western and Chinese approaches. I do so to highlight the distinct contribution of a Marxist approach to human rights, primarily because this approach is not so well known in some other parts of the world.

In order to explicate this argument, the chapter has four parts. The first part introduces the distinction between false and rooted universals. A false universal forgets the conditions of its emergence and asserts that its assumptions apply to all irrespective of context, while a rooted universal is always conscious of and factors into analysis contextual origins, with their possibilities and limitations. With this distinction in mind, the next part deals with the Western European approach to human

R. Boer, *Socialism with Chinese Characteristics*,
https://doi.org/10.1007/978-981-16-1622-8_7

rights, not in terms of a false universal (which it always risks becoming), but as a rooted universal with its own history of emergence, possibilities, and limitations. This approach is predicated on an individual's mastery over private property (in which slavery plays an initial and not insignificant role), so much so that the civil and political rights that became a hallmark of this Western tradition are inevitably seen as forms of individual private property.

The third and fourth parts of the presentation are closely related, for they seek to explicate precisely what a Chinese Marxist approach to human rights entails. This requires a treatment of state sovereignty, initially with regard to Europe. The standard narrative of this development has two main phases: the initial Westphalian definition (1648) and its significant restriction after the Second World War. The main problem with this narrative is that it largely neglects what drove the shift: the success of anti-colonial struggles in the first half of the twentieth century. In light of this global perspective, it becomes clear that in formerly colonised and semi-colonised countries the definition of sovereignty is transformed into a quite distinct anti-colonial and anti-hegemonic form—a form that resists the efforts of former colonial powers to assert their dominance by other means. This discussion of anti-hegemonic sovereignty leads us to the Chinese Marxist approach to human rights, for which such sovereignty is a prerequisite. This situation produces a distinct rooted universal in which the right to socio-economic well-being is the core human right. I track the development of this emphasis through Hegel, Marx and Engels, the Soviet Union, and then into China, while also noting the contribution of the Chinese tradition. In order to explicate what this core human right means, I recast a number of policies so as to highlight the way they are underpinned by the drive to socio-economic well-being: liberating the forces of production; poverty alleviation; Belt and Road Initiative; and minority nationalities policy. I close by asking how civil, political, cultural, and environmental rights relate to the right to socio-economic well-being, and how the two rooted universals—the Western and the Chinese—emerge in key statements from the United Nations.

7.2 On Universals, False and Rooted

7.2.1 False Universals

To begin with a story (Bell 2006, 1–2): in 2002, the United States' legal theorist Ronald Dworkin gave a series of lectures in China on human rights, having been invited by Chinese universities and scholars keen for mutual learning between 'East' and 'West'. Addressing crowded lecture rooms, Dworkin began by 'conceding' that the terminology of 'human rights' is uniquely European, but he suggested that the specific history of the idea is irrelevant to its normative and universal status. Not only do such human rights concern civil and political rights, but they are also underpinned by the individual values of moral equality and self-direction. Dworkin then challenged his audience to produce 'Asian values' that might contribute to civil and political rights. The audience remained silent, confirming the visitor's assumption that no such 'values' could be found. Yet Dworkin felt that his lectures were a raging success, based on the numbers attending and the praise of his hosts. Nothing could have been further from the truth. The hosts and audiences may have given him due deference as a 'famous scholar', but they found him distinctly rude and hectoring. They had hoped for genuine engagement, some robust self-criticism and a desire to listen to other perspectives. Instead, Dworkin appeared as an uncritical spokesperson for Euro-American values, using this platform to judge the rest of the world.

What went wrong? Dworkin manifested a common move by those immersed in liberal Western contexts. It may be called a false universal. By this is not meant that it is false to universalise—or find common ground—from a specific situation. Instead, it is false to universalise by means of neglecting or denying the specific context in which a universal arises, asserting that it is absolute, singular, unchangeable, and applicable to all situations. False universals most often arise in the context of a hegemonic power, most typically those that were involved in European colonialism from the fifteenth century onward. Through colonial conquest and the imposition of a distinct framework on those colonised (Hou 2014, 121–124), the first steps to a false universal are made. Specific ideas relating to forms of governance, culture, and human nature become assumed norms, promoted as 'universal' and 'abstract' in a way that entails discarding the context in which they arose.[1] By now we can see the trap into which Dworkin fell. He is one of many who assume that the Western liberal tradition's concern with civil and political rights constitutes 'human rights' per se, without taking into account the way such an assumption has been shaped by this tradition through education, social formation, culture, and a history of colonialism.

7.2.2 Rooted Universals

To this false universal we may contrast a rooted universal, or contextualised commonality. Once again, contradiction analysis (Chapter 3) comes to the fore: it is not a case of either universality or particularity, but that a universal can be a universal only through its particularity. Thus, a rooted universal always factors into account its specific genesis and the conditions under which it arose. Only when this happens is it a genuine universal. This is not to say that the universal in question is relativised—an either-or opposition (Sun P. 2014, 132–135)—but that a universal can be so when its history, conditions, and specificity are present in the very nature of its universality.

I have drawn this concept from the work of the philosopher Sun Xiangchen,[2] who seeks to avoid the dual trap of hegemonic universalism and a regionalism that rejects such universalism. The background to this argument is the concept of a 'dual

[1] Sun Xiangchen argues that a crucial part of the process was a rationalisation of these specific developments so that they could assume the mantle of a universal (Sun X. and Lu 2017, 182).

[2] Sun Xiangshen, of Fudan University, initially proposed this concept to me in a conversion some years ago, which led me to engage in careful research of his writings.

ontology [*shuangchong benti*]', which Sun defines as containing two related problems (Sun X. 2015; Sun X. and Lu 2017, 179). The first is between ancient and modern, which so often boils down to debates over whether to negate the classical in light of the modern, or vice versa. The second is closely related and very pertinent in China: adopting Western 'centralism [*zhongxinzhuyi*]' or 'universalism [*pubianxing*]'—which is often equated with 'modernity'—and having contempt for local traditions; or adopting 'selfish departmentalism [*benweizhuyi*]' and rejecting the modern world. The problem with the latter, whether one finds it in Europe, China, or in other traditions, is that the perspective remains limited and unable to speak outside its own situation.[3]

Further, through many years of in-depth research into the Western and Chinese traditions of philosophy, Sun Xiangchen has argued for the both the contextual differences of traditions and the need to seek commonalities. For example, the contextual reality of the West includes the inescapable roles of Christianity and Judaism, which have shaped—through a process of secularising rationalisation—core questions of 'being (towards death)', 'individual', 'freedom', 'transcendence', and politics. The Chinese situation is quite different. For example, Chinese thought has, at least since the Song Dynasty, already been 'secularised' for a very long time. Except to put it this way is to use Western categories. Instead, Confucian and indeed Daoist traditions play the key role, with Buddhism acceptable only in terms of its adaptation to the main paradigm. The implication is that rationalisation does not entail a history of secularisation; 'continuous regeneration [*shengshengbuxi*]' is the reality rather that 'being'; transcendence does not rely on an outer and imagined reality, but is very much inner; the individual is not an entity unto itself, but is inescapably collective, whether in terms of the relatedness of 'family' and society, or through cultural codes of virtue and self-cultivation (Sun X. 2014, 2017b, 2018, 2019, 2020a; see also Xu 2016).

At the same time, commonality must be sought in the modern world, for which Sun proposes a 'mutual coordination [*hu wei zuobiao*]' between dual ontologies. What does this mean?

> On the one hand, we are Chinese, with our own cultural traditions and logical worldview. On the other hand, as modern Chinese, we live in the modern world, which also has its own logic. Each system of meaning is itself an ontology … In fact, today's Chinese people live in a world of 'dual ontologies'. Therefore, it is necessary to let these 'dual ontologies' coordinate with each other … Modernity is indispensable in the study of Chinese problems, and a Chinese perspective is also necessary in the study of Western learning. (Sun X. and Lu 2017, 181)

Sun's project has moved from studying Western philosophy so as to understand the West and how it has a bearing on China in the modern world, to developing proposals from a Chinese perspective so as to contribute to the realities of the modern world. Thus, the mutual coordination of dual ontologies; or, as he puts more recently, the

---

[3]In an online article for the Central Institute of Socialism, Sun identifies three relevant traditions in China: China's cultural tradition, that of modernity, and the socialist tradition (Sun X. 2017a).

need for a 'framework contrast' of different traditions so as to produce the conditions for such a mutual coordination (Sun X. 2020b).

What is the implication for universals or commonalities (the Chinese *pubianxing* has both senses)? A universal thus becomes the outcome of the mutual coordination of distinct ontologies or cultural logics.[4] Given the focus of this chapter, let us take the example of human rights. The concept of human rights may have initially arisen in a European context, but it can be a universal that applies elsewhere only when its history, promises, and limitations are kept in mind (see also Li B. et al. 2015, 62–65; Wan 2017, 34–35, 48–49). As Tom Zwart (2020a) puts it, human rights entail a dialectic of universality and contextuality. Thus, a contextual universal is open to contributions from other traditions and other contexts, enabling the universal to be enhanced and become multi-faceted. It follows that such a universal applies with different emphases in distinct contexts. To use the plant metaphor once more: it is a universal not with a singular root, but with multiple roots.

7.3 The Western Liberal Tradition of Human Rights

With the concept of rooted universals in mind, I would like to deal initially—and relatively briefly—with the Western liberal approach to human rights. As mentioned earlier, the focus of this tradition is on the civil and political rights of an individual human being. But how did this tradition come to have such a focus? The origins of what is now known as human rights in a European context emerged in the twelfth century, when the Latin term *ius* began to assume a distinct sense: it primarily meant a natural innate force or power that leads a human being to act rightly.[5] Further, this 'natural' force arose from the innate power of reason. Here are the seeds of what would later come to be defined as 'subjective rights', those that pertain to a human being as an individual. Crucially, *ius* was intimately connected with another Latin term, *dominium*, which means mastery. Or more fully, it designates the mastery of a rational and free-willing individual over his or her actions. Thus, *ius* was exercised through *dominium*: a right can work only if an individual has power to enact it.

These meanings did not arise in a vacuum, for they were part of the rediscovery and application of ancient Roman law by the 'lawyer popes' of the eleventh century (Gianaris 1996, 20; Miéville 2005, 95–97).[6] Central to this rediscovery was the idea of absolute private property, which the Romans called *dominium*. It entailed

[4]Some readers may be drawn to compare this approach with that of Alain Badiou's very Western proposal, for whom the context of a universal is necessary but not determinative (Badiou 2006). Needless to say, Badiou's approach leads to another version of a Western false universal.

[5]I summarise here the detailed work of Tierney (1997) and Kilcullen (2011).

[6]By adapting Roman law to feudalism, the popes—through their legal representatives (*legates*)—sought to clear up the murky question of property in terms of land claims and due process for every minute aspect of daily life. This rediscovery fed into many strands, including the Enlightenment, the French civil code of Napoleon, and the first stirrings of capitalism in the sixteenth century—a development first noted by none other than Proudhon (1840).

in the first instance mastery—by a *dominus*—over a thing (*res*). But the 'thing' in question was a slave; thus, private property begins with an effort to provide a legal and economic framework for slavery, which was eventually applied to all private property. As Graeber observes:

> In creating a notion of *dominium*, then, and thus creating the modern principle of absolute private property, what Roman jurists were doing first of all was taking a principle of domestic authority, of absolute power over people, defining some of those people (slaves) as things, and then extending the logic that originally applied to slaves to geese, to chariots, barns, jewelry boxes, and so forth – that is, to every other sort of thing that the law had anything to do with. (Graeber 2011, 201)[7]

Thus far, we have the connection between slavery and private property, embodied in the term *dominium*. But how is this history pertinent for understanding the nature of human rights in Europe, for the connection between *dominium* and *ius*? Here the Dutch lawyer Hugo Grotius (1583–1645) is of assistance, especially because he was responsible for a major step in developing the European tradition of human rights. Not only did he emphasise a shift from the singular 'right [*ius*]' to the plural 'rights [*iures*]', but he also argued that a human right is simultaneously the power exercised over ourselves *and* over others, such as slaves. A '*Right properly, and strictly taken*', he wrote, means a 'Power either over our selves, which is term'd Liberty; or over others, such as that of a *Father over his Children*, or *a Lord over his Slave*' (Grotius 1625, I.1.5; see further Boer and Petterson 2014, 36–43).[8] For Grotius, such a power was the very definition of liberty.

Thus, human rights in a European context are inescapably connected with individual mastery, slavery, and the freedom to exercise control over one's private property. Not only would these features become constitutive of what we now know as liberalism (Losurdo 2011), but they would also develop into the idea that human rights entail individual mastery over life itself, individual speech, political expression, religious belief—in short, all of the features associated with bourgeois civil society (Lin 2013, 74). For this tradition, such rights are seen to be God-given and inalienable.

In order to illustrate the dynamics of this tradition, a diagram is helpful (Diagram 7.1).

---

[7]Or, as Patterson writes: 'It can be no accident that the shift in the meaning of "*dominium*" from slaveholding to the holding of all objects of property in an absolute sense perfectly correlates with the changeover of Roman economy from one in which slaves were simply one of many objects of property to a society in which slaves became one of the two most important sources of wealth and objects of property' (Patterson 1982, 32; see also Wolff 1951, 67).

[8]Much to the chagrin of his liberal admirers, Grotius also argued with impeccable logic that an individual also has the power to give up or sell freedom and become a slave, and indeed that a people as a whole can give up their freedom and become colonial subjects: 'It is lawful for any Man to engage himself as a Slave to whom he pleases; as appears both by the Hebrew and Roman Laws. Why should it not therefore be as lawful for a People that are at their own Disposal, to deliver up themselves to any one or more Persons, and transfer the Right of governing them upon him or them, without reserving any Share of that Right to themselves?' (Grotius 1625, I.3.8).

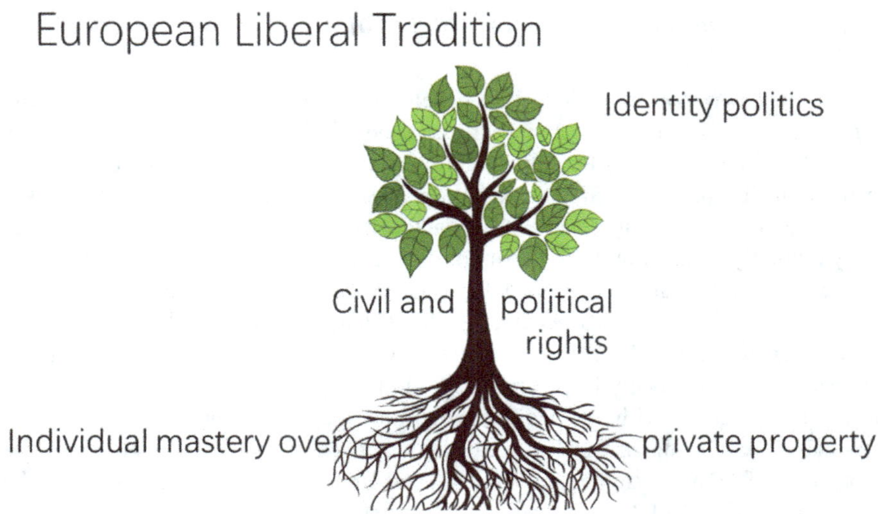

Diagram 7.1 Western liberal tradition of human rights

The roots and trunk should be clear, with the core feature of civil and political rights based on mastery of private property by an individual—embodied now in the United Nations' *International Covenant on Civil and Political Rights* (1966a). But this tradition also leads to a development that is beyond my remit: the flourishing and indeed end-run of the whole tradition in identity politics. Now an individual can 'choose' from an almost unlimited number of identities, whether in terms of sexual preference, ethnicity, religious tradition, or even one's age. They can be appropriated as yet another type of private property, over which one has dominion. In many respects, such identity politics and the fault lines they generate in terms of political persuasion are the ultimate expression of this Western liberal tradition.

7.4 Sovereignty: From Westphalia to Anti-colonialism

Thus far, I have sought to present the European tradition's emphasis on civil and political rights as a rooted universal by emphasising its specific history of emergence and defining contextual features. This emphasis runs against the tendency to claim that this specific approach constitutes human rights as such and should be used as a yardstick to measure any other part of the world—in other words, a false universal. My main concern in this chapter, however, is to present the material concerning a quite distinct tradition and approach to human rights, that of the Marxist tradition and especially the form it has taken in a Chinese context. This approach is based on the principle of anti-hegemonic sovereignty, so we need to spend some time on the question of sovereignty.

7.4.1 Westphalia and Secularised Theology

A dominant narrative concerning the development of sovereignty in a European context is that its initial articulation arose in the conflicts—particularly the Thirty Years War (1618–1648)—that led to the Peace of Westphalia in 1648 and the rise of modern European nation-states (Jackson 2007; Grimm 2015). Sovereignty was assumed to mean that a ruler had supreme authority within a defined territory and did so by mutually respecting the authority of other rulers in other territories. Supported by theorists such as Jean Bodin and Thomas Hobbes, this Westphalian assumption dominated until its excesses became apparent, particularly with the Third Reich. Thus, after the Second World War, sovereignty was gradually restricted, becoming subject to the 'universally held' criteria of human rights and principles that would be used to grant or withhold legitimacy to any state claiming sovereignty. Here we find the evolution of the European Union, the European Convention for the Protection of Human Rights and Fundamental Freedoms, the United Nations, the International Court of Justice, and other trans-state bodies that began both to cut back the earlier Westphalian sense and justified interventions in states that were judged to have contravened the criteria.

A notable feature of this narrative is the role of Christian theology, specifically in the way state and trans-state bodies have appropriated for themselves what was once seen as a divine role: the sanction for sovereignty or the lack thereof. The theological justifications took a number of forms. In a Roman Catholic framework, it was argued that all states must be subject to the Church's mandate, in which the pope functioned as God's representative on earth. Even in the twentieth century there were efforts to reclaim this idea as criticisms of the older model of European sovereignty grew (Maritain 1951; Jouvenal 1957). From Lutheran and Reformed perspectives, the sovereign was always subject to divine approval or its abrogation. This is particularly so with Calvin's argument that even though an unpopular monarch rules with divine sanction, this is always subject to the ruler in question following God's laws. If not, then God would appoint an agent to remove the ruler and even allow the people to disobey (Calvin 1559; Boer 2019, 75–90). We find the same emphasis in a somewhat more muted manner in Luther's 'two kingdoms' hypothesis, with its transfer of secular power from Rome to the prince (Luther 1523). Even so, Luther never urged a complete separation between the two kingdoms: the monarch was to ensure not merely proper conduct of religious observance, but of all relevant divine laws. If not, the sanction would be removed. This emphasis even applies to absolute monarchies: the monarch may be the determinant of and thereby above state law—'There is no authority except from God, and those authorities that exist have been instituted by God' (Romans 13:1–7)—but such a monarch rules only on the basis of divine sanction (Bodin 1576; Hobbes 1651). It follows that the sanction can also be removed from an absolute monarch.

This was all very well during the heyday of the overt theological dominance over European culture and political realities, but what happened during the long and peculiarly European experience of secularisation? Here I draw on Adorno's argument that—in the process of conceptual secularisation—the effort to empty theological terms of their content and fill them with new and secularised concepts results not in the development of a whole new framework but in a pattern of thought and practice that has none of the former controls that had been developed over millennia (Adorno 1964a, 1964b). Thus, systems of theological ideas may be sublated into cultural, philosophical, or political systems of thought, but this process renders the latter far more pernicious. Adorno's examples are many, but I would like to focus on the way modern political thought may seek to retain the external forms of theology, but in doing so it discards the old theological authority structures and replaces them with other actors—especially the European nation-states that became the arbiters of right and wrong. Thus, in relation to the European development of sovereignty, state actors and trans-state institutions have produced new principles and laws with which they seek to judge other sovereign states as to their viability.[9] In appropriating this quasi-divine role, these bodies increasingly seek to use civil and political rights as a new form of 'universal' law. To return to the distinction between false and rooted universals: if such a development were to remain 'a regional theory and a regional model' (Yang W. 2017, 18), and from this basis cautiously seek to contribute to global commonalities concerning sovereignty, it may be regarded as a rooted universal. But if—as has happened—the new approach to adjudicating sovereignty is seen as an extra-territorial and global 'responsibility', then it has become a false universal.

7.4.2 Anti-colonial Sovereignty

The narrative I have summarised is one that comes from the western peninsula of the Eurasian landmass (Diakonoff 2003, 157), but let us see what happens to the narrative in light of a global situation. The crucial determinant here concerns anti-colonial struggles in the many parts of the world that were dominated by European colonialism. Thus, 'Westphalia'—shorthand for a distinctly European notion of sovereignty—developed in the wake of initial European colonisation of significant parts of the globe. The Portuguese, Spanish, and especially the Dutch with the first capitalist colonial empire, set the early pace, but other European powers would follow, culminating in the British Empire that collapsed by the mid-twentieth century. Obviously, if European powers tried their best to observe a somewhat 'Westphalian' understanding of sovereignty amongst themselves (not without frequent wars that had to be 'justified' in light of such a framework), they completely ignored it when dealing with states outside Europe, states they sought to colonise or semi-colonise. The phase of curtailment that followed the Second World War was triggered by the successful liberation of one colonised country after another from its European coloniser (or its surrogates, such as the United States, Australia, and New Zealand).

[9] A pertinent example here is Carl Schmitt's effort to remove territory from the concept of sovereignty (Schmitt 1922).

Faced with a loss of global power, the former colonial club set about to debunk the idea of state sovereignty and to establish a series of trans-state institutions in their own image and imbued with quasi-divine power.[10] They would decide the legitimacy or illegitimacy of a state, and use such criteria as the basis of intervention.

By contrast, in an anti-colonial context sovereignty was appropriated and redefined. A key moment was in the 1950s, when the Soviet Union proposed what became the 'Declaration on the Granting of Independence to Colonial Countries and Peoples'. It was adopted on 14 December, 1960, in a version authorised by a coalition of Asian and African states, and approved by an overwhelming majority of the member states of the United Nations. But why did the Soviet Union first propose this document? As part of the anti-capitalist and anti-imperialist struggle of communism, the Soviet Union was the main supporter of anti-colonial struggles around the world, culminating in a swathe of successful declarations of independence.

Notably, the abstentions from the vote on the declaration in 1960 were Australia, Belgium, France, Portugal, Spain, South Africa, the United Kingdom, and the United States.[11] All were former and some were—at the time—current colonial powers. Whereas previously they had voted against anti-colonial resolutions, for some stood much to lose, now they opted for abstention. Is this mere coincidence, predicated on an anti-communist platform since the declaration was initially proposed by the Soviet Union? In part this may be true, but at a deeper level it was precisely these countries that were also behind the post-Westphalian downgrading of sovereignty and the favouring of intervention in light of what were asserted to be 'universal' human rights (Wan 2017, 41).

I would like to pay a little more attention to the UN declaration, especially in the way it reframes the question of sovereignty. First, sovereignty itself is a right, for it is equated again and again with the 'inalienable right' to freedom. Thus, the 'subjection of peoples to alien subjugation, domination and exploitation constitutes a denial of fundamental human rights'. Second, sovereignty provides the conditions for the exercise of human rights, for the latter can take place only in the context of the 'self-determination of all peoples'. Thus, colonialism is an 'impediment' to freedom, to 'the social, cultural and economic development of dependent peoples'. Crucially, territorial integrity is an inescapable feature of this redefinition of sovereignty, so much so that 'any attempt aimed at the partial or total disruption of the national unity and the territorial integrity of a country is incompatible with the purposes and principles of the Charter of the United Nations' (United Nations General Assembly 1960).

---

[10]Notably, many of the works that seek to dismantle the concept and practice of sovereign states largely ignore the anti-colonial question (Bartelson 1995; Krasner 1999; Pogge 2008, 177–189; Teschke 2009; Kalmo and Skinner 2010; Haldén 2011; Pavel 2014).

[11]The Dominican Republic also abstained, under pressure from the United States.

7.4.3 *Anti-hegemony, Non-interference, and Peaceful Coexistence*

The ramifications of these three points in the specific Chinese situation are as follows. To begin with, while the concept of sovereignty was drawn from the European tradition, with all is benefits and traps, it was not a global extension of a Westphalian definition but thoroughly transformed in an anti-colonial context (contra Philpott 2001, 161–164; Gottwald and Duggan 2012, 42). We may already see this transformation in the Chinese term *zhuquan* (主权): *quan* (权) is the key, for it means to weigh, a power, authority, and thus a right. Combined with *zhu* (主–to be in charge of), *zhuquan* means that one has the right to be in charge of one's situation. Further, the absence of this right means that a country cannot exercise any other rights whatsoever. This was particularly the case during the struggle against colonialism—the time of 'humiliation'—which is usually put in terms of the three mountains: imperialism, feudalism and its relics, and bureaucratic capitalism (Wan 2017, 36). Only when these three were overcome, with Liberation in 1949, could sovereignty begin to be exercised and rights enacted. Finally, this approach to sovereignty entails both non-interference and resolute opposition to efforts at hegemony (within which territorial integrity plays an important role). Obviously, the two terms are closely related, albeit with different emphases. On the one hand, the principle of non-interference appears again and again in China's responses to the efforts by other states and even trans-state bodies to interfere in China's internal affairs (Deng 1990b, 1990a). From the long experience of resisting semi-colonial occupation, through negotiations over Hong Kong and Macao, to the need to block efforts to stir up trouble in China's border areas (Xi L. 1995, 13–15), the constant need to reassert anti-colonial sovereignty as non-interference in China's affairs is a reality.

The other side of the coin is the resolute opposition to efforts at hegemony. I have been much persuaded by Lorsurdo's argument that China's long road to rejuvenation should be seen as a major feature of the ongoing anti-colonial struggle (Losurdo 2013; Zhang S. and Ni 2017, 75). However much true, this is not the terminology used in China. Up to the 1970s, the Chinese struggle to construct socialism was seen as resistance to colonialism and imperialism, but by the 1980s the preferred term became 'anti-hegemonism [*fandui baquanzhuyi*]'. For example, in the 1981 resolution by the CPC Central Committee, we find reference to the continued need to oppose 'imperialism, hegemonism, colonialism, and racism' for the sake of safeguarding world peace (CPC Central Committee 1981, 2, 9). Here imperialism, colonialism, and racism are clearly present, but there is also the inclusion of 'hegemonism'. At the same time, the document marks a shift by focusing more clearly on the need to oppose hegemonism:

> While upholding our own independence, we respect other people's right to independence. The road of revolution and construction suited to the characteristics of a country has to be explored, decided on and blazed by its own people. No one has the right to impose his views on others. Only under these conditions can there be genuine internationalism. Otherwise, there can only be hegemonism. We will always adhere to this principled stand in our international relations. (CPC Central Committee 1981, 7)

'*Baquan*' (霸权), translated here as 'hegemony', is a word rich with connotations. The semantic field of '*ba* (霸)' includes a leader of feudal lords, a tyrant or despot, a hegemonic power, and to dominate and tyrannise—in short, to rule by might rather than right. It is arguably an even stronger term than 'colonialism', and is seen as more appropriate to what some would call the 'post-colonial' period when the heyday of European colonialism has faded, or what in China is seen as the internationalisation of class conflict (see Sect. 4.5.2) in terms of capitalist opposition to socialist countries like China. It should be no surprise that one of Deng Xiaoping's signature international emphases was to counter 'hegemonism [*baquan*]' or to 'struggle against hegemony [*fanba douzheng*]' (Deng 1978b, 112; 1978a, 123; 1980c, 239–240; 1980d, 241; 1980b, 275; 1980a, 274; 1982b, 415–417; 1982a, 407–409).

What is the alternative to hegemony and anti-hegemonism? The seeds can already be found in the 1950s, with the 'Five Principles for Peaceful Coexistence' being promoted: 'mutual respect for sovereignty and territorial integrity, mutual non-aggression, non-interference in each other's internal affairs, equality and mutual benefit, and peaceful coexistence' (Zhou 1953b, 113; 1953a, 128). These arose in the context of much activity, including the Bandung—or Asian-African—Conference of the following year, which focused on sovereignty, world peace, and economic and cultural co-operation, as well as the moves by Soviet Union in promoting the United Nations' declaration mentioned earlier. In short, if one opposes hegemony by other states, then one does not seek to impose hegemony on anyone else (Zwart 2020a). Initially, the principles of peaceful co-existence were focused primarily on recently—or indeed still—colonised and developing countries. Even today, China has much closer relations with such countries, understanding and working with them in a way that is simply beyond the understanding of the former colonisers known as the 'West'. At the same time, China is willing to extend such an approach even to the latter countries, should they be ready and able to put aside their hegemonic assumptions and work together with developing countries. At the time of writing, we may see the developments of this anti-hegemonic and peaceful coexistence approach manifested in the Belt and Road Initiative, the Shanghai Cooperation Organisation, BRICS, and so on. In each case, the resolute assumption remains: non-interference in the affairs of other countries, in the name of anti-hegemonic sovereignty.

7.5 The Chinese Marxist Approach to Human Rights

7.5.1 The Prerequisite of Anti-hegemonic Sovereignty

For Chinese scholars, anti-hegemonic sovereignty is the prerequisite for a Chinese Marxist approach to human rights (Li B. and Wang 1995; Wan 2017, 42; Jiang K. 2018, 36; Wu F. 2018, 17). This point relates not merely to the fact that individual states need to ratify and enact international treaties and declarations, especially from the United Nations, but to the more important fact that a colonised country cannot exercise any rights. One may object: from the perspective of the 'Western' tradition it is asserted that 'rights' are not granted by a sovereign state, for then they can be removed. Thus far, I have indicated that the post-Westphalian phase in Europe has sought to restrict the exercise of sovereignty in the name of a universal 'human rights', which are restricted to civil and political rights. I also indicated that the proponents of this position did so in response to anti-colonial liberation, as an alternative method for asserting dominance. A further factor may now be added: 'inalienable' rights. For example, Thomas Paine declared in *Rights of Man* (1791) that any notion that rights are granted, by a charter or otherwise, is a perversion of the very idea of what he called 'natural rights'. Like the old theological doctrine of original sin, such rights are—for this tradition—the property of the private individual at birth.

In contrast to such a secularised theological approach to human rights—as 'natural' and 'inalienable'—a Chinese Marxist approach stresses that rights are historical rather than innate, are granted by society rather than by nature, and are practical rather than ideal (Fang 2015, 107–111). In particular, the unfolding of human rights is closely connected with the development of the rule of law (Li L. 2018, 6; F. Wu 2018, 14; Wang X. and Cui 2019). As for the role of a sovereign state, the argument is dialectical: sovereignty—as a right—is the prerequisite and even foundation for any other rights. Is sovereignty then determinative of human rights? No: sovereignty is an inescapable basis, for 'without independent sovereignty, there cannot be a complete guarantee of human rights'. Sovereignty is therefore a prerequisite but not determinative, for 'human rights are the most essential and at the highest level' (Sun P. 2014, 121).[12] Thus, when one struggles against colonial domination, anti-hegemonic sovereignty is the primary concern; when one has sovereignty, human rights become determinative.

7.5.2 The Right to Socio-Economic Well-Being

This is only a beginning, for the core of this rooted universal is the right to economic well-being for all, which includes the rights to development and work (Lin 2013, 76–78; Wan 2017, 42–43; Guo W. and Zhao 2018, 27–28; Jiang K. 2018, 37–38; Li L. 2018, 3–5; F. Wu 2018, 13–14).[13] To understand this difference from the Western European liberal tradition, we need to dig back into the Marxist and Chinese traditions. Let us begin with Marxism, where we find that the precursor to the Marxist

[12]By far the best work in English on Chinese Marxist human rights is By Sun Pinghua (2014), while in Chinese the study by Wan Qianhui (2017) is even better. I also recommend the full range of online English resources at the website of the China Society for Human Rights Studies (chinahumanrights.org), as well as the recent volume edited by Chang et al. (2020). Of non-Chinese scholars, the best is the work by Tom Zwart (2011, 2014, 2018, 2019, 2020a, 2020b), who has developed a cross-cultural approach to human rights, although he does not take much account of Marxism.

[13]This emphasis on economic and social rights is not seen as a 'second generation' of human rights, with civil and political rights as the 'first generation' (Vasak 1977), since the idea of such generations arises from a European context.

emphasis is already found with Hegel. As Losordo argues, Hegel's resolute emphasis was on 'material rights', which it is the task of the state to ensure (Hegel 1986, 109; Losurdo 2004, 69, 89). In order to understand what this means, let us use the concrete example of the starving person:

> A man who is starving has the absolute right to violate another person's property, since he is violating property only in a limited fashion: the right of necessity [*Notrecht*][14] requires him not to violate another person's right as such: he is only interested in a piece of bread, he is not treating the other person as an individual without rights. Abstract intellect is prone to consider any legal violation as absolute, but a starving man only violates the particular, he does not violate right per se. (Hegel 1974, Vol. 4, 341; see also Losurdo 2004, 155)

In this case, the right to property is clearly limited (a distinct challenge to liberal assertions), while the right of a person in life-threatening need is an absolute right. For Hegel, the starving person draws nigh to and is equated with the slave, whose right to freedom overcomes any specific right over property (Losurdo 2004, 169–172). One person has the 'absolute right' to freedom from hunger, while the other person has the 'absolute right' to freedom itself (Hegel 1974, Vol. 3, 251). Both are forms of the core *material right*, which is manifested in terms of self-preservation, subsistence, freedom from want, work, and thus socio-economic well-being. As 'positive rights' they all embody what Hegel means by the 'right to life' (Losurdo 2004, 186).

I have drawn on Losurdo's explication of Hegel's material rights for a reason, since this renders Hegel a forerunner of Marx and Engels. While Marx in particular was scathing about the severe limitations of bourgeois approaches to rights (Marx 1875b, 14–15; 1875a, 86–87), both he and Engels consistently maintained the fundamental importance of proletarian action, revolution, and a socialist system that would focus on managing production and watching over the true interests of society (Engels 1873a, 86; 1873b, 425; Boer, in press). As we will see in Chapter 9, the Soviet Union developed this basic assumption further in the 1930s, with an emphasis on proactive rights that depend upon the basic right of freedom from exploitation (Weatherley 1999, 97–98; Lin 2013, 75–76).

At this point, we make the transition to China, but before focusing on Marxist developments I would like to consider briefly the influence of the long Chinese tradition. In this case, the approach is to refer to a distinct saying that sums up an emphasis of thousands of years: 'When the granaries are full, the people follow appropriate rules of conduct, and when there is enough to eat and wear, the people know honour and shame' (Sima 2014, 2595, 3952).[15] The saying, as recorded by Sima Qian, is attributed to Guan Zhong (720–645 BCE), an influential reformer of

[14]Understood as the 'right of extreme need', *Notrecht* in Hegel undergoes a significant reinterpretation of the old *ius necessitas*. Even for Kant, this was a right outside the law, in a state of nature; for Hegel, it was a right within society, within the state. But for Hegel, 'the traditional *ius necessitatis* has turned into something different: *Notrecht* is now the right of extreme need, the right of the poor struggling to survive' (Losurdo 2004, 160).

[15]The sentence appears on two occasions in Sima Qian's *Shiji*, once in the *Guanyan liezhuan* section, and once in the *Huozhi liezhuan* section.

the State of Qi during the Warring States Period.[16] The later Confucian tradition would debate whether ethics arose naturally from such a material basis, or whether they also required the 'cultivation of moral character [*xiushen*]'. The latter became the dominant position under the influence of Mencius,[17] but I would like to emphasise here the Confucian idea of *xiaokang*. Since I have analysed this concept in the previous chapter (Sect. 6.4), there is no need to repeat that material here, save to point out that through its reinterpretation in light of the Marxist tradition—initially by Deng Xiaoping—it came to refer to the whole project of socialism with Chinese characteristics. At its foundation, the idea of a moderately well-off, healthy, and peaceful society is primarily one concerned with economic well-being. This is the core emphasis, but it is by no means enough: already with Deng Xiaoping and even more with those who followed, it was very clear that cultural, social, and ethical matters are also very much needed.

7.5.3 Policy Implications: From the Belt and Road Initiative to Minority Nationalities

By now we have returned to the Marxist framework, within which—as I have emphasised on a number of occasions—the rich Chinese tradition is consistently reinterpreted.[18] Given that the core human right in a Chinese Marxist context is that of socio-economic well-being, I would like to undertake an exercise in which a range of Chinese programs and policies—some already presented in earlier chapters—can be understood as manifestations of such a right. To begin with, a signature emphasis of the Reform and Opening-Up is on liberating the forces of production (see Sects. 2.4 and 5.3.1). This is not for the sake of enriching a few at the expense of the many, but for the sake of 'serving the community [*gongtongti fuwu*]' so that all may benefit (Huang 1994). Closely related is the long-term poverty alleviation project, which achieved its goal of raising more than 800 million people out of poverty and thus abolishing absolute poverty by the early weeks of 2021 (see also Yang Z. and Qin

[16]Some readers may be reminded of Engels's observation at Marx's funeral: 'humankind must first of all eat, drink, have shelter and clothing, before it can pursue politics, science, art, religion, etc' (Engels 1883, 407). Note also Bertolt Brecht's aphorism from *The Threepenny Opera*—'Food comes first, then morality' (Brecht and Weill 1968, 54).

[17]Mencius observed that if the people 'have not a certain livelihood, it follows that they will not have a fixed heart'. But the steady 'heart' in question required more: people must have more than food and shelter, for without the cultivation of virtue they would be little better than animals (Mencius 1895, 147, 251). Beyond my remit here is a debate in China concerning the differences and possible similarities between cultivating one's moral character (*xiushen*) in a collective context and the Western liberal emphasis on the private individual (Yu 1998; Mou 1999; Li M. 2005; Sun X. 2017b; Li B. et al. 2015, 66–68).

[18]While the Marxist framework is a consistent emphasis of Chinese scholarship, foreign scholars tend to ignore or downplay it (Bell 2000, 49–105; Angle 2002, 200–204, 240–249; Freeman and Geeraerts 2012, 100; Biddulph 2015).

2018, 7).[19] This aim became one of the defining features of the achievement of a *xiaokang* society by 2021 and is clearly one of the most significant human rights achievements in human history (Zwart 2018; 2020a).

Another example concerns international projects, especially the landmark Belt and Road Initiative from 2013, within which a whole range of other agreements and projects are now located.[20] As one would expect with an initiative of such global and epoch-making significance, the amount of research is growing exponentially, even if I restrict myself to the Marxist principles at work in the BRI.[21] My concern here is quite specific: how the BRI manifests at a global level the right to socio-economic well-being. As we saw earlier, the BRI and its related initiatives function in terms of mutual anti-hegemonic sovereignty, but it is primarily founded on the need to improve the economic base of the countries involved. Thus, one of the major concerns is with liberating the forces of production in each of the countries involved precisely through their interaction and cooperation. This emphasis is, of course, drawn directly from the Chinese experience of the Reform and Opening-Up and the development of a socialist market economy alongside a planned economy. It should be no surprise that BRI projects are primarily infrastructural, seeking to improve transport, communications, facilities, environmental protection, and so on. Further, the focus of these initiatives is not on an exclusive club (like the G7) but primarily on developing countries, which account for 80% of the world's population. As mentioned earlier, it is precisely with these countries that China shares a deep understanding and much common ground in terms of earlier experiences of colonialism and the consequent articulation of anti-hegemonic sovereignty.

More specifically, when Xi Jinping launched the Belt and Road Initiative in September of 2013, he did so in Kazakhstan, which was not only a major corridor of the ancient Silk Route, but also shares—along other Central Asian countries—mutual concerns focused on development, economic improvement, and thus socio-economic well-being. In that landmark speech, Xi spoke of what are now called the 'five links [*wu tong*]': policy communication, transport integration, unimpeded trade, currency circulation, and people-to-people ties—all based on the 'principle of seeking common ground while reserving differences' (Xi J. 2013).[22] As one would expect, from the very beginning of the BRI the small club of former colonisers

[19]In a global perspective, this means that 75% of people lifted out of poverty around the globe were in China.

[20]These include, but are not limited to, the Shanghai Cooperation Organisation, Asia Infrastructure Investment Bank, Forum of China-Africa Cooperation, China-ASEAN '10+1', APEC, Asia-Europe Meeting, Asian Cooperation Dialogue, CICA, China-Arab Cooperation Forum, Greater Mekong Sub-regional Economic Cooperation, and Central Asian Regional Economic Cooperation, Boao Forum for Asia, and the Qianhai Cooperation Forum (Cui 2019, 107–108).

[21]Instead of multiple references at every turn, I cite here the key works from which I have drawn the main points in this paragraph (Dong and Bai 2016; Guo J. and Lin 2016; Zhang F. 2016; Zhang X. and He 2016; Wang Z. 2017; Zhang Z. and Liu 2017; Ba 2018; Li D. 2018; Yang Z. and Qin 2018; Cui 2019).

[22]Or, as Zhuang and Wu put it, projects of the BRI operate with 'we' rather than 'I', in which each country is the 'host [*zhuren*]' of a project and not a 'guest [*keren*]' of another country on its own soil (Zhuang and Wu 2017, 111).

known as the 'West' have both misunderstood and sought to disparage the BRI. Of course, they do so from a worldview shaped by crusades, colonialism, a zero-sum approach, and the structural imbalances of international capitalism that have appeared most recently in 2008 and 2020. Here the Danish proverb is apt: a thief always thinks every one else steals. Against such headwinds, there have been even further Chinese efforts to articulate the alternative vision embodied in the BRI: the most common is the 'community with a shared future for humankind', with its distinct vision of global human rights (Li L. 2018, 1–3; Liao 2018; F. Wu 2018, 18).[23] Indeed, Tom Zwart (2020b) anticipates that as this approach gains international traction, it will reform and thus save the faltering international human rights system. Other expressions follow in the same vein, deploying variations on the core character *gong* (共) with the sense of 'in common'. Here we find the 'three commons [*san gong*]': 'consultation [*gongshang*]', 'co-construction [*gongjian*]', and 'mutual enjoyment [*gongxiang*].[24] These concepts provide some more detail to what is more widely known as 'win-win [*gongying*]'.

The right to socio-economic well-being also underlies policies in relation to all of the minority nationalities, especially since most of them live in remote border regions where poverty has been an endemic problem. It applies as much to Inner Mongolia, Ningxia, Yunnan, Guangxi, and small minority nationalities in other areas such as Heilongjiang, as it does to Tibet and Xinjiang (Zhu 2012). Those who are fond of promoting Western human rights and interfering with the sovereignty of other countries (see above) have focused on Tibet and Xinjiang with greater intensity in the last two or three decades. But these efforts come in waves and have done so ever since the founding of the People's Republic. Let us consider Tibet and Xinjiang for a moment, for here the problem is compounded with the three evils of separatism, extremism, and terrorism (aided by foreign forces). What is the Chinese response? The immediate focus is on combating terrorism for the sake of safety, peace, and social harmony—three basic social imperatives in Chinese culture and governance. Apart from ensuring that no further terrorist attacks occur, this task also entails sustained efforts to eradicate extremist thought and propaganda. However, the deeper assessment is that these problems have arisen due to poverty and the uneven development of China's varied regions. Thus, the way to overcome the dangers of separatism, extremism, and terrorism is to focus on measures to ensure the right to socio-economic well-being. We may already see such an emphasis with Jiang Zemin's push in the 1990s to develop the western and central regions since they were already lagging behind in the process of socialist modernisation (Jiang Z. 1995b, 465–467; 1995a, 454–456). However, the most successful project continues to be the Belt and Road Initiative,

---

[23]The phrase 'community of shared future for humankind [*renlei mingyun gongtongti*]', along with 'win-win [*gong ying*]', first appeared in Hu Jintao's final report as general secretary at the eighteenth congress of the CPC (Hu 2012, 31).

[24]Commonalities, yes, global Communism, not yet; but some argue that the focus on common concerns may be seen as a small foretaste of what global Communism might be. There are also the 'four substantives [*si ti*]': beneficial, responsible, future, and development commonalities and communities—*gongtongti*, a word coined to translate *Gemeinschaft* in the works of Marx and Engels, can mean both commonality and community.

since the regions in question have become vital nodes in fostering economic interaction across the Eurasian landmass, but especially with Russia and Central Asia. As I write, the economies of Xinjiang, Tibet, Inner Mongolia, Ningxia, Gansu, and so on, have been booming, precisely as an outcome of BRI integration. Obviously, this is the result of the Marxist emphasis on the economic base and thus on the right to socio-economic well-being.

A question remains: what about civil and political rights, let alone cultural and environmental rights? Are they to be delayed until economic well-being is achieved for all? If one is starving then the immediate concern is food rather that the niceties of freedom of expression or political representation. But it is a long way from emerging from poverty and achieving moderate prosperity, let alone the prosperity needed for the transition from socialism to communism. From a Chinese Marxist perspective, socio-economic rights are closely connected with civil, political, and cultural rights. You cannot focus on socio-economic rights and dispense with the rest, but you also cannot have civil and political rights without the core socio-economic rights. It is precisely these rights that are absolutely necessary for the exercise of civil, political, and cultural rights. To follow another path in a developing country is a recipe for chaos. Thus, as the right to socio-economic well-being has been realised gradually, so have the rights that flow from it. That said, the civil and political rights in question take place within a socialist system. They are not the same as Western liberal notions. We may see how such rights are exercised when we consider the full panoply of the socialist democratic system, with its electoral, consultative, and grassroots democratic practices (see the next chapter). Indeed, it is possible to claim that the more comprehensive approach to democracy within a socialist system entails a fuller realisation of civil and political rights than can be found elsewhere.

Once again, I use an image to illustrate Diagram 7.2.

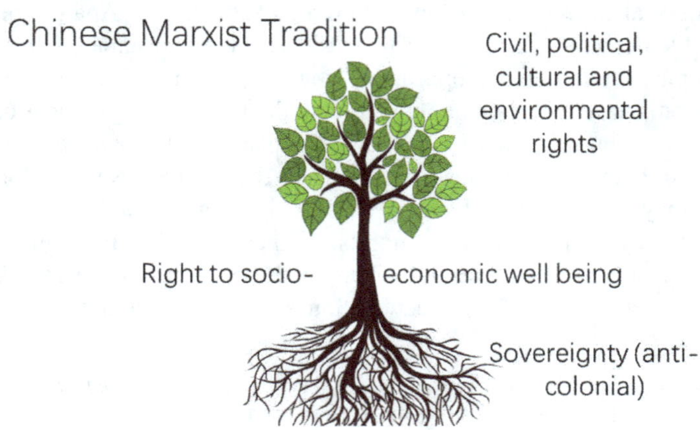

Diagram 7.2 Chinese Marxist Tradition of Human Rights

7.5.4 *The Rooted Universal of Chinese Marxist Human Rights*

In this light may we understand the claim by Sun Pinghua with which I began this chapter: 'The history of the Communist Party of China is the history of its struggle for human rights on behalf of Chinese people' (Sun P. 2014, 56). But has this approach to human rights been recognised as a rooted universal outside China, or indeed outside developing countries that share such an emphasis? Indeed it has, especially in terms of the United Nations' *International Covenant on Economic, Social, and Cultural Rights* (1966b). This is by no means the only resolution of the United Nations. Alongside the declaration on granting independence to colonial nations and peoples, mentioned earlier, there is also the landmark *Declaration on the Right to Development* (United Nations General Assembly 1986; see further Zwart 2019).[25] While the latter text notes the 'inalienable right' to development, the covenant from 1966 speaks of state parties recognising 'the rights of everyone to an adequate standard of living for himself and his family, including adequate food, clothing, and housing, and to the continuous improvement of living conditions'.

In fact, the rooted universal of the Chinese approach to human rights has also been recognised by none other than the Vatican. As Marcelo Sánchez Sorondo, who is chancellor of the Vatican's Academy of Social Sciences, observes:

> Right now, those who are best implementing the social doctrine of the Church are the Chinese. They seek the common good, subordinating things to the general good ... The dignity of the person is defended ... Liberal thought has liquidated the concept of the common good, not even wanting to take it into account, asserting that it is an empty idea, without any interest. By contrast, the Chinese focus on work and the common good. (quoted in Álvarez 2018)

This statement did not arise in a vacuum, for it should be seen in light of the current pope's—Pope Francis—emphasis on the common ground between Communists and Christians, and in the context of the long-overdue agreement between the Vatican and China over the appointment of bishops and the reunification of the two branches of the Chinese Roman Catholic Church (Pope Francis 2016; Faggioli 2018). But I have quoted the text here since it indicates a recognition even at the heart of the old Christendom of the rooted universal of the Chinese Marxist approach to human rights.

7.6 Conclusion: Mutual Recognition in a Multi-polar World

By now it should be clear that there is a distinct tradition of human rights arising from the Chinese Marxist context, a tradition that is well-developed and well-articulated. By way of conclusion, I would like to return to the idea of rooted universals and see

[25]One may also usefully consult the *ASEAN Human Rights Declaration* (ASEAN 2012).

if it is possible to identify not so much common ground but a basis for mutual understanding and contributions to the universal of human rights from different contexts and perspectives. True, the way I have presented the material above was more sceptical of the Western liberal approach, especially in light of its imperialist pretensions, and more favourable in dealing with the Chinese Marxist approach, largely because the latter remains so little known in some corners of the world. However, Chinese colleagues encourage me to seek what is beneficial from the Western tradition, while appreciating the contribution from Chinese Marxism.

In order to see how this might work, let us consider two crucial documents from the United Nations that I have mentioned earlier. These are the *International Covenant on Civil and Political Rights* and the *International Covenant on Economic, Social, and Cultural Rights*. They were initially conceived as one document, but in light of disagreements over emphasis they were divided into two, albeit with significant overlaps. Initially published in 1966, they both came into effect in 1976. In many respects, these two documents reflect the emphases of the two traditions I have examined. Noticeably, former colonisers from Europe and North America as well as Australia and New Zealand ratified the first, while countries liberated from colonialism quickly ratified the second. Further, we may consider the responses of China and the United States to the two documents. Thus, while China signed the covenant on civil and political rights in 1998, it has yet to ratify it, wary of the way it has been weaponised and used for hegemonic purposes. At the same time, the United States has failed to ratify the covenant on economic, social, and cultural rights (it also has so many reservations about the other covenant so as to render it ineffective).

Clearly, we still have some distance to go for mutual recognition of the distinct rooted traditions of human rights. There is little progress in mutual 'East-West' oppositions or accusations, with one side accusing the other of colonial and anti-communist motives, or the other side seeking to impose a false universal on the rest of the world for the sake of its own agenda. Instead, it is noticeable that Chinese scholars and policy advisers in particular have been advocating greater progress to a globally recognised universal with distinct emphases depending on the specific conditions (Sun P. 2014; Li B. et al. 2015, 68–69; see also Zwart 2020a). Realistically, this situation will emerge only with the mutual recognition borne of a robust multi-polar world, in which some states are no longer able to impose hegemony on others.

References

Adorno, Theodor W. 1964a. *Jargon der Eigentlich: Zur deutschen Ideologie*. In *Gesammelte Schriften*, vol. 6. Frankfurt am Main: Suhrkamp, 2003.

Adorno, Theodor W. 1964b. *The jargon of authenticity*. Translated by Knut Tarnowski. Evanston: Northwestern University Press, 1973.

Álvarez, Andrés Beltramo. 2018. Chinos, quienes mejor realizan la doctrina social de la Iglesia. *La Stampa*, 2 February 2018. Available at http://www.lastampa.it/2018/02/02/vaticaninsider/es/vaticano/chinos-quienes-mejor-realizan-la-doctrina-social-de-la-iglesia-mBmGrdwCpUt2VVswtlkeuN/pagina.html.

Angle, Stephen. 2002. *Human rights and Chinese thought: A cross-cultural inquiry*. Cambridge: Cambridge University Press.
ASEAN. 2012. *ASEAN human rights declaration*. Osaka: Asia-Pacific Human Rights Center.
Ba, Yanfeng. 2018. Tuijin 'yidai yilu' changyi de sikao – jiyu makesizhuyi shehui kexue fangfalun de shijiao. *Xin xibu* 2018 (21): 56–57.
Badiou, Alain. 2006. *Being and event*. Translated by Oliver Feltham. London: Continuum.
Bartelson, Jens. 1995. *A genealogy of sovereignty*. Cambridge: Cambridge University Press.
Bell, Daniel. 2000. *East meets west: Human rights and democracy in East Asia*. Princeton: Princeton University Press.
Bell, Daniel. 2006. *Beyond liberal democracy: Political thinking for an East Asian context*. Princeton: Princeton University Press.
Biddulph, Sarah. 2015. *The stability imperative: Human rights and law in China*. Vancouver: UBC Press.
Bodin, Jean. 1576. *Les six livres de la république*. Paris: Librairie générale française, 1993.
Boer, Roland. In press. *Friedrich Engels and the foundations of socialist governance*. Singapore: Springer.
Boer, Roland. 2019. *Red theology: On the Christian Communist tradition*. Leiden: Brill.
Boer, Roland, and Christina Petterson. 2014. *Idols of nations: Biblical myth at the origins of capitalism*. Minneapolis: Fortress.
Brecht, Bertolt, and Kurt Weill. 1968. *Die Dreigroschenoper*. Frankfurt am Main: Suhrkamp.
Calvin, John. 1559. *Institutes of the Christian religion*. Translated by Ford Lewis Battles. Louisville: Westminster John Knox, 2006.
Chang, Jian, Li Ruoyu, Zhang Chong, and Shi Hui, eds. 2020. *Human rights and the concept of a human community with a shared future*. Chinese Perspectives on Human Rights and Good Governance. Leiden: Brill.
CPC Central Committee. 1981. Guanyu jianguo yilai dang de ruogan lishi wenti de jueyi (1981 nian 6 yue 27 ri Zhongguo gongchandang di shiyi jie zhongyang weiyuanhui di liu ci quanti huiyi tongguo). *Renmin ribao*, 27 June 1981: 1–9.
Cui, Chentao. 2019. 'Yidai yilu': makesizhuyi zhexue shijian guan de dangdai luoji. *Hanjiang shifan xueyuan xuebao* 2019 (2): 104–110.
Deng, Xiaoping. 1978a. Realise the four modernisations and never seek hegemony (7 May 1978). In *Selected works of Deng Xiaoping*, vol. 2:122–123. Beijing: Foreign Languages Press, 1995.
Deng, Xiaoping. 1978b. Shixian sihua, yongbu chengba (1978.05.07). In *Deng Xiaoping wenxuan*, vol. 2:111–112. Beijing: Renmin chubanshe, 2008.
Deng, Xiaoping. 1980a. Adhere to the Party line and improve methods of work (29 February 1980). In *Selected works of Deng Xiaoping*, vol. 2:273–282. Beijing: Foreign Languages Press, 1995.
Deng, Xiaoping. 1980b. Jianchi dang de luxian, gaijin gongzuo fangfa (1980.02.29). In *Deng Xiaoping wenxuan*, vol. 2:274–283. Beijing: Renmin chubanshe, 2008.
Deng, Xiaoping. 1980c. Muqian de xingshi he renwu (1980.01.16). In *Deng Xiaoping wenxuan*, vol. 2:239–273. Beijing: Renmin chubanshe, 2008.
Deng, Xiaoping. 1980d. The present situation and the tasks before us (16 January 1980). In *Selected works of Deng Xiaoping*, vol. 2:241–272. Beijing: Foreign Languages Press, 1995.
Deng, Xiaoping. 1982a. China's foreign policy (21 August 1982). In *Selected works of Deng Xiaoping*, vol. 2:407–409. Beijing: Foreign Languages Press, 1995.
Deng, Xiaoping. 1982b. Zhongguo de duiwai zhengce (1982.08.21). In *Deng Xiaoping wenxuan*, vol. 2:415–417. Beijing: Renmin chubanshe, 2008.
Deng, Xiaoping. 1990a. China will never allow other countries to interfere in its internal affairs (11 July 1990). In *Selected works of Deng Xiaoping*, vol. 3:346–348. Beijing: Foreign Languages Press, 1994.
Deng, Xiaoping. 1990b. Zhongguo yongyuan bu yunxu bieguo ganshe neizheng (1990.07.11). In *Deng Xiaoping wenxuan*, vol. 3:359–361. Beijing: Renmin chubanshe, 2008.
Diakonoff, Igor. 2003. *The paths of history*. Cambridge: Cambridge University Press.

Dong, Yukun, and Bai Baoli. 2016. 'Yidai yilu' zhanlüe de zhengzhijingjixue fenxi – makesizhuyi zhengzhijingjixue de fengfu yu fazhan. *Shaanxi shifan daxue xuebao (zhexue shehui kexue ban)* 46 (3): 18–26.

Engels, Friedrich. 1873a. Dell' autorità. In *Marx Engels Gesamtausgabe*, vol. I.24:82–86. Berlin: Dietz, 1984.

Engels, Friedrich. 1873b. On authority. In *Marx and Engels collected works*, vol. 23:422–425. Moscow: Progress Publishers, 1988.

Engels, Friedrich. 1883. Das Begräbnis von Karl Marx. In *Marx Engels Gesamtausgabe*, vol. I:25:407–413. Berlin: Dietz, 1985.

Faggioli, Massimo. 2018. China-Vatican talks uphold historical legacy. *Global Times*, 21 February 2018. http://www.globaltimes.cn/content/1090048.shtml.

Fang, Ning. 2015. *China's democratic path*. Translated by Wu Yisheng and Liu Aiyun. Springer Insights. Singapore: Springer.

Freeman, Duncan, and Gustaaf Geeraerts. 2012. Europe, China and expectations for human rights. In *Conceptual gaps in China–EU relations: Global governance, human rights and strategic partnerships*, ed. Pan Zhongqi, 98–112. Houndmills: Palgrave Macmillan.

Gianaris, Nicholas. 1996. *Modern capitalism: Privatization, employee ownership, and industrial democracy*. Westport: Greenwood.

Gottwald, Joern-Carsten, and Niall Duggan. 2012. Diversity, pragmatism and convergence: China, the European Union and the issue of sovereignty. In *Conceptual gaps in China–EU relations: Global governance, human rights and strategic partnerships*, ed. Pan Zhongqi, 35–49. Houndmills: Palgrave Macmillan.

Graeber, David. 2011. *Debt: The first 5,000 years*. New York: Melville House.

Grimm, Dieter. 2015. *Sovereignty: The origin and future of a political and legal concept*. Translated by Belinda Cooper. New York: Columbia University Press.

Grotius, Hugo. 1625. *The rights of war and peace*. Translated by John Clarke. Indianapolis: Liberty Fund, 2005.

Guo, Jianbiao, and Lin Fang. 2016. 'Yidai yilu' yu makesizhuyi huayu tixi jiangou yanjiu. *Jimei daxue xuebao (zhe she ban)* 2016 (4): 69–73.

Guo, Wei, and Zhao Shifa. 2018. Xinshidai Zhongguo tese shehuizhuyi renquan guan jiqi shijian. *Lilun shiye* 2018 (7): 27–31.

Haldén, Peter. 2011. *Sovereignty without statehood: Lessons from Europe's history before the sovereign state*. New York: Palgrave Macmillan.

Hegel, G.W.F. 1974. *Vorlesungen über Rechtsphilosophie 1818–1831*. Stuttgart-Bad Cannstatt: Friedrich Frommann Verlag.

Hegel, G.W.F. 1986. Berliner Schriften 1818–1831. In *Werke*, vol. 11. Frankfurt am Main: Suhrkamp.

Hobbes, Thomas. 1651. *Leviathan*. Cambridge: Cambridge University Press, 1996.

Hou, Huiqin. 2014. On the power of ideological discourse. *Marxist studies in China* 2014: 118–135.

Hu, Jintao. 2012. *Jianding bu yi yanzhe Zhongguo tese shehui zhuyi daolu, qianjin wei quanmian jiancheng xiaokang shehui er fendou (2012.11.08)*. Beijing: Renmin chubanshe.

Huang, Nansen. 1994. Shehuizhuyi shichang jingji lilun de zhexue jichu. *Makesizhuyi yu xianshi* 1994 (11): 1–6.

Jackson, Robert. 2007. *Sovereignty: Evolution of an idea*. Cambridge: Polity.

Jiang, Kai. 2018. Makesizhuyi renquan guan de zhongguohua yu dangdai jiangou. *Xibu xuekan* 2018 (11): 34–38.

Jiang, Zemin. 1995a. Correctly handle certain major relationships in the socialist modernization drive (28 September 1995). In *Selected works of Jiang Zemin*, vol. 1:449–464. Beijing: Foreign Languages Press, 2010.

Jiang, Zemin. 1995b. Zhengque chuli shehuizhuyi xiandaihua jianshe zhong de ruogan zhongda guanxi (1995.09.28). In *Jiang Zemin wenxuan*, vol. 1:460–475. Beijing: Renmin chubanshe, 2006.

Jouvenal, Bertrand de. 1957. *Sovereignty: An inquiry into the political good.* Translated by J. F. Huntingdon. Chicago: University of Chicago Press.

Kalmo, Hent, and Quentin Skinner. 2010. *Sovereignty in fragments: The past, present and future of a contested concept.* Cambridge: Cambridge University Press.

Kilcullen, John. 2011. Natural rights. In *Encyclopedia of medieval philosophy: Philosophy between 500 and 1500*, ed. Henrik Lagerlund, 867–873. Dordrecht: Springer.

Krasner, Stephen. 1999. *Sovereignty: Organized hypocrisy.* Princeton: Princeton University Press.

Li, Buyun, Chen Youwu, Yang Songcai, Liu Zhiqiang, and Yuan Bingxi. 2015. Zhongguo tese shehuizhuyi renquan lilun tixi lun gang. *Faxue yanjiu* 2015 (2): 56–79.

Li, Buyun, and Wang Xuejing. 1995. Renquan guoji baohu yu guojia zhuquan. *Faxue yanjiu* 1995: 19–23.

Li, Danjing. 2018. Makesizhuyi yu 'yidai yilu' jianshe. *Mao Zedong sixiang yanjiu* 2018 (5): 123–128.

Li, Long. 2018. Goujian renlei mingyun gongtongti shi shijie renquan shiye de weida chuangju. *Wuhan keji daxue xuebao (shehui kexue ban)* 20 (1): 1–7.

Li, Minghui. 2005. *Rujia shiye xia de zhengzhi sixiang.* Taibei: Taiwan daxue chuban zhongxin.

Liao, Fan. 2018. 'Renlei mingyun gongtongti' de renquan yu zhuquan neihan. *Jilin daxue shehui kexue xuebao* 2018 (6): 25–35.

Lin, Yuchuan. 2013. Pubian renquan de jeigou yu Zhongguo renquan moshi de jiazhi – jiyu makesizhuyi renquan lilun zhongguohua de fenxi. *Jiangsu shehui kexue* 2013 (2): 73–78.

Losurdo, Domenico. 2004. *Hegel and the freedom of the moderns.* Translated by Marella Morris and Jon Morris. Durham: Duke University Press.

Losurdo, Domenico. 2011. *Liberalism: A counter-history.* Translated by Gregory Elliott. London: Verso.

Losurdo, Domenico. 2013. Le libéralisme, ennemi le plus acharné du droit à vivre à l'abri. Interviewed by Anna Musso. *l'Humanité*, 16 August, 2013. https://www.humanite.fr/tribunes/domenico-losurdo-le-liberalisme-ennemi-le-plus-ach-547299.

Luther, Martin. 1523. Temporal authority: To what extent it should be obeyed. In *Luther's works*, ed. Walther Brandt, vol. 45:81–129. Minneapolis: Fortress, 1962.

Maritain, Jacques. 1951. *Man and the state.* Chicago: University of Chicago Press.

Marx, Karl. 1875a. Critique of the Gotha programme. In *Marx and Engels collected works*, vol. 24:75–99. Moscow: Progress Publishers, 1989.

Marx, Karl. 1875b. Kritik des Gothaer Programms. In *Marx Engels Gesamtausgabe*, vol. I.25:3–25. Berlin: Dietz, 1985.

Mencius. 1895. *The works of Mencius.* Translated by James Legge. Oxford: Clarendon.

Miéville, China. 2005. *Between equal rights: A Marxist theory of international law.* Leiden: Brill.

Mou, Zongsan. 1999. *Xinti yu xingti.* Shanghai: Shanghia guji chubanshe.

Paine, Thomas. 1791. *Rights of man: Being an answer to Mr. Burke's attack on the French revolution.* London: J. S. Jordan.

Patterson, Orlando. 1982. *Slavery and social death: A comparative study.* Cambridge: Harvard University Press.

Pavel, Carmen. 2014. *Divided sovereignty: International institutions and the limits of state authority.* Oxford: Oxford University Press.

Philpott, Daniel. 2001. *Revolutions in sovereignty: How ideas shaped modern international relations.* Princeton: Princeton University Press.

Pogge, Thomas. 2008. *World poverty and human rights.* Cambridge: Polity.

Pope Francis. 2016. Pope Francis: 'Trump? I do not judge. I care only if he makes the poor suffer'. Interviewed by Eugenio Scalfari. Translated by Kathryn Wallace. *La Repubblica*, 11 November 2016. Available at https://www.repubblica.it/vaticano/2016/11/11/news/pope_francis_trump-151810120/.

Proudhon, Pierre-Joseph. 1840. *Qu'est ce que la propriété? Recherches sur le principe du droit et du gouvernement.* In *Œvres Complètes de P.J. Proudhon.* vol. 1. Paris: Librairie Internationale, 1873.

Schmitt, Carl. 1922. *Politische Theologie*, 2015. Vier Kapitel zur Lehre von der Souveränität. Berlin: Duncker & Humblot.

Sima, Qian. 2014. *Shiji*. Beijing: Zhonghua shuju.

Sun, Pinghua. 2014. *Human rights protection system in China*. Heidelberg: Springer.

Sun, Xiangchen. 2014. Xiangsi er sheng yu shengshengbuxi – Zhongguo wenhua chuantong de shengcun lun jiegou. *Zongjiao yu zhexue* 2014: 223–235.

Sun, Xiangchen. 2015. Shuangchong benti: xingsu xiandai Zhongguo jiazhi xingtai de jichu. *Xueshu yuekan* 2015 (6): 20–34.

Sun, Xiangchen. 2017a. Jiazhi xingtai fenxi. *Zhongyang shehuizhuyi xueyuan wangzhan* 2017 (09). http://www.zysy.org.cn/a1/a-XCX9GND70AD609EC5E1AD6.

Sun, Xiangchen. 2017b. Xiandai geti quanli yu rujia chuantong zhong de 'geti'. *Wen shi zhe* 2017 (3): 90–105, 166–167.

Sun, Xiangchen. 2018. Shengsheng: zai shidai zhi shang cunzai. *Zhexue yanjiu* 2018 (9): 113–125, 128.

Sun, Xiangchen. 2019. *Lun jia: geti yu qinqin*. Shanghai: Huadong shifan daxue chubanshe.

Sun, Xiangchen. 2020a. Jia: Zhongguo wenhua zui qiejin de dangdai xingshi. *Zhongyang shehuizhuyi xueyuan xuebao* 2020 (5): 116–123.

Sun, Xiangchen. 2020b. Zai xifang jiang Zhongguo zhexue. *Wenhua zongheng* 2020 (4): 86–97, 142.

Sun, Xiangchen, and Lu Xinyu. 2017. Xiandaixing bushi minmie zishen de chuantong – Sun Xiangchen jiaoshou fangtan. *Xueshu yuekan* 2017 (4): 178–184.

Teschke, Benno. 2009. *The myth of 1648: Class, geopolitics, and the making of modern international relations*. London: Verso.

Tierney, Brian. 1997. *The idea of natural rights: Studies on natural rights, natural law and church law 1150–1625*. Atlanta: Scholar's Press.

United Nations General Assembly. 1960. *Declaration on the granting of independence to colonial countries and peoples (Resolution 1514)*. New York: United Nations.

United Nations General Assembly. 1966a. *International covenant on civil and political rights (Resolution 2200A (XXI))*. New York: Office of the United Nations Human Rights High Commissioner.

United Nations General Assembly. 1966b. *International covenant on economic, social, and cultural rights (Resolution 543)*. New York: Office of the United Nations Human Rights High Commissioner.

United Nations General Assembly. 1986. *Declaration on the right to development*. A/RES/41/128. New York: Office of the United Nations Human Rights High Commissioner.

Vasak, Karel. 1977. Human rights: A thirty-year struggle: The sustained efforts to give force of law to the universal declaration of human rights. *UNESCO Courier* 30 (11): 29–32.

Wan, Qianhui. 2017. Zhongguo tese renquan guan de lishi fazhan yu neizai luoji. *Renquan* 2017 (5): 33–52.

Wang, Xigen, and Cui Yang. 2019. Gaige kaifang 40 nian Zhongguo renquan lilun yu shijian de chuangxin fazhan. *Faxue zazhi* 40 (199): 1–8.

Wang, Zhaoming. 2017. 'Yidai yilu': makesizhuyi shijie lishi lilun de zuixin fazhan. *Zhonggong Nanchang shiwei dangxiao xuebao* 2017 (4): 2–5.

Weatherley, Robert. 1999. *The discourse of human rights in China: historical and ideological perspectives*. Houndmills: Macmillan.

Wolff, Hans Julius. 1951. *Roman law: An historical introduction*. Norman: University of Oklahoma Press.

Wu, Fan. 2018. Lun xinshidai Zhongguo tese shehuizhuyi renquan sixiang chuangxin. *Lilun yuekan* 2018 (12): 13–19.

Xi, Jinping. 2013. Hongyang renmin youyi, gong chuang meihao weilai – zai Nazha'erbayefu daxue de yanjiang (2013.09.07). *Xinhua wang* 2013: 1–3.

Xi, Li. 1995. Guojia liyi yu guojia guanxi. *Gaoxiao lilun zhanxian* 1995 (3): 12–15.

Xu, Tao. 2016. Zhongxi zhexue huitong shiyu zhong de 'neizaichaoyue' yu 'tianren heyi'. *Xueshu yuekan* 2016 (6): 166–176.

Yang, Weimin. 2017. Zhongguo tese zhengdang zhidu de youshi ji dui shijie gongxian – 'wei renlei dui genghao shehui zhidu de tansuo tigong Zhongguo fang'an' zhi guanjian. *Tongyi zhanxian xue yanjiu* 2017 (1): 15–31.

Yang, Zhi, and Qin Zhen. 2018. 'Yidai yilu' changyi shi makesizhuyi zhongguohua de weida chuangxin. *Jiaoxue yu yanjiu* 2018 (1): 5–14.

Yu, Yingshi. 1998. *Xiandai ruxue lun*. Shanghai: Shanghai renmin chubanshe.

Zhang, Feng. 2016. Makesi Engesi de guoji jiaowang lilun yu 'yidai yilu' jianshe. *Makesizhuyi yanjiu* 2016 (5): 68–75.

Zhang, Shuangli, and Ni Yisi. 2017. Jintian weishenme yao chongdu Heige'er de Fazhexue – Yidali zhexuejia Duominike·Luosu'erduo fangtan lu. *Tansuo yu zhengming* 2017 (5): 69–75.

Zhang, Xuezhong, and He Hanxia. 2016. 'Yidai yilu': gong hui chongman huoli xin yuanjing – zhongguohua makesizhuyi fazhan sixiang yanjiu. *Shengchanli yanjiu* 2016 (6): 6–9, 23.

Zhang, Zhonghua, and Liu Fei. 2017. Makesizhuyi kaifang jingji sixiang yu 'yidai yilu' zhanlüe. *Zhonggong Qingdao shiwei dangxiao, Qingdao xingzheng xueyuan xuebao* 2017 (1): 34–36.

Zhou, Enlai. 1953a. Five principles for peaceful coexistence (31 December 1953). In *Selected works of Zhou Enlai*, vol. 2:128. Beijing: Foreign Languages Press, 1989.

Zhou, Enlai. 1953b. Heping gongchu wu xiang yuanze (1953.12.31). In *Zhou Enlai wenji*, vol. 2:113. Beijing: Renmin chubanshe, 1980.

Zhu, Yufu. 2012. Zhongguo fuchi renkou jiao shao minzu de chengjiu, jingyan he duice. *Heilongjiang minzu congkan* 2012 (5): 37–45.

Zhuang, Mu, and Wu Meichuan. 2017. Makesi gonggongxing sixiang shiyu xia 'yidai yilu' de sikao. *Makesizhuyi yanjiu* 2017 (7): 110–117.

Zwart, Tom. 2011. Rethinking human rights in China: Towards a receptor approach. In *Human rights in the Asia-Pacific region: Towards institution building*, ed. Hitoshi Nasu and Ben Saul, 249–263. London: Routledge.

Zwart, Tom. 2014. Realizing the Chinese dream: Letting the outside world better understand Chinese stories and Chinese voices on human rights. In *Collected papers of the seventh Beijing forum on human rights 2014 paper collection*, ed. Zhang Wei, 357–366. Beijing: China Society for Human Rights Studies.

Zwart, Tom. 2018. Getting the stories and voices of China heard: Promoting targeted poverty alleviation and 'putting people first' at the international level. In *Beijing forum on human rights 2018 paper collection*, ed. Zhang Wei, 466–474. Beijing: China Society for Human Rights Studies.

Zwart, Tom. 2019. The declaration on the right to development as a first step towards a comprehensive southern vision on human rights. *The Journal of Human Rights* 16 (1): 50–61.

Zwart, Tom. 2020a. The contribution of China to the development of international human rights during the past seventy years. *The Journal of Human Rights* 19 (1): 116–125.

Zwart, Tom. 2020b Building a human community with a shared future: The consequences for the international human rights system. In *Human rights and the concept of a human community with a shared future*, ed. Chang Jian, Li Ruoyu, Zhang Chong, and Shi Hui, 212–218. Chinese Perspectives on Human Rights and Good Governance. Leiden: Brill.

Chapter 8
Socialist Democracy in Practice

8.1 Opening Remarks

> What is the democracy that the Chinese people need today? The democracy that the Chinese people need today can only be socialist democracy or people's democracy, not bourgeois individualistic democracy. (Deng 1979, 175)

The topic of this chapter is socialist democracy, and with this topic we move from—to use Marxist terminology—the economic base (*jingji jichu*) to features of the superstructure (*shangceng jianzhu*), the latter of which includes the matter of governance. In China, socialist democracy has a number of integrated components: electoral democracy; consultative democracy; grassroots democracy; minority nationalities policy; rule of law; leadership role of the Communist Party; and human rights. Since I have dealt with human rights in the previous chapter, here I address the remaining components, which together form what is regarded as a 'highly democratic [*gaodu minzhu*] socialist political system [*zhidu*]' (CPC Central Committee 1981, 8), albeit one that is constantly a work in progress.

In researching this chapter, I have delved deeply into Chinese Marxist scholarship.[1] Socialist democracy in China is a subject of massive research, and each of the sub-topics is worthy of detailed study in its own right. Thus, the chapter is long and heavily referenced. Even so, I have had to exercise an even stricter discipline than other chapters: I cite only the most important and influential works. The chapter is long for another reason: as China steps onto the centre of the world stage, there is greater international attention and scrutiny devoted to its political system (less so its economic system). Most of this attention is actually positive, given what the system has achieved, but those who are part of the relatively few countries that make up the 'West' do not view China's political system so favourably, not least because they are quite misinformed and seek to see the world in their own image. Thus,

[1]For those unable to read Chinese and who seek a useful overview, see Fang Ning's *China's Democratic Path*, and the relevant section of Han Zhen's and Zhang Weiwen's *Contemporary Value Systems in China* (Fang N. 2015; Han F. and Zhang 2018).

R. Boer, *Socialism with Chinese Characteristics*,
https://doi.org/10.1007/978-981-16-1622-8_8

Western European liberal democracy has become the myth of 'democracy' as such and continues to be used as a model to assess other and quite different forms (Li S. 2009, 266–278; Yang G. 2009, 5–8). This is a classic case of '*yixi jiezhong*' (see Sect. 1.4.2), seeking to understand China according to a Western approach. Works that propagate such an approach are particularly unhelpful for understanding the realities of socialist democracy in China.[2] Instead, objective and scientific information is needed, and those best placed to provide that information are Chinese scholars. This chapter primarily concerns the actual practice of socialist democracy in China; the next chapter focuses on the theoretical development of socialist democracy in the Marxist tradition.[3]

Before proceeding with the presentation of the various components of China's socialist democratic system, we need to ask: what does 'democracy [*minzhu*]' mean in China? Historically, China's democratic struggle began with the anti-colonial Opium Wars and came to fruition with Liberation in 1949 (Fang N. 2015, 14–15). The key term used to explicate democracy is 'people as masters of the country [*renmin dangjia zuozhu*]'—a longer explication of Chinese *minzhu*, the people in charge, as masters. In a little more detail, the phrase 'people as masters of the country' means more literally that the people (*renmin*) act as the master of (*zuozhu*), or take responsibility for, the affairs of the house (*dangjia*)—the 'house [*jia*]' in question being the country as whole. The term already appeared in the new constitution of 1954, although one can trace earlier variations on the idea at least back to Sima Qian (c.145–c.86 BCE) in his *Shiji*, or *Historical Records*, from the time of the Han Dynasty.[4] Of course, in a Marxist framework, the meaning of the phrase is quite distinct. A couple of other terms also relate to 'people as masters of the country', the first being 'people oriented' or 'putting people first [*yiren weiben*]'—literally being focused on the people as the basis, principle, and priority.[5] A little later, the term was clarified in light the Marxist focus on concrete, flesh-and-blood people, rather than an abstract

---

[2]Examples include the authoritarian-democratic distinction, with any system that does not follow the model of capitalist democracy labelled as 'undemocratic' and 'authoritarian', as well as the 'China doomers', who predict with wearying frequency the imminent 'collapse' of China's political system since it is not following a process of bourgeois liberalisation (Lipset 1959; Lieberthal and Lampton 1992; Dickson 2003; Weatherley 2006; Tsai 2007; Wright 2010; Fewsmith 2012, 52–55; Landry 2012; Weller 2012; Huang Y. 2013; Nathan, Diamond, and Plattner 2013; Wu G. 2013; Lampton 2014; Miranda 2017). It should be no surprise that these misguided efforts are met with a well thought-through rejection by those subjected to the propaganda (Ogden 2007, 50; Xie 2009). Further, a few suggest that China is making a transition to a Confucian-inspired meritocracy, or a 'nonliberal elitist democracy' of the type found in other Asian societies (Bell 2006; Peerenboom 2007, 233–81). While these very Western approaches at least attempt to understand China, there is a glaring omission: the centrality of China's socialist system.

[3]Since I have dealt with economic democracy in the chapter on Deng Xiaoping, I will not discuss this feature here (Xie 2009, 21–22).

[4]In relation to first emperor of the Qin Dynasty, who unified China, Sima Qian writes: 'Today, it has been decreed, the law is issued, the common people manage the house as peasants and workers [*baixing dangjia ze li nonggong*], and the scholars learn the laws and bans' (Sima 2014, Vol. 1, 325). The text may also be found in chapter 6, stanza 38, at ctext.org/shiji/qin-shi-huang-ben-ji/ens.

[5]This phrase initially appeared in a decision from the third plenary session of the sixteenth central committee of the CPC (2003, 2).

'human being' (Zhao J. 2018, 12). From the CPC's eighteenth congress onward, we also find 'people centred', or more fully 'according to the people as centre [*yi renmin wei zhongxin*]' (Hu Jintao 2012, 21; CPC Central Committee 2014, 6; Zhonggong zhongyang xuanchuanbu 2019, 40–48). While the reference of these terms concerns all aspects of the construction of socialism in China (Chen X. 2015, 2), they may also be seen further explications of the meaning of *demokratia, minzhu*, rule and mastery by the people. It is precisely the reality and practice of socialist democracy that I examine in what follows.

8.2 Electoral Democracy and the People's Congresses

The first component concerns electoral democracy and its manifestation in the people's congresses. These have a longer history, as Mao Zedong's observation from 1940 indicates: 'China may now adopt a system of people's congresses, from the national people's congress down to the provincial, county, district and township people's congresses, with all levels electing their respective governmental bodies' (Mao 1940b, 677; 1940a, 352). Clearly, people's congresses were not only envisaged early in the process, but had already been practised in the Red Areas during the revolutionary struggle. The initial stipulation as to how they would work after Liberation appears with the Electoral Law of 1953, which has subsequently been revised on a number of occasions (National People's Congress 2015). The practice today has five levels of people's congresses: (1) the supreme legislative body of the National People's Congress, which first met on 15 September, 1954; (2) people's congresses in provinces, autonomous regions, and municipalities directly administered by the central government; (3) people's congresses in sub-districts of larger cities and in autonomous prefectures; (4) people's congresses of cities not sub-divided, municipal districts, counties, and autonomous counties; (5) people's congresses in villages, minority nationality townships, and towns.

This approach is called electoral democracy in the sense that elections pertain to the people's congresses as representative legislative bodies (this is apart from inner-Party elections). The crucial distinction is between direct and indirect elections. To return to the five levels of people's congresses, at levels four and five elections are direct. Every citizen over the age of 18 has the right to vote, and such a right is not restricted by any factor, whether ethnicity, sex, occupation, education, occupation, or religion. Further, every such citizen may stand for direct elections. Levels one, two, and three of the people's congresses have indirect elections: this simply means that delegates are elected from the people's congresses at levels four and five. All very well, but do people actually vote and stand for election? Here the further regulations are important: an election is valid only when more than 50% of eligible voters in a district actually vote, and the candidate who receives the majority of votes is elected. As for candidates, anyone may stand for election, and candidates may be nominated by all political parties and mass organisations. Further, a candidate may be nominated by ten eligible voters in direct elections and by ten delegates in indirect elections.

The number of such candidates must be more than the number of delegates to be elected. In direct elections, the number of candidates must be 30–100% more than the number of delegates elected; in indirect elections, the excess of candidates to delegates elected should be 20–50%.

These are basic facts concerning China's electoral democracy, but they need to be reiterated since there is considerable ignorance outside China concerning such practices. The outcome of this system is that China has more elections every year than any capitalist democracy. But there is another feature of China's electoral democracy that reveals an even greater difference: the assumed need for constant reform and improvement of socialist democracy. In critical Chinese research, we find emphases on improving the system of elections to people's congresses, including the principle of the same vote in urban and rural areas; strengthening the role of the standing committees of the people's congresses so that they may carry on the work of the congresses when the latter are not meeting; the need for increased education in how the system works so that citizens can participate in a more informed manner; ensuring that all eligible voters can in fact vote, with a particular focus on migrant workers from the countryside; and the need for constantly improving the supervision of the organs of governance so that they can eliminate bribery and function more smoothly and efficiently (Yang H. 2008, 20–21; Xiao and Yu 2012, 16–17).

Clearly, China's electoral democracy is not a given but a constant work in progress. One does not rely on a system established decades or even centuries ago, but constantly seeks improvements in light of practice and the need to resolve problems that have emerged. The reason for this constant need for criticism and improvement already appears in Mao Zedong's observation from 1940. Following the text quoted at the beginning of this section, Mao speaks of a 'genuinely democratic system [*zhenzheng de minzhu zhidu*]' in which there is 'really universal and equal suffrage, irrespective of sex, creed, property or education'. This democratic system, which fully expresses the 'will of all the revolutionary people' is none other than 'democratic centralism' (Mao 1940b, 677; 1940a, 532).

8.3 Consultative Democracy

Electoral democracy is usually paired with consultative democracy, with the two practices seen as distinct but complementary (Zhuang 2006, 81; Zhang Y. 2012; Xu Y. 2017, 11).[6] Lin Shangli explains the two approaches as follows:

> One is the democratic form in which people in different regions participate in the country's political life at different levels through their representatives, namely the People's Congress system; the second is a democratic form in which people from different sectors participate

[6]As a 2006 CPC document points out: 'The two important forms of socialist democracy in China are that the people exercise their rights through elections and voting, and that all sectors of the people engage in full consultation before making major decisions and reach as much consensus as possible on issues of common interest' (CPC Central Committee 2006, 1).

> in national political life through their functional representative organisations or representatives, namely, the system of the People's Political Consultative Conferences. The former is the system customised by national decision-making, while the latter is the system of social participation in the deliberation and administration of state affairs. Although these two systems are different in nature, their logical starting point is the same, that is, the organic unity of Party leadership and multi-class alliance. (Lin S. 2007, 18)

Given that consultative democracy focuses on discussion and consensus, some readers may be reminded of Western proposals for 'deliberative democracy'. The latter has been promoted assiduously ever since Bessette (1981) coined the term, to the point where we now have the inevitable Oxford 'handbook' (Bächtiger et al. 2018). Chinese researchers have studied this development in detail, since it promotes rational, consensus-based decisions. However, they note that this Western research indicates clearly the profound shortcomings of antagonistic capitalist democracy, against which 'deliberative democracy' is seen as an antidote. This reality entails that 'deliberative democracy' in capitalist societies has a thin basis, precisely because it is reactive and has not been put into widespread and state-level practice (Han F. and Zhang 2015, 48–49). The contrast with Chinese consultative democracy is stark: the latter has a solid basis in China's cultural and socialist tradition, along with extensive experience in consultation from the revolutionary period onward (Ma Y. 2015, 9–12).[7] Ultimately, the Chinese approach—with the givens of its socialist system and leadership of the Communist Party—is quite distinct from what is really a variation on capitalist democracy.

The Chinese foundations are philosophical and historical. Philosophically, we need to recall the emphasis on non-antagonistic contradictions within a socialist system (see Sect. 3.4.1), with the result that the political system that arises from this situation must of necessity reflect the elimination of class conflict and the priority of non-antagonistic class relations. Contradiction analysis also applies to the paradigms of electoral and consultative democracy, in which the two are not in an either-or but in a both-and relation: they complement one another through their strengths and are able to resolve respective limitations (Qi 2013; Dong 2017, 57–58; Ma Y. 2017, 27; Zhang M. and Yi 2017). Votes in the elected NPC—the supreme legislative body—provide an excellent manifestation of the process. While Western eyes superficially see the NPC as a 'rubber stamp' for the will of the CPC, the process for legislation to reach the NPC is long and arduous. Multiple consultations take place, with differences in public opinion aired, tensions and arguments presented and debated, until a broad consensus is reached by the time the legislation arrives at the NPC for a vote. Thus, the process entails the integration of electoral and consultative democratic practices (Lin S. 2007, 25).[8]

---

[7] As is so often the case, Chinese analysis of Western 'deliberative democracy' far outweighs genuine efforts from foreign scholars to understand China's consultative democracy. When the latter on occasion mention China, they assume that China is 'learning from' this Western development, and try to fit China's path into a Western model (Fishkin 2009, 106–111; Dryzek 2011, 135–154).

[8] As Zhou Enlai already observed in 1949, the key to China's approach to democracy lies 'not in the final vote, but mainly in prior consultation and repeated discussion' (Zhou E. 1949, 134).

8.3.1 Philosophical and Historical Foundations: Non-Antagonistic Contradictions and the Mass Line

Historically, some scholars point out that long-standing cultural assumptions of harmony (*hexie*), the common good (*tianxia wei gong*), and actual practices of governmental consultation, indicate deep roots in China's history (Zhuang 2006, 82; Wang Xuejian 2015; Yang W. 2017, 18–19; Zhou X. 2017; Fang L. and Meng 2019, 31). In terms of Communist roots, we may identify precursors in the 'three-thirds' principle during the War of Resistance Against Japan,[9] and especially in the 'mass line [*qunzhong luxian*]' that was developed and honed during the long revolutionary struggle. While the former has been long surpassed due to historical developments, the latter continues to be a foundational feature of Chinese democracy (Lin S. 2007, 19; Jiangxi sheng shehuikexue xueyuan ketizu 2011; Ou and Wang 2013; Ma S. 2014). Initially developed in the process of land reform in liberated areas before 1949, the mass line has the following features: 'it is inclusive, as the opinions of the broad mobilized masses are listened to; it is guided by reason, as the views of the masses are studied and become the views of the central system; it achieves balance through reflection, as opinions are constantly tested through the actions of the masses; and it links consultation and decision-making, as the views of the masses are elevated into action' (Ma Y. 2017, 27).[10] Initially, the mass line provided the mechanism for turning the Communist Party's project into a mass movement for liberation, with obvious historical success. But the mass line also provided the foundations of consultative democracy, understood in terms of constant process of consultation-based self-adjustment that ensures the government's decisions are based on mass participation.[11] The mass line would in time need to be institutionalised into rule-of-law procedures appropriate for a socialist democratic system, but it also provides an insight into the term 'mass organisation'.[12] These are not simply

[9] According to the 'three-thirds principle', the government was composed of one-third Communists, one-third Left progressives, and one-third middle-of-the-roaders and other elements.

[10] Or as Mao Zedong put it in his important text on leadership from 1943: 'In all the practical work of our Party, all correct leadership is necessarily "from the masses, to the masses". This means: take the ideas of the masses (scattered and unsystematic ideas) and concentrate them (through study turn them into concentrated and systematic ideas), then go to the masses and propagate and explain these ideas until the masses embrace them as their own, hold fast to them and translate them into action, and test the correctness of these ideas in such action. Then once again concentrate ideas from the masses and once again go to the masses so that the ideas are persevered in and carried through. And so on, over and over again in an endless spiral, with the ideas becoming more correct, more vital and richer each time. Such is the Marxist theory of knowledge' (Mao 1943a, 899; 1943b, 119; see also Ma S. 2014, 200–202).

[11] As Xi Jinping observes, 'Consultative democracy is a unique form and distinctive advantage of China's socialist democracy, and an important embodiment of the Party's mass line in the political field' (Xi 2013, 82; see also 2014c, 281–283; Weng and Liu 1993).

[12] The term 'masses [*qunzhong*]' has a rich semantic field in China, meaning the union of rural and urban workers who form the bedrock of the Communist Party, but also overlapping significantly with 'people'. Thus, the phrase 'the Party leads the people' means 'the Party leads the masses'. As an example, see the 2015 speech by Xi Jinping on mass organisations (Xi 2015a).

social organisations, characteristic of bourgeois civil society and in opposition to the state,[13] but specific organisations bearing a 'mass character [*qunzhongxing*]'. They have deep political roots, going back in many cases to the period of revolutionary struggle, and are representative of public matters not directly connected with governance. Obviously, these mass organisations have a distinct role in consultative democracy, and they have in many cases become part of the structure of people's political consultative conferences.

8.3.2 Chinese People's Political Consultative Conferences

The clearest and earliest institutionalisation of consultative democracy was in the people's political consultative conferences. Here we find the eight political parties apart from the CPC,[14] as well as 'personages without party affiliation' (Li C. 2008, 8–10). The primary location of these parties is in the various levels of people's conferences, from regional to national levels, most notably in the country-wide Chinese People's Political Consultative Conference (CPPCC), which meets every year at the same time as the NPC. Why these eight political parties, most of which were established in the first half of the twentieth century? Historically, they were part of the multi-party struggle against imperialism and feudalism, explicitly supporting the CPC in its struggle to establish a New China.[15] Thus, they responded enthusiastically to the invitation to participate in the (new) CPPCC,[16] which had its first plenary session on 21–30 September, 1949. Note the date: it was before the official declaration of the People's Republic on 1 October of the same year. It was at this inaugural meeting of the CPPCC that the 'Common Program' and organic laws were passed for the New China, as well as decisions concerning the capital, new flag and the name, People's Republic of China. The implication should be obvious: the very shape of the People's Republic was formed not as a one-party state—which was attempted by the Guomindang—but as a cooperative multi-party political system (Yang W. 2017, 19; Zhang S. 2018).

As regards the CPPCC's working methods in our time, consultation covers an ever-expanding range of topics, all the way from the Constitution and laws, through

[13]This means that the terminology of 'bourgeois civil society [*bürgerliche Gesellschaft*]' in tension with the capitalist state is not appropriate in a Chinese context (Boer 2018).

[14]The eight parties are: Revolutionary Committee of the Chinese Kuomintang (81,000 members); China Democratic League (181,000 members), China National Democratic Construction Association (108,000 members); China Association for Promoting Democracy (103,000 members); Chinese Peasants and Workers Democratic Party (99,000 members); China Zhi Gong Party (28,000 members); Jiusan Society (105,000 members); and the Taiwan Democratic Self-Government League (2,100 members) (State Council 2007b, 9–10; 2007a, 16–18).

[15]For a detailed history of this multi-party struggle, see the insightful account by Zhang Shiwei (2018).

[16]On the 'old' and short-lived CPPCC of 1946, based on the CPC and Guomindang, see Fang Ning (2015, 95).

budgets and development projects, to social and cultural matters. And the process covers all aspects, including drafting of proposals, decision-making, implementation, and assessment. More specifically, as the prime consultative body, all other organisations—including the CPC and NPC—submit topics to the CPPCC, which organises sessions for consultation and determines their scope and who will participate. Those involved must be sent all of the relevant documents one week beforehand, and at the consultation robust debate is encouraged and respected; no one is to hold back from expressing a position. After the consultation, those responsible—usually the CPPCC Standing Committee—write a report of the meeting and, taking on board all relevant suggestions, present a draft to all of the meeting participants for approval. The results of the decision are then submitted to the NPC and CPC. The responsibilities and expectations are high: 'CPPCC members should study hard, dig deep into the realities of life, engage in investigation and study, keep in close contact with the parties, organisations and people of relevant parties they represent, actively reflect the opinions and demands of the people, and better play their proper role in participating in and discussing state affairs' (CPPCC 1995, 2).[17]

8.3.3 Comprehensive Consultation and Democratic Supervision

However, restricting ourselves to the CPPCC, and even the lower levels of people's political consultative conferences, gives a somewhat limited presentation of the practice of consultative democracy. In order to gain a more comprehensive picture, I draw on the long and influential article by Han Fuguo and Zhang Kaiping (2015).[18] They identify at least five levels of consultation: state, society, economy, administrative policy-making, and base-level or grassroots. Obviously, these concern all levels of Chinese society,[19] although we should note the grassroots level, for this is my concern in the next section. Han and Zhang also identify participants in consultative democracy based on assessments of actual practice. These participants include mass and social organisations, multi-level people's congresses, Party organisations at all levels (which are also concerned with Party building), rural and urban community self-government organisations, and—notably—migrant labourers from the countryside.

[17]The preceding description is actually drawn from a key document from 1995 that stipulates the range of involvement, topics to be covered, and processes for consultation for which the CPPCC is responsible.

[18]Many are the studies one may consult, with their assessments and proposals for improvements in consultative democracy. Due to the sheer number, I can provide only a sample of the more relevant (Zhuang 2006, 85; Li C. 2008, 16–19; Yang H. 2008; Shi and Cui 2012; Xiao and Yu 2012; Han F. 2018).

[19]This should be no surprise, since the 2015 decision of the CPC Central Committee on promoting the construction of consultative democracy indicates how extensive it has become (2015b). Other scholars distinguish between political, policy or administrative, and social consultation (Li X. and Yan 2018).

To complete the picture, Han and Zhang write of the way consultative democracy has had an influence on the domains of urban and rural governance, on policy agendas (especially budgets, but also now with respect to the national five-year plans), on the structure of direct elections at the grassroots level, and on the pressing question of labour-management relations, not least in terms of labour security. As is the way of Chinese research, constructive criticism concludes their study, with a notable emphasis on the need for a nation-wide approach that embraces the dialectic of unity-in-diversity—given that the vastly different contexts require specific forms of consultative democracy.

By now it should be obvious that consultative democracy is extraordinarily widespread in China, but let me close this section with the observation that consultation entails not only cooperation and co-existence, but also supervision—of the work of the CPC and state organs through investigation, suggestion, and criticism (Zhuang 2006, 83).[20] This is not supervision of, but supervision *by* the democratic process. Or rather, it entails what Wang Puqu (2013, 37) describes as the 'dialectical unity of democratic decision-making and democratic supervision'. Already in 1957, Zhou Enlai observed that the risks of being in power included becoming 'dizzy with success' and divorced from the masses, or even becoming individual careerists who betray the masses. How to deal with this problem? At one level, such supervision should be undertaken by the CPC itself, through 'criticism and self-criticism [*piping he ziwo piping*]', but this is not enough. External supervision is also needed, especially by the other democratic parties, but also by mass organisations and people in different walks of life, not least for the sake or curbing dominant groups and protecting the vulnerable. 'As long as we dare to face reality', Zhou Enlai observes, 'dare to expose, criticise and correct mistakes, we should not be afraid of supervision'. Zhou goes further, for ultimately it is the masses who provide the best supervision: 'without the people, what can the Communist Party do? … If you do right, the people will support you. If you do wrong, the people will not support you' (Zhou E. 1957, 348–349; see also Mao 1956a, 278–280; 1956b, 296–297; Deng 1957a, 1957b). It is nothing less than supervision by the 'broad masses of the people [*guangda renmin qunzhong*]' (CPC Central Committee 1989, 1).

8.4 Grassroots Democracy

A major subset of consultative democracy is base-level (*jiceng*) or grassroots democracy, or—in full—'grassroots consultative democracy' (CPC Central Committee 2015b, 2015a). However, grassroots democracy has some features that give it distinct characteristics, most notably the integration with local governance structures of CPC

[20]Initially, this was expressed in an eight-character saying, 'long-term coexistence, mutual supervision', but in 1989 this was expanded to a sixteen-character saying, 'long-term coexistence, mutual supervision, sincere treatment of one another, and sharing weal and woe [*changqi gongcun, huxiang jiandu, gandan xiangzhao, rongru yugong*]' (CPC Central Committee 1989, 1).

committees, people's congresses, people's political consultative conferences, mass organisations, and—importantly—a significant degree of autonomy in decision-making (Lin X. 2017, 18–20). If we rely on foreign observers who became interested in the development of grassroots democracy over the last couple of decades, we may gain the impression that this form of democracy is a new phenomenon. Of course, these observers have tried to understand grassroots democracy in Western terms, vainly hoping that bourgeois liberalisation would follow, only to be flummoxed by the growth of grassroots democracy and its difference from Western models (Dryzek 2011, 135–154; Weller 2012; Wang Guohui 2014).

8.4.1 History: From Engels to Pre-Liberation Red Areas

But did grassroots democracy suddenly emerge at some time in the early twenty-first century?[21] Not at all. We may take two historical perspectives, one in terms of Marxist historiography in relation to political forms, and the other in terms of China's own development. The first draws us back to the question of 'baseline democracy', which Engels was the first to identify in his studies of the state and socialist governance. Although the material permeates his research of the 1880s, the best expression appears in 'The Mark' (Engels 1882a, 1882b), which was addressed to German peasants and sought to recover the pre-state democratic practices of the 'Mark association [*Markgenossenschaft*]'. Not merely recover, for Engels sought a dialectical transformation (*Aufhebung*) of this form of governance—in which the organs of governance stood in the midst of society—for the sake of communism (Boer In press). In this light, grassroots or base-level democracy is an old practice indeed.

When we turn to specifically Chinese studies, there is an emphasis of tracing the development of grassroots democracy in the period of revolutionary struggle and the political structures of the Red Areas, as well as the 'small parliaments [*xiao yihui*]' typical of rural areas and the mostly spontaneous urban committees in the 1950s. These developments had to be recalibrated with the introduction of the household responsibility system at the beginning of the Reform and Opening-Up, leading to a clear statement in the 1982 Constitution, which designated urban and rural committees as 'mass organisations of self-governance at the grassroots level' (National People's Congress 1982, art. 111). The path from the 'The Organic Law of the Villagers' Committees of the People's Republic of China (Trial)' (National People's Congress 1987), through Jiang Zemin's proposals (1997a, 30; 1997b, 31), until the newer developments of the last two decades in light of the Reform and Opening-Up, has been long, full of trial and error, expansion and improvement (Bu 2015, 45–47; Zhao X. 2016, 44–45; Fang L. and Meng 2019).

[21] This is the unfortunate impression from the well-intentioned but ill-informed collection edited by Leib and He (2006).

8.4.2 Two Case Studies: Miaoba and Dengzhou

My main concern, however, is to provide an overview of a couple of examples of grassroots democracy in action. These case studies are now myriad and the research on them equally plentiful. Thus, the examples given here are not isolated occurrences but increasingly common across China.[22] Of the three main types—rural, urban, and enterprise (Xiao and Yu 2012, 17)—I draw on two examples, one from the mountains of Yunnan and the other from the fertile plains of Henan. The first—from Miaoba township—is quite specific, focusing on the processes of participatory budgeting that were instituted in 2012 (Huang J. 2016, 109–110).

In Miaoba, they select a total of 50 people for terms of three years through recommendation from each village in the area. They also select household representatives and include a random pool of representatives. All of these people undergo training so they can get a grip on the budget, financial knowledge, and the needed reforms.

The process:

(a) Budget draft. Representatives may propose budget items in the draft stage. If seven representatives jointly submit a proposal it must be included in the draft. This approach seeks to enhance the autonomy of representatives over the budget. Further, 30% of the draft budget must include costs for public participation.

(b) Democratic consultation. Meetings are held twice a year to study and decide on the preparation and adjustment of next year's budget. Before each meeting, 25 people are randomly selected from 50 people's representatives to attend the meetings. The budget preparation group is composed of the mayor, deputy mayors, and the finance director, and this group reports to the public representatives. Further, any representatives who have made proposals for the draft may speak, as well as the Party branch secretary of the village or community that benefits from the project. At the meetings, people's representatives put forward opinions, make suggestions, and ask questions about the project.

(c) Project evaluation. Each proposal arising from discussion is debated and put to the vote. If the vote is more than two-thirds of the participants, the item must be included in the budget. If the approved budget exceed available funds, items will are implemented according to the ranking of votes.

(d) Approval by the local People's Congress. The final step of the process is to submit the draft budget to the local People's Congress or its presidium. If it

[22]One may find studies of many districts, towns, and villages in Wenling city (Zhejiang), Xinhe, Yueqing and Linhai cities (Zhejiang), Shangcheng and Yuhang districts of Hangzhou city (Zhejiang), Pengzhou city and Qionglai new village (Sichuan), Rizhao rural district (Shandong), Minhang district (Shanghai), Xinmi and Nanyang cities (Henan), Wuxi city (Jiangsu), Harbin city (Heilongjiang), Yanjin county (Yunnan), Shunde district in Foshan city (Guangdong), Chaoyang district (Beijing), Baodi district (Tianjin), Longkeng town (Guizhou). Given the sheer number of such studies, I can provide only a sample of references (Zhu S. 2014; Huang J. 2016; Li Y. 2016, 125–126; Shen and Tan 2016, 24–26; Feng and Luo 2017; Han F. and Xiao 2017; Lin X. 2017; Qian and Jiang 2017; Han F. 2018, 75–77; Ma D. and Zhang 2018; Wang Guoqin and Tao 2018; Yan and Lui 2018).

is approved, the budget will be implemented. Items not approved at this level may be held over and included in the following year's budget.

The second example comes from Dengzhou, a small county-level city in Henan province, with a focus on primary industries (Bu 2015, 48–49). Here the range of subjects for grassroots participation are impressive: long-term and annual work plans for rural construction; contract and lease of collective village lands; the raising and managing of funds for public welfare projects; establishment and contracting of collective economic projects and public welfare undertakings; purchase, construction, and disposal of collective assets; collective lending and restructuring of collective enterprises; construction planning, land requisition, and distribution of compensation; implementing policies on family planning, rural subsistence allowances, and rural cooperative medical care; distribution of funds and goods for disaster relief; and so on.

Participants for consultation are elected on the basis of reputations for honest and fair dealings, as well as political consciousness, and a quota system applies to ensure representation from new interest groups and emerging social organisations. Of particular note is that Dengzhou, and then Nanyang city as a whole (of which Dengzhou is a part), has developed since the early 2000s what is called the '4 + 2' approach: 'four meetings and two publications'. In more detail:

(a) Preliminary proposals by the village Party branch (first meeting), based on listening widely to the masses, detailed investigations, and direct suggestions.
(b) Discussion by the village's 'two committees' (which together comprise the second meeting). The preliminary opinions of the village Party branch are submitted to the 'two committees' of the village for discussion, and the opinions are deliberated according to the principle that the minority submits to the majority.
(c) Deliberation at the general meeting of Party members (third meeting). Agreed-upon opinions from the village's 'two committees' are submitted to the meeting of all village Party members, who will solicit further opinions, discuss, and deliberate.
(d) Villagers' representative meeting or villagers' resolution meeting (fourth meeting). Opinions discussed and adopted by all Party members are submitted to the villagers' representative meeting for discussion and voting.
(e) Disclosure of resolutions. Resolutions adopted by the villagers' meeting are made public for no less than seven days.
(f) Disclosure of implementation results. The results of the implementation of the resolution are announced to all villagers in good time.

These two examples indicate the development of the working methods of grassroots democracy that have led to a significant increase not only in participation in decision-making on a wide range of matters, but have also enabled significantly higher levels of public supervision and accountability. Needless to say, it ensures a distinct sense of ownership of the whole process and its results.

8.4.3 Improving Targeted Grassroots Democracy

Proposals for analysing these developments in grassroots democracy range from more practical matters such as improving the mechanisms to theoretical matters. Many are the proposals for improvements, especially in terms of the level of participation and inclusion of groups such a migrant workers, as well as the quality and decision-making input of participants, with resultant reforms in existing structures of local governance (Shen and Tan 2016; Zhao X. 2016, 48–52; Feng and Luo 2017; Li Z. and Du 2018; Xu K. and Zhu 2018). More theoretical issues concern the relations between unified leadership and multiple processes (democratic centralism), between top-down design and bottom-up initiative, CPC leadership and genuine mass participation, formal and informal processes of consultation, representation and consultation, rural and urban concerns, and the optimum democratic method for improving people's livelihoods (Bu 2015, 49–52; Han F. and Zhang 2015; Huang J. 2016; Tan 2018; Yin and Qiu 2018).

Out of these studies, I would like to emphasise three points. First, the very possibility for a new stage of grassroots democracy in the last couple of decades has a distinct material basis. As Zhao Xiuling (2016, 41–42) observes in an influential study, the vast bulk of rural residents have been lifted out of absolute poverty, which provides them the wherewithal to engage in local democratic practices. Yet, the process has generated a series of new contradictions, with socialist market economy relations, complex chains of economic interests, and all that goes with fostering entrepreneurial endeavours in light of local conditions. These economic shifts have generated corresponding social changes, requiring thorough reforms of local governance and democratic practices. Second, while the recent uptick in grassroots democracy may be attributed to responses to pressure for accountability or even to the reality of social conflict (typically in cases of corrupt acquisition of collectively-owned village land),[23] this is by no means always the case. As Li Yaoyao (2016) points out, the impetus for renewed local practices of grassroots democracy has also appeared incidentally (due to local initiative) and then developed by trial-and-error, or they have arisen through a process of absorbing local desires and appropriating practices from elsewhere, thereby enabling a fusion of local governance and democratic participation. Both impetuses are notable for an absence of any pressure for grassroots democracy, but are due to a desire to implement procedures. The third point concerns the nature of 'pilot' programs, or—better—targeted measures. Given the sheer diversity of China's landscape, settlement patterns, and economic activity, the forms of grassroots democracy must reflect the diversity of local conditions. For example, a measure that works in a sparsely populated rural area northwest of the Aihui-Tengchong line[24] may not be appropriate for a residential district in Shanghai.

---

[23]As Bu Wanhong (2015, 47) observes, by 2005 careful assessments had identified 30,000 'difficult villages [*nandian cun*]', or six percent of villages country-wide. Judging by the level of complaints, a major problem was corruption at the local level—a relic of the 'wild 90s'.

[24]The Aihui-Tengchong line was initially proposed by Hu Huanyong (1935). On the basis of population data, Hu found that more than 90% of the Chinese population has historically flourished

Thus, each development needs to take into account local realities and be tailored in such a way that one may speak of a continuing series of targeted programs appropriate for each situation.

8.5 Minority Nationalities

Although the question of nationalities is a topic in its own right (Mackerras 2003; Boer 2019; Hao S. 2020), I deal with it here as another important component of the overall system of socialist democracy. While the minority nationalities policy is usually seen as part of consultative democracy, it has the specific focus of ensuring the incorporation of minorities within the very structures of governance (Li C. 2008, 12). That said, the topic does require some background so as to understand how it fits within the socialist democratic framework.

8.5.1 Defining 'Minzu'

To begin with, *minzu* is best translated as 'nationality' and not as 'ethnic group', for which *zuqun* is the proper term.[25] Why? A nationality is not determined by ethnicity.[26] A range of determining features play a role, such as cultural or regional commonality, religion, or the appropriation of an identity initially proposed by government agencies.[27] To give an example: the nationality now known as the Hui (a Muslim

south-east of a line that runs from Aihui (Heilongjiang province in the northeast) to Tengchong (Yunnan province in the southwest). Political power too has historically been located in the same zone, but there is a problem: most of the mineral resources and headwaters of the major rivers are northwest of the line, as also are border regions such as Inner Mongolia, Xinjiang, and Tibet. The outcome: from earlier forms of the state until today, the focus remains on the unification of diverse areas (with wars fought only for securing such unification), state-directed redistribution of resources, stability and—especially—continuity (Fang N. 2015, 42–46). With the Reform and Opening-Up, development took place first in the southeast, with the northwest lagging.

[25] The semantic field of *zuqun* also includes 'race'.

[26] At this point a divergence appears with Western scholarship on 'ethnicity' and 'nation' (Ma R. 2011, 16). While Chinese scholars are fully conversant with Western scholarship on such matters, seeking to draw insights where useful, they also emphasise the distinctness of China's millennia-long cultural continuity. The difference may be captured by the contrast between a Western 'multicultural' state and a Chinese or indeed socialist 'multinational' state. As Wang Xi'en (2010c) argues, the latter is richer and stronger, in terms of both theory and practice.

[27] The origin of *minzu* is complex. The *Cihai* (Xia and Chen 2009, 2734) observes that *minzu* first appeared in the Southern Song dynasty (1127–1279 CE), referring to different types of people in a crowd or a state, but not with the modern sense. In the modern period, the word has attained two meanings, one under influence from debates at the turn of the twentieth century and the Soviet Union, according to which a nationality is a distinct group within a state, and the other from the West and referring to a country as whole, as in *Zhongguo minzu* (Ma R. 2007, 15). In terms of the first and dominant meaning, *minzu* translates Russian *natsional'nost'*, which designates a particular

group) has its roots in the era of the Tang Dynasty more than a millennium ago (Dillon 1999). The Tang emperors began to invite Muslim peoples from further west to come to Chang'an (now Xi'an), due to their reputation for hard work and trade. Over time, especially with the later Song and Yuan dynasties, more were encouraged to come to China and they spread across the country. A long history of intermarriage with Han people, as well converts among the Han, led eventually to a distinct nationality. Now for the twist: the Hui have become strongly conscious of being a nationality. This means that the long history of the Hui, with migration, intermarriage, state decisions and policies, has led to, if not produced, a strong sense of a distinct identity (Gladney 1991, 323). This example can be multiplied across nationalities, which throughout China's long and continuous history have developed through constant interaction with others (Ma R. 2007, 26). But let me summarise with the point that a nationality is distinct group within a state, a group defined by language, location, cultural history, economic shape, and at times religion.[28]

8.5.2 Preferential Policies (youhui zhengce): Economics, Culture, and Governance

How do the 'preferential policies [*youhui zhengce*]' work in China? After an intense process of research and identification in the 1950s (Ma R. 2012), the government eventually came to identify 56 official *minzu,* including the majority Han and 55 other groups, ranging in size from almost 20 million to a few thousand.[29] The policies are among the earliest enacted, since the realities of nationalities is one of the basic structural features of Chinese governance. Already in 1941 we find the establishment of the Mongolian and Hui autonomous regions within the Red Areas (Fang N. 2015, 53–54).[30] By the time of the 'Common Program' in 1949, the

group within a state that has overlaid common characteristics. The Russian terminology was itself the result of long debates and deliberations—from the turn to the twentieth century—concerning what was called the 'national question' in countries with significant diversity, such as Austria and Russia (Suny 1993, 2001; Egry 2005; Boer 2017, 142–156).

[28]The basis for such policies was Stalin's (1913a, 164; 1913b, 307) much-studied definition of a nation or nationality: "A nation is a historically constituted, stable community of people, formed on the basis of a common language, territory, economic life, and psychological storehouse manifested in a common culture'. This was, of course, only a beginning, for much research has been undertaken since (Ma R. 2000, 133; 2007, 14).

[29]By far the best works in English on China's nationalities are by Mackerras and Hao (Mackerras 2003; Hao S. 2020). One may also usefully consult Sautman (1998). In Chinese, the programmatic study by Ma Rong from 2007 has set the agenda for a whole new level of research, but see also the lengthy interview from a few years later (Ma R. 2007, 2013).

[30]While acknowledging the influence of the Soviet Union's model (Ma R. 2007, 27–28; 2011, 18–19), as also on all subsequent socialist states, Chinese scholars also emphasise the distinctness of China's path (Wang Xi'en 2010b), which is embodied in Mao Zedong's observation already in 1938: 'give the Meng, Hui, Zang, Miao, Yao, Yi, Fan, and all the other nationalities equal rights with the Han. Under the principle of joint resistance to Japan, they have the right to manage their

emphasis was on the equality and unity of all nationalities, with the need to establish autonomous regions where nationalities are concentrated. Above all, note article 53 of the Common Program: 'All minority nationalities have the freedom to develop their spoken and written languages, to maintain or reform their customs and religious beliefs. The people's governments shall assist the people of the minority nationalities in developing the construction of their political, economic, cultural and educational institutions' (CPPCC 1949, art. 53; see also National People's Congress 2018, art. 4). As with the Soviet Union, nationalities have been an integral part of the political structure from the beginning—in contrast to Western liberal states and their 'identity politics'.[31]

Let us focus on four features of the nationalities policy: economic development; cultural autonomy, with a focus on language, customs, and education; political autonomy; and the inviolability of China's borders. I begin with economic development, since the underlying Marxist approach to the minority nationalities policy focuses heavily on the economic base (Hao S. 2020). Since most minority nationalities live west of the Aihui-Tengchong line (see above) and usually in mountainous areas, they have typically lagged behind in economic development, especially during the Reform and Opening-Up. To compensate, economic policies entail central government incentives and investment—especially in infrastructure and transport—along with encouraging targeted projects and enterprises suited to local conditions and proclivities. These two elements—central and local—are particularly notable in large-scale projects such as the Belt and Road Initiative (for which Xinjiang in particular has become a major hub) and in targeted poverty alleviation (Wu X. and Hao 2017, 5).

Culturally, local languages continue to be fostered, which entails media, education, and literature. Local customs, rituals, festivals, and especially religions are not merely permitted but actively supported,[32] with temples, churches, and mosques constructed and maintained with state funds—so much so that minority peoples are far more religious than the Han nationality. In terms of education, school children receive classes in their local language, alongside the obligatory classes in Mandarin—needed for communication across China and for work. At university level, not only are there *minzu* universities in all regions, but students are also assisted—through quotas and extra points—for the all-important university entrance examinations, or *gaokao*. While these cultural policies are well-established in China, with significant resources devoted to enhancing their effectiveness, they are not fixed and unchangeable. This is particularly so in light of the rapid changes brought about by the Reform and Opening-Up. Ma Rong (2010) puts the tension in terms of 'protecting the traditional culture' and 'realising the modernisation' of minorities, especially in terms of

own affairs, while at the same time uniting with the Han to establish a unified state' (Mao 1938a, 619; 1938b, 506).

[31] Contrast the effort by Jiang Jieshi (Chiang Kai-shek) to see only 'tribes' or 'clans [*zongzu*]' apart from the Han (Chiang 1947, 39–40; in reply, see Mao 1945a, 1083–1084; 1945b, 305).

[32] The most authoritative and comprehensive study in English of the religious faith of the Chinese is by Zhuo Xinping (2018).

the mobility of labour and participation in the political, cultural, and economic life of China.

In light of this outline of the preferential policies for minority nationalities, we may return to the question of governance and socialist democracy. One the one hand, autonomous regions and prefectures now number almost 160 in China, with significant autonomy in policy development. On the other hand, all minority nationalities are represented in the CPPCC, along with people who may—through initial direct elections and then higher-level indirect elections—become delegates in the annual NPC. Thus, when issues arise relating directly to minority nationalities, the consultative role of the CPPCC comes into full force. I would add that minority membership of the CPC has been steadily growing: for example, in 1980 only three percent of the total number of members were from minority nationalities; at the time of writing, the percentage of members is drawing ever closer to the percentage of minority nationalities among the population as a whole, which is 8.14% (Mackerras 2003, 42).

8.5.3 Autonomy and Unity

It is precisely at the level of governance that a tension arises between autonomy and unity, concerning which three points are relevant. First, ever since the founding of the People's Republic, there have been efforts—usually coming in waves—to break up the country, with a particular focus on autonomous regions. Already in 1949, Zhou Enlai observed that every country has the right to self-determination, so that the New China should be on its guard: 'Today the imperialists want to split Tibet, Taiwan, and even Xinjiang; in this case, we hope that all ethnic groups do not listen to the provocation of imperialists' (Zhou E. 1949, 140). Over the decades since 1949, we can see how these efforts have unfolded: the United States' focus on Taiwan island and turning it into an 'unsinkable aircraft carrier' (Deng 1984b, 86; 1984a, 93); attempts to foster counter-revolutions in Tibet so as to undo its progress in economic improvement and democratic reform (State Council 2019c, 2019a); funnelling arms, trained fighters, and drugs into Xinjiang, while promoting 'atrocity propaganda' (see Sect. 1.4.1) and downplaying the real problems of terrorism promoted by such acts (Davis 2013, 102–103, 108; State Council 2019d, 2019b)[33]; revisiting the old practice from the nineteenth century of trying to use Hong Kong SAR as a lever to destabilise the mainland.[34] All of these externally supported efforts are of course framed in terms of the empty slogan of 'freedom and democracy' (which is seen in China as a Western neo-imperialist agenda), all the while peddling a line that

[33]On Xinjiang, it is worth noting that Muslim-majority countries support China's efforts to counter Islamic extremism and terrorism in Xinjiang, since they too have similar problems and work with China to deal with them.

[34]As far as English-language material is concerned, the best studies on Tibet and Xinjiang are by Sautman (1998, 2003, 2006, 2010), while one must consult Losurdo (2007, 249–250) in regard to Hong Kong SAR and Taiwan island. One may also usefully consult Norbu (2001) and Davis (2013).

completely ignores the fact that such regions have been part of China for centuries, as well as avoiding any recognition of China's minority nationalities policy and its significant achievements. In all of these cases, the observation of Mackerras (2003, 46), based on the experiences of those who actually live in such regions, is pertinent: 'what strikes me most forcefully about the period since 1980 or so is not how much the Chinese have harmed Tibetan culture, but how much they have allowed, even encouraged it to revive; not how weak it is, but how strong'. The same can be said of Xinjiang, Inner Mongolia, Ningxia, and many other minority areas.

Second, the approach to dealing with such problems draws heavily on a Marxist approach, with short-term and long-term solutions. In the short term, the need is to ensure safety, stability, and harmony, which entails strict measures to clamp down on the 'three evils' of separatism, extremism, and terrorism—the three are on a continuum—and counter the waves of foreign interference. In the long term, the underlying economic lag in development is the focus, with programs—all the way from education to economic incentives—focused on improving socio-economic well-being. Given that such improvement is the core human right in China (see Sect. 7.5.2), it is very clear that China has always sought to promote human rights among its minority nationalities.

The third point entails returning to contradiction analysis, specifically in terms of how to manage the contradiction of unity and diversity (Hao S. 2020, 95, 217–218). On the this matter, there is some debate, which is still influenced by the aftermath of the disintegration of the Soviet Union. Chinese assessments concluded that a significant part of the problem was that although the Soviet Union pioneered preferential policies for nationalities, it was unable to continue reforming the system so as ensure the state's unity while fostering the diversity of nationalities. At a point of weakness, some of the Soviet Union's autonomous regions began to declare independence, spurred on and assisted by Western forces keen to break up the country. The question arises: how to manage a unitary socialist republic with multinational diversity? Two main answers are embodied in a difference of opinion between two leading scholars of minority nationalities: Ma Rong draws more on Western materials and argues that nationalities should have even greater support for economic, cultural, and linguistic development, but that political autonomy should be reserved for the state as a whole, for which the term 'nation' should be used (Ma R. 2007, 2011; see also Zhang Jijiao and Wei 2018). By contrast, Wang Xi'en (2009, 2010a) argues that China should continue to follow its own path, determined by Marxist analysis. Thus, the approach to managing this complex contradiction is not in terms of emphasising one element and playing down the other, not a delicate balance and constant readjustment, but rather a full dialectical move: the greater the autonomy, the greater the unity; the more people's lives are improved through the preferential policies, the more do they see themselves as part of the whole. To integrate means to diversify, and vice versa. This approach has indeed become the dominant position and is promoted by the CPC and the government (Xi 2014b, 300; Wu X. and Hao 2017, 4).[35]

[35]This approach also embodies the spirit of Zhou Enlai, who emphasised that the People's Republic is not a federal state, but a republic that entails 'advocating regional nationalities autonomy and

As a footnote to this approach, I would like to return to consultative democracy, now going beyond the institutionalised role of minority nationalities in the political consultative conferences. As Lin Shangli (2007, 24) observes, safeguarding the rights of nationalities entails enabling them to express their interests and participate on an equal footing through consultation and interaction. Only when they are full able to do so, through the channels of democratic practice discussed earlier, will their rights be enhanced and so also China's unity.

8.6 Rule of Law

Rule of law is another necessary component of China's socialist democratic system (Xie 2009, 29), although it is also—like minority nationalities—a topic in its own right.[36] Let us begin with a small but significant amendment to the Chinese Constitution. On the eleventh of March, 2018, at the thirteenth National People's Congress, a specific phrase in the preamble to the Constitution was amended: 'improve the socialist legal system [*fazhi*]' became 'improve the socialist rule of law [*fazhi*]'. The change was only in the final character of the phrase, from 制 to 治—although they have exactly the same pronunciation: *zhì*. The amendment may seem simple enough, but there was a long history—with intricate legal debate—of development to get to this point.[37]

8.6.1 Legal System and Rule of Law

Three parallel debates influenced the change from 'legal system' to 'rule of law', the first of which concerned these two terms. Some background: 'legal system' is

exercising the powers of national autonomy' (Zhou E. 1949, 140). Relevant here is the influential proposal of a leading anthropologist, Fei Xiaotong (1989), who coined the phrase '*duoyuan yiti*', stressing the dialectical notion of 'diversity in unity' as it has emerged in China's long history of multiple nationalities. Further, if we compare the initial law on Nationalities Autonomy of 1984 with the revised version of 2001, we find that autonomy at all levels has not been reduced but enhanced—economically, culturally, and politically (National People's Congress 1984, 2001; see also State Council 2005). At the same time, the revised law stresses even more that the borders of the country are inviolable.

[36]Many Chinese scholars also see rule of law as integral to the other major components of China's reform process, such as modernisation, *xiaokang* society, harmonious society, planned and market economies, and so on. The most comprehensive history of the development and meaning of rule of law in English is by Li Lin (2018), while in Chinese one may also consult Zhang Wenxian (2018).

[37]For useful surveys, with copious references, of developments in Chinese jurisprudence since the beginning of the Reform and Opening-Up, see Liu, Li and Feng (2008), and Chen and Li (2018). One of the few English works that at least attempts to understand rule of law on Chinese terms is by Peerenboom (2002), although the work is notable for its complete misunderstanding of the central role of Marxism.

an ancient term in China, while 'rule of law'—in its modern sense—is a relatively recent term, appropriated from Western discourse and sinified. In more detail, 'legal system' appears already in the *Yueling* chapter of the *Book of Rites*: 'restore the legal system [*xiu fazhi]'*.[38] Further, 'legal system' appears with two overlapping senses: a static meaning with reference to the existing laws and regulations of a country; a dynamic sense, which includes formulating legislation, revision, enforcement, and supervision—all of which comprise components of the overall legal system.[39] In this light, 'legal system' seems like a neutral term, designating the reality that every country has a legal system, in both static and dynamic dimensions.

By contrast, 'rule of law' in its modern sense is not attested in the Chinese tradition,[40] and Chinese scholars acknowledge the influence of the Western tradition in spurring the development of a distinct Chinese approach.[41] Further, the Reform and Opening-Up, with its myriad economic and social transformations, has generated the need for a robust rule of law to ensure the smooth working of the socialist market economy (Li L. 2011, 75–77; Gong 2015, 36–39). However, Chinese scholars are very clear that the concept of 'rule of law' should not be appropriated in its liberal and capitalist sense, since this would be an ill fit indeed in China's socialist system (Yao and Huang 2012, 11–13; Fu and Zhu 2015, 23–24, 27–28; Zhang W. 2017b, 11). Instead, 'rule of law' needs to sinified in two related ways. The first is China's long legal tradition, specifically in terms of the intersections between the Legalist and Confucian traditions (see more at Sect. 8.6.2 below). The second type of sinification involves the Marxist tradition. This is where the full term 'socialist rule of law [*shehuizhuyi fazhi*]' comes into play, which entails not only in-depth research on Marxist jurisprudence all the way from the classics of the Marxist tradition to the implications of the sinification of Marxism in light of China's concrete conditions and the Reform and Opening-Up, but also the insistence that a rule of law developed in China should arise from and undergird its socialist system (Fu and Zhu 2015, 19–21; Chen Youwu and Li 2018, 73).[42]

In light of this brief exposition, it remains unclear why there was a distinct shift in the constitutional amendment of 2018, from 'legal system' to 'rule of law'. On

---

[38]The Chinese text may be found at ctext.org/liji/yue-ling. For further examples, see He and Qi (2018, 7).

[39]The *Cihai* (Xia and Chen 2009, 560) distinguishes three senses of 'legal system': the widest, which incorporates all the laws (written and unwritten) of a state and its various political, economic, and cultural components; a medium sense, which incorporates legal system and legal order; and the narrowest, the legal system itself (*falü zhidu*). The narrowest is the most common usage.

[40]The term itself appears in the Chinese tradition, but with the combined sense of 'law-and-governance'. A good example is the *Huainanzi* (compiled in the second century BCE), in the *Fanlun* chapter: 'If you understand from whence law-and-governance [法治] arise, then you can respond to the times and alter. If you do not understand the origin of law-and-governance [法治], even if you accord with antiquity, you will end up in disorder' (Liu An 2010, 611). The Chinese text may be found at ctext.org/huainanzi/fan-lun-xun. For further examples, see He and Qi (2018, 8).

[41]He Qinhua (2011, 2015, 34–36), a leading legal scholar, has particularly emphasised this aspect, albeit always with a need to 'localise' such an influence in light of Chinese conditions.

[42]For a detailed overview of scholarship on this emphasis, see Yao and Huang (2012, 5–9).

initial appearances, there appears to be little conflict between the two terms. 'Legal system' is ancient, with static and dynamic senses, while 'rule of law' is more recent, undergoing a full sinification in terms of Chinese Marxism. Why then make the shift? In the 1990s, there was considerable debate over the two terms, with positions taken falling into three main types (Sun S. 2006, 43–44). The first was that 'legal system' and 'rule of law' are identical, with the same basic sense of following or working according the law. The second position was that the two terms are related but distinct: assuming that 'legal system [*fazhi*]' is an abbreviation of 'a system of laws [*falü zhidu*]', scholars argued that a legal system concerns the reality of an overall system with its components, such as constitution, laws, judiciary, enforcement, and legal profession, while rule of law concerns the underlying principles of the legal system, such as the supreme authority of law, justice, stability, universality, openness and equality of law, checks on political power, and protection of human rights. It follows that while all countries have a legal system, they do not necessarily have the rule of law. The third position was that the two terms are dissimilar. In contrast to a legal system, rule of law entails that governance, society, economy, and ecology are all subject to the law, and that a country cannot develop a democratic system—of whatever type—without a rule of law in which everyone is equal.

The outcome of these debates was a combination of the second and third positions: legal system and rule of law are different, in the sense that they concern distinct realms of meaning, but they relate to one another precisely through such a demarcation: rule of law provides the principled framework for the functioning of a concrete legal system (Liu H. and Li 1998).

8.6.2 Rule of Law and Rule of Virtue

This debate was by no means the end of the matter, for the distinctly sinified version of 'rule of law' was influenced by the Chinese tradition. Earlier, I mentioned that the term itself—in its modern sense—does not appear in the tradition. But Chinese scholars have been wary of simply appropriating the Western sense of the term, since that sense is a superstructural feature of a capitalist system.

On this matter, we need to go back to the intersections between Legalism (*fajia*) and Confucianism (*ruxue* and *rujia*). It is not my task here to delve into the vast complexities of these two lines in relation to jurisprudence,[43] since my purpose is to draw out a dialectical point. Thus, He Qinhua (2015, 36–38) identifies two lines or emphases. The loose collection of pre-Qin legal scholars who later became known as the Legalists emphasised that governance should work 'according to law as the basis [*yifaweiben*]' and that all, from highest to lowest, should follow the law. This approach, however, was predicated on the assumption that 'human nature is evil [*xing'elun*]' and thus required strong punishments and appropriate rewards

[43] For an excellent overview in English, see Zhang Jinfan (2013), while one may also consult in Chinese the works of He Qinhua (2017, 2018).

for the sake of social order. The Legalists are often maligned as instigating harsh punishments, and the adoption of Legalism by the initial dynasty that unified China—the Qin Dynasty—is often given as a reason for its relative brevity (221–206 BCE). The sheer harshness of the laws soon led to revolt and the dynasty's overthrow. At the same time, scholars are keen to point out that whenever a government has needed to root out corruption and ensure stability for the sake of economic and social improvement, it has resorted to the Legalist tradition.

The other emphasis is Confucian, which sought 'both hands [*liangshou*]' of legal sanction and virtue, albeit with a distinct emphasis on the latter: benevolence, righteousness, ritual (propriety), wisdom, and faithfulness (*renyilizhixin*) are the five key virtues, which would ensure stability and harmony—and indeed a concern with the common people's livelihood (so Mencius). As the *Analects* (1993, 2.3) put it: 'If the people are guided by law, and kept in order by punishment, they may try to avoid crime, but have no sense of shame. If they are guided by virtue, and kept in order by the rules of propriety, they will have a sense of shame, and moreover will come to be good'. In short, the Confucian emphasis is both 'rule of virtue [*dezhi*]' and 'rule of propriety [*lizhi*]'. As we will see in a moment, there is a danger within this Confucian emphasis that virtue, as embodied in the ruler, would mean the diminution of law. Indeed, it was precisely this risk that led to an explicit dialectical connection between law and virtue through the work of Dong Zhongshu (179–104 BCE), who was instrumental in establishing Confucianism as the state system for the Han Dynasty (202 BCE–220 CE). He did so by drawing on the Daoist tradition of yin-yang: the two lines are inescapably connected in governance, in which the positive yang is virtue and the negative yin is punishment. Thus, while 'virtue is more vital than punishment [*rende bu renxing*]', it would be vain to imagine that one can do without the sanction of law.

In light of this tradition, there are those in recent debates who have argued that rule of virtue is a feature of feudal and patriarchal society and is thus not appropriate for modern China (Sun L. 2002; Sun S. 2006). Theirs is not the view held by the majority of scholars, who argue not that the rule of law embodies the Legalist emphasis and that rule of virtue is a Confucian addition, but that in a Chinese context the modern sense of rule of law itself includes both law and virtue.

8.6.3 Rule of Law Versus Rule of a Person

Yet, it was not the law-virtue debate that was the primary trigger for the 2018 constitutional amendment from 'legal system' to 'rule of law'. The key was a third debate—usually interwoven with the preceding two debates—concerning the rule of law and rule of a person (*renzhi*). This opposition was the main impetus for emphasising the rule of law, for specific historical reasons in relation to the Cultural Revolution. Chinese scholars generally agree that the initial foundations for China's modern 'legal revolution' go back to Liberation in 1949 (Gong 2015, 30–32; Zhang W. 2017b, 6–7).[44] However, the deviation of the Cultural Revolution disrupted this process, with Mao Zedong raised to a whole new level as the leader who would keep matters on the correct path.[45] The twist is that during the Cultural Revolution Mao unwittingly embodied a tendency in Confucianism to emphasise the virtuous ruler—the risk of pushing virtue too far. As the *Zhongyong* section of the *Book of Rites* puts it, 'governance depends on a human being [*weizheng zairen*]'; indeed, 'if a person exists, the government will flourish; if a person dies, the government will cease'.[46] This emphasis came to be known as 'a person of virtue rules the country [*xianren zhiguo*]'. In short, left to its own devices the emphasis on virtue can lead to the 'rule of a person', which may produce 'evil fruit [*eguo*]' (He and Qi 2018, 14).[47] It is this historical background that Deng Xiaoping (1986a, 177; 1986b, 178–179) had in mind when he observed: 'through the reform, we intend to straighten out the relationship between the rule of law [*fazhi*] and the rule of a person [*renzhi*]'.[48]

But I have leapt ahead in the narrative, for Deng's usage of 'rule of law [*fazhi*]' appeared in 1986, in the midst of a significant debate. Back in 1978, he did not use such terminology, finding that reforming and strengthening the 'socialist legal system' was sufficient.[49] However, 'legal system' would soon prove to be insufficient in light of a debate that turned on the question of rule of law and rule of a person.[50] In this debate, which ran from 1978 to 1997, three main positions were argued (Chen Youwu and Li 2018, 67–68; Liu Xuebin, Li, and Feng 2008, 15). First, laws are made and carried out by human beings, which in a Marxist framework entails the

[44] Article 17 of the 'Common Program' (1949) reads: 'Abolish all laws, decrees and judicial systems of the reactionary Guomindang government that oppress the people, enact laws and decrees to protect the people and establish the people's judicial system [*sifa zhidu*]'.

[45] For a detailed account of struggles leading up the Cultural Revolution, in which 'rule of a person' gradually came to the forefront, see Hao Tiechuan (2015).

[46] The Chinese text may be found at ctext.org/liji/zhong-yong.

[47] Note also Deng Xiaoping's observation (1989b, 325; 1989a, 314–315) as he was planning retirement: 'I have never believed in exaggerating the role of any one individual, because that is dangerous and makes it difficult for others to carry on. The stability of a country and a party cannot be based merely on the prestige of one or two persons. That tends to create problems'.

[48] See also Xi Jinping's (2015b, 12) observation: 'The rule of law and the rule of a person is a basic problem in the history of human political civilisation, and also a major problem that all countries must face and solve in the process of modernisation. Looking at the modern history of the world, no country that has successfully realised modernisation has failed to solve the problems of the rule of law and the rule of a person. On the contrary, although some countries achieved rapid development for a time, they did not reach the threshold of modernisation smoothly, but fell into one or another "trap," resulting in stagnation or even retrogression in economic and social development. The latter situation is largely related to the lack of rule of law'.

[49] For example, in the key document from the Third Plenary of the CPC's Eleventh Central Committee we find 'turn the socialist legal system into a powerful instrument for protecting the rights of the people' (CPC Central Committee 1981, 8).

[50] A trigger for this debate was Deng's observation (1978b, 146; 1978a, 156): 'Democracy has to be institutionalised and written into law, so as to make sure that institutions and laws do not change whenever the leadership [*lingdaoren*] changes, or whenever the leaders change their views or shift the focus of their attention'.

proletariat, Communist Party, and indeed the whole people. Thus, all a socialist country needs is a legal system developed by human beings; it does not need rule of law. Second, the opposition between rule of law and rule of a person is a false one, for a country requires both. Third, the rule of law is clearly superior to the rule of a person. Thus, the rule of a person risks emphasising that it matters not whether the law is good or bad, but rather that the ruler is wise and virtuous. By contrast, the rule of law is inseparable from socialist democracy: democracy is the basis of rule of law and rule of law is the guarantee of socialist democracy.

The third position came to be accepted by the end of the 1990s, but a question remains: what happened to 'legal system'? It came to be seen as inadequate on its own. As mentioned earlier, it was agreed that every country may have a legal system, but not every country has a rule of law. Indeed, a legal system could be used by a few, or even one person, to advance their own agenda. 'Legal system' left to its own devices risks becoming 'rule by law'—a common translation of the term *fazhi*—in which the legal system becomes an instrument deployed in the rule of a person. This is not to say that a 'legal system' should be abandoned, but it needs a rule of law to prevent its deployment under rule by a person (He and Qi 2018, 11). Thus, the legal system requires rule of law to enable its improvement; at the same time, rule of law is meaningless without a legal system in which rule of law can be embodied. In other words, the legal system is the basis of the rule of law, but rule of law constitutes the goal and value of the legal system.

8.6.4 Governing the Country According to Law

The practical implications of all this legal debate are embodied in the phrase 'law-based governance', or—better—'governing the country according to law [*yifazhiguo*]'. This phrase indicates the connection between theory and practice: the development of the theory of rule of law is inescapably related to the practice of governing the country according to law. The key moment came in Jiang Zemin's (1997a, 28; 1997b, 29) report to the CPC's Fifteenth National Congress: here he spoke for the first time of 'governing the country according to law' and building a—literally—'socialist rule of law country [*shehuizhuyi fazhi guojia*]'—a phrase that was incorporated into the constitutional amendments of 1999. Over the next couple of decades, we find Hu Jintao (2012, 18) speaking of 'the rule of law' as the 'fundamental way of ruling the country', the CPC's Central Committee (2014) issuing a major statement on promoting the rule of law as one of the 'four comprehensives [*si ge quanmian*]',[51] and the constitutional amendment of 2018, which laid the foundation for a whole new stage of development.

[51] The other three 'comprehensives' are building a *xiaokang* society, deepening reform, and strict Party discipline (Wang Yujue 2015). As Xi Jinping's observations (2014a, 2–3) make clear, the decision by the Eighteenth Central Committee was based on extensive consultations and soliciting of opinions and proposals—as one would expect in terms of consultative democracy.

This is all very well, but I have not yet addressed directly how it is a Marxist or indeed socialist rule of law. On this matter, the leading Chinese legal scholars are keen to offer their perspectives,[52] so let me draw from their work the following key points. First, rule of law ensures and promotes the people as masters of the country. This entails both rights before the law—understood in terms of the Chinese Marxist approach to human rights (see the previous chapter)—and responsibilities, such as ensuring social fairness and justice, and promoting common prosperity. It also includes a transparent and well-administered legal system subject to high standards. Second, rule of law means equality before the law. It applies uniformly and strictly to everyone, from the Central Committee to the common person working hard for the advancement of China. As Xi Jinping (2017a, 16; 2017b, 35) points out in his major speech at the CPC's Nineteenth Congress: 'We must promote the rule of law and work to ensure sound lawmaking, strict law enforcement, impartial administration of justice, and the observance of law by everyone'. Third, rule of law ensures not merely that every component of the socialist democratic system works, but also that electoral and consultative democracy (including grassroots democracy) have a substantive—rather than merely formal—influence on decisions. Fourth, rule of law functions as the most comprehensive level of checks on and supervision of the exercise of power by the CPC, but also of the NPC and CPPCC, so as to ensure transparency and institutionalised processes. Fifth, rule of law must include the rule of virtue.[53] Let us recall the earlier observations on the Chinese tradition and quote Xi Jinping (2012b, 141; 2012a, 170): 'law is written morality [*daode*], while morality is inner [*neixin*] law. We should persist in combining the rule of law with the rule of virtue'—or, as the Chinese text puts it, 'ruling the country according to law [*yifazhiguo*] and ruling the country according to virtue [*yidezhiguo*]'.[54] Sixth, rule of law is forward-looking and dynamic. Not only does it release social vitality, maintain social fairness and justice, and promote social harmony and stability, but it is part and parcel of the whole process of socialist modernisation and Chinese rejuvenation. Finally, and most importantly, rule of law relies on and ensures the leadership of the CPC, which includes comprehensive legal structures within the Party. But a question lingers: is the Communist Party above the law or is the law above the Party? This is a false question, framed in a Western form as 'either-or'. Instead, as Li Lin observes, there is an organic unity between rule of law and the Communist Party: 'the Party's leadership is the basic guarantee of ruling the country by law whereas ruling the country by law is the basic strategy by which the Party

---

[52]In drawing up the following points, I have consulted a number of leading scholars (Sun G. and Huang 1998; Li L. 2011, 2015; Fu and Zhu 2015; Ma Y. 2015; Zhang W. 2017a, 2017b; Chen Youwu and Li 2018; Hu Jianmiao 2018; Liu S. 2018). See also the important decision on from the Fourth Plenary of the CPC's Eighteenth Central Committee (2014), along with Xi Jinping's observations (2014a) on the decision. For an in-depth study of the development of Xi Jinping's approach to rule of law, see Xu Hanming (2017).

[53]For significant debates concerning this pairing in a modern context, see Liu, Li and Feng (2008, 16–17).

[54]The combination of rule of law and rule of virtue in the current context was initially made by Jiang Zemin (2000, 91). He came to deploy the combination on many occasions afterwards.

leads the people to administer state affairs and the basic mode by which the Party rules the country' (Li L. 2018, 310). In short, it is 'both-and': they complement rather than oppose one another.

8.7 Leadership of the Communist Party

It is precisely the leadership of the Communist Party as an inescapable feature of socialist democracy that provides one of the sharpest differences from capitalist democracy. 'Democratic centralism' is the shorthand for this reality, so what follows seeks to describe how it is practised. The next chapter will deal with the development of the theory of democratic centralism.

The CPC's leadership is predicated on the fact that it represents the vast majority of the people, initially rural and urban workers and now also the middle-income group that has arisen as a result of the thorough poverty alleviation program. But this basis is simply a beginning. To go further, Chinese scholars distinguish between founding and ruling.[55] The initial reference is historical, in the sense that the foundation of the New China was impossible without the CPC, but also that the Communist Party has become responsible for the construction of socialism and thus ruling the country. The technical Marxist term for the latter is the dictatorship of the proletariat and peasantry.

8.7.1 From Historical to Practical Legitimacy

More substantially, the distinction between founding and ruling relates to the CPC's legitimacy: the CPC's core role in founding the New China provides it with historical legitimacy, while the shift to governing the country entails practical legitimacy.[56] Of course, any political system and indeed any political party requires legitimacy to function, let alone to rule. In this respect, the CPC is no different. But the question of legitimacy is raised to another level by the fact that the very definition of socialist democracy requires the Communist Party in question to be the ruling party. Two questions are relevant: how does a Communist Party enable the transition from historical to practical legitimacy? And how does practical legitimacy work? In answering these questions, I need to follow the sequential dictates of writing, but it should be remembered that they are closely entwined in the whole process. The transition from historical to practical legitimacy relies on the legitimacy generated by the inherent Communist practice of consultation and the mass line. Initially, this consultative legitimacy provided the groundwork for Liberation and establishing the

[55] The following draws from two insightful and very useful articles by Ma Yide (2015, 2017).

[56] We may see this distinction in the preamble to the Constitution, with historical legitimacy emphasised in the first four paragraphs, and practical legitimacy in the tenth paragraph.

New China, but it also provided the necessary background for the transition to the practical legitimacy of ruling.

8.7.2 The Statutory Procedures of Practical Legitimacy

In regard to practical legitimacy, can the Communist Party simply enact its decisions and simultaneously maintain legitimacy among the people? Obviously, the answer is no.[57] Instead, the CPC's 'will is sublimated into that of the state through the state's organs of power by virtue of a specific logic and the systemic structure directed thereby' (Ma Y. 2015, 15; see also Guo 2009, 6). In other words, any proposal or decision by the CPC does not automatically and directly become law: it must go through a complete statutory procedure in order to become a decision of the state as such, finalised by the NPC. Thus, the CPC's leadership is indirect rather than direct. A shorthand for this statutory procedure is 'ruling the country according to law', but it actually includes all of the components of the socialist democratic system—electoral, consultative, and grassroots democracy, minority nationalities policy, rule of law, and human rights.

I have summarised some complex and detailed arguments, but my summary should show how the Communist Party's leadership is integrally connected with all of the features of China's socialist democratic system. Let me quote Ma Yide's insightful summary of the basic logic of China's system of governance:

> First, the Party's leadership is political leadership, and the Party's views are a combination of historical and practical legitimacy based on multi-party cooperation and political consultation. Second, the Party's views, which have solid legitimacy, are transformed into the will of the state through people's congresses, and the concrete expression of the will of the state is democratic legislation. During this process, the people re-examine and substantiate the Party's views through the system of people's congresses. Third, as the legal procedure for transforming the will of the Party, democratic legislation constitutes the basis for governing the country according to law, and is the governance basis for the direct links between the modern state and citizens. Fourth, the leadership of the Party should advance with the times through consultations between the Party and the masses and social consultation, thereby entering the logical chain of direct governance consisting of legitimization of the Party's views and their transformation into the will of the state and thence into the rule of law, thus successfully coordinating state governance and social development. (Ma Y. 2017, 31)

---

[57]At this point, Western observers abysmally fail to understand: deploying a Western bourgeois framework, they assume that the Communist Party arbitrarily imposes its will and therefore has no legitimacy.

8.7.3 The Mutual Strength of Communist Party Leadership and Socialist Democracy

All of this leads to a dialectical point: it is precisely by means of the robust exercise of governance through socialist democracy that the CPC's leadership is strengthened, not weakened. Conversely, it is only through the Party's leadership that the institutions of socialist democracy are strengthened (Jiang Z. 1990b, 112–113; 1990a, 107). Further, it is because of the CPC's founding and systemic role in socialist democracy that supervision, transparency, clean governance, and legitimacy are enhanced exponentially—far more than in capitalist democracy. Thus, inner-Party democracy must be even more rigorously practised by all members so that all views are aired and rigorous criticism exercised so as to ensure mistakes are not made, or, if they are made, they are corrected. Indeed, the CPC's inner-Party democracy functions as a vanguard for democratic practices in the country as a whole (CPC Central Committee 2009, 4; Ren Z. 2011, 20–22). That the CPC has not always lived up to this high calling is obvious. We may mention the 'Cultural Revolution' and its 'rule of a person', or the deep corruption that became evident during the 'wild 90s' and persisted for a decade later. To recall a distinction I mentioned in the chapter on the Reform and Opening-Up: these phases were not manifestations of a systemic problem, but incidental or cyclical. The fact that the excesses of the 'Cultural Revolution' could be corrected, and that the gap between Party and people that led to the problem of corruption has been addressed in the most consistent anti-corruption campaign since Mao Zedong, indicates a democratic self-correcting process that lives up to the high calling of 'governing the country according to law'. That the CPC's esteem is higher than it has been for a long time—as witnessed in one international survey after another—is clear testament to this reality (Yang W. 2017, 20).

It should be no surprise that a constituent feature of speeches and texts by CPC leaders typically conclude with a section dealing with improving the Party's functioning, mass line, unity, and representative nature. This feature was already found in the Soviet Union, where it became part of the genre, so to speak. They may, depending on the circumstances, focus on improving inner-party democracy, dealing with excess and corruption, promoting clean living and hard work, or on Party unity (Xiao and Yu 2012, 18). Is all this merely window-dressing, a ritual invocation due to the tradition? At times this may have been the case, but they also require a leader who is a 'needle hidden in silk floss [*mianli cangzhen*]', who has 'firmness cloaked beneath gentleness [*rouzhong yougang*]', as Mao advised Deng Xiaoping (Zhonggong zhongyang wenxian yanjiushi 2003, 1674). In other words, it needs a leader who can be tough when needed and so can ensure that the measures are enacted through systemic, law-based procedures. Ultimately, the point is that a Communist Party simply cannot continue to lead without a robust democratic system—democratic centralism.

8.8 Conclusion: The Superiority of a Work in Progress

> People's democracy is the life of socialism. Without democracy, there can be no socialism, no socialist modernisation, and no great rejuvenation of the Chinese nation. (Xi 2014d, 5)

By now its should be obvious that the 'unitary multinational People's Republic of China cannot be judged by the Western pattern of national states' (Jiang L. 2011, 83). In the preceding material, I have described the background and practice of all but one of the components of China's socialist democratic system, beginning with electoral democracy, running through consultative and grassroots democracy, minority nationality policies, and ending with rule of law and democratic leadership by CPC. Given its importance in international debates, I have already dealt with the Chinese Marxist approach to human rights in the previous chapter.

By way of conclusion, I would like to address three points. The first is to pick up a point made a few times concerning the constant emphasis on socialist democracy as a work in progress, especially since the construction of a normative democratic system based on Marxist political philosophy is a massive project (Ren P. and Wang 2010, 108). Although there is a clear recognition that forms of the state in China predate those found in most other parts of the world, the development of socialist governance and democracy began in the mid-twentieth century from a distinctly 'backward' condition. Of course, this condition is inescapably connected with China's economic condition, which made it one of the poorest countries in the world in 1949. Given the extraordinary development since that time, especially with the Reform and Opening-Up, it follows that forms of governance also need to develop according to the times, albeit in a way that ensures stability rather than chaos (Wei 2016, 68). Thus, socialist democracy is not a given in China, is not a complete form, but is recognisably incomplete and needs constant development and deepening of reform (Li S. 2009, 282; Li J. 2013; Liu Xiaowei and Yang 2013, 33–34; Wang Yan and Wei 2017, 16–17). Many are the pilot and targeted projects, the adjustments and refinements; 'Step by step [*zhubu*]' is a favoured phrase, or 'crossing the stream by feeling the stones [*mozhe shitou guohe*]' (Chen Yun 1980, 279).

Second, a Western-style competitive capitalist democracy would simply not work in China. This reality is not due to a supposedly stubborn refusal of the CPC to adopt a system that would lead to its own destruction, but because such a system would not suit China's historical and socialist conditions (Lin S. 2009, 7–9; Fang N. and Zhou 2010, 14; Wang C. 2010). This is a specifically Marxist point, in that political systems arise from their socio-economic base, and are determined by the overall system in place (Zhu J. 2016, 26–27).[58] Thus, to impose a competitive superstructural political system on a socialist system that functions with non-antagonistic contradictions would be an ill fit indeed, leading to chaos and disorder (Lu, Zhang, and Sun 2009, 14–16; Xie 2009, 28; Jiang H. and Zhao 2010, 4; Hou 2015, 7–9). In fact, this competitive capitalist democracy, which arose in specific conditions during the expansion of

[58] As Li Lin (2017, 7) puts it, China's democratic system is a 'superstructure deeply rooted in China's economic, social, and cultural soil'.

capitalism in Europe, is increasingly emerging as a crude and ineffective form of the state (Zhonggong zhongyang xuanchuanbu lilun ju 2009, 9–10; Qiu 2010; Yang W. 2017, 16).

A third theme is the superiority of the socialist system, and thus of its democratic approach (Fang N. and Zhou 2010; Sun C. 2010; Jin and Tao 2018; Xin 2019). As the 2013 decision on deepening reform puts it, conditions should be established to give full play to or 'fully bring out the latent potentialities [*chongfen fahui*] of the superiority [*youyuexing*] of the socialist political system in China' (CPC Central Committee 2003, 5; 2013, 17). I must admit that I have always been wary of such a claim, especially since it was also common in the Soviet Union and in Eastern Europe. The risk is that the claim will lead people to expect not merely an adequate life, with the basics of food, shelter, work, medical care, and education, but that life will in fact be better under a socialist system in comparison to all other systems. If this claim turns out not to be the case, the task of explanation becomes so much more difficult. However, in China they are bold enough to make precisely this claim, seeking to overcome the lingering connotation of 'the West [*xifang*]' as 'better', and the results are beginning to show in terms of increasing 'cultural confidence', of the sense that China's socialist democracy is in fact superior to the antagonistic chaos of Western capitalist democracy. Indeed, in a detailed and comparative study, Yang Weimin (2017) argues not merely that China's political system is superior, but that it may and actually is providing an alternative model for those—particularly in developing countries where they have had more than their fill of Western impositions—seeking a more stable, disciplined, and efficient form of governance. It goes without saying that such a model is not hegemonic, but needs to be adapted in light of local characteristics.

References

Bell, Daniel. 2006. *Beyond liberal democracy: Political thinking for an East Asian context*. Princeton: Princeton University Press.

Bessette, Joseph. 1981. Deliberative democracy: The majority principle in republican government. In *How democratic is the constitution?*, ed. Robert Goldwin and William Shambra, 102–116. Washington: American Enterprise Institute.

Boer, Roland. In press. *Friedrich Engels and the foundations of socialist governance*. Singapore: Springer.

Boer, Roland. 2017. *Stalin: From theology to the philosophy of socialism in power*. Beijing: Springer.

Boer, Roland. 2018. Civil society or bourgeois society? An alternative history, from Hegel to Losurdo. *Berlin Journal of Critical Theory* 2 (4): 5–32.

Boer, Roland. 2019. The state and minority nationalities (Ethnic groups) in China. In *The Palgrave handbook of ethnicity*, edited by Steven Ratuva, 93–107. Singapore: Palgrave Macmillan (Springer).

Bu, Wanhong. 2015. Lun woguo jiceng xieshang shi zhili tansuo de chengjiu yu jingyan—jiyu minzhu kentanhui yu 'si yi liang gongkai' gongzuo fa de fenxi. *Henan daxue xuebao (shehui kexue ban)* 55 (5): 45–52.

Bächtiger, Andre, John Dryzek, Jane Mansbridge, and Mark Warren (eds.). 2018. *The Oxford handbook of deliberative democracy*. Oxford: Oxford University Press.

Chen, Xueming. 2015. Zhongguo daolu dui makesizhuyi de fazhan—lun Zhongguo daolu de makesizhuyi yiyi zhi san. *Nanjing zhengzhi xueyuan xuebao* 2015 (6): 1–12.

Chen, Youwu, and Li Buyun. 2018. Zhongguo fazhi lilun sishi nian: fazhan, chuangxin ji qianjing. *Zhengzhi yu falü* 2018 (12): 64–75.

Chen, Yun. 1980. Jingji xingshi yu jingyan jiaoxun (1980.12.16). In *Chen Yun wenxuan*, Vol. 3:276–82. Beijing: Renmin chubanshe, 1986.

Chiang, Kai-Shek. 1947. *China's destiny and Chinese economic theory*. New York: Roy Publishers.

Confucius. 1993. *Lunyu jinyi—The Analects of Confucius (Chinese-English Bilingual Edition)*. Translated by Yang Bojun, Wu Shuping, Pan Fu'en, and Wen Shaoxia. Jinan: Qilu shushe chuban gongsi.

CPC Central Committee. 1981. Guanyu jianguo yilai dang de ruogan lishi wenti de jueyi (1981 nian 6 yue 27 ri Zhongguo gongchandang di shiyi jie zhongyang weiyuanhui di liu ci quanti huiyi tongguo). *Renmin ribao*, 27 June 1981: 1–9.

CPC Central Committee. 1989. *Zhonggong zhongyang guanyu jianchi he wanshan Zhongguo gongchandang lingdao de duodang hezuo he zhengzhi xieshang zhidu de yijian*. Beijing: Zhongguo gongchandang zhongyang weiyuanhui.

CPC Central Committee. 2003. *Zhonggong zhongyang guanyu wanshan shehuizhuyi shichang jingji tizhi ruogan wenti de jueding*. Beijing: Zhongguo gongchandang zhongyang weiyuanhui.

CPC Central Committee. 2006. *Zhonggong zhongyang guanyu jiaqiang renmin zhengxie gongzuo de yijian*. Beijing: Zhongguo gongchandang zhongyang weiyuanhui.

CPC Central Committee. 2009. *Zhonggong zhongyang guanyu jiaqiang he gaijin xin xingshi xia dang jianshe ruogan zhongda wenti de jueding*. Beijing: Zhongguo gongchandang zhongyang weiyuanhui.

CPC Central Committee. 2013. *Decision of the central committee of the communist party of China on some major issues concerning comprehensively deepening the reform*. Beijing: Zhongguo gongchandang zhongyang weiyuanhui.

CPC Central Committee. 2014. *Zhonggong zhongyang guanyu quanmian tuijin yifazhiguo ruogan zhongda wenti de jueding*. Beijing: Zhongguo gongchandang zhongyang weiyuanhui.

CPC Central Committee. 2015a. *Guanyu jiaqiang chengxiang shequ xieshang de yijian*. Beijing: Zhongguo gongchandang zhongyang weiyuanhui.

CPC Central Committee. 2015b. *Guanyu jiaqiang shehuizhuyi xieshang minzhu jianshe de yijian*. Beijing: Zhongguo gongchandang zhongyang weiyuanhui.

CPPCC. 1949. *Zhongguo renmin zhengzhi xieshang huiyi gongtong gangling*. Beijing: CPPCC.

CPPCC. 1995. *Zhengxie quanguo weiyuanhui guanyu zhengzhi xieshang, renmin jiandu, canzheng yizheng de guiding*. Beijing: CPPCC. www.cppcc.gov.cn/2011/09/06/ARTI1315304860593209.shtml.

Davis, Elizabeth Van Wie. 2013. *Ruling, resources and religion in China: Managing the multiethnic state in the 21st century*. Houndmills: Palgrave Macmillan.

Deng, Xiaoping. 1957a. Gongchandang yao jieshou jiandu (1957.04.08). In *Deng Xiaoping wenxuan*, Vol. 1:270–274. Beijing: Renmin chubanshe, 2008.

Deng, Xiaoping. 1957b. The communist party should accept supervision (8 April 1957). In *Selected works of Deng Xiaoping*, Vol. 1:267–271. Beijing: Foreign Languages Press, 1995.

Deng, Xiaoping. 1978a. Emancipate the mind, seek truth from facts and unite as one in looking to the future (13 December, 1978). In *Selected works of Deng Xiaoping*, Vol. 2:150–163. Beijing: Foreign Languages Press, 1995.

Deng, Xiaoping. 1978b. Jiefang sixiang, shishiqiushi, tuanjieyizhi xiangqian kan (1978.12.13). In *Deng Xiaoping wenxuan*, Vol. 2:140–153. Beijing: Renmin chubanshe, 2008.

Deng, Xiaoping. 1979. Jianchi sixiang jiben yuanze (1979.03.30). In *Deng Xiaoping wenxuan*, Vol. 2:158–184. Beijing: Renmin chubanshe, 2008.

Deng, Xiaoping. 1984a. Speech at the third plenary session of the central advisory commission of communist party of China (22 October, 1984). In *Selected works of Deng Xiaoping*, Vol. 3:90–99. Beijing: Foreign Languages Press, 1994.

Deng, Xiaoping. 1984b. Zai zhongyang guwen weiyuanhui disanci quanti huiyi shang de jianghua (1984.10.22). In *Deng Xiaoping wenxuan*, Vol. 3:83–93. Beijing: Renmin chubanshe, 2008.
Deng, Xiaoping. 1986a. Guanyu zhengzhi tizhi gaige wenti (1986.09–11). In *Deng Xiaoping wenxuan*, Vol. 3:176–180. Beijing: Renmin chubanshe, 2008.
Deng, Xiaoping. 1986b. On reform of the political structure (September–November, 1986). In *Selected works of Deng Xiaoping*, Vol. 3:178–181. Beijing: Foreign Languages Press, 1994.
Deng, Xiaoping. 1989a. We are confident that we can handle China's affairs well (16 September, 1989). In *Selected works of Deng Xiaoping*, Vol. 3:314–317. Beijing: Foreign Languages Press, 1994.
Deng, Xiaoping. 1989b. Women you xinxin ba zhongguo de shiqing zuo de geng hao (1989.09.16). In *Deng Xiaoping wenxuan*, Vol. 3:324–327. Beijing: Renmin chubanshe, 2010.
Dickson, Bruce. 2003. *Red capitalists in China: The party, private entrepreneurs and prospects for political change*. Cambridge: Cambridge University Press.
Dillon, Michael. 1999. *China's muslim Hui community: Migration, settlement and sects*. London: Routledge.
Dong, Shubin. 2017. Xi Jinping shehuixhuyi xieshang minzhu sixiang de lilun jiagou. *Gaoxiao makesizhuyi lilun yanjiu* 2017 (1): 55–62.
Dryzek, John. 2011. *Foundations and frontiers of deliberative governance*. Oxford: Oxford University Press.
Egry, Gábor. 2005. Social democracy and the nationalities question. In *Regimes and transformations: Hungary in the twentieth century*, ed. Istvan Feitl and Balázs Sipos, 95–118. Budapest: Napvilág Kiadó.
Engels, Friedrich. 1882a. Die Mark. In *Marx Engels Gesamtausgabe*, Vol. I.27:628–643. Berlin: Dietz, 1988.
Engels, Friedrich. 1882b. The mark. In *Marx and Engels collected works*, Vol. 24:439–456. Moscow: Progress Publishers, 1989.
Fang, Lei, and Meng Yan. 2019. Xin Zhongguo chengli 70 nianlai jiceng xieshang minzhu fazhan de lishi luoji. *Zhonggong zhongyang dangxiao (guojia xingzheng xueyuan) xuebao* 2019 (5): 30–38.
Fang, Ning. 2015. *China's democratic path*. Translated by Wu Yisheng and Liu Aiyun Liu. Springer Insights. Singapore: Springer.
Fang, Ning, and Zhou Shaolai. 2010. Zhongguo tese shehuizhuyi minzhu de tedian yu youshi. *Qiushi* 2010 (6): 14–17.
Fei, Xiaotong. 1989. Zhonghua minzu duoyuan yiti geju. *Beijing daxue xuebao (zhexue shehui kexue ban)* 1989 (4): 1–12.
Feng, Zhifeng, and Luo Jiawei. 2017. Difang canyushi yusuan de shijian jingyan, wenti jianshi yu pojie zhi dao—yige jiceng xieshang minzhu de bijiao fenxi shijiao. *Difang zhili yanjiu* 2017 (4): 48–61.
Fewsmith, Joseph. 2012. China politics twenty years later. In *Socialism vanquished, socialism challenged: Eastern Europe and China, 1989–2009*, ed. Nina Bandelj and Dorothy Solinger, 44–59. Oxford: Oxford University Press.
Fishkin, James. 2009. *When people speak: Deliberative democracy and public consultation*. Oxford: Oxford University Press.
Fu, Zitang, and Zhu Linfang. 2015. Zhongguo tese shehuizhuyi fazhi lilun de jiben goucheng. *Fazhi yu shehui fazhan* 2015 (3): 17–31.
Gladney, Dru. 1991. *Muslim Chinese: Ethnic nationalism in the people's republic*. Cambridge: Council on East Asian Studies, Harvard University.
Gong, Pixiang. 2015. Zhongguo tese shehuizhuyi fazhi daolu de shidai jincheng. *Zhongguo faxue* 2015 (5): 29–52.
Guo, Dingping. 2009. Dangdai Zhongguo zhengdang yu guojia guanxi moshi de chonggou: bijiao de shiye. *Shehui kexue yanjiu* 2009 (1): 1–11.
Han, Fuguo. 2018. Chaoyue 'zhiding daibiao' he 'suiji chaoyang': Zhongguo shehuizhuyi fushi xieshang minzhu de chengxu sheji. *Tansuo* 2018 (5): 71–81.

Han, Fuguo, and Xiao Yingmin. 2017. Xieshang minzhu de jiceng shijian chengxu yu xiaoneng jianyan—Zhejiang Wenling canyushi gonggong yusuan de zhidu fenxi. *Xi'an jiaotong daxue xuebao (shehui kexue ban)* 37 (5): 59–70.

Han, Fuguo, and Zhang Kaiping. 2015. Shehui zhili de 'xieshang' lingyu yu 'minzhu' jizhi—dangxia Zhongguo jiceng xieshang minzhu de zhidu tezheng, shijian jiegou he lilun pipan. *Zhejiang shehui kexue* 2015 (10): 48–61.

Han, Zhen, and Zhang Weiwen. 2018. *Contemporary value systems in China*. Translated by Zhao Chaoyong. China Insights. Singapore: Springer.

Hao, Shiyuan. 2020. *China's solution to its ethno-national issues*. Translated by Zhang Jianping and Ke Mingxing. China Insights. Singapore: Springer.

Hao, Tiechuan. 2015. Fazhi yu renzhi linian yu duikang yu chongtu—xin Zhongguo chengli chuqi fazhi jianshe ruogan zhongda zhengyi wenti shuping. *Dongfang faxue* 2015 (1): 2–20.

He, Qinhua. 2011. Fa de guojihua yu bentuhua: yi Zhongguo jindai yizhi waiguo fa shijian wei zhongxin de sikao. *Zhongguo faxue* 2011 (4): 43–52.

He, Qinhua. 2015. Lun Zhongguo tese shehuizhuyi fazhi daolu. *Fazhi yu shehui fazhan* 2015 (3): 32–45.

He, Qinhua. 2017. Yi gudai Zhongguo yu Riben wei zhongxin de zhonghua faxi zhi lüjia kao. *Zhongguo faxue* 2017 (5): 196–215.

He, Qinhua. 2018. Zhongguo faxi zhi falü xueshu kao: yi gudai Zhongguo lüxue yu riben de mingfa dao wei zhongxin. *Zhongwai faxue* 30 (1): 7–36.

He, Qinhua, and Qi Kaiyue. 2018. Fazhi chengwei fazhi: xianfa xiugai tuijin shehuizhuyi fazhi jianshe. *Shandong shehui kexue* 2018 (7): 5–15.

Hou, Huiqin. 2015. Lun Zhongguo tese shehuizhuyi minzhu zhidu jianshe. *Makesizhuyi yanjiu* 2015 (12): 5–11.

Hu, Huanyong. 1935. Zhongguo renkou zhi fenbu—fu tongjibiao yu midu tu. *Dili xuebao (Acta Geographica Sinica)* 1935 (2): 33–74.

Hu, Jianmiao. 2018. Xi Jinping xinshidai Zhongguo tese shehuizhuyi sixiang dui yifazhiguo jiben fanglüe de quanmian shenhua. *Guojia xingzheng xueyuan xuebao* 2018 (1): 9–13.

Hu, Jintao. 2012. *Jianding bu yi yanzhe Zhongguo tese shehui zhuyi daolu, qianjin wei quanmian jiancheng xiaokang shehui er fendou (2012.11.08)*. Beijing: Renmin chubanshe.

Huang, Junyao. 2016. 'Qianrushi' yihuo 'tixihua': jiceng xieshang minzhu de tuijin lujing fenxi. *Zhonggong Zhejiang shengwei dangxiao xuebao* 2016 (6): 107–113.

Huang, Yasheng. 2013. Democratize or die: Why China's communists face reform or revolution. *Foreign Affairs* 92 (1): 47–54.

Jiang, Hui, and Zhao Peijie. 2010. Shuli kexue de makesizhuyi minzhu guan. *Zhengzhixue yanjiu* 2010 (3): 3–9.

Jiang, Liu. 2011. The marxist national theory and the Chinese nation theory. *Marxist Studies in China* 2011: 75–83.

Jiang, Zemin. 1990a. Adhere to and improve the system of people's congresses (18 March, 1990). In *Selected works of Jiang Zemin*, Vol. 1:106–111. Beijing: Foreign Languages Press, 2010.

Jiang, Zemin. 1990b. Jianchi he wanshan renmin daibiao dahui zhidu (1990.03.18). In *Jiang Zemin wenxuan*, Vol. 1:111–116. Beijing: Renmin chubanshe, 2006.

Jiang, Zemin. 1997a. Gaoju Deng Xiaoping lilun weida qizhi, ba jianshe you Zhongguo tese shehuizhuyi shiye quanmian tui xiang ershiyi shiji (1997.09.12). In *Jiang Zemin wenxuan*, Vol. 2:1–49. Beijing: Renmin chubanshe, 2006.

Jiang, Zemin. 1997b. Hold high the great banner of Deng Xiaoping theory and comprehensively advance the cause of building socialism with Chinese characteristics into the 21st century (12 September, 1997). In *Selected works of Jiang Zemin*, Vol. 2:1–50. Beijing: Foreign Languages Press, 2012.

Jiang, Zemin. 2000. Zai zhongyang sixiang zhengzhi gongzuo huiyi shang de jianghua (2000.06.28). In *Jiang Zemin wenxuan*, Vol. 3:74–100. Beijing: Renmin chubanshe, 2006.

Jiangxi sheng shehuikexue xueyuan ketizu. 2011. Makesizhuyi qunzhong guan yu dangdai Zhongguo minzhu zhengzhi jianshe. *Jiangxi shehui kexue* 2011 (2): 14–20.

Jin, Wei, and Tao Di. 2018. Zhengque renshi he lijie Zhongguo tese shehuizhuyi minzhu de youyuexing. *Xuexiao dangjian yu sixiang jiaoyu* 2018 (11): 4–8.
Lampton, David. 2014. *Following the leader: Ruling China, from Deng Xiaoping to Xi Jinping*. Berkeley: University of California Press.
Landry, Pierre. 2012. *Decentralized authoritarianism in China: The communist party's control of local elites in the post-Mao era*. New York: Cambridge University Press.
Leib, Ethan, and He Baogang (eds.). 2006. *The search for deliberative democracy in China*. Houndmills: Palgrave Macmillan.
Li, Changjian. 2008. Guanyu Zhongguo de xieshang minzhu zhidu. *Zhongguo renmin zhengxie lilun yanjiu hui huikan* 2008 (3): 4–20.
Li, Junru. 2013. Jiji wentuo de tuijin zhengzhi tizhi gaige. *Mao Zedong Deng Xiaoping lilun yanjiu* 2013 (8): 1–11.
Li, Lin. 2011. Dangdai Zhongguo de yifazhiguo yu yifa zhizheng. *Xueshu tansuo* 2011 (2): 74–88.
Li, Lin. 2015. Zhongguo tese shehuizhuyi fazhi qiangguo zhilu—quanmian yifazhiguo de zhanlüe buju he xitong siwei. *Xueshu qianyan* 2015 (7): 52–66.
Li, Lin. 2017. Kaiqi xinshidai Zhongguo tese shehuizhuyi fazhi xin zhengcheng. *Huanqiu falü pinglun* 2017 (6): 5–29.
Li, Lin. 2018. *The Chinese road of the rule of law*. Translated by Bi Xiaoqing. China Insights. Singapore: Springer.
Li, Shenming. 2009. Some thoughts on democracy and universal democracy. *Marxist Studies in China* 2009: 253–285.
Li, Xiuke, and Yan Jirong. 2018. Zhongguo xieshang minzhu de cengcixing—jiyu luoji, changyu he yiti fenxi. *Guojia xingzheng xueyuan xuebao* 2018 (5): 23–29.
Li, Yaoyao. 2016. Jiceng xieshang zhili de shengcheng luoji yu yanjin jizhi. *Shehuizhuyi yanjiu* 2016 (3): 123–130.
Li, Zupei, and Du Jiao. 2018. Fenpeixing xieshang minzhu: 'xiangmu jin cun' zhong cun ji minzhu de shijian luoji jiqi jieshi. *Quanguo xinzheng gunali* 2018 (3): 76–84.
Lieberthal, Kenneth, and David Lampton. 1992. *Bureaucracy, politics, and decision making in post-Mao China*. Berkeley: University of California Press.
Lin, Shangli. 2007. Xieshang zhengzhi: Zhongguo tese minzhu zhengzhi de jiben xingtai. *Mao Zedong Deng Xiaoping lilun yanjiu* 2007 (9): 17–26.
Lin, Shangli. 2009. Zhengdang, zhengdang zhidu yu xiandai guojia—dui Zhongguo zhengdang zhidu de lilun fansi. *Zhongguo Yan'an ganbu xueyuan xuebao* 2009 (5): 5–14.
Lin, Xuefei. 2017. Dang difang zhili tizhi yudao xieshang minzhu—jiyu Wenling 'minzhu kentan' zhidu de chang shiduan yanhua yanjiu. *Gonggong guanli xuebao* 14 (1): 14–26.
Lipset, Seymour. 1959. Some social requisites of democracy: Economic development and political legitimacy. *The American Political Science Review* 53: 69–105.
Liu, An. 2010. *The Huainanzi: A guide to the theory and practice of government in early Han China*. Translated by John Major, Sarah Queen, Andrew Meyer, Harold Roth, Michael Puett, and Judson Murray. New York: Columbia University Press.
Liu, Han, and Li Lin. 1998. Kaichuang kua shiji falixue yanjiu de xin jumian—jinnian lai Zhongguo falixue yanjiu de huigu yu qianzhan. *Falü kexue* 1998 (2): 3–5.
Liu, Shaojun. 2018. Lun Xi Jinping xinshidai Zhongguo tese shehuizhuyi fazhi sixiang. *Hunan shehui kexue* 2018 (5): 10–14.
Liu, Xiaowei, and Yang Anni. 2013. 'Zhongguo tese shehuizhuyi zhengzhi fazhan daolu' yanjiu shuping. *Renda yanjiu* 2013 (4): 31–37.
Liu, Xuebin, Li Yongjun, and Feng Fei. 2008. Gaige kaifang sanshi nian de Zhongguo falixue: 1978–2008. *Fazhi yu shehui fazhan* 2008 (5): 3–36.
Losurdo, Dominico. 2007. Lenin and *Herrnvolk* democracy. In *Lenin reloaded: Towards a politics of truth*, ed. Sebastian Budgen, Stathis Kouvelakis, and Slavoj Žižek, 239–252. Durham: Duke University Press.

Lu, Jining, Zhang Hai, and Sun Cunliang. 2009. Weishenme bixu jianchi Zhongguo gongchandang lingdao de duodang hezuo he zhengzhi xieshang zhidu, er buneng gao xifang de duodangzhi. *Sixiang lilun jiaoyu dao kan* 2009 (5): 10–16.

Ma, Deyong, and Zhang Hua. 2018. Zhidu chuangxin zhong de jiazhi yu xijie: san ge jiceng minzhu chuangxin anli de shizheng fenxi. *Tansuo* 2018 (1): 38–51.

Ma, Rong. 2000. Guanyu minzu yanjiu de ji ge wenti. *Beijing daxue xuebao (zhexue shehui kexue ban)* 2000 (4): 132–143.

Ma, Rong. 2007. Dangqian Zhongguo minzu wenti yanjiu de xuanti yu silu. *Zhongyang minzu daxue xuebao (zhexue shehui kexue ban)* 2007 (3): 12–38.

Ma, Rong. 2010. Guanyu Zhongguo xiaoshu minzu jiaoyu de ji dian sikao. *Xinjiang shifan daxue xuebao (zhexue shehui kexue ban)* 31 (1): 6–18.

Ma, Rong. 2011. Zhongguo minzu wenti de lishi yu xianzhuang. *Yunnan minzu daxue xuebao (zhexue shehui kexue ban)* 28 (5): 15–20.

Ma, Rong. 2012. Zhongguo de minzu wenti yu 20 shiji 50 niandai de 'minzu shibie'. *Xibei minzu yanjiu* 2012 (3): 13–28.

Ma, Rong. 2013. Dui dangdai Zhongguo minzu zhengce de fansi. *Qinghai minzu yanjiu* 2013 (4): 42–58.

Ma, Shaomeng. 2014. Observing the mass line and implementing democratic centralism. *Marxist Studies in China* 2014: 195–219.

Ma, Yide. 2015. The role of consultative democracy in a constitutional system and the rule of law in China. *Social Sciences in China* 36 (4): 5–23.

Ma, Yide. 2017. The role of consultative democracy under the constitutional framework and the associated rule of law. *Social Sciences in China* 38 (2): 21–38.

Mackerras, Colin. 2003. *China's ethnic minorities and globalisation.* London: RoutledgeCurzon.

Mao, Zedong. 1938a. Lun xin jieduan (1938.10.12–14). In *Zhonggong zhongyang wenjian xuanji*, Vol. 11:557–662. Beijing: Zhonggang zhongyang xuexiao chubanshe, 1991.

Mao, Zedong. 1938b. On the new stage (12–14 October, 1938). In *Mao's road to power: Revolutionary writings 1912–1949*, Vol. 6:458–541. Armonk: M. E. Sharpe, 2004.

Mao, Zedong. 1940a. On new democracy (January, 1940). In *Selected works of Mao Tse-tung*, Vol. 2:339–384. Beijing: Foreign Languages Press, 1965.

Mao, Zedong. 1940b. Xin minzhuzhuyi lun (1940.01.15). In *Mao Zedong xuanji*, Vol. 2:662–711. Beijing: Renmin chubanshe, 2009.

Mao, Zedong. 1943a. Guanyu lingdao fangfa de ruogan wenti (1943.06.01). In *Mao Zedong xuanji*, Vol. 3:897–902. Beijing: Renmin chubanshe, 2009.

Mao, Zedong. 1943b. Some questions concerning methods of leadership. In *The Selected works of Mao Tse-Tung*, Vol. 3:117–122. Beijing: Foreign Language Press, 1965.

Mao, Zedong. 1945a. Lun lianhezhengfu (1945.04.24). In *Mao Zedong xuanji*, Vol. 3:1029–1100. Beijing: Renmin chubanshe, 2009.

Mao, Zedong. 1945b. On coalition government (24 April, 1945). In *Selected works of Mao Tse-Tung*, Vol. 3:255–320. Beijing: Foreign Languages Press, 1965.

Mao, Zedong. 1956a. Lun shi da guanxi (1956.04.25). In *Mao Zedong xuanji*, Vol. 5:267–288. Beijing: Renmin chubanshe, 1977.

Mao, Zedong. 1956b. On the ten major relationships (25 April, 1956). In *Selected works of Mao Tse-Tung*, Vol. 5:284–307. Beijing: Foreign Languages Press, 1977.

Miranda, Marina. 2017. The issue of political reform and the evolution of the so-called 'Deng Xiaoping model' in Hu Jintao and Xi Jinping's China. In *Understanding China today: An exploration of politics, economics, society, and international relations*, ed. Silvio Beretta, Axel Berkofsky, and Zhang Lihong, 263–274. Cham: Springer.

Nathan, Andrew, Larry Diamond, and Marc Plattner. 2013. *Will China democratize?*. Baltimore: Johns Hopkins University Press.

National People's Congress. 1982. *Zhongguo renmin gongheguo xianfa.* Beijing: NPC.

National People's Congress. 1984. *Zhonghua renmin gongheguo minzu quyu zizhi fa.* Beijing: NPC.

National People's Congress. 1987. *Zhonghua renmin gongheguo cunmin weiyuanhui zuzhi fa (shixing)*. Beijing: NPC.

National People's Congress. 2001. *Zhonghua renmin gongheguo minzu quyu zizhi fa*. Beijing: NPC.

National People's Congress. 2015. *Zhongguo renmin gongheguo quanguo renmin daibiao dahui he difang geji renmin daibiao dahui xuanjufa*. Beijing: NPC.

National People's Congress. 2018. *Zhongguo renmin gongheguo xianfa*. Beijing: NPC.

Norbu, Dawa. 2001. *China's Tibet policy*. Richmond: Curzon.

Ogden, Suzanne. 2007. Don't judge a country by its cover: Governance in China. In *China in the twenty-first century: Challenges and opportunities*, ed. Hua Shiping and Guo Sujian, 49–85. New York: Palgrave Macmillan.

Ou, Liming, and Wang Yunqiang. 2013. Zhongguo tese shehuizhuyi minzhu zhengzhi shiye zhong de qunzhong luxian. *Yunnan xingzheng xueyuan xuebao* 2013 (2): 79–83.

Peerenboom, Randall. 2002. *China's long march toward rule of law*. Cambridge: Cambridge University Press.

Peerenboom, Randall. 2007. *China modernizes: Threat to the west or model for the rest?* Oxford: Oxford University Press.

Qi, Weiping. 2013. Xieshang minzhu zhidu yu Zhongguo tese shehuizhuyi zhengzhi fazhan. *Guihua luncong* 2013 (1): 11–15.

Qian, Zaijian, and Jiang Yijin. 2017. Jiceng xieshang minzhu: shengcheng jizhi, chengzhang zhi kun he fazhan zhi dao—yi zhejiang wenling 'minzhu kentan' wei li. *Guancha yu sikao* 2017 (7): 101–106.

Qiu, Shi. 2010. Zhongguo tese shehuizhuyi minzhu zhengzhi de zhidu youshi yu jiben tezheng—huaqing Zhongguo tese shehuizhuyi minzhu tong xifang zibenzhuyi minzhu de jiexian. *Qiushi* 2010 (18): 6–9.

Ren, Ping, and Wang Jianming. 2010. Lun chayixing shehui yu Zhongguo tese shehuizhuyi minzhu zhengzhi de weilai. *Makesizhuyi yanjiu* 2010 (5): 102–110.

Ren, Zhongping. 2011. Dangnei minzhu yu renmin minzhu, guojia minzhu yu shehui minzhu de guanxi bianxi ji fazhan zouxiang. *Yunnan shehui kexue* 2011 (2): 19–23.

Sautman, Barry. 1998. Preferential policies for ethnic minorities in China: The case of Xinjiang. *Nationalism and Ethnic Politics* 4 (1–2): 86–118.

Sautman, Barry. 2003. 'Cultural genocide' and Tibet. *Texas International Law Journal* 38 (2): 173–246.

Sautman, Barry. 2006. Colonialism, genocide, and Tibet. *Asian Ethnicity* 7 (3): 243–265.

Sautman, Barry. 2010. 'Vegetarian between meals': The Dalai Lama, war, and violence. *Positions* 18 (1): 89–143.

Shen, Jianlin, and Tan Shizan. 2016. Canyushi yusuan de Zhongguo shijian, xieshang moshi jiqi zhuanxing. *Hubei shehui kexue* 2016 (3): 23–29.

Shi, Xuehua, and Cui Heng. 2012. Lun Zhongguo renmin zhengzhi xieshang huiyi gongneng zhongxin de tiaozheng. *Zhongguo tese shehuizhuyi yanjiu* 2012 (1): 36–46.

Sima, Qian. 2014. *Shiji*. Beijing: Zhonghua shuju.

Stalin, I. V. 1913a. Marksizm i natsional′nyĭ vopros. In *Trudy*, Vol. 5:159–228. Moscow: Prometeĭ Info, 2014.

Stalin, I. V. 1913b. Marxism and the national question. In *Works*, Vol. 2:300–381. Moscow: Foreign Languages Publishing House, 1953.

State Council Information Office of the PRC. 2005. *Zhongguo de minzu quyu zizhi*. Beijing: Guowuyuan xinwen bangongshi.

State Council Information Office of the PRC. 2007a. *China's political party system*. Beijing: Guowuyuan xinwen bangongshi.

State Council Information Office of the PRC. 2007b. *Zhongguo de zhengdang zhidu*. Beijing: Guowuyuan xinwen bangongshi.

State Council Information Office of the PRC. 2019a. *Democratic reform in Tibet—Sixty years on*. Beijing: Guowuyuan xinwen bangongshi.

State Council Information Office of the PRC. 2019b. *The fight against terrorism and extremism and human rights protection in Xinjiang*. Beijing: Guowuyuan xinwen bangongshi.

State Council Information Office of the PRC. 2019c. *Weida de kuayue: Xizang minzhu gaige 60 nian*. Beijing: Guowuyuan xinwen bangongshi.

State Council Information Office of the PRC. 2019d. *Xinjiang de fankong, qu jiduanhua douzheng yu renquan baozhang*. Beijing: Guowuyuan xinwen bangongshi.

Sun, Cunliang. 2010. Xuanju minzhu yu xieshang minzhu xiang jiehe shi Zhongguo tese shehuizhuyi minzhu de zhongyao youshi. *Sixiang lilun jiaoyu dao kan* 2010 (5): 38–41.

Sun, Guohua, and Huang Wenyi. 1998. Lun shehuizhuyi de yifazhiguo. *Zhongguo faxue* 6: 10–20.

Sun, Li. 2002. Dezhi yu fazhi zhengdangxing fenxi—jian ji Zhongguo yu dongya fa wenhua chuantong zhi jian sheng. *Zhongguo shehui kexue* 2002 (6): 95–104.

Sun, Shoujuan. 2006. Guanxi lun shijiao xia de fazhi bianxi—jian lun fazhi yu renzhi, fazhi, dezhi de guanxi. *Shandong shehui kexue* 2006 (12): 41–46, 49.

Suny, Ronald Grigor. 1993. *The revenge of the past: Nationalism, revolution, and the collapse of the Soviet Union*. Stanford: Stanford University Press.

Suny, Ronald Grigor. 2001. The empire strikes out: Imperial Russia, 'national' identity, and theories of empire. In *A state of nations: Empire and nation-making in the age of Lenin and Stalin*, edited by Ronald Grigor Suny and Terry Martin, 23–66. Oxford: Oxford University Press.

Tan, Huosheng. 2018. Hunheshi daibiao jizhhi: Zhongguo jiceng xieshang de zhidu chuangxin. *Zhejiang shehui kexue* 2018 (2): 35–42.

Tsai, Lily. 2007. *Accountability without democracy: Solidarity groups and public goods provision in rural China*. Cambridge: Cambridge University Press.

Wang, Chuanzhi. 2010. Zhongguo tese shehuizhuyi minzhu yu xifang minzhu de jiexian. *Xueshujie* 2010 (4): 43–49.

Wang, Guohui. 2014. *Tamed village 'democracy': Elections, governance and clientelism in a contemporary Chinese village*. Heidelberg: Springer.

Wang, Guoqin, and Tao Zhengxuan. 2018. Wenling minzhu kentan de zhidu yanjin yu lilun fazhan. *Zhili yanjiu* 2018 (6): 111–120.

Wang, Puqu. 2013. Zhongguo xieshang zhili de jiben tedian. *Qiushi* 2013 (10): 36–38.

Wang, Xi'en. 2009. Ye tan zai woguo minzu wenti shang de 'fansi' yu 'shishi qiushi'—yu Ma Rong jiaoshou de ji dian shangque. *Xinan minzu daxue xuebao (renwen sheke ban)* 2009 (1): 1–17.

Wang, Xi'en. 2010a. Duoyuan wenhuazhuyi yu makesizhuyi minzu lilun de liang dian bijiao. *Kexue shehuizhuyi* 2010 (2): 8–12.

Wang, Xi'en. 2010b. Guanyu minzu de zai sikao. *Xibei shida daxue (shehui kexue ban)* 47 (1): 55–58.

Wang, Xi'en. 2010c. Zhongguo minzu shibie de yiju. *Minzu yanjiu* 2010 (5): 1–15.

Wang, Xuejian. 2015. Shilun Zhongguo tese shehuizhuyi xieshang minzhu de si da jichu. *Zhongguo zhengxie lilun yanjiu* 2015 (2): 26–30.

Wang, Yan, and Wei Chonghui. 2017. The Chinese logic of consultative governance. *Social Sciences in China* 38 (3): 5–24.

Wang, Yujue. 2015. 'Si ge quanmian' zhanlüe sixiang: Zhongguo tese shehuizhuyi lilun tixi de xin fazhan. *Sichuan ligong xueyuan xuebao (shehui kexue ban)* 2015 (2): 1–10.

Weatherley, Robert. 2006. *Politics in China since 1949: Legitimizing authoritarian rule*. Abingdon: Routledge.

Wei, Bo. 2016. Goujian Zhongguo tese shehuizhuyi zhili tizhi. *Xinjiang shifan daxue xuebao (zhexue shehui kexue ban)* 37 (1): 68–73.

Weller, Robert. 2012. Responsive authoritarianism and blind-eye governance in China. In *Socialism vanquished, socialism challenged: Eastern Europe and China, 1989–2009*, ed. Nina Bandelj and Dorothy Solinger, 83–99. Oxford: Oxford University Press.

Weng, Shisheng, and Liu Minghui. 1993. Xi Jinping tan lingdao. *Lingdao wencui* 1: 8–11.

Wright, Theresa. 2010. *Accepting authoritarianism: State-society relations in China's reform era*. Stanford: Stanford University Press.

Wu, Guoguang. 2013. Politics against science: Reflections on the study of Chinese politics in contemporary China. In *Political science and Chinese political studies: The state of the field*, ed. Guo Sujian, 215–236. Heidelberg: Springer.

Wu, Xiaohua, and Hao Nan. 2017. Zhongguo tese makesizhuyi minzu lilun de xin fazhan—Xi Jinping minzu gongzuo sixiang jiedu. *Minzu yanjiu* 2017 (4): 1–10.

Xi, Jinping. 2012a. Commemorate the 30th Anniversary of the promulgation and implementation of the current constitution (4 December, 2012). In *The governance of China*, Vol. 1:163–172. Beijing: Foreign Languages Press, 2014.

Xi, Jinping. 2012b. Zai shoudu gejie jinian xianxing xianfa gongbu shixing 30 zhounian dahui shang de jianghua (2012.12.04). In *Tan zhiguolizheng*, Vol. 1:135–143. Beijing: Waiwen chubanshe, 2014.

Xi, Jinping. 2013. Guanyu 'Zhonggong zhongyang guanyu quanmian shenhua gaige ruogan zhongda wenti de jueding' de shuoming (2013.11.09). In *Tan zhiguolizheng*, Vol. 1:70–89. Beijing: Waiwen chubanshe, 2014.

Xi, Jinping. 2014a. *Guanyu 'Zhonggong zhongyang guanyu quanmian tuijin yifazhiguo ruogan zhongda wenti de jueding' de shuoming (2014.10.20)*. Beijing: Renmin chubanshe.

Xi, Jinping. 2014b. Quanmian guanche dang de minzu zhengce he zongjiao zhengce (2014.04.22, 2014.09.28). In *Tan zhiguolizheng*, Vol. 2:299–302. Beijing: Waiwen chubanshe, 2017.

Xi, Jinping. 2014c. Tuijin xieshang minzhu guangfan duoceng zhiduhua fazhan (2014.09.21). In *Tan zhiguolizheng*, Vol. 2:291–298. Beijing: Waiwen chubanshe, 2017.

Xi, Jinping. 2014d. *Zai qingzhu quanguo renmin daibiao dahui chengli 60 zhounian dahui shang de jianghua*. Beijing: Renmin chubanshe.

Xi, Jinping. 2015a. Baochi he zengqiang dang de quntuan gongzuo he quntuan zuzhi zhengzhixing xianjinxing qunzhongxing (2015.07.06). In *Tan zhiguolizheng*, Vol. 2:306–312. Beijing: Waiwen chubanshe, 2017.

Xi, Jinping. 2015b. *Guanyu quanmian yifazhiguo lunshu zhaibian*. Beijing: Zhongyang wenxian chubanshe.

Xi, Jinping. 2017a. *Juesheng quanmian jiancheng xiaokang shehui, duoqu xinshidai Zhongguo tese shehuizhuyi weida shengli (2017.10.18)*. Beijing: Renmin chubanshe.

Xi, Jinping. 2017b. *Secure a decisive victory in building a moderately prosperous society in all respects and strive for the great success of socialism with Chinese characteristics for a new era: Report to the 19th national congress of the communist party of China, October 18, 2017*. Beijing: Foreign Languages Press.

Xia, Zhengnong, and Chen Zhili (eds.). 2009. *Cihai*, 6th ed. Shanghai: Shanghai cishu chubanshe.

Xiao, Guiqing, and Yu. Jiangtao. 2012. Gaige kaifang yilai zhongguo tese shehuizhuyi zhidu de tansuo he chuangxin. *Dangdai zhongguo shi yanjiu* 19 (5): 13–19.

Xie, Zhikui. 2009. Cuowu de minzhu guannian yu xianshi de minzhu lujing—dui Zhongguo tese shehuizhuyi minzhu daolu de lilun sikao. *Zhengzhixue yanjiu* 2009 (6): 21–30.

Xin, Xiangyang. 2019. Zhongguo tese shehuizhuyi zhengzhi zhidu de youyuexing. *Lingdao kexue luntan* 2019 (12): 3–24.

Xu, Hanming. 2017a. Xi Jinping shehui zhili fazhi sixiang yanjiu. *Faxue zazhi* 2017 (10): 1–27.

Xu, Kaiyi, and Zhu Chenchen. 2018. Jiceng xieshang minzhu de zhidu rentong lun xi. *Zhengzhixue yanjiu* 2018 (4): 80–89.

Xu, Yaotong. 2017b. Shiba da yilai Zhongguo tese shehuizhuyi zhengzhi jianshe de xin fazhan. *Dangzheng yanjiu* 2017 (6): 5–12.

Yan, Xia, and Liu Hui. 2018. Nongcun jiceng xieshang minzhu de dianxing tansuo yu shijian lujing yanjiu. *Xuexi luntan* 2018 (2): 38–43.

Yang, Guangbin. 2009. Minzhu de shehuizhuiyi zhi wei—jian ping zichan jieji yu minzhu zhengzhi shenhua. *Zhongguo shehui kexue* 2009 (3): 4–18.

Yang, Haijiao. 2008. 30 nianlai Zhongguo tese shehuizhuyi minzhu zhengzhi jianshe huigu. *Xuexi yu tansuo* 2008 (6): 20–26.

Yang, Weimin. 2017. Zhongguo tese zhengdang zhidu de youshi ji dui shijie gongxian—'wei renlei dui genghao shehui zhidu de tansuo tigong Zhongguo fang'an' zhi guanjian. *Tongyi zhanxian xue yanjiu* 2017 (1): 15–31.

Yao, Jianzong, and Huang Wenyi. 2012. Zhongguo tese shehuizhuyi faxue lilun tixi yanjiu. *Fazhi yu shehui fazhan* 2012 (2): 3–13.

Yin, Limin, and Qiu Guanlin. 2018. Minzhu cu minsheng: jingying yinling xia de jiceng xieshang minzhu zhili shijian—jiyu SQ cun xieshang minzhu shijian anli yanjiu. *Zhongguo xingzheng guanli* 2018 (2): 58–64.

Zhang, Jijiao, and Wei Jianwen. 2018. San lun 'guojia—minzu' guanxi—guoji shiye yu Zhongguo jingyan. *Yunnan minzu daxue xuebao (zhexue shehui kexue ban)* 35 (5): 49–54.

Zhang, Jinfan. 2013. Ancient China's legal tradition and legal thought. *Social Sciences in China* 34 (2): 134–151.

Zhang, Mingjun, and Yi Chengzhi. 2017. Zhongguo fuhe minzhu de jiazhi jiqi youhua luoji. *Zhengzhixue yanjiu* 2017 (2): 14–29.

Zhang, Shiwei. 2018. Zhongguo gongchandang lingdao de duodang hezuo he zhengzhi xieshang zhidu de zhengzhi jichu yu lishi shengcheng. *Xueshujie* 2018 (11): 46–56.

Zhang, Wenxian. 2017a. Xin sixiang yinling fazhi xin zhengcheng—Xi Jinping xinshidai Zhongguo tese shehuizhuyi sixiang dui yifazhiguo he fazhi jianshe de zhidao yiyi. *Faxue yanjiu* 2017 (6): 3–20.

Zhang, Wenxian. 2017b. Xinshidai quanmian yifazhiguo sixiang, fanglüe he shijian. *Zhongguo faxue* 2017 (6): 5–28.

Zhang, Wenxian. 2018. Zhongguo fazhi 40 nian: licheng, guiji he jingyan. *Jilin daxue shehui kexue xuebao* 2018 (5): 5–25.

Zhang, Yi. 2012. Lun Zhongguo tese shehuizhuyi minzhu: xuanju minzhu yu xieshang minzhu. *Changchun shiwei dangxiao xuebao* 2012 (5): 43–47.

Zhao, Jianying. 2018. Zhongguohua makesizhuyi zhexue yinling gaige kaifang de weida lishi jincheng. *Shehui kexue zhanxian* 2018 (11): 7–13.

Zhao, Xiuling. 2016. Xieshang minzhu yu Zhongguo nongcun zhili xiandaihua. *Qinghua daxue xuebao (zhexue shehui kexue ban)* 2016 (1): 40–52.

Zhonggong zhongyang wenxian yanjiushi. 2003. *Mao Zedong zhuan 1949–1976*. Beijing: Zhongyang wenxian chubanshe.

Zhonggong zhongyang xuanchuanbu. 2019. *Xi Jinping xinshidai Zhongguo tese shehuizhuyi sixiang xuexi gangyao*. Beijing: Xuexi chubanshe.

Zhonggong zhongyang xuanchuanbu lilun ju. 2009. Juyou qiangda shengmingli de zhengdang zhidu—weishenme bixu jianchi Zhongguo gongchandang lingdao de duodang hezuo he zhengzhi xieshang zhidu, er buneng gao xifang de duodangzhi. *Dangjian* 2009 (7): 7–10.

Zhou, Enlai. 1949. Guanyu renmin zhengxie de jige wenti (1949.09.07). In *Zhou Enlai tongyi zhanxian wenxuan*, 129–143. Beijing: Renmin chubanshe, 1984.

Zhou, Enlai. 1957. Changqi gongcun, huxiang jiandu (1957.04.24). In *Zhou Enlai tongyi zhanxian wenxuan*, 345–349. Beijing: Renmin chubanshe, 1984.

Zhou, Xiulong. 2017. Woguo xieshang minzhu zhidu de fa zhexue sikao. *Tianjin daxue xuebao (shehui kexue ban)* 19 (5): 444–449.

Zhu, Jiamu. 2016. Advancing the construction of the discourse system of Marxist theory of historiography with Chinese characteristics in the struggle with historical nihilism. *Marxist Studies in China* 2016: 18–52.

Zhu, Shengming. 2014. Jiceng minzhu xieshang de shijian yu tansuo—yi zhejiang wenling kentan wei li. *Zhongguo tese shehuizhuyi yanjiu* 2014 (2): 59–64.

Zhuang, Congsheng. 2006. Xieshang minzhu: Zhongguo tese shehuizhuyi minzhu de zhongyao xingshi. *Makesizhuyi yanjiu* 2006 (7): 81–85.

Zhuo, Xinping. 2018. *Religious faith of the Chinese*. Translated by Dong Zhao. China Insights. Singapore: Springer.

Chapter 9
Socialist Democracy in Theory

9.1 Opening Remarks

> China's socialist democracy is the broadest, most genuine, and most effective democracy to safeguard the fundamental interests of the people. (Xi 2017a, 15)

Theory arises from practice—for this reason the present chapter on the theory of socialist democracy follows the chapter concerning practice. In pursuing this theory, I dig back into the Marxist tradition, beginning with Marx and especially Engels, and run through to its current development in China. This is a tradition rich in theoretical developments that arose from the actual practices of constructing socialist democracy. While there are some overlaps with the previous two chapters, my primary concern is the theory of socialist democracy from places in the world where a Communist revolution was successful and where it became possible to construct forms of socialist democracy.[1] Of course, Marx and Engels were not in such a position, so their proposals are sparse and cautious, for they were fully aware that one can engage in scientific analysis only on the basis of actual experience. This experience would come with the Soviet Union, so I turn to Lenin and then Stalin, where we find initial articulations of democratic centralism and the necessary organic leadership of the Communist Party for any viable form of socialist democracy.

My main concern, however, is with China. Mao Zedong is crucial, with his three overlapping categories of new democracy, democratic dictatorship, and democratic centralism. While new democracy, with its multi-party cooperation, pertained to the period of revolutionary struggle and the anti-Japanese struggle, it carried on in the New China in the form of political consultative conferences and multi-party

[1]For this reason, I do not deal with ideal and impractical theories of what socialist democracy might be (found particularly in some forms of 'Western' Marxism), nor in 'rightist' or moderating tendencies in which it is argued that Communist Parties must work within the parliamentary systems of capitalist democracy and eschew revolutionary politics. Social democracy, Eurocommunism, 'weak' communism—call it what you will, it is not socialist democracy.

R. Boer, *Socialism with Chinese Characteristics*,
https://doi.org/10.1007/978-981-16-1622-8_9

consultative democracy. As for the people's democratic dictatorship, this was a reinterpretation of the dictatorship of the proletariat, now seen in terms of dictatorship over counter-revolutionaries within and especially outside a new socialist country, and democracy for the vast numbers of urban and rural workers. Most significant is Mao's development of the dialectical category of democratic centralism, for this would become the defining feature of socialist democracy in China. At the same time, Mao bequeathed a problem in relation to democratic centralism: by and large he assumed that its initial practice in inner-Party governance could simply be extended to country-wide governance. Mao did not as yet see the necessary difference between the two forms of democratic centralism. This would be the problem that Deng Xiaoping and those who followed sought to solve. Apart from correcting the breakdown of democratic centralism seen during the Cultural Revolution, Deng Xiaoping stressed the separation of the Communist Party and governance of the country, with the consequence that a socialist country like China is not—as some suggest—a 'party-state'. This emphasis by Deng would unfold with the articulation of the components of the socialist democratic system (Jiang Zemin) and the need for 'statutory processes [*fading chengxu*]' so that the proposals of the Communist Party become the will of the country's governing structures (Hu Jintao). However, they still did not identify these developments with democratic centralism, preferring to use that term for inner-Party governance. The breakthrough comes with Xi Jinping, who clearly identifies democratic centralism as the definition of both the overall socialist political system with its components and the statutory processes needed for relations between the Communist Party and the country's government.

9.1.1 Historical Forms of Democracy

Before proceeding, I would like to set the scene by surveying the distinct historical forms of democracy that have appeared in human history—given that there is no pure and abstract form of 'democracy as such' (Jiang H. and Zhao 2010, 4; Lenin 1919e, 489–499; 1919d, 464).[2] The first is baseline—a better term than 'primitive'—democracy, which Engels described so well in his piece called 'The Mark' (1882a, 1882c). Characteristic of pre-state formations, its basic feature was that the organs of governance were not separated from but stood in the midst of society. Second is ancient Greek democracy, practised in a few city-states with small populations in which only adult 'free' males partook in the assembly. Given that the very idea of 'freedom' in this context relies on a constitutive un-freedom, the vast majority—such as slaves, women, and foreigners—were excluded in what Chinese researchers call

[2]As Engels put it sharply in a letter to August Bebel in 1884, 'pure democracy' often becomes a slogan for counter-revolutionary reaction: 'At the moment of revolution … the entire reactionary mass … will act as though they were democrats … At all events, on the crucial day and the day after that, our only adversary will be *collective reaction centred round pure democracy* and this, I think, ought never to be lost from view' (Engels 1884a, 253; 1884b, 234).

'slave-owner democracy' (Cai 2011, 144).[3] The third is capitalist or liberal democracy, which emerged slowly in Europe after the bourgeois revolutions. Since the parliaments were shaped by political parties based on classes, this form of democracy is highly antagonistic. All manner of items, including health and environment, become 'political footballs', with the result that common welfare, internal order, and justice for the majority have not been attained. It is understandable why Chinese researchers depict this model as 'competitive democracy [*jingzhengxing minzhu*]' (Xie Z. 2009, 24). This form of democracy was fully established only in Europe and in its former colonies where European colonists largely obliterated indigenous populations. Otherwise, it does not transplant very well, as we see with illiberal and colonial democracies. As for illiberal democracy, it takes some of the outward forms of liberal democracy, such as periodic elections and parliamentary terms, but it ensures that a specific political party remains in power. The first such modern example is the city-state of Singapore, but it has spread to eastern Europe, Russia, and many other parts of the world. Colonial democracies were—as the name suggests—initially transplanted in undeveloped former European colonies where the local population remained dominant. The result has largely been chaos: the inherent antagonisms of capitalist democracy have been transformed in light of religious partisanship and the interests of 'ethnic groups' and clans. We can see these developments in countries such as Malaysia, Indonesia, and India, where religion has become the determining feature, and in many African countries, where each ethnic group and clan has its own political party. It should be no surprise that many such places are not only raising profound questions about the colonial democracy imposed upon them, but also seeking alternative models that can actually provide efficient, disciplined, and stable governance (Yang W. 2017, 16–17).

The final historical form is socialist democracy, which developed initially in the Soviet Union, was dominant in Eastern Europe, and is now the form of democracy found in socialist states from Cuba to China. To summarise its basic features: it arises from within a socialist system and its economic base; it deploys democratic centralism, in which Communist Party leadership is the key; the Party represents the vast majority—rural and urban workers—who are disenfranchised in other forms of democracy, especially liberal democracy; as seen in the previous chapter, it typically has more elections than other forms of democracy, relies on consultation rather than antagonism, and develops a transformed (*Aufhebung*) type of baseline democracy that is described as 'grassroots'. It is the theory of this type of democracy that I analyse in what follows.

[3]Given that political forms arise from the economic base, some Chinese scholars also speak of European feudal democracy, limited to the aristocracy (Li S. 2009, 282; Xie Z. 2009, 26).

9.2 Engels and Marx

It was primarily Engels who began to work out the rudimentary framework of what socialist democracy might mean, although he was always clear that neither he nor Marx could foresee what the reality might be.[4] Engels's important research that has a bearing on socialist governance took place in the 1880s and early 1890s. During this time, he prepared a series of earlier manuscripts by Marx for publication and dug deep into European and particularly German history to produce the outlines—often in notes and unpublished texts—concerning the state (Engels 1882d; 1882b; 1884c). My concern is how this research relates to socialist democracy.[5]

9.2.1 Equating the Paris Commune with the Dictatorship of the Proletariat

The context for this work was a moderating or 'rightist' tendency in the large German Social-Democratic Party, of which the elected delegates in the Reichstag sought to retreat from the need for revolution and distance themselves from any notion of the proletarian dictatorship. Here we see the beginning of a process of elevating Marx's depiction of the Paris Commune as a well-nigh utopian image of socialist democracy and putting aside the proletarian dictatorship—a deviation that continues to bedevil Western Marxism. Engels would have none of it, dusting off articles and unpublished texts by Marx where the dictatorship of the proletariat was mentioned, as well as writing introductions to some of those texts (Marx 1875c, 1875a; Engels 1891c, 1891d, 1891e, 1891a, 1895a, 1895b).[6] The crucial move came in the introduction to the third edition of Marx's *The Civil War in France*, where Engels writes: 'do you want to know what this dictatorship looks like? Look at the Paris Commune. That was the Dictatorship of the Proletariat [*Das war die Diktatur des Proletariats*]' (Engels 1891c, 16; 1891d, 191). The commune is the proletarian dictatorship—this is a distinct step beyond Marx, who did not have the energy to think through the problem. In this text, Engels argues that the Paris Commune did in fact begin the process of lopping off more and more pieces of the capitalist state, although the commune failed in the end since it did not go far enough.

[4]Marx made a few initial moves in relation to the Paris commune and the dictatorship of the proletariat, but he left the relation between the two unresolved (Boer 2019).

[5]The following summarises material from a monograph entitled *Friedrich Engels and the Foundations of Socialist Governance* (Boer In press).

[6]The 1895 introduction was for a collection of Marx's articles that Engels edited and entitled *The Class Struggles in France* (Marx 1895). See also the 1890 letter to Conrad Schmitt, where Engels writes: 'Otherwise why should we be fighting for the political dictatorship of the proletariat if political power [*die politische Macht*] is economically powerless [*ohnmächtig*]? *Gewalt* (i.e. state power [*Staatsmacht*]) is also an economic force [*ökonomische Potenz*]!' (Engels 1890, 493).

9.2.2 The Seeds of Democratic Centralism

This equation of the dictatorship of the proletariat with communist democracy is the first significant principle that may be drawn from Engels's works. In time, it would come to have profound implications for what came to be known as democratic centralism. Let me put it this way: in the 'Communist Manifesto', both Engels and Marx stipulate that strong centralising moves are needed after the seizure of the power through a proletarian revolution. These include the centralisation of and monopoly over communication, transport, and credit in a national bank, the abolition of private property in land and inheritance, the control and expansion of agriculture and industry as the instruments of production owned by the state, the 'establishment of labour armies' and the 'equal liability' of all adults to labour (Marx and Engels 1848a, 481–482; 1848b, 505–506). This centralised control over the means of production is explicitly identified a couple of years later as the dictatorship of the proletariat (Marx and Engels 1850a, 354; 1850b, 387–388).

At the same time, the exercise of governance after a proletarian revolution would be based on decentralising democratic measures. Governance would take place through a 'working, not a parliamentary, body' that is to be 'executive and legislative at the same time'. These political forms were to be based on universal suffrage and recall, and would be replicated across the land, even in 'the smallest country hamlet', with local bodies administering 'their common affairs by an assembly of delegates in the central town'. They would also elect delegates to participate in the national body, but the point is that governance would be 'restored to the responsible agents of society' (Marx 1871, 139–141). I have quoted here from the well-known pages concerning the Paris Commune in Marx's *The Civil War in France*, which are so often cited as a model for socialist democratic governance. But it was precisely this text for which Engels wrote the introduction mentioned earlier, where he took a step beyond Marx and identified the commune with the proletarian dictatorship. In doing so, he makes an implicitly dialectical point: socialist governance would be both centralising and democratic, both repressive against the remnants of the bourgeois dictatorship and a free association of workers as the vast majority. In short, democratic centralism.

9.2.3 Principles of Socialist Democracy

A number of further philosophical principles, arising from Engels's later works, are relevant for this study: (1) public power (*Gewalt*) continues but loses its 'political character'; (2) governance entails the administration of things and the management of the processes of production for the sake of the true interests of society; (3) the many organs of governance would not be separated from society but stand in the midst of society; (4) this reality may be seen as a dialectical transformation, an *Aufhebung*, of baseline communism.[7]

Already in the Manifesto, both Engels and Marx specified that in the process of socialist construction 'public power [*öffentliche Gewalt*] will lose its political character [*den politischen Charakter*]' (Marx and Engels 1848a, 482; 1848b, 505). To explain: the state as it had become known is defined by Engels as a 'separated [*getrennte*]' power set over against society. This form of the state would not continue, but a 'public power' would continue. What type of public power? It and its 'public functions [*funzioni pubbliche*] will lose their political character [*carattere politico*]' (Engels 1873a, 86; 1873c, 425). For both Engels and Marx, 'political character' means the reality of class struggle and its manifestation in the state (Marx and Engels 1848a, 482; 1848b, 505). Thus, if public *Gewalt* loses its political character, it ceases to be a manifestation of class struggle and instrument of coercion. The implications are far-reaching: without political character based on class struggle, antagonistic struggle between different political parties would no longer exist, so much so that 'elections have nothing [*hat nichts*] of today's political character [*politischen Charakter*]' (Marx 1875b, 635; 1875d, 519–520). In other words, elections themselves—seen by those saturated in the Western liberal tradition as the very definition of democracy—would cease to be politicised. And if this applies to elections, then it also applies to all other forms of governance under socialism.

The remaining three principles indicate how a depoliticised public power may work. To begin with, the matters of life and the economy can be managed for the benefit of society (Marx and Engels 1872b, 49–50; 1872a, 121; Engels 1894, 535; see also Wang and Wei 2017, 10). No longer functioning as 'political footballs' that can be tossed from one political party to another, with the one constantly seeking to undo the policies of the other, policies in all areas can be enacted in terms of 'watching over the true interests of society' (Engels 1873a, 86; 1873c, 425). As the Chinese translation of this text puts it, the purpose is to safeguard social interests and benefits—'*weihu zhenzheng shehui liyi*' (Engels 1873b, 338).[8] Further, instead of antagonism and conflict between state and society, the organs of governance 'stand in the midst of society [*steht eben mitten in der Gesellschaft*]' (Engels 1892a, 265; 1892b, 275).[9] The quotation comes from Engels's detailed study of the comprehensive pre-state governing roles in *The Origin of the Family,* with their democratic councils, elected positions, and significant administrative functions. But the point here is that governance and society are seen as cooperative rather than conflict-ridden, consultative rather than antagonistic (Liu W. 2002). How are these pre-state forms of baseline democracy relevant for socialist democracy? The clearest answer may be found in

---

[7]See also the useful study by Jia Jianfang (2014, 3–6).

[8]Or, as another Chinese term puts it, to 'serve the community [*gongtongti fuwu*]'. *Gongtongti* is a word that arose in Chinese through the translation of the works of Engels and Marx, especially *The German Ideology* (Marx and Engels 1846). It is a rendering of *Gemeinschaft* and *Gemeinwesen*, but the *fuwu* (服务) is crucial, for it means to be in the service of society or the collective as whole (Boer and Zang 2019).

[9]I quote here from the most widely used fourth and revised edition of 1892. The first edition of *The Origin of the Family* was published in 1884.

'The Mark', a study that sought to appeal to German peasants by outlining the history of the 'Mark-association [*Markgenossenschaft*]', with its common ownership of the means of production and its democratic assemblies. The point, however, is that the Communist movement does not seek to restore such a practice, for this would not be possible. Instead—and here Engels directly addresses the rural workers—by a 'rebirth [*Wiedergeburt*] of the mark, not in its old, outdated [*überlebten*] form, but in a rejuvenated [*verjüngten*] form' that entails all of the latest technological improvements administered by the community itself (Engels 1891b, 330; 1882c, 456).[10] In other words, this baseline communism and its democratic practices would require a thorough dialectical transformation (*Aufhebung*) in the new society.

In summing up, let me address the implications of these early and undeveloped thoughts by Engels and Marx. I have already indicated the implicit dialectical point concerning democratic centralism, so here I add that governing functions continue under socialism (a 'public power'); these functions are depoliticised and stand in the midst of society, which entails the importance of cooperation and consultation in democratic processes, instead of antagonism and class conflict; and to gain a sense of how socialist democracy might work, Engels argues that one component would entail an *Aufhebung* of baseline democracy. The latter would eventually become one of the inspirations for 'base-level [*jiceng*]' or grassroots consultative democracy.

9.3 Lenin and the 'Highest Form of Democracy'

In contrast to Engels and Marx, it was Lenin and then Stalin who developed the initial framework of a theory of socialist democracy arising from actual practice. Since no one had tried socialism before at a state level, they were seeking a 'correct road to the unknown' (Yermakov 1975, 107). But they did so by constantly returning to the texts of Engels and Marx for insights and principles, since—as Lenin observed—'A state more democratic, in the true sense of the word, one more closely connected with the working and exploited people, has *never yet existed*' (Lenin 1919m, 29; 1919a, 433).

9.3.1 Three Meanings of Democracy

Lenin occupies a unique position, both 'before October' and 'after October', struggling for a proletarian revolution and engaged in the early construction of socialism after a successful revolution. His reflections on socialist democracy may also been

[10] I have quoted from the *Werke* (MEW) version, since the final sentences were penned later and included in the 1891 appendix to the German edition of *Socialism: Utopian and Scientific*. The sentences appeared in all subsequent editions, but are not included in the text provided by *Gesamtaugabe*, or MEGA (Engels 1882a).

in terms of this distinction, although his experience of actual socialist democracy was limited by the few years left to him. Chinese researchers tend to distinguish between the more idealistic expectations Lenin had for socialist democracy before the October revolution and the sober modifications made in light of the immense difficulties of constructing socialism (Rong and Lai 2000, 16–18; Liu Sicang and Lu 2004; Cai 2011; Yan 2014). Further, Lenin's thoughts on socialist democracy were very much a work in progress, seeking to find the best approach in light of rapidly changing circumstances.

Democracy has three main and overlapping senses in Lenin's texts. First, it is bourgeois democracy and is seen as part and parcel of the 'bourgeois-democratic revolution', which was agreed to have emerged in Russia between the 1905 revolution and the February revolution of 1917. Lenin saw the historical value of bourgeois democracy in terms of the struggle against the relics of feudalism and absolutism, the need to make the most of bourgeois reforms—by means of the press and freedom of assembly—to promote the Bolshevik platform (Lenin 1894a, 300–301; 1894b, 290–291; 1919n, 21; 1919i, 272), and in the way a democratic republic would sharpen class conflict and bring about a proletarian revolution. It was precisely in this context of heightened class conflict that Lenin came to distinguish even more sharply between the illusory and deceptive promises of bourgeois democracy and socialist democracy (Lenin 1905h, 7–19; 1905g, 281–292; 1905b, 1905l).

Second, democracy is more commonly connected with the broader socialist project and has a distinct class and thus revolutionary character. More generally, the loan word 'democracy' tended to be associated with the labouring masses of workers and peasants, especially during the revolutionary period from 1905 to 1917. Democracy became synonymous with the range of socialist parties, while those of the bourgeoisie (Kadets) and the old aristocracy (Octobrists and others) were anti-democratic (Kolonitskii 2004). Using 'democracy' in this sense, Lenin advocated a coalition with other socialist parties in the initial phases of the proletarian revolution, arguing that the democratic and socialist struggles—as class based—are inseparably connected in the political struggle (Lenin 1897b, 445–451; 1897a, 328–333; see also 1902a, 78–95; 1902d, 421–435; 1905e, 318; 1905c, 187).[11] During the tumultuous year of 1917, such democracy was embodied in the Soviets of Workers', Soldiers' and Peasants' Deputies—hence the slogan 'all power to the Soviets'. Needless to say, the Bolsheviks should take the vanguard role in leading such a coalition of revolutionary-democratic parties in completing the democratic revolution, since true revolutionary democracy should lead to a socialist revolution and should not be seduced by the

[11] In the compressed time of revolutionary developments, when years were compressed into weeks and even days, Lenin made use of a number of positions and terms that he would later leave aside. These include: elements of bourgeois democracy at a minimum level of socialist democracy (Lenin 1902c, 206–207; 1902b, 27–28); the shorthand of 'democratic revolution' to refer to the range of socialist parties pushing for revolution (Lenin 1906f, 1906a); and 'revolutionary-democratic' parties and even a 'revolutionary-democratic dictatorship of the proletariat and peasantry', which was seen to be distinct from the 'socialist dictatorship of the proletariat and peasantry' (Lenin 1905f, 1905j, 1905d, 126–141; 1905k, 382–395).

compromises entailed in 'bourgeois democratic phrases' (Lenin 1905a, 1905i, 1917b, 190–194; 1917c, 360–364).

9.3.2 *The Superiority of Socialist Democracy*

The third sense is the one that interests me here: 'democracy' is itself a socialist project, although now in terms of full, complete, and consistent democratisation that would lead to its own demise. Thus, socialist democracy in Lenin's hands has a minimum and a maximum sense: at the minimum level, it designates all socialist parties and their struggle against the old aristocracy and especially the bourgeoisie with its form of bourgeois democracy; in its maximum sense, proletarian or socialist democracy means the democracy advocated by Communists. The latter is my concern, but what did socialist democracy come to mean after the proletarian revolution?

As mentioned, the answer is not provided by Lenin in a neat summary, for he made his points mostly in response to developments on the ground and in the context of often sharp debates,[12] so I draw the following points from moments in his writings. To begin with, socialist democracy is predicated on '*radical* change in the entire political system' (Lenin 1912b, 199; 1912a, 417), entailing that it is quantitatively and qualitatively distinct (Cai 2011, 144). In terms of quantity, socialist democracy is the rule by and expresses the will of the rural and urban workers, who are the vast majority that had been exploited by and thereby excluded from the benefits of capitalist democracy (Lenin 1919h, 90–91; 1919c, 106–107). Thus, socialist democracy is partisan and openly so, for the sake of the majority. As Lenin observed after the October Revolution: '"Liberties" and democracy *not* for all, but *for* the working and exploited masses, to emancipate them from exploitation; ruthless suppression of exploiters' (Lenin 1918e, 73; 1918a, 155).

Further, socialist democracy is qualitatively distinct, for it is the 'highest form of democracy'—as Soviet or proletarian democracy (Lenin 1919l, 304; 1919k, 308; 1919h, 89–96; 1919c, 105–112)—in which the working class and other workers are the masters of the country. The distinct formulation for this qualitative difference appears clearly in the exegesis of Marx and especially Engels that is found in *The State and Revolution* (Lenin 1917a, 1917d; see also 1919g, 264–266; 1919j, 99–101). Here Lenin deploys two terms that develop implications found in Marx and Engels: the proletarian state; and a distinct stage of socialism in which this state arises. The proletarian state is by definition the dictatorship of the proletariat, which means the highest form of democracy (Wen and Huang 1998).[13] Clearly, this is a development

[12]That said, we do find occasional fuller and programmatic statements, such as the one found in the draft program of the Russian Communist Party from early 1919 (Lenin 1919h, 89–96; 1919c, 105–112). Even here, we find a distinct emphasis on 'first steps', on the need to take time in transforming the whole system.

[13]With the proletariat as the ruling class, the tasks of this democracy are both to smash bourgeois remnants and lead the masses towards socialism.

of Engels's point that the proletarian dictatorship is one and same with the commune. Lenin observes: 'The dictatorship of the proletariat alone can emancipate humanity from the oppression of capital, from the lies, falsehood and hypocrisy of bourgeois democracy—democracy *for the rich*—and establish democracy *for the poor*, that is, make the blessings of democracy *really* accessible to the workers and poor peasants' (Lenin 1919f, 390; 1919b, 370).[14]

9.3.3 Democratic Centralism

In 1904–1905, a new principle with profound ramifications for the global Communist movement appeared: the dialectical concept of democratic centralism (Li W. 2010; Ma 2014, 208–209; Li Z. and Wang 2018). As we saw earlier, the concept itself is implicit in the centralising and democratic emphases of proletarian power as outlined by Engels and Marx, but it was not explicitly articulated as a distinct principle. For Lenin and the Bolsheviks, democratic centralism was initially concerned with inner-Party structures, in terms of full freedom to criticise so as to maintain unity of action: 'The principle of democratic centralism and autonomy for local Party organisations implies universal and full *freedom to criticise*, so long as this does not disturb the unity *of a definite action*; it rules out *all* criticism which disrupts or makes difficult the *unity* of an action decided on by the Party' (Lenin 1906e, 129; 1906c, 443; see also 1906f, 237; 1906a, 163; Harding 2009, vol. 2, 172–179).[15] However, the major step was to apply democratic centralism to the new state as a whole, initially in terms of nationalities and autonomous regions, and then in relation to economic developments and the governmental structure (Lenin 1917a, 74; 1917d, 453; see also 1913b, 143–149; 1913a, 45–51; 1918c, 151–153; 1918b, 207–209).[16] Herein lies a problem that would take some time—well beyond Lenin—to resolve: the Bolsheviks assumed that democratic centralism could simply be extended from its principal deployment in inner-Party governance to governing the country as a whole. They did not realise

[14] See also: 'During this period, the state must inevitably be a state that is democratic *in a new way* (for the proletariat and the propertyless in general) and dictatorial *in a new way* (against the bourgeoisie)' (Lenin 1917a, 35; 1917d, 417).

[15] See also his observation on 'the principle of democratic centralism, on guarantees for the rights of all minorities and for all loyal opposition, on the autonomy of every Party organisation, on recognising that all Party functionaries must be elected, accountable to the Party and subject to recall. We see the observance in practice of these principles of organisation, their sincere and consistent application, as a guarantee against splits, a guarantee that the ideological struggle in the Party can and must prove fully consistent with strict organisational unity' (Lenin 1906d, 399–400; 1906b, 314).

[16] When it came to the new Communist International, Lenin emphasised the centralist dimension: 'Parties belonging to the Communist International must be organised on the principle of democratic *centralism*. In this period of acute civil war, the Communist parties can perform their duty only if they are organised in a most centralised manner, are marked by an iron discipline bordering on military discipline, and have strong and authoritative party centres invested with wide powers and enjoying the unanimous confidence of the membership' (Lenin 1920b, 209; 1920a, 210).

that such a move required significant institutional transformations to make it work for country-wide governance.

Finally, the form of socialist democracy envisaged by Lenin does not happen in an instant, immediately after a proletarian revolution. As Chinese scholars emphasise (Cai 2011, 144), it is a long term term project, connected with the eventual dying away of the state: 'victorious socialism cannot consolidate its victory and bring humanity to the withering away of the state without implementing full democracy' (Lenin 1916b, 128; 1916a, 74). But Lenin goes a step further, invoking the dialectical argument that since democracy is based on class struggle even in a proletarian state, it will disappear with the realisation of Communism. In *The State and Revolution*, Lenin engages closely with Engels's famous text from the third edition of *Anti-Dühring* (1894, 534–535) to argue that a proletarian state—which would destroy and replace the preceding capitalist state—is the 'most complete form of democracy' and as such would over a long period of time die away. In other words, democracy as embodied in such a proletarian state would, with that form of the state, eventually wither or die away: 'Communism alone is capable of providing really complete democracy, and the more complete it is, the sooner it will become unnecessary and wither away of its own accord' (Lenin 1917a, 90; 1917d, 468). In this process, democracy would become not a goal for which one must strive but an everyday habit of freedom (Lenin 1917a, 89, 102; 1917d, 467, 479; 1918d, 251; 1918f, 242).

To sum up: while Lenin did not have all of the material from Marx and especially Engels at hand (since some of Engels's notes and drafts had not yet been published), his exegesis of relevant texts both develops some of the implications and goes a step further. Democratic centralism is a clear case of developing implications, while Lenin also took to heart Engels's identification of the proletarian dictatorship with the commune to argue that the dictatorship of the proletariat—embodied in the soviets—was highest stage of democracy achieved thus far. Lenin went a distinct step further by arguing that Marx's initial phase of communism was the stage of socialism. During this long period, there would be a need for a proletarian state that embodied democratic centralism and the higher stage of democracy through the dictatorship of the proletariat. What has happened to Engels's arguments for the organs of governance standing in the midst of society and the *Aufhebung* of baseline democracy? It would seem that Lenin saw these developments as part of the final stage of Communism, when even socialist democracy would eventually die away, along with classes and the state of which it was an inescapable part.

9.4 Stalin and the Leadership of the Communist Party

The very newness of these concepts and their practice took some time to gain traction, especially in light of Western polemic against the new Soviet model and its inability to understand how Lenin's nascent dialectical formulations were beginning to work in practice. It fell to Stalin's long tenure to consolidate socialist democracy in light of Russian conditions. Given Stalin's immersion in the writings of Lenin, as well as those of Marx and Engels, it should be no surprise that there is significant common ground and continuity: the quantitative and qualitative difference of socialist democracy, so much so that such democracy is the 'most all-embracing and most democratic state organisation of all possible state organisations' (Stalin 1924c, 120; 1924d, 124; see also 1924b, 256–257; 1924f, 268–269); the dictatorship of the proletariat and peasantry as socialist democracy, to the point that Stalin coined the term 'democratic dictatorship', which would have resonance in China (Stalin 1927a, 251; 1927b, 256)[17]; and the assumption of a distinct stage of socialism with its socialist state form and qualitatively superior socialist democracy.

However, Stalin went further than Lenin on a couple of points, while preferring to avoid the terminology of 'democratic centralism'. Let me begin with the last point: the term appears soon after its promulgation (Stalin 1906a, 371; 1906b, 205) and it lies behind debates over the nature of a unitary state and self-determination of autonomous regions in the 1910s, but it is not used again until relatively late in the piece in relation to the workings of the Communist Party itself and the need for democratic supervision of the leadership (Stalin 1937d, 179; 1937c, 282–283; 1938b, 190; 1938a, 198). A major reason for its avoidance lies in the drawn-out struggle with Trotsky and his ilk, for one of the groupings around Trotsky included the 'Democratic Centralism' group (Stalin 1938b, 240–242; 1938a, 251–253). We should not read too much into this situation, especially not in terms of Trotsky's wayward accusations of 'dictatorship of the Party' rather than of the workers and peasants, if not a dictatorship of the small circle of leaders at the expense of the Party (Trotsky 1937, 94–100, 265–272). In light of the struggle, Stalin would not accept the weakening effect of factionalism and ultimately multiple political parties that would be the outcome of Trotsky's fostering of unlimited debate and different groupings.

9.4.1 Organic Leadership of the Communist Party

This struggle led Stalin to emphasise even more than Lenin the organic leadership of the Communist Party.[18] To this question Stalin devoted considerable energy, developing a complex dialectic of 'from below' and 'from above', and of the need for an organic connection between the Party and the masses, while constantly guarding against separation or divorce. In his key text, 'The Foundations of Leninism', Stalin draws from Lenin's thought six theses concerning the nature of the Communist Party, which is: (1) an advanced detachment of the working class; (2) an organised detachment; (3) the highest form of class organisation of the proletariat; (4) an instrument

[17]For Stalin, this 'genuine democracy' is the power of the 'majority over the minority', by which he means the 'dictatorship of the lower classes' (Stalin 1918b, 36–37; 1918a, 37–38; see also 1937a, 239–40; 1937b, 307–308).

[18]I have analysed this material in-depth in an earlier study, where one may find comprehensive references (Boer 2017, 115–139).

of the dictatorship of the proletariat; (5) the embodiment of the unity of will that is incompatible with factions; (6) strong precisely because it purges opportunist elements (Stalin 1924c, 169–186; 1924d, 175–193). Of these theses, I would like to emphasise the idea that the Party is a 'detachment' of the working class. For Stalin, the Party is inescapably part of the working class, 'closely bound up with it by all the fibres of its being', existing only through this 'bond' and the 'moral and political credit' granted by the masses. In relation to the dictatorship of the proletariat, Stalin stresses once again that the Party is not an end to itself, not a self-sufficient force. By contrast, it is a 'weapon' or 'instrument [*orudie*] in the hands of the proletariat', a tool that seeks to achieve the proletarian dictatorship and expand it when achieved (Stalin 1924c, 179–180; 1924d, 187).

In this light, socialist democracy means for Stalin not the exercise of multiple parties or factions, but rather the close and organic bond between the Party and the workers, peasants, and—from the 1930s—communist intellectuals.[19] This emphasis lays a hard task upon the Party, which must always ensure prestige, respect, and 'moral capital [*moral'nyi kapital*]' among the non-Party masses (Stalin 1924a, 313; 1924e, 327). Without such a connection any 'democracy' is worthless and the Party is doomed: 'The Party is part of the class; it exists for the class, not for itself' (Stalin 1924h, 227; 1924g, 238). The nature of the leadership of a Communist Party in the context of socialist democracy was by no means solved by Stalin, but his main contribution was to indicate the profound importance of this question.

9.4.2 *Proactive Human Rights Based on Freedom from Economic Exploitation*

Another contribution that would have significant ramifications is a major step towards a distinctly Marxist approach to human rights. This question came to the fore with the 1936 Constitution, in which multiple rights were clearly stipulated (Stalin 1936b, 1936a). In his reflections on the Constitution, Stalin inevitably contrasts the situation in the Soviet Union with capitalist democracies. What is missing from the latter form of democracy and its constitutions, he argues, is an emphasis on freedom from economic exploitation: 'there cannot be real equality between employer and workman, between landlord and peasant, if the former possess wealth and political weight in society while the latter are deprived of both—if the former are exploiters while the latter are exploited' (Stalin 1936c, 130; 1936d, 169). By contrast, this is precisely what socialism emphasises: freedom from economic exploitation.

Further, Stalin distinguishes between formal and proactive rights, or between abstract and exercised rights. The former are found in bourgeois constitutions, which simply state the limited rights in question—civil and political freedoms—without stipulating the more basic question of freedom from economic exploitation. The

[19] The reality of classes in a socialist system would also give rise to the category of non-antagonistic contradictions (see Sect. 3.3).

outcome is that the civil and political rights characteristic of bourgeois democracy appear in merely formal or abstract statements. By contrast, socialist rights are proactive and exercised, precisely because they are based on freedom from economic exploitation. With this foundation, the rights in question can be enacted and insured. As we saw in the preceding two chapters, human rights are another inescapable component of socialist democracy.

To sum up: Stalin's distinct contribution to the tradition of socialist democracy in practice concerns the leadership of the Communist Party and a Marxist approach to human rights. Both emphases would become abiding features of socialist democracy wherever it has been practised. Only through the Party's leadership can socialist democracy function; only through such a leadership can socio-economic well-being be ensured, as well as preferential policies for minority nationalities, universal education in socialism, and much more.

By way of transition to the next section, Chinese researchers emphasise two sides of the Soviet experience. On the one side are the those characteristics specific to the Soviet Union due to its own situation, while on the other side are common themes that carry through and indeed provided inspiration for China's own path. The former include the restriction to one political party, to the exclusion of all others, as the representative of rural and urban workers, as well as the structure of the Soviet state that constitutionally allowed self-determination and secession by Soviet states and autonomous regions. The common themes include the qualitative and quantitative difference of socialist democracy, democratic centralism, the leadership of the Communist Party, the seeds of a Marxist approach to human rights, and the implicit development of direct and indirect democracy (Ren 1995; Wen and Huang 1998; Cai 2011; Li M. and Liu 2011; Ouyang 2019). Obviously, it is the latter from which Chinese researchers draw for the sake of developing socialist democracy in light of Chinese conditions.

9.5 Mao Zedong

In relation to China, I begin with Mao Zedong's reflections on three forms of democracy: new democracy; democratic dictatorship; and democratic centralism. The first was inspired by Lenin and arose in the context of the United Front against Japanese imperialism and colonial occupation, the second was a term already coined by Stalin and entailed a translation of the proletarian dictatorship in light of the realities of power, and the third was drawn more directly from Lenin and made a centrepiece of primarily inner-Party structures, but also of Red Areas before 1949 as a model for the whole country afterwards. However, Mao left unresolved precisely how democratic centralism would make the transition from inner-Party to country-wide governance.

9.5.1 *New Democracy*

New democracy has obvious affinities with Lenin's united-front version of socialist democracy,[20] which sought to draw together all of the revolutionary parties under Communist leadership so as to complete the revolutionary process.[21] However, Mao reshapes the approach in two respects: contradiction analysis and the anti-colonial and anti-feudal struggle. Already in his lectures on dialectical materialism from 1937, Mao had observed that the principal contradiction during times of imperialist aggression is between the country concerned and imperialism. All other contradictions within a country—especially those between classes—temporarily become secondary. His specific examples include the anti-Japanese struggle under way as he gave the lectures (Mao 1937a, 259–260; 1937f, 643–644). Over the following few years, Mao reiterated the point in relation to the nature of the military struggle, but also in relation to developing the concept of new democracy.

As a way of examining how he did so, I turn to the second—and obviously related—framework of anti-colonial and anti-feudal struggle. In a word, new democracy entails a united front by *all* parties and groups in such a struggle.[22] Mao's argument is double-edged. To begin with, this revolution is a bourgeois-democratic revolution by nature, since it is directed at the feudal and semi-feudal leftovers in China under the Guomindang.[23] However, this revolution and its democracy is not of the old and obsolete type found in Europe and North America. The change in nature is due to the following reasons: after the turning point of the October Revolution in Russia, what was initially a bourgeois-democratic revolution became part of the global revolutionary movement; this revolution takes place in a semi-colonised country that had suffered waves of imperialist depredation and is thereby

---

[20]Mao also shared Lenin's assumption that democracy is equivalent with socialism. By the 1950s Mao was commonly using 'people's democracy'—a term coined by Tito in 1945—and 'democratic camp' as synonymous with socialism, which was contrasted with capitalist countries (Mao 1954a, 1954b).

[21]The following analysis is drawn from some key works from the late 1930s to the mid-1940s, in which Mao dealt with new democracy at some length (Mao 1939d, 646–649; 1939a, 326–329; 1940f, 1940d, 1940e, 1940c, 1945a, 1055–1062; 1945b, 278–285). Precursors may also be found in the new United Front against Japanese colonial occupation from 1937 onward (Mao 1937l, 256–262; 1937h, 267–273; 1937j, 274–275; 1937k, 288–289; 1945a, 1090–1092; 1945b, 311–313; 1948b, 1948a). A useful summing up may be found in the 1945 resolution of the Seventh Plenary Session of the CPC's Sixth Central Committee (CPC Central Committee 1945a, 1945b).

[22]In this sense can they be seen as part of a 'joint dictatorship' under the leadership of the Communist Party.

[23]Mao argues that the long process of this democratic revolution began with the Opium War in 1840, although he distinguishes between an older period of about 80 years and then a new period in light of the impetus of the May Fourth Movement and the Russian Revolution (Mao 1939c, 1939b, 1940f, 666–667; 1940d, 342–343). In the late 1920s, Mao adhered more closely to the Comintern's position that the distinct stage of a bourgeois-democratic revolution, as a precursor to the socialist revolution, had begun in 1924–1927 (Mao 1928a, 77–78; 1928b, 97–98; 1935a, 159–160; 1935b, 169–170).

part of the global anti-colonial struggle.[24] Indeed, these reasons are inextricably connected: after the October Revolution, the anti-colonial struggle became a major part of the global Communist movement.[25] Thus, the 'new-democratic revolution' focuses simultaneously on liberation from colonial oppression and from feudal left-overs.[26] In this sense, new democracy can include bourgeois political parties in their struggle against feudalism, but they too must be focused on the anti-colonial struggle. At the same time, Mao stipulates that the new-democratic revolution will not lead to the dead end of bourgeois dictatorship,[27] even if capitalist elements in China are left intact.[28] How so? Once again Mao deploys contradiction analysis: while he follows conventional Marxist analysis in delineating two revolutionary stages, the first bourgeois-democratic and the second socialist, he also argues that the initial bourgeois-democratic revolution—in the context of anti-colonial and anti-imperial struggle—has become a part of, or a transition to, the socialist revolution. 'Everybody knows', Mao observes, 'that the Communist Party has an immediate and a future program, a minimum and a maximum program, with regard to the social system it advocates'. He continues: 'For the present period, New Democracy, and for the future, socialism; these are two parts of an organic whole, guided by one and the same communist ideology' (Mao 1939d, 686; 1939a, 361).

A few further points need to be addressed. To begin with, Mao delineates three types of republics that have been or might be constituted: bourgeois dictatorship with its capitalist democracy, which is characteristic of the old bourgeois revolutions in Europe and North America; a one-party proletarian dictatorship, which emerged in the Soviet Union; and the joint dictatorship of several revolutionary classes. In light of my earlier treatment of Lenin and Stalin, we can see that the second and third types were actually both present in Russia and then the Soviet Union. During the 1905–1917 period, Lenin too advocated a transitional united-front joint dictatorship of

[24]In regard to the latter, Mao draws heavily on Sun Zhongshan's manifesto at the first national congress of the Guomindang, as well as 'Three Principles of the People [*sanminzhuyi*]' (Sun 1924b, 1924a; see also Rong and Lai 2000, 6–7).

[25]Mao acknowledges the important breakthrough made by Stalin in connecting the Russian Revolution's focus on the national question and the global anti-colonial struggle (Mao 1940f, 669–672; 1940d, 345–347; see further Boer 2017, 168–172).

[26]Note how the two aspects are interrelated: 'Unless imperialist rule is overthrown, the rule of the feudal landlord class cannot be terminated, because imperialism is its main support. Conversely, unless help is given to the peasants in their struggle to overthrow the feudal landlord class, it will be impossible to build powerful revolutionary contingents to overthrow imperialist rule, because the feudal landlord class is the main social base of imperialist rule in China and the peasantry is the main force in the Chinese revolution. Therefore the two fundamental tasks, the national revolution and the democratic revolution, are at once distinct and united' (Mao 1939d, 637; 1939a, 318). Further, the complexity of China's situation is summed up in the following: 'China today is colonial in the Japanese-occupied areas and basically semi-colonial in the Guomindang areas, and it is predominantly feudal or semi-feudal in both' (Mao 1940f, 664–665; 1940d, 341).

[27]China had already experienced a single-party bourgeois dictatorship with Jiang Jieshi's commandeering of the Guomindang in a reactionary direction.

[28]Mao and Deng, among others, reiterate frequently that capitalist elements would not be eliminated under a new-democratic framework, not merely for the sake of economic reconstruction, but primarily because this was not yet a full socialist revolution.

revolutionary-democratic parties under the leadership of the Communist Party so as to bring the revolutionary process to completion with a proletarian revolution. After 1917 and especially in light of the internal struggles of the 1920s and 1930s, Lenin and especially Stalin focused on the Communist Party as the sole representative of rural and urban workers, as well as the Communist intelligentsia. While Mao adheres to the transitional nature of the united-front approach, he also indicates the differences in the context of the anti-feudal and anti-colonial struggle:

> The third kind is the transitional form of state to be adopted in the revolutions of the colonial and semi-colonial countries. Each of these revolutions will necessarily have specific characteristics of its own, but these will be minor variations on a general theme. So long as they are revolutions in colonial or semi-colonial countries, their state and governmental structure will of necessity be basically the same, i.e., a new-democratic state under the joint dictatorship of several anti-imperialist classes. In present-day China, the anti-Japanese united front represents the new-democratic form of state. It is anti-Japanese and anti-imperialist; it is also a united front, an alliance of several revolutionary classes. (Mao 1940f, 676; 1940d, 351)

How transitional? There was, of course, the culmination of the revolutionary process with Liberation in 1949 and the establishment of the People's Republic. But unlike the Soviet Union, China did not dispense with the united-front approach. Not only did Mao continue to advocate the program of new democracy up to the eve of Liberation (Mao 1948b, 1948a), but also—as we saw in the previous chapter (Sect. 8.3.2)—the Communist Party along with the eight other revolutionary parties, leading political personages, and minority nationalities, met as the CPPCC in September of 1949 in order to make crucial decisions concerning the structure of the New China (Mao 1949n, 1949i). And in line with Mao's advice from the 1950s (Mao 1956a, 278–280; 1956b, 296–297), all nine political parties continue to work together today, under the leadership of the Communist Party.

9.5.2 Democratic Dictatorship

The idea of democratic dictatorship constitutes a reinterpretation of the proletarian dictatorship in Chinese conditions. It has two overlapping senses in Mao's texts, one focusing on the composition of this democratic dictatorship and the other on its purpose. In the framework of new democracy, it would entail a 'joint dictatorship' of workers, peasants, and intellectuals, as well as uniting with as many of the petty-bourgeoisie and even 'national bourgeoisie' who support the project of new democracy (Mao 1939d, 747–748; 1939a, 327; 1949l, 1436–1437; 1949h, 372). Thus, Mao invokes the 'people's democratic dictatorship' at his opening and closing speeches at the first meeting of the new CPPCC in September of 1949 (Mao 1949n, 5–6; 1949i, 17–18; 1949m, 9; 1949e, 20). This 'worker-peasant dictatorship' or 'united-front dictatorship' is seen as a counterpoint not merely to the bourgeois dictatorship and its associated 'democratic individualism',[29] but especially to the feudal-fascist one-party dictatorship of the Guomindang.

As far as the purpose of the democratic dictatorship is concerned, its focus is on the continued presence of class struggle in the early period after the proletarian revolution: 'democracy for the people and dictatorship over the reactionaries' (Mao 1949f, 1475; 1949g, 418; see also 1950b, 28; 1950a, 40). How should one treat the reactionaries and former ruling classes? The state machinery that used to be in the hands of the reactionaries can now be used by the people as an 'instrument for the oppression of antagonistic classes', whether inside China or outside. The purpose is to protect the people, to maintain state power, and to assist in the development of Communism. If this requires violence, then so be it—but only as a last resort, only if reactionaries seek to restore their rule. In fact, if they avoid rebellion and sabotage, and if they are willing to work under the new arrangement, then they will have the opportunity to do so. Alongside propaganda and education, the new situation may require force in order to get them to do what they have never done—work.

The key statement from which I have drawn these points, 'On the People's Democratic Dictatorship', was written on the eve of Liberation in 1949 (Mao 1949f; 1949g; see also 1957d, 366–367; 1957e, 387–388). While it looks ahead to the process of consolidating power, of establishing the new government, of economic and social reconstruction, it also raises two questions. First, what happens if the primacy of this class struggle is directed at the people? This was the mistake of the Cultural Revolution, when Mao identified class struggle as the primary contradiction and forgot his emphasis on managing non-antagonistic contradictions among the people (Mao 1957d, 1957e), as well as the need for democratic centralism. Second, why replace the proletarian dictatorship with democratic dictatorship? To be sure, Mao and indeed Chinese Marxism continue to deploy the dictatorship of the proletariat (urban and rural), but the shift to 'people' in this case has a distinct point: it may include the petty-bourgeoisie and even the 'national bourgeoisie [*minzu zichanjieji*]' who had been remoulded and made their peace with the Communist Party and the project of socialist construction, and who no longer harboured a desire for counter-revolution.

9.5.3 Democratic Centralism

In contrast to democratic dictatorship, democratic centralism concerns the internal form of governance appropriate for socialism, especially after the transitional new democracy has achieved its task (Mao 1953a, 1953b). As we have seen, this was Lenin and the Bolsheviks' distinct contribution to the question of socialist governance (less so from Stalin for reasons already discussed). Mao would take democratic centralism a significant step further by seeing its foundation in the mass line. More of that in

[29] In response to a nervous United States' 'white paper' that sought to promote 'democratic individualism', Mao stresses the collective form of democratic dictatorship in China (Mao 1949c, 1949b, 1949a, 1949d, 1949j, 1949k).

a moment, since I would like to begin with an answer given by Mao to the English journalist James Bertram. Mao speaks of bringing together 'in a certain form' the two seeming opposites of democracy and centralisation.

> There is no impassable gulf between democracy and centralism, both of which are essential for China. On the one hand, the government we want must be truly representative of the popular will; it must have the support of the broad masses throughout the country and the people must be free to support it and have every opportunity of influencing its policies. This is the meaning of democracy. On the other hand, the centralisation of administrative power is also necessary, and once the policy measures demanded by the people are transmitted to their own elected government through their representative body, the government will carry them out and will certainly be able to do so smoothly, so long as it does not go against the policy adopted in accordance with the people's will. This is the meaning of centralism. (Mao 1937d, 383; 1937e, 57)

Notably, this description refers to the united-front government that Mao defined at the time as new democracy (see also Mao 1940f, 677; 1940d, 352; 1940b, 751; 1940a, 428). Even at this time, Mao begins to apply democratic centralism not merely to the CPC, but to the whole country. As we saw earlier, Lenin had seen democratic centralism primarily in terms of the Communist Party, later applying it to the form of governance emerging after the October Revolution. This distinction also applies in China (Lin 2007, 19), so much so that when Chinese Communists engaged in democratic centralism in the Red Areas before liberation or in proposals for country-wide governance in conjunction with other political parties, they tended to see such democratic centralism in terms of an extension of inner-Party practices.[30]

Democratic centralism would, of course, become the defining feature of socialist democracy after Liberation in 1949, but I would like to address two further points. To begin with, the text quoted above implicitly invokes the 'mass line' discussed in the preceding chapter (Sect. 8.3.1) in relation to consultative democracy, especially in terms of transmitting the policy measures demanded by the people to the government, which would then enact them only insofar as they express the people's will. Valuable and deep-rooted experience of the mass line was gained in the Red Areas over a couple of decades before Liberation, but the most detailed discussion of the practical workings of democratic centralism in light of the mass line comes from a speech delivered to an enlarged Central Committee work conference from the early 1960s (Mao 1962, 290–298). In this insightful text, three categories are closely linked: the mass line, criticism and self-criticism, and democratic centralism. In regard to the mass line, Mao observes: 'It is a democratic centralist method; it is a mass line method'. Further, 'first democracy, then centralism; coming from the masses, returning to the masses; the unity of leadership and the masses' (Mao 1962, 290; see also Ma 2014, 204–205). In terms of criticism, Mao points out that many cadres, even with decades of experience in the Party, are still afraid of democratic criticism by the masses. Inside and outside the Party, he observes, 'we must live a fully democratic

[30] For example, see Mao's treatments of democratic centralism in relation to the Red Area of Jinggang Shan in the late 1920s, as well as his proposals for a national government in 1937 and afterwards in light of experience in anti-Japanese base areas (Mao 1928a, 72; 1928b, 91; 1937b, 347; 1937g, 17; 1937i, 355; 1937c, 26–27).

life, that is to say, we must conscientiously practice democratic centralism'. In other words, 'we must open our hearts to the masses and let them truly speak their opinions', so as to lead to criticism and self-criticism among cadres (Mao 1962, 291, 293). And if the initial effort is unsatisfactory, it must be undertaken again and again until there is nothing left to say. In most of this discussion, Mao emphasises the role of democratic participation by the masses, but how does centralism work? He observes that even in the Central Committee decisions are made collectively. If he as chairman puts forward a proposal and the others disagree, he must submit to their opinion. In other words, robust criticism and self-criticism are at work here too. All of this leads to the dialectical formulation: 'without a high degree of democracy, it is impossible to have a high degree of centralism' (Mao 1962, 297).

At a number of points in this text, Mao observes that such a democratic approach is appropriate for dealing with contradictions among the people, which brings me to the question of contradiction analysis. In the answer given to the British journalist, Mao offers a necessary conjunction of two terms, but does not address their internal and dialectical unity (Lin 2007, 20). Some 20 years later, Mao does focus on precisely this question:

> Both democracy and freedom are relative, not absolute, and they come into being and develop in specific historical conditions. Within the ranks of the people, democracy is correlative with centralism and freedom with discipline. They are the two opposites of a single entity, contradictory as well as united, and we should not one-sidedly emphasise one to the exclusion of the other. Within the ranks of the people, we cannot do without freedom, nor can we do without discipline; we cannot do without democracy, nor can we do without centralism. This unity of democracy and centralism, of freedom and discipline, constitutes our democratic centralism. (Mao 1957d, 368; 1957e, 389)[31]

No 'golden mean' here, but rather an explicit invocation of contradiction analysis (Mao 1957d, 372; 1957e, 392–393).[32] Mao speaks of 'the two opposites of a single unity, contradictory as well as united [*shi maodun de, you shi tongyi de*]'.

To sum up: given Mao's status in the New China, it should be no surprise that each of his three proposals continue to have influence, albeit in slightly different ways. Multi-party cooperation—initially proposed with 'new democracy' and later with 'coalition government' and the need to engage democratically with the non-Party masses—continues in revised form today in terms of consultative democracy and the CPPCC. More substantially, both 'democratic dictatorship' and 'democratic centralism' appear in the Chinese Constitution, with the former clearly identified as in essence the proletarian dictatorship[33] and the latter as the 'principle [*yuanze*]' of

[31] Note also the stylistic interchange of terms when Mao speaks of inner-Party democratic centralism: 'the minority is subordinate to the majority, the lower level to the higher level, the part to the whole and the entire membership to the Central Committee' (Mao 1942b, 821; 1942a, 44).

[32] Given my earlier treatment of contradiction analysis (Sect. 3.4), there is no need to repeat that material here.

[33] Already in 1949, Mao had made this definition clear: 'the people's democratic dictatorship under the leadership of the working class (through the Communist Party) and based upon the alliance of workers and peasants. This dictatorship must unite as one with the international revolutionary forces' (Mao 1949f, 1480; 1949g, 422).

governance as a whole. Yet, Mao never really resolved precisely how the principle of democratic centralism would actually work in country-wide governance. It is to this problem that I now turn.

9.6 From Deng Xiaoping to Xi Jinping: The Problem of Democratic Centralism

Out of all the material I have examined thus far with its many developments, democratic centralism has emerged as the core philosophical principle for socialist democracy. However, there remained a problem: by and large, it was assumed that this principle of inner-Party governance could be applied directly to the country as a whole. Let me put it this way: in terms of the Communist Party, democratic centralism concerns the relations between the cadres (and local branches) and the Central Committee; in regard to the country as a whole, it concerns the role of the Communist Party in relation to country-wide governance. The transition from the former to the latter had as yet not been clarified. In seeking the basis for such a move in a Chinese context, we may focus on the 'mass-line' dating back to the 1940s (Ma 2014). However, these policy-making practices remained relatively informal, so much so that Lin Shangli (2007, 20–21) has argued that the problem of democratic centralism as a principle of country-wide governance is still in the process of being solved. While democratic centralism is the basic principle and prevails in all aspects of political life, Lin argues that there is a difference between the highly disciplined structure of the Communist Party and the democratic institutional structures of country-wide governance. It is not enough to assert the dialectical unity of the two terms or assume that democratic centralism can simply be applied from the Party to the country. Both of these moves we find in the statements by Lenin and Mao on democratic centralism, with little to no elaboration on how it may actually be done. It would fall to Deng Xiaoping to begin the process of describing how democratic centralism could work for country-wide governance, specifically in terms of the separation between the Communist Party and governance, mediated through rule of law. But it was not until Xi Jinping that this problem came closer to being resolved.

9.6.1 *Inner-Party Democratic Centralism*

Initially, Deng Xiaoping's main problem was to deal with the legacy of the Cultural Revolution, which entailed restoring the strength of democratic centralism—the emphasis of Mao Zedong Thought up to the late 1950s before it was derailed by the Maoism of the Cultural Revolution (Deng 1977c, 1977a).[34] More specifically, he

[34]This emphasis entails extensive common ground with Mao on issues such as democratic centralism, the people's democratic dictatorship as the means for ensuring socialist democracy

argued that it required greater democratisation so as to liberate thought, foster initiative, and thus provide the basis for a genuine centralism based on democracy. Deng's emphasis was on the axis of democracy and centralism, moving from the former to the latter. Let us recall Mao's observation that without democracy one cannot have full centralism, that without robust initiative and criticism from the masses, there would be no discipline and unity of purpose.[35] It is precisely this dialectical relationship that fell apart during the Cultural Revolution (Fang 2010), when 'centralism was divorced from democracy and there was too little democracy' (Deng 1978b, 144; 1978a, 154).

On this matter, I would like to consider an earlier text that may be seen as a harbinger of what was to come. At an enlarged Central Committee Work Conference, both Mao and Deng gave speeches in which they discussed democratic centralism (Mao 1962; Deng 1962b).[36] Earlier, I discussed Mao's contribution to this conference, so my concern here is what Deng proposes. On many points Deng reinforces Mao's position, but he also goes a step further. To begin with, Deng reiterates Mao's observation that 'without democracy, there can be no centralism, and centralism cannot be truly or correctly realised unless it is based on democracy' (Deng 1962b, 304; 1962a, 300). The movement is from the full realisation of democracy so as to reinforce centralism. But what is the role of centralism? While Mao's concern in his concurrent speech was with democratic dictatorship, dealing with reactionaries, and developing a socialist economic system, Deng stresses that centralism entails that the Party is united and combat-effective: 'Without democracy it would not have centralism and unity; without centralism and unity it would not be combat-effective' (Deng 1962b, 307; 1962a, 302; see also 1965b, 1965a). The crucial term here is 'combat-effective [*zhandouli*]': democracy produces centralised unity, and centralised unity leads to combat-effectiveness.

The third point of Deng's speech is the most pertinent and is not mentioned by Mao: Deng observes that the lack of democratic centralism leads to decentralisation and authoritarianism. This dialectical emphasis may come as a surprise to those who assume that democracy is equivalent to decentralisation, and that centralism equates with authoritarianism. Deng's point is far more dialectical. 'In dealing with many matters', he observes, 'we seem to be exercising more centralisation than before, when in fact decentralisation has become a serious problem'. Further, 'in many other matters we seem to be practising more democracy than before, when in fact authoritarian practices, arbitrary decisions made and peremptory actions taken by a few people or an individual are all too common' (Deng 1962b, 305; 1962a, 301). In other words, decentralisation means here the absence of democratic practices based on the mass line and thus an increase in arbitrary and authoritarian decisions. A weakening

---

and social stability for the people, the need to work together with other revolutionary democratic parties, the foundations of socialist democracy in the mass line, and the supervisory role of other democratic parties and the masses.

[35]This was a reasonably common refrain in the late 1950s (Mao 1957f, 468; 1957a, 485; 1957c, 451; 1957b, 467).

[36]Earlier elaborations of democratic centralism, in relation to the Party and governance, already appear in the 1950s (Deng 1956a, 225–235; 1956b, 228–237).

of democracy leads to authoritarianism and thus a weakening of centralism.[37] In hindsight, this warning was quite prescient, for only a few years later they would be realised in the Cultural Revolution. It would require much hard work after the Cultural Revolution to recover the theory and practice of democratic centralism, entailing a 'unity of personal interests and collective interests, of the interests of the part and those of the whole, and of immediate and long-term interests'. For Deng, this was 'precisely why Comrade Mao Zedong said that our aim is to create a political situation in which we have both centralism and democracy, both discipline and freedom, both unity of will and personal ease of mind and liveliness' (Deng 1979a, 175–176; 1979c, 183–184).[38]

Even so, Deng's emphasis tended to be on inner-Party practices, an emphasis we also find in the material from Liu Shaoqi (1945a, 358–370; 1945b, 353–364; 1962b, 373–394; 1962a, 351–373) and Jiang Zemin. The latter observes that democratic centralism is an 'embodiment of dialectical materialism and historical materialism' (Jiang Z. 1989, 97), but his primary concerns are with elaborating the principle that individual Party members are subordinate to the Party, the minority to the majority, the lower to the higher, and all organisations to the National Congress and the Central Committee (Jiang Z. 1992, 250–342; 1994, 409–410; 2001b, 287–288). When Jiang does gesture toward country-wide governance, he assumes that the Party itself is now the centralising feature of such governance (Jiang Z. 2000b, 188–189; 2001a, 226).

A step further—beyond assertions of dialectical interaction and the extension of inner-Party practices—begins to appear with Zhou Enlai. Often, he too assumes an extension of the principle, with a brief mention of people's congresses and political consultative conferences (Zhou E. 1949a, 140–142; 1949b, 147; 1950, 163; 1957, 349), but at one point Zhou pauses to say a little more. The year was 1953, at the very early stages of the New China. It does not matter, Zhou observes, whether it is the working class or the Communist Party, for they 'must exercise leadership through the state, through the people's congresses, through government organs and through economic leadership organs'. Here we have an early indication of the need for mediated leadership through the structures of socialist democracy. For example, economic leadership can go only through the state organs, or educational leadership can work only through the ministry or education and school organs. 'This', observes Zhou, 'is called democratic centralism, that is, everything is collected from the masses and then carried out among the masses'. Indeed, only in this way can the 'whole country built in a planned, organised and methodical way' (Zhou E. 1953, 248–249). In hindsight, this proposal by Zhou Enlai—in which democratic centralism entails processes through governing organs—was both embryonic and anticipatory.

[37]Looking back on the Cultural Revolution, Deng would add a number of other factors: the weight of bureaucracy; lack of experience in democratic practices; over-centralisation that became individualised; life tenure for older comrades, which stifled younger talent; the persistence of feudal and patriarchal assumptions; and the influx of individualised bourgeois assumptions (Deng 1980a, 320–338; 1980c, 319–337).

[38]Elsewhere, Deng urged that democratic centralism should be practised in politics, in the military, and in economic activities (Deng 1977d, 83; 1977b, 96). See also the treatment of economic democracy in Chapter 1.

Embryonic in the sense that how such a process might actually work would take quite some time to clarify; anticipatory in the sense that it would be only with Xi Jinping that the nature of democratic centralism for country-wide governance would be articulated.

9.6.2 Separation of Party and Government

Zhou Enlai may have provided some preliminary indications as to how democratic centralism would actually function in country-wide governance, specifically through the mediation of what were then the rudimentary structures of socialist democracy, but some further steps were required. The first step was the separation between the Communist Party and the government. This was actually an abiding emphasis by Deng, as we already see in a text from 1941 and its lengthy elaboration on the role of the Party and government (Deng 1941a, 1941b). The context is in many respects quite different: the concern is coalition government based on the 'three-thirds principle', thereby falling into the framework of new democracy (Deng 1941d, 24; 1941c, 34). But the reason why this piece was included as one of the first in Deng Xiaoping's selected works is that it already expresses a signature emphasis, so much so that it was one of the enabling factors for the CPC's ability to turn from historical to practical legitimacy—to the rule-of-law statutory process whereby the will of the Party becomes the will of the people.

How does Deng envisage such a process in the early 1940s? First, the mass line is crucial: 'we should chiefly rely on the political prestige our Party enjoys as a result of its correct views that are endorsed, supported and trusted by the masses' (Deng 1941a, 9; 1941b, 20). Second, this is a thoroughly democratic process, involving honest, open, and friendly engagement with the masses and non-Party people, patiently taking in their viewpoints and acting upon them. Third, it is indirect. It is not a case of 'ruling the country by the Party [*yi dang zhiguo*]', of monopolising and interfering in all levels of governance and issuing commands that must be followed (as was the practice of the Guomindang), but of guidance and supervision. Deng articulates a process that would eventually come to fruition with the rule-of-law statutory processes of socialist democracy found today in China: the Party 'should carefully study policies, formulate correct ones and, through the leading Party members' groups in the administrative organs and people's representative bodies, turn its policies into the decrees and administrative policies of the government' (Deng 1941a, 13; 1941b, 24; see also Rong and Lai 2000, 7–8).

Fast forward to 1986 and Deng's speech 'On Reform of the Political Structure' (Deng 1986a, 1986b). The key point in this speech is to ensure the Party's leadership, and that its 'functions should be separated [*fenkai*] from those of the government' (Deng 1986a, 177; 1986b, 179). In Deng's eyes, this distinction would not only ensure more effective leadership by the Party, but also foster socialist democracy and stimulate initiatives from the people. As is his wont, these proposals have a practical focus that which turns on clearly demarcating the roles of the government and the Party, all the way from state-wide governance to workplace practices (see also Deng 1980a, 339–343; 1980c, 337–341). But how is the Party's leadership to be strengthened in such a reform? As is characteristic of Deng, one sentence sums up his position: 'we intend to straighten out the relationship between the rule of law and the rule of a person and between the Party and the government' (Deng 1986a, 177; 1986b, 178–179). I have already quoted this text on a couple of occasions, although now I include the last clause as well. The point is that a robust rule of law (*fazhi*) would become the structural framework for clarifying and streamlining the relation between Party and government, thereby ensuring the Party's leadership and sponsoring the development of socialist democracy (Rong and Lai 2000, 9–10).[39] In short, this is the realisation in an established socialist system of the vanguard role of the Party.

9.6.3 The Statutory Procedures of Socialist Democracy

By the time Deng Xiaoping stepped down completely in 1992, we find the beginnings of a solution as to how democratic centralism should function country-wide. For Deng Xiaoping, the key was the separation of Party and government, while for Zhou Enlai it also included the components of a socialist democratic system. The years that followed in many ways entailed more detailed articulations of the integrated components of socialist democracy (Xiao and Yu 2012, 16). For example, Jiang Zemin too stressed the need for Party-government separation as a way to strengthen Party leadership (Jiang Z. 1989, 92–93). More substantively, Jiang began to elaborate on the crucial role of a robust legal system, which would soon become 'rule of law', and the need for electoral, consultative, and grassroots democracy as parts of a larger whole (Jiang Z. 1992, 235–237; 2000a, 574–576). The most complete articulation appears at the close of his tenure as general secretary of the CPC:

> To develop socialist democracy, it is essential to integrate adherence to the leadership of the Party, the position of the people as masters of the country, and the rule of law. The leadership of the Party is the fundamental guarantee for the people's position as masters of the country and the rule of law; the people's position as masters of the country is the essential requirement of socialist democracy; and the rule of law is the basic strategy for the Party to lead the people in running the country'. (Jiang Z. 2002, 553; see also Lin 2007, 20)

Hu Jintao would continue the path, identifying more clearly the components of the overall system: electoral democracy through the people's congresses; consultative democracy through the people's political conferences and minority nationalities; grassroots democracy; leadership of the CPC; governing the country according to law; and promoting socialist human rights. Indeed, by 2007 he could claim that

---

[39] In a brief and earlier piece, Deng boils the question down to the necessary relationship between socialist democracy and—in terms he was using at the time before 'rule of law' came into common parlance—the legal system. Both are 'like two hands, neither of which can be weakened' (Deng 1979b, 189; see also 1980b, 359–360).

steady progress had been made in developing this system and that it had 'basically taken shape [*jiben xingcheng*]' (Hu 2007, 3).

In all this, Hu Jintao's most crucial observation is that this overall system would ensure that 'the Party's proposals become the will of the country through statutory procedures [*fading chengxu*]' (Hu 2007, 13; see also 2012, 17). How so? The leadership of the Party will be enhanced by ensuring that the people are the masters of the country, in the sense that all governing power belongs to the people, and that this reality is to be underpinned by the 'basic strategy of governing the country according to law [*yifazhiguo*], fostering the socialist concept of rule of law [*fazhi*], and bringing all the country's work under the rule of law' (Hu 2007, 13). Or as Hu puts it in 2012, the 'basic strategy by which the party leads the people in governing the country is through governing the country according to law [*yifazhiguo*]', for rule of law is the 'fundamental way [*jiben fangshi*] to govern the country' (Hu 2012, 9, 18).

In many respects, the task bequeathed to Xi Jinping has been to enhance these insights. But let us pause for a moment before dealing with Xi Jinping's contribution. Thus far, I have followed the clarification as to how Party and government have been separated since the time of Deng Xiaoping. This initially entailed establishing a robust legal system, which then became defined as rule of law. Further, the various components of China's socialist democratic system were articulated and analysed in terms of their integration. By the time of Hu Jintao, we find the emergence of the principle of statutory procedures, in which the will of the Party becomes government law—since the whole process is determined by strengthening the leadership of the Communist Party. However, none of the leaders thus far has explicitly identified these developments in terms of democratic centralism. They have largely stuck to the tradition since Lenin and used 'democratic centralism' to speak of inner-Party governance.

9.6.4 *Xi Jinping: Democratic Centralism and Country-Wide Governance*

It is Xi Jinping's distinct contribution to deploy 'democratic centralism' to speak not merely of inner-Party governance,[40] but also of distinct processes required for country-wide governance. Let us see how he does so. To begin with, Xi also emphasises the need to improve even further the CPC's indirect leadership through the legal

[40]For example: 'Democratic centralism and the system of inner-Party organisation activities are important institutions of the Party and must be fully implemented. Leading bodies and officials at all levels must rigorously follow the reporting system. We must reinforce organisational management of Party members, and guide all Party members and officials in developing a correct attitude towards the Party organisation, matching our deeds to our words, speaking the truth, and embracing the Party organisation's education and oversight. Party organisations at all levels must fully observe organisational discipline, make no exceptions in this regard, and have the moral fibre to denounce and rectify violations of Party discipline to preserve it as a high-tension line of deterrence' (Xi 2014b, 396).

or statutory procedures of rule of law governance (Xi 2012, 142; 2015, 17; 2019, 3). When the Party's policies become state laws, 'the implementation of the law is the implementation of the Party's will, and the implementation of the party's policies is to act in accordance with the law' (Xi 2015, 18). All of this entails that the organs of state power are independent, proactive, and responsible in terms of adhering to the Constitution and relevant laws. Now we come the explicit connection with democratic centralism, which is predicated on the fact that the 'authority of both Party and state' are distinct (Xi 2015, 20; 2017b, 28). More fully:

> Adhering to the principle of democratic centralism, the system of state power and the standards of action defined in the Constitution, we should exercise state power through the people's congresses, ensure that decision-making power, executive power and oversight power function independently but are coordinated with each other, ensure that government agencies exercise their power and perform their duties in accordance with statutory mandates and procedures [*fading quanxian he chengxu*], and ensure that government agencies organise all undertakings concertedly and effectively. (Xi 2012, 139; see also 2014a, 290)[41]

In this text, Xi uses a fuller phrase, 'statutory mandates and procedures [*fading quanxian he chengxu*]'. The term *quanxian* (权限) has the senses of the limits of authority, extent of power, and thus jurisdiction or mandates. In other words, 'statutory procedures [*fading chengxu*]' entail that all decisions should be undertaken within the limits of authority. A little later in the same text, Xi specifies what such statutory procedures mean for turning the Party's will into government decisions and statutes. Here he speaks of 'foundational [*jiben*]' way of 'exercising power according to law [*yifa zhizheng*]' and 'governing the country according to law [*yifazhiguo*]' (Xi 2012, 142). All of these clarify the definition of democratic centralism in the context of country-wide governance.

Is the process complete? Hu Jintao may have claimed in 2007 that the socialist democratic system is basically in place, but Xi Jinping observes that there are still many 'weak links [*boruo huanjie*]' in legislation, law enforcement, the judiciary, and compliance with the law (Xi 2019, 1). So he has set the year 2035—halfway between the 'two centenary goals'—as the target for fully establishing the socialist democratic system and its core practice of democratic centralism.

9.7 Conclusion: Stability and Social Health

This chapter has offered an overview of developments in the theory of socialist democracy, beginning with Engels (and Marx) and ending with Xi Jinping. In contrast to the previous two chapters, where I focused on Chinese Marxist scholarship, this chapter has primarily been concerned in canonical fashion with the views of recognised leaders of the Communist movement. The risk, of course, is that the development of ideas is seen as the task of individuals. This is by no means the case, since

[41] In subsequent elaborations, Xi connects multi-level consultative democracy with democratic centralism, including minority groups, religions, classes, and overseas Chinese (Xi 2014c, 294, 296; see also Lin 2007).

the theories discussed here were the result of collective leadership, consultation, and debate. It may seem like quite a distance from the succinct formulations of Engels and Marx to the comprehensive theory of socialist democracy in China, running all the way from depoliticised governance that stands in the midst of society to the dialectical relation of the people as masters and the leadership of the Communist Party, embodied in the statutory processes of democratic centralism.

Chinese researchers take a number of overlapping approaches to this process. One is to point out that Marx and Engels themselves were clear that their brief prescriptions for Communist society could be verified only through scientific inquiry, for they were fully aware that they had not experienced the reality of socialist construction and thus the practice of socialist democracy. Another approach is to point out implied concepts in Marx and Engels, such as democratic centralism in the dialectical connection between the proletarian dictatorship and the commune, or in the structure of the First International, which sought to avoid the extremes of anarchism and individual dictatorship and thus embodied early practices of democratic centralism (Ma 2014, 207–208). A third and very common approach is to see the tradition in terms of clarification. In light of actual experience in different contexts, the theory of socialist democracy was gradually clarified in light of earlier principles, successes, and mistakes. Thus, the initial speculations by Engels and Marx were grounded and clarified after the Russian Revolution, only to be clarified further in light of the specificity of Chinese conditions. A specific example here is the red thread of democratic centralism: the concept has moved from an implicit presence in the thought of Marx and Engels, through its articulation by Lenin and indeed Mao as primarily an inner-Party practice, to the clarification of statutory processes between the Communist Party and the government from Deng Xiaoping through to Xi Jinping. From a Chinese perspective, this long process is one of gradual clarification in light of practice.

9.7.1 Why Not Social Democracy?

I would like to close on a slightly different note, on the question of stability and social health, which in China is regarded as an absolute necessity for socialist democracy. Let me begin by asking a question that may arise for some readers: instead of democratic centralism, why not democratic socialism (or, as it is sometimes called, social democracy)?[42] Those wedded to capitalist parliamentary systems may feel that democratic socialism is more desirable. In China, the debate over democratic socialism has come in waves, initially after the dismantling of socialist states in the

[42]For a careful study of the history of the two terms, social democracy and democratic socialism, see Yin Xuyi's two studies (2001a, 2001b). He points that while social democracy has a longer history with its roots in nineteenth-century socialism (with Marx and Engels very much involved), democratic socialism marks the revisionist turn after the Second World War and particularly after 1989 in Europe. The twist is that this revisionism also claims the title of 'social democracy'—hence the clear difference with scientific socialism.

Soviet Union and Eastern Europe,[43] and once again after a provocative article by Xie Tao (2007), who advocated a shift to this model in China's political development. Many have been the responses, which usually include in-depth assessments of the history, philosophical foundations, and transformations of democratic socialism and social democracy, along with comparisons with scientific socialism. However, the overwhelming response is that democratic socialism is not Marxist and certainly not scientific socialism, and that it would lead to the end of China's socialist system (Gao 2007; Luo and Wu 2009; Dai and Zhao 2010; Lv 2010; Xu 2010; Jia Z. and Li 2011; Lu 2012; Yang Y. 2012; Xue 2014; Zhou X. 2018). Underlying this debate is the system-component distinction, which we have already encountered on a number of occasions. Thus, an overall socialist democratic system (*zhidu*) has a number of integrated components (*tizhi* or *tixi*), such as electoral, consultative, and grassroots democracy, as well as minority nationalities, rule of law, human rights, and the leadership of the Communist Party. By contrast, democratic socialism is a component of the capitalist democratic system with its unresolvable antagonisms. Democratic socialism may attempt to ameliorate the excesses and antagonisms of capitalism, offering a few socialist-like policies, but it is ultimately unable to change the overall system. Indeed, since 1989 Western social democracy has noticeably abandoned any pretence to transformation and become 'social capitalism' (Zheng 2006; Liu Y. 2008). The conclusion is that any move to democratic socialism would entail bourgeois liberalisation, adopting a capitalist democratic system, and abolishing China's socialist democratic system. Clearly, this is an unacceptable move, but also a distinctly poor fit with China's socialist system. As Xi Jinping observes, 'the most reliable and effective system is one that takes root in its own soil and draws on abundant nutrients'. Further, the reason why socialist democracy with Chinese characteristics is 'feasible, viable and efficient is that it grew out of the soil of Chinese society', and 'to continue to thrive in the future, it must be deeply rooted in China's social soil' (Xi 2014a, 286).

9.7.2 *Stability and Social Health*

What would happen if China adopted an alien, Western-style system of capitalist democracy, of which social democracy is a component. Again and again, from Deng Xiaoping to Xi Jinping, we find the warning that it would lead to chaos and anarchy. Socialist democracy, predicated on the dialectical relation between the people as masters and the leadership of the Communist Party, is the reason why China has maintained 'long-term stability, without chaos' (Xi 2019, 1). Harking back to Engels's initial insights, Chinese researchers argue that socialist democracy is predicated not

[43]Earlier Chinese studies were devoted to countering efforts to promote democratic socialism as an alternative in Eastern Europe (Chen 1991; Zai 1991; Liu Shulin 2003). One may ask: what about Lenin and Russian Social-Democratic Party? A careful study by Wu Wei and Xia Yinping (2016) shows how Lenin's thought and practice moved towards a clearer distinction between Communism and the European path of social democracy.

on an opposition between state and society, but on mutual and non-antagonistic interaction so that it is conducive to social health and stability (Liu W. 2002; Yang H. 2008, 24–25). On this matter, and in anticipation of the next chapter, let me give Xi Jinping the last word:

> Actually, how to govern a socialist society, a completely new society, has not been clearly addressed by world socialism so far... Our Party has worked on the same question steadily ever since it came to national power, and, in spite of serious setbacks, has accumulated rich experience and achieved great success in improving our governance system and enhancing our governance capacity. The success has been particularly resounding since we adopted the policy of Reform and Opening-Up. Enjoying political stability, economic growth, social harmony and unity of nationalities, today's China poses a striking contrast to many regions and countries that suffer constant chaos. This shows that our national governance system and capacity are on the whole quite sound and suited to our national conditions and development needs. (Xi 2013, 91)

References

Boer, Roland. In press. *Friedrich Engels and the foundations of socialist governance*. Singapore: Springer.

Boer, Roland. 2017. *Stalin: From theology to the philosophy of socialism in power*. Beijing: Springer.

Boer, Roland. 2019. Marx's ambivalence: State, proletarian dictatorship and commune. *International Critical Thought* 9 (1): 109–127.

Boer, Roland, and Zang Fengyu. 2019. Renlei mingyun gongtongti de lilun neihan yu xianshi jiazhi. *Zhongyang shehuizhuyi xueyuan xuebao* 2019 (4): 9–17.

Cai, Yazhi. 2011. Liening shehuizhuyi minzhu sixiang yu Zhongguo tese shehuizhuyi minzhu zhengzhi jianshe. *Kexue shehuizhuyi* 2011 (1): 144–147.

Chen, Xianda. 1991. Lun 'liang ge biranxing' – jian ping minzhu shehuizhuyi de zhexue ping. *Zhongguo renmin daxue xuebao* 1991 (3): 8–15, 24.

CPC Central Committee. 1945a. Guanyu ruogan lishi de wenti jueyi (1945.04.20). In *Mao Zedong xuanji*, vol. 3:953–1003. Beijing: Renmin chubanshe, 2009.

CPC Central Committee. 1945b. Resolution on certain questions in the history of our party (20 April, 1945). In *Selected works of Mao Tse-Tung*, vol. 3:177–225. Beijing: Foreign Languages Press, 1965.

Dai, Xiaojun, and Zhao Chengwen. 2010. Kexue shehuizhuyi yu minzhu shehuizhuyi zai jiazhi tixi shang de qubie. *Lilun xuekan* 2010 (6): 22–26.

Deng, Xiaoping. 1941a. Dang yu kangri minzhu zhengquan (1941.04.15). In *Deng Xiaoping wenxuan*, vol. 1:7–19. Beijing: Renmin chubanshe, 2008.

Deng, Xiaoping. 1941b. The party and the anti-Japanese democratic government (15 April, 1941). In *Selected works of Deng Xiaoping*, vol. 1:19–32. Beijing: Foreign Languages Press, 1995.

Deng, Xiaoping. 1941c. The principles, tasks and orientation for cultural work in the 129th division (May, 1941). In *Selected works of Deng Xiaoping*, vol. 1:33–39. Beijing: Foreign Languages Press, 1995.

Deng, Xiaoping. 1941d. Yi er jiu shi wenhua gongzuo de fangzhen renwu jiqi nuli fangxiang (1941.05). In *Deng Xiaoping wenxuan*, vol. 1:22–29. Beijing: Renmin chubanshe, 2008.

Deng, Xiaoping. 1956a. Guanyu xiugai dang de zhangcheng de baogao (1956.09.16). In *Deng Xiaoping wenxuan*, vol. 1:212–256. Beijing: Renmin chubanshe, 2008.

Deng, Xiaoping. 1956b. Report on the revision of the constitution of the Communist Party of China (16 September, 1956). In *Selected works of Deng Xiaoping*, vol. 1:217–255. Beijing: Foreign Languages Press, 1995.

Deng, Xiaoping. 1962a. Speech delivered at an enlarged working conference of the Party Central Committee (6 February, 1962). In *Selected works of Deng Xiaoping*, vol. 1:294–311. Beijing: Foreign Languages Press, 1995.

Deng, Xiaoping. 1962b. Zai kuoda de zhongyang gongzuo huiyi shang de jianghua (1962.02.06). In *Deng Xiaoping wenxuan*, vol. 1:297–317. Beijing: Renmin chubanshe, 2008.

Deng, Xiaoping. 1965a. Build a mature and combat-effective party (June and December, 1965). In *Selected works of Deng Xiaoping*, vol. 1:332–342. Beijing: Foreign Languages Press, 1995.

Deng, Xiaoping. 1965b. Jianshe yige chengshu de you zhandouli de dang (1965.06.12). In *Deng Xiaoping wenxuan*, vol. 1:338–348. Beijing: Renmin chubanshe, 2008.

Deng, Xiaoping. 1977a. Mao Zedong thought must be correctly understood as an integral whole (21 July, 1977). In *Selected works of Deng Xiaoping*, vol. 2:55–60. Beijing: Foreign Languages Press, 1995.

Deng, Xiaoping. 1977b. Speech at a plenary meeting of the military commission of the Central Committee of the CPC (28 December, 1977). In *Selected works of Deng Xiaoping*, vol. 2:85–97. Beijing: Foreign Languages Press, 1995.

Deng, Xiaoping. 1977c. Wanzheng de zhunque de lijie Mao Zedong sixiang (1977.07.21). In *Deng Xiaoping wenxuan*, vol. 2:42–47. Beijing: Renmin chubanshe, 2008.

Deng, Xiaoping. 1977d. Zai zhongyang junwei quanti huiyi shang de jianghua (1977.12.28). In *Deng Xiaoping wenxuan*, vol. 2:72–84. Beijing: Renmin chubanshe, 2008.

Deng, Xiaoping. 1978a. Emancipate the mind, seek truth from facts and unite as one in looking to the future (13 December, 1978). In *Selected works of Deng Xiaoping*, vol. 2:150–163. Beijing: Foreign Languages Press, 1995.

Deng, Xiaoping. 1978b. Jiefang sixiang, shishiqiushi, tuanjieyizhi xiangqian kan (1978.12.13). In *Deng Xiaoping wenxuan*, vol. 2:140–153. Beijing: Renmin chubanshe, 2008.

Deng, Xiaoping. 1979a. Jianchi sixiang jiben yuanze (1979.03.30). In *Deng Xiaoping wenxuan*, vol. 2:158–184. Beijing: Renmin chubanshe, 2008.

Deng, Xiaoping. 1979b. Minzhu he fazhi liangshou dou buneng xueruo (1979.06.28). In *Deng Xiaoping wenxuan*, vol. 2:189. Beijing: Renmin chubanshe, 2008.

Deng, Xiaoping. 1979c. Uphold the four cardinal principles (30 March, 1979). In *Selected works of Deng Xiaoping*, vol. 2:168–191. Beijing: Foreign Languages Press, 1995.

Deng, Xiaoping. 1980a. Dang he guojia lingdao zhidu gaige (1980.08.18). In *Deng Xiaoping wenxuan*, vol. 2:320–343. Beijing: Renmin chubanshe, 1995.

Deng, Xiaoping. 1980b. Guanche tiaozheng fangzhen, baozheng anding tuanjie (1980.12.25). In *Deng Xiaoping wenxuan*, vol. 2:354–374. Beijing: Renmin chubanshe, 2008.

Deng, Xiaoping. 1980c. On the reform of the system of party and state leadership (18 August, 1980). In *Selected works of Deng Xiaoping*, vol. 2:319–341. Beijing: Foreign Languages Press, 1995.

Deng, Xiaoping. 1986a. Guanyu zhengzhi tizhi gaige wenti (1986.09-11). In *Deng Xiaoping wenxuan*, vol. 3:176–180. Beijing: Renmin chubanshe, 2008.

Deng, Xiaoping. 1986b. On reform of the political structure (September – November, 1986). In *Selected works of Deng Xiaoping*, vol. 3:178–181. Beijing: Foreign Languages Press, 1994.

Engels, Friedrich. 1873a. Dell' autorità. In *Marx Engels Gesamtausgabe*, vol. I.24:82–86. Berlin: Dietz, 1984.

Engels, Friedrich. 1873b. Lun quanwei. In *Makesi Engesi wenji*, vol. 3:335–338. Beijing: Renmin chubanshe, 2009.

Engels, Friedrich. 1873c. On authority. In *Marx and Engels collected works*, vol. 23:422–425. Moscow: Progress Publishers, 1988.

Engels, Friedrich. 1882a. Die Mark. In *Marx Engels Gesamtausgabe*, vol. I.27:628–643. Berlin: Dietz, 1988.

Engels, Friedrich. 1882b. Fränkische Zeit. In *Marx Engels Gesamtausgabe*, vol. I:25:352–696. Berlin: Dietz, 1985.

Engels, Friedrich. 1882c. The mark. In *Marx and Engels collected works*, vol. 24:439–456. Moscow: Progress Publishers, 1989.

Engels, Friedrich. 1882d. Zur Urgeschichte der Deutschen. In *Marx Engels Gesamtausgabe*, vol. I:25:308–341. Berlin: Dietz, 1985.
Engels, Friedrich. 1884a. Engels an August Bebel in Leipzig, London, 11/12.Dez. 1884. In *Marx Engels Werke*, 36:250–254. Berlin: Dietz, 1979.
Engels, Friedrich. 1884b. Engels to August Bebel in Leipzig, London, 11–12 December, 1884. In *Marx and Engels collected works*, 47:231–235. Moscow: Progress Publishers, 1995.
Engels, Friedrich. 1884c. Über den Verfall des Feudalismus und das Aufkommen der Bourgeoisie. In *Marx Engels Gesamtausgabe*, vol. I:30:43–53. Berlin: Akademie Verlag, 2011.
Engels, Friedrich. 1890. Engels an Conrad Schmidt in Berlin, London, 27.Oktober 1890. In *Marx Engels Werke*, vol. 37:488–495. Berlin: Dietz, 1974.
Engels, Friedrich. 1891a. A critique of the draft social-democratic programme of 1891. In *Marx and Engels collected works*, vol. 27:217–232. Moscow: Progress Publishers, 1990.
Engels, Friedrich. 1891b. Die Mark. In *Marx Engels Werke*, vol. 19:315–330. Berlin: Dietz, 1987.
Engels, Friedrich. 1891c. Einleitung zur dritten deutschen Auflage (1891) von Karl Marx, 'Der Bürgerkrieg in Frankreich'. In *Marx Engels Gesamtausgabe*, vol. I.32:3–16. Berlin: Akademie Verlag, 2010.
Engels, Friedrich. 1891d. Introduction to Karl Marx's *The civil war in France*. In *Marx and Engels collected works*, vol. 27:179–191. Moscow: Progress Publishers, 1990.
Engels, Friedrich. 1891e. Zur Kritik des sozialdemokratischen Programmentwurfs 1891. In *Marx Engels Gesamtausgabe*, vol. I.32:42–54. Berlin: Akademie Verlag, 2010.
Engels, Friedrich. 1892a. *Der Ursprung der Familie, des Privateigentums und des Staats. Im Anschluß an Lewis H. Morgans Forschungen. 4. Auflage. Stuttgart 1892.* In *Marx Engels Gesamtausgabe*, vol. 1:29:125–271. Berlin: Dietz, 1990.
Engels, Friedrich. 1892b. The origin of the family, private property and the state. In the light of the researches by Lewis H. Morgan. In *Marx and Engels collected works*, vol. 26:129–276. Moscow: Progress Publishers, 1990.
Engels, Friedrich. 1894. Herrn Eugen Dührings Umwälzung der Wissenschaft. 3. Auflage. In *Marx Engels Gesamtausgabe*, vol. I:27:485–538. Berlin: Dietz, 1988.
Engels, Friedrich. 1895a. Einleitung (1895) zu Karl Marx's 'Klassenkämpfe in Frankreich 1848 bis 1850'. In *Marx Engels Gesamtausgabe*, vol. I.32:330–351. Berlin: Akademie Verlag, 2010.
Engels, Friedrich. 1895b. Introduction to Karl Marx's *The class struggles in France*. In *Marx and Engels Collected Works*, vol. 27:506–524. Moscow: Progress Publishers, 1990.
Fang, Ning. 2010. Inspiration from Mao Zedong's thought on democracy for modern times. *Marxist Studies in China* 2010: 167–180.
Gao, Fang. 2007. Bainian lai kexue shehuizhuyi yu minzhu shehuizhuyi guanxi de yanbian – jian tan 'zhiyou shehuizhuyi minzhu caineng jiu Zhongguo'. *Lilun xuekan* 2007 (6): 15–22.
Harding, Neil. 2009. *Lenin's political thought*. Chicago: Haymarket.
Hu, Jintao. 2007. *Gaoju Zhongguo tese shehuizhuyi weida qizhi, wei daoqu quanmian jianshe xiaokang shehui shengli er fendou (2007.10.15)*. Beijing: Renmin chubanshe.
Hu, Jintao. 2012. *Jianding bu yi yanzhe Zhongguo tese shehui zhuyi daolu, qianjin wei quanmian jiancheng xiaokang shehui er fendou (2012.11.08)*. Beijing: Renmin chubanshe.
Jia, Jianfang. 2014. Makesizhuyi shehui yu guojia guanxi lilun jiqi qishi. *Shehuizhuyi yanjiu* 2014 (4): 1–18.
Jia, Zhonghai, and Li Juan. 2011. Minzhu shehuizhuyi de jiazhi tixi: yuanzhi, pipan yu xuanze. *Zhengzhixue yanjiu* 2011 (4): 28–34.
Jiang, Hui, and Zhao Peijie. 2010. Shuli kexue de makesizhuyi minzhu guan. *Zhengzhixue yanjiu* 2010 (3): 3–9.
Jiang, Zemin. 1989. Wei ba dang jianshe cheng gengjia jianqiang de gongrenjieji xianfengdui er douzheng (1989.12.29). In *Jiang Zemin wenxuan*, vol. 1:87–104. Beijing: Renmin chubanshe, 2006.
Jiang, Zemin. 1992. Jiakuai gaige kaifang he xiandaihua jianshe bufa, duoqu you Zhongguo tese shehuizhuyi shiye de geng da shengli (1992.10.12). In *Jiang Zemin wenxuan*, vol. 1:210–254. Beijing: Renmin chubanshe, 2006.

Jiang, Zemin. 1994. Tuijin dang de jianshe xin de weida gongcheng (1994.09.28). In *Jiang Zemin wenxuan*, vol. 1:403–412. Beijing: Renmin chubanshe, 2006.

Jiang, Zemin. 2000a. Tongbao zhongyang zhengzhiju dangwei 'sanjiang' qingkuang de jianghua (2000.01.20). In *Jiang Zemin wenxuan*, vol. 2:519–586. Beijing: Renmin chubanshe, 2006.

Jiang, Zemin. 2000b. Tuidong dangfeng lianzheng jianshe he fan fubai douzheng shenru kaizhan (2000.12.26). In *Jiang Zemin wenxuan*, vol. 3:173–195. Beijing: Renmin chubanshe, 2006.

Jiang, Zemin. 2001a. Guanyu jianchi si xiang jiben yuanze (2001.04.02). In *Jiang Zemin wenxuan*, vol. 3:214–232. Beijing: Renmin chubanshe, 2006.

Jiang, Zemin. 2001b. Zai qingzhu Zhongguo gongchandang chengli bashi zhounian dahui shang de jianghua (2001.07.01). In *Jiang Zemin wenxuan*, vol. 3:264–299. Beijing: Renmin chubanshe, 2006.

Jiang, Zemin. 2002. Quanmian jianshe xiaokang shehui, kaichuang zhongguo tese shehuizhuyi shiye xin jumian (2002.11.08). In *Jiang Zemin wenxuan*, vol. 3:528–575. Beijing: Renmin chubanshe, 2006.

Kolonitskii, Boris Ivanovich. 2004. 'Democracy' in the political consciousness of the February revolution. In *Revolutionary Russia: New approaches*, ed. Rex Wade, 75–90. New York: Routledge.

Lenin, V.I. 1894a. Chto takoe 'druz′ia naroda' i kak oni voiuiut protiv otsial-demokratov? (Otvet na stat′i 'Russkogo Bogatstva' protiv marksistov). Vesno-letom 1894 g. In *Polnoe sobranie sochinenii*, vol. 1:125–346. Moscow: Izdatel'stvo politicheskoi literatury, 1967.

Lenin, V.I. 1894b. What the 'friends of the people' are and how they fight the social-democrats (a Reply to articles in *Russkoye Bogatstvo* opposing the marxists). In *Collected works*, vol. 1:129–332. Moscow: Progress Publishers, 1960.

Lenin, V.I. 1897a. The tasks of the Russian social-democrats. In *Collected works*, vol. 2:323–251. Moscow: Progress Publishers, 1960.

Lenin, V.I. 1897b. Zadachi russkikh sotsial-demokratov. Konets 1897 g. In *Polnoe sobranie sochinenii*, vol. 2:433–470. Moscow: Izdatel'stvo politicheskoi literatury, 1967.

Lenin, V.I. 1902a. Chto delat′? Nabolevshie voprosy nashego dvizheniia. Osen′ 1901–fevral′ 1902 g. In *Polnoe sobranie sochinenii*, vol. 6:1–192. Moscow: Izdatel'stvo politicheskoi literatury, 1963.

Lenin, V.I. 1902b. Material for the preparation of the programme of the R.S.D.L.P. In *Collected works*, vol. 6:15–76. Moscow: Progress Publishers, 1961.

Lenin, V.I. 1902c. Materialy k vyrabotke programmy RSDRP. Ianvare–aprele 1902 g. In *Polnoe sobranie sochinenii*, vol. 6:193–256. Moscow: Izdatel'stvo politicheskoi literatury, 1961.

Lenin, V.I. 1902d. What is to be done? Burning questions of our movement. In *Collected works*, vol. 5:347–529. Moscow: Progress Publishers, 1961.

Lenin, V.I. 1905a. Demokraticheskie zadachi revoliutsionnogo proletariata. 4 (17) iiunia 1905 g. In *Polnoe sobranie sochinenii*, vol. 10:270–277. Moscow: Izdatel'stvo politicheskoi literatury, 1967.

Lenin, V.I. 1905b. Dve taktiki sotsial-demokratii v demokraticheskoi revoliutsii. Iiune–iiule 1905 g. In *Polnoe sobranie sochinenii*, vol. 11:1–131. Moscow: Izdatel'stvo politicheskoi literatury, 1967.

Lenin, V.I. 1905c. General plan of the third congress decisions. In *Collected works*, vol. 8:184–189. Moscow: Progress Publishers, 1962.

Lenin, V.I. 1905d. III s"ezd RSDRP 12–27 aprelia (25 aprelia–10 maia) 1905 g. In *Polnoe sobranie sochinenii*, vol. 10:87–192. Moscow: Izdatel'stvo politicheskoi literatury, 1967.

Lenin, V.I. 1905e. Obshchii plan rabot i reshenii III s"ezda RSDRP. Fevrale 1905 g. In *Polnoe sobranie sochinenii*, vol. 9:311–324. Moscow: Izdatel'stvo politicheskoi literatury, 1967.

Lenin, V.I. 1905f. Revoliutsionnaia demokraticheskaia diktatura proletariata i krest'ianstva. 30 marta (12 aprelia) 1905 g. In *Polnoe sobranie sochinenii*, vol. 10:20–31. Moscow: Izdatel'stvo politicheskoi literatury, 1967.

Lenin, V.I. 1905g. Social-democracy and the provisional revolutionary government. In *Collected works*, vol. 8:275–292. Moscow: Progress Publishers, 1962.

Lenin, V.I. 1905h. Sotsial-demokratiia i vremennoe revoliutsionnoe pravitel′stvo. 23 i 30 marta (5 i 12 aprelia) 1905 g. In *Polnoe sobranie sochinenii*, vol. 10:1–19. Moscow: Izdatel'stvo politicheskoi literatury, 1967.

Lenin, V.I. 1905i. The democratic tasks of the revolutionary proletariat. In *Collected works*, vol. 8:511–518. Moscow: Progress Publishers, 1962.

Lenin, V.I. 1905j. The revolutionary-democratic dictatorship of the proletariat and the peasantry. In *Collected works*, vol. 8:293–303. Moscow: Progress Publishers, 1962.

Lenin, V.I. 1905k. The third congress of the R.S.D.L.P., April 12 (25) – April 27 (May 10), 1905. In *Collected works*, vol. 8:359–424. Moscow: Progress Publishers, 1962.

Lenin, V.I. 1905l. Two tactics of social-democracy in the democratic revolution. In *Collected works*, vol. 9:15–140. Moscow: Progress Publishers, 1962.

Lenin, V.I. 1906a. A tactical platform for the unity congress of the R.S.D.L.P. In *Collected works*, vol. 10:147–163. Moscow: Progress Publishers, 1962.

Lenin, V.I. 1906b. An appeal to the party by delegates to the unity congress who belonged to the former 'Bolshevik' group. In *Collected works*, vol. 10:310–315. Moscow: Progress Publishers, 1962.

Lenin, V.I. 1906c. Freedom to criticise and unity of action. In *Collected works*, vol. 10:442–443. Moscow: Progress Publishers, 1962.

Lenin, V.I. 1906d. Obrashchenie k partii delegatov ob"edinitel′nogo s"ezda, prinadlezhavshikh k byvshei fraktsii 'bol′shevikov'. 25–26 aprelia (8–9 maia) 1906 g. In *Polnoe sobranie sochinenii*, vol. 12:395–400. Moscow: Izdatel'stvo politicheskoi literatury, 1968.

Lenin, V.I. 1906e. Svoboda kritiki i edinstvo deistvii. 20 maia 1906 g. In *Polnoe sobranie sochinenii*, vol. 13:128–130. Moscow: Izdatel'stvo politicheskoi literatury, 1971.

Lenin, V.I. 1906f. Takticheskaia platforma k ob"edinitel′nomu s"ezdu RSDRP. Proekt rezoliutsii k ob"edinitel′nomu s"ezdu RSDRP. 20 marta (2 aprelia) 1906 g. In *Polnoe sobranie sochinenii*, vol. 12:221–238. Moscow: Izdatel'stvo politicheskoi literatury, 1968.

Lenin, V.I. 1912a. Concerning certain speeches by workers' deputies. In *Collected works*, vol. 18:413–419. Moscow: Progress Publishers, 1964.

Lenin, V.I. 1912b. K voprosu o nekotorykh vystupleniiakh rabochikh deputatov. Noiabr′, pozdnee 11 (24), 1912 g. In *Polnoe sobranie sochinenii*, vol. 22:197–201. Moscow: Izdatel'stvo politicheskoi literatury, 1968.

Lenin, V.I. 1913a. Critical remarks on the national question. In *Collected Works*, vol. 20:17–51. Moscow: Progress Publishers, 1964.

Lenin, V.I. 1913b. Kriticheskie zametki po natsional′nomu voprosu. Oktiabre–dekabre 1913 g. In *Polnoe sobranie sochinenii*, vol. 24:113–150. Moscow: Izdatel'stvo politicheskoi literatury, 1974.

Lenin, V. I. 1916a. A caricature of marxism and imperialist economism. In *Collected works*, vol. 23:28–76. Moscow: Progress Publishers, 1964.

Lenin, V.I. 1916b. O karikature na marksizm i ob 'imperialisticheskom ėkonomizme.' Avguste–oktiabre 1916 g. In *Polnoe sobranie sochinenii*, vol. 30:77–130. Moscow: Izdatel'stvo politicheskoi literatury, 1973.

Lenin, V.I. 1917a. Gosudarstvo i revoliutsiia. Uchenie marksizma o gosudarstve i zadachi proletariata v revoliutsii. Avguste–sentiabre 1917 g.; ranee 17 dekabria 1918 g. In *Polnoe sobranie sochinenii*, vol. 33:1–120. Moscow: Izdatel'stvo politicheskoi literatury, 1969.

Lenin, V.I. 1917b. Groziashchaia katastrofa i kak s nei borot′sia. 10–14 (23–27) sentiabria 1917 g. In *Polnoe sobranie sochinenii*, vol. 34:151–199. Moscow: Izdatel'stvo politicheskoi literatury, 1969.

Lenin, V.I. 1917c. The impending catastrophe and how to combat it. In *Collected works*, vol. 25:323–369. Moscow: Progress Publishers, 1964.

Lenin, V.I. 1917d. The state and revolution: The marxist theory of the state and the tasks of the proletariat in the revolution. In *Collected works*, vol. 25:385–497. Moscow: Progress Publishers, 1964.

Lenin, V.I. 1918a. Extraordinary seventh congress of the R.C.P.(B.), March 6–8, 1918. In *Collected works*, vol. 27:85–158. Moscow: Progress Publishers, 1965.

Lenin, V.I. 1918b. Original version of the article 'the immediate tasks of the Soviet Government.' Verbatim Report. In *Collected works*, vol. 27:203–218. Moscow: Progress Publishers, 1965.
Lenin, V.I. 1918c. Pervonachal'nyi variant stat'i 'Ocherednye zadachi Sovetskoi vlasti.' Mezhdu 23 i 28 marta 1918 g. In *Polnoe sobranie sochinenii*, vol. 36:127–164. Moscow: Izdatel'stvo politicheskoi literatury, 1969.
Lenin, V.I. 1918d. Proletarskaia revoliutsiia i renegat Kautskii. 10 noiabria 1918 g. In *Polnoe sobranie sochinenii*, vol. 37:235–338. Moscow: Izdatel'stvo politicheskoi literatury, 1969.
Lenin, V.I. 1918e. Sed'moi ėkstrennyi s"ezd RKP (b) 6-8 marta 1918 g. In *Polnoe sobranie sochinenii*, vol. 36:1–76. Moscow: Izdatel'stvo politicheskoi literatury, 1969.
Lenin, V.I. 1918f. The proletarian revolution and the renegade Kautsky. In *Collected works*, vol. 28:227–325. Moscow: Progress Publishers, 1965.
Lenin, V.I. 1919a. A great beginning: Heroism of the workers in the rear: 'Communist subbotniks'. In *Collected works*, vol. 29:409–434. Moscow: Progress Publishers, 1965.
Lenin, V.I. 1919b. 'Democracy' and dictatorship. In *Collected works*, vol. 28:368–372. Moscow: Progress Publishers, 1965.
Lenin, V.I. 1919c. Draft programme of the R.C.P.(B.). In *Collected works*, vol. 29:97–140. Moscow: Progress Publishers, 1965.
Lenin, V.I. 1919d. First Congress of the Communist International. In *Collected works*, vol. 28:455–477. Moscow: Progress Publishers, 1965.
Lenin, V.I. 1919e. I kongress Kommunisticheskogo Internatsionala 2–6 marta 1919 g. In *Polnoe sobranie sochinenii*, vol. 37:487–511. Moscow: Izdatel'stvo politicheskoi literatury, 1969.
Lenin, V.I. 1919f. O 'demokratii' i diktature. In *Polnoe sobranie sochinenii*, vol. 37:388–393. Moscow: Izdatel'stvo politicheskoi literatury, 1969.
Lenin, V.I. 1919g. O diktature proletariata. Sentiabre–oktiabre 1919 g. In *Polnoe sobranie sochinenii*, vol. 39:259–268. Moscow: Izdatel'stvo politicheskoi literatury, 1970.
Lenin, V.I. 1919h. Proekt programmy RKP (b). Fevralia, ranee 23; 23–25 fevralia 1919 g.. In *Polnoe sobranie sochinenii*, vol. 38:81–124. Moscow: Izdatel'stvo politicheskoi literatury, 1969.
Lenin, V.I. 1919i. The constituent assembly elections and the dictatorship of the proletariat. In *Collected works*, vol. 30:253–275. Moscow: Progress Publishers, 1965.
Lenin, V.I. 1919j. The dictatorship of the proletariat. In *Collected works*, vol. 30:93–106. Moscow: Progress Publishers, 1965.
Lenin, V.I. 1919k. The third international and its place in history. In *Collected works*, vol. 29:305–313. Moscow: Progress Publishers, 1965.
Lenin, V.I. 1919l. Tretii Internatsional i ego mesto v istorii. 15 aprelia 1919 g. In *Polnoe sobranie sochinenii*, vol. 38:301–309. Moscow: Izdatel'stvo politicheskoi literatury, 1969.
Lenin, V.I. 1919m. Veliki pochin (O geroizme rabochikh v tylu. Po povodu 'kommunisticheskikh subbotnikov'). 28 iiunia 1919 g. In *Polnoe sobranie sochinenii*, vol. 39:1–29. Moscow: Izdatel'stvo politicheskoi literatury, 1970.
Lenin, V.I. 1919n. Vybory v Uchreditel'noe sobranie i diktatura proletariata. 16 dekabria 1919 g. In *Polnoe sobranie sochinenii*, vol. 40:1–24. Moscow: Izdatel'stvo politicheskoi literatury, 1974.
Lenin, V.I. 1920a. The terms of admission into the Communist International. In *Collected works*, vol. 31:206–211. Moscow: Progress Publishers, 1966.
Lenin, V.I. 1920b. Usloviia priema v kommunisticheskii internatsional. In *Polnoe sobranie sochinenii*, vol. 41:204–211. Moscow: Izdatel'stvo politicheskoi literatury, 1981.
Li, Man, and Liu Congde. 2011. Liening guanyu renquan baozhang de zhengzhi tansuo: shehuizhuyi minzhu. *Xueshu luntan* 2011 (2): 1–4, 10.
Li, Shenming. 2009. Some thoughts on democracy and universal democracy. *Marxist Studies in China* 2009: 253–285.
Li, Weidong. 2010. Lun Liening minzhujizhongzhi sixiang zai Sulian de lishi yanbian jiqi xianshi. *Shehuizhuyi yanjiu* 2010 (2): 31–34.
Li, Zhijun, and Wang Yizhe. 2018. Zhongguo gongchandang minzhujizhongzhi sixiang de lishi yanjin. *Makesizhuyi yanjiu* 2018 (6): 117–123 + 160.

Lin, Shangli. 2007. Xieshang zhengzhi: Zhongguo tese minzhu zhengzhi de jiben xingtai. *Mao Zedong Deng Xiaoping lilun yanjiu* 2007 (9): 17–26.

Liu, Shaoqi. 1945a. Lun dang (1945.05.14). In *Liu Shaoqi xuanji*, vol. 1:314–370. Beijing: Renmin chubanshe, 1981.

Liu, Shaoqi. 1945b. On the party (14 May, 1945). In *Selected works of Liu Shaoqi*, vol. 1:314–364. Beijing: Foreign Languages Press, 1984.

Liu, Shaoqi. 1962a. Report to an enlarged working conference of the central committee (27 January, 1962). In *Selected works of Liu Shaoqi*, vol. 2:328–396. Beijing: Foreign Languages Press, 1991.

Liu, Shaoqi. 1962b. Zai kuoda de zhongyang gongzuo huiyi shang de baogao (1962.01.27). In *Liu Shaoqi xuanji*, vol. 2:349–417. Beijing: Renmin chubanshe, 1985.

Liu, Shulin. 2003. Guanyu minzhu shehuizhuyi sichao qiyuan de kaocha yu lunbian. *Makesizhuyi yu xianshi* 2003 (4): 55–76.

Liu, Sicang, and Lu Zhengyan. 2004. Shiyue geming hou dui eguo shixing shehuizhuyi minzhu de tansuo. *Qianyan* 2004 (8): 25–29.

Liu, Wanhong. 2002. Guojia yu shehui: fa zhexue yanjiu fanshi de pipan yu chongjian. *Faxue yanjiu* 2002 (6): 15–37.

Liu, Yu'an. 2008. Cong minzhu shehuizhuyi dao shehui minzhuzhuyi – sudong jubian hou xi'ou shehui minzhudang de zhanlüe tiaozheng. *Dangdai shijie shehuizhuyi wenti* 2008 (4): 60–74.

Lu, De'an. 2012. Minzhu shehuizhuyi moshi yu Zhongguo moshi bijiao fenxi. *Qiushi* 2012 (2): 67–73.

Luo, Xianhua, and Wu Zhuo. 2009. Lun minzhu shehuizhuyi yu kexue shehuizhuyi de zhexue jichu. *Sixiang lilun jiaoyu* 2009 (7): 48–53.

Lv, Weizhou. 2010. Minzhu shehuizhuyi de liubian jiqi yu Zhongguo tese shehuizhuyi de benzhi qubie. *Hongqi wengao* 2010 (4): 10–15.

Ma, Shaomeng. 2014. Observing the mass line and implementing democratic centralism. *Marxist Studies in China* 2014: 195–219.

Mao, Zedong. 1928a. Jinggang shan de douzheng (1928.11.25). In *Mao Zedong Quanji*, vol. 1:57–84. Beijing: Renmin chubanshi, 1976.

Mao, Zedong. 1928b. The struggle in the Chingkang mountains (25 November, 1928). In *Selected works of Mao Tse-Tung*, vol. 1:73–104. Beijing: Foreign Languages Press, 1965.

Mao, Zedong. 1935a. Lun fandui Riben diguozhuyi de celüe (1935.12.27). In *Mao Zedong xuanji*, vol. 1:142–169. Beijing: Renmin chubanshe, 2009.

Mao, Zedong. 1935b. On tactics against Japanese imperialism (27 December, 1935). In *Selected works of Mao Tse-Tung*, vol. 1:153–178. Beijing: Foreign Languages Press, 1965.

Mao, Zedong. 1937a. Bianzheng weiwu lun. In *Mao Zedong ji, Bujuan*, ed. Minoru Takeuchi, vol. 5:187–280. Tokyo: Sōsōsha, 1983–1986.

Mao, Zedong. 1937b. Fandui Riben jingong de fangzhen, banfa he qiantu (1937.07.23). In *Mao Zedong xuanji*, vol. 2:343–351. Beijing: Renmin chubanshe, 2009.

Mao, Zedong. 1937c. For the mobilization of all the nation's forces for victory in the war of resistance (25 August, 1937). In *Selected works of Mao Tse-tung*, vol. 2:23–30. Beijing: Foreign Languages Press, 1965.

Mao, Zedong. 1937d. He Yingguo jizhe Beitelan de tanhua (1937.10.25). In *Mao Zedong xuanji*, vol. 2:373–386. Beijing: Renmin chubanshe, 2009.

Mao, Zedong. 1937e. Interview with the British journalist James Bertram (25 October, 1937). In *Selected works of Mao Tse-tung*, vol. 2:47–60. Beijing: Foreign Languages Press, 1965.

Mao, Zedong. 1937f. On dialectical materialism (Lecture notes). In *Mao's road to power: Revolutionary writings 1912–1949*, vol. 6:573–667. Armonk: M. E. Sharpe, 2004.

Mao, Zedong. 1937g. Policies, measures and perspectives for resisting the Japanese invasion (23 July, 1937). In *Selected works of Mao Tse-tung*, vol. 2:13–22. Beijing: Foreign Languages Press, 1965.

Mao, Zedong. 1937h. The tasks of the Chinese Communist Party in the period of resistance against Japan (3 May, 1937). In *Selected works of Mao Tse-Tung*, vol. 1:263–284. Beijing: Foreign Languages Press, 1965.

Mao, Zedong. 1937i. Wei dongyuan yiqie liliang zhengqu kangzhan shengli er douzheng (1937.08.25). In *Mao Zedong xuanji*, vol. 2:352–358. Beijing: Renmin chubanshe, 2009.

Mao, Zedong. 1937j. Wei zhengqu qian baiwan qunzhong jinru kangri minzu tongyi zhanxian (1937.05.07). In *Mao Zedong xuanji*, vol. 1:271–281. Beijing: Renmin chubanshe, 2009.

Mao, Zedong. 1937k. Win the masses in their millions for the Anti-Japanese United Front (7 May, 1937). In *Selected works of Mao Tse-Tung*, vol. 1:285–294. Beijing: Foreign Languages Press, 1965.

Mao, Zedong. 1937l. Zhongguo gongchandang zai kangri shiqi de renwu (1937.05.03). In *Mao Zedong wenji*, vol. 1:252–270. Beijing: Renmin chubanshe, 2009.

Mao, Zedong. 1939a. The Chinese revolution and the Chinese Communist Party (December, 1939). In *Selected works of Mao Tse-tung*, vol. 2:305–334. Beijing: Foreign Languages Press, 1965.

Mao, Zedong. 1939b. The May 4th Movement (1 May, 1939). In *Selected works of Mao Tse-tung*, vol. 2:237–239. Beijing: Foreign Languages Press, 1965.

Mao, Zedong. 1939c. Wusi yundong (1939.05.01). In *Mao Zedong xuanji*, vol. 2:558–560. Beijing: Renmin chubanshe, 2009.

Mao, Zedong. 1939d. Zhongguo geming he Zhongguo gongchandang (1939.12). In *Mao Zedong xuanji*, vol. 2:621–656. Beijing: Renmin chubanshe, 2009.

Mao, Zedong. 1940a. Current problems of tactics in the Anti-Japanese United Front (11 March, 1940). In *Selected works of Mao Tse-tung*, vol. 2:421–430. Beijing: Foreign Languages Press, 1965.

Mao, Zedong. 1940b. Muqian kangri tongyi zhanxian zhong de celüe wenti (1940.03.11). In *Mao Zedong xuanji*, vol. 2:744–752. Beijing: Renmin chubanshe, 2009.

Mao, Zedong. 1940c. New-democratic constitutional government (20 February, 1940). In *Selected works of Mao Tse-tung*, vol. 2:407–410. Beijing: Foreign Languages Press, 1965.

Mao, Zedong. 1940d. On new democracy (January, 1940). In *Selected works of Mao Tse-tung*, vol. 2:339–384. Beijing: Foreign Languages Press, 1965.

Mao, Zedong. 1940e. Xin minzhuzhuyi de xianzheng (1940.02.20). In *Mao Zedong xuanji*, vol. 2:731–740. Beijing: Renmin chubanshe, 2009.

Mao, Zedong. 1940f. Xin minzhuzhuyi lun (1940.01.15). In *Mao Zedong xuanji*, vol. 2:662–711. Beijing: Renmin chubanshe, 2009.

Mao, Zedong. 1942a. Rectify the party's style of work (1 February, 1942). In *Selected works of Mao Tse-Tung*, vol. 3:35–51. Beijing: Foreign Languages Press, 1965.

Mao, Zedong. 1942b. Zhengdun dang de zuofeng (1942.02.01). In *Mao Zedong xuanji*, vol. 3:811–829. Beijing: Renmin chubanshe, 2009.

Mao, Zedong. 1945a. Lun lianhezhengfu (1945.04.24). In *Mao Zedong xuanji*, vol. 3:1029–1100. Beijing: Renmin chubanshe, 2009.

Mao, Zedong. 1945b. On coalition government (24 April, 1945). In *Selected works of Mao Tse-Tung*, vol. 3:255–320. Beijing: Foreign Languages Press, 1965.

Mao, Zedong. 1948a. Speech at a conference of cadres in the Shansi-Suiyuan liberated area (1 April, 1948). In *Selected works of Mao Tse-Tung*, vol. 4:227–239. Beijing: Foreign Languages Press, 1961.

Mao, Zedong. 1948b. Zai Jin-Sui ganbu huiyi de jianghua (1948.04.01). In *Mao Zedong xuanji*, vol. 4:1305–1317. Beijing: Renmin chubanshe, 2009.

Mao, Zedong. 1949a. Bie le, Situ Leideng (1949.08.18). In *Mao Zedong xuanji*, vol. 4:1491–98. Beijing: Renmin chubanshe, 2009.

Mao, Zedong. 1949b. Cast away illusions, prepare for struggle (14 August, 1949). In *Selected works of Mao Tse-Tung*, vol. 4:425–432. Beijing: Foreign Languages Press, 1961.

Mao, Zedong. 1949c. Duidiao huanxiang, zhunbei douzheng (1949.08.14). In *Mao Zedong xuanji*, vol. 4:1483–1490. Beijing: Renmin chubanshe, 2009.

Mao, Zedong. 1949d. Farewell, Leighton Stuart! (18 August, 1949). In *Selected works of Mao Tse-Tung*, vol. 4:433–440. Beijing: Foreign Languages Press, 1961.

Mao, Zedong. 1949e. Long live the great unity of the Chinese people! (30 September, 1949). In *Selected works of Mao Tse-Tung*, vol. 5:19–21. Beijing: Foreign Languages Press, 1977.

Mao, Zedong. 1949f. Lun renmin minzhu zhuanzheng: jinian Zhongguo gongchandang ershi ba zhounian (1949.06.30). In *Mao Zedong xuanji*, vol. 4:1468–1482. Beijing: Renmin chubanshe, 2009.

Mao, Zedong. 1949g. On the people's democratic dictatorship: In commemoration of the twenty-eighth anniversary of the Communist Party of China (30 June, 1949). In *Selected works of Mao Tse-Tung*, vol. 4:411–424. Beijing: Foreign Languages Press, 1961.

Mao, Zedong. 1949h. Report to the second plenary session of the Seventh Central Committee of the Communist Party (5 March, 1949). In *Selected works of Mao Tse-Tung*, vol. 4:361–375. Beijing: Foreign Languages Press, 1969.

Mao, Zedong. 1949i. The Chinese people have stood up (21 September, 1949). In *Selected works of Mao Tse-Tung*, vol. 5:15–18. Beijing: Foreign Languages Press, 1977.

Mao, Zedong. 1949j. Weishenme yao taolun baipishu? (1949.08.28). In *Mao Zedong xuanji*, vol. 4:1499–1504. Beijing: Renmin chubanshe, 2009.

Mao, Zedong. 1949k. Why it is necessary to discuss the white paper (28 August, 1949). In *Selected works of Mao Tse-Tung*, vol. 4:441–446. Beijing: Foreign Languages Press, 1961.

Mao, Zedong. 1949l. Zai Zhongguo gongchandang di qi jie zhongyang weiyuanhui di er ci quanti huiyi shang de baogao (1949.03.05). In *Mao Zedong xuanji*, vol. 4:1424–1439. Beijing: Renmin chubanshe, 2009.

Mao, Zedong. 1949m. Zhongguo renmin datuanjie wansui (1949.09.30). In *Mao Zedong xuanji*, vol. 5:8–10. Beijing: Renmin chubanshe, 1977.

Mao, Zedong. 1949n. Zhongguo renmin zhanqilai le (1949.09.21). In *Mao Zedong xuanji*, vol. 5:3–7. Beijing: Renmin chubanshe, 1977.

Mao, Zedong. 1950a. Be a true revolutionary (23 June, 1950). In *Selected works of Mao Tse-Tung*, vol. 5:37–40. Beijing: Foreign Languages Press, 1977.

Mao, Zedong. 1950b. Zuo yige wanquan de geming pai (1950.06.23). In *Mao Zedong wenji*, vol. 5:25–29. Beijing: Renmin chubanshe, 1999.

Mao, Zedong. 1953a. Pipan likai zongluxian de youqing guandian (1953.06.15). In *Mao Zedong xuanji*, vol. 5:81–82. Beijing: Renmin chubanshe, 1977.

Mao, Zedong. 1953b. Refute right deviationist views that depart from the general line (15 June, 1953). In *Selected works of Mao Tse-Tung*, vol. 5:93–94. Beijing: Foreign Languages Press, 1977.

Mao, Zedong. 1954a. Guanyu Zhonghua renmin gongheguo xianfa cao'an (1954.06.14). In *Mao Zedong wenji*, vol. 6:324–331. Beijing: Renmin chubanshe, 2009.

Mao, Zedong. 1954b. On the draft constitution of the People's Republic of China (14 June, 1954). In *Selected works of Mao Tse-Tung*, vol. 5:141–147. Beijing: Foreign Languages Press, 1977.

Mao, Zedong. 1956a. Lun shi da guanxi (1956.04.25). In *Mao Zedong xuanji*, vol. 5:267–288. Beijing: Renmin chubanshe, 1977.

Mao, Zedong. 1956b. On the ten major relationships (25 April, 1956). In *Selected works of Mao Tse-Tung*, vol. 5:284–307. Beijing: Foreign Languages Press, 1977.

Mao, Zedong. 1957a. Be activists in promoting the revolution (9 October, 1957). In *Selected works of Mao Tse-Tung*, vol. 5:483–497. Beijing: Foreign Languages Press, 1977.

Mao, Zedong. 1957b. Beat back the attacks of the bourgeois rightists (9 July, 1957). In *Selected works of Mao Tse-Tung*, vol. 5:457–472. Beijing: Foreign Languages Press, 1977.

Mao, Zedong. 1957c. Datui zichanjieji youpai de jingong (1957.07.09). In *Mao Zedong xuanji*, vol. 5:440–555. Beijing: Renmin chubanshe, 1977.

Mao, Zedong. 1957d. Guanyu zhengque chuli renmin neibu maodun de wenti (1957.02.27). In *Mao Zedong xuanji*, vol. 5:363–402. Beijing: Renmin chubanshe, 1977.

Mao, Zedong. 1957e. On the correct handling of contradictions among the people (27 February, 1957). In *Selected works of Mao Tse-Tung*, vol. 5:384–421. Beijing: Foreign Languages Press, 1977.

Mao, Zedong. 1957f. Zuo geming de cujinpai (1957.10.09). In *Mao Zedong xuanji*, vol. 5:466–479. Beijing: Renmin chubanshe, 1977.

Mao, Zedong. 1962. Zai kuoda de zhongyang gongzuo huiyi shang de jianghua (1962.01.30). In *Mao Zedong wenji*, vol. 8:289–314. Beijing: Renmin chubanshe, 2009.

Marx, Karl. 1871. The civil war in France. In *Marx and Engels Gesamtausgabe*, vol. I.22:119–162. Berlin: Dietz, 1978.
Marx, Karl. 1875a. Critique of the Gotha programme. In *Marx and Engels collected works*, vol. 24:75–99. Moscow: Progress Publishers, 1989.
Marx, Karl. 1875b. Konspekt von Bakunins Buch 'Staatlichkeit und Anarchie'. In *Marx Engels Werke*, vol. 18:597–642. Berlin: Dietz, 1973.
Marx, Karl. 1875c. Kritik des Gothaer Programms. In *Marx Engels Gesamtausgabe*, vol. I.25:3–25. Berlin: Dietz, 1985.
Marx, Karl. 1875d. Notes on Bakunin's book *Statehood and anarchy*. In *Marx Engels collected works*, vol. 24:485–526. Moscow: Progress Publishers, 1989.
Marx, Karl. 1895. *Die Klassenkämpfe in Frankreich 1848 bis 1850. Abdruck aus der 'Neuen Rheinischen Zeitung', Politisch-ökonomische Revue, Hamburg 1850, mit Einleitung von Friedrich Engels.* Berlin: Verlag der Expedition des 'Vorwärts' Berliner Volksblatt.
Marx, Karl, and Friedrich Engels. 1846. *Deyizhi yishi xingtai. Dui Fei'erbaha, Bu·baowei'er he Shidina suo daibiao de xiandai deguo zhexue yiji ge shi ge yang xianzhi suo daibiao de deguo shehuizhuyi de pipan.* In *Makesi Engesi quanji*, vol. 3:11–640. Beijing: Renmin chubanshe, 1972.
Marx, Karl, and Friedrich Engels. 1848a. Manifest der Kommunistischen Partei. In *Marx Engels Werke*, vol. 4:459–493. Berlin: Dietz Verlag, 1974.
Marx, Karl, and Friedrich Engels. 1848b. The manifesto of the Communist Party. In *Marx and Engels collected works*, vol. 6:477–519. Moscow: Progress Publishers, 1976.
Marx, Karl, and Friedrich Engels. 1850a. Erklärungen an den Redakteur der 'Neuen Deutschen Zeitung'. In *Marx Engels Gesamtausgabe*, I.10:354–355. Berlin: Dietz.
Marx, Karl, and Friedrich Engels. 1850b. Statement: To the editor of the *Neue Deutsche Zeitung*. In *Marx and Engels collected works*, vol. 10:387–388. Moscow: Progress Publishers.
Marx, Karl, and Friedrich Engels. 1872a. Fictitious splits in the international. Private circular from the general council of the International Working Men's Association. In *Marx and Engels collected works*, vol. 23:79–123. Moscow: Progress Publishers, 1988.
Marx, Karl, and Friedrich Engels. 1872b. Les prétendues scissions dans l'Internationale: Circulaire privée du Conseil Général de l'Associalion Internationale des Travailleurs. In *Le mouvement socialiste: Revue de critique sociale, littéraire et artistique*, 34, No. 253–254:5–50. Paris: M. Giard & E. Brière, 1913.
Ouyang, Qiong. 2019. Liening de shehuixhuyi minzhu sixiang jiqi xianshi yiyi. *Dongyue luncong* 2019 (9): 129–136.
Ren, Weide. 1995. Liening lun shehuizhuyi minzhu yu fazhi jianshe. *Neimenggu daxue xuebao (zhexue shehui kexue ban)* 1995 (1): 101–108.
Rong, Jingben, and Lai Hairong. 2000. Guanyu xian xiang liang ji zhengzhi tizhi gaige de bijiao yanjiu – cong cun dao xiangzhen minzhu zhidu jianshe de fazhan. *Jingji shehui tizhi bijiao* 2000 (4): 1–53.
Stalin, I.V. 1906a. Dve skhvatki (Po povodu 9 ianvaria). In *Trudy*, vol. 2:365–73. Moscow: Prometeĭ Info, 2013.
Stalin, I.V. 1906b. Two clashes (concerning January 9). In *Works*, vol. 1:198–207. Moscow: Foreign Languages Publishing House, 1954.
Stalin, I.V. 1918a. Speech delivered at the third all-Russian congress of Soviets of Workers', Soldiers' and Peasants' Deputies, 10–18 January 1918. In *Works*, vol. 4:31–38. Moscow: Foreign Languages Publishing House, 1953.
Stalin, I.V. 1918b. Vystupleniia na III Vserossiiskom s"ezde Sovetov rabochikh, soldatskikh i krest′ianskikh deputatov 10–18 ianvaria 1918 g. In *Sochineniia*, vol. 4:30–37. Moscow: Gosudarstvennoe izdatel′stvo politicheskoi literatury, 1947.
Stalin, I.V. 1924a. O zadachakh partii v derevne: Rech′ na plenume TSK RKP(b), 26 oktiabria 1924 g. In *Sochineniia*, vol. 6:313–320. Moscow: Gosudarstvennoe izdatel′stvo politicheskoi literatury, 1947.

Stalin, I.V. 1924b. Ob itogakh XIII s"ezda RKP(b): Doklad na kursakh sekretarei ukomov pri TSK RKP(b), 17 iiunia 1924 g. In *Sochineniia*, vol. 6:234–260. Moscow: Gosudarstvennoe izdatel´stvo politicheskoi literatury, 1947.

Stalin, I.V. 1924c. Ob osnovakh leninizma: Lektsii, chitannye v Sverdlovskom universitete. In *Sochineniia*, vol. 6:69–188. Moscow: Gosudarstvennoe izdatel´stvo politicheskoi literatury, 1947.

Stalin, I.V. 1924d. The foundations of Leninism: Lectures delivered at the Sverdlov University. In *Works*, vol. 6:71–196. Moscow: Foreign Languages Publishing House, 1953.

Stalin, I.V. 1924e. The party's tasks in the countryside: Speech delivered at a the plenum of the Central Committee of the R.C.P. (B.), 26 October 1924. In *Works*, vol. 6:327–34. Moscow: Foreign Languages Publishing House, 1953.

Stalin, I.V. 1924f. The results of the thirteenth congress of the R.C.P.(B.): Report delivered at the C.C., R.C.P.(B.) courses for secretaries of Uyezd Party committees, 17 June 1924. In *Works*, vol. 6:246–73. Moscow: Foreign Languages Publishing House, 1953.

Stalin, I.V. 1924g. Thirteenth conference of the R.C.P.(B.), 16–18 January 1924. In *Works*, vol. 6:3–46. Moscow: Foreign Languages Publishing House, 1953.

Stalin, I.V. 1924h. XIII s"ezd RKP(b) 23–31 maia 1924 g. In *Sochineniia*, vol. 6:191–233. Moscow: Gosudarstvennoe izdatel´stvo politicheskoi literatury, 1947.

Stalin, I.V. 1927a. Beseda so studentami Universiteta imeni Sun Iat-sena, 13 maia 1927 g. In *Sochineniia*, vol. 9:239–268. Moscow: Gosudarstvennoe izdatel´stvo politicheskoi literatury, 1948.

Stalin, I.V. 1927b. Talk with students of the Sun Yat-Sen University, 13 May 1927. I *Works*, vol. 9:243–73. Moscow: Foreign Languages Publishing House, 1954.

Stalin, I.V. 1936a. Constitution (Fundamental Law) of the Union of Soviet Socialist Republics, with amendments adopted by the First, Second, Third, Sixth, Seventh and Eighth Sessions of the Supreme Soviet of the U.S.S.R., Kremlin, Moscow, December 5, 1936. In *Works*, vol. 14:199–239. London: Red Star Press, 1978.

Stalin, I.V. 1936b. *Konstitutsiia (osnovnoĭ zakon) soiuza sovetskikh sotsialisticheskikh respublik (utverzhdena postanovleniem chrezvychaĭnogo VIII s"ezda sovetov soiuza sovetskikh sotsialisticheskikh respublik ot 5 dekabria 1936 g.)*. Moscow: Garant, 2015.

Stalin, I.V. 1936c. O proekte konstitutsii soiuza SSR: Doklad na chrezvychaĭnom VIII vsesoiuznom s"ezde sovetov, 25 noiabria 1936 goda. In *Sochineniia*, vol. 14:119–147. Moscow: Izdatel′stvo "Pisatel′", 1997.

Stalin, I.V. 1936d. On the draft constitution of the U.S.S.R.: Report delivered at the extraordinary eighth congress of Soviets of the U.S.S.R., November 25, 1936. In *Works*, vol. 14:151–97. London: Red Star Press, 1978.

Stalin, I.V. 1937a. Rech′ na predvybornom sobranii izbirateleĭ Stalinskogo izbiratel′nogo okruga goroda Moskvy, 11 dekabria 1937 goda. In *Sochineniia*, vol. 14:238–243. Moscow: Izdatel′stvo "Pisatel′", 1997.

Stalin, I.V. 1937b. Speech delivered by Comrade J. Stalin at a meeting of voters of the Stalin Electoral Area, 11 December 1937. In *Works*, vol. 14:305–313. London: Red Star Press, 1978.

Stalin, I.V. 1937c. Speech in reply to debate, 5 March 1937. In *Works*, vol. 14:275–296. London: Red Star Press, 1978.

Stalin, I.V. 1937d. Zakliuchitel′noe slovo na Plenume TSK VKP(b), 5 marta 1937 goda. In *Sochineniia*, vol. 14:174–188. Moscow: Izdatel′stvo "Pisatel′", 1997.

Stalin, I.V. 1938a. *History of the Communist Party of the Soviet Union (Bolsheviks): Short course*. New York: International Publishers.

Stalin, I.V. 1938b. *Istoriia Vsesoiuznoĭ Kommunisticheskoĭ Partii (Bol′shevikov): Kratkii kurs*, 1946. Moscow: OGIZ Gospolitizdat.

Sun, Zhongshan. 1924a. Sanminzhuyi (1924.01-08). In *Sun Zhongshan juan*, ed. Zhang Ping and Zhang Lei, 257–436. Beijing: Zhongguo renmin daxue chubanshe, 2015.

Sun, Zhongshan. 1924b. Zhongguo guomindang di yi ci quanmian daibiao dahui xuanyan (1924.01.23). In *Sun Zhongshan juan*, ed. Zhang Ping and Zhang Lei, 248–256. Beijing: Zhongguo renmin daxue chubanshe, 2015.

Trotsky, Leon. 1937. *The revolution betrayed: What is the Soviet Union and where is it going?*, trans. Max Eastman. New York: Pathfinder.

Wang, Yan, and Wei Chonghui. 2017. The Chinese logic of consultative governance. *Social Sciences in China* 38 (3): 5–24.

Wen, Yong, and Huang Sikai. 1998. Shehuizhuyi minzhu gaoyu zibenzhuyi minzhu – xuexi Liening 'Guojia yu geming' yi shu de tihui. *Guangxi shifan daxue xuebao (zhexue shehui kexue ban)* 1998 (S3): 10–12.

Wu, Wei, and Xia Yinping. 2016. Liening yu 'shehui minzhuzhuyi'. *Dangdai shijie yu shehuizhuyi* 2016 (3): 39–47.

Xi, Jinping. 2012. Zai shoudu gejie jinian xianxing xianfa gongbu shixing 30 zhounian dahui shang de jianghua (2012.12.04). In *Tan zhiguolizheng*, vol. 1:135–143. Beijing: Waiwen chubanshe, 2014.

Xi, Jinping. 2013. Qieshi ba sixiang tongyi dao dang de shiba jie zhong quanhui jingshen shanglai (2013.11.12). In *Tan zhiguolizheng*, vol. 1:90–99. Beijing: Waiwen chubanshe, 2014.

Xi, Jinping. 2014a. Jianding dui Zhongguo tese shehuizhuyi zhengzhi zhidu de zixin (2014.09.05). In *Tan zhiguolizheng*, vol. 2:285–290. Beijing: Waiwen chubanshe, 2017.

Xi, Jinping. 2014b. Shenru tuijin dangfeng lianzheng jianshe he fan fubai douzheng (2014.01.14). In *Tan zhiguolizheng*, vol. 1:393–396. Beijing: Waiwen chubanshe, 2014.

Xi, Jinping. 2014c. Tuijin xieshang minzhu guangfan duoceng zhiduhua fazhan (2014.09.21). In *Tan zhiguolizheng*, vol. 2:291–298. Beijing: Waiwen chubanshe, 2017.

Xi, Jinping. 2015. *Guanyu quanmian yifazhiguo lunshu zhaibian*. Beijing: Zhongyang wenxian chubanshe.

Xi, Jinping. 2017a. *Juesheng quanmian jiancheng xiaokang shehui, duoqu xinshidai Zhongguo tese shehuizhuyi weida shengli (2017.10.18)*. Beijing: Renmin chubanshe.

Xi, Jinping. 2017b. Zhongguo gongchandang shi Zhongguo tese shehuizhuyi zui benzhi de tezheng (2014.09-05 – 2017.02.13). In *Tan zhiguolizheng*, vol. 2:28–30. Beijing: Waiwen chubanshe, 2017.

Xi, Jinping. 2019. Jiaqiang dang dui quanmian yifazhiguo de lingdao. *Qiushi* 2019 (4): 1–4.

Xiao, Guiqing, and Yu. Jiangtao. 2012. Gaige kaifang yilai Zhongguo tese shehuizhuyi zhidu de tansuo he chuangxin. *Dangdai zhongguo shi yanjiu* 19 (5): 13–19.

Xie, Tao. 2007. Minzhu shehuizhuyi moshi yu Zhongguo qiantu. *Yanhuang chunqiu* 2007 (2): 1–8.

Xie, Zhikui. 2009. Cuowu de minzhu guannian yu xianshi de minzhu lujing – dui Zhongguo tese shehuizhuyi minzhu daolu de lilun sikao. *Zhengzhixue yanjiu* 2009 (6): 21–30.

Xu, Chongwen. 2010. Ruhe renshi minzhu shehuizhuyi. *Mao Zedong Deng Xiaoping lilun yanjiu* 2010 (4): 62–71.

Xue, Xinguo. 2014. Lun minzhu shehuizhuyi yu kexue minzhuzhuyi de guanxi. *Makesizhuyi yanjiu* 2014 (5): 84–89.

Yan, Beibei. 2014. Liening shehuizhuyi minzhu zhengzhi jianshe sixiang zai tan. *Henan shifan daxue xuebao (zhexue shehui kexue ban)* 2014 (6): 57–61.

Yang, Haijiao. 2008. 30 nianlai Zhongguo tese shehuizhuyi minzhu zhengzhi jianshe huigu. *Xuexi yu tansuo* 2008 (6): 20–26.

Yang, Weimin. 2017. Zhongguo tese zhengdang zhidu de youshi ji dui shijie gongxian – 'wei renlei dui genghao shehui zhidu de tansuo tigong Zhongguo fang'an' zhi guanjian. *Tongyi zhanxian xue yanjiu* 2017 (1): 15–31.

Yang, Yang. 2012. Chayi, jiejian yu chaoyue: Zhongguo tese shehuizhuyi yu minzhu shehuizhuyi de bijiao. *Henan shehui kexue* 20 (1): 60–63.

Yermakov, A. 1975. *A. Lunacharsky*. Moscow: Novosti.

Yin, Xuyi. 2001a. Shehui minzhuzhuyi he minzhu shehuizhuyi (shang) – gainian de qiyuan he lishi yanbian. *Dangdai shijie shehuizhuyi wenti* 2001 (3): 3–21.

Yin, Xuyi. 2001b. Shehui minzhuzhuyi he minzhu shehuizhuyi (xia) – gainian de qiyuan he lishi yanbian. *Dangdai shijie shehuizhuyi wenti* 2001 (4): 3–18.

Zai, Douyong. 1991. Xi 'minzhu shehuizhuyi' de zhexue jichu. *Xiandai zhexue* 1991 (3): 31–36.

Zheng, Baiqiong. 2006. Cong zhidu shehuizhuyi dao jiazhi shehuizhuyi – minzhu shehuizhuyi zai dangdai de fazhan. *Shehuizhuyi yanjiu* 2006 (5): 18–21.

Zhou, Enlai. 1949a. Guanyu renmin zhengxie de jige wenti (1949.09.07). In *Zhou Enlai tongyi zhanxian wenxuan*, 129–143. Beijing: Renmin chubanshe, 1984.

Zhou, Enlai. 1949b. Renmin zhengxie gongtong gangling cao'an de tedian (1949.09.22). In *Zhou Enlai tongyi zhanxian wenxuan*, 144–149. Beijing: Renmin chubanshe, 1984.

Zhou, Enlai. 1950. Chuli hao renmin minzhu tongyi zhanxian zhong de si ge guanxi (1950.04.12). In *Zhou Enlai tongyi zhanxian wenxuan*, 159–164. Beijing: Renmin chubanshe, 1984.

Zhou, Enlai. 1953. Minzhu dangpai chengyuan xuexi he canjia jianshe de wenti (1953.06.04). In *Zhou Enlai tongyi zhanxian wenxuan*, 244–51. Beijing: Renmin chubanshe, 1984.

Zhou, Enlai. 1957. Changqi gongcun, huxiang jiandu (1957.04.24). In *Zhou Enlai tongyi zhanxian wenxuan*, 345–349. Beijing: Renmin chubanshe, 1984.

Zhou, Xincheng. 2018. Renqing minzhu shehuizhuyi de benzhi, huaqing kexue shehuizhuyi yu minzhu shehuizhuyi de jiexian – jinian 'Gongchandang xuanyan' fabiao 170 zhounian. *Mao Zedong Deng Xiaoping lilun yanjiu* 2018 (9): 58–65.

Chapter 10
Xi Jinping on Marx and Engels

10.1 Setting the Scene: Why Xi Jinping's Thought is Important

Only the wearer knows whether the shoes fits or not. (Xi 2013e, 273)

The specific concern of this chapter is Xi Jinping's engagement with Marx and Engels. I do so primarily through an important speech delivered at the celebration of the 200th anniversary of Marx's birth (5 May 2018), although I will also refer to other important material. In the introduction chapter (Sect. 1.2), I dealt with three interrelated pieces by Xi Jinping on Marxist philosophy and analysis, along with their implications for the CPC and education.[1] By contrast, here my focus is on the way Xi Jinping draws upon the works of Marx and Engels for the Chinese context. By now the reason for such a focus should be clear: it is precisely Xi Jinping's emphasis on Marxism as the heart and soul of the Chinese project that enables one to navigate an increasingly voluminous collection of speeches and publications. Before dealing with the Marx speech in some detail, we need to step back a moment to consider the wider and indeed global scene.

In this context, there are two problems: first, it took some parts of the world quite some time to realise that Xi Jinping and the CPC are absolutely serious about Marxism and thus that China is not following a capitalist road; second, one finds that Western observers have a constitutive inability to understand the importance of a Communist leader's thought. The two problems are related but distinct. In terms of the time-lag, it was only with Xi Jinping's major speech at the nineteenth congress of the CPC in late 2017—when 'Xi Jinping Thought' was established—that observers in some Western parts came to the delayed realisation that China is clearly not following a path of Western bourgeois liberalisation. Until then, it was not so uncommon to hear

[1]The three texts concern philosophy and the social sciences, dialectical materialism, and historical materialism (Xi 2016c, 2019a, 2020b). Two other texts that focus extensive on Marxism are the speech at the 90th anniversary of the CPC and a text that reasserts the centrality of Marxist political economy (Xi 2011, 2020a).

R. Boer, *Socialism with Chinese Characteristics*,
https://doi.org/10.1007/978-981-16-1622-8_10

that China had given up on Marxism and replaced it with nationalism, that China was well down the 'capitalist road', indeed that it would soon adopt capitalist democracy. However, by the end of 2017, and indeed by the time of the Marx speech in May of 2018, it had became clear that such an assumption was quite erroneous. One might ask: what took so long to realise this? After all, Xi Jinping had been elected general secretary of the CPC in 2012 and president of the People's Republic in early 2013. And anyone who had bothered to take the time to study Xi's path until that point would have been under no delusions about his Marxist credentials.[2] Perhaps this delay was due to the persistence of ideological assumptions concerning China, of 'using the West to understand China [*yixi jiezhong*]', indeed of 'using the West to understand Marx [*yixi jiema*]' (see Sect. 1.4.2).

This brings us to the second and perhaps deeper problem: virtually no-one in the relatively small number of Western countries takes the thought of a leader seriously—let alone a current leader. I have addressed this problem in the introductory chapter (Sect. 1.2.3), indicating the distinct shortcomings of the Western liberal tradition in terms of political analysis and the role of a political leader's thoughts. Thus, it should be no surprise that there is in a Western context virtually no serious engagement with Xi Jinping's thought, let alone his extensive engagements with Marxism. Indeed, if one consults the growing number of Western works on Xi Jinping, one will note a—to put it politely—constitutive failure to deal adequately with Xi's emphasis on Marxism (Brown 2016, 2018; Garrick and Bennett 2016; Li Cheng 2016; Bougon 2018; Economy 2018; Magnus 2018).[3] By contrast, those familiar with the Communist tradition will know that the general secretary of the Communist Party is also expected to be a thinker and a writer. Of course, the thinking takes place in a collective context, in study, rigorous debate, and the search for solutions in light of Marxism, but it means that the general secretary's thought deserves and indeed demands careful study. This is the reality in China today, and it would be negligent to the extreme not to take seriously the speeches and writings of Xi Jinping, particularly those concerning Marx and Engels. We need to keep reminding ourselves: here is a leader of a major global power, if not the strongest socialist country in human history, quoting and drawing extensively from the founders of the Marxist tradition. A final warning before we plunge into the Marx speech: anyone looking for hidden codes and subtle signals will be disappointed. I know this is a game of some, even if it is futile. With Xi Jinping, what you see is what you get.

[2]No-one in China, or indeed in other parts of the world where people pay proper attention to such matters, is at all surprised as to Xi Jinping's Marxist credentials. These have been obvious from the beginning (Xi 2006, 2011, 2012, 2013a, 2013b, 2016a; Wang H. 2016; Yang 2016; Yuan and Li 2016; Liu Y. 2017; Zhonggong zhongyang xuanchuanbu 2016, 277–282).

[3]On occasion, one finds a writer who is noticeably frustrated and even angry that Xi Jinping has upset a pet narrative concerning China's path to bourgeois liberalisation.

10.2 The Biography of an Engaged Intellectual

Xi Jinping's Marx speech has not as yet been translated into other languages. This may seem somewhat curious given its programmatic importance for not merely Xi's tenure as general secretary but for China's project as it steadily draws closer to the goal of a 'strong socialistically modernised country'. One may of course find full texts—in Chinese—of the speech on quite a number of internet sites, along with audio recordings. But let us note where the speech was first published: it was in a journal called *Gongchandangyuan*, 'Communist Party Member' (Xi 2018a). The speech was also published in full in a separate booklet (Xi 2018b),[4] as well as being republished in about ten journals, although note the following: *Dangjian* (Party Building), *Beijing renda* (Beijing Standing Committee of the National People's Congress), *Dangdai bingtuan* (Army Today), and *Dangdai dangyuan* (Party Member Today). These journals are focused on Party building: clearly, the prime audience for the speech and its subsequent publication are the 100 million or so CPC members, and the speech has been studied in detail by the monthly study groups that are required for all Party members. One effect of this emphasis is that the text has not as yet been translated into other languages,[5] although I would suggest—and this chapter is evidence of such a position—that it is in fact of profound interest and importance not merely for all members of Communist Parties around the world, but also for anyone seeking to understand China's direction and its crucial role in the international arena (Liu J. 2018, 12).[6]

The speech itself has three sections, after an introduction that elaborates briefly on Marx's continued influence on the world. Here Xi already identifies a recurring theme: the world may have changed much since Marx's time, but this context makes Marxism not less but more relevant than ever. The first section focuses on Marx's biography, which is both appropriate but also significant in a Chinese context. The second section introduces the basic premises before leading to the situation in China. The third and final section is the longest and most significant, for it develops nine topics concerning the importance of Marxism for China. Each of these nine topics begins by quoting texts from both Marx and Engels, which are then used to explicate the developments of Chinese Marxism. Notably, it is an interpretation that takes place after 70 years of socialism in power. As Lenin and Mao said repeatedly, it is relatively easy to gain power through a Communist revolution, but the task of

---

[4]This booklet form is the text I cite in what follows. Where a quotation appears without an immediate source cited, it comes from the Marx speech.

[5]By contrast, the widely studied collection *The Governance of China*—now at three volumes—has been translated into many languages.

[6]As one might expect, the Chinese scholarly literature on Xi Jinping's increasingly voluminous output is immense, even if we restrict our focus to Marxism. For this reason, I exercise a very strict discipline in citations. I draw on only widely read items that focus on the background in Marx and Engels, and have been published in journals that are 'core [*hexin*] journals' and are on the CSSCI list of quality journals. As for the Marx speech as a whole, I cite here the most authoritative and widely read analyses (Liu H. 2018; Liu J. 2018).

constructing socialism, let alone Communism, is infinitely more complex. This is Xi's perspective.

Marx's biography takes up the initial part of the speech, where Xi hits the main points of Marx's ideas, the meeting with Engels, the development of the first outline of historical materialism in *The German Ideology*, the profound influence of the 'Communist Manifesto' and the detailed labour involved in *Capital*. So much is well-known, but I am intrigued by a particular emphasis: Marx came from a situation—a lawyer's family of Jewish background in the Rhineland-Palatinate town of Trier—that may have set him up for a comfortable and unremarkable life. But he and Jenny did not do so. They found themselves exiles and pariahs, mostly through circumstances beyond their control but also due to the direction of their thought and action. Xi stresses the hardship of a life on the run, all for the sake of what became the Communist cause. Why this emphasis? Is it a species of 'hero worship'? Not really, for it draws on two themes in Chinese culture, themes that stand in tension with one another. On the one hand, one desires a life of good fortune and opportunity, not least for the benefit of the children, but also so that one may care adequately for one's parents in their dotage. On the other hand, one's calling is not merely to the family, however wide it may be. It is ultimately and more importantly to society as a whole. Thus, even though one may aspire to a quiet and secure life, Karl and Jenny's path is by far the more admirable calling (Jin 2018).[7]

10.3 Marxism in China

As the speech unfolds, Xi identifies four premises of Marxism: it is scientific and not utopian; it is a theory of the people's hope for a society without oppression and exploitation, and not a ruling-class theory; it is a theory of practice, specifically the practice of liberation; it is an open and developing theory, a guide to action rather than a dogma (*jiaotiao*). These four premises are what one would expect in light of the Marxist tradition, and they will unfold as the speech progresses.

10.3.1 Scientific Socialism

Let me emphasise here scientific rather than utopian socialism, which is also expressed as seeking truth from facts (Cai 2018, 7). This emphasis is drawn from Engels's well-known pamphlet (Engels 1880b, 1880a) which sought to acknowledge the prior influence of European utopian socialism (Saint-Simon, Fourier, Proudhon, and so on), but also marks out the difference of the method he and Marx had hammered

[7]Given the way Marx's life resonates so deeply with Chinese assumptions, it should be no surprise that by far the most visitors to the tiny two-room apartment in Dean Street, Soho, should be Chinese. Or indeed that Trier, Marx's birthplace, was a prime destination for Chinese people in 2018.

out: this was to put the whole movement on a thoroughly scientific basis. In China, such a scientific emphasis is seen to be even more necessary 'after October', after the proletarian revolution led by the Communist Party, and in the long and arduous task of constructing socialism. Of course, science needs philosophy, as Xi emphasised in an earlier speech—which I have discussed in detail in the introductory chapter—where he quotes Engels: 'a nation that wants to climb the pinnacles of science cannot possibly manage without theoretical thought for a moment' (Xi 2016c, 2; Engels 1882e, 437; 1882b, 332; 1882a, 340). These emphases stand in contrast to the constant danger in Western Marxism of falling back on utopian tendencies, especially in light of the specific religious background of European culture and the long history of seeking revolutionary transformation but never achieving it (Losurdo 2008, 2017). But does this mean that Chinese Marxism eschews all forms of what Ernst Bloch called the 'warm stream' of Marxism, the appeal to the heart as well as to the mind (Bloch 1985, 235–241; 1995, 205–210; see further Boer 2016)? Not at all, although it takes a specific form in China. As we will see later, Xi Jinping in particular has emphasised 'faith' and 'trust [*xinyang*]' in Marxism, which is the 'spiritual calcium [*jingshen zhigai*]' of Communists (Yuan and Li 2016, 18–19; Liu J. 2018, 10). This is far from the type of utopian socialism—in Chinese literally 'empty-thought socialism [*kongxiang shehuizhuyi*]'—that relies on a form of ontological transcendence (see Sect. 6.3.2).

10.3.2 Marxism and Anti-colonial Struggles

Another significant emphasis of the speech is that Marxism is a 'guide to action' rather than a dogma. I will address this emphasis in the conclusion, but here I would like to connect it the next step in Xi's speech: the development of the Marxist tradition, which he identifies as beginning with 'The Manifesto of the Communist Party'. The way he presents it is crucial: initially, the theory of Marx and Engels inspired global workers' movements and political parties, which took hold of their own destiny; with Lenin and the October Revolution, there was a crucial shift from theory to practice, in revolution and the construction of socialism; after the Second World War, more revolutions—such as China—developed yet another level of global socialist development; crucially, Marxism through Lenin inspired national liberation movements in colonised and semi-colonised countries, with more and more countries achieving liberation from colonial masters in the second half of the twentieth century. As one would expect, Xi has a particular interest in how these developments relate to China, observing that Marx wrote a dozen or so articles denouncing Western invasions of China, defending justice for the Chinese people, and even speaking of 'Chinese socialism' and the 'Chinese republic' (Xi 2018b, 6; Marx and Engels 1850a, 265; 1850c, 220; 1850b, 267).[8] But it was not that Marxism simply happened in China,

[8]The articles in question were published between 1853 and 1860 in English in the *New York Daily Tribune* (Marx 1853, 1857a, 1857b, 1857c, 1857d, 1857e, 1858b, 1858c, 1858d, 1858e; Marx and

or that it was imposed on the country. Xi reiterates a point made many times before: Marxism was the specific choice of the Chinese people and the Communist Party, since it was the only way to overcome a century of colonial humiliation and begin the path to a New China (see also Liu J. 2018, 8).

Although I have discussed the importance of anti-colonial struggles for the Communist movement in the chapter on human rights (Sect. 7.4.2), some further observations are needed here, especially since a number of Western Marxists have unfortunately forgotten or neglected this important point. This neglect is quite surprising, for Marx and Engels addressed the question directly and on many occasions. As Losurdo emphasises, class struggle is clearly not restricted in their works to the bourgeoisie and proletariat, but includes in its very structure and articulation anti-colonial struggles against capitalist imperialism (Losurdo 2013, 2016). So too with Lenin on imperialism and the national question, but especially with clear insight by Stalin in the Soviet Union of the 1930s. It became apparent not only that the October Revolution was also a revolution of national liberation, but also that the global anti-colonial struggle was the logical outcome and that the Soviet Union should be supporting struggles as a new form of global class struggle and revolution (Boer 2017, 168–172). In other words, Marxism in its focus on overthrowing capitalist imperialism is also a deeply anti-colonial project or, as is the preferred terminology in China now, the struggle against hegemony.

As Xi Jinping puts it, the Marxist-inspired anti-colonial struggles and the liberation that followed ‘completely disrupted the imperial colonial system’. In many respects, China today—with other socialist states and indeed developing countries that were formerly colonised—carries on this project (Liu H. 2018, 81). The eventual achievement of this project is cast in terms of a ‘great rejuvenation [*fuxing*]’ and a ‘strong socialistically modernised country [*shehuizhuyi xiandaihua qiangguo*]’, which entails three great leaps: the ‘great leap [*weida feiyue*]’ China undertook, under Communist Party leadership, from being the ‘sick man [*bingfu*]’ of Asia to a liberated country; the ‘great leap’ of the Reform and Opening-Up, which has led to China becoming a country of abundance; and the ‘great leap’ of the new era, which will lead to China being not only abundant, but also strong.[9] As I write, it is common to speak in China of the ‘leap from prosperity to strength [*cong fu qilai dao qiang qilai*]’, or as one may also put it, a dialectical leap that entails not simply ‘catching up’ with developed countries, but of undertaking a leap that follows its own socialist path.

Engels 1858; Marx 1859a; 1859b; 1860). One may also consult a collection entitled *Marx on China*, where most of the articles are gathered (Marx 1951). To be added here are a couple of further articles by Engels (Engels 1857a, 1857b), although he was also responsible for actually writing a number of the articles on China, even though they are attributed to Marx.

[9]The fuller phrase for this leap is ‘the great Chinese dream of rejuvenation [*weida fuxing de Zhongguo meng*]’ or ‘renaissance’ (Xi 2017c, 1, 5, 12, 28; Shi 2013).

10.4 Study Marx

After a section on China's longer history in light of Marxism—from its ancient civilisation, through humiliation at the hands of foreign powers, to liberation and rejuvenation through the Communist Party—Xi comes to his main topic: why Marx and Engels should be studied today.[10] Here we find the reason why the text of this speech was initially published in a number of Party-building journals, for Xi urges all Party members, and indeed all people, to study Marx once again in the new era. One may ask: should not Communist Party members always study Marx and Engels, let alone the Marxist tradition? Of course, but if you ask an old Party member in China, they will tell you that there was a time in the early 2000s and before Xi's tenure when this was not always the case. Indeed, it was not so uncommon for even senior Party leaders to have only a rudimentary knowledge of Marxism. I can add here that I have met more than a decade ago the occasional Party member who opined that 'Marxism is rubbish'. Fully aware of what was becoming a parlous situation, one of the signature emphases by Xi Jinping and the collective leadership has been on the need to enhance one's knowledge of Marxism not merely through formal education, but also throughout one's life (Liu J. 2018, 11).

In this speech, Xi focuses on nine topics, each beginning with a quotation or two from Marx and Engels, followed by an elaboration of the point in a Chinese context. Why these nine? As Liu Jianjun (2018, 9) observes, the purpose of the speech is 'neither to build a theoretical system, nor for the sake of pure theoretical research, but to guide the cause of socialist construction in China'. In what follows, I begin each point by identifying and—if necessary—providing some background to the quotations from Marx and Engels, after which I analyse Xi's interpretation in a Chinese context.

*10.4.1 Development of Human Society (*renlei shehui fazhan*)*

The first quotation comes from the Communist Manifesto, where Marx and Engels speak of a future society, beyond bourgeois society, which will be 'an association, in which the free development of each is the condition for the free development of all'. And in the words of the final flourish of the Manifesto, 'The proletarians have nothing to lose but their chains. They have a world to win' (Marx and Engels 1848a,

[10]I cite here the most comprehensive and widely-read studies of the Marxist foundations of what is now called 'Xi Jinping Thought on Socialism with Chinese Characteristics in a New Era' (Wang W. 2014, 2015, 2017; Cai 2018; Guo and Liu 2018; Jia 2018), although we need to note the warning of Wang Xinyan (2018, 12–13) that Xi Jinping's approach does not arise simply from Marx and Engels—as though it were a type of Western reform movement seeking the 'original'—but that it must be understood in light of the whole development of the sinification of Marxism.

53; 1848b, 482; 1848c, 506).[11] The Chinese translation of '*Assoziation*' is '*lianheti*', which designates an organic whole, a connectivity of all parts. It is, of course, another way of speaking of Communism.

Clearly, Xi does not shy away from the task of achieving Communism, specifically from within the realities of constructing socialism in China today (Wei 2018, 141). Communism is the final goal of the process, although one may identify glimpses in the here and now. But this emphasis does raise a question: is the Communism Xi mentions a utopian and transcendent ideal, forever delayed because it is ultimately unachievable? It may be all very well to uphold an ideal from the core text of the whole Marxist tradition, but is it merely a rhetorical flourish characteristic of politicians? If one comes from the Western political tradition, these may be one's assumptions: politicians are not to be trusted, for they like to speak empty and meaningless phrases that have little connection with the everyday lives of common people. We may add here a suspicion in some quarters of an emphasis on stages—with socialism in its preliminary and mature stages and then finally Communism—as a way to avoid Communism as such since it is so far in the future.

Once again, we need to put aside the tendency to deploy *yixi jiezhong*, using Western approaches to understand China. Recall the analysis in the chapter on *xiaokang* society (Sect. 6.3.2), where I pointed out that in the Chinese tradition the world of *datong*, the Great Harmony, is not one of speculation, imagination, and rumour, a world determined by ontological transcendence and thus unknowable by ordinary human abilities. For a Chinese approach, this world is not one that is beyond our knowledge and expertise, not an imagined utopia or 'no-place'. Instead, it is a verifiable and recorded society; one can see it and read about it in reliable records. In other words, it will be an empirical reality.

In Xi Jinping's hands, this emphasis becomes the inevitable process of human history, of mastering the development of human society, of confidence in and adherence to the ideals and beliefs of Communism. Let us see how this works. Some key phrases provide an insight: Xi speaks of realising the goal 'step by step [*yibuyibu*]'; the constantly changing 'actual [*xiancun*] movement of the existent [*xiancun*] situation'; and that the historical process of actualising Communism entails 'one-by-one phased goals [*yige yige jieduanxing mubiao*]' and is 'reached [*dacheng*]' progressively or 'step by step [*zhubu*]'. In other words, the achievement of Communism requires careful planning, implementation, and assessment. One does not simply sit back and dream about it; instead, one gets to work and seeks to achieve what is possible in the here and now, setting in place yet more foundations upon which generations to come are able to build. I cannot emphasise this point enough, for it is difficult indeed for Westerners to understand: the eventual achievement of Communism needs careful planning, much testing, trial and error, considerable effort—in short, it entails 'struggle for all one's life [*fendou zhongshen*]', as Xi puts it at the close of this first point.

---

[11] Given the importance of the citations in this section, I cite them in this order: Chinese text, original language, and English translation. With one exception, all of the Chinese quotations are drawn from the authoritative scholarly edition, *Makesi Engesi wenji*, published in 2009.

10.4.2 *Sticking to the People's Standpoint* (jianshou renmin lichang*)*

On this point, the key quotation comes from *The Holy Family*: 'Historical activity is the activity of the masses' (Marx and Engels 1845c, 287),[12] which becomes the basis for a resolute focus on the people and the mass line. Earlier, I discussed the importance of the mass line and the emphasis on a 'people-centred [*yi renmin wei zhongxin*]' approach, which is also expressed in terms of 'putting the people first [*yiren weiben*]', or 'people as masters of the country [*renmin dangjia zuozhu*]'. As I pointed out there (Sect. 8.1), in many respects this is the essence of a Chinese approach to socialist democracy, but here Xi points out that the 'people's standpoint' is one of the fundamental features of the Communist Party and socialist governance, based upon the work of Marx and Engels (see also Xi 2013b, 27–28; 2020b, 4–5; Xiao and Tian 2016; Yuan and Li 2016, 18; Guo and Liu 2018, 38; Xiong 2019). It may be seen as the underlying factor for a range of projects, such as poverty alleviation, ecological civilisation, and the drive to a *xiaokang* society. But let us see how Xi develops the point.

For Xi, the people's standpoint (*lichang*) is basic and foundational (*genben*). Three times does Xi use *genben*—foundational—to indicate the Party's stand, mission, and purpose. What mission? The people's well-being and happiness. What purpose? Serving the people with one's whole heart and whole mind (*quanxin quanyi*). This is followed by the invocation not only of Mao—in terms of the mass line and keeping flesh-and-blood ties (*xuerou lianxi*)—but also of a slogan Xi had already stressed at the nineteenth congress of the CPC (November 2017): 'forget not the original desire, keep in mind the mission [*bu wang chuxin, laoji shiming*]' (see also Xi 2016a). The original desire and the mission are, of course, one and the same: Communism.

This is all very well, but is it really the case? I could draw upon an impressive array of internationally collated surveys on confidence in the direction China is going, on trust in governance and public institutions, or in approval of the way the COVID-19 pandemic was handled in China (Ipsos 2019; Edelman 2020; Cunningham et al. 2020). In all such surveys, we repeatedly find a percentage range from the 80s to the 90s for confidence, trust, and approval among the common people for governance as such. But I would like to add some anecdotal evidence from reasonably extensive engagement with common people (*laobaixing*), with urban and rural workers. Perhaps a decade ago, the joke among such people was that the government might say it is focused on the *renmin*, the people, but that it was actually concerned with the *renminbi*, the alternative name for the Chinese yuan. In the last few years, I have noticed a distinct change: now people increasingly feel Xi is 'pretty good [*bucuo*]'.

---

[12]The quotation is actually the first part of an effort to render a somewhat difficult sentence in the original German, which may be translated as: 'Together with the thoroughness of the historical action [*geschichtlichen Aktion*], the size of the mass whose action it is [*der Masse … deren Aktion sie ist]* will therefore increase' (Marx and Engels 1845b, 86).

How so? He invokes Mao Zedong and is felt to have the common people's interests at heart.[13]

10.4.3 *Productive Forces and Relations of Production* (shengchanli he shengchan guanxi)

The quotation around which this important point turns comes from Marx and Engels's *The German Ideology*: 'the amount of productive forces accessible to human beings determines the condition of society' (Marx and Engels 1846a, 533; 1845a, 30; 1846b, 43). I hardly need to point out that this is a well-known feature of dialectical and historical materialism: not only is the 'base [*jichu*]' determinative, but the economic base and superstructure—or the productive forces and the realms of society, culture, politics, and philosophy—act in a dialectical manner of mutual constraint and advance, so as to become the motor of development. As an inheritor of Marxist dialectical analysis, Xi Jinping reasserts such an approach (see also Xi 2020b, 2–3; Cai 2018, 6; Guo and Liu 2018, 40).

But now he makes a crucial move: Marxist political economy also provides the basis for socialist construction in terms of liberating (*jiefang*) and advancing (*fazhan*) the productive forces, as well as the constant need to adjust the relationship between productive forces and relations of production (Wei 2018).[14] I have presented in some detail this emphasis in the chapters on Deng Xiaoping (whom Xi invokes) and the on socialist market economy, so I have no need to repeat that material here. But I do want to observe that too many Marxists have taken the method from Marx and Engels and applied it mostly to the capitalist market economy. But this move is actually a retreat from their work: thus, it is not for nothing that Xi quotes from the opening section of *The German Ideology*, for here we also find the first real outline of the history of modes of production. And if this works for earlier history, it also works for future history, namely, the construction of socialism. Further, Xi stresses the insight from Deng Xiaoping that the liberation of the productive forces is the core project of socialism, so as to provide the economic foundation for Communism. This emphasis may have lifted China from being one of the poorest countries in the world to being a serious global economic force, but the process is by no means over, for—as he does on many occasions—Xi stresses that further liberation is needed, that the relations between base and superstructure need constant refining and adjusting, and that the Reform and Opening-Up—as a revolutionary socialist project—must be deepened (see Sect. 4.3.1).

[13]On the importance of 'gripping the masses'—to allude to Marx's famous formulation—and the concrete reality of people's everyday in the popularisation of Marxism and the need to move beyond the 'simple worship of textual propaganda', see Gong and Qiao (2018).

[14]For a detailed analysis of how Marxist political economy is the key to China's socialist development in the eyes of Xi Jinping, see Fang Yumei's careful analysis in light of the work of Marx and Engels (Fang 2018).

This is all very well, but one may ask: what has happened to the other side of the socialist dialectic, to the ownership of the means of production? Marx and Engels may have emphasised the liberation of the forces of production (an emphasis recovered by Deng Xiaoping), but they also stressed ownership of these means by the proletariat. I use again a quotation from the 'Communist Manifesto': 'The proletariat will use its political supremacy to wrest, by degrees, all capital from the bourgeoisie, to centralise all instruments of production in the hands of the State, i.e., of the proletariat organised as the ruling class; and to increase the total of productive forces as rapidly as possible [*kuai de zengjia shengchanli*]' (Marx and Engels 1848a, 52; 1848b, 481; 1848c, 504).[15] The socialist project—as I have emphasised earlier (Sects. 2.3 and 5.3.1)—involves both liberation and ownership, both the means and relations of production, albeit always recalibrated in light of changing circumstances.[16]

To answer my earlier question, we need to turn to another piece by Xi on Marxist political economy (Xi 2020a, 2020c; see also Cheng 2018, 6–7).[17] In the introduction to this text, Xi reiterates the increased relevance of Marxist political economy for understanding the repeated crises of capitalist systems, especially the contradiction between socialised production and private ownership of the means of production, and he outlines the history of Marxist political economy in China's own development path. But his main emphasis is on how Marxist political economy, and not other economic theories, remains the guide for plotting China's development in the current situation. He does so through six points, but let us focus on the third point: 'ownership of the means of production is the core of the relations of production' (Xi 2020a, 4; 2020c, 3). Note the emphasis: when speaking of the relations of production, ownership of the means of production is the key and determines the nature of a society and its development path. Thus, a dominance of private ownership means a capitalist society and basic economic system, while public ownership indicates a 'basic socialist economic system [*shehuizhuyi jiben jingji zhidu*]'. Why, then, does China's current system allow private ownership? In assessing the realities of the long period of the primary stage of socialism, the policy is to stress public ownership as the mainstay and allowing—and indeed nurturing—other forms of ownership to exist alongside. Ideally, they should support and reinforce one another. Lest one think that this is the beginning of a slippery slope to the dominance of privatised ownership of the means of production (as has been asserted with wearying frequency by some foreign 'observers' since the 1980s), Xi is unequivocal: 'we must be extremely clear that our nation's basic economic system is an important pillar of the Chinese socialist

[15]Engels would repeat this dual emphasis on a number of occasions (Engels 1877a, 460; 1877b, 109; 1877c, 193; 1894b, 299; 1894c, 536; 1894a, 269–270).

[16]Elsewhere, I have analysed the differences between Marxism in developed economies, where ownership of the means of production is (over-)emphasised, and in 'backward' and developing economies, where the project after a proletarian revolution was more concerned with liberating the productive forces so as to overcome endemic poverty (Boer 2020).

[17]The article was originally a speech given in November of 2015 at a CPC Central Committee Politburo study session. Xi has had an abiding interest in Marxist political economy at least since his Doctor of Laws thesis at Tsinghua University (Xi 2001; see also 2016c, 8; 2021b; Jiang 2016; Gu 2019).

system and the basis of the socialist market economy, and therefore the dominant role of public ownership and the leading role of the state sector must not change' (Xi 2020a, 4; 2020c, 4).

Has Xi Jinping shifted, then, from emphasising the liberation of the forces of production to public ownership? Not at all, for the text on Marxist political economy acknowledges the importance of Deng Xiaoping's emphasis on liberating the forces of production, as well as stressing the need to uphold reforms so as to develop the socialist market economy. Not only is this a 'great pioneering effort' in leveraging the strengths of a market economy and of a socialist system, but it is a market economy that has developed in the context of a socialist system. Thus, the 'term "socialist" is the key descriptor, and this is something that we must never lose sight of'. Further, 'we call our economy a socialist market economy because we are committed to maintaining the strengths of our system while effectively avoiding the deficiencies of a capitalist market economy' (Xi 2020a, 5; 2020c, 4). The text addresses other questions, such as a 'people centred [*yi renmin wei zhongxin*]' approach (see above), the new development philosophy that is innovative, coordinated, green, open, and shared, and the importance of opening up and distribution so as to address wealth inequalities (see also Dong and Bai 2018). But my concern here has been to focus on the necessary dialectical interplay of both liberating the forces of production and common ownership.

*10.4.4 People's Democracy (*renmin minzhu*)*

Much has already been said in Chapters 7–9 on the whole system of China's socialist democracy, so here I focus on Xi's emphases. As this point in his speech indicates, Xi Jinping has for some time been emphasising socialist democracy, but he has also given the implicit go ahead—in light of the urging to tell China's story well throughout the world—for Chinese speakers to address this question directly in international contexts (as I have experienced with increasing frequency within and outside China).[18] On this occasion, Xi quotes two texts by Marx and Engels, the first from the 'Communist Manifesto': 'The proletarian movement is the independent movement of the immense majority, in the interest of the immense majority' (Marx and Engels 1848a, 42; 1848b, 472; 1848c, 495). And: 'The working class, once come to power, could not go on managing with the old state machine', for it requires a 'replacement by a new and truly democratic state power [*guojia zhengquan*]' (Engels 1891b, 110–111; 1891a, 14–15; 1891c, 189–190). While the first text focuses on the quantitative superiority of socialist democracy in terms of giving genuine voice to the vast majority of rural and urban workers, the second concerns the qualitative

[18]By now, the occasions on which Xi Jinping has spoken of socialist democracy are quite numerous. For example, one may usefully consult the three volumes of *The Governance of China*, as well as some more specific texts within those volumes (for example, Xi 2014a, 2014b).

difference of the new system, which requires a new and 'truly democratic [*zhenzheng minzhu*]' system.

I would like to dwell on the second quotation for a few moments, for it is the more intriguing and extremely important. It comes from Engels's 1891 introduction to the third edition of Marx's *The Civil War in France*. Why this text and not the one we find in *The Civil War in France* itself, which has—in the original English—'But the working class cannot simply lay hold of the ready-made State machinery, and wield it for its own purposes' (Marx 1871, 137)? Why indeed, for they seem to say largely the same? Let me draw some material from the previous chapter and set the context. In the 1890s, Engels was struggling against both the moderating trend of the German Social-Democratic Party and an entrenched anarchist position (first clearly articulated in the 1870s). The moderates wanted to dispense with any notion of violent revolution and dictatorship of the proletariat after such a revolution, while the Anarchists insisted that the first act after the seizure of power should be an active 'abolition [*Abschaffung*]' of the state. Thus, the moderate right-wing sought to work within the structures of the bourgeois state and the Anarchists trenchantly asserted that any type of state was an evil. Engels would have nothing of either position: in a series of crucial texts (Engels 1890a, 1891a, 1891d, 1895a), he argued, on the one hand, that the Paris commune was also very much the proletarian dictatorship, and, on the other, that the ensuing structure would have many complex governing functions. One feature of this new structure was that it would be 'truly democratic'.

Given its importance, the specific text by Engels introducing Marx's *The Civil War in France* needs some more attention, especially the second sentence from which Xi Jinping quotes. Engels writes: 'This shattering [*Sprengung*] of the former state power [*Staatsmacht*] and its replacement by a new and truly democratic one [*eine neue, in Wahrheit demokratische*] is described in detail in the third section of *The Civil War*' (Engels 1891a, 14–15). Understanding this sentence is crucial. Notably, Engels does not say explicitly that it would be a new form of a 'state': the word itself is left out when he writes of a 'new and truly democratic …'. Given his earlier definition of the state as a 'separated public power' in *The Origin of the Family*, he could not use 'state' to speak of the new form of governance after a proletarian revolution. However, as we saw in the previous chapter (Sect. 9.2.3), both he and Marx do write of the continuance of a 'public power [*die öffentliche Gewalt*]' that would not be separated but stand in the midst of society and would lose its 'political character', by which they mean the realities of class struggle and politicisation of all aspects of life in light of such struggle. Further, this non-politicised public power, which is enmeshed within society, would entail a whole range of sophisticated governing functions, with a focus on managing the economy and watching out for the true interests of society (Engels 1873a, 86; 1873c, 425; see further Boer, in press).

Back to the sentence on which we have been focusing: its logic leads to the position that a new and truly democratic form of enmeshed governance will arise. Engels may have been reluctant to call this new form of governance a 'state' as such, but Lenin would take the step: drawing on Marx's comments on a 'future state' and even a 'workers' state [*gongren guijia*]', Lenin spoke explicitly of a 'proletarian state', while Stalin was even clearer, speaking of an 'entirely new, Socialist state (*sotsialisticheskoe gosudarstvo*), without precedent in history' (Marx 1875c, 444; 1875e, 21; 1875b, 94; 1875a, 407; 1875d, 635; 1875f, 520; Lenin 1917b, 1917a, 1917c; Stalin 1939c, 264; 1939a, 336; 1939b, 421–422). This development in the Marxist tradition leads Xi to identify already in Engels words the outlines of such a new 'state political power [*guojia zhengquan*]' (Engels 1891b, 111; Xi 2018b, 10).[19] From this basis, Xi argues that China must continue to build 'socialist democratic politics [*shehuizhuyi minzhu zhengzhi*]'. What does this mean? It entails an 'organic unity [*youji tongyi*]' of the components of socialist democracy that I have discussed in some detail in the previous three chapters (see also Xi 2014a, 287–288, 290). Or, as Xi sums up, socialist democracy entails that the people are masters in the house (*dengjia zuozhu*), supervising the servants of society (*shehui gongpu*) through the socialist rule of law and institutional guarantees. Elsewhere, Xi emphasises a number of related themes, such as the fact that democracy comes in a variety of forms and that there is no universal form of democracy that should be rigidly imposed everywhere (Xi 2014b, 291), or the related need to develop a political system appropriate to a country's history, culture, and system and not simply import a model that may have worked elsewhere for a time but would lead to chaos in China (Xi 2014a, 285–286),[20] or the complementary roles of electoral and consultative democracy (Xi 2014b, 293), or—as we saw in the previous chapter—the specific identification of the overall democratic system in China as 'democratic centralism'.[21] As this point of the speech makes clear, ultimately all of the these aspects are framed in terms of developing a new and truly democratic form of socialist governance.

*10.4.5 Cultural Construction (*wenhua jianshe*)*

Here Xi Jinping does not quote Marx or Engels directly. Instead, he points out that Marx 'held that in different [*butong*] economic and social environments, people produce different thoughts [*sixiang*] and cultures'. This awareness actually entailed some struggle on Marx's part, for he had assumed that the positions he had developed in a Western European context were universal. Only late in life, as he engaged more with developments in other parts of the world, did he come to realise that his insights were in many cases 'expressly limited [*expressément restreinte*] to the countries of

---

[19] The Chinese translations offer, in both the *Wenji* and *Xuanji*, '*xin de zhenzheng minzhu de guojia zhengquan* [state political power]', and, in the earlier (1972) *Quanji*, '*xin de zhenzheng minzhu de guojia quanli* [state power]'.

[20] In terms of the earthy metaphors of which Xi is fond: 'The reason why the socialist political system with Chinese characteristics is feasible, viable, and efficient is that it grew out of the soil of Chinese society. The political system of socialism with Chinese characteristics has been and is growing in China's social soil, and it must be deeply rooted in China's social soil if it is to continue to thrive in the future' (Xi 2014d, 12).

[21] At times, Xi goes further and argues that mutual non-interference (and thus multi-polarity) in international relations is democratic, and the opposite of an international imperialist dictatorship or oligarchy by former colonial powers (Xi 2017a, 540).

Western Europe' (Marx 1881e, 589; 1881f, 241; 1881g, 71). This observation comes from a letter to Vera Zasulich, which was finally sent after four drafts, the first three much longer than the final letter (Marx 1881h, 1881a, 1881j, 1881i). In these drafts, we find a Marx struggling in light of his growing awareness of different histories and developments. Like a good old German philosopher, he had assumed that German philosophy, if not Western European philosophy, was 'philosophy' per se. Now he finds increasingly that this is not the case.

The specific question Zasulich[22] had asked Marx concerned a topic of significant debate among the various socialist circles in Russia at the time: would the agricultural or village commune, with its relics of collective property and practices of field shares, enable a different path to socialism, or did Russia too have to undergo all of the stages of capitalism found in Western Europe before the possibility of a proletarian revolution arose and the construction of socialism might begin. Initially, Marx tackled the specific question concerning the village commune, drawing on research in which Engels was engaged at the time (Engels 1882c, 1882d), and arguing that the village commune too would inevitably be drawn into capitalist relations. As the drafts proceed, Marx realises that the more substantial question concerned the historical path to socialism: did Russia have to follow the same path as Western Europe? Drawing from *Capital*—which was widely studied in Russia at the time—and his research into the thorough expropriation of the agricultural producer that had been and was still being undertaken in Western Europe, Marx comes to his conclusion: no, these capitalist processes are expressly limited to Western Europe. By implication: economic and social conditions, in light of their histories, are in fact not the same. This means that their potential paths to socialism will also have distinct differences. It should be no surprise that these letter drafts and the succinct letter itself are the subject of continuing study in China since there has always been a great awareness of the distinctness of Chinese history, political development, and culture (Marx 1881b, 1881c, 1881d, 1881e; Feng 2009; Sha 2010; Yu 2013).

To return to the Marx speech: in order to explicate how China's context works for the sake of cultural construction, Xi draws on a Marxist staple, which runs from Marx and Engels onward through the whole tradition. While ideology and culture are ultimately determined by the economic base, they also respond to and influence the base. Marxist theory is the obvious example, for it comes—through the Communist Party—to grip the masses and become a material force (see also Xi 2011, 20). But only advanced theory, advanced Marxist philosophy and culture, can become such a force. By contrast, if culture and ideology are backward, they become fetters on social development.

But what culture? Here I reiterate some points made earlier: the Chinese term *wenhua* (文化), culture, is a much broader concept than 'culture' in English. It embraces all of the dimensions of what may be called the 'superstructure', but also history, politics, and philosophy.[23] The term combines *wen* (文), with the senses of

[22]The letter from Zasulich was originally published in Russian in 1924, with an English translation eventually available (Zasulich 1881b, 1881a).

[23]For a very useful overview of Chinese culture, see Gan Chunsong's recent book, which has been translated into English (Gan 2019).

language, script, literature, and thus culture, and *hua* (化), which means to transform, to make into, and thus to '...ise', as in 'Sinicisation' or perhaps better 'Sinification [*zhongguohua*]'. Thus *wenhua* means the constant transformation and renewal of a cultural tradition, a tradition that tends to be understood as a written tradition. Tao Delin can put it better than I:

> Culture seems the 'softest' at the first glance, but actually it is the 'hardest'. It ... refers to tenacious vitality, extensive coverage, and strong penetration. Culture is the spiritual pillar, i.e., the soul and backbone often mentioned by the people, to maintain the human community (including nation and state). The culture of any community will develop and change with the living environment and social system, but a lot of things will be necessarily deposited and turn into relatively stable characteristics. (Tao 2014, 247)

In this light, it is common to distinguish between Chinese culture and 'Western' culture, but one also finds—admittedly to a lesser extent—contrasts with Russian, or Latin American, or Pacific cultures. This is all very well, but what has Marxism got to do with it? Historical examples are useful, such as the mutual transformation of Confucian and Daoist emphases, or the whole process of Neo-Confucianism that arose initially during the Tang Dynasty (from the eight century CE) and flourished during the Northern Song Dynasty, especially in the eleventh century CE. In this case, the conjunction of philosophical reflection, moral self-cultivation, and social service came primarily as a response to the more esoteric and spiritual dimensions of both Buddhism and Daoism.[24] Analogously, we see how Marxism has been reshaping and renewing Chinese culture in the last century or so. This has been a renewed emphasis by Xi Jinping, who clearly sides with the Communist tradition's emphasis on drawing upon and transforming what is best of earlier cultural traditions rather than simply abolishing them for the sake of the new (Bao 2017, 31–33; Zhang Z. 2017). As he pointed out at the 2565th anniversary of Confucius: 'Chinese Communists are Marxists, adhering to Marxist scientific theories and upholding and developing socialism with Chinese characteristics, but Chinese Communists are neither historical nihilists nor cultural nihilists'. Instead, 'Marxism must be closely integrated with China's actual conditions', arming itself with and treating in a scientific manner China's fine cultural traditions as well as those of other countries (Xi 2014c, 12; see also 2016c, 8). In this light do we find the promotion of a socialist 'spiritual civilisation [*jingshen wenming*]', an emphasis on 'core socialist values [*shehuizhuyi hexin jiazhiguan*]',[25] the importance of 'rule of virtue [*dezhi*]' in conjunction with 'rule of law' (see Sects. 8.6.2 and 8.6.4), all for the sake of developing an 'advanced socialist culture'. For Xi and many others, socialist culture is increasingly seen as

[24] Conversely, Buddhism too and even the earlier Christianity brought by Matteo Ricci had to become 'sinified' in order to be accepted in China (Tao 2014, 253–254).

[25] The core socialist values, which have now been assiduously promoted for the last few years, are: prosperity and strength (*fuqiang*); democracy (*minzhu*); civilisation (*wenming*); harmony (*hexie*); freedom (*ziyou*); equality (*pingdeng*); justice (*gongzheng*); rule of law (*fazhi*); love of country (*aiguo*); dedication (*jingye*); honesty and trustworthiness (*chengxin*); friendship (*youshan*). Apart from the key statement by the CPC Central Committee, I cite here the most important and widely-read studies (CPC Central Committee 2013; Tao 2014; Han and Zhang 2018).

central to a 'creative transformation' and 'innovative development' of this long-standing and constantly changing tradition of Chinese culture.

*10.4.6 Social Construction (*shehui jianshe*)*

On the question of social construction—as distinct from but obviously related to productive forces, the people's standpoint, and culture—Xi Jinping quotes from three texts. Note the emphasis in these quotations: for all, of all, by all, and to all. The first comes from Marx's economic manuscripts of 1857–1858 (also known as the *Grundrisse*), where Marx observes that 'production will now be calculated to provide wealth for all' (Marx 1858f, 200; 1858g, 584; 1858a, 94).[26] The second is a well-known text in China—Engels's Communist catechism, which became a major basis for the later 'Communist Manifesto'. Here Engels observes that a communist society would enable 'the participation of all in the material benefits created by all' (Engels 1847a, 689; 1847b, 377; 1847c, 354). The third text—originally in English—sums up the direction of the previous two, if not the aims of Communism itself: a socialist society should 'give healthy and useful labour to all, ample wealth and leisure to all, and the truest and fullest freedom to all' (Engels 1887a, 570; 1887b, 482).[27]

As mentioned earlier, the emphasis is clearly on all people—*suoyou de ren*—which is repeated in each quotation. Or as Xi puts it in terms of the new primary contradiction in China, people long for a 'beautiful and good life [*meihao shenghuo*]'.[28] What does this mean? Abstractly, it means improving livelihood, social justice and better education; practically, Xi identifies adequate income for labour, medical care for the sick, support for the aged, housing in which to live, and support for the frail. In short, it entails not so much a 'welfare safety net' found in some capitalist market economies, but 'common prosperity [*gongtong fuyu*] for the whole people' and not merely for a few (Zhou H. 2017). The full achievement of such a system is one of the key targets of the Fourteenth Five-Year Plan, launched in 2021. I would add that one needs a strong economic foundation to ensure such a system, for the liberation of the productive forces is the key, leading to the current situation in

[26] This is an intriguing quotation, for Marx is analysing the exacerbation of contradictions under the capitalist market economy, but as he does so, he provides glimpses of the potential of socialist society. This and other texts from the 1857–1858 manuscripts, which offer comparable glimpses, have been analysed in detail by Chinese scholars.

[27] Intriguingly, this text is not directly from Engels's hand, but from the program of the North of England Socialist Federation. Engels was asked to comment on the program, which he did at some points while approving the rest. Xi quotes from one part that Engels approved.

[28] Although I have presented in some detail the material on contradiction analysis in Chapter 3, let me quote the new primary contradiction again: 'What we now face is the contradiction between unbalanced and inadequate development and the people's ever-growing needs for a better life' (Xi 2017c, 5).

which more than 800 million urban and rural workers have been lifted out of poverty since the beginning of the Reform and Opening-Up.[29]

*10.4.7 Human-Nature Relationship (***ren yu ziran guanxi***)*

Xi Jinping has been promoting for some time the concept and practice of 'ecological civilisation [*shengtai wenming*]' (Xi 2013c). The relevant text here comes from Marx's 'Economic and Philosophic Manuscripts' of 1844. Simply put: 'Human beings live on nature' (Marx 1844a, 161; 1844c, 240; 1844d, 368; 1844b, 276). Alluding to the rest of this sentence from Marx, Xi observes that it is an interactive (*hudong*) relationship: if human beings treat nature well (*shandai*), nature will present gifts (*kuizeng*) of food—an old agricultural assumption. But—and here Xi quotes an important text by Engels—'if human beings, by dint of their knowledge and inventive genius, have subdued the forces of nature, the latter avenge themselves upon them' (Engels 1873b, 336; 1873a, 85; 1873c, 423).[30] All of this requires not simply the protection of the natural environment, as though human beings are separate from it, but working in terms of 'harmonious symbiosis [*hexie gongsheng*]' in the 'community of life [*shengming gongtongti*]', or taking seriously an organism's relation to its environment (the meaning of *shengtai*).[31]

This is all very well, one might say, but one of the standard tropes in the few countries that make up the 'West' is that China is supposedly one of the world's worst polluters, if not engaged in a 'war on nature'. At a pinch, one may focus on the 'wild 90s' (see Sect. 4.3.3) with its resolute emphasis on economic development in order to lift as many out of poverty as possible, and the attendant environmental problems that arose as China became the 'world's factory'. In fact, this is precisely the problem, since Western media outlets and others even now tend to dwell on this period as in some way normative. Witness, for example, the standard image of a day of polluted air in Beijing, which was trotted not so long ago on a regular basis, so much so that people in the West believed that it was always like this in Beijing. However, unlike the empty words of Western politicians, in China 'words have power', or, as Austin Farrar (1962) observed, words can function as 'performative acts'. So when Xi Jinping speaks of 'ecological civilisation', or that 'lucid waters and lush mountains are invaluable assets [*lüshui qingshan jiu shi jinshan yinshan*]' (Xi 2016b), or that the new philosophy of development is 'innovative, coordinated, green, open, and shared' (Xi 2020a, 3; 2020c, 3), these words have concrete effects. And as I emphasised in the chapter on a *xiaokang* society, not only

[29]For an insightful analysis of how Marx and Engels's concern with poverty and its alleviation through Communism is relevant for China and Xi Jinping's emphasis, see Zhang and Fan (2018).

[30]Scholars also refer to Engels's treatment of such matters in the section of *Dialectics of Nature* entitled 'The Part Played by Labour in the Transition from Ape to Man' (Li Chongfu 2009, 158; Engels 1882e, 550–563; 1882b, 444–455; 1882a, 452–464).

[31]There are a few insightful and systematic analyses of the roots of Xi Jinping's emphasis in the works of Marx and Engels (Zhou G. and Hu 2015; Li G. and Chen 2017; Huang 2018).

is such a society simply unachievable without ecological civilisation, it also requires immense planning, implementation, and assessment of achievements and mistakes. To restrict myself to a sample of English language publications on this matter, there is the multi-volume series published by Brill Press entitled 'Chinese Research Perspectives on the Environment', the Springer series on technical aspects of environmental improvement and energy, entitled 'Energy and Environment Research in China', and a number of other publications (Pan 2016; Su and Thomson 2016b, 2016a; Pang et al. 2018). These items are merely a sample in English; Chinese studies on environmental matters are myriad.[32]

I could also list a string of achievements in the last few years, whether in terms of afforestation (actually a much longer achievement), green power, ecological living space, and so on. But allow me to make a personal observation and return to my earlier reference to Beijing: when I first arrived in Beijing in 2009, people used to joke that they saw the sun and blue skies in the previous year of the Olympics, but that such sights were no longer possible. In 2013 I began to work in Beijing and there were regular 'yellow alerts' for smog, but also quite a few clear blue days. By 2019 I was ready to move on, but as a way of saying farewell to Beijing, I walked its length and breadth, from the mountains in the west to the plains in the east. Again and again, I encountered green projects: the waters in the many parks had been thoroughly restored, with plants and animal life; the green belts around Beijing were plentiful, so that most of my hiking—often 15–20 kms a day—was along green belts. The air? Of all the days of hiking, only one or two had moderately polluted air. The rest were clear. I was witnessing what may be called 'the greening of Beijing'. The point: ecological civilisation is not merely discussed, but enacted.

*10.4.8 World History (*shijie lishi*)*

As for world history, Xi quotes from *The German Ideology*: 'the more the original isolation of the separate nationalities is destroyed by the advanced mode of production, by intercourse and by the natural division of labour between various nations arising as a result, the more history becomes world history' (Marx and Engels 1846a, 540–541; 1845a, 45; 1846b, 50–51). This text is often used in Chinese Marxist scholarship and in the CPC, with the sense that this prediction by Marx and Engels has already come about today in an integrated world, where the one who rejects such a world will be rejected by it. Here we find phrases and slogans that have become common parlance: win–win (*gongying*—more literally 'win in common'),[33] and

[32]I cite here some of the major works from a Marxist perspective (Liu S. 2006; Du 2011; Xu and Liu 2012).

[33]The full phrase used on some occasions is 'both win, many win, all win [*shuangying, duoying, gongying*]'.

'community of common destiny for humankind [*renlei mingyun gongtongti*]' (Xi 2017a, 2021a; see further Boer and Zang 2019).[34]

Let me focus on a few items in a little more detail. I begin with Xi's observation: 'neither dependent [*yifu*] on others, nor plundering [*lüeduo*] others'. This is of course an allusion not only to the era of European colonialism, but also to hegemonic efforts that continue today by some countries. In reply, Xi draws on and maps further the long anti-colonial—or better, anti-hegemonic—project (see above). It may be seen today in the Belt and Road Initiative, as well as the Asia Infrastructure Development Bank, and the Shanghai Cooperation Organisation, if not also BRICS. Some may ask: but is not China engaged in a new form of colonialism, a 'creditor colonialism' if you will? Apart from observing that it is little rich for former colonisers to accuse China of colonialism, I am reminded of the Danish proverb: a thief always thinks everyone else is a thief. Others may ask: what about the 'global' opposition to China, so much so that today it has few if any friends? It all depends on what one means by 'global'? Somewhere between 12 and 15 'Western' countries—former colonisers all—have been ramping up the 'China threat' to some degree, although even here relatively few of even these countries are playing along with the game. The number is small indeed. If fact, even if we take the number of 'Western' countries at their full count, their combined populations comprise only 14% of the global population. More than 80% of peoples in the world live in developing countries, China included. It is precisely the experience—still in living memory in China—of grinding poverty and the need for development that provides a level of mutual understanding with other developing countries that is well-nigh impossible to appreciate among the former colonisers. It is noteworthy here that the 'community of shared future for humankind' was in 2017 written into a number United Nations resolutions and then into the resolutions of the UN Security Council and the UN Human Rights Council.

Let me put it this way: we are currently witnessing—somewhat paradoxically—a global contest between two models of globalisation, between 'zero-sum' and 'win–win'. The former has been the dominant model ever since the era of European colonialism, when Europe arose from its backwardness and engaged in primitive capitalist accumulation through colonial plunder, slavery, and domination of other parts of the world. In this light, the USA is the last European colonial power, constantly interfering in other countries, bombing them, invading them, and seeking 'regime change' to suit its interests. The USA may be an empire in decline, and it may be that now all its tricks simply hasten the decline, but it is still attempts to dictate to other countries how they should act. This model has a distinct cultural and philosophical background, predicated on ontological transcendence, on religious intolerance between different forms of Christianity (let alone against Islam or Judaism), and the constant wars between small European states as they sought to dominate one another. In short, it is a cultural tradition in which 'either-or' dominates. The peak of this tradition and

[34]For a comprehensive study of the foundations of this concept in the work of Marx and Engels, especially in terms of the false or 'illusory community [*xuhuan de gongtongti*]' and the 'true community [*zhenzheng gongtongti*]' (Marx and Engels 1846a, 536–537, 571;1845a, 33, 74), see Zhou et al. (2017).

its approach to globalisation may well have been Fukuyama's now infamous 'end of history', in which the Western liberal order was to be the last world order. Now, of course, we can see that the claim was a historical irony (Hou 2009, 18), for it was actually the signal of the sunset of the West.[35]

By contrast, the Chinese model of 'win–win' arises from a very different historical experience. China's vast territory includes many different regions (think of the Aihui-Tengchong line), multiple nationalities that have arisen over time, and a vast population. The main focus in this long history has been—after the 'Warring States' period (475–221 BCE)—consolidation of its territory and relations among the many regions and nationalities. With very rare exceptions, the wars fought have concerned the border areas, with the need either to deal with threats to the borders or to incorporate border regions (the last being Xinjiang in the 1750s) in the country as a whole. It is not for nothing that one finds a long historical emphasis on stability and harmony. But it also provides a model for international relations, in which one seeks cooperation while being aware of differences. Culturally and philosophically, we must return to contradiction analysis (see Chapter 3), which is not so much either-or, but both-and; as the old Chinese proverb has it, things that oppose one another also complement one another; or, as dialectical materialism puts, in the struggle of opposites one also finds a unity of opposites.

Is there really an alternative to the liberal capitalist model of globalisation, in which countries—through the dictates of bodies such as the World Bank and the International Monetary Fund—must change their internal workings to be accepted? The Chinese approach suggests that there is an alternative. As scholars point out, it is based on the need for contradiction analysis and dialectical materialism—'win–win' is still in contradiction with 'zero-sum'—but it also seeks to move beyond the antagonistic contradictions of a capitalist approach, not least because the latter is by no means globally monolithic since socialist systems exist even now (Hao and Zhou 2018, 10–11; Liu H. 2018, 82; Mao 2019, 37). Further, it is an explicit realisation of what the Russians are fond of calling a 'multi-polar' world with many distinct cultural traditions and civilisations, a world that has already emerged in many respects. Now I am returning to material covered in the chapter on human rights, but let me point out that this alternative model of globalisation is increasingly being adopted by countries that have found that the Western liberal model has left them mired in poverty and political corruption, and who see a distinct benefit for themselves in such an approach. In short, it is increasingly favoured by developing countries in Africa, Eurasia, Central Asia, Latin America, and the Pacific.[36]

---

[35]Indeed, Fukuyama himself has been backtracking ever since *The End of History and the Last Man* (1992), with the observation after Donald Trump was elected president that the USA was becoming a 'failed state' (Fukuyama 2016).

[36]For example, see the most recent 'Arab Barometer' report, which tracks public opinion in the MENA countries (Middle East and North Africa). On three crucial counts—favourability, threat to national interests, and foreign policy—China doubles and even trebles the score of the United States. The report notes that changing regimes in the United States make no difference, since this is a long-term trend (Robbins 2021).

Arising from all this is a consistent emphasis in China that the objective path of world history is for greater integration, following the model of globalisation outlined above. Those who seek to isolate themselves from this global path of history, or who seek to impose a 'zero-sum' agenda, will be left behind.[37] This leads to the final observation, which concerns the sentence: 'All things are nourished together without their injuring one another [*wanwu bing yu er bu xiang hai, dao bingxing er bu xiangbei*]'. This saying has been used by Xi on a number of occasions, but it is not original to him. Instead it comes from the Confucian *Book of Rites*, in the 'Zhongyong' section (Legge 1885, 326).[38] This is by no means the first, nor will it be the last time, Xi has quoted from the Chinese classics.

*10.4.9 Marxist Party Building (***makesizhuyi zhengdang jianshe***)*

A characteristic feature of speeches by Communist Party leaders since the time of the Soviet Union is to conclude a major address with a discussion of 'Party building [*dangjian*]'. This speech also does so, but the question here is what Marx and Engels might have to say on the matter of Marxist Party building. More than one might initially expect, especially in the second section of the Manifesto, which is, after all 'The Manifesto of the Communist Party'. Xi offers no less than four quotations: (1) 'In the various stages of development which the struggle of the working class against the bourgeoisie has to pass through, they [the Communists][39] always and everywhere represent the interests of the movement as a whole' (Marx and Engels 1848a, 44; 1848b, 474; 1848c, 497); (2) 'They have no interests separate and apart from those of the proletariat as a whole' (Marx and Engels 1848a, 44; 1848b, 474; 1848c, 497); (3) The Party works 'in the interest of the immense majority' (Marx and Engels 1848a, 42; 1848b, 472; 1848c, 495); (4) And the Communist Party has 'to set up milestones [*lichengbei*][40] before the whole world, by which people can measure the level of the Party movement' (Marx 1875c, 426; 1875e, 6; 1875b, 70).

[37]Indeed, anyone who travels between Western countries and China will notice an increasing—and for some a rather astounding—gap: these Western countries are now increasing falling behind on all counts, whether economic activity, political systems, or culture, so much so that they feel more and more 'backward'. By contrast, when one spends some time in China will feel—if coming from a Western country—that one is stepping into the future.

[38]The online bilingual version, with James Legge's translation, may be found at https://ctext.org/liji/zhong-yong.

[39]As is the tendency in Chinese, one repeats the subject rather than using a pronoun, especially where ambiguity may arise. Thus, the translation here clarifies 'they' with 'Communists', or, literally, 'Communist Party people [*gongchandangren*]'.

[40]I have provided an English rendering of the Chinese translation here, which uses 'milestones [*lichengbei*]' for the German *Marksteine* (compared to 'bench marks' in MECW), and 'measure the level [*hengliang shuiping*]' for the German '*die Höhe … misst*' (compared to 'gauge … progress' in MECW).

In explicating Xi Jinping's interpretation, let me begin with a small but significant linguistic point: the Chinese for 'Communist'—the noun—is '*gongchandangren*' (also '*gongchandangyuan*'). Literally, it means a 'Communist Party person' and thus a 'Communist Party member'. In other words, to be a Communist is not so much an existential political choice or an individual faith. It means primarily that one is a member of a Communist Party. Indeed, one is able to call someone else a genuine 'comrade [*tongzhi*]' only if that person is also a Party member. Of course, one also needs the element of 'belief', 'trust', 'confidence' and 'faith'—all parts of the semantic field surrounding *xin* (信) as in *xinxin, xinnian* and *xinyang*—but it takes place within the collective context. Conversely, the idea that one can 'be' a Communist as a matter of existential choice without Party membership is a very 'Western' idea, where the primacy of the autonomous individual has determined culture, politics, and even religion. Ideally, of course, a recognition of both the collective and existential senses of a 'Communist' is needed for international cooperation, as I have found when enabling such cooperation across different parts of the world.

Further, in each of the quotations from Marx and Engels, the emphasis is clearly on the interests of the proletariat and movement as a whole, if not the interests of the immense majority (see also Xi 2013d).[41] Xi has not chosen these quotations at random, for they emphasise that the basis of the Communist Party, and indeed its difference from other political parties, is that it works with and fights for rural and urban workers, the vast majority. Everything flows from this primary premise. But it also raises the crucial question as to how the Party maintains such a focus and continues to have the trust and confidence of the people after seven decades in power.

Before Xi Jinping became general secretary (*zongshuji*), there were grave concerns that the Party was losing this trust (Zhao 2016). As I have mentioned in the discussion of the 'wild 90s' (see Sect. 4.3.3), Party discipline had become relatively lax, knowledge of Marxism even by leading cadres was superficial at best, corruption was widespread, companies and enterprises were regularly flouting the law, exploiting workers and dispossessing the collectively-owned land of villages, and factional strife within the Party had become a distinct problem. If Xi had not fixed the Party, many felt they would have been doomed. That the Party of 100 million members has not fallen apart and that trust in government and public institutions is now at all time highs (see above), is testament to the effect of Xi Jinping's reforms. It should be no surprise that we find at this point of the Marx speech a summary of emphases found on many other occasions: Party unity and strength, strict management, correcting mistakes, political and theoretical knowledge of Marxism, and the unity of the Party's central authority—these have produced a Communist Party in China that is now stronger than it has been for a very long time, arguably since the time of Mao Zedong (Hao and Zhou 2018, 7–8).[42] In typical fashion, Xi uses two four-character sayings to conclude this point: 'tested by wind and waves [*fenglang*

[41] Although there is a significant amount of scholarly literature on the implications of Xi's thought for Party building, I recommend Wang and Guo (2018, 14–15).

[42] For an insight into the state of Marxist education and the CPC, see my recent study (Boer 2021).

kaoyan]' and 'full of youthful spirit and vitality [*zhaoqi pengbo*]'. These are the characteristics of a Marxist Party in power.

10.5 Conclusion: An Original Contribution to the Development of Marxism

As this speech should make clear, Marxism is core and centre of the Chinese project. For foreigners, this emphasis may be surprising, frightening, or heartwarming—depending upon one's political persuasions. In terms of yet another four-character saying that I have mentioned in the introductory chapter (Sect. 1.2), Marxism is China's special and honed skill, or the 'skill with which one looks after the house [*kanjia benling*]' (Xi 2013f, 404; 2020b, 5; Wang W. 2014). This is not 'rhetoric' or 'spin', not a label conjured up from the past to which one pays lip-service. Instead, it is the Marxism that has its foundations in the thought of Marx and Engels, as should by now be clear. This centrality of Marxism applies to both theory and practice (Liu H. 2018, 83–84; Liu J. 2018, 11; Wang Xisen 2018). On the one hand, the speech urges Party members and indeed all Chinese people to make the study of Marx a 'life habit' and even a vigorous and 'spirited [*jingshen*] pursuit'.[43] Why? As a 'powerful theoretical weapon [*qiangda sixiang wuqi*]', Marxism has from beginning to end been the 'guiding thought [*sixiang*] of our Party and country'. But it is not merely thought, for in providing the means to understand the world, it enables one to 'transform [*gaizao*] the world'. The echo of Marx's eleventh thesis on Feuerbach should be obvious.

Here Engels is even more direct. Xi quotes Engels's letter to Werner Sombart in 1895: 'Marx's whole world outlook [*shijieguan*] is not a doctrine [*jiaoyi*], but a method. What it provides is not ready-made dogmas [*jiaotiao*], but a starting point for further research and a method for such research' (Engels 1895d, 691; 1895b, 428; 1895c, 461; see also Xi 2011, 16–17; 2016c, 7).[44] This is a well-known text, which became in Lenin's hands the slogan that Marxism is 'not a dogma, but a guide for action'.[45] It is difficult to find a Communist who would not agree with this

[43] A survey of the critical literature (too many to cite here) reveals implications for all aspects of the Chinese project, ranging from news media, through science, education, literature and the arts, to the all-important economic and social policies, as well as governance itself.

[44] I have provided here a rendering of the Chinese text. One may compare a careful English rendering of the German: 'Marx's whole way of conceptualising [*Auffassungsweise*] is not so much a doctrine [*Doctrin*] as a method. It provides not so much ready-made dogmas [*Dogmen*], as reference points [*Anhaltspunkte*] for further investigation and the method *for* such investigation'.

[45] Or, as Lenin put it in the preface to the second edition of *The Development of Capitalism in Russia*: 'only hopeless pedants could set about solving the peculiar and complex problems arising merely by quoting this or that opinion of Marx about a different historical epoch' (Lenin 1899a, 16; 1899b, 33).

slogan, for no-one wishes to be seen as a dogmatic Marxist.[46] But now Xi Jinping challenges us with his second quotation from Engels, from *Dialectics of Nature*: 'In every epoch, and therefore also in ours, theoretical thought is a historical product, which at different times assumes very different forms and, therewith, very different contents' (Engels 1882e, 436; 1882b, 330; 1882a, 338). Engels is speaking of the history of scientific thought, but if one assumes that Marxism too is a science, then the point applies to historical and dialectical materialism as well. But how? Here Xi follows in the Marxist tradition: the basic principles of scientific socialism can never be lost, but at the same time they cannot become an 'immutable and frozen [*yicheng bubian*]' dogma. Thus, the complex process of the construction of socialism is neither an 'original edition' of Chinese history and culture, nor a 'template' applied from the classic Marxist texts, nor a 'second edition' of efforts to construct socialism in other countries, nor a 'reprint' of the process of modernisation elsewhere.[47] Instead, one must take into account a country's specific conditions, its history and culture, and always be aware of concrete requirements of the present.[48] This is nothing less than a 'scientific approach to Marxism', which requires a careful and proper handling of the dialectical and unified relationship between upholding Marxism and developing it, between holding to the consistent line of Marxism and deploying the method to solve current problems. So much so, in fact, that it is Xi's hope that the substantial history of experience in China will lead to a recognition of 'China's original contribution to the development of Marxism' (Xi 2017b, 66).[49]

In other words, Marxism is a work in progress; or in terms of the Chinese idiom, '*yushi jujin*', one needs to keep abreast of the times (Xi 2011, 20; 2013b, 26–27; 2019b, 3; Bao 2017, 23–24; Guo and Liu 2018, 39–40; Zou and Wang 2018, 45–46). On this matter, the following observation from Engels is well-known in China: 'So-called "socialist society" is not, in my view, to be regarded as something that remains crystallised for all time [*allemal fertiges Ding*], but rather being in process of constant change and transformation [*in fortwährender Verändrung und Umbildung*] like all other social conditions' (Engels 1890d, 588; 1890c, 18; 1890b, 447; see also Wang S. and Guo 2018, 15). More specifically, it is a Marxism that is at the core of an ongoing project of constructing socialism, led by a Communist Party for which Marxism is its 'special skill' (Peng and Liang 2018, 15–17). In the context of such

[46]Engels's observations on some Marxists from North America are also pertinent. In a letter to Friedrich Adolf Sorge, he writes: 'they themselves do not for the most part understand the theory and treat it in doctrinaire and dogmatic fashion as something which, having once been learnt by rote, is sufficient as it stands for any and every need. To them it is a credo, not a guide to action' (Engels 1886a, 578; 1886b, 531–532).

[47]I have tried to render Xi's complex wordplay here: 'original edition [*muban*]', 'template [*moban*]', 'second edition [*zaiban*]' and 'reprint' [*fanban*]' (see also Xi 2016c, 11).

[48]In another work, Xi quotes Marx on this dialectical point: 'Men make their own history, but they do not make it just as they please; they do not make it under circumstances chosen by themselves, but under circumstances directly encountered, given and transmitted from the past (Xi 2019b, 2; Marx 1852b, 470–471; 1852a, 96–97; 1852c, 103).

[49]Not a bad achievement given the dire straights in which the world-wide Communist cause found itself in the 1990s, as Ren Xiaowei's insightful study shows (2019).

construction Marxism is a living tradition and not locked in the past. Now Xi comes to his arresting conclusion: all this means that Marxism is even more important now! And it should be developed in new, creative, and energetic ways. To do so is the 'sacred duty [*shensheng zhize*]' of every Communist. To quote Engels one last time: 'The prospect[50] of a gigantic revolution, the most gigantic revolution that has ever taken place, therefore presents itself to us as soon as we pursue our materialist thesis further and apply it to the present time' (Engels 1859a, 597–598; 1859c, 470; 1859b, 469–470). Lest anyone should harbour the illusion that China has in some way given up on the goal of Communism, Xi reminds his listeners and readers that the 'lofty ideal [*yuandalixiang*]' of Communism should never be abandoned, especially by Communist Party members. After all, the 'faith [*xinyang*] in Marxism, the belief [*xinnian*] in socialism and Communism is the political soul [*zhengzhi linghun*] of Communists and the spiritual pillar [*jingshen zhizhu*] for them to withstand any test' (Xi 2019b, 3).

To finish on a slightly different note: throughout the text and especially when Xi is elaborating on the nine core points, he begins each point with 'study Marx'. The Chinese word for 'study' is '*xuexi*'. This usage has led to a pun used frequently today: the character *xi* (习) is the same as the family name for Xi Jinping. So now it is common to use '*xuexi* [学习]' to mean 'study Xi'.[51] Given Xi Jinping's in-depth engagement with the texts of Marx and Engels, such study is at least worth the energy.

References

Bao, Xinjian. 2017. Makesizhuyi zhongguohua de xin chengguo xin feiyue – lun Xi Jinping zhiguolizheng de luoji qidian, zhuti zhuxian, jiazhi shiye he lishi diwei. *Jinan daxue xuebao (shehui kexue ban)* 27 (1): 22–35.

Bloch, Ernst. 1985. *Das Prinzip Hoffnung*. In *Ernst Bloch Werkausgabe*, vol. 5. Frankfurt am Main: Suhrkamp Verlag.

Bloch, Ernst. 1995. *The principle of hope*, trans. Neville Plaice, Stephen Plaice, and Paul Knight. Cambridge: MIT Press.

Boer, Roland. 2016. Concerning the 'warm stream' within Marxism. *International Critical Thought* 6 (1): 13–28.

Boer, Roland. 2017. *Stalin: From theology to the philosophy of socialism in power*. Singapore: Springer.

Boer, Roland. 2020. What is comparative Marxist philosophy? In *Jointly building a community with a shared future for humankind and improving the well-being of people around the world: Proceedings of the Cloud Workshop, School of Marxism Studies, Dalian University of Technology, 17–19 December 2020*, edited by Yan Ping, Fang Yumei, and Roland Boer, 20–32. Dalian: Dalian University of Technology.

[50]The Chinese translation of '*Die Perspepktive*' is '*yuanjing*', a long-range view, prospect, or even vision.

[51]Not only do we find a whole section of the Chinese version of the CPC newspaper, the'People's Daily', entitled 'study Xi [*xuexi*]', but there is also a series of study books produced for the monthly study sessions of all CPC members in their local branches (Zhonggong zhongyang xuanchuanbu 2016, 2019).

Boer, Roland. 2021. Domenico Losurdo in China: An insight into the state of Marxist education and the CPC. *Socialism and Democracy* 34: 1–23.
Boer, Roland. in press. *Friedrich Engels and the foundations of socialist governance*. Singapore: Springer.
Boer, Roland, and Zang Fengyu. 2019. Renlei mingyun gongtongti de lilun neihan yu xianshi jiazhi. *Zhongyang shehuizhuyi xueyuan xuebao* 2019 (4): 9–17.
Bougon, François. 2018. *Inside the mind of Xi Jinping*, trans. Vanessa Lee. London: Hurst.
Brown, Kerry. 2016. *CEO, China: The rise of Xi Jinping*. London: I.B. Tauris.
Brown, Kerry. 2018. *The world according to Xi: Everything you need to know about the new China*. London: I.B. Tauris.
Cai, Yongsheng. 2018. Lun dangdai Zhongguo xianhuo de makesizhuyi de hexin yaoyi – Xi Jinping xinshidai Zhongguo tese shehuizhuyi sixiang yanjiu. *Nanjing shida xuebao (shehui kexue ban)* 2018 (1): 5–12.
Cheng, Enfu. 2018. Makesizhuyi jiqi zhongguohua lilun de juda chengjiu – Xi Jinping xinshidai Zhongguo tese shehuizuyi jingji sixiang shu lun. *Dongnan xueshu* 2018 (5): 1–8.
CPC Central Committee. 2013. *Guanyu peiyu he jianxing shehuizhuyi hexin jiazhiguan de yijian (2013.12.23)*. Beijing: Zhongguo gongchandang zhongyang weiyuanhui.
Cunningham, Edward, Tony Saich, and Jessie Turiel. 2020. *Understanding CCP Resilience: Surveying Chinese public opinion through time*. Cambridge: Ash Center for Democratic Governance and Innovation.
Dong, Yukun, and Bai Baoli. 2018. Xi Jinping xinshidai Zhongguo tese shehuizhuyi shouru fenpei lilun tantao – makesizhuyi zhengzhijingjixue de fengfu yu fazhan. *Xi'an caijing xueyuan xuebao* 31 (4): 5–12.
Du, Xiujuan. 2011. *Makesizhuyi shengtai zhexue sixiang lishi fazhan yanjiu*. Beijing: Beijing shifan daxue chubanshe.
Economy, Elizabeth. 2018. *The third revolution: Xi Jinping and the Chinese state*. Oxford: Oxford University Press.
Edelman. 2020. *2020 Edelman trust barometer: Global report*. Los Angeles: Edelman.
Engels, Friedrich. 1847a. Gongchanzhuyi yuanli. In *Makesi Engesi wenji*, vol. 1:676–693. Beijing: Renmin chubanshe, 2009.
Engels, Friedrich. 1847b. Grundsätze des Kommunismus. In *Marx Engels Werke*, vol. 4:361–380. Berlin: Dietz, 1972.
Engels, Friedrich. 1847c. Principles of communism. In *Marx and Engels collected works*, vol. 6:341–357. Moscow: Progress Publishers, 1976.
Engels, Friedrich. 1857a. A new English expedition to China. In *Marx and Engels collected works*, vol. 15:243–246. Moscow: Progress Publishers, 1986.
Engels, Friedrich. 1857b. Persia-China. In *Marx and Engels collected works*, vol. 15:278–283. Moscow: Progress Publishers, 1986.
Engels, Friedrich. 1859a. Ka'er·makesi 'Zhengzhijingjixue pipan. Diyi fence'. In *Makesi Engesi wenji*, vol. 2:595–606. Beijing: Renmin chubanshe, 2009.
Engels, Friedrich. 1859b. Karl Marx, *A contribution to the critique of political economy*. In *Marx and Engels collected works*, vol. 16:465–477. Moscow: Progress Publishers, 1980.
Engels, Friedrich. 1859c. Karl Marx, 'Zur Kritik der Politischen Ökonomie'. In *Marx Engels Werke*, vol. 13:468–477. Berlin: Dietz, 1974.
Engels, Friedrich. 1873a. Dell' autorità. In *Marx Engels Gesamtausgabe*, vol. I.24:82–86. Berlin: Dietz, 1984.
Engels, Friedrich. 1873b. Lun quanwei. In *Makesi Engesi wenji*, vol. 3:335–338. Beijing: Renmin chubanshe, 2009.
Engels, Friedrich. 1873c. On authority. In *Marx and Engels collected works*, vol. 23:422–425. Moscow: Progress Publishers, 1988.
Engels, Friedrich. 1877a. Ka'er·Makesi. In *Makesi Engesi wenji*, vol. 3:451–462. Beijing: Renmin chubanshe, 2009.

Engels, Friedrich. 1877b. Karl Marx. In *Marx Engels Gesamtaugabe*, vol. I.25:100–111. Berlin: Dietz, 1985.

Engels, Friedrich. 1877c. Karl Marx. In *Marx and Engels collected works*, vol. 24:183–195. Moscow: Progress Publishers, 1989.

Engels, Friedrich. 1880a. Socialism: Utopian and scientific. In *Marx and Engels collected works*, vol. 24:281–325. Moscow: Progress Publishers, 1989.

Engels, Friedrich. 1880b. Socialisme utopique et socialisme scientifique. In *Marx Engels Gesamtaugabe*, vol. I.27:541–582. Berlin: Dietz, 1985.

Engels, Friedrich. 1882a. *Dialectics of nature*. In *Marx and Engels collected works*, vol. 25:313–588. Moscow: Progress Publishers, 1987.

Engels, Friedrich. 1882b. *Dialektik der Natur*. In *Marx Engels Werke*, vol. 20:305–570. Berlin: Dietz, 1973.

Engels, Friedrich. 1882c. Die Mark. In *Marx Engels Gesamtausgabe*, vol. I.27:628–643. Berlin: Dietz, 1988.

Engels, Friedrich. 1882d. The mark. In *Marx and Engels collected works*, vol. 24:439–456. Moscow: Progress Publishers, 1989.

Engels, Friedrich. 1882e. *Ziran bianzhengfa (jiexuan)*. In *Makesi Engesi wenji*, vol. 9:399–563. Beijing: Renmin chubanshe, 2009.

Engels, Friedrich. 1886a. Engels an Friedrich Adolph Sorge in Hoboken, London, 29.November 1886. In *Marx Engels Werke*, vol. 36:578–581. Berlin: Dietz, 1973.

Engels, Friedrich. 1886b. Engels to Friedrich Adolph Sorge in Hoboken, 29 November 1886. In *Marx and Engels collected works*, vol. 47:531–534. Moscow: Progress Publishers, 1995.

Engels, Friedrich. 1887a. Engesi dui yingguo beifang shehuizhuyi lianmeng gangling de xiuzheng. In *Makesi Engesi quanji*, vol. 21:569–570. Beijing: Renmin chubanshi, 1972.

Engels, Friedrich. 1887b. Notes to the programme of the North of England Socialist Federation. In *Marx and Engels Gesamtausgabe*, vol. I.31:481–482. Berlin: Akademie Verlag, 2002.

Engels, Friedrich. 1890a. Engels an Conrad Schmidt in Berlin, London, 27.Oktober 1890. In *Marx Engels Werke*, vol. 37:488–495. Berlin: Dietz, 1974.

Engels, Friedrich. 1890b. Engels an Otto v. Boenigk in Breslau, Folkestone bei Dover, 21./8./90. In *Marx Engels Werke*, vol. 37:447–448. Berlin: Dietz, 1968.

Engels, Friedrich. 1890c. Engels to Otto von Boenigk in Breslau, Folkestone near Dover, 21 August 1890. In *Marx and Engels collected works*, vol. 49:18–20. Moscow: Progress Publishers, 2001.

Engels, Friedrich. 1890d. Engesi zhi Autuo·feng·boníke, Buleisilao 1890 nian 8 yue 21 ri. In *Makesi Engesi wenji*, vol. 10:588–590. Beijing: Renmin chubanshe, 2009.

Engels, Friedrich. 1891a. Einleitung zur dritten deutschen Auflage (1891) von Karl Marx, 'Der Bürgerkrieg in Frankreich'. In *Marx Engels Gesamtausgabe*, vol. I.32:3–16. Berlin: Akademie Verlag, 2010.

Engels, Friedrich. 1891b. 'Falanxi neizhan': Engesi xie de 1891 nian ban daoyan. In *Makesi Engesi wenji*, vol. 3:99–112. Beijing: Renmin chubanshe, 2009.

Engels, Friedrich. 1891c. Introduction to Karl Marx's *The Civil War in France*. In *Marx and Engels collected works*, vol. 27:179–191. Moscow: Progress Publishers, 1990.

Engels, Friedrich. 1891d. Zur Kritik des sozialdemokratischen Programmentwurfs 1891. In *Marx Engels Gesamtausgabe*, vol. I.32:42–54. Berlin: Akademie Verlag, 2010.

Engels, Friedrich. 1894a. *Anti-Dühring: Herr Eugen Dühring's revolution in science*. In *Marx and Engels collected works*, vol. 25:3–309. Moscow: Progress Publishers, 1987.

Engels, Friedrich. 1894b. *Fan Dulin lun (Ougen·Dulin xiansheng zai kexue zhong shixing de biange)*. In *Makesi Engesi wenji*, vol. 9:3–398. Beijing: Renmin chubanshe, 2009.

Engels, Friedrich. 1894c. *Herrn Eugen Dührings Umwälzung der Wissenschaft. 3. Auflage*. In *Marx Engels Gesamtausgabe*, vol. I:27:485–538. Berlin: Dietz, 1988.

Engels, Friedrich. 1895a. Einleitung (1895) zu Karl Marx's 'Klassenkämpfe in Frankreich 1848 bis 1850'. In *Marx Engels Gesamtausgabe*, vol. I.32:330–351. Berlin: Akademie Verlag, 2010.

Engels, Friedrich. 1895b. Engels an Werner Sombart in Breslau, London, 11.März 1895. In *Marx Engels Werke*, 39:427–429. Berlin: Dietz, 1973.

Engels, Friedrich. 1895c. Engels to Werner Sombart in Breslau, London, 11 March 1895. In *Marx and Engels collected works*, 50:460–462. Moscow: Progress Publishers, 2004.
Engels, Friedrich. 1895d. Zhi Wei'erna·Sangbate, Buleisilao, 1895 nian 3 yue, 11 ri yu Lundun xibei qu. In *Makesi Engesi wenji*, vol. 10:689–692. Beijing: Renmin chubanshe, 2009.
Fang, Yumei. 2018. Xi Jinping xinshidai Zhongguo tese jingji sixiang luoji lilu – jiyu makesizhuyi zhengzhijingjixue de fenxi kuangjia. *Shehuizhuyi yanjiu* 2018 (6): 1–7.
Farrar, John. 1962. *How to do things with words*. Oxford: Oxford University Press.
Feng, Jingyuan. 2009. Makesi kuayue 'kafuding xiagu' lilun de zhiding – zai du 'gei Wei·yi·chasuliqi de xin.' *Dongnan xueshu* 2009 (4): 114–123.
Fukuyama, Francis. 1992. *The end of history and the last man*. New York: Free Press.
Fukuyama, Francis. 2016. America: The failed state. *Prospect Magazine*, 13 December,. Available at www.prospectmagazine.co.uk/magazine/america-the-failed-state-donald-trump.
Gan, Chunsong. 2019. *A concise reader of Chinese culture*, trans. Yu Shiyi. China Insights. Singapore: Springer.
Garrick, John, and Yan Chang Bennett, eds. 2016. *China's socialist rule of law reforms under Xi Jinping*. London: Routledge.
Gong, Jianqing, and Qiao Yaozhang. 2018. Cong 'huadazhong' dao 'dazhonghua': Makesizhuyi dazhonghua de di erjiexing – jian lun Zi Jinping xinshidai Zhongguo tese shehuizhuyi sixiang dazhonghua de lujing zhuanxiang. *Guangxi shehui kexue* 2018 (7): 25–30.
Gu, Hailiang. 2019. Zhongguo tese shehuizhuyi zhengzhijingjixue de 'daoyan' – Xi Jinping 'Buduan kaituo dangdai Zhongguo makesizhuyi zhengzhijingjixue xin jingjie' yanjiu. *Jingji xuejia* 2019 (3): 5–16.
Guo, Yunze, and Liu Tongfang. 2018. Xi Jinping xinshidai Zhongguo tese shehuizhuyi sixiang dui makesizhuyi zhexue de jicheng yu fazhan. *Sixiang Lilun Jiaoyu* 2018 (8): 37–43.
Han, Zhen, and Zhang Weiwen. 2018. *Contemporary value systems in China*, trans. Zhao Chaoyong. China Insights. Singapore: Springer.
Hao, Lixin, and Zhou Kanglin. 2018. Makesizhuyi xindaihua de xin feiyue – xuexi Xi Jinping xinshidai Zhongguo tese shehuizhuyi sixiang. *Zhongguo gaoxiao shehui kexue* 2018 (1): 4–12.
Hou, Huiqin. 2009. A common destiny for China's reform and opening-up and scientific socialism: Commemorating the 160th anniversary of the publication of the Communist Manifesto. *Marxist Studies in China* 2009: 16–30.
Huang, Chengliang. 2018. Lun Xi Jinping shengtai wenming sixiang dui makesizhuyi shengtai wenming xueshuo de lishixing gongxian. *Xibei shida xuebao (shehui kexue ban)* 55 (5): 5–11.
Ipsos. 2019. *What worries the world—November 2019*. Paris: Ipsos Public Affairs.
Jia, Pengfei. 2018. Xi Jinping xinshidai Zhongguo tese shehuizhuyi dui makesizhuyi lichang guandian fangfa de chuangzao. *Dalian ligong daxue xuebao (shehui kexue ban)* 39 (3): 1–7.
Jiang, Qian. 2016. Fazhan dangdai Zhongguo makesizhuyi zhengzhijingjixue de kexue zhinan – xuexi Xi Jinpng zongshuji zai zhexue shehui kexue gongzuo zuotanhui shang de zhongyao jianghua. *Lilun shiye* 2016 (8): 9–11.
Jin, Xiaoping. 2018. Jianghao xianhuo de Makesi, chuanbo makesizhuyi zhenli – xuexi Xi Jinping 'zai jinian Makesi danchen 200 zhounian dahui shang de jianghua' jingshen de tihui. *Sixiang lilun jiaoyu dao kan* 2018 (8): 34–37.
Legge, James. 1885. *The sacred books of China: The texts of confucianism. Part IV: The Li Ki, X-XLVI*. Oxford: Clarendon.
Lenin, V.I. 1899a. *Razvitie kapitalizma v Rossii. Protsess obrazovaniia vnutrennego rynka dlia krupnoĭ promyshlennosti*. In *Polnoe sobranie sochinenii*, 3:1–609. Moscow: Izdatel'stvo politicheskoi literatury.
Lenin, V.I. 1899b. *The development of capitalism in Russia: The process of the formation of a home market for large-scale industry*. In *Collected works*, 3:21–607. Moscow: Progress Publishers.
Lenin, V.I. 1917a. Gosudarstvo i revoliutsiia. Uchenie marksizma o gosudarstve i zadachi proletariata v revoliutsii. Avgust–sentiabr' 1917 g.; ranee 17 dekabria 1918 g. In *Polnoe sobranie sochinenii*, vol. 33:1–120. Moscow: Izdatel'stvo politicheskoi literatury, 1969.
Lenin, V.I. 1917b. Guojia yu geming (1917.08-09). In *Liening xuanji*, vol. 3:109–221. Beijing: Renmin chubanshe, 1972.

Lenin, V.I. 1917c. The state and revolution: The marxist theory of the state and the tasks of the proletariat in the revolution. In *Collected works*, vol. 25:385–497. Moscow: Progress Publishers.

Li, Cheng. 2016. *Chinese politics in the Xi Jinping era: Reassessing collective leadership*. Washington: Brookings Institution.

Li, Chongfu. 2009. Creative application and deepened development of historical materialism in the great practice of reform and opening-up. *Marxist Studies in China* 2008–2009: 144–164.

Li, Guojun, and Chen Mengxi. 2017. Xi Jinping lüse fazhan linian: makesizhuyi shengtai wenming guan de lilun chuangxin. *Xueshu jiaoliu* 2017 (12): 53–57.

Liu, Han. 2018. Xi Jinping xinshidai makesizhuyi guan chutan. *Hainan daxue xuebao (renwen shehui kexue ban)* 36 (6): 78–85.

Liu, Jianjun. 2018. Yi pian guanghui makesizhuyi ganglingxing wenxian – Xi Jinping 'Zai jinian Makesi danchen 200 zhounian dahui shang de jianghua'shenceng jiedu. *Xibei daxue xuebao (zhexue shehui kexue ban)* 48 (5): 5–12.

Liu, Sihua. 2006. *Shengtai makesizhuyi jingjixue yuanli*. Beijing: Renmin chubanshe.

Liu, Yongling. 2017. Lun Xi Jinping de makesizhuyi guan. *Xuexi yu tansuo* 2017 (11): 15–21.

Losurdo, Domenico. 2008. Wie der 'westliche Marxismus' geboren wurde und gestorben ist. In *Die Lust am Widerspruch. Theorie der Dialektik – Dialektik der Theorie. Symposium aus Anlass des 80. Geburtstag von Hans Heinz Holz*, ed. Erich Hahn and Silvia Holz-Markun, 35–60. Berlin: Trafo.

Losurdo, Domenico. 2013. *La lotta di classe: Una storia politica e filosofica*. Roma-Bari: Laterza.

Losurdo, Domenico. 2016. *Class struggle: A political and philosophical history*. New York: Palgrave Macmillan.

Losurdo, Domenico. 2017. *Il marxismo occidentale: Come nacque, come morì, come può rinascere*. Rome: Editori Laterza.

Magnus, George. 2018. *Red flags: Why Xi's China is in jeopardy*. New Haven: Yale University Press.

Mao, Lina. 2019. Xi Jinping waijiao sixiang zhong de makesizhuyi zhexue siwei. *Dangjian* 2019 (2): 37–38.

Marx, Karl. 1844a. 1844 nian jingjixue zhexue shougao. In *Makesi Engesi wenji*, vol. 1:109–248. Beijing: Renmin chubanshe, 2009.

Marx, Karl. 1844b. Economic and philosophic manuscripts of 1844. In *Marx and Engels collected works*, vol. 3:229–346. Moscow: Progress Publishers, 1975.

Marx, Karl. 1844c. Ökonomisch-philosophische Manuskripte (Erste Wiedergabe). In *Marx Engels Gesamtausgabe*, vol. I.2:187–322. Berlin: Akademie Verlag, 2009.

Marx, Karl. 1844d. Ökonomisch-philosophische Manuskripte (Zweite Wiedergabe). In *Marx Engels Gesamtausgabe*, vol. I.2:323–463. Berlin: Akademie Verlag, 2009.

Marx, Karl. 1852a. Der achtzehnte Brumaire des Louis Bonaparte. In *Marx Engels Gesamtausgabe*, vol. I.11:96–189. Berlin: Dietz, 1985.

Marx, Karl. 1852b. Luyi·Bonaba de wu yue shiba ri. In *Makesi Engesi wenji*, vol. 2:461–578. Beijing: Renmin chubanshe, 2009.

Marx, Karl. 1852c. The Eighteenth Brumaire of Louis Bonaparte. In *Marx and Engels collected works*, vol. 11:99–197. Moscow: Progress Publishers, 1979.

Marx, Karl. 1853. Revolution in China and Europe. In *Marx Engels Gesamtausgabe*, vol I.12:147–153. Berlin: Dietz, 1984.

Marx, Karl. 1857a. Defeat of the Palmerston ministry. In *Marx and Engels collected works*, vol. 15:213–218. Moscow: Progress Publishers, 1986.

Marx, Karl. 1857b. English atrocities in China. In *Marx and Engels collected works*, vol. 15:232–235. Moscow: Progress Publishers, 1986.

Marx, Karl. 1857c. Parliamentary debates on the Chinese hostilities. In *Marx and Engels collected works*, vol. 15:207–212. Moscow: Progress Publishers, 1986.

Marx, Karl. 1857d. Russian trade with China. In *Marx and Engels collected works*, vol. 15:223–225. Moscow: Progress Publishers, 1986.

Marx, Karl. 1857e. The Anglo-Chinese conflict. In *Marx and Engels collected works*, vol. 15:158–163. Moscow: Progress Publishers, 1986.

Marx, Karl. 1858a. *Economic manuscripts of 1857–58 (First Version of Capital) [Grundrisse]*. In *Marx and Engels collected works*, vol. 29. Moscow: Progress Publishers, 1987.

Marx, Karl. 1858b. History of the opium trade (first article). In *Marx Engels Gesamtausgabe*, vol. I.16:396–398. Berlin: Walter de Gruyter, 2018.

Marx, Karl. 1858c. History of the opium trade (second article). In *Marx Engels Gesamtausgabe*, vol. I.16:399–401. Berlin: Walter de Gruyter, 2018.

Marx, Karl. 1858d. The Anglo-Chinese treaty. In *Marx Engels Gesamtausgabe*, vol. I.16:409–413. Berlin: Walter de Gruyter, 2018.

Marx, Karl. 1858e. The British and Chinese treaty. In *Marx Engels Gesamtausgabe*, vol. I.16:433–437. Berlin: Walter de Gruyter, 2018.

Marx, Karl. 1858f. *Zhengzhijingjixue pipan (1857–1858 nian shougao) zhai xuan*. In *Makesi Engesi wenji*, vol. 8:37–209. Beijing: Renmin chubanshe, 2009.

Marx, Karl. 1858g. *Ökonomische Manuskripte 1857/1858*. In *Marx Engels Gesamtausgabe*, vol. II.1. Berlin: Dietz, 1976.

Marx, Karl. 1859a. The new Chinese war. In *Marx and Engels collected works*, vol. 16:508–524. Moscow: Progress Publishers, 1980.

Marx, Karl. 1859b. Trade with China. In *Marx Engels Gesamtausgabe*, vol. I.18:18–21. Berlin: Dietz, 1984.

Marx, Karl. 1860. English politics. In *Marx Engels Gesamtausgabe*, vol. I.18:38–42. Berlin: Dietz, 1984.

Marx, Karl. 1871. The civil war in France. In *Marx and Engels Gesamtausgabe*, vol. I.22:119–162. Berlin: Dietz, 1978.

Marx, Karl. 1875a. Bakuning 'Guojia zhidu he wuzhengfu zhuangtai' – shu zhaiyao (zhailu). In *Makesi Engesi wenji*, vol. 3:403–409. Beijing: Renmin chubanshe, 2009.

Marx, Karl. 1875b. Critique of the Gotha programme. In *Marx and Engels collected works*, vol. 24:75–99. Moscow: Progress Publishers, 1989.

Marx, Karl. 1875c. Geda gangling pi. In *Makesi Engesi wenji*, vol. 3:419–450. Beijing: Renmin chubanshe, 2009.

Marx, Karl. 1875d. Konspekt von Bakunins Buch 'Staatlichkeit und Anarchie'. In *Marx Engels Werke*, vol. 18:597–642. Berlin: Dietz, 1973.

Marx, Karl. 1875e. Kritik des Gothaer Programms. In *Marx Engels Gesamtausgabe*, vol. I.25:3–25. Berlin: Dietz, 1985.

Marx, Karl. 1875f. Notes on Bakunin's book *Statehood and anarchy*. In *Marx Engels collected works*, vol. 24:485–526. Moscow: Progress Publishers, 1989.

Marx, Karl. 1881a. Deuxième projet de la lettre à Vera Ivanovna Zassoulitch. In *Marx Engels Gesamtausgabe*, vol. I.25:231–234. Berlin: Dietz, 1985.

Marx, Karl. 1881b. Gei wei·yi·chasuliqi de fuxin caogao: chugao. In *Makesi Engesi quanji*, vol. 19:430–441. Beijing: Renmin chubanshi, 1972.

Marx, Karl. 1881c. Gei wei·yi·chasuliqi de fuxin caogao: ergao. In *Makesi Engesi quanji*, vol. 19:442–446. Beijing: Renmin chubanshi, 1972.

Marx, Karl. 1881d. Gei wei·yi·chasuliqi de fuxin caogao: sangao. In *Makesi Engesi quanji*, vol. 19:447–452. Beijing: Renmin chubanshi, 1972.

Marx, Karl. 1881e. Gei wei·yi·chasuliqi de fuxin [fuxin]. In *Makesi Engesi wenji*, vol. 3:589–590. Beijing: Renmin chubanshi, 2009.

Marx, Karl. 1881f. Lettre à Vera Ivanovna Zassoulitch résidant à Genève, Londres, le 8 mars 1881. In *Marx Engels Gesamtausgabe*, vol. I.25:241–242. Berlin: Dietz, 1985.

Marx, Karl. 1881g. Marx to Vera Zasulich, Geneva, 8 March 1881. In *Marx and Engels collected works*, 46:71–72. Moscow: Progress Publishers.

Marx, Karl. 1881h. Premier projet de la lettre à Vera Ivanovna Zassoulitch. In *Marx Engels Gesamtausgabe*, vol. I.25:219–230. Berlin: Dietz, 1985.

Marx, Karl. 1881i. Quatrième projet de la lettre à Vera Ivanovna Zassoulitch. In *Marx Engels Gesamtausgabe*, vol. I.25:240. Berlin: Dietz, 1985.

Marx, Karl. 1881j. Troisième projet de la lettre à Vera Ivanovna Zassoulitch. In *Marx Engels Gesamtausgabe*, vol. I.25:235–239. Berlin: Dietz, 1985.

Marx, Karl. 1951. *Marx on China, 1853–1860. Articles from the New York Daily Tribune with an introduction and notes by Dona Toor*, ed. Dona Toor. London: Lawrence & Wishart.

Marx, Karl, and Friedrich Engels. 1845a. *Die deutsche Ideologie. Kritik der neuesten deutschen Philosophie in ihren Repräsentanten Feuerbach, B. Bauer und Stirner und des deutschen Sozialismus in seinen verschiedenen Propheten*. In *Marx Engels Werke*, 3:9–530. Berlin: Dietz.

Marx, Karl, and Friedrich Engels. 1845b. *Die heilige Familie oder Kritik der kritischen Kritik*. In *Marx Engels Werke*, vol. 2:3–223. Berlin: Dietz, 1974.

Marx, Karl, and Friedrich Engels. 1845c. *Shensheng jiazu, huo dui pipan de pipan suo zuo de pipan, bo bulunuo·baowei'er ji qi huoban*. In *Makesi Engesi quanji*, 2:3–268. Beijing: Renmin chubanshe.

Marx, Karl, and Friedrich Engels. 1846a. *Deyizhi yishi xingtai. Dui Fei'erbaha, Bu·baowei'er he Shidina suo daibiao de xiandai deguo zhexue yiji ge shi ge yang xianzhi suo daibiao de deguo shehuizhuyi de pipan (jiexuan)*. In *Makesi Engesi wenji*, vol. 1:507–591. Beijing: Renmin chubanshe, 2009.

Marx, Karl, and Friedrich Engels. 1846b. *The German ideology: Critique of modern German philosophy according to its representatives Feuerbach, B. Bauer and Stirner, and of German socialism according to its various prophets*. In *Marx and Engels collected works*, vol. 5:19–539. Moscow: Progress Publishers, 1976.

Marx, Karl, and Friedrich Engels. 1848a. Gongchandang xuanyan. In *Makesi Engesi wenji*, vol. 2:3–67. Beijing: Renmin chubanshe, 2009.

Marx, Karl, and Friedrich Engels. 1848b. Manifest der Kommunistischen Partei. In *Marx Engels Werke*, vol. 4:459–493. Berlin: Dietz Verlag, 1974.

Marx, Karl, and Friedrich Engels. 1848c. The manifesto of the Communist Party. In *Marx and Engels collected works*, vol. 6:477–519. Moscow: Progress Publishers, 1976.

Marx, Karl, and Friedrich Engels. 1850a. Guoji shuping (1). In *Makesi Engesi quanji*, vol. 7:254–268. Beijing: Renmin chubanshe, 1972.

Marx, Karl, and Friedrich Engels. 1850b. Review, January–February 1850. In *Marx and Engels collected works*, vol. 10:257–270. Moscow: Progress Publishers, 1978.

Marx, Karl, and Friedrich Engels. 1850c. Revue. Januar/Februar 1850. In *Marx Engels Gesamtausgabe*, I.10:211–223. Berlin: Dietz, 1977.

Marx, Karl, and Friedrich Engels. 1858. Russia in China. In *Marx Engels Gesamtausgabe*, vol. I.16:467–470. Berlin: Walter de Gruyter, 2018.

Pan, Jiahua. 2016. *China's environmental governing and ecological civilisation*. Heidelberg: Springer.

Pang, Ruizhi, Bai Xuejie, and Knox Lovell, eds. 2018. *Energy, environment and transitional green growth in China*. Singapore: Springer.

Peng, Fuyang, and Liang Ye. 2018. Xi Jinping chuangxin sixiang de makesizhuyi zhexue yiyun jiqi shidai jiazhi. *Hexiang luntan* 2018 (5): 12–19.

Ren, Xiaowei. 2019. Xi Jinping xhinshidai zhongguo tese shehuizhuyi sixiang zai makesizhuyi fazhan shishang de diwei. *Dangdai shijie yu shehuizhuyi* 2019 (1): 88–94.

Robbins, Michael. 2021. U.S. and China's competition extends to MENA, 12 January. Online report. Princeton: Arab Barometer. Available at www.arabbarometer.org/2021/01/u-s-chinas-competition-extends-to-mena.

Sha, Jiansun. 2010. Lunshu Eguo nongcun gongshe mingyun he shehui fazhan qianjing de zhongyao zhuzuo – xuexi makesi 'gei Wei·yi·chasuliqi de fuxin' zhaji. *Gaoxiao lilun zhanxian* 2010 (9): 10–16.

Shi, Zhongquan. 2013. 'Zhongguo meng' sixiang: cong Mao Zedong dao Xi Jinping. *Mao Zedong Deng Xiaoping lilun yanjiu* 2013 (10): 1–7.

Stalin, I.V. 1939a. Otchetnyi doklad na XVIII s"ezde partii o rabote TSK VKP(b), 10 marta 1939 goda. In *Sochineniia*, vol. 14:290–341. Moscow: Izdatel'stvo "Pisatel'", 1997.

Stalin, I.V. 1939b. Report on the work of the central committee to the eighteenth congress of the C.P.S.U.(B.) (Delivered March 10, 1939). In *Works*, vol. 14:355–429. London: Red Star Press, 1978.

Stalin, I.V. 1939c. Zai dang de shiba ci daibiao dahui shang guanyu liangong (bu) zhongyang gongzuao zongjie baogao (1939.03.10). In *Sidalin quanji*, vol. 14:221–269. Beijing: Renmin chubanshe, 2005.

Su, Bin, and Elspeth Thomson, eds. 2016a. *China's energy efficiency and conservation: Household behaviour, legislation, regional analysis and impacts*. Singapore: Springer.

Su, Bin, and Elspeth Thomson, eds. 2016b. *China's energy efficiency and conservation: Sectoral analysis*. Singapore: Springer.

Tao, Delin. 2014. A study on cultivation and practice of core socialist values from the perspective of cultural construction. *Marxist Studies in China* 2014: 245–268.

Wang, Hongbo. 2016. Jianchi makesizhuyi zhidao, kaichuang Zhongguo fazhan xin jingjie – xuexi Xi Jinping xilie jianghua jingshen tihui. *Xi'an jiaotong daxue xuebao (shehui kexue ban)* 36 (5): 7–14, 121.

Wang, Shiguo, and Guo Gaosheng. 2018. Xi Jinping xinshidai Zhongguo tese shehuizhuyi sixiang yu makesizhuyi zhongguohua de xin fazhan. *Qiushi* 2018 (4): 4–19.

Wang, Weiguang. 2014. Xuehao yonghao makesizhuyi zhexue, nuli zhangwo kanjia benling – xuexi Xi Jinping tongzhe xilie zhongyao jianghua jingshen de tihui. *Zhexue yanjiu* 2014 (6): 3–18.

Wang, Weiguang. 2015. Makesizhuyi zhongguohua de dangdai lilun chengguo – xuexi Xi Jinping zongshuji xilie zhongyao jianghua jingshen. *Zhongguo Shehui Kexue* 2015 (10): 4–28.

Wang, Weiguang. 2017. Dangdai Zhongguo makesizhuyi de zuixin lilun chengguo – Xi Jinping xinshidai Zhongguo tese shehuizhuyi sixiang xuexi tihui. *Zhongguo shehui kexue* 2017 (12): 4–30.

Wang, Xinyan. 2018. Xi Jinping xinshidai shehuizhuyi sixiang de zhexue jichu yanjiu shuping. *Wuhan daxue xuebao (zhexue shehui kexue ban)* 71 (2): 5–15.

Wang, Xisen. 2018. Xi Jinping goujian makesizhuyi yishixingtai huayuquan sixiang chuyi. *Sixiang zhengzhi jiaoyu yanjiu* 34 (1): 28–33.

Wei, Jian. 2018. Xi Jinping xinshidai Zhongguo tese shehuizhuyi jingji sixiang: makesizhuyi zhengzhijingjixue guanyu shehuizhuyi xiandaihua jianshe de chuangxin fazhan. *Gaige* 2018 (11): 139–146.

Xi, Jinping. 2001. *Zhongguo nongcun shichanghua yanjiu*. Boshi lunwen, Beijing: Tsinghua University.

Xi, Jinping. 2006. *Gan zai shichu, zou zai qianlie – tuijin Zhejiang xin fazhan de sikao yu shijian*. Beijing: Zhonggong zhongyang dangxiao chubanshe.

Xi, Jinping. 2011. Zhongguo gongchandang 90 nianlai zhidao sixiang he jiben lilun de yushijujin ji lishi qishi – zai jinian Zhongguo gongchandang chengli 90 zhounian dangjian yantaohui shang de jianghua (2011.06.20). *Dangjian yanjiu* 2011 (7): 16–21.

Xi, Jinping. 2012. Jinjin weirao jianchi he fazhan Zhongguo tese shehuizhuyi, xuexi xuanchuan guanche dang de shibada jingshen (2012.11.17). In *Tan zhiguolizheng*, vol. 1:6–20. Beijing: Waiwen chubanshe, 2014.

Xi, Jinping. 2013a. Haobu dongyao jianchi he fazhan Zhongguo tese shehuizhuyi (2013.01.05). In *Tan zhiguolizheng*, vol. 1:21–24. Beijing: Waiwen chubanshe, 2014.

Xi, Jinping. 2013b. Jianchi he yunyong hao Mao Zedong sixiang huo de linghun (2013.12.26). In *Tan zhiguolizheng*, vol. 1:25–31. Beijing: Waiwen chubanshe, 2014.

Xi, Jinping. 2013c. Nuli zouxiang shehuizhuyi shengtai wenming xinshidai (2013.05.24). In *Tan zhiguolizheng*, vol. 1:208–210. Beijing: Waiwen chubanshe, 2014.

Xi, Jinping. 2013d. Qunzhong luxian dang de shengmingxian he genben gongzuo luxian (2013.06.18). In *Tan zhiguolizheng*, vol. 1:365–372. Beijing: Waiwen chubanshe, 2014.

Xi, Jinping. 2013e. Shunying shidai qianjin chaoliu, cujin shijie heping fazhan (2013.03.23). In *Tan zhiguolizheng*, vol. 1:271–278. Beijing: Waiwen chubanshe, 2014.

Xi, Jinping. 2013f. Yikao xuexi zouxiang weilai (2013.03.01). In *Tan zhiguolizheng*, vol. 1:401–408. Beijing: Waiwen chubanshe, 2014.

Xi, Jinping. 2014a. Jianding dui Zhongguo tese shehuizhuyi zhengzhi zhidu de zixin (2014.09.05). In *Tan zhiguolizheng*, vol. 2:285–290. Beijing: Waiwen chubanshe, 2017.

Xi, Jinping. 2014b. Tuijin xieshang minzhu guangfan duoceng zhiduhua fazhan (2014.09.21). In *Tan zhiguolizheng*, vol. 2:291–298. Beijing: Waiwen chubanshe, 2017.

Xi, Jinping. 2014c. *Zai jinian Kongzi danchen 2565 zhounian guoji xueshu yantaohui ji guoji ruxue lianhehui di wu jie huiyuan dahui kaimu hui shang de jianghua (2014.09.24)*. Beijing: Renmin chubanshe.

Xi, Jinping. 2014d. *Zai qingzhu quanguo renmin daibiao dahui chengli 60 zhounian dahui shang de jianghua*. Beijing: Renmin chubanshe.

Xi, Jinping. 2016a. Bu wang chuxin, jixu qianjin (2016.07.01). In *Tan zhiguolizheng*, vol. 2:32–46. Beijing: Waiwen chubanshe, 2017.

Xi, Jinping. 2016b. Shuli 'lüshui qingshan jiu shi jinshan yinshan' de qianglie yishi (2016.11.28). In *Tan zhiguolizheng*, vol. 2:393. Beijing: Waiwen chubanshe, 2017.

Xi, Jinping. 2016c. *Zai zhexue shehui kexue zuotanhui shang de jianghua (2016.05.17)*. Beijing: Renmin chubanshe.

Xi, Jinping. 2017a. Gongtong goujian renlei mingyun gongtongti (2017.01.18). In *Tan zhiguolizheng*, vol. 2:537–550. Beijing: Waiwen chubanshe, 2017.

Xi, Jinping. 2017b. Jixu tuijin makesizhuyi zhongguohua shidaihua dazhonghua (2017.09.29). In *Tan zhiguolizheng*, vol. 2:65–70. Beijing: Waiwen chubanshe, 2017.

Xi, Jinping. 2017c. *Juesheng quanmian jiancheng xiaokang shehui, duoqu xinshidai Zhongguo tese shehuizhuyi weida shengli (2017.10.18)*. Beijing: Renmin chubanshe.

Xi, Jinping. 2018a. Zai jinian makesi danchen 200 zhounian dahui shang de jianghua. *Gongchandangyuan (Hebei)* 2018 (8): 1, 4–9.

Xi, Jinping. 2018b. *Zai jinian makesi danchen 200 zhounian dahui shang de jianghua (2018.05.04)*. Beijing: Renmin chubanshe.

Xi, Jinping. 2019a. Bianzheng weiwuzhuyi shi Zhongguo gongchandangren de shijieguan he fangfalun. *Qiushi* 2019 (1): 1–3.

Xi, Jinping. 2019b. Guanyu jianchi he fazhan Zhongguo tese shehuizhuyi de jige wenti. *Qiushi* 2019 (7): 1–4.

Xi, Jinping. 2020a. Buduan kaituo dangdai makesizhuyi zhengzhijingjixue xin jingjie. *Qiushi* 2020 (16): 1–6.

Xi, Jinping. 2020b. Jianchi lishi weiwuzhuyi buduan kaipi dangdai Zhongguo makesizhuyi fazhan xin jingjie (2020.01.15). *Qiushi* 2020 (2): 1–5.

Xi, Jinping. 2020c. Opening up new frontiers for Marxist political economy in contemporary China. *Qiushi Journal (English Edition)* 2020 (6): 1–6.

Xi, Jinping. 2021a. Gongtong goujian renlei mingyun gongtongti. *Qiushi* 2021 (1): 1–14.

Xi, Jinping. 2021b. Zhengque renshi he bawo zhong–changqi jingji shehui fazhan zhongda wenti (2020.08.24). *Qiushi* 2021 (2): 1–6.

Xiao, Guiqing, and Tian Qiao. 2016. Renmin zhuti diwei: Xi Jinping zhiguolizheng sixiang de hexin linian. *sixiang lilun jiaoyu* 2016 (12): 4–12.

Xiong, Zhidong. 2019. Makesi renmin zhuti sixiang jiti dangdai jiazhi – jian lun Xi Jinping xinshidai 'yi renmin wei zhongxin' sixiang de makesizhuyi zhiyuan. *Henan daxue xuebao (shehui kexue ban)* 59 (1): 23–29.

Xu, Minhua, and Liu Xigang. 2012. *Makesizhuyi shengtai zhexue sixiang yanjiu*. Beijing: Zhongguo shehui kexue chubanshe.

Yang, Mingwei. 2016. 'Ba makesizhuyi zhexue zuowei kanjia benling' – Xi Jinping tan xuexi he yunyong makesizhuyi zhexue de ji ceng yiyun. *Dang de wenxian* 2016 (6): 42–49.

Yu, Liangzao. 2013. Makesi dui Eguo zou xinshi shehui fazhan daolu kenengxing de pinggu – yandu 'gei Wei·yi·Chasuliqi de fuxin (chugao).' *Henan shifan daxue shehui kexue xuebao* 2013 (2): 5–12.

Yuan, Tingting, and Li. Guoquan. 2016. Lun Xi Jinping de makesizhuyi guan. *Shehuizhuyi yanjiu* 2016 (6): 16–22.

Zasulich, Vera. 1881a. A letter to Marx, 16. Feb., 1881, Genéve. In *Late Marx and the Russian road: Marx and the 'peripheries of capitalism'*, ed. Teodor Shanin, 98–99. New York: Monthly Review Press, 1983.

Zasulich, Vera. 1881b. V. Zasulich – K. Marksa, 16. Fevralia, 1881 g., Zheneva. In *Arkhiv K. Marksa i F. Engel'sa*, vol. 1:269–270. Moskva: Gosudarstvennoe izdatel'stvo, 1924.

Zhang, Qiao, and Fan Hongda. 2018. Xi Jinping dui makesizhuyi fanpinkun lilun zhongguohua de xin gongxian. *Zhonggong Fujian shengwei dangxiao xuebao* 2018 (7): 20–25.

Zhang, Zhaoduan. 2017. Zhengque renshi he kexue duidai zhonghua youxiu chuantong wenhua – lun Xi Jinping de makesizhuyi chuantong wenhua guan. *Dongbei shida xuebao (zhexue shehui kexue ban)* 2017 (1): 47–53.

Zhao, Jianying. 2016. On the CPC's theoretical innovation in ideology since the 18th CPC National Congress. *Marxist Studies in China* 2016: 113–126.

Zhonggong zhongyang xuanchuanbu. 2016. *Xi Jinping zongshuji xilie zhongyao jianghua duben.* Beijing: Xuexi chubanshe, Renmin chubanshe.

Zhonggong zhongyang xuanchuanbu. 2019. *Xi Jinping xinshidai Zhongguo tese shehuizhuyi sixiang xuexi gangyao.* Beijing: Xuexi chubanshe.

Zhou, Guangxun, and Hu. Qian. 2015. Cong renlei mingyun de hongkuo shiye shenshi shengtai wenming – Xi Jinping dui makesizhuyi shengtai zhexue sixiang de jicheng yu fazhan lun lüe. *Ziran bianzhengfa yanjiu* 31 (4): 105–111.

Zhou, Hong. 2017. *Towards a society with social protection for all: A concise history of social security transformation in modern China*, trans. Hui Jia. China Insights. Singapore: Springer.

Zhou, Wenwen, Lin Meiqing, and Zhao Jinke. 2017. Lun Xi Jinping 'renlei mingyun gongtongti' sixiang de kexue neihan he zhongda yiyi – jiyu makesizhuyi lilun shijiao. *Lilun dao kan* 2017 (1): 80–84.

Zou, Zhikun, and Wang Yilin. 2018. Xi Jinping xinshidai Zhongguo tese shehuizhuyi sixiang shi makesizhuyi zhongguohua zhongda lilun chuangxin. *Fujian luntan (renwen shehui kexue ban)* 2018 (7): 44–49.

Chapter 11
Conclusion: On the Socialist System and Cultural Confidence

11.1 A Guide for Foreigners

This book is subtitled 'A Guide for Foreigners'. It may be a somewhat longish guide, but this has been necessary in order to present a full range of materials relating to China's socialist system. Some of this material is not known as well as it should be outside China, especially the chapters on Deng Xiaoping and Xi Jinping, or the central role that Marxist philosophy and contradiction analysis plays in the CPC and in country-wide policy-making, or indeed the maturing socialist democratic system in China. Other material is woefully distorted and misrepresented in some circles outside China. I think here of the socialist market economy and its interweaving with a planned economy, as well as minority nationalities policies and the Chinese Marxist approach to human rights in which the right to socio-economic well-being is the core right—the latter is actually a common approach to human rights in many developing countries. A comparable misrepresentation relates to the way the CPC leads China. This leadership is clearly not in terms of a 'party-state' structure; instead, the CPC's leadership functions indirectly, through statutory processes in light of rule of law so that the will of the Party becomes governmental decisions and laws. Understanding all of this will be easier for those who have been brought up in socialist countries past and present. But for those who have been brought up in the small number of countries known as the 'West', the task of understanding will be more difficult. In their case, a more complete washing of the brain is required (as Mao put it), or a liberation of thought (as Deng emphasised). To use an image I have used earlier: the process requires big ears and a small mouth, a need to listen and learn so as to understand what Chinese Marxists have to say about their socialist system. In fact, it is precisely out of this image that I would like draw out two final topics, the first concerning the meaning of 'socialist system' and the second 'cultural confidence'.

R. Boer, *Socialism with Chinese Characteristics*,
https://doi.org/10.1007/978-981-16-1622-8_11

11.2 Socialist System

On a few occasions I have spoken of an overall socialist system that has a number of structural components or institutional forms—to borrow a term from *Régulation* theory (Boyer and Saillard 2002). However, the word 'system' in English can lead to some misunderstanding. In the overly politicised context of Western countries, 'system' usually means a political system, in the sense that the form of the state determines all other factors. This is not the sense of 'system' used in Chinese Marxist scholarship. Two terms are important: *zhidu* (制度) is generally used for an overall system, while *tizhi* (体制) and at times *tixi* (体系) means a structural component or institutional form within the overall system.[1] At the widest level, such a system includes economic, political, social, educational and cultural components. It is in this sense that we may distinguish between a capitalist system and a socialist system.

Now it becomes a little more complicated, for there are sub-systems withing the overall system. For example, since there are a number of components that make up socialist democracy in China—including electoral, consultative, and grassroots democracy, along with human rights, minority nationalities policy, rule of law, and leadership of the Communist Party—one may also speak of a socialist democratic system. Similarly, since education comprises primary, middle, and high schools, as well as universities, research centres, academies, journals, and presses, it is also possible to speak of an educational system with its components. What about economic matters? In this case one may speak of a 'basic socialist economic system [*shehuizhuyi jiben jingji zhidu*]' that has the institutional forms of markets and planning. In sum, there is the overall socialist system within which are a number of subs-systems. These sub-systems can be seen at two levels: when one considers the overall system, the sub-systems are its components; when one focuses on a sub-system, it has its own specific institutional forms or structural components.

A question remains: since the economic base (*jingji jichu*) is—according to Marxist analysis and in contrast to Western assumptions noted above—the ultimately determining factor for a system, how should we understand the economic realities of China's socialist system? The answer has three parts. First, the combination of planning and markets constitutes a basic socialist economic system (see above). Second, we need to keep in mind the dialectical relation between ownership and the liberation of the productive forces (see Sect. 2.4 and 10.4.3). These two sides of the socialist project are found in Marx and Engels (1848a, 52; 1848b, 481; 1848c, 504). Both are necessary, but their relationship needs to be constantly recalibrated. For example, in Western Marxist contexts there is a tendency to a one-sided definition of socialism as the ownership of the means of production (leading at times to a mistaken assessment of actual socialist construction such as that in China). By contrast, proletarian revolutions have been successful overwhelmingly in places that had undeveloped productive forces, so one finds that (eventually in some cases) that

[1]As we saw in the chapter on the socialist market economy, the terminology has become quite specific and consistent in relation economic matters, although one stills finds some fluidity between the terms in more common usage.

there is greater attention to liberating productive forces. This was Deng Xiaoping's particular emphasis, although one can also find occasional mentions in Mao's writings. The risk here is to over-emphasise such liberation at the expense of ownership, which has actually led in the last decade or more to a renewed emphasis in China on the latter, along with associated categories such as justice and equality.

The third part of my answer concerns the specific features that make the system socialist. Here I would like to copy the points listed earlier (see Sect. 5.4.2): (1) the system contains a multiplicity of components, but public ownership remains the core economic driver; (2) while both state owned and private enterprises must be viable, their main purpose is not profit at all costs, but social benefit and meeting the needs of all people—in short 'people-centred [*yi renmin wei zhongxin*]'; (3) it deploys the old socialist principle of from each according to ability and to each according to work, limiting exploitation and wealth polarisation, and seeking common prosperity; (4) the guide for action always remains Marxism; (5) the primary value should always be 'socialist collectivism [*shehuizhuyi de jitizhuyi*]' rather than bourgeois individualism (Huang 1994, 5).

Lest one feel that all this talk of systems, sub-systems, and components entails unneeded complexity, perhaps we should recall Engels's observation:

> Political, juridical, philosophical, religious, literary, artistic, etc., development is based upon economic development. But each of these also reacts the others and upon the economic base. This is not to say that the economic situation is the *cause* and that it *alone* is *active* and that everything else is mere passive effect, but rather that there is reciprocal action based, *in the final analysis*, on economic necessity which invariably prevails. (Engels 1894a, 206; 1894b, 265)[2]

Engels was of course speaking in his own context of the capitalist system, but the crucial philosophical and methodological insight applies just as much to understanding a socialist system. While economic realities—and in China these are socialist—ultimately determine the whole in the final analysis, the relationship between the components of the overall socialist system is not in terms of active and passive, but in terms of reciprocal action between all the components. As Engels writes to Joseph Bloch: 'It is in the interaction of all these factors and amidst an unending multitude of fortuities [*alle die unendliche Menge von Zufälligkeiten*] … that the economic trend ultimately asserts itself as something inevitable' (Engels 1890a, 463; 1890b, 35). Thus, in a Chinese situation the ultimately determining factor is the economic base, with its basic socialist economic system of planned and market economies. But all of the other institutional forms—political, juridical, philosophical, cultural, and so on—are also part of the overall socialist system and

[2]Note also: 'According to the materialistic view of history, the determining fact in history is, *in the final analysis*, the production and reproduction of life. More than that was never maintained either by Marx or myself … The economic situation is the basis, but the various factors of the superstructure … also have a bearing upon the course of the historical struggles of which, in many cases, they largely determine the *form*. It is in the interaction of all these factors and amidst an unending multitude of fortuities … that the economic trend ultimately asserts itself as something inevitable' (Engels 1890a, 463; 1890b, 34–35).

interact upon one another in a reciprocal fashion. It is precisely in this vein that we should understand a well-known observation by Xi Jinping:

> Socialism with Chinese characteristics is socialism, and not any other kind of '-ism'. We must not abandon the basic principles of scientific socialism; if they are abandoned, it is not socialism. Our Party has always emphasised that socialism with Chinese characteristics not only adheres to the basic principles of scientific socialism, but also endows it with distinctive Chinese characteristics in accordance with the conditions of the times. That is to say, socialism with Chinese characteristics is socialism, not any other '-ism'. (Xi 2019, 1; see also 2013b, 22)

11.3 Cultural Confidence

I would like to conclude with a few observations on cultural confidence (*wenhua zixin*). This became an important topic about a decade ago, and through the debate and discussion a number of key points arose.[3] The beginning point is an awareness that China's economic and political strength is not commensurate with its cultural strength. In the introductory chapter to this book (see Sect. 1.2.2), I mentioned Xi Jinping's concern that the status and quality of China's philosophy and social sciences is incommensurate with China's global status, and noted that he urged those responsible to do all they could to address this imbalance. But cultural confidence is wider than philosophy and social sciences, wider than academic work as such (Qin 2012), for it embraces the whole range of what is understood to be culture—*wenhua* (文化)—in China. These include the material, spiritual, systemic, life, and value assumptions of society as a whole, as well as a history that spans five millennia (Zhou 2017, 82). It is precisely confidence, or self-belief, in this rich and long cultural tradition that is at issue.

Further, there are the lingering effects of the century of humiliation, from the first Opium War that began in 1839 to Liberation in 1949. As a result of multiple invasions, the imposition of opium on China by a British Empire that was fostering empire-wide drug trafficking, and colonial occupation by the Japanese, China became one of the poorest countries in the world, with the threat of becoming a failed state. The sense grew in China that its once proud cultural tradition was worth little, and that the 'West' was in many, if not all, ways superior. These experiences still have have a lingering cultural effect in China, leading to the assumption that 'the West is strong and we are weak, poor, and speechless' (Chen 2018, 11). Younger people these days no longer share such an assumption, but I continue to encounter older people who still think in such a manner.

A major shift has begun to take place during the tenure of Xi Jinping as general secretary of the CPC and as the country's president. Early in this tenure, he was

[3] The reader may find a collection of journal and newspaper articles on the topic of cultural confidence and the Chinese discursive mode (*huayu tixi*) on the website of the Chinese Academy of Social Sciences: www.cssn.cn/zt/zt_xkzt/xkzt_yyxzt/zghy. In what follows, I draw on the major contributions to the discussion (Zhang Y. 2013; Xu 2014; Zhang W. 2014; Zhou 2017; Chen 2018; Gao 2018; Wang and Wang 2020).

already stressing the need to 'explain clearly the historical origin, evolution, and basic tendency of the outstanding traditional Chinese culture and its uniqueness, values, and distinctive features, so as to enhance our cultural confidence [*wenhua zixin*] and our confidence in our core values [*jiazhiguan hexin*]' (Xi 2014, 164).[4] The lingering effects of humiliation were clearly over, although the long path to cultural confidence had really only just begun. But let me emphasise the use of 'explain clearly [*jiang qingchu*]', as well as an equally common phrase 'tell China's story well [*jianghao Zhongguo gushi*]',[5] for this applies not merely to internal dynamics within China, but especially to international realities.

All the same, there remains a disjuncture or lag between the internal and the external. Internal to China, it has been clear for some time that the 'China model'—socialism with Chinese characteristics—is a superior model to others. As revealed in survey after survey, there is a distinct confidence in the direction in which China is going, in the nature of its economy, structures of governance, and its rich cultural tradition.[6] In short, it is a confidence in the socialist system, which has been tested time and again and stood up to and learned from such tests (Gao 2018). But cultural confidence is all very well within China, and indeed for non-Chinese citizens who make China their home. The key problem is how to ensure this distinctly Chinese Marxist way of speaking about the Chinese path can gain traction in an international arena.

All of this brings me to the crucial question: how does China tell its story well (*jianghao Zhongguo gushi*), how does it engage internationally at a cultural level so that its own distinct discursive mode (*huayu tixi*) can be understood, appreciated, and debated? One approach would be to adopt Western categories and assumptions, and this has been a temptation in the past. As an insightful study by Chen Shuguang observes, not so long ago the reality was that the 'discourse stage is controlled by the West, topics are proposed by the West, the agenda is dominated by the West, standards are set by the West, content is provided by the West, and discourse is judged by the West' (Chen 2018, 11). As a cultural by-product of European colonialism and imperialism, this discursive mode was a closed system, which viewed the rest of the world through its own lens and in its own image, attempted to force the rest of the world to fit into this image, and if this did not happen, rejected the world. In short, such a discursive mode was the means by which 'the Western world studied itself, explained its own functioning, the better to control what was happening' (Wallerstein

[4]Note also: 'We need to have greater confidence in the path, theory, system and, ultimately, in the culture of socialism with Chinese characteristics. Cultural confidence is a more fundamental, deeper and more enduring force. Both history and reality show that a nation that abandons or betrays its own history and culture is not only impossible to develop, but also likely to stage a historical tragedy' (Xi 2016, 9; see further Zhou 2017).

[5]The full phrase is 'tell China's story well and making our voice heard [*jianghao Zhongguo gushi, chuanbo hao Zhongguo shengyin*]', which Xi has used on many occasions (Xi 2013a, 156; see further Xu 2014).

[6]These strengths are sometimes cast in terms of the 'four supers' and the 'four particulars': the 'four supers' refer to population, territory, history, and culture, and the 'four particulars' or 'unique characteristics' refer to language, politics, society, and economy (Zhang W 2014, 20).

2011, 264). How things change. As the last European colonial power—the United States—fragments and falls apart due to its own internal contradictions and as the 14 percent of the global population found in Western countries realises belatedly that the whole Western project is in its sunset phase, the appeal of its discursive mode had markedly declined (Zhang Y. 2013). In Russia, they speak of the end of the liberal project, in Africa and Central Asia they seek an alternative path to the economic plunder and corrupt political structures imposed upon them in the 'post-colonial' era, in Latin America they are more and more shaking off the effects of United States intervention, in Western and Southeast Asia, Muslim-majority countries have clearly indicated their rejection, and in Eastern Asia the strengths of its own cultural traditions and histories are becoming apparent. In light of all of these developments, it would be foolhardy in the extreme to 'use Western categories to understand China [*yixi jiezhong*]'.

Other approaches to cultural confidence have appeared in debates. One option is to bide one's time, waiting for the cultural sphere to catch up to China's economic and political status (Zhang W. 2014). Given China's natural, historical, and Marxist strengths, it will only be a matter of time before international standards and discourses are shaped in light of Chinese contributions. While there is some truth in this point, the risk in such an approach is that it may come to be seen as a replacement of an existing international discursive mode with one that is shaped and determined by China. Another approach is to treat the question of cultural confidence as a strategic issue in terms of China's place in the world. Alongside comprehensive planning and execution across the full range of academic, cultural and governmental institutions, it also entails the use of both 'soft power' and 'hard power' to ensure China's voice is heard fully—and not in a distorted and misrepresented manner—in international debates (Xu 2014). Obviously, this is a clear necessity: you cannot have cultural confidence and a robust discourse system in an international context without significant economic and political power.

It is in this light that we should understand a further approach, which is to emphasise the need to find a way to communicate across dual or even multiple 'ontologies'. In the chapter on sovereignty and human rights (see Sect. 7.2.2), I presented some of the work of Sun Xiangchen, who seeks a way to communicate across the cultural ontologies of the West and China (Sun 2015; Sun and Lu 2017, 179). The risk here, however, is to see these cultural ontologies as a duality, between the fading global dominance of Western discourse and the increasing importance of Chinese discourse. Instead, there are multiple discursive modes, multiple cultural ontologies, all the way from Russia through Africa. For example, in the robust and growing Chinese-Russian engagements there is a distinct sense of the civilisational and cultural distinctness of both traditions, the one Eurasian and the other East Asian. But there is also an ongoing effort at mutual understanding of these cultural ontologies, at times in terms of a common past-and-present in terms of Marxism and socialist construction, at others in terms of a greater emphasis on stability and harmony, and at other times in relation to mutual interests in the current global situation. In short, the mode of engagement does not take place only in light of a shared opposition to the West, but in a way that remains faithful to one's own culture and its discursive system and yet

finds ways to communicate in ways that are non-hegemonic. As Yang Weimin puts it, 'the greatest confidence is cultural confidence, but cultural confidence is neither arrogant nor narcissistic' (Yang 2017, 18).[7]

We may also deploy the Marxist distinction between base and superstructure, which I have discussed in an earlier piece in *Guangming Daily* (Boer 2020). By now it is clear that China has stepped onto the centre of the world stage. This reality entails that everyone has an opinion about China, that China is open to much greater international scrutiny than ever before, and that Chinese approaches to international relations—such as 'win-win' and a 'community of common destiny for humankind'—are gaining more and more traction, especially with developing countries with whom China shares deep connections through common experience. However, such international engagement is easier at the level of the economic base. I think not merely of China's central role in global economics, but also of a growing series of trade deals, and of course the BRI and its host of related organisations. At the superstructural level of culture, and indeed of philosophy, politics, values, and social patterns, the process of international engagement is much more complex. Understanding, trust, and then mutual debate takes time at this level. This is particularly so if one does not seek a hegemonic imposition of one cultural framework upon another, but follows an approach in which—as the Confucian *Book of Rites* puts it—'All things are nourished together without their injuring one another [*wanwu bing yu er bu xiang hai, dao bingxing er bu xiangbei*]'. In short, cultural confidence entails mutual respect for cultural sovereignty.

Finally, what is the bearing of this for Marxism, which has been the consistent concern of this book as a whole? As I have mentioned, historical and theoretical reasons have led to the terms 'sinified Marxism' and 'socialism with Chinese characteristics'. While these terms are perfectly valid and embody the Marxist method itself—seeking truth from facts, becoming concrete in specific situations—they can give the impression of a certain peculiarity that pertains to Chinese Marxism. Thus, we find an increasing confidence that Chinese Marxism is Marxism, that socialism with Chinese characteristics is socialism, so much so that it is part of the mainstream and will be recognised as an 'original contribution to the development of Marxism' (Xi 2017, 66).

References

Boer, Roland. 2020. Women xuedao le shenme, shijie jiang hui zenyang? *Guangming ribao*, 12 May 2020. http://news.gmw.cn/2020-05/12/content_33821736.htm.

Boyer, Robert, and Yves Saillard (eds.). 2002. *Régulation theory: The state of the art*. London: Routledge.

Chen, Shuguang. 2018. Zhongguo makesizhuyi yanjiu 40 nian: 1978–2018. *Jiaoxue yu yanjiu* 2018 (10): 5–16.

[7] By now it should be clear that this approach is not to be confused with a liberal notion of 'tolerance', which is another way of seeking hegemony.

Engels, Friedrich. 1890a. Engels an Joseph Bloch in Königsberg. London, 21–22 September 1890. In *Marx Engels Werke*, Vol. 37:462–465. Berlin: Dietz, 1968.
Engels, Friedrich. 1890b. Engels to Joseph Bloch in Königsberg, London, 21–22 September, 1890. In *Marx and Engels collected works*, Vol. 49:33–37. Moscow: Progress Publishers, 2001.
Engels, Friedrich. 1894a. Engels an W. Borgius in Breslau, London, 25 Januar 1894. In *Marx Engels Werke*, Vol. 39:205–207. Berlin: Dietz, 1973.
Engels, Friedrich. 1894b. Engels to W. Borgius in Breslau, London, 25 January 1894. In *Marx and Engels collected works*, Vol. 50:264–267. Moscow: Progress Publishers, 2004.
Gao, Zhonghua. 2018. Zhongguo tese shehuizhuyi zhidu zixin yanjin de lishi luoji. *Ha'erbin shiwei dangxiao xuebao* 2018 (11): 12–18.
Huang, Nansen. 1994. Shehuizhuyi shichang jingji lilun de zhexue jichu. *Makesizhuyi yu xianshi* 1994 (11): 1–6.
Marx, Karl, and Friedrich Engels. 1848a. Gongchandang xuanyan. In *Makesi Engesi wenji*, Vol. 2:3–67. Beijing: Renmin chubanshe, 2009.
Marx, Karl, and Friedrich Engels. 1848b. Manifest der Kommunistischen Partei. In *Marx Engels Werke*, Vol. 4:459–493. Berlin: Dietz Verlag, 1974.
Marx, Karl, and Friedrich Engels. 1848c. The manifesto of the communist party. In *Marx and Engels collected works*, Vol. 6:477–519. Moscow: Progress Publishers, 1976.
Qin, Xuan. 2012. Zhongguo tese xueshu huayu tixi goujian silu. *Renmin luntan* 2012 (11): 11–17.
Sun, Xiangchen. 2015. Shuangchong benti: xingsu xiandai Zhongguo jiazhi xingtai de jichu. *Xueshu yuekan* 2015 (6): 20–34.
Sun, Xiangchen, and Lu Xinyu. 2017. Xiandaixing bushi minmie zishen de chuantong—Sun Xiangchen jiaoshou fangtan. *Xueshu yuekan* 2017 (4): 178–184.
Wallerstein, Immanuel. 2011. *The modern World-system IV: Centrist liberalism triumphant, 1789–1914*. Berkeley: University of California Press.
Wang, Hailiang, and Wang Yonggui. 2020. Xi Jinping guanyu wenhua zixin zhongyao lunshu shengcheng de so chong zhuti weidu. *Sixiang zhengzhi jiaoyu yanjiu* 2020 (6): 6–11.
Xi, Jinping. 2013a. Ba xuanchuan sixiang gongzuo zuo de geng hao (2013.08.19). In *Tan zhiguolizheng*, Vol. 1:153–157. Beijing: Waiwen chubanshe, 2014.
Xi, Jinping. 2013b. Haobu dongyao jianchi he fazhan Zhongguo tese shehuizhuyi (2013.01.05). In *Tan zhiguolizheng*, Vol. 1:21–24. Beijing: Waiwen chubanshe, 2014.
Xi, Jinping. 2014. Peiyu he hongyang shehuizhuyi hexin jiazhiguan (2014.02.24). In *Tan zhiguolizheng*, Vol. 1:163–165. Beijing: Waiwen chubanshe, 2014.
Xi, Jinping. 2016. *Zai zhexue shehui kexue zuotanhui shang de jianghua (2016.05.17)*. Beijing: Renmin chubanshe.
Xi, Jinping. 2017. Jixu tuijin makesizhuyi zhongguohua shidaihua dazhonghua (2017.09.29). In *Tan zhiguolizheng*, Vol. 2:65–70. Beijing: Waiwen chubanshe, 2017.
Xi, Jinping. 2019. Guanyu jianchi he fazhan Zhongguo tese shehuizhuyi de jige wenti. *Qiushi* 2019 (7): 1–4.
Xu, Zhanchen. 2014. Jianghao Zhongguo gushi de xianshi kunnan yu pojie zhi ce. *Shehuizhuyi yanjiu* 2014 (3): 20–26.
Yang, Weimin. 2017. Zhongguo tese zhengdang zhidu de youshi ji dui shijie gongxian—'wei renlei dui genghao shehui zhidu de tansuo tigong Zhongguo fang'an' zhi guanjian. *Tongyi zhanxian xue yanjiu* 2017 (1): 15–31.
Zhang, Weiwei. 2014. Zhongguo moshi he Zhongguo huayu de shijie yiyi. *Jingji daokan* 2014 (3): 14–21.
Zhang, Yiongjin. 2013. Zhongguo dui quanqiu zhixu de shexiang didai mingque. *Renmin luntan* 2013 (25): 52–55.
Zhou, Yinzhen. 2017. Xi Jinping zongshuji wenhua zixin jiqi dangdai yiyi yanjiu—jiyu makesizhuyi zhexue shijiao. *Jianghan daxue xuebao (shehui kexue ban)* 34 (6): 82–87.

GPSR Compliance
The European Union's (EU) General Product Safety Regulation (GPSR) is a set of rules that requires consumer products to be safe and our obligations to ensure this.

If you have any concerns about our products, you can contact us on

ProductSafety@springernature.com

In case Publisher is established outside the EU, the EU authorized representative is:

Springer Nature Customer Service Center GmbH
Europaplatz 3
69115 Heidelberg, Germany

www.ingramcontent.com/pod-product-compliance
Lightning Source LLC
Chambersburg PA
CBHW062251280426
44090CB00003B/36
* 9 7 8 9 8 1 1 6 1 6 2 1 1 *